VOLUME II:
SINCE THE SIXTEENTH CENTURY

THE WESTERN EXPERIENCE

THE WESTERN EXPERIENCE

Ninth Edition

MORTIMER CHAMBERS
University of California, Los Angeles

BARBARA HANAWALT
The Ohio State University

THEODORE K. RABB
Princeton University

ISSER WOLOCH
Columbia University

RAYMOND GREW
University of Michigan

LISA TIERSTEN
Barnard College

Boston   Burr Ridge, IL   Dubuque, IA   Madison, WI   New York   San Francisco   St. Louis
Bangkok   Bogotá   Caracas   Kuala Lumpur   Lisbon   London   Madrid   Mexico City
Milan   Montreal   New Delhi   Santiago   Seoul   Singapore   Sydney   Taipei   Toronto

Higher Education

THE WESTERN EXPERIENCE, VOLUME II: SINCE THE SIXTEENTH CENTURY
Published by McGraw-Hill, a business unit of The McGraw-Hill Companies, Inc., 1221 Avenue of the Americas, New York, NY, 10020.

Some ancillaries, including electronic and print components, may not be available to customers outside the United States.

This book is printed on acid-free paper.

1 2 3 4 5 6 7 8 9 0 DOW/DOW 0 9 8 7 6

ISBN-13: 978-0-07-325082-3
ISBN-10: 0-07-325082-1

Vice President and Editor-in-Chief: *Emily Barrosse*
Publisher: *Lyn Uhl*
Senior Sponsoring Editor: *Monica Eckman*
Director of Development: *Lisa Pinto*
Developmental Editor: *Angela W. Kao*
Permissions Coordinator: *The Permissions Group*
Marketing Manager: *Katherine Bates*
Managing Editor: *Jean Dal Porto*
Project Manager: *Emily Hatteberg*
Art Director: *Jeanne Schreiber*
Art Editor: *Ayelet Arbel*
Lead Designer: *Gino Cieslik*
Cover and Interior Designer: *Ellen Pettengell*
Cover credit: *Charles Ginner*, Piccadilly Circus, *1912; Tate Gallery, London, Great Britain/Art Resource, NY*
Senior Photo Research Coordinator: *Alexandra Ambrose*
Photo Research: *Photosearch, Inc., New York*
Senior Production Supervisor: *Carol A. Bielski*
Lead Media Producer: *Sean Crowley*
Media Project Manager: *Kate Boylan*
Composition: *9.5/12 Trump, by Carlisle Publishing Services*
Printing: *45 # Pub Matte Plus, R.R. Donnelley & Sons*

Credits: The credits section for this book begins on page C-1 and is considered an extension of the copyright page.

Library of Congress Cataloging-in-Publication Data

The Western experience / Mortimer Chambers ... [et al,].—9th ed. [main text]
    6 v. cm.
   Includes bibliographical references and index.
   ISBN-13: 978-0-07-288369-5 (alk. paper)
   ISBN-10: 0-07-288369-3 (alk. paper)
   1. Civilization—History. 2. Civilization, Western—History. I. Chambers, Mortimer.
CB59.W38 2007
909'.09821—dc22

                                 2006041940

The Internet addresses listed in the text were accurate at the time of publication. The inclusion of a Web site does not indicate an endorsement by the authors or McGraw-Hill, and McGraw-Hill does not guarantee the accuracy of the information presented at these sites.

www.mhhe.com

About the Authors

Mortimer Chambers is Professor of History at the University of California at Los Angeles. He was a Rhodes Scholar from 1949 to 1952 and received an M.A. from Wadham College, Oxford, in 1955 after obtaining his doctorate from Harvard University in 1954. He has taught at Harvard University (1954–1955) and the University of Chicago (1955–1958). He was Visiting Professor at the University of British Columbia in 1958, the State University of New York at Buffalo in 1971, the University of Freiburg (Germany) in 1974, and Vassar College in 1988. A specialist in Greek and Roman history, he is coauthor of *Aristotle's History of Athenian Democracy* (1962), editor of a series of essays entitled *The Fall of Rome* (1963), and author of *Georg Busolt: His Career in His Letters* (1990) and of *Staat der Athener*, a German translation and commentary to Aristotle's *Constitution of the Athenians* (1990). He has edited Greek texts of the latter work (1986) and of the *Hellenica Oxyrhynchia* (1993). He has contributed articles to the *American Historical Review* and *Classical Philology* as well as to other journals, both in America and in Europe. He is also an editor of *Historia*, the international journal of ancient history.

Barbara Hanawalt holds the King George III Chair of British History at The Ohio State University and is the author of numerous books and articles on the social and cultural history of the Middle Ages. Her publications include *The Middle Ages: An Illustrated History* (1999), *'Of Good and Ill Repute': Gender and Social Control in Medieval England* (1998), *Growing Up in Medieval London: The Experience of Childhood in History* (1993), *The Ties That Bound: Peasant Life in Medieval England* (1986), and *Crime and Conflict in English Communities, 1300–1348* (1979). She received her M.A. in 1964 and her Ph.D. in 1970, both from the University of Michigan. She has served as president of the Social Science History Association and the Medieval Academy of America and has been on the Council of the American Historical Association and the Medieval Academy of America. She was a fellow of the Netherlands Institute for Advanced Study (2005–2006), a fellow of the Guggenheim Foundation (1998–1999), an ACLS Fellow in 1975–1976, a fellow at the National Humanities Center (1997–1998), a fellow at the Wissenschaftskolleg in Berlin (1990–1991), a member of the School of Historical Research at the Institute for Advanced Study, and a senior research fellow at the Newberry Library in 1979–1980.

Theodore K. Rabb is Professor of History at Princeton University. He received his Ph.D. from Princeton in 1961 and subsequently taught at Stanford, Northwestern, Harvard, and Johns Hopkins universities. He is the author of numerous articles and reviews in journals such as *The New York Times* and the *Times Literary Supplement*, and he has been editor of *The Journal of Interdisciplinary History* since its foundation. Among his books are *The Struggle for Stability in Early Modern Europe* (1975), *Renaissance Lives* (1993), and *Jacobean Gentleman* (1999). He has won awards from the Guggenheim Foundation, the National Endowment for the Humanities, the American Historical Association, and the National Council for History Education. He was the principal historian for the PBS series *Renaissance*, which was nominated for an Emmy.

Isser Woloch is Moore Collegiate Professor of History at Columbia University. He received his Ph.D. (1965) from Princeton University in the field of eighteenth- and nineteenth-century European history. He has taught at Indiana University and at the University of California at Los Angeles, where, in 1967, he received a Distinguished Teaching Citation. He has been a fellow of the ACLS, the National Endowment for the Humanities, the Guggenheim Foundation, and the Institute for Advanced Study at Princeton. His publications include *Jacobin Legacy: The Democratic Movement under the Directory* (1970), *The Peasantry in the Old Regime: Conditions and Protests* (1970), *The French Veteran from the Revolution to the Restoration* (1979), *Eighteenth-Century Europe: Tradition and Progress, 1715–1789* (1982), *The New Regime: Transformations of the French Civic Order, 1789–1820s* (1994), *Revolution and the Meanings of Freedom in the Nineteenth Century* (1996), and *Napoleon and His Collaborators: The Making of a Dictatorship* (2001).

Raymond Grew is Professor of History Emeritus at the University of Michigan. He has also taught at Brandeis University, Princeton University, and at the Écoles des Hautes Études en Sciences Sociales in Paris. He earned both his M.A. and Ph.D. from Harvard University in the field of modern European history. He has been a Fulbright Fellow to Italy and a Fulbright Travelling Fellow to Italy and to France, a Guggenheim Fellow, and a Fellow of the National Endowment for the Humanities. In 1962 he received the Chester Higby Prize from the American Historical Association, and in 1963 the Italian government awarded him the Unità d'Italia Prize; in 1992 he received the David Pinkney Prize of the Society for French Historical Studies and in 2000 a citation for career achievement from the Society for Italian Historical Studies. He has twice served as national chair of the Council for European Studies, was for many years the editor of the international quarterly *Comparative Studies in Society and History*, and is one of the directors of the Global History Group. His recent publications include essays on historical comparison, global history, Catholicism in the nineteenth century, fundamentalism, and Italian culture and politics. His books include *A Sterner Plan for Italian Unity* (1963),

Crises of Development in Europe and the United States (1978), *School, State, and Society: The Growth of Elementary Schooling in Nineteenth-Century France* (1991), with Patrick J. Harrigan, and two edited volumes: *Food in Global History* (1999) and *The Construction of Minorities* (2001).

Lisa Tiersten is Associate Professor of History at Barnard College, Columbia University. She received her Ph.D. (1991) at Yale University and has taught at Wellesley College and Barnard College. She has been the recipient of a Chateaubriand Fellowship, a French Historical Studies Society Fellowship, and a Getty Fellowship. She also received the Emily Gregory Teaching Award at Barnard College in 1996. Her publications include *Marianne in the Market: Envisioning Consumer Society in Fin-de-Siècle France* (2001). She is currently at work on a history of bankruptcy and the culture of credit in modern France, entitled *Terms of Trade: The Capitalist Imagination in Modern France*, and on an edited volume on the comparative history of children's rights in twentieth-century Europe. Her research interests include modern France, gender, consumer culture, empire, and the comparative culture of capitalism.

This book is dedicated to the memory of David Herlihy, whose erudition and judgment were central to its creation and whose friendship and example continue to inspire his coauthors.

Brief Contents

Contents

Chapter 15

WAR AND CRISIS 429

Chapter 16

CULTURE AND SOCIETY IN THE AGE OF THE SCIENTIFIC REVOLUTION 459

Chapter 17

THE EMERGENCE OF THE EUROPEAN STATE SYSTEM 491

Chapter 18

THE WEALTH OF NATIONS 527

Chapter 19

THE AGE OF ENLIGHTENMENT 555

Chapter 20

THE FRENCH REVOLUTION 581

Chapter 21

THE AGE OF NAPOLEON 615

Chapter 22

FOUNDATIONS OF THE NINETEENTH CENTURY: POLITICS AND SOCIAL CHANGE 641

Chapter 29
THE NIGHTMARE: WORLD WAR II 901

Chapter 30
THE NEW EUROPE 941

Maps

Boxes

Primary Source Boxes

Historical Issues Boxes

Chronological Boxes

Global Moment Boxes

Preface

When *The Western Experience* was originally conceived, we sought to write a textbook that would introduce students to the growing field of social history and exciting new ways of thinking about history. We wanted the textbook not merely to set forth information but to serve as an example of historical writing. That means we cared a lot about the quality of the writing itself and also that we wanted the chapters to be examples of a historical essay that set up a historical problem and developed arguments about that problem using historical evidence. We also recognized that for American students the Western Civilization textbook needed to provide an overview of that civilization, giving students an introduction to the major achievements in Western thought, art, and science as well as the social, political, and economic context for understanding them. And lastly, we were determined that our book would treat all these various aspects of history in an integrated way. Too many books, we felt, dealt with cultural or social change entirely separately, even in separate chapters, and we sought to demonstrate and exemplify the connections. To that end, *The Western Experience* is designed to provide an analytical and reasonably comprehensive account of the contexts within which, and the processes by which, European society and civilization evolved.

Now in the ninth edition, this book has evolved with the strength of prior revisions, including Barbara Hanawalt's impressive rewriting and reordering of the six chapters that cover the Middle Ages for the seventh edition. To continue that evolution, we are proud to welcome another distinguished scholar, Lisa Tiersten of Barnard College, to our author team. She has written a new chapter on nineteenth-century empires (chapter 26), one of the first among western civilization textbooks, and she has undertaken the substantial revision and reorganization of chapters 25 and 27. With a fresh voice and lucid approach, Dr. Tiersten has greatly enriched the coverage in these chapters by incorporating recent research on gender, bourgeois and consumer culture, imperialism, technology, and globalization.

EXPERIENCING HISTORY

Everyone uses history. We use it to define who we are and to connect our personal experience to the collective memory of the groups to which we belong, including a particular region, nation, and culture. We invoke the past to explain our hopes and ambitions and to justify our fears and conflicts. The Charter of the United Nations, like the American Declaration of Independence, is based on a view of history. When workers strike or armies march, they cite the lessons of their history. Because history is so important to us psychologically and intellectually, historical understanding is always shifting and often controversial.

Historical knowledge is cumulative. Historians may ask many of the same questions about different periods of history or raise new questions or issues; they integrate the answers, and historical knowledge grows. The study of history cannot be a subjective exercise in which all opinions are equally valid. Regardless of the impetus for a particular historical question, the answer to it stands until overturned by better evidence. We now know more about the past than ever before, and we understand it as the people we study could not. Unlike them, we know the outcome of their history; we can apply methods they did not have, and often we have evidence they never saw.

Humans have always found pleasure in the reciting and reading of history. The poems about the fall of Troy or the histories of Herodotus and Thucydides entertained the ancient Greeks. The biographies of great men and women, dramatic accounts of important events, colorful tales of earlier times can be fascinating in themselves. Through these encounters with history we experience the common concerns of all people; and through the study of European history, we come to appreciate the ideals and conflicts, the failures and accidents, the social needs and human choices that formed the Western world in which we live. Knowing the historical context also enriches our appreciation for the achievements of European culture, enabling us to see its art, science, ideas, and politics in relationship to real people, specific interests, and burning issues.

We think of Europe's history as the history of Western civilization because the Greeks gave the names east and west to the points on the horizon at which the sun rises and sets. Because the Persian Empire and India lay to their east, the Greeks labeled their own continent, which they called Europe, the west. However, we need to be cautious about the view that Western civilization is a united whole, entirely distinct from other civilizations, except perhaps in its cultural development. We will see many occasions when a larger context is appropriate.

The Western Experience thus gives primary attention to a small part of the world and honors a particular cultural tradition. Yet the concentration on Europe does allow us to explore contrasts of worldwide significance; between city and rural life; among empires and monarchies and republics; in life before and after industrialization; among societies that organized labor through markets, serfdom, and slavery; between cultures little concerned with science and those that used changing scientific knowledge; among different ways of creating and experiencing forms of literature and the arts; and among Christian and non-Christian religions and all the major forms of Christianity.

A college course alone cannot create an educated citizen. Moreover, Western history is not the only history a person should know, and an introductory survey is not necessarily the best way to learn it. Yet, as readers consider and then challenge interpretations offered in this text, they will exercise critical and analytical skills. They can begin to overcome the parochialism that attributes importance only to the present. To learn to think critically about historical evidence and know how to formulate an argument on the bases of this evidence is to experience the study of history as one of the vital intellectual activities by which we come to know who and where we are.

A BALANCED, INTERPRETIVE, AND FLEXIBLE APPROACH

At the same time, we recognize that the professional scholar's preference for new perspectives over familiar ones makes a distinction that students may not share. For them, the latest interpretations need to be integrated with established understandings and controversies, with the history of people and events that are part of our cultural lore. We recognize that a textbook

should provide a coherent presentation of the basic information from which students can begin to form their historical understanding. We believe this information must be part of an interpretive history but also that its readers—teachers, students, and general readers—should be free to use it in many different ways and in conjunction with their own areas of special knowledge and their own interests and curiosity.

USE OF THEMES

Throughout this book, from the treatment of the earliest civilizations to the discussion of the present, we pursue certain key themes. These seven themes constitute a set of categories by which societies and historical change can be analyzed.

Social Structure   In early chapters, social structure involves how the land was settled, divided among its inhabitants, and put to use. Later discussions of how property is held must include corporate, communal, and individual ownership, then investment banking and companies that sell shares. Similarly, in each era we treat the division of labor, noting whether workers are slave or free, male or female, and when there are recognized specialists in fighting or crafts or trade. The chapters covering the ancient world, the Middle Ages, and the early modern period explore social hierarchies that include nobles, clergy, commoners, and slaves or serfs; the treatments of the French Revolution, the Industrial Revolution, and twentieth-century societies analyze modern social classes.

The Body Politic   Another theme we analyze throughout this book is what used to be called the body politic. Each era contains discussions of how political power is acquired and used and of the political structures that result. Students learn about the role of law from ancient codes to the present, as well as problems of order, and the formation of governments, including why government functions have increased and political participation of the population has changed.

Technology   From cultivation in the plains of the Tigris and Euphrates to the global economy, we follow changes in the organization of production and in the impact of technology. We note how goods are distributed, and we observe patterns of trade as avenues of cultural exchange in addition to wealth. We look at the changing economic role of governments and the impact of economic theories.

Gender Roles and Family   The evolution of the family and changing gender roles are topics fundamental to every historical period. Families give form to daily life and kinship structures. The history of demography, migration, and work is also a history of the family. The family has always been a central focus of social organization and religion, as well as the principal instrument by which societies assign specific practices, roles, and values to women and men. Gender roles have changed from era to era, differing according to social class and between rural and urban societies. Observing gender roles across time, the student discovers that social, political, economic, and cultural history are always interrelated; that the present is related to the past; and that social change brings gains and losses rather than evolution in a straight line—three lessons all history courses teach.

War   No history of Europe could fail to pay attention to war, which, for most polities, has been their most demanding activity. Warfare has strained whatever resources were available from ancient times to the present, leading governments to invent new ways to extract wealth and mobilize support. War has built and undermined states, stimulated science and consumed technology, made heroes, and restructured nobility, schooling, and social services. Glorified in European culture and often condemned, war in every era has affected the lives of all its peoples. This historical significance, more than specific battles, is one of the themes of *The Western Experience.*

Religion   Religion has been basic to the human experience, and our textbook explores the different religious institutions and experiences that societies developed. Religion affects and is affected by all the themes we address, creating community and causing conflict, shaping intellectual and daily life, providing the experiences that bind individual lives and society within a common system of meaning.

Cultural Expression   For authors of a general history, no decision is more difficult than the space devoted to cultural expression. In this respect, as elsewhere, we have striven for a balance between high and popular culture. We present as clearly and concisely as possible the most important formal ideas, philosophies, and ideologies of each era. We emphasize concepts of recognized importance in the general history of ideas and those concepts that illuminate behavior and discourse in a given period. We pay particular attention to developments in science that we believe are related to important intellectual, economic, and social trends. Popular culture appears both in specific sections and throughout the book. We want to place popular culture within its social and historical con-

text but not make the gulf too wide between popular and high or formal culture. Finally, we write about many of the great works of literature, art, architecture, and music. Because of the difficulties of selection, we have tried to emphasize works that are cultural expressions of their time but that also have been influential over the ages and around the globe.

Attention to these seven themes occasions problems of organization and selection. We could have structured this book around a series of topical essays, perhaps repeating the series of themes for each of the standard chronological divisions of European history. Instead, we chose to preserve a narrative flow that emphasizes interrelationships and historical context. We wanted each chapter to stand as an interpretive historical essay, with a beginning and conclusion. As a result, the themes emerge repeatedly within discussions of a significant event, an influential institution, an individual life, or a whole period of time. Or they may intersect in a single institution or historical trend. Nevertheless, readers can follow any one of these themes across time and use that theme as a measure of change and a way to assess the differences and similarities between societies.

CHANGES TO THE NINTH EDITION

For us the greatest pleasure in a revision lies in the challenge of absorbing and then incorporating the latest developments in historical understanding. From its first edition, this book included more of the results of quantitative and social history than most general textbooks of European history, an obvious reflection of our own research. Each subsequent edition provided an occasion to incorporate current methods and new knowledge, such as the rise of gender studies: a challenge that required reconsidering paragraphs, sections, and whole chapters in the light of new theories and new research, sometimes literally reconceptualizing part of the past.

Newly Revised Chapter 25: "Progress and Its Discontents"

From the last edition, chapters 25 and 26, "European Power: Wealth, Knowledge, and Imperialism" and "The Age of Progress," have been combined into a new chapter 25, "Progress and Its Discontents." Relevant material on imperial Europe has been moved to chapter 26. This new chapter 25 treats late-nineteenth-century economic transformations that brought the bourgeoisie to power along with the intellectual developments that both reinforced that power and raised doubts about its bases and its legitimacy. It also explores the class identity of the new ruling elite and examines both the pleasures and anxieties evoked by the mass commercial culture it created.

New Chapter 26: "Nineteenth-Century Empires"

In the past fifteen years, European historians increasingly have acknowledged the centrality of imperial experience to European history. Spanning a long nineteenth century from 1780 to 1914, this chapter not only explores the impact of major European economic, cultural, and political developments on imperial practice and attitudes, but also explores the profound impact of imperialism on Europe itself (making use of new scholarship on gender and popular culture, for example, to show how empire increasingly touched upon the lives of everyday Europeans). The chapter thus argues that empire did not happen "out there," but at the center of nineteenth-century European society and culture. This chapter includes fresh new illustrations and photographs, primary source boxes, and a Global Moment box on the Indian Rebellion of 1857.

Newly Revised Chapter 27: "World War I and the World It Created"

The revised chapter 27 brings to bear new scholarship on the war, including research on gender relations and the home front and on the imperial dimension of war. It emphasizes in particular how the military mobilization of the colonies—combined with the postwar rhetoric of national self-determination—raised expectations of colonial reform and gradual self-government. When these hopes were disappointed in the postwar period, the chapter shows, colonial reform movements were transformed into militant movements for colonial independence.

Streamlined Narrative throughout the Book

All of the chapters in the ninth edition have been substantially shortened and streamlined. We have worked to make difficult concepts more understandable and to remove material that interfered with the general flow of the text.

New Global Moment Features

The process whereby worldwide connections have intensified in the past two centuries, usually referred to as globalization, has caused a revision in the way we think about the histories of individual states and regions. Although revolutions in communications and transport have made the interconnections inescapable since the 1800s, it is important to see them in perspective and to pay attention to early signs of cross-cultural activity. Five Global Moment boxed essays highlight significant occasions when Europeans had to come to terms with neighbors in other continents. And we have tried, throughout, to keep students aware of the larger context within which European history has developed.

PEDAGOGICAL FEATURES

Each generation of students brings different experiences, interests, and training into the classroom—changes that are important to the teaching-learning process. The students we teach have taught us what engages or confuses them, what impression of European history they bring to college, and what they can be expected to take from a survey course. Current political, social, and cultural events also shape what we teach and how we teach. Our experience as teachers and the helpful comments of scores of other teachers have led to revisions and new additions throughout the book as we have sought to make it clearer and more accessible without sacrificing our initial goal of writing a reasonably sophisticated, interpretive, and analytic history.

Primary Source Boxes

These excerpts from primary sources are designed to illustrate or supplement points made in the text, to provide some flavor of the issues under discussion, and to allow beginning students some of that independence of judgment that comes from a careful reading of historical sources.

"THEY HAVE A MASTER CALLED LAW"

As King Xerxes leads his army into Greece in 480 B.C., he asks a former king of Sparta, who is accompanying him, whether the Greeks will really fight against the Persians.

"Now, Demaratus, I will ask you what I want to know. You are a Greek and one from no minor or weak city. So now tell me, will the Greeks stand and fight me?" Demaratus replied, "Your Majesty, shall I tell you the truth, or say what you want to hear?" The king ordered him to tell the truth, saying that he would respect him no less for doing so.

"Your Majesty," he said, "I am not speaking about all of them, only about the Spartans. First, I say they will never accept conditions from you that would enslave Greece; second, that they will fight you in battle even if all the other Greeks join your side."

Xerxes said, "Demaratus, let's look at it in all logic: why should a thousand, or ten thousand, or fifty thousand men, if they are all free and not ruled by a single master, stand up against such an army as mine? If they were ruled by one man, like my subjects, I suppose they might, out of fear, show more bravery than usual and, driven into battle by the lash, go up against a bigger force; but if allowed their freedom, they wouldn't do either one."

Demaratus said, "Your Majesty, I knew from the beginning that if I spoke the truth you wouldn't like my message, but, since you ordered me to do so, I told you about the Spartans. They are free men, but not wholly free: They have a master called Law, whom they fear far more than your soldiers fear you. And his orders are always the same—they must not run away from any army no matter how big, but must stand in their formation and either conquer or die. But, your Majesty, may your wishes be fulfilled."

From *Herodotus*, book VII, M. H. Chambers (tr.).

Historical Issues Boxes

These boxes explain major controversies over historical interpretations so that students can see how historical understanding is constructed. They encourage students to participate in these debates and formulate their own positions.

New *Global Moment Boxes*

These boxes focus on particularly vivid occasions when Europeans encountered other world civilizations, in order to suggest the broader context within which Western history unfolded.

HISTORICAL ISSUES: TWO VIEWS OF LOUIS XIV

Implicit in any assessment of the reign of Louis XIV in France is a judgment about the nature of absolutism and the kind of government the continental European monarchies created in the late seventeenth and eighteenth centuries. From the perspective of Frenchman Albert Sorel, a historian of the French Revolution writing at the end of the nineteenth century, the Revolution had been necessary to save France from Louis' heritage. For the American John Rule, a historian who concerned himself primarily with the development of political institutions during the seventeenth century, the marks of Louis XIV's rule were caution, bureaucracy, and order.

Sorel: "The edifice of the state enjoyed incomparable brilliance and splendor, but it resembled a Gothic cathedral in which the height of the nave and the arches had been pushed beyond all reason, weakening the walls as they were raised ever higher. Louis XIV carried the principle of monarchy to its utmost limit, and abused it in all respects to the point of excess. He left the nation crushed by war, mutilated by banishments, and impatient of the yoke which it felt to be ruinous. Men were worn-out, the treasury empty, all relationships strained by the violence of tension, and in the immense framework of the state there remained no institution except the accidental appearance of genius. Things had reached a point where, if a great king did not appear, there would be a great revolution."

From Albert Sorel, *L'Europe et la révolution française*, 3rd ed., Vol. 1, Paris, 1893, p. 199, as translated in William F. Church (ed.), *The Greatness of Louis XIV: Myth or Reality?*, Boston: D. C. Heath, 1959, p. 63.

Rule: "As Louis XIV himself said of the tasks of kingship, they were at once great, noble, and delightful. Yet Louis' enjoyment of his craft was tempered by political prudence. At an early age he learned to listen attentively to his advisers, to speak when spoken to, to ponder evidence, to avoid confrontations, to dissemble, to wait. He believed that time and tact would conquer. Despite all the evidence provided him by his ministers and his servants, Louis often hesitated before making a decision; he brooded, and in some instances put off decisions altogether. As he grew older, the king tended to hide his person and his office. Even his officials seldom saw the king for more than a brief interview. And as decision-making became centralized in the hands of the ministers, [so] the municipalities, the judges, the local estates, the guilds and at times the peasantry contested royal encroachments on their rights. Yet to many in the kingdom, Louis represented a modern king, an agent of stability whose struggle was their struggle and whose goal was to contain the crises of the age."

From John C. Rule, "Louis XIV, *Roi-Bureaucrate*," in Rule (ed.), *Louis XIV and the Craft of Kingship*, Columbus: Ohio State University Press, 1969, pp. 91–92.

Global Moment

THREE EMPIRES AND AN ELEPHANT

Although trade and diplomatic ties between the West and the East diminished in the period of the seventh through the tenth centuries, merchants, pilgrims, envoys, and religious officials still traveled extensively and spread news. If we look at events surrounding the year 800, we find that diplomatic missions among the Franks (a Germanic kingdom), the Byzantines (the Eastern Roman Empire), and the Abbasid caliphate (an Arabic-speaking Muslim empire) continued. The main actors in these negotiations and contacts were Charles the Great or Charlemagne (r. 768–814), king of the Franks and, as of Christmas Day 800, Roman emperor in the West; Irene (r. 796–802), who became empress of Roman Empire in the East after she blinded her son, who subsequently died; and the Caliph Harun al-Rashid (786–809), heir to the Abbasid Dynasty, centered in Baghdad in Persia.

These three rulers dominated the area around the Mediterranean, but their empires were vastly different in terms of economic sophistication, religion, and in-

the scholars were the world's leaders in medicine and science. A great hospital flourished in this period. Harun al-Rashid was said to have sponsored the "golden age" for the Arabic world. It took centuries for Arab learning in geography, astronomy, and medicine to reach the West. Charlemagne's court in Aachen was a long way from this intellectual achievement and cultural splendor.

The three empires had a history of clashes. The Arabic expansions had left the Eastern Roman Empire with far less territory. The Franks and other Germanic tribes had taken over the Western Empire and established independent kingdoms, with the Franks conquering most of them. Charlemagne, as King of the Franks, wanted the title of emperor. But before 800, no other Germanic ruler had the audacity to take the title of emperor of the Romans, and he had some trepidation over assuming the title without permission or blessings of the real successor to the title in Constantinople. The Franks and the Arabs also had considerable conflicts. After all, Charlemagne's grandfather, Charles Martel, had defeated the Arabs 70 years before (732) and he,

Among the many exotic gifts that Harun al-Rashid gave to Charlemagne was, perhaps, this crystal pitcher. It is certainly a piece of late eighth or early ninth century craftsmanship from Persia. It has long been assumed that this pitcher was among the gifts.
To come

was a rash hope, if he ever had it. He could not, as a Christian, make a real alliance with Arabs. The Church forbade such treaties with non-Christians. What did Charlemagne hope to achieve and what did Harun al-Rashid hope to gain with such a diplomatic overture?

Although the Arabic sources are silent about the exchange, Carolingian sources speak of diplomatic mis-

and the governor of Egypt back with a white elephant named Abu l'-Abbas from India. The elephant and Isaac took four years to travel from Baghdad to Jerusalem and then on to Carthage. From there they went by ship to Italy. It is not clear what ship would have been large enough to hold an elephant in 800. Waiting until spring to cross the Alps, Isaac and the Abu l'-Abbas arrived in

---

New *Chapter-Opening Timelines*

Each chapter now opens with a new timeline. These timelines are meant to offer students a visual aid with which to track simultaneous developments and important dates to remember. Ultimately, we hope that they will help give readers a grounded sense of chronology.

1800	1820	1840	1860	1880	1900

- Indian Rebellion 1857
- Taiping Rebellion in China 1850–1864
- The Great Trek of the Afrikaners in southern Africa 1835–1845
- Britain abolishes slavery 1834
- 1807 Britain abolishes the slave trade
- 1804–1825 Latin American liberation from colonial rule
- 1791 Haitian Revolution
- 1859 Darwin, *On the Origin of Species*
- 1869 Opening of the Suez Canal
- 1884–1885 Berlin Conference
- 1885 Indian National Congress established
- 1894–1895 zz War
- 1896 Ethiopian defeat of the Italians at Adowa
- 1898 Fashoda Crisis
- 1900 Boxer Rebellion in China
- 1899–1902 Boer War in southern Africa
- 1904–1905 Russo-Japanese War

Chapter Twenty

THE FRENCH REVOLUTION

REFORM AND POLITICAL CRISIS • 1789: THE FRENCH REVOLUTION •
THE RECONSTRUCTION OF FRANCE • THE SECOND REVOLUTION

Well into the eighteenth century, the long-standing social structures and political institutions of Europe were securely entrenched. Most monarchs still claimed to hold their authority directly from God. In cooperation with their aristocracies, they presided over realms composed of distinct orders of citizens, or *estates* as they were sometimes known. Each order had its particular rights, privileges, and obligations. But pressures for change were building during the century. In France, the force of public opinion grew increasingly potent by the 1780s. A financial or political crisis that could normally be managed by the monarchy threatened to snowball in this new environment. Such vulnerability was less evident in Austria, Prussia, and Russia, however, where strong monarchs instituted reforms to streamline their governments. Similarly, in Britain the political system proved resilient despite explosions of discontent at home and across the Atlantic.

Unquestionably, then, the French Revolution constituted the pivotal event of European history in the late eighteenth century. From its outbreak in 1789, the Revolution transformed the nature of sovereignty and law in France. Under its impetus, civic and social institutions were renewed, from local government and schooling to family relations and assistance for the poor. Soon its ideals of liberty, equality, and fraternity resonated across the borders of other European states, especially after war broke out in 1792 and French armies took the offensive.

The French Revolution's innovations defined the foundations of a liberal society and polity. Both at home and abroad, however, the new regime faced formidable opposition, and its struggle for survival propelled it in unanticipated directions. Some unforeseen turns, such as democracy and republicanism, became precedents for the future even if they soon aborted. Other developments, such as the Reign of Terror, seemed to nullify the original liberal values of 1789. The bloody struggles of the Revolution thus cast a shadow over this transformative event as they dramatized the brutal dilemma of means versus ends.

New *Chapter-Opening Outlines*

Each chapter now opens with a short outline to give students a sense of what's to come in each chapter.

New *Glossary and Key Terms*

Reviewers of the last edition requested this new feature. Glossary words are bolded in each chapter and compiled in the end-of-book glossary.

Cahiers and Elections   For the moment, however, patriot spokesmen stood far in advance of c[...] grass roots. The king had invited all citize[...] their local parishes to elect delegates to [...] toral assemblies and to draft grievan[...] (***cahiers***) setting forth their views. The gre[...] rural cahiers were highly traditional in t[...] plained only of particular local ills or hi[...] pressing confidence that the king would [...]

Anabaptists Individuals who, citing that the Bible nowhere mentions infant baptism, argued that the sacrament was effective only if the believer understood what was happening and that therefore adults ought to be rebaptized. Opponents argued that infant baptism was necessary so that a baby would not be denied salvation if it died young.

anarchists Radical activists who called for the abolition of the state, sometimes by violent means.

The Art

The ninth edition of *The Western Experience* continues the precedent of earlier editions, with more than four hundred full-color reproductions of paintings and photographs and over one hundred clearly focused maps.

The Maps

The maps in *The Western Experience* are already much admired by instructors. Each carries an explanatory caption that enhances the text coverage to help students tackle the content without sacrificing subtlety of interpretation or trying to escape the fact that history is complex. In the ninth edition, each caption has been further improved with a thought question.

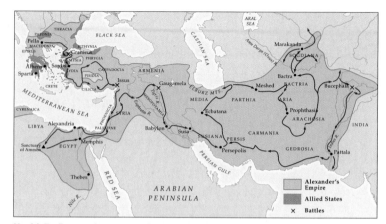

MAP 3.2 THE EMPIRE OF ALEXANDER THE GREAT AND THE ROUTE OF HIS CONQUESTS
Alexander formed the largest empire known down to his own time. He even conquered some territory across the Indus River in India. What were the two major Persian cities near the Persian Gulf?
◆ For an online version, go to www.mhhe.com/chambers9 > chapter 3 > book maps

---

QUESTIONS FOR FURTHER THOUGHT

1. The Greeks invented historical writing. In looking at the past, what are the most important questions a historian should ask?

2. The Greek city-states and their system of alliances gave way to the rising power of Macedonia. How might the Greek states have preserved their strength and political power?

Questions for Further Thought

To encourage students to move beyond rote learning of historical "facts" and to think broadly about history, the authors have added "Questions for Further Thought" at the end of each chapter. These are too broad to be exam questions; instead, they are meant to be questions that stimulate the students to think about history and social, political, and economic forces. Some are comparative, some require students to draw on knowledge of a previous chapter, some ask about the role of great leaders in politics, and some ask about how the less famous people living at the time perceived the events surrounding them.

More Heading Levels

We have given particular attention to adding more descriptive content guides, such as the consistent use of three levels of headings. We believe these will help students identify specific topics for purposes of study and review as well as give a clear outline of a chapter's argument.

Chronological Charts

Nearly every chapter employs charts and chronological tables that outline the unfolding of major events and social processes and serve as a convenient reference for students.

CHRONOLOGY
The Persian Wars
(All dates B.C.)

499, autumn	Greek cities of Ionia in Asia Minor revolt from Persian Empire.
498	Athens and Eretria (on island of Euboea) take part in burning Sardis in Persian Empire.
496	Persians besiege Miletus, the leading city in the revolt.
494	Fall of Miletus.
493	End of Ionian revolt.
492, spring	Persian expedition to northern Greece suffers heavy losses in storms.
490, mid-August	Battle of Marathon near Athens; Persians defeated.
486, November	Death of King Darius of Persia; accession of Xerxes.
484, spring–480, spring	Xerxes prepares for new invasion of Greece.
480, spring	Persian army sets out from Sardis.
480, late August	Battles of Thermopylae and Artemisium.
480, late September	Battle of Salamis.
479, early August	Battle of Plataea.

AVAILABLE FORMATS

To provide an alternative to the full-length hardcover edition, *The Western Experience* Ninth Edition, is available in two-volume and three-volume paperbound editions.

- Volume I includes chapters 1–17 and covers material through the eighteenth century.
- Volume II includes chapters 15–30 and covers material since the sixteenth century.
- Volume A includes chapters 1–12, Antiquity and the Middle Ages.
- Volume B includes chapters 11–21, The Early Modern Era.
- Volume C includes chapters 19–30, The Modern Era.

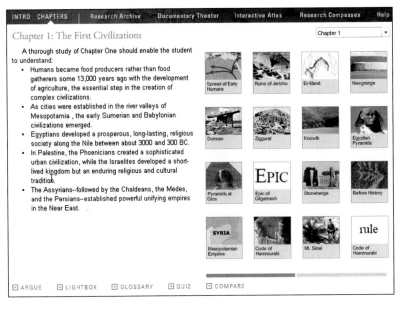

SUPPLEMENTARY INSTRUCTIONAL MATERIALS

McGraw-Hill offers instructors and students a wide variety of ancillary materials to accompany *The Western Experience*. Please contact your local McGraw-Hill representative for details concerning policies, prices, and availability.

For the Instructor

Instructor's Resource CD-ROM The Instructor's Resource CD-ROM (IRCD) contains several instructor tools on one easy CD-ROM. For lecture preparation, teachers will find an Instructor's Manual with PowerPoint samples by chapter. For quizzes and tests, the IRCD contains a test bank and *EZ Test*, McGraw-Hill's flexible and easy-to-use electronic testing program. Extras on the IRCD also include map images from the book as well as extra photographs and art images.

Online Learning Center for Instructors At www.mhhe.com/chambers9. At this home page for the text-specific website, instructors will find a series of online tools to meet a wide range of classroom needs. The Instructor's Manual, PowerPoint presentations, and blank maps can be downloaded by instructors, but are password protected to prevent tampering. Instructors can also create an interactive course syllabus using McGraw-Hill's *PageOut* (www.mhhe.com/pageout).

Overhead Transparency Acetates This expanded full-color transparency package includes all the maps and chronological charts in the text.

For the Student

McGraw-Hill's Primary Source Investigator (PSI) CD-ROM This CD-ROM, bound into each copy of *The Western Experience*, provides students with instant access to hundreds of world history documents, images, artifacts, audio recordings, and videos. PSI helps students practice the art of "doing history" on a real archive of historical sources. Students follow the three basic steps of *Ask, Research,* and *Present* to examine sources, take notes on them, and then save or print copies of the sources as evidence for their papers or presentations. After researching a particular theme, individual, or time period, students can use PSI's writing guide to walk them through the steps of developing a thesis, organizing their evidence, and supporting their conclusion.

More than just a history or writing tool, the PSI is also a student study tool that contains interactive maps, quiz questions, and an interactive glossary with audio pronunciation guide.

Student Study Guide/Workbook with Map Exercises, Volumes I and II Includes the following features for each chapter: chapter outlines, chronological diagrams, four kinds of exercises—map exercises, exercises in document analysis, exercises that reinforce the book's important overarching themes, exercises in matching important terms with significant individuals—and essay topics requiring analysis and speculation.

The Online Learning Center At www.mhhe.com/chambers9. The Online Learning Center is a fully interactive, book-specific website featuring numerous student study tools such as multiple-choice and true-false practice quizzes; interactive, drag-and-drop games about significant individuals and chronologies; key

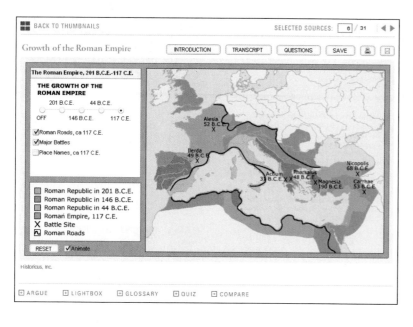

terms with correct identifications; an audio function to help students pronounce difficult terms; and drag-and-drop map exercises. Animated maps from the book are also available through the site. These maps carry a specific URL in their caption.

ACKNOWLEDGMENTS

Manuscript Reviewers, Ninth Edition

Robert Bast, University of Tennessee; Stephen Blumm, Montgomery County Community College; Nathan Brooks, New Mexico State University; Susan Carrafiello, Wright State University; Steven Fanning, University of Illinois at Chicago; Betsy Hertzler, Mesa Community College; Paul Hughes, Sussex County Community College; Mary Kelly, Franklin Pierce College; Paul Lockhart, Wright State University; Eileen Moore, University of Alabama at Birmingham; Penne Prigge, Rockingham Community College; William Roberts, Fairleigh Dickinson University; Steven Ross, Louisiana State University; Charles Sullivan, University of Dallas; Robert Thurston, Miami University.

Manuscript Reviewers, Eighth Edition

Tyler Blethen, West Carolina University; Owen Bradley, University of Tennessee; Dan Brown, Moorpark College; Richard Cole, Luther College; Vickie Cook, Pima Community College; Mary DeCredico, U.S. Naval Academy; Gunar Freibergs, Los Angeles Valley College; Ron Goldberg, Thomas Nelson Community College; Neil Heyman, San Diego State University; Elizabeth McCrank, Boston University; Edrene Stephens McKay, Northwest Arkansas Community College; George Monahan, Suf-

folk Community College; Fred Murphy, Western Kentucky University; Laura Pintar, Loyola University; Anne Quartararo, U.S. Naval Academy; Thomas Rowland, University of Wisconsin–Oshkosh; Charles Steen, University of New Mexico; Sig Sutterlin, Indian Hills Community College; John Tanner, Palomar College; Valentina Tikoff, DePaul University; Guangquin Xu, Northwest Arkansas Community College.

Manuscript Reviewers, Seventh Edition

Frank Baglione, Tallahassee Community College; Paul Goodwin, University of Connecticut; Robert Herzstein, University of South Carolina; Carla M. Joy, Red Rocks Community College; Kathleen Kamerick, University of Iowa; Carol Bresnahan Menning, University of Toledo; Eileen Moore, University of Alabama at Birmingham; Frederick Murphy, Western Kentucky University; Michael Myers, University of Notre Dame; Robert B. Patterson, University of South Carolina at Columbia; Peter Pierson, Santa Clara University; Alan Schaffer, Clemson University; Marc Schwarz, University of New Hampshire; Charles R. Sullivan, University of Dallas; Jack Thacker, Western Kentucky University; Bruce L. Venarde, University of Pittsburgh.

Manuscript Reviewers, Sixth Edition

S. Scott Bartchy, University of California, Los Angeles; Thomas Blomquist, Northern Illinois University; Nancy Ellenberger, U.S. Naval Academy; Steven Epstein, University of Colorado at Boulder; Laura Gellott, University of Wisconsin at Parkside; Drew Harrington, Western Kentucky University; Lisa Lane, Mira Costa College; William Matthews, S.U.N.Y. at Potsdam; Carol Bresnahan Menning, University of Toledo; Sandra Norman, Florida Atlantic University; Peter Pierson, Santa Clara University; Linda Piper, University of Georgia; Philip Racine, Wofford College; Eileen Soldwedel, Edmonds Community College; John Sweets, University of Kansas; Richard Wagner, Des Moines Area Community College.

Focus Group Reviewers from Spring 1992

Michael DeMichele, University of Scranton; Nancy Ellenberger, U.S. Naval Academy; Drew Harrington, Western Kentucky University; William Matthews, S.U.N.Y. at Potsdam.

We would like to thank Lyn Uhl, Monica Eckman, Angela Kao, and Emily Hatteberg of McGraw-Hill for their considerable efforts in bringing this edition to fruition.

THE WESTERN EXPERIENCE

Francois Dubois
THE MASSACRE OF ST. BARTHOLOMEW'S DAY
Although it makes no attempt to depict the massacre realistically, this painting by a Protestant does convey the horrors of religious war. As the victims are hanged, disemboweled, decapitated, tossed from windows, bludgeoned, shot, or drowned, their bodies and homes are looted. Dubois may have intended the figure dressed in widow's black and pointing at a pile of corpses near the river at the back to be a portrait of Catherine de Medici, who many thought inspired the massacre.
Musée Cantonal des Beaux-Arts, Lausanne

WAR AND CRISIS

RIVALRY AND WAR IN THE AGE OF PHILIP II • FROM UNBOUNDED WAR TO
INTERNATIONAL CRISIS • THE MILITARY REVOLUTION • REVOLUTION IN ENGLAND •
REVOLTS IN FRANCE AND SPAIN • POLITICAL CHANGE IN AN AGE OF CRISIS

In the wake of the rapid and bewildering changes of the early sixteenth century—the Reformation, the rises in population and prices, the overseas discoveries, and the dislocations caused by the activities of the new monarchs—Europe entered a period of fierce upheaval. So many radical alterations were taking place that conflict became inevitable. There were revolts against monarchs, often led by nobles who saw their power dwindling. The poor launched hopeless rebellions against their social superiors. And the two religious camps struggled relentlessly to destroy each other. From Scotland to Russia, the century following the Reformation, from about 1560 to 1660, was dominated by warfare; and the constant military activity had widespread effects on politics, economics, society, and thought. The fighting, in fact, helped bring to an end the long process

whereby Europe came to terms with the revolutions that had begun about 1500. As we will see, two distinct periods of ever more destructive warfare—the age of Philip II from the 1550s to the 1590s, and the age of the Thirty Years' War from the 1610s to the 1640s, with a decade of uneasy peace in between—led to a vast crisis of authority throughout Europe in the mid-1600s. From the struggles of that crisis there emerged fundamental economic, political, social, and religious changes, as troubled Europeans at last found ways to accept their altered circumstances. Interestingly, there were peasant revolts in Russia and China at the same time as those in Western Europe in the mid-seventeenth century, and they, too, reflected unease with state power, which was growing in Russia, but declining in China as the Ming Dynasty came to an end.

Thirty Years' War **1618–1648** ■

Reign of Gustavus Adolphus in Sweden **1611–1632** ■

Revolt of the Netherlands **1572–1648** ■

1562–1598 French Wars of Religion

1558–1603 Reign of Elizabeth I in England

1556–1598 Reign of Philip II in Spain

RIVALRY AND WAR IN THE AGE OF PHILIP II

The wars that plagued Europe from the 1560s to the 1650s involved many issues, but religion was the burning motivation, the one that inspired fanatical devotion and the most vicious hatred. A deep conviction that heresy was dangerous to society and hateful to God made Protestants and Catholics treat one another brutally. Even the dead were not spared: Corpses were sometimes mutilated to emphasize how dreadful their sins had been. These emotions, which shaped politics in this period, especially the decades dominated by Philip II, gave the fighting a brutality unprecedented in European history.

Philip II of Spain

During the second half of the sixteenth century, international warfare was ignited by the leader of the Catholics, Philip II of Spain (r. 1556–1598), the most powerful monarch in Europe. A stern defender of the Catholic faith, who is looked back on by Spaniards as a model of prudence, self-discipline, and devotion, he was also a tireless administrator, building up and supervising a vast and complex bureaucracy. It was needed, he felt, because of the far-spreading territories he ruled: the Iberian Peninsula, much of Italy, the Netherlands, and a huge overseas empire. Yet his main concern was to overcome the two enemies of his church, the Muslims and the Protestants.

Against the Muslims in the Mediterranean area, Philip's campaigns seemed to justify the financial strains they caused. In particular, his naval victory over the Ottomans at Lepanto, off the Greek coast, in 1571 made him a Christian hero at the same time that it re-

duced Muslim power. Although the Ottomans remained a considerable force in the eastern half of the Mediterranean, and indeed were able to besiege Vienna again in 1683, Philip was unchallenged in the west. He dominated the rich Italian peninsula; in 1580 he inherited the kingdom of Portugal; and his overseas wealth, passing through Seville, made this the fastest-growing city in Europe. The sixteenth century was the last age in which the Mediterranean was the heart of the European economy, but its prosperity was still the chief pillar of Philip's power.

Further north, Philip fared less well. He tried to prevent a Protestant, Henry IV, from inheriting the French crown and continued to back the losing side in France's civil wars even though Henry converted to Catholicism. Philip's policy toward England and the Netherlands was similarly ineffective. After the Protestant Queen Elizabeth I came to the English throne in 1558, Philip remained uneasily cordial toward her for about ten years. But relations deteriorated as England's sailors and explorers threatened Philip's wealthy New World possessions. Worse, in 1585 Elizabeth began to help the Protestant Dutch, who were rebelling against Spanish rule. Though their countries were smaller than Spain, the English and Dutch were able to inflict on Philip the two chief setbacks of his reign; and in the years after his death they were to wrest the leadership of Europe's economy away from the Mediterranean.

Elizabeth I of England

In a struggle with Spain, England may have seemed an unlikely victor: a relatively poor kingdom that had lost its continental possessions and for some time had played a secondary role in European affairs. Yet its people were united by such common bonds as the institution of Parliament and a commitment to the international Protes-

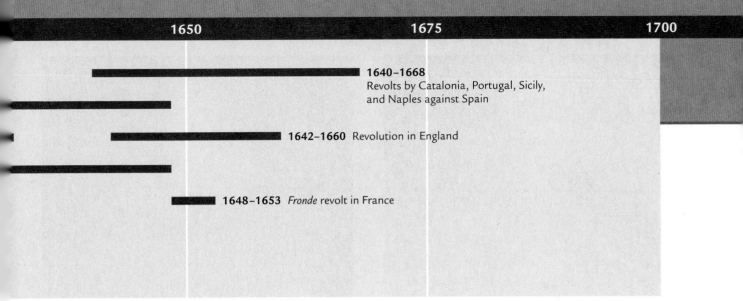

1640–1668
Revolts by Catalonia, Portugal, Sicily, and Naples against Spain

1642–1660 Revolution in England

1648–1653 *Fronde* revolt in France

tant cause that was carefully promoted by Queen Elizabeth I (r. 1558–1603).

Elizabeth is an appealing figure because she combined shrewd hardheadedness with a disarming appearance of frailty. Her qualities were many: her dedication to the task of government; her astute choice of advisers; her civilizing influence at court, where she encouraged elegant manners and the arts; her tolerance of religious dissent as long as it posed no political threat; and her ability to feel the mood of her people, to catch their spirit, to inspire their enthusiasm. Although social, legal, and economic practices usually subordinated women to men in this age, inheritance was respected; thus, a determined woman with a recognized claim to authority could win complete acceptance. Elizabeth was the most widely admired and most successful queen of her time, but she was by no means alone; female rulers also shaped the histories of France, Sweden, and the southern Netherlands in the sixteenth and seventeenth centuries.

Royal Policy Elizabeth could be indecisive, notably where the succession was concerned. Her refusal to marry caused serious uncertainties, and it was only the shrewd planning of her chief minister, Robert Cecil, that enabled the king of Scotland, James Stuart, to succeed her without incident in 1603. Similar dangers arose from her indecisive treatment of England's remaining Catholics. They hoped that Mary Queen of Scots, a Catholic, would inherit the throne; and since she was next in line, they were not above plotting against Elizabeth's life. Eventually, in 1587, Elizabeth had Mary executed and the plots died away. Despite her reluctance to take firm positions, Elizabeth showed great skill in balancing policy alternatives, and her adroit maneuvering assured her of her ministers' loyalty at all times. She also inspired the devotion of her subjects by traveling

throughout England to make public appearances; by delivering brilliant speeches (see "Queen Elizabeth's Armada Speech," p. 433); and by shaping her own image, even regulating how she was to be depicted in portraits. She thus retained her subjects' allegiance despite the profound social changes that were eroding traditional patterns of deference and order. England's nobility, for instance, no longer dominated the military and the government; nearly all Elizabeth's ministers were new in national life; and the House of Commons was beginning to exert more political influence within Parliament than the House of Lords. All groups in English society, however, shared a resentment of Spanish power, and Elizabeth cultivated this sentiment astutely as a patriotic and Protestant cause.

The Dutch Revolt

The same cause united the people living in the provinces in the Netherlands that Philip inherited from his father, the Emperor Charles V. Here his single-minded promotion of Catholicism and royal power provoked a fierce reaction that grew into a successful struggle for independence: the first major victory in Western Europe by subjects resisting royal authority.

Causes of Revolt The original focus of opposition was Philip's reorganization of the ecclesiastical structure so as to gain control over the country's Catholic Church, a change that deprived the aristocracy of important patronage. At the same time, the **billeting** of troops aroused the resentment of ordinary citizens. In this situation, the local nobles, led by William of Orange, warned of mass disorder, but Philip kept up the pressure: He put the Inquisition to work against the Calvinists, who had begun to appear in the Netherlands, and also summoned the Jesuits to combat the

William Segar (attrib.)
PORTRAIT OF ELIZABETH I, 1585
Elizabeth I was strongly aware of the power of propaganda, and she used it to foster a dazzling public image. Legends about her arose in literature. And in art she had herself portrayed in the most elaborate finery imaginable. Here, she is every inch the queen, with her magnificent dress, the trappings of monarchy, and the symbol of virginity, the ermine.
By courtesy of The Marquess of Salisbury

El Greco
THE DREAM OF PHILIP II, 1578
Characteristic of the mystical vision of El Greco is this portrayal of the devout, black-clad figure of Philip II. Kneeling alongside the doge of Venice and the pope, his allies in the victory of Lepanto over the Turks, Philip adores the blazing name of Jesus that is surrounded by angels in heaven, and he turns his back on the gaping mouth to hell.
Reproduced by courtesy of the Trustees, © The National Gallery, London (NG6260)

heretics. These moves were disastrous because they further undermined local autonomy and made the Protestants bitter enemies of the king.

Philip's aggressiveness provoked violence in 1566. Although the Protestants were still a tiny minority, they formed mobs in a number of cities, assaulted Catholics, and sacked churches. In response, Philip tightened the pressure, appointing as governor the ruthless duke of Alba, who used his Spanish troops to suppress opposition. Protestants were hanged in public, rebel groups were hunted down, and two nobles who had been guilty of nothing worse than demanding that Philip change his policy were executed.

Full-Scale Rebellion   Organized revolt broke out in 1572, when a small group of Dutch sailors flying the flag of William of Orange seized the fishing village of Brill, on the North Sea. The success of these "sea beggars," as the Spaniards called them, stimulated uprisings in towns throughout the Low Countries. The banner of William of Orange became the symbol of resistance, and under his leadership full-scale rebellion erupted. By 1576, when Philip's troops mutinied and rioted in Antwerp, sixteen of the seventeen provinces in the Netherlands had united behind William. The next

Queen Elizabeth's Armada Speech

Elizabeth's ability to move her subjects was exemplified by the speech she gave to her troops as they awaited the fight with the Spanish Armada. She understood that they might have doubts about a woman leading them in war, but she turned that issue to her own advantage in a stirring cry to battle that enhanced her popularity at the time and her legendary image thereafter.

"My loving People: We have been persuaded by some that are careful of our safety, to take heed how we commit ourselves to armed multitudes, for fear of treachery; but I assure you, I do not desire to live to distrust my faithful and loving people.

"Let tyrants fear; I have always so behaved myself, that, under God, I have placed my chiefest strength and safeguard in the loyal hearts and good will of my subjects, and therefore I am come amongst you, as you see, at this time, not for my recreation . . . but being resolved in the midst and heat of the battle, to live or die amongst you all, to lay down for my God, and for my kingdoms, and for my people, my honour and my blood, even in the dust.

"I know I have the body of a weak and feeble woman; but I have the heart and stomach of a king, and of a king of England too; and think foul scorn that . . . Spain, or any prince of Europe should dare to invade the borders of my realm; to which rather than any dishonour shall grow by me, I myself will take up arms, I myself will be your general, judge, and rewarder of every one of your virtues in the field. . . . By your concord in the camp, and your valour in the field, we shall shortly have a famous victory over those enemies of my God, of my kingdoms, and of my people."

Walter Scott (ed.), *A Collection of Scarce and Valuable Tracts, on the Most Interesting and Entertaining Subjects: But Chiefly Such as Relate to the History and Constitution of These Kingdoms,* Vol. 1, London, 1809, pp. 429–430.

Anonymous
Engraving of the Spaniards in Haarlem
This engraving was published to arouse horror at Spanish atrocities during the Dutch revolt. As the caption indicates, after the Spanish troops (on the right) captured the city of Haarlem, there was a great bloodbath (*ein gross bluit batt*). Blessed by priests, the Haarlemites were decapitated or hung, and then tossed in a river so that the city would be cleansed of them. The caption states that even women and children were not spared.
New York Public Library

Pieter Brueghel the Elder
THE MASSACRE OF THE INNOCENTS, **1565**
Probably to avoid trouble, Brueghel hid his critique of the Spanish rulers of the Netherlands in this supposed portrayal of a biblical event. It would have been clear to anyone who saw it, however, that this was a scene of Spanish cruelty toward the local inhabitants in the harsh days of winter, as soldiers tear babies from their mothers and kill them.
Erich Lessing/Art Resource, NY

year, however, Philip offered a compromise to the Catholic nobles, and the ten southern provinces returned to Spanish rule.

The United Provinces In 1579 the remaining seven provinces formed the independent United Provinces. Despite the assassination of William in 1584, they managed to resist Spain's army for decades, mainly because they could open dikes, flood their country, and thus drive the invaders back. Moreover, Philip was often diverted by other wars and, in any case, never placed total confidence in his commanders. The Calvinists formed the heart of the resistance; though still a minority, they had the most to lose, because they sought freedom for their religion as well as their country. William never showed strong religious commitments, but his son, Maurice of Nassau, a brilliant military commander who

won a series of victories in the 1590s, embraced Calvinism and helped make it the country's official religion. Unable to make any progress, the Spaniards agreed to a twelve-year truce in 1609, but they did not recognize the independence of the United Provinces until the Peace of Westphalia in 1648.

The Armada In 1588 Philip tried to end his troubles in northern Europe with one mighty blow. Furious that the English were interfering with his New World empire (their traders and raiders had been intruding into Spain's American colonies for decades) and that Elizabeth was helping Dutch Protestants, he sent a mammoth fleet—the Armada—to the Low Countries. Its task was to pick up a Spanish army, invade England, and thus undermine Protestant resistance. By this time, however, English mariners were among the best in the world, and their

MAP 15.1 THE NETHERLANDS, 1579–1609
The seventeen provinces making up the Netherlands, or the
Low Countries, were detached from the Holy Roman Empire
when Charles V abdicated in 1556. As the map indicates,
their subsequent division into two states was determined
not by the linguistic differences between French-speaking
people of the south and Dutch-speaking people of the north
but rather by geography. The great river systems at the
mouth of the Rhine eventually proved to be the barrier
beyond which the Spaniards could not penetrate. Notice the
shifting boundaries. Did the United Provinces gain more
between 1590 and 1648 than they lost after 1579?
◆ For an online version, go to www.mhhe.com/chambers9 >
chapter 15 > book maps

---

ships had greater maneuverability and firepower than
did the Spaniards'. After several skirmishes in the Channel, the English set fire to a few of their own vessels with
loaded cannons aboard and sent them drifting toward the
Spanish ships, anchored off Calais. The Spaniards had to
raise anchor in a hurry, and some of the fleet was lost.
The next day the remaining Spanish ships retreated up
the North Sea. The only way home was around Ireland;
and wind, storms, and the pursuing English ensured that
less than half the fleet returned safely to Spain. This
shattering reversal was comparable in scale and unex-
pectedness only to Xerxes' disaster at Salamis more than
two thousand years earlier. More than any other single
event, it doomed Philip's ambitions in England, the
Netherlands, and France and signaled a northward shift
in power in Europe.

Civil War in France

The other major power of Western Europe, France, was
rent apart by religious war in this period, but it too felt
the effects of the Armada's defeat. By the 1550s Calvinism was gaining strength among French peasants and
in the towns of the south and southwest, and its leaders had virtually created a small semi-independent
state. To meet this threat, a great noble family, the
Guises, assumed the leadership of the Catholics; in response, the Bourbons, another noble family, champi-
oned the Calvinists, about a twelfth of the population.
Their struggle split the country apart.

It was ominous that in 1559—the year that Henry II,
France's last strong king for a generation, died—the
Calvinists (known in France as Huguenots) organized
their first national synod, an indication of impressive
strength. During the next thirty years, the throne was
occupied by Henry's three ineffectual sons. The power
behind the crown was Henry's widow, Catherine de
Medici (see "The Kings of France in the Sixteenth Century," p. 436), who tried desperately to preserve royal
authority. But she was often helpless because the religious conflict intensified the factional struggle for
power between the Guises and the Bourbons, both of
whom were closely related to the monarchy and hoped
one day to inherit the throne.

The Wars Fighting started in 1562 and lasted for
thirty-six years, interrupted only by short-lived peace
agreements. Catherine switched sides whenever one
party became too powerful; and she may have approved
the notorious massacre of St. Bartholomew's Day—
August 24, 1572—which started in Paris, spread through
France, and destroyed the Huguenots' leadership.
Henry of Navarre, a Bourbon, was the only major figure
who escaped. When Catherine switched sides again and
made peace with the Huguenots in 1576, the Guises
formed the Catholic League, which for several years
dominated the eastern half of the country. In 1584 the
league allied with Spain's Philip II to attack heresy in
France and deny the Bourbon Henry's legal right to inherit the throne.

The defeat of the Armada in 1588 proved to be the
turning point in the French civil wars, for Spain could
not continue helping the duke of Guise, who was soon
assassinated, and within a few months Henry of
Navarre inherited the throne as Henry IV (r.
1589–1610). He had few advantages as he began to reassert royal authority, because the Huguenots and
Catholics ran almost independent governments in large
sections of France. In addition, the royal administration
was in a sorry state because the crown's oldest rivals,
the great nobles, could now resist all outside interference in their domains.

Anonymous
THE ARMADA
This depiction suggests the sheer splendor of the scene as Philip II's fleet sailed through the Channel on its way to invading England. The opposing ships were never this close, but the colorful flags (red cross English, yellow cross Spanish) and the elaborate coats of arms must have been dazzling. The firing cannon and the sinking ship remind us that, amidst the display, there was also death and destruction.
National Maritime Museum, Greenwich, London

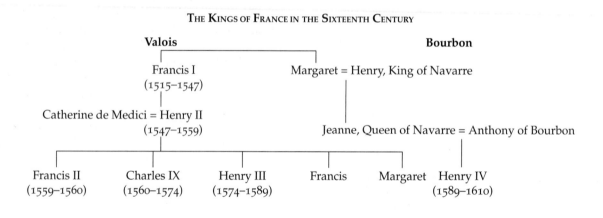

THE KINGS OF FRANCE IN THE SIXTEENTH CENTURY

Valois　　　　　　　　　　　　　　　**Bourbon**

Francis I　　　　　　　Margaret = Henry, King of Navarre
(1515–1547)

Catherine de Medici = Henry II
(1547–1559)　　　　　　　　　Jeanne, Queen of Navarre = Anthony of Bourbon

Francis II　　Charles IX　　Henry III　　Francis　　Margaret　Henry IV
(1559–1560)　(1560–1574)　(1574–1589)　　　　　　　　　(1589–1610)

Peace Restored　Yet largely because of the assassination of the duke of Guise, Henry IV was able to restore order. The duke had been a forceful leader and a serious contender for the throne. His replacement was a Spanish candidate for the crown who had little chance of success. The distaste for a possible foreign ruler, combined with war weariness, destroyed much of the support for the Catholic League, which finally collapsed as a result of revolts against it in eastern France in the 1590s. These up-risings, founded on a demand for peace, increased in frequency and intensity after Henry IV renounced Protestantism in 1593 in order to win acceptance by his Catholic subjects. The following year Henry had himself officially crowned, and all of France rallied to the king as he beat back a Spanish invasion—Spain's final, rather weak, attempt to put its own candidate on the throne.

When Spain finally withdrew and signed a peace treaty in 1598, the fighting came to an end. To complete

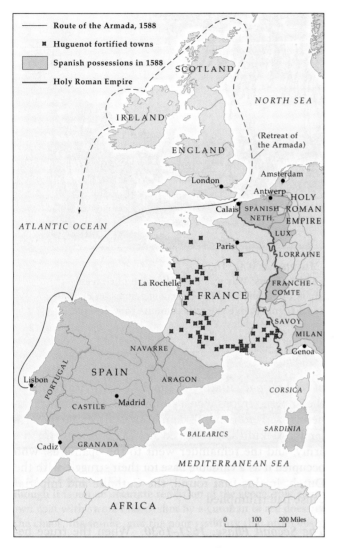

**MAP 15.2 CATHOLIC AND PROTESTANT POWERS IN THE LATE
SIXTEENTH CENTURY**
The heart of the Catholic cause in the wars of religion was
the Spain of Philip II. Spanish territories surrounded France
and provided the route to the Netherlands, where the
Protestant Dutch had rebelled against the Spaniards (see map
15.1). The Armada was launched to help that cause by
crushing the ally of the Dutch, Protestant England. In the
meantime, the surrounded French had problems of their own
with the Huguenots, who protected their Protestantism in a
network of fortified towns. Why did the Armada follow the
route shown on the map?
◆ For an online version, go to www.mhhe.com/chambers9 >
chapter 15 > book maps

the reconciliation, Henry issued (also in 1598) the Edict
of Nantes, which granted limited toleration to the
Huguenots. Although it did not create complete religious liberty, the edict made Calvinist worship legal,
protected the rights of the minority, and opened public
office to Huguenots.

FROM UNBOUNDED WAR TO INTERNATIONAL CRISIS

During the half century after Philip II's death, warfare
spread throughout Europe. There was a brief lull in the
early 1600s, but then the slaughter and the devastations
began to multiply. For a while it seemed that nothing
could bring the fighting to an end, and a feeling of irre-
solvable crisis descended on international affairs. Not
until an entirely new form of peacemaking was devised,
in the 1640s, was the fighting brought under control.

The Thirty Years' War

The new arena in which the warfare erupted was the
Holy Roman Empire. Here religious hatreds were especially disruptive because the empire lacked a central
authority and unifying institutions. Small-scale fighting broke out repeatedly after the 1550s, always inspired by religion. Although elsewhere the first years of
the seventeenth century were a time of relative peace
that seemed to signal a decline of conflict over faith, in
the empire the stage was being set for the bloodiest of
all the wars fired by religion.

Known as the Thirty Years' War, this ferocious
struggle began in the Kingdom of Bohemia in 1618 and
continued until 1648. The principal battleground, the
empire, was ravaged by the fighting, which eventually
involved every major ruler in Europe. At first it was a
renewed struggle between local Protestants and
Catholics, but eventually it became a fight among political rivals who were eager to take advantage of the
fragmentation of the empire to advance their own ambitions. As the devastation spread, international relations seemed to be sinking into total chaos; but the
chief victims were the Germans, who, like the Italians
in the sixteenth century, found themselves at the
mercy of well-organized states that used another country as a place to settle their quarrels.

The First Phase, 1618–1621   The immediate problem
was typical of the situation in the empire. In 1609 the
Habsburg Emperor Rudolf II promised toleration for
Protestants in Bohemia. When his cousin Ferdinand, a
pious Catholic, succeeded to the Bohemian throne in
1617, he refused to honor Rudolf's promise, and the Bo-
hemians rebelled in 1618. They declared Ferdinand de-
posed, replacing him with the leading Calvinist of the
empire, Frederick II of the Palatinate. Frederick accepted the crown, an act of defiance whose only possible outcome was war.

The first decade or so of the war was a time of victories for the Catholics. When Ferdinand became emperor (r. 1619–1637), the powerful Catholic Maximilian

Gerard Terborch
THE PEACE OF WESTPHALIA, **1648**
The artist was an eyewitness to this scene, the formal signing of peace between the United Provinces and Spain in Münster on May 15, 1648. The two leaders of the Spanish delegation on the right put their hands on a Bible as they swear to uphold the terms of the treaty, and the Dutch on the left all raise their hands as they declare "So help me God." Terborch himself, dressed in brown, is looking out at the viewer on the far left.
Reproduced by courtesy of the Trustees, © The National Gallery, London (NG896)

The Fourth Phase, 1632–1648   Gustavus' success opened the final phase of the war, as political ambitions—the quest of the empire's princes for independence and the struggle between the Habsburgs and their enemies—almost completely replaced religious aims. The Protestant princes began to raise new armies, and by 1635 Ferdinand had to make peace with them. In return for their promise of assistance in driving out the Swedes, Ferdinand agreed to suspend the Edict of Restitution and to grant amnesty to all but Frederick of the Palatinate and a few Bohemian rebels. Ferdinand was renouncing most of his ambitions, and it seemed that peace might return at last.

But the French could not let matters rest. In 1635 they finally declared war on Ferdinand. For the next thirteen years, the French and Swedes rained unmitigated disaster on Germany. Peace negotiations began in 1641, but not until 1648 did the combatants sign the treaties of Westphalia. Even thereafter the war between France and Spain, pursued mainly in the Spanish Netherlands, continued for another eleven years; and hostilities around the Baltic among Sweden, Denmark, Poland, and Russia, which had started in 1611, did not end until 1661.

The Effect of War   The wars and their effects (such as the diseases spread by armies) killed off more than a third of Germany's population. The conflict caused serious economic dislocation because a number of princes—

already in serious financial straits—sharply debased their coinage. Their actions worsened the continent-wide trade depression that had begun around 1620 and had brought the great sixteenth-century boom to an end, causing the first drop in prices since 1500. Few contemporaries perceived the connection between war and economic trouble, but nobody could ignore the drain on men and resources, the crisis in international relations, or the widespread destruction caused by the conflict.

The Peace of Westphalia

By the 1630s it was becoming apparent that the fighting was getting out of hand and that it would not be easy to bring the conflicts to an end. There had never been such widespread or devastating warfare, and many diplomats felt that the settlement had to be of far greater scope than any negotiated before. And they were right. When at last the treaties were signed in 1648, after seven years of negotiation in the German province of Westphalia, a landmark in international relations was passed—remarkable not only because it brought an anarchic situation under control but because it created a new system for dealing with wars.

The most important innovation was the gathering at the peace conference of all the participants in the Thirty Years' War, rather than the usual practice of bringing only two or three belligerents together. The presence of delegations from 109 interested parties

MAP 15.3 TERRITORIAL CHANGES, 1648–1661
**This map shows the territorial changes that took place after the Thirty Years' War. The treaties of Westphalia (1648)
and the Pyrenees (1659) arranged the principal transfers, but the settlements in the Baltic were not confirmed until
the treaties of Copenhagen, Oliva (both 1660), and Kardis (1661). Who were the main winners and losers in the
territorial changes of this period?**
◆ For an online version, go to www.mhhe.com/chambers9 > chapter 15 > book maps

made possible, for the first time in European history, a
series of all-embracing treaties that dealt with nearly
every major international issue at one stroke. Visible at
the meetings was the emergence of a state system.
These independent states recognized that they were
creating a mechanism for controlling their relations
with one another. Although some fighting continued,
the Peace of Westphalia in 1648 became the first comprehensive rearrangement of the map of Europe in
modern times.

Peace Terms   The principal beneficiaries were France
and Sweden, the chief aggressors during the last decade
of the war. France gained the provinces of Alsace and
Lorraine, and Sweden obtained extensive territories in
the Holy Roman Empire. The main loser was the
House of Habsburg, since both the United Provinces
and the Swiss Confederation were recognized as independent states, and the German princes, who agreed
not to join an alliance against the emperor, were otherwise given almost complete independence.

The princes' autonomy was formally established in 1657, when they elected as emperor Leopold I, the head of the House of Habsburg, in return for two promises. First, Leopold would give no help to his cousins, the rulers of Spain; and second, the empire would be a state of princes, in which each ruler would be free from imperial interference. This freedom permitted the rise of Brandenburg-Prussia and the growth of absolutism—the belief that the political authority of the ruler was unlimited—within the major principalities. Moreover, the Habsburgs' capitulation prepared the way for their reorientation toward the east along the Danube River—the beginnings of the Austro-Hungarian Empire.

The Effects of Westphalia   For more than a century, the settlement reached at Westphalia was regarded as the basis for all international negotiations. Even major new accords, such as the one that ended yet another series of wars in 1713, were seen mainly as adjustments of the decisions of 1648. In practice, of course, multinational conferences were no more effective than brief, limited negotiations in reducing tensions among states. Wars continued to break out, and armies grew in size and skill. But diplomats did believe that international affairs were under better control and that the chaos of the Thirty Years' War had been replaced by something more stable and more clearly defined.

This confidence was reinforced as it became clear after 1648 that armies were trying to improve discipline and avoid the excesses of the previous thirty years. As religious passions waned, combat became less vicious and the treatment of civilians became more orderly. On battlefields, better discipline reduced the casualty rate from one death per three soldiers in the 1630s to one death in seven, or even one in twenty, during the early 1700s. The aims of war also changed significantly.

Changed International Relations   The most obvious differences after the Peace of Westphalia were that France replaced Spain as the continent's dominant power and that northern countries—especially England and the Netherlands, where growth in population and in commerce resumed more quickly than elsewhere—took over Europe's economic leadership. But behind this outward shift a more fundamental transformation was taking place. What had become apparent in the later stages of the Thirty Years' War was that Europe's states were prepared to fight only for economic, territorial, or political advantages. Dynastic aims were still important, but supranational goals like religious causes could no longer determine a state's foreign policy.

The Thirty Years' War was the last major international conflict in Europe in which two religious camps organized their forces as blocs. After 1648 such connections gave way to purely national interests; it is no surprise that the papacy denounced the peace vehemently. For this shift marked the decisive stage of a process that had been under way since the Late Middle Ages: the emergence of the state as the basic unit and object of loyalty in Western civilization. That it had taken a major crisis, a descent into international anarchy, to bring about so momentous a change is an indication of how profoundly the upheavals of the mid-seventeenth century, this age of crisis, affected European history.

THE MILITARY REVOLUTION

The constant warfare of the sixteenth and seventeenth centuries brought about dramatic changes in the ways that battles were fought and armies were organized.

Weapons and Tactics

The Use of Gunpowder   Though it had been known since the 1330s, gunpowder became central to warfare only around 1500. The result was the creation of a new type of industry, cannon and gun manufacture, and also a transformation of tactics. Individual castles could no longer be defended against explosives; even towns had to build heavy and elaborate fortifications if they were to resist the new firepower. Sieges became expensive, complex operations whose purpose was to bring explosives right up to a town wall so that it could be blown up. This process required an intricate system of trenches, because walls were built in star shapes so as to multiply angles of fire and make any approach dangerous. Although they became increasingly costly, sieges remained essential to the strategy of warfare until the eighteenth century.

New Tactics   In open battles, the effects of gunpowder were equally expensive. The new tactics that appeared around 1500, perfected by the Spaniards, relied on massed ranks of infantry, organized in huge squares, that made the traditional cavalry charge obsolete. Interspersed with the gunners were soldiers carrying pikes. They fended off horses or opposing infantry while the men with guns tried to mow the enemy down. The squares with the best discipline usually won, and for more than a century after the reign of Ferdinand of Aragon, the Spaniards had the best army in Europe. Each square had about three thousand troops, and to maintain enough squares to fight all of Spain's battles required an army numbering approximately forty thousand. The cost of keeping that many men clothed, fed, and housed, let alone equipped and paid, was enormous. But worse was to come: New tactics emerged in the early seventeenth century that required even more soldiers.

Anonymous
WAFFENHANDLUNG, ENGRAVING AFTER JACQUES DE GHEYN
The expansion of armies and the professionalization of war in the seventeenth century were reflected in the founding of military academies and in the growing acceptance of the notion that warfare was a science. There was now a market for published manuals, especially if they had illustrations like this one, which shows how a pikeman was supposed to crouch and hold his weapons (stabilizing his pike against his foot) when facing a cavalry charge.
Deutsches Historisches Museum, Berlin, Germany

Since nobody could outdo the Spaniards at their own methods, a different approach was developed by their rivals. The first advance was made by Maurice of Nassau, in the Dutch revolt against Spain. He relied not on sheer weight and power but on flexibility and mobility. Then Sweden's Gustavus Adolphus, one of the geniuses of the history of warfare, found a way to achieve mobility on the field without losing power. His main invention was the salvo: Instead of having his musketeers fire one row at a time, like the Spaniards, he had them all fire at once. What he lost in continuity of shot he gained in a fearsome blast that, if properly timed, could shatter enemy ranks. Huge, slow-moving squares were simply no match for smaller, faster units that riddled them with well-coordinated salvos.

The Organization and Support of Armies

These tactical changes brought about steady increases in the size of armies, because the more units there were, the better they could be placed on the battlefield. Although the Spanish army hardly grew between 1560 and 1640, remaining at 40,000 to 60,000 men, the Swedes had 150,000 by 1632; and at the end of the century, Louis XIV considered a force of 400,000 essential to maintain his dominant position in Europe.

This growth had far-reaching consequences. One was the need for **conscription,** which Gustavus introduced in the late 1620s. At least half his army consisted of his own subjects, who were easier to control than foreign mercenaries. Because it also made sense not to disband such huge forces each autumn, when the campaigning season ended, most armies were kept permanently ready. To strengthen discipline, new mechanisms were developed: drilling, combat training, uniforms, and the various officer ranks we still have. And the need to maintain so many soldiers the year round caused a rapid expansion of supporting administrative personnel. Taxation mushroomed. All levels of society felt the impact, but especially the lower classes, who paid the bulk of the taxes and provided most of the recruits.

The Life of the Soldier

Some soldiers genuinely wanted to join up. They had heard stories of adventure, booty, and comradeship, and they were tempted by free food and clothing. But many "volunteers" did not want to go, for they had also heard of the hardship and danger. Unfortunately for them, recruiting officers had quotas, and villages had to provide the numbers. Community pressure, bribery, enlistment of drunken men, and even outright kidnapping helped fill the ranks.

Joining an army did not necessarily mean cutting oneself off from friends or family. Men from a particular area enlisted together and, in some cases, wives and even children came along. There were dozens of jobs to do aside from fighting, because soldiers needed cooks, launderers, peddlers, and other tradespeople. An army in the field often needed five people for every soldier. Few barracks were built, and therefore, unless they were on the march or out in the open on a battlefield, troops were housed (or billeted) with ordinary citizens. Since soldiers almost never received their wages on time—delays could be as long as a year or more—they rarely could pay for their food and housing. Local civilians, therefore, had to supply their needs or risk the thievery that was universal. It was no wonder that the approach of an army was a terrifying event.

Discomforts of Military Life Military life was not easy. Soldiers suffered constant discomfort. A garrison might be able to settle into a town in reasonable conditions for a long stretch, but if it was besieged, it became hungry, fearful, and vulnerable. Days spent on the march could be grim, exhausting, and uncertain; even in camps soldiers were often filthy and wet. Real danger

Sebastian Vrancx
A Military Camp
**Vrancx was himself a soldier, and the many military scenes he painted during the Thirty Years' War give us a
sense of the life of the soldier during the long months when there were no campaigns or battles. Conditions could
be grim, but there were many hours during which a soldier could simply nap, chat, or play dice.**
Hamburg/Hamburger Kunsthalle/The Bridgeman Art Library

was not common, though it was intense during battles
and occasionally during sieges. Even a simple wound
could be fatal, because medical care was generally appalling. Despite traditional recreations—drink, gam-
bling, and the brawls common among soldiers—the
attractions of army service were limited; most military
men had few regrets when they returned to civilian life.

REVOLUTION IN ENGLAND

In the 1640s and 1650s the growing burdens of war and
taxation, and the mounting assertiveness of governments, sparked upheavals throughout Europe that were
the equivalent in domestic politics of the crisis in international relations. In country after country, people
rose up in vain attempts to restore the individual and
regional autonomies that were being eroded by power-

ful central governments. Only in England, however, did
the revolt become a revolution—an attempt to overturn the social and political system and create a new
structure for society.

Pressures for Change

The Gentry The central figures in the drama were the
gentry, a social group immediately below the nobles at
the head of society. They ranged from people considered great in a parish or other small locality to courtiers
considered great throughout the land. Although in Elizabeth's reign there were never more than sixty nobles,
the gentry numbered close to twenty thousand. Most
of the gentry were doing well economically, profiting
from agricultural holdings and crown offices. A number also became involved in industrial activity, and
hundreds invested in new overseas trading and colonial

ventures. The gentry's participation in commerce made them unique among the landed classes of Europe, whose members were traditionally contemptuous of business affairs, and it testified to the enterprise and vigor of England's social leaders. Long important in local administration, they flocked to the House of Commons to express their views on public matters. Their ambitions eventually posed a serious threat to the monarchy, especially when linked with the effects of rapid economic change.

Economic Advance   In Elizabeth's reign, thanks to a general boom in trade, England's merchants, aided by leading courtiers, had begun to transform the country's economy. They opened commercial links throughout Europe and parts of Asia and promoted significant industrial development at home. Mining and manufacture developed rapidly, and shipbuilding became a major industry. The production of coal increased fourteen-fold between 1540 and 1680, creating fortunes and an expertise in industrial techniques that took England far ahead of its neighbors.

The economic vigor and growth that ensued gave the classes that benefited most—gentry and merchants—a cohesion and a sense of purpose that made it dangerous to oppose them when they felt their rights infringed. They were coming to see themselves as leaders of the nation, almost alongside the nobility. They wanted respect for their wishes, and they bitterly resented the economic interference and political high-handedness of Elizabeth's successors.

The Puritans   Heightening this unease was the sympathy that many of the gentry felt toward a small but vociferous group of religious reformers, the **Puritans.** Puritans believed that the Protestant Anglican Church established by Elizabeth was still too close to Roman Catholicism, and they wanted further reductions in ritual and hierarchy. Elizabeth refused, and although she tried to avoid a confrontation, in the last years of her reign she had to silence the most outspoken of her critics. As a result, the Puritans became a disgruntled minority. By the 1630s, when the government tried to repress religious dissent more vigorously, many people in England, non-Puritan as well as Puritan, felt that the monarchy was leading the country astray and was ignoring the wishes of its subjects. Leading parliamentarians in particular soon came to believe that major changes were needed to restore good government in England.

Parliament and the Law

The place where the gentry made their views known was Parliament, the nation's supreme legislative body.

Three-quarters of the House of Commons consisted of gentry. They were better educated than ever before, and nearly half of them had legal training. Since the Commons had to approve all taxation, the gentry had the leverage to pursue their grievances.

The monarchy was still the dominant force in the country when Elizabeth died in 1603, but Parliament's demand to be heard was gathering momentum. Although the queen had been careful with money, in the last twenty years of her reign her resources had been overtaxed by war with Spain and an economic depression. Thus, she bequeathed to her successor, Scotland's James Stuart, a huge debt—£400,000, the equal of a year's royal revenue; his struggle to pay it off gave the Commons the means to seek changes in royal policy.

James I's Difficulties   Trouble began during the reign of James I (r. 1603–1625), who had a far more exalted view of his own powers than Elizabeth and who did not hesitate to tell his subjects that he considered his authority almost unlimited. In response, gentry opposed to royal policies dominated parliamentary proceedings, and they engaged in a running battle with the king. They blocked the union of England with Scotland that James sought. They drew up an "Apology" explaining his mistakes and his ignorance, as a Scotsman, of English traditions. They forced two of his ministers to resign in disgrace. And they wrung repeated concessions from him, including the unprecedented right for Parliament to discuss foreign policy.

Conflict over the Law   The Commons used the law to justify their resistance to royal power. The basic legal system of the country was the common law—justice administered on the basis of precedents and parliamentary statutes and relying on the opinions of juries. This system stood in contrast to Roman law, prevalent on the Continent, where royal edicts could make law and decisions were reached by judges without juries. Such practices existed in England only in a few royal courts of law, such as Star Chamber, which, because it was directly under the crown, came to be seen as an instrument of repression.

The common lawyers, whose leaders were also prominent in the Commons, resented the growing business of the royal courts and attacked them in Parliament. Both James and his successor were accused of pressuring judges, particularly after they won a series of famous cases involving a subject's right to criticize the monarch. Thus, the crown could be portrayed as disregarding not only the desires of the people but the law itself. The king still had broad powers, but when he exercised them contrary to Parliament's wishes, his actions seemed to many to be taking on the appearance of tyranny.

OLIVER CROMWELL'S AIMS

When Parliament in late 1656 offered to make Oliver Cromwell the king of England as a way of restoring political stability, he hesitated before replying. When he finally came to Parliament with his response on April 13, 1657, he turned down the offer of a crown and explained in a long speech—from which a passage follows—why he felt it would be wrong to reestablish a monarchy in England.

"I do think you ought to attend to the settling of the peace and liberties of this Nation. Otherwise the Nation will fall in pieces. And in that, so far as I can, I am ready to serve not as a King, but as a Constable. For truly I have, before God, often thought that I could not tell what my business was, save comparing myself to a good Constable set to keep the peace of the parish. And truly this hath been my content and satisfaction in the troubles I have undergone . . . I was a person who, from my first employment, was suddenly lifted up from lesser trusts to greater. . . . The Providence of God hath laid aside this Title of King; and that not by sudden humor, but by issue of ten or twelve years Civil War, wherein much blood hath been shed. I will not dispute the justice of it when it was done. But God in His severity hath eradicated a whole Family, and thrust them out of the land. And God hath seemed providential not only in striking at the family but at the Name [of king]. It is blotted out. God blasted the very Title. I will not seek to set up that which Providence hath destroyed, and laid in the dust: I would not build Jericho again."

From Thomas Carlyle (ed.), *Oliver Cromwell's Letters and Speeches*, Vol. 3, London, 1908, pp. 230, 231, and 235.

years of his life he tried desperately to lay down a new constitutional structure for his government.

Cromwell was driven by noble aspirations, but in the end he had to rule by military dictatorship. From 1653 on he was called lord protector and ruled through eleven major generals, each responsible for a different district of England and supported by a tax on the estates of royalists. To quell dissent, he banned newspapers; to prevent disorder, he took such measures as enlisting innkeepers as government spies. Cromwell was always a reluctant revolutionary; he hated power and sought only limited ends. Some revolutionaries, like Lenin, have a good idea of where they would like to be carried by events; others, like Cromwell, move painfully, hesitantly, and uncertainly to the extremes they finally reach. It was because he sought England's benefit so urgently and because he considered the nation too precious to abandon to irreligion or tyranny that Cromwell remained determinedly in command to the end of his life.

The End of the Revolution Gradually, more traditional political forms reappeared. The Parliament of 1656 offered Cromwell the crown, and, though he refused, he took the title of "His Highness" and ensured that the succession would go to his son. Cromwell was monarch in all but name, yet only his presence ensured stability (see "Oliver Cromwell's Aims," above). After he died, his quiet, retiring son Richard proved no match for the scheming generals of the army, who created political turmoil. To bring an end to the uncertainty, General George Monck, the commander of a well-disciplined force in Scotland, marched south in 1660, assumed control, and invited the son of Charles I, Charles II, to return from exile and restore the monarchy.

Results of the Revolution Only the actions taken during the first months of the Long Parliament—the abolition of royal courts, the prohibition of taxation without parliamentary consent, and the establishment of the writ of habeas corpus—persisted beyond the revolution. Otherwise, everything seemed much the same as before: Bishops and lords were reinstated, religious dissent was again repressed, and Parliament was called and dissolved by the monarch. But the tone and balance of political relations had changed for good.

Henceforth, the gentry could no longer be denied a decisive voice in politics. In essence, this had been their revolution, and they had succeeded. When in the 1680s a king again tried to impose his wishes on the country without reference to Parliament, there was no need for another major upheaval. A quiet, bloodless coup reaffirmed the new role of the gentry and Parliament. The crisis of authority that had arisen from a long period of growing unease and open conflict had been resolved, and the English could settle into a system of rule that with only gradual modification remained in force for some two centuries.

Anonymous
The Seine from the Pont Neuf, CA. 1635
Henry IV of France, celebrated in the equestrian statue overlooking the Seine that stands in Paris to this day, saw the physical reshaping of his capital as part of the effort to restore order after decades of civil war. He laid out the first squares in any European city, and under the shadow of his palace, the Louvre, he built the Pont Neuf (on the right)—the first open bridge (without houses on it) across the Seine.
Giraudon/Art Resource, NY

REVOLTS IN FRANCE AND SPAIN

The fact that political upheaval took place not only in England but in much of Europe in the 1640s and 1650s is the main reason that historians have come to speak of a "general crisis" during this period. Political institutions and political authority were being challenged in many countries, and although only England went through a revolution, the disruptions and conflicts were also significant in the two other major states of the age, France and Spain.

The France of Henry IV

In the 1590s Henry IV resumed the strengthening of royal power, which had been interrupted by the civil wars that had begun in the 1560s. He mollified the traditional landed aristocracy, known as the nobility of the sword, with places on his Council of Affairs and with large financial settlements. The principal bureaucrats, known as the nobility of the robe, controlled the country's administration, and Henry made sure to turn their interests to his benefit. Because all crown offices had to be bought, he used the system both to raise revenues and to guarantee the loyalty of the bureaucrats. He not only accelerated the sales of offices but also invented a new device, an annual fee known as the *paulette*, which ensured that an officeholder's job would remain in his family when he died. This increased royal profits and also reduced the flow of newcomers, thus strengthening the commitment of existing officeholders to the crown.

By 1610 Henry had imposed his will throughout France, and he was secure enough to plan an invasion of the Holy Roman Empire. Although he was assassinated before he could join his army, and the invasion was called off, his heritage, especially in economic affairs, long outlived him. France's rich agriculture may have had one unfortunate effect—successful merchants abandoned commerce as soon as they could afford to move to the country and buy a title of nobility (and thus gain exemption from taxes)—but it did ensure a solid basis for the French economy. Indeed, agriculture suffered little during the civil wars, though the violence and the rising taxes did cause uprisings of peasants (the main victims of the tax system) almost every year from the 1590s to the 1670s.

Mercantilism   By restoring political stability, Henry ended the worst economic disruptions, but his main legacy was the notion that his increasingly powerful government was responsible for the health of the country's economy. This view was justified by a theory

RICHELIEU ON DIPLOMACY

The following passages are taken from a collection of the writings of Cardinal Richelieu that was put together after his death and published in 1688 under the title Political Testament. *The book is presented as a work of advice to the king and summarizes what Richelieu learned of politics and diplomacy as one of Europe's leading statesmen during the Thirty Years' War.*

"One cannot imagine how many advantages States gain from continued negotiations, if conducted wisely, unless one has experienced it oneself. I admit I did not realize this truth for five or six years after first being employed in the management of policy. But I am now so sure of it that I say boldly that to negotiate everywhere without cease, openly and secretly, even though one makes no immediate gains and future gains seem unlikely, is absolutely necessary for the good of the State. . . . He who negotiates all the time will find at last the right moment to achieve his aims, and even if he does not find it, at least it is true that he can lose nothing, and that through his negotiations he knows what is happening in the world, which is of no small consequence for the good of the State. . . . Important negotia-tions must not be interrupted for a moment. . . . One must not be disheartened by an unfortunate turn of events, because sometimes it happens that what is undertaken with good reason is achieved with little good fortune. . . . It is difficult to fight often and always win. . . . It is often because negotiations are so innocent that one can gain great advantages from them without ever faring badly. . . . In matters of State one must find an advantage in everything; that which can be useful must never be neglected."

From Louis Andrè (ed.), *Testament Politique* (Editions Robert Laffont, 1947), pp. 347–348 and 352; translated by T. K. Rabb.

developed mainly in France: **mercantilism,** which became an essential ingredient of absolutism. Mercantilism was more a set of attitudes than a systematic economic theory. Its basic premise—an erroneous one—was that the world contained a fixed amount of wealth and that each nation could enrich itself only at the expense of others. To some thinkers, this theory meant hoarding bullion (gold and silver); to others, it required a favorable balance of trade—more exports than imports. All mercantilists, however, agreed that state regulation of economic affairs was necessary for the welfare of a country. Only a strong, centralized government could encourage native industries, control production, set quality standards, allocate resources, establish tariffs, and take other measures to promote prosperity and improve trade. Thus, mercantilism was as much about politics as economics and fit perfectly with Henry's restoration of royal power. In line with their advocacy of activist policies, the mercantilists also approved of war. Even economic advance was linked to warfare in this violent age.

Louis XIII

Unrest reappeared when Henry's death left the throne to his nine-year-old son, Louis XIII (r. 1610–1643). The widowed queen, Marie de Medici, served as regent and soon faced revolts by Calvinists and disgruntled nobles. In the face of these troubles, Marie summoned the Es-tates General in 1614. This was their last meeting for 175 years, until the eve of the French Revolution; and the weakness they displayed, as various groups within the Estates fought one another over plans for political reform, demonstrated that the monarchy was the only institution that could unite the nation. The session revealed the impotence of those who opposed royal policies, and Marie brought criticism to an end by declaring her son to be of age and the regency dissolved. In this absolutist state, further protest could be defined as treason.

Richelieu   For a decade, the monarchy lacked energetic direction; but in 1624, one of Marie's favorites, Armand du Plessis de Richelieu, a churchman who rose to be a cardinal through her favor, became chief minister and took control of the government. Over the next eighteen years, this ambitious and determined leader resumed Henry IV's assertion of royal authority (see "Richelieu on Diplomacy," above).

The monarchy had to manage a number of vested interests as it concentrated its power, and Richelieu's achievement was that he kept them under control. The strongest was the bureaucracy, whose ranks had been swollen by the sale of offices. Richelieu always paid close attention to the views of the bureaucrats, and one reason he had such influence over the king was that he acted as the head and representative of this army of royal servants. He also reduced the independence of traditional nobles by giving them positions in the regime as diplomats, soldiers, and officials without significant administrative responsibility. Finally, he took on the Huguenots in a military campaign. After he defeated them, he abolished most of the guarantees in the Edict of Nantes and ended the Huguenots' political independence.

Royal Administration   Under Richelieu the sale of offices broke all bounds: By 1633 it accounted for approximately one-half of royal revenues. Ten years later more than three-quarters of the crown's direct taxation was needed to pay the salaries of the officeholders. It was a vicious circle, and the only solution was to increase the taxes on the lower classes. As this financial burden grew, Richelieu had to improve the government's control over the realm to obtain the revenue he needed. He increased the power of the **intendants,** the government's chief agents in the localities, and established them (instead of the nobles) as the principal representatives of the monarchy in each province of France. Unlike the nobles, the *intendants* depended entirely on royal favor for their position; consequently, they enthusiastically recruited for the army, arranged billeting, supervised the raising of taxes, and enforced the king's decrees. They soon came to be hated figures, both because of the rising taxes and because they threatened the power of the nobles. The result was a succession of peasant uprisings, often led by local notables who resented the rise of the *intendants* and of royal power.

Political and Social Crisis

France's foreign wars made the discontent worse, and it was clear that eventually the opponents of the central government would reassert themselves. But the centralization of power by the crown had been so successful that when trouble erupted, in a series of revolts known as the *Fronde* (or "sling," the simple weapon of the rebels), there was no serious effort to reshape the social order or the political system. The principal actors in the Fronde came from the upper levels of society: nobles, townsmen, and members of the regional courts and legislatures known as parlements. Only rarely were these groups joined by peasants, who may have been resentful of taxes and other government demands and vulnerable to starvation when harvests failed, but the Fronde never raised issues that connected with the peasants' uprisings. These focused on issues like food scarcities, which often brought women into prominent roles, especially since soldiers were reluctant to shoot them. But without noble support, such disorders remained fairly low-scale; they never reached the level of disruption that was to overtake France in the Revolution.

Mazarin   The death of Louis XIII in 1643, followed by a regency because Louis XIV was only five years old, offered an opportunity to those who wanted to reverse the rise of absolutism. Louis XIII's widow, Anne of Austria, took over the government and placed all the power in the hands of an Italian, Cardinal Giulio Mazarin. He used his position to amass a huge fortune, and he was therefore a perfect target for the anger caused by the encroachment of central government on local authority.

Early in 1648 Mazarin sought to gain a respite from the monarch's perennial financial trouble by withholding payment of the salaries of some royal officials for four years. In response, the members of various institutions in Paris, including the Parlement, drew up a charter of demands. They wanted the office of *intendant* abolished, no new offices created, power to approve taxes, and enactment of a habeas corpus law.

The Fronde   Mazarin reacted by arresting the Paris Parlement's leaders, thus sparking a popular rebellion in the city that forced him and the royal family to flee from the capital—an experience the young Louis XIV never forgot. In 1649 Mazarin promised to redress the *parlementaires'* grievances, and he was allowed to return to Paris. But the trouble was far from over; during that summer, uprisings spread throughout France, particularly among peasants and in the old Huguenot stronghold, the southwest.

The next three years were marked by political chaos, mainly as a result of intrigues and shifting alliances among the nobility. As it became clear that the perpetual unrest was producing no results, Mazarin was able to take advantage of disillusionment among nobles and *parlementaires* to reassert the position of the monarchy. He used military force and threats of force to subdue Paris and most of the rebels in the countryside, and he brought the regency to an end by declaring the fourteen-year-old Louis of age in 1652. Although the nobles were not finally subdued until the following year, and peasants continued their occasional regional uprisings for many years to come, the crown now established its authority as the basis for order in the realm. As surely as England, France had surmounted its crisis and found a stable solution for long-standing conflicts.

Sources of Discontent in Spain

For Spain the crisis that swept much of Europe in the mid-seventeenth century—with revolt in England and France and war in the empire—meant the end of the country's international power. Yet the difficulties the monarchy faced had their roots in the sixteenth century. Philip II had already found it difficult to hold his sprawling empire together despite his elaborate bureaucracy. Obsessively suspicious, he maintained close

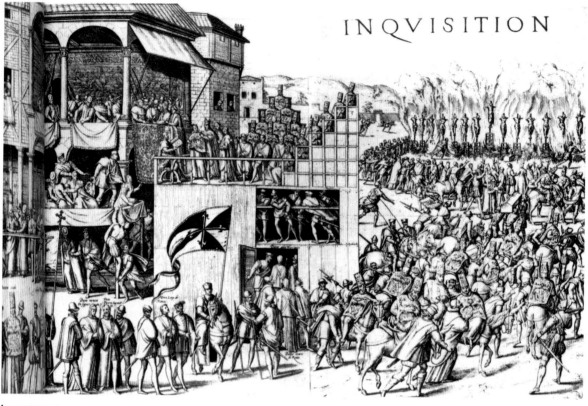

Anonymous
ENGRAVING OF THE SPANISH INQUISITION, 1560
The burning of heretics was a major public event in sixteenth-century Spain. Aimed mainly at people who practiced Judaism or Islam secretly and in a few cases at Protestants, the Inquisition's investigations usually led to imprisonment or lesser punishments. The occasional executions of those who determinedly refused to accept Catholic teachings, even after torture, were carried out by secular authorities, and they attracted huge crowds.
Bibliothèque Nationale de France, Paris

control over all administrative decisions, and government action was, therefore, agonizingly slow. Moreover, the bureaucracy was run by Castilian nobles, who were resented as outsiders in other regions of the empire. And the standing army, though essential to royal power, was a terrible financial drain.

Philip did gain wide admiration in Spain for his devoutness. His commitment to religion undoubtedly promoted political cohesion, but the economic strains caused by relentless religious warfare eventually undermined Spanish power.

Economic Difficulties   Spain was a rich country in Philip's reign, but the most profitable activities were monopolized by limited groups. Because royal policy valued convenience above social benefit, the city of Seville (dominated by foreign bankers) received a monopoly over shipping to and from the New World; other lucrative pursuits, such as wool and wine production, were also controlled by a small coterie of insiders. The

only important economic activities that involved large numbers of Spaniards were shipping and the prosperous Mediterranean trade, centered in Barcelona, which brought wealth to much of Catalonia. Thus, the influx of silver into Spain was not profitably invested within the country. Drastically overextended in foreign commitments, Philip had to declare himself bankrupt three times. For a while it seemed that the problems might ease because there was peace during the reign of Philip's son, Philip III (r. 1598–1621). But in fact, Philip III's government was incompetent and corrupt, capable neither of dealing with the serious consequences of the spending on war nor of broadening the country's exports beyond wool and wine. And when the flow of treasure from the New World began to dwindle after 1600, the crown was deprived of a major source of income that it was unable to replace (see "Imports of Treasure to Spain . . . ," p. 453). The decline was caused partly by a growing use of precious metals in the New World colonies but also by depletion of the mines.

IMPORTS OF TREASURE TO SPAIN FROM THE NEW WORLD, 1591–1660	
Decade	*Total Value**
1591–1600	85,536,000
1601–1610	66,970,000
1611–1620	65,568,000
1621–1630	62,358,000
1631–1640	40,110,000
1641–1650	30,651,000
1651–1660	12,785,000

*In ducats.

Adapted from J. H. Elliott, *Imperial Spain, 1469–1716*, Edward Arnold, Hodder Neadling PLC Group, 1964, p. 175.

In the meantime, tax returns at home were shrinking. The most significant cause of this decrease was a series of severe plagues, which reduced the population of Castile and Aragon from 10 million in 1590 to 6 million in 1700. No other country in Europe suffered a demographic reversal of this proportion during the seventeenth century. In addition, sheep farming took over huge tracts of arable land, and Spain had to rely increasingly on imports of expensive foodstuffs to feed its people. When Spain resumed large-scale fighting against the Dutch and French under Philip IV (r. 1621–1665), the burdens became too much to bear. The effort to maintain the commitment to war despite totally inadequate finances was to bring the greatest state in Europe to its knees.

Revolt and Secession

The final crisis was brought about by the policies of Philip IV's chief minister, the count of Olivares. His aim was to unite the realm so that all the territories shared equally the burden of maintaining Spanish power. Although Castile would no longer dominate the government, it would also not have to provide the bulk of the taxes and army. Olivares' program was called the Union of Arms, and while it seemed eminently reasonable, it caused a series of revolts in the 1640s that split Spain apart.

The reason was that Castile's dominance had made the other provinces feel that local independence was being undermined by a centralized regime. They saw the Union of Arms, imposed by Olivares, as the last straw. Moreover, the plan appeared at a time when Spain's military and economic fortunes were in decline. France had declared war on the Habsburgs in 1635, the funds to support an army were becoming harder to raise, and in desperation Olivares pressed

more vigorously for the Union of Arms. But all he accomplished was to provoke revolts against Castile in the 1640s by Catalonia, Portugal, Naples, and Sicily. By 1641 Catalonia and Portugal had declared themselves independent republics and placed themselves under French protection. Plots began to appear against Olivares, and Philip dismissed the one minister who had understood Spain's problems but who, in trying to solve them, had made them worse.

The Revolts   The Catalonian rebellion continued for another eleven years, and it was thwarted in the end only because the peasants and town mobs transformed the resistance to the central government into an attack on the privileged and wealthy classes. When this happened, the Catalan nobility abandoned the cause and joined the government side. About the same time, the Fronde forced the withdrawal of French troops from Catalonia. When the last major holdout, Barcelona, fell to a royal army in 1652, the Catalan nobles could regain their rights and powers, and the revolt was over.

The Portuguese had no social upheaval; as a result, though not officially granted independence from Spain until 1668, they defended their autonomy easily and even invaded Castile in the 1640s. But the revolts that the people of Sicily and Naples directed at their Castilian rulers in 1647 took on social overtones. In Naples the unrest developed into a tremendous mob uprising led by a local fisherman. The poor turned against all representatives of government and wealth they could find, and chaos ensued until the leader of the revolt was killed. The violence in Sicily, the result of soaring taxes, was aimed primarily at government officials. But in both Naples and Sicily the government was able to reassert its authority by force within a few months.

Consequences   The effect of this unrest was to end the Spanish government's international ambitions and, thus, the worst of its economic difficulties. Like England and France, Spain found a new way of life after its crisis: It became a stable second-level state, heavily agricultural, run by its nobility.

POLITICAL CHANGE IN AN AGE OF CRISIS

Although the level of violence was highest in England and Spain, almost all of Europe's countries experienced the political upheavals of this era of "general crisis." In some cases—for instance, Sweden—the conflict was minor and did little to disturb the peace of the land. But everywhere the basic issue—Who should hold political authority?—caused some degree of strife. And

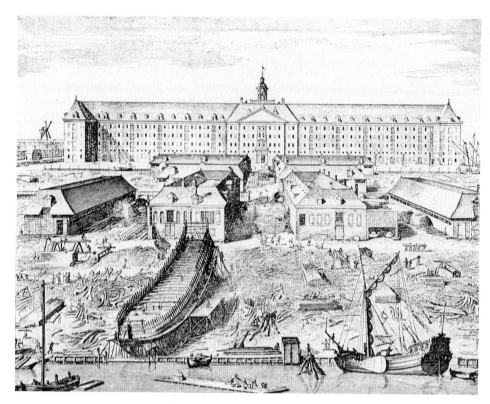

Anonymous
ENGRAVING OF A DUTCH SHIPYARD
The Dutch became the best shipbuilders in Europe in the seventeenth century; the efficiency of their ships, which could be manned by fewer sailors than those of other countries, was a major reason for their successes in trade and commerce.
The Granger Collection, New York

each state had to find its own solutions to the competing demands of governments and their subjects.

The United Provinces

The Dutch did not escape the struggles against the power of centralized governments that created an atmosphere of crisis in much of Europe during the middle decades of the seventeenth century. Despite the remarkable fluidity of their society, the Dutch, too, became embroiled in a confrontation between a ruling family seeking to extend its authority and citizens defending the autonomy of their local regions. The outcome determined the structure of their government for more than a century.

The United Provinces were unique in a number of ways. Other republics existed in Europe, but they were controlled by small oligarchies; the Dutch, who had a long tradition of a strong representative assembly, the Estates General, had created a nation in which many citizens participated in government through elected delegates. Although powerful merchants and a few aristocrats close to the House of Orange did create a small elite, the social differentiation was less than elsewhere in Europe. The resulting openness and homogeneity underlay the economic mastery and cultural brilliance of the United Provinces.

Commerce and Tolerance   The most striking accomplishment of the Dutch was their rise to supremacy in the world of commerce. Amsterdam displaced Antwerp as the Continent's financial capital and gained control of the trade of the world's richest markets. In addition, the Dutch rapidly emerged as the cheapest international shippers. As a result, by the middle of the seventeenth century they had become the chief carriers of European commerce.

The openness of Dutch society permitted the freest exchange of ideas of the time. The new state gave refuge to believers of all kinds, whether extreme Protestant radicals or Catholics who wore their faith lightly, and Amsterdam became the center of a brilliant Jewish community. This freedom attracted some of the greatest minds in Europe and fostered remarkable artistic creativity. The energy that produced this outpouring reflected the pride of a tiny nation that was winning its independence from Spain.

Two Political Parties   There was, however, a basic split within the United Provinces. The two most urbanized and commercial provinces, Holland and Zeeland, dominated the Estates General because they supplied a majority of its taxes. Their representatives formed a mercantile party, which advocated peace abroad so that their trade could flourish unhampered, government by the Estates General so that they could make their influence felt, and religious toleration so that their cities could attract enterprising people of all faiths. In opposition to this mercantile interest was the House of Orange: the descendants of William of Orange, who sought to establish their family's leadership of the Dutch. They were supported by the more rural provinces and stood for war because their authority and popularity derived from their command of the army, for centralized power to enhance the position of the family, and for the strict Calvinism that was upheld in the rural provinces.

The differences between the two factions led Maurice of Nassau to use religion as a pretext to execute his chief opponent, Jan van Oldenbarneveldt, the representative of the province of Holland, in 1618. Oldenbarneveldt was against war with Spain, and his removal left the House of Orange in control of the country. Maurice resumed the war in 1621, and for more than twenty years, his family remained in command, unassailable because it led the army in wartime. Not until 1648—when a new leader, William II, tried to prolong the fighting—did the mercantile party reassert itself by insisting on peace. As a result, the Dutch signed the Treaty of Westphalia, which recognized the independence of the United Provinces. It now seemed that Holland and Zeeland had gained the upper hand. But their struggle with the House of Orange continued (there was even a threat by Orange troops to besiege Amsterdam) until William II suddenly died in 1650, leaving as his successor a baby son, William III.

Jan De Witt   The mercantile interest now assumed full power, and Jan De Witt, the representative of the province of Holland, took over the government in 1653. De Witt's aims were to leave as much authority as possible in the hands of the provinces, particularly Holland; to weaken the executive and prevent a revival of the House of Orange; to pursue trading advantage; and to maintain peace so that the economic supremacy of the Dutch would not be endangered. For nearly twenty years he guided the country in its golden age. But in 1672 French armies overran the southern provinces, and De Witt lacked the military instinct to fight a dangerous enemy. The Dutch at once turned to the family that had led them to independence; a mob murdered De Witt; and the House of Orange, under William III, resumed the centralization that henceforth was to characterize the political structure of the United Provinces. The country had not experienced a midcentury upheaval as severe as those of its neighbors, but it had nevertheless been forced to endure unrest and violence before the form of its government was securely established.

CHRONOLOGY
An Age of Crisis
1618–1660

1618	Revolt in Bohemia, beginning of Thirty Years' War.
1621	Resumption of war between Spanish and Dutch.
1629	Edict of Restitution—high point of Habsburg power.
1630	Sweden enters war against Habsburgs.
1635	France declares war on Habsburgs.
1639	Scots invade England.
1640	Revolts in Catalonia and Portugal against Spanish government.
1642	Civil War in England.
1647	Revolts in Sicily and Naples against Spanish government.
1648	Peace of Westphalia ends Thirty Years' War. Outbreak of *Fronde* in France. Coup by nobles in Denmark. Revolt of Ukraine against Poland. Riots in Russian cities.
1650	Constitutional crisis in Sweden. Confrontation between William of Orange and Amsterdam in Netherlands.
1652	End of Catalan revolt.
1653	End of *Fronde*.
1655	War in Baltic region.
1659	Peace of the Pyrenees between France and Spain.
1660	End of English revolution. Treaties end war in Baltic.

Sweden

The Swedes, too, settled their political system in the mid-seventeenth century. In 1600 Sweden, a Lutheran country of a million people, was one of the backwaters of Europe. A feudal nobility dominated the countryside, a barter economy made money almost unknown, and both trade and towns were virtually nonexistent. Moreover, the country lacked a capital, central institutions, and government machinery. The royal administration consisted of the king and a few courtiers; other officials were appointed only to deal with specific problems as they arose.

Gustavus Adolphus (r. 1611–1632) transformed this situation. He won over the nobles by giving them dominant positions in a newly expanded bureaucracy, and he reorganized his army. Thus equipped both to govern and to fight, Gustavus embarked on a remarkable series of conquests abroad. By 1629 he had made Sweden the most powerful state in the Baltic area. He then entered the Thirty Years' War, advancing victoriously through the Holy Roman Empire until his death, in 1632, during the showdown battle with Wallenstein. Without their great general, the Swedes could do little more than hang on to their gains, but they were now a force to be reckoned with in international affairs.

Government and Economy The highly efficient system of government established by Gustavus and his chief adviser, Axel Oxenstierna, was to be the envy of other countries until the twentieth century. At the heart of the system were five administrative departments, each led by a nobleman, with the most important—the Chancellery, for diplomacy and internal affairs—run by Oxenstierna. An administrative center emerged in Stockholm, and the new bureaucracy proved that it could run the nation, supply the army, and implement policy even during the last twelve years of Gustavus' reign, when the king himself was almost always abroad.

A major cause of Sweden's amazing rise was the development of the domestic economy, stimulated by the opening up of copper mines and the development of a major iron industry. The country's traditional tar and timber exports were also stepped up, and a fleet was built. By 1700 Stockholm had become an important trading and financial center, growing in the course of the century from fewer than five thousand to more than fifty thousand inhabitants.

The Nobles The one source of tension amidst this remarkable progress was the position of the nobles. After Gustavus died, they openly challenged the monarchy for control of government and society. Between 1611 and 1652 they more than doubled the proportion of land they owned in Sweden, and much of this growth was at the expense of the crown, which granted away or sold lands to help the war effort abroad. Both peasants and townspeople viewed these developments with alarm, because the nobility usually pursued its own, rather than public, interests. The concern intensified when, in 1648, the nobles in neighboring Denmark took advantage of the death of a strong king to gain control of their government. Two years later the showdown came in Sweden.

Political Confrontation The monarch now was Gustavus' daughter Christina, an able but erratic young queen who usually allowed Oxenstierna to run the government. For some time, she had hoped to abdicate her throne, become a Catholic, and leave Sweden—an ambition she fulfilled in 1654. She wanted her cousin Charles recognized as her successor, but the nobles threatened to create a republic if she abdicated. The queen, therefore, summoned the Riksdag, Sweden's usually weak representative assembly, in 1650; she encouraged the townspeople and peasants to raise their grievances and allowed them to attack the aristocracy. Soon these groups were demanding the return of nobles' lands to the crown, freedom of speech, and real power; under this pressure, the nobility gave way and recognized Charles X as successor to the throne.

The political upheaval of 1650 was short-lived. Once Christina had her way, she turned against the Riksdag and rejected the lower estates' demands. Only gradually did power shift away from the great nobles toward a broader elite of lesser nobles and bureaucrats, but the turning point in Sweden, as elsewhere, was during the crisis years of the mid-seventeenth century.

Eastern Europe and the Crisis

In Eastern Europe, too, long-term patterns became clear in this period. The limits of Ottoman rule were reconfirmed when an attack on Vienna failed in 1683. Although the Ottomans' control of the Balkans did not immediately waver, their government was increasingly beset by internal problems, and their retreat from Hungary was under way by 1700. Further north, Poland's weak central government lost all claim to real authority in 1648 when it proved unable to stop a group of nobles in the rich province of the Ukraine from switching allegiance from the king of Poland to the tsar in Moscow. And in Russia, following a period of disorder known as the Time of Troubles (1584–1613), the new Romanov **Dynasty** began consolidating its power. The nobility was won over; the last possibilities for escaping serfdom were closed; the legal system was codified; the church came under the tsar's control; and the revolts that erupted against these changes between 1648 and 1672—involving peasants and Cossacks (marauding horsemen, mainly from the South), and often looking like rural revolts in the West, especially France—were brutally suppressed. As elsewhere in Europe, long-standing conflicts between centralizing regimes and their opponents were resolved, and a new political system, supported by the government's military power, was established for centuries to come. Further east, the Ming Dynasty of China was overthrown by the new Ch'ing Dynasty in 1644, a shift that was also accompanied by peasant revolts. That parallel suggests that this was a time of upheaval throughout much of the world, possibly because of a cooling in climate that affected food crops. But everywhere the outcome was a return to stability: crisis there may have been, but the restoration of order was a worldwide phenomenon, too.

Summary

Because these struggles were so widespread, historians have called the midcentury period an age of "general crisis." In country after country, people tried to resist the growing ambitions of central governments. These confrontations reached crisis proportions in almost all cases during the 1640s and 1650s and then subsided at the very time that the anarchy of warfare and international relations was resolved by the Peace of Westphalia. As a result, the sense of settlement after 1660 contrasted sharply with the turmoil of the preceding decades. Moreover, the progression in politics from turbulence to calm had its analogs in the cultural and social developments of the sixteenth and seventeenth centuries.

QUESTIONS FOR FURTHER THOUGHT

1. Are the social benefits of warfare so minimal, compared to its destructive effects, that one can dismiss them as unimportant?

2. Why are there differences in the ways warfare changes domestic politics?

RECOMMENDED READING

Sources

Bodin, Jean. *On Sovereignty.* Julian H. Franklin (ed. and tr.). 1992. An abridgment of Bodin's *Six Books of the Republic.*

Kossmann, E. H., and A. E. Mellink. *Texts Concerning the Revolt of the Netherlands.* 1974. A collection of Spanish and Dutch documents that reveal the different political and religious goals of the two sides.

Studies

*Aston, Trevor (ed.). *Crisis in Europe, 1560–1660: Essays from Past and Present.* 1965. This is a collection of the essays in which the "general crisis" interpretation was initially put forward and discussed.

Braudel, Fernand. *The Mediterranean and the Mediterranean World in the Age of Philip II.* S. Reynolds (tr.). 2 vols. 1972 and 1973. A pioneering and far-ranging work of social history.

Coward, Barry. *The Cromwellian Protectorate.* 2002.

*Duplessis, Robert R. *Transitions to Capitalism in Early Modern Europe.* 1997.

*Elliott, J. H. *Richelieu and Olivares.* 1984. A comparative study of the two statesmen who dominated Europe in the 1620s and 1630s; also analyzes the changing nature of political authority.

*Hale, J. R. *War and Society in Renaissance Europe, 1450–1620.* 1985. A vivid account of what it meant to be a soldier.

Kishlansky, Mark A. *A Monarchy Transformed: Britain, 1603–1714.* 1997.

MacCaffrey, Wallace. *Elizabeth I.* 1994.

*Mattingly, Garrett. *The Armada.* 1959. This beautifully written book, which was a best seller when it first appeared, is a gripping account of a major international crisis.

Moote, A. Lloyd. *The Revolt of the Judges: The Parlement of Paris and the Fronde, 1643–1652.* 1971. The most detailed account of the causes of the Fronde and its failures.

Parker, Geoffrey. *The Army of Flanders and the Spanish Road, 1567–1659: The Logistics of Spanish Victory and Defeat in the Low Countries' Wars.* 2004.

———. *The Dutch Revolt.* 1977. This brief book gives a good introduction to the revolt of the Netherlands and the nature of Dutch society in the seventeenth century.

———. *The Thirty Years' War.* 1984. The most up-to-date history of the war.

Parker, Geoffrey, and Lesley M. Smith (eds.). *The General Crisis of the Seventeenth Century.* 1997.

Pierson, Peter. *Philip II of Spain.* 1975. A clear and lively biography of the dominant figure of the second half of the sixteenth century.

*Rabb, Theodore K. *The Struggle for Stability in Early Modern Europe.* 1975. An assessment of the "crisis" interpretation, including extensive bibliographic references.

Rogers, Clifford, J. *The Military Revolution Debate: Readings on the Military Transformation of Early Modern Europe.* 1995.

*Available in paperback.

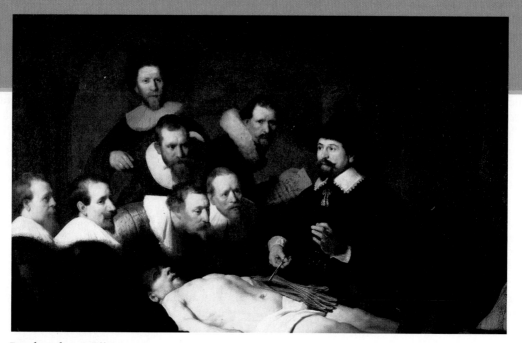

Rembrandt van Rijn
THE ANATOMY LESSON OF DR. NICOLAAS TULP, **1632**
Among the many representations of the public anatomy lessons so popular in seventeenth-century Holland, the most famous is one of Rembrandt's greatest paintings, *The Anatomy Lesson of Dr. Nicolaas Tulp*. Here art reflects the new fascination with science.
Mauritshuis, The Hague

Chapter Sixteen

CULTURE AND SOCIETY IN THE AGE OF THE SCIENTIFIC REVOLUTION

SCIENTIFIC ADVANCE FROM COPERNICUS TO NEWTON • THE EFFECTS OF THE
DISCOVERIES • THE ARTS AND LITERATURE • SOCIAL PATTERNS AND POPULAR CULTURE

Of all the many changes of the sixteenth and seventeenth centuries, none had a more far-reaching impact than the scientific revolution. By creating a new way of understanding how nature worked—and by solving long-standing problems in physics, astronomy, and anatomy—the theorists and experimenters of this period gave Europeans a new sense of confidence and certainty. They also began to set their civilization apart from those of the rest of the world, where the outlook of the scientist did not take hold for centuries. Although the revolution began with disturbing questions, but few clear answers, about the physical world, it ended by offering a promise of knowledge and truth that was eagerly embraced by a society racked by decades of religious and political turmoil and uncertainty. Indeed, it is remarkable how closely intellectual and cultural patterns paralleled the progression from struggle and doubt to stable resolution that marked the political developments of these years. In the mid-seventeenth century, just as Europe's states were able to create more settled conditions following a major crisis, so in the realms of philosophy and the study of nature a long period of searching, anxiety, and dispute was resolved by scientists whose discoveries and self-assurance helped restore a sense of order in intellectual life. And in literature, the arts, and social relations, a time of insecurity and doubt also gave way to an atmosphere of confidence and calm.

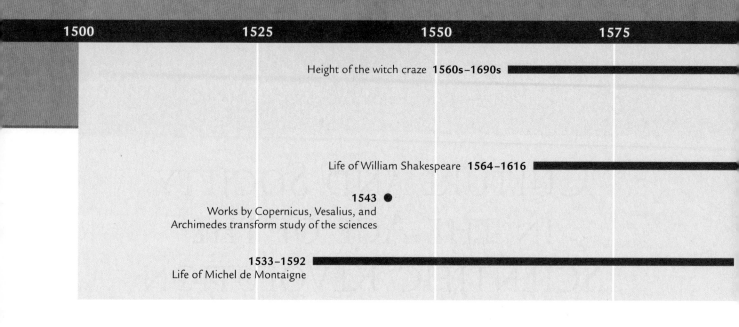

Height of the witch craze **1560s–1690s**

Life of William Shakespeare **1564–1616**

1543 ●
Works by Copernicus, Vesalius, and
Archimedes transform study of the sciences

1533–1592
Life of Michel de Montaigne

SCIENTIFIC ADVANCE FROM COPERNICUS TO NEWTON

Fundamental to the transformation of Europe in the seventeenth century were advances in the knowledge of how nature worked. At first the new discoveries added to the uncertainties of the age, but eventually the scientists were seen as models of orderly thought, who had at last solved ancient problems in convincing fashion.

Origins of the Scientific Revolution

The Importance of Antiquity   Until the sixteenth century, the study of nature in Europe was inspired by the ancient Greeks. Their work shaped subsequent research in three main fields: Aristotle in physics, Ptolemy in astronomy, and Galen in medicine. The most dramatic advances during the **scientific revolution** came in these fields, to some extent because it was becoming evident that the ancient theories could not account for new observations without highly complicated adjustments. For instance, Ptolemy's picture of the heavens, in which all motion was circular around a central earth, did not readily explain the peculiar motion that observers noticed in some planets, which at times seemed to be moving backward. Similarly, dissections often showed Galen's anatomical theories to be wrong.

Despite these problems, scientists (who in the sixteenth and seventeenth centuries were still known as "natural philosophers," or seekers of wisdom about nature) preferred making adjustments rather than beginning anew. And it is unlikely they would have abandoned their cherished theories if it had not been for other influences at work in this period. One such

stimulus to rethinking was the Humanists' rediscovery of a number of previously unknown ancient scientists, who had not always agreed with the theories of Aristotle or Ptolemy. A particularly important rediscovery was the work of Archimedes, whose writings on dynamics helped inspire new ideas in physics.

The Influence of "Magical" Beliefs   Another influence was a growing interest in what we now dismiss as "magic," but which at the time was regarded as a serious intellectual enterprise. There were various avenues of magical inquiry, many of which had been pursued in other civilizations, as well as Europe, for centuries. Alchemy was the belief that matter could be understood and transformed by mixing substances and using secret formulas. A famous sixteenth-century alchemist, Paracelsus, suggested that metals as well as plants might have medicinal properties, and he helped demonstrate that mercury (if carefully used) could cure syphilis. Another favorite study was astrology, which claimed that natural phenomena could be predicted if planetary movements were properly interpreted.

What linked these "magical" beliefs was the conviction that the world could be understood through simple, comprehensive keys to nature. The theories of Neoplatonism—an influential school of thought during the Renaissance, based on Plato's belief that truth lay in essential but hidden "forms"—supported this conviction, as did some of the mystical ideas that attracted attention at this time. One of the latter, derived from a system of Jewish thought known as *cabala*, suggested that the universe might be built around magical arrangements of numbers. The ancient Greek mathematician Pythagoras had also suggested that numerical patterns might connect all of nature, and his ideas now gained new attention. For all its irrational elements, it

1606–1669 Life of Rembrandt van Rijn

1607 Premier of Monteverdi's opera *Orfeo*

● **1633** Condemnation of Galileo by the Inquisition

● **1637** Descartes, *Discourse on Method*

● **1660** Founding of the Royal Society in London

● **1687** Newton, *Principia*

was precisely this interest in new and simple solutions for long-standing problems that made natural philosophers capable, for the first time, of discarding the honored theories they had inherited from antiquity, trying different ones, paying greater attention to mathematics, and eventually creating an intellectual revolution.

Observations, Experiments, and Instruments Two other influences deserve mention. The first was Europe's fascination with technological invention. The architects, navigators, engineers, and weapons experts of the Renaissance were important pioneers of a new reliance on measurement and observation that affected not only how domes were built or heavy cannons were moved but also how problems in physics were addressed. A second, and related, influence was the growing interest in experiment among anatomists. In particular, the medical school at the University of Padua became famous for its dissections and direct observations of nature; many leading figures in the scientific revolution were trained there.

It was not too surprising, therefore, that during the sixteenth and seventeenth centuries important new instruments were invented, which helped make scientific discovery possible: the telescope, the vacuum pump, the thermometer, the barometer, and the microscope. These instruments encouraged the development of a scientific approach that was entirely new in the seventeenth century: It did not go back to the ancients, to the practitioners of magic, or to the engineers. This approach rested on the belief that in order to make nature reveal its secrets, it had to be made to do things it did not do normally. What this meant was that one did not simply observe phenomena that occurred normally in nature—for instance, the way a stick seems to bend when it is placed in a glass of water—but created

Pieter Brueghel the Elder
THE ALCHEMIST
This down-to-earth portrayal, typical of Brueghel's art, shows the alchemist as an undisciplined figure. He is surrounded by a chaos of instruments and half-finished experiments, and his helpers resemble witches. Like Brueghel, most people thought it unlikely that this disorganized figure would make a major contribution to the understanding of nature.
Pen and brown ink on paper, Kd Z 4399. Kupferstichkabinett, Staatliche Museen zu Berlin, Germany. Bildarchiv Preussischer Kulturbesitz/Art Resource, NY

conditions that were not normal. With the telescope, one saw secrets hidden to the naked eye; with the vacuum pump, one could understand the properties of air.

The Breakthroughs

Vesalius   The earliest scientific advances came in anatomy and astronomy, and by coincidence they were announced in two books published in 1543, which was also the year when the earliest printed edition of Archimedes appeared. The first book, *The Structure of the Human Body* by Andreas Vesalius (1514–1564), a member of the Padua faculty, pointed out errors in the work of Galen, the chief authority in medical practice for over a thousand years. Using dissections, Vesalius produced anatomical descriptions that opened a new era of careful observation and experimentation in studies of the body.

Copernicus   The second book, *On the Revolutions of the Heavenly Spheres* by Nicolaus Copernicus (1473–1543), a Polish cleric who had studied at Padua, had far greater consequences. A first-rate mathematician, Copernicus believed that the calculations of planetary movements under Ptolemy's system had grown too complex. In Ptolemaic astronomy, the planets and the sun, attached to transparent, crystalline spheres, revolved around the earth. All motion was circular, and irregularities were accounted for by **epicycles**—movement around small revolving spheres that were attached to the larger spheres. Influenced by Neoplatonic ideas, Copernicus believed that a simpler picture would reflect more accurately the true structure of the universe. In sound Neoplatonic fashion, he argued that the sun, as the most splendid of celestial bodies, ought rightfully to be at the center of an orderly and harmonious universe. The earth, no longer immobile, would thus circle the sun.

Copernicus' system was, in fact, scarcely simpler than Ptolemy's—the spheres and epicycles were just as complex—and he had no way of demonstrating the superiority of his theory. But he was such a fine mathematician that his successors found his calculations of planetary motions indispensable. His ideas thus became part of intellectual discussion, drawn on when Pope Gregory XIII decided to reform the calendar in 1582. The Julian calendar, in use since Roman times, counted century years as leap years, thus adding extra days that caused Easter—whose date is determined by the position of the sun—to drift farther and farther away from its normal occurrence in late March. The reform produced the Gregorian calendar, which we still use. Ten days were simply dropped: October 5, 1582, became October 15; and since then only one out of every four century years has been counted as a leap year (1900 had no February 29, but 2000 did). The need

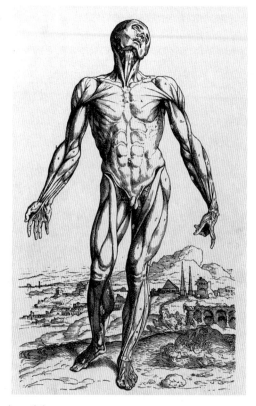

Titian (attrib.)
ENGRAVING ILLUSTRATING THE STRUCTURE OF THE HUMAN BODY BY ANDREAS VESALIUS, 1543
Almost as remarkable as the findings themselves were these illustrations of the results of Vesalius' dissections. Traditionally, professors of anatomy read from textbooks to their students while lowly barber-surgeons cut up a cadaver and displayed the parts being discussed. Vesalius did his dissections himself and thus could observe directly such structures as the musculature. Here his illustrator displays the muscles on a gesturing figure and places it in a stretch of countryside near Padua, where Vesalius taught.

for calendar reform had been one of the motives for Copernicus' studies, which thus proved useful even though his theories remained controversial.

Theories in Conflict   For more than half a century, the effect of *Revolutions* was growing uncertainty, as the scholarly community argued over the validity of the new ideas. The leading astronomer of the period, the Dane Tycho Brahe (1546–1601), produced the most remarkable observations of the heavens before the invention of the telescope by plotting the paths of the moon and planets every night for decades. But the only theory he could come up with was an uneasy compromise between the Ptolemaic and Copernican systems. There was similar indecision among anatomists, who admired Vesalius but were not ready to discard Galen.

Kepler and Galileo Address the Uncertainties

As late as 1600, it seemed that scientists were creating more problems than solutions. But then two brilliant discoverers—the German Johannes Kepler (1571–1630) and Galileo Galilei, an Italian professor of mathematics—made major advances on the work of Copernicus and helped resolve the uncertainties in the field of astronomy.

Kepler and the Laws of Planetary Motion

Like Copernicus, Kepler believed that only the language of mathematics could describe the movements of the heavens. He was a famous astrologer and an advocate of magical theories, but he was also convinced that Copernicus was right. He threw himself into the task of confirming the sun-centered (heliocentric) theory, and by studying Brahe's observations, he discovered three laws of planetary motion (published in 1609 and 1619) that opened a new era in astronomy. Kepler was able to prove that the orbits of the planets are ellipses and that there is a regularity, based on their distance from the sun, which determines the movements of all planets. So revolutionary were these laws that few astronomers accepted them until Isaac Newton used them fifty years later as the basis for a new system of the heavens.

Galileo and a New Physics

A contemporary of Kepler's, the Italian Galileo Galilei (1564–1642), made further advances when he became the first to perceive the connection between planetary motion and motion on earth. His studies revealed the importance to astronomy not only of observation and mathematics but also of physics. Moreover, Galileo's self-consciousness about technique, argument, and evidence marks him as one of the first investigators of nature to approach his work in essentially the same way as a modern scientist.

The study of motion inspired Galileo's most fundamental scientific contributions. When he began his investigations, the Aristotelian view that a body is naturally at rest and needs to be pushed constantly to keep moving dominated the study of dynamics. Galileo broke with this tradition, developing instead a new type of physical explanation that was perfected by Isaac Newton half a century later. Much of Galileo's work was based on observation. From watching how workers at the Arsenal in Venice used pulleys and other devices to lift huge weights, he gained insights into physics; adapting a Dutch lens maker's invention, he built a primitive telescope that was essential to his studies of the heavens; and his seemingly mundane experiments, such as swinging a pendulum or rolling balls down inclined planes, were crucial means of testing his theo-

CHRONOLOGY
The Scientific Revolution

1543	Publication of Copernicus' *On the Revolutions of the Heavenly Spheres*.
	Publication of Vesalius' *The Structure of the Human Body*.
	First printing of the work of Archimedes.
1582	Pope Gregory XIII reforms the calendar.
1609	Publication of Kepler's first two laws of planetary motion.
1610	Publication of Galileo's *Starry Messenger*.
1619	Publication of Kepler's third law of planetary motion.
1627	Publication of Bacon's *New Atlantis*.
1628	Publication of Harvey's *On the Motion of the Heart*.
1632	Publication of Galileo's *Dialogue on the Two Great World Systems*.
1633	Condemnation of Galileo by the Inquisition.
1637	Publication of Descartes' *Discourse on Method*.
1639	Pascal's theorem concerning conic sections.
1660	Founding of the Royal Society of London for Improving Natural Knowledge.
1666	Founding of the French Royal Academy of Sciences.
1687	Publication of Newton's *Mathematical Principles of Natural Philosophy*.

ries. Indeed, it was by moving from observations to abstraction that Galileo arrived at the first wholly new way of understanding motion since Aristotle: the principle of inertia.

This breakthrough could not have been made by observation alone, for the discovery of inertia depended on mathematical abstraction, the ability to imagine a situation that cannot be created experimentally: the motion of a perfectly smooth ball across a perfectly smooth plane, free of any outside forces, such as friction. Galileo's conclusion was that "any velocity once imparted to a moving body will be rigidly maintained as long as external causes of acceleration and retardation are removed. . . . If the velocity is uniform, it will not be diminished or slackened, much less destroyed." This insight overturned the Aristotelian view. Galileo had demonstrated that only mathematical language could describe the underlying principles of nature.

A New Astronomy   Galileo's most celebrated work was in astronomy. He first became famous in 1610, when he published his discoveries, made with the telescope, that Jupiter has satellites and the moon has mountains. Both these revelations were further blows to traditional beliefs, which held that the earth is changing and imperfect while the heavens are immutable and unblemished. Now, however, it seemed that other planets had satellites, just like the earth, and that these satellites might have the same rough surface as the earth. This was startling enough, but Galileo also argued that the principles of terrestrial physics could be used to explain phenomena in the heavens. He calculated the height of the mountains on the moon by using the geometric techniques of surveyors, and he described the moon's secondary light—seen while it is a crescent—as a reflection of sunlight from the earth. Galileo was treating his own planet simply as one part of a uniform universe. Every physical law, he was saying, is equally applicable on earth and in the heavens, including the laws of motion. As early as 1597 Galileo had admitted that some of his discoveries in physics could be explained only if the earth were moving, and during the next thirty years he became the most famous advocate of Copernicanism in Europe (see "Galileo and Kepler on Copernicus," p. 465).

Galileo Galilei
THE MOON, 1610
This sketch of the moon's surface appeared in Galileo's *Starry Messenger* (1610). It shows what he had observed through the telescope and had interpreted as proof that the moon had a rugged surface because the lighted area within the dark section had to be mountains. These caught the light of the setting sun longer than surrounding lower terrain and revealed, for example, a large cavity in the lower center of the sketch.
New York Public Library

Galileo made a powerful case. Why, he asked, was it necessary to say that the entire universe revolved around the earth when all celestial motions could be explained by the rotation of a single planet, the earth? When academic and religious critics argued that we would feel the earth moving or pointed out that the Bible said Joshua made the sun stand still, he reacted with scorn. In response to religious objections, he asserted that "in discussions of physical problems we ought to begin not from the authority of scriptural passages, but from sense experience and necessary demonstrations."

Conflict with the Church   For all the brilliance of his arguments, Galileo was now on dangerous ground. Although traditionally the Catholic Church had not concerned itself with investigations of nature, in the early seventeenth century the situation was changing. The Church was deep in the struggle with Protestantism, and it responded to the challenge to its authority by trying to control potentially questionable views. And Galileo's biting sarcasm toward other scientists antagonized Jesuit and Dominican astronomers. These two orders were the chief upholders of orthodoxy in the Church. They referred Galileo's views to the Inquisition and then guided the attack on Copernicanism by seeking to condemn the brilliant advocate who had made the theory famous throughout Europe.

The Book and the Trial   In 1616 the Inquisition forbade Galileo, within certain limits, to teach the heretical doctrine that the earth moves. When one of his friends was elected pope in 1623, however, Galileo thought he would be safe in writing a major work on astronomy. The result was his *Dialogue on the Two Great World Systems*, published in 1632 (with the approval, probably accidental, of the Church). A marvelously witty, elegant book, the *Dialogue* is one of the few monuments in the history of science that the layperson can read with pleasure. And so it was intended. Galileo wrote it in Italian, not the Latin that had always been used for scholarly works, because he wanted to reach the widest possible audience.

In April 1633 he was brought before the Inquisition for having defied the order not to teach Copernicanism. In a trial that has caused controversy ever since, the aged astronomer, fearing excommunication, abjured the "errors and heresies" of believing that the earth moved. But he did not remain docile for the remainder of his life, though he was kept under house arrest and progressively lost his eyesight. Many of his letters ridiculed his opponents, and in 1638 he published (in tolerant Holland) his principal work on physics, the *Two New Sciences*.

GALILEO AND KEPLER ON COPERNICUS

In 1597 Kepler sent Galileo a copy of his New Astronomy, *which argued for the Copernican theory of the heavens, and asked the Italian for his opinion. The exchange of letters that followed, with Galileo cautious and Kepler urging him on, reflects an age when the new ideas were not yet proved and also gives a hint, in Kepler's last comments, of the troubles that lay ahead.*

Galileo to Kepler: "Like you, I accepted the Copernican position several years ago. I have written up many reasons on the subject, but have not dared until now to bring them into the open. I would dare publish my thoughts if there were many like you; but, since there are not, I shall forbear."

Kepler's Reply: "I could only have wished that you, who have so profound an insight, would choose another way. You advise us to retreat before the general ignorance and not to expose ourselves to the violent attacks of the mob of scholars. But after a tremendous task has been begun in our time, first by Copernicus and then by many very learned mathematicians, and when the assertion that the Earth moves can no longer be considered something new, would it not be much better to pull the wagon to its goal by our joint efforts, now that we have got it under way, and gradually, with powerful voices, to shout down the common herd? Be of good cheer, Galileo, and come out publicly! If I judge correctly, there are only a few of the distinguished mathematicians of Europe who would part company with us, so great is the power of truth. If Italy seems a less favorable place for your publication, perhaps Germany will allow us this freedom."

From Giorgio de Santillana, *The Crime of Galileo*, Chicago: University of Chicago Press, 1955, pp. 11, 14–15.

Galileo's Legacy   The condemnation of Galileo discouraged further scientific activity by his compatriots. Italy had been a leader of the new investigations, but now major further advances were made by the English, Dutch, and French. Yet this shift showed merely that the rise of science, once begun, could not be halted for long. By the late 1630s, no self-respecting astronomer could deny the correctness of the Copernican theory.

Assurance Spreads   The new studies of nature may have caused tremendous bewilderment at first, as scientists struggled with the ideas of pioneers like Copernicus and Vesalius. But in the end these investigations created a renewed sense of certainty about the physical world, which was to have a far-reaching influence. This was true not only in physics and astronomy but also in anatomy, where, in 1628, another genius of the scientific revolution, the English doctor William Harvey, revolutionized the understanding of the human body when he identified the function of the heart and proved that the blood circulates.

The Climax of the Scientific Revolution: Isaac Newton

The culmination of the scientific revolution was the work of Isaac Newton (1642–1727), who made decisive contributions to mathematics, physics, astronomy, and optics and brought to a climax the changes that had begun with Copernicus. He united physics and astronomy into a single system to explain all motion, he helped transform mathematics by developing the calculus, and he established some of the basic laws of modern physics.

Part of the explanation of his versatility lies in the workings of the scientific community at the time. Newton was a retiring man who nevertheless got into fierce arguments with prominent contemporaries, such as the learned German scholar and scientist Wilhelm von Leibniz, who was working on the calculus. If not for his active participation in meetings of scientists at the recently founded Royal Society of London (see p. 468), Newton might never have pursued his researches to their conclusion. He disliked the give-and-take of these discussions, but he felt forced, in order to prove that he had solved various problems, to prepare some of his most important papers for the Royal Society. Such institutions were now being established throughout Europe to promote the advance of science, and their creation indicates how far the scientific community had come since the days of Copernicus, who had worked largely in isolation.

The Principia   Newton's masterpiece, *The Mathematical Principles of Natural Philosophy* (1687)—usually referred to by the first word of its Latin title, the *Principia*—was the last widely influential book to be written in Latin, the traditional language of scholarship. Latin was still useful to Newton, who wanted as many experts as possible to read the book, which claimed that everything he said was proved by experiment or by mathematics.

The most dramatic of Newton's findings was the solution to the ancient problem of motion. Building on Galileo's advances and overturning Aristotle's theories once and for all, Newton defined his system in three laws: first, in the absence of force, motion continues in a straight line; second, the rate of change of the motion is determined by the forces acting on it (such as friction); and third, action and reaction between two bodies are equal and opposite. To arrive at these laws, he defined the concepts of mass, inertia, and force in relation to velocity and acceleration as we know them today.

Newton extended these principles to the entire universe by demonstrating that his laws govern the motions of the moon and planets too. Using the concept of gravity, he provided the explanation of the movement of objects in space that is the foundation for current space travel. There is a balance, he said, between the earth's pull on the moon and the forward motion of the satellite, which would continue in a straight line were it not for the earth's gravity. Consequently, the moon moves in an elliptical orbit in which neither gravity nor inertia gains control. The same pattern is followed by the planets around the sun (as Kepler had shown).

The Influence of Newton The general philosophical implication of the uniformity that Newton described—that the world was stable and orderly—was as important as his specific discoveries in making him one of the idols of his own and the next centuries. The educated applauded Newton's achievements, and he was the first scientist to receive a knighthood in England. Only a few decades after the appearance of the *Principia*, the poet Alexander Pope summed up the public feeling:

> Nature and nature's law lay hid in night;
> God said, "Let Newton be!" and all was light.

So overpowering was Newton's stature that in physics and astronomy the remarkable advances of 150 years slowed down for more than half a century after the publication of the *Principia*. There was a general impression that somehow Newton had done it all, that no important problems remained. There were other reasons for the slowdown—changing patterns in education, an inevitable lessening of momentum—but none was so powerful as the reverence for Newton, who became the intellectual symbol of his own and succeeding ages.

THE EFFECTS OF THE DISCOVERIES

The scientists' discoveries about the physical universe made them famous. But it was the *way* they proved their case that made them so influential. The success of their reasoning encouraged a new level of confidence in human powers that helped end the doubts and uncertainties of the previous age.

A New Epistemology

Galileo had stressed that his discoveries rested on a way of thinking that had an independent value, and he refused to allow traditional considerations, such as common sense or theological teachings, to interfere with his conclusions. Scientists were now moving toward a new **epistemology**, a new theory of how to obtain and verify knowledge. They stressed experience, reason, and doubt; they rejected all unsubstantiated authority; and they developed a revolutionary way of determining what was a true description of physical reality.

Scientific Method The process the scientists said they followed, after they had formulated a hypothesis, consisted of three parts: first, observations; second, a generalization induced from the observations; and third, tests of the generalization by experiments whose outcome could be predicted by the generalization. A generalization remained valid only as long as it was not contradicted by experiments specifically designed to test it. The scientist used no data except the results of strict observation—such as the time it took balls to roll down Galileo's inclined planes—and scientific reasoning uncovered the laws, principles, or patterns that emerged from the observations. Since measurement was the key to the data, the observations had a numerical, not a subjective, value. Thus, the language of science came to be mathematics.

In fact, scientists rarely reach conclusions in the exact way this idealized scheme suggests. Galileo's perfectly smooth balls and planes, for instance, did not exist, but Galileo understood the relevant physical theory so well that he knew what would happen if one rolled across the other, and he used this "experiment" to demonstrate the principle of inertia. In other words, experiments as well as hypotheses can occur in the mind; the essence of scientific method is a special way of looking at and understanding nature.

The Wider Influence of Scientific Thought

The principles of scientific inquiry received attention throughout the intellectual community only gradually; it took time for the power of the scientists' method to be recognized. If the new methods were to be accepted, their effectiveness would have to be demonstrated to more than a few specialists. This wider understanding was eventually achieved by midcentury, as much through the efforts of ardent propagandizers as through the writings of the great innovators themselves. Gradually, they convinced a broad, educated public that science, after first causing doubts by challenging ancient truths, now offered a promise of certainty that was not to be found anywhere else in an age of general crisis.

Bacon and Descartes

Bacon's Vision of Science   Although he was not an important scientist himself, Francis Bacon was the greatest of science's propagandists, and he inspired a whole generation with his vision of what it could accomplish for humanity. His description of an ideal society in the *New Atlantis*—published in 1627, the year after his death—is a vision of science as the savior of the human race. It predicts a time when those doing research at the highest levels will be regarded as the most important people in the state and will work on vast government-supported projects to gather all known facts about the physical universe. By a process of gradual **induction**, this information will lead to universal laws that, in turn, will enable people to improve their lot on earth. Bacon's view of research as a collective enterprise inspired a number of later scientists, and by the mid-seventeenth century, his ideas had entered the mainstream of European thought.

Descartes and the Principle of Doubt   The Frenchman René Descartes (1596–1650) made the first concentrated attempt to apply the new methods of science to theories of knowledge, and, in so doing, he laid the foundations for modern philosophy. The impulse behind his work was his realization that, for all the importance of observation and experiment, people can be deceived by their senses. In order to find some solid truth, therefore, he decided to apply to all knowledge the principle of doubt—the refusal to accept any authority without strict verification. He began with the assumption that he could know unquestionably only one thing: that he was doubting. This assumption allowed him to proceed to the observation "I think, therefore I am," because the act of doubting proved he was thinking, and thinking, in turn, demonstrated his existence.

From the proof of his own existence he derived a crucial statement: That whatever is clearly and distinctly thought must be true. This assertion in turn enabled him to construct a proof of God's existence. We cannot fail to realize that we are imperfect, he argued, and we must therefore have an idea of perfection

Frans Hals
PORTRAIT OF DESCARTES**, 1649**
The increasingly common portraits of scientists in the seventeenth century testify to their growing fame. In this case, Descartes sat for one of the Netherlands' most renowned artists, and because the painting was copied in a number of engravings, his face became as well known as that of many kings and princes.
Erich Lessing/Art Resource, NY

against which we may be measured. If we have a clear idea of what perfection is, then it must exist; hence, there must be a God.

The Discourse on Method   Descartes' proof may have served primarily to show that the principle of doubt did not contradict religious belief, but it also reflected the emphasis on the power of the mind in his major work, *Discourse on the Method of Rightly Conducting the Reason and Seeking Truth in the Sciences* (1637). Thought is a pure and unmistakable guide, he said, and only by relying on its operations can people hope to advance their understanding of the world. Descartes developed this view into a fundamental proposition about the nature of the world—a proposition that philosophers have been wrestling with ever since. He stated that there is an essential divide between thought and extension (tangible objects) or, put another way, between spirit and matter. Bacon and Galileo had insisted that science, the study of nature, is separate from and unaffected by faith. But Descartes turned this distinction into a far-reaching principle, dividing not only science from faith but even the reality of the world from our perception of that reality. There is a difference, in other words, between a chair and how we think of it as a chair.

The Influence of Descartes Descartes' emphasis on the operations of the mind gave a new direction to epistemological discussions. A hypothesis gained credibility not so much from external proofs as from the logical tightness of the arguments used to support it. Descartes thus applied what he considered the methods of science to all of knowledge. Not only the phenomena of nature but all truth had to be investigated according to the methods of the scientist.

Descartes' contributions to scientific research were theoretical rather than experimental. In physics, he was the first to perceive the distinction between mass and weight; and in mathematics, he was the first to apply algebraic notations and methods to geometry, thus founding analytic geometry. Above all, his emphasis on the principle of doubt undermined forever traditional assumptions such as the belief in the hierarchical organization of the universe.

Pascal's Protest Against the New Science

At midcentury only one important voice still protested against the new science and, in particular, against the philosophy of Descartes. It belonged to a Frenchman, Blaise Pascal, a brilliant mathematician and experimenter. Pascal's investigations of probability in games of chance produced the theorem that still bears his name, and his research in conic sections helped lay the foundations for integral calculus. He also helped discover barometric pressure and invented a calculating machine. In his late twenties, however, Pascal became increasingly dissatisfied with scientific research, and he began to wonder whether his life was being properly spent. Moved by a growing concern with faith, Pascal had a mystical experience in November 1654 that made him resolve to devote his life to the salvation of his soul.

The Pensées During the few remaining years of his life, Pascal wrote a collection of reflections—some only a few words long, some many pages—that were gathered together after his death and published as the *Pensées* (or "Reflections"). These writings revealed not only the beliefs of a deeply religious man but also the anxieties of a scientist who feared the growing influ-

ence of science. He did not wish to put an end to research; he merely wanted people to realize that the truths uncovered by science were limited and not as important as the truths perceived by faith. As he put it in one of his more memorable *pensées*, "The heart has its reasons that reason cannot know."

Pascal's protest was unique, but the fact that it was put forward at all indicates how high the status of the scientist and his methods had risen by the 1650s. Just a quarter-century earlier, such a dramatic change in fortune would have been hard to predict. But now the new epistemology, after its initial disturbing assault on ancient views, was offering one of the few promises of certainty in an age of upheaval and general crisis. In intellectual matters as in politics, turmoil was gradually giving way to assurance.

Science Institutionalized

Many besides Bacon realized that scientific work should be a cooperative endeavor and that information should be exchanged among all its practitioners. A scientific society founded in Rome in 1603 made the first major effort to apply this view, and it was soon followed up in France, where in the early seventeenth century a friar named Marin Mersenne became the center of an international network of correspondents interested in scientific work. He also spread news by bringing scientists together for discussions and experiments. Contacts that were developed at these meetings led eventually to a more permanent and systematic organization of scientific activity.

The Royal Society In England, the first steps toward such organization were taken at Oxford during the Civil War in the 1640s, when the revolutionaries captured the city and replaced those at the university who taught traditional natural philosophy. A few of the newcomers formed what they called the Invisible College, a group that met to exchange information and discuss each other's work. The group included only one first-class scientist, the chemist Robert Boyle; but in 1660 he and eleven others formed an official organization, the Royal Society of London for Improving Natural Knowledge, with headquarters in the capital. In 1662 it was granted a charter by Charles II—the first sign of a link with political authority that not only boosted science but also indicated the growing presence of central governments in all areas of society.

The Royal Society's purposes were openly Baconian. Its aim for a few years—until everyone realized it was impossible—was to gather all knowledge about nature, particularly if it had practical uses. For a long time the members offered their services for the public good, helping in one instance to develop for the government

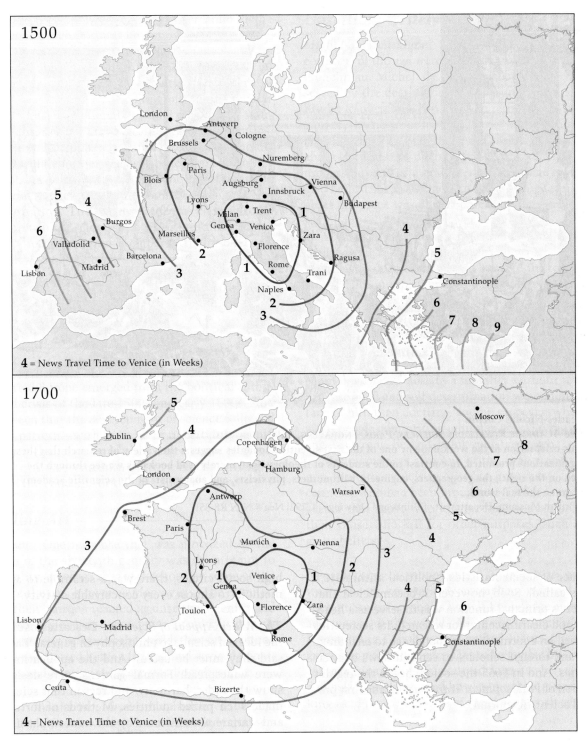

MAP 16.1 SPEED OF NEWS TRAVELING TO VENICE IN 1500 AND 1700
Although the dramatic advances in communications lay in the future, by 1700 improved roads and canals and more efficient shipping did bring about significant advances in the distance news could travel in two or three weeks. How much faster could news get from Madrid to Venice in 1700 than in 1500? What about from Constantinople to Venice? Why might communication across Western Europe have speeded up more than across Eastern Europe?

◆ For an online version, go to www.mhhe.com/chambers9 > chapter 16 > book maps

knight who was ready to tilt at windmills, though he obviously admired the sincerity of his well-meaning hero and sympathized with him as a perennial loser. On another level, the author brought to life the Europe of the time—the ordinary people and their hypocrisies and intolerances—with a liveliness rarely matched in literature. Cervantes avoided politics, but he was clearly directing many of his sharpest barbs at the brutality and disregard for human values that were characteristic of his fanatical times. And in England another towering figure was grappling with similar problems.

Shakespeare For the English-speaking world, the most brilliant writer of this and all other periods was William Shakespeare (1564–1616), whose characters bring to life almost every conceivable mood: searing grief, airy romance, rousing nationalism, uproarious humor. Despite his modest education, his imagery shows a familiarity with subjects ranging from astronomy to seamanship, from alchemy to warfare. It is not surprising, therefore, that some have doubted that one man could have produced this amazing body of work. During most of his writing career, Shakespeare was involved with a theatrical company, where he often had to produce plays on short notice. He thus had the best of all possible tests—audience reactions—as he gained mastery of theatrical techniques.

Shakespeare's plays made timeless statements about human behavior: love, hatred, violence, sin. Of particular interest to the historian, however, is what he tells us about attitudes that belong especially to his own era. Again and again, legality and stability are shown as fundamental virtues amidst turbulent times. Shakespeare's expressions of patriotism are particularly intense; when in *Richard II* the king's uncle, John of Gaunt, lies dying, he pours out his love for his country in words that have moved the English ever since:

> This royal throne of kings, this scepter'd isle,
> This earth of majesty, this seat of Mars,
> This other Eden, demi-paradise, . . .
> This happy breed of men, this little world,
> This precious stone set in the silver sea, . . .
> This blessed plot, this earth,
> This realm, this England.
>
> *Richard II*, act 2, scene 1

As in so much of the art and writing of the time, instability is a central concern of Shakespeare's plays. His four most famous tragedies—*Hamlet, King Lear, Macbeth,* and *Othello*—end in disillusionment: The heroes are ruined by irresoluteness, pride, ambition, and jealousy. Shakespeare was exploring a theme that had absorbed playwrights since Euripides—the fatal flaws that destroy the great—and producing dramas of revenge that were popular in his day; but the plays also demonstrate his deep understanding of human nature. Whatever one's hopes, one cannot forget human weakness, the inevitability of decay, and the constant threat of disaster. The contrast appears with compelling clarity in a speech delivered by Hamlet:

> What a piece of work is man! How noble in reason! how infinite in faculties! in form and moving how express and admirable! in action how like an angel! in apprehension how like a god! the beauty of the world, the paragon of animals! And yet to me what is this quintessence of dust? Man delights not me.
>
> *Hamlet*, act 2, scene 2

Despite such pessimism, despite the deep sense of human inadequacy, the basic impression Shakespeare gives is of immense vigor, of a restlessness and confidence that recall the many achievements of the sixteenth century. Yet a sense of decay is never far absent. Repeatedly, people seem utterly helpless, overtaken by events they cannot control. Nothing remains constant or dependable, and everything that seems solid or reassuring, be it the love of a daughter or the crown of England, is challenged. In this atmosphere of ceaseless change, where landmarks easily disappear, Shakespeare conveys the tensions of his time.

The Return of Assurance in the Arts

The Baroque After 1600, the arts began to move toward the assurance and sense of settlement that was descending over other areas of European civilization. A new style, the **Baroque,** sought to drown the uneasiness of Mannerism in a blaze of grandeur. Passion, drama, mystery, and awe were the qualities of the Baroque: Every art form—from music to literature, from architecture to opera—had to involve, arouse, and uplift its audience.

The Baroque style was closely associated with the Counter-Reformation's emphasis on gorgeous display in Catholic ritual. The patronage of leading Church figures made Rome a magnet for the major painters of the period. Elsewhere, the Baroque flourished primarily at the leading Catholic courts of the seventeenth century, most notably the Habsburg courts in Madrid, Prague, and Brussels, and remained influential well into the eighteenth century in such Catholic areas as the Spanish Empire. Few styles have conveyed so strong a sense of grandeur, theatricality, and ornateness.

Caravaggio The artist who first shaped the new aesthetic, Caravaggio (1571–1610), lived most of his life in Rome. Although he received commissions from high Church figures and spent time in a cardinal's household, he was equally at home among the beggars and petty criminals of Rome's dark back streets. These

Caravaggio
THE SUPPER AT EMMAUS, CA. **1597**
By choosing moments of high drama and using sharp contrasts of light, Caravaggio created an immediacy that came to be one of the hallmarks of Baroque painting. Here he shows the moment during the supper at Emmaus when his disciples suddenly recognized the resurrected Christ. The force of their emotions and their almost theatrical gestures convey the intensity of the moment, but many at the time objected to the craggy, tattered appearance of the disciples. These were not idealized figures, as was expected, but ordinary people at a humble table.
Reproduced by courtesy of the Trustees, © The National Gallery, London (NG172)

ordinary people served as Caravaggio's models, which shocked those who believed it inappropriate for such humble characters to represent the holy figures of biblical scenes. Yet the power of Caravaggio's paintings—their depiction of highly emotional moments, and the drama created by their sharp contrasts of light and dark—made his work much prized. He had to flee Rome after he killed someone in a brawl, but he left behind an outpouring of work that influenced an entire generation of painters.

Rubens Among those who came to Rome to study Caravaggio's art was Peter Paul Rubens (1577–1640), the principal ornament of the brilliant Habsburg court at Brussels. His major themes typified the grandeur that came to be the hallmark of Baroque style: glorifi-

cations of great rulers and also of the ceremony and mystery of Catholicism. Rubens' secular paintings convey enormous strength; his religious works overwhelm the viewer with the majesty of the Church and excite the believer's piety by stressing the power of the faith.

Velázquez Other artists glorified rulers through idealized portraiture. The greatest court painter of the age was Diego Velázquez (1599–1660). His portraits of members of the Spanish court depict rulers and their surroundings in the stately atmosphere appropriate to the theme. Yet occasionally Velázquez hinted at the weakness of an ineffective monarch in his rendering of the face, even though the basic purpose of his work was always to exalt royal power. And his celebration of a notable Habsburg victory, *The Surrender of Breda,*

Artemisia Gentileschi
JUDITH SLAYING HOLOFERNES, CA. **1620**
Female artists were rare in the seventeenth century because they were not allowed to become apprentices. But Artemisia (1593–1652) was the daughter of a painter who happened to be a friend of Caravaggio, and she had the opportunity to become a gifted exponent of Baroque style. Known throughout Europe for her vivid portrayals of dramatic scenes (she painted the murder of Holofernes by the biblical heroine Judith at least five times), she practiced her chosen profession with considerable success, despite the trauma of being raped at age seventeen by a friend of her father's—an act of violence that may be reflected (and avenged) in this painting.
Uffizi, Florence, Italy. Scala/Art Resource, NY

Peter Paul Rubens
DESCENT FROM THE CROSS, **1612**
This huge altarpiece was one of the first pictures Rubens painted upon returning to his native Antwerp after spending most of his twenties developing his art in Italy. The ambitious scale, the strong emotions, the vivid lighting, and the dramatic action showed the artist's commitment to the Baroque style that had recently evolved in Italy. The powerful impact of the altarpiece helped make him one of the most sought-after painters of the day.
Center panel. Scala/Art Resource, NY

Diego Velázquez
THE SURRENDER OF BREDA, **1635**
The contrasting postures of victory and defeat are masterfully captured by Diego Velázquez in *The Surrender of Breda*. The Dutch soldiers droop their heads and lances, but the victorious Spaniards hardly show triumph, and the gesture of the victorious general, Ambrogio Spinola, is one of consolation and understanding.
Oroñoz

managed to suggest the sadness and emptiness as much as the glory of war.

Bernini GianLorenzo Bernini (1598–1680) brought to sculpture and architecture the qualities that Rubens brought to painting, and like Rubens he was closely associated with the Counter-Reformation. Pope Urban VIII commissioned him in 1629 to complete both the inside and the outer setting of the basilica of St. Peter's in Rome. For the interior, Bernini designed a splendid papal throne that seems to float on clouds beneath a burst of sunlight. For the exterior, he created an enormous plaza, surrounded by a double colonnade, that is the largest such plaza in Europe. Similarly, his dramatic religious works reflect the desire of the Counter-

Reformation popes to electrify the faithful. The sensual and overpowering altarpiece dedicated to the Spanish mystic St. Teresa makes a direct appeal to the emotions of the beholder that is the epitome of the excitement and confidence of the Baroque.

New Dimensions in Music The seventeenth century was significant, too, as a decisive time in the history of music. New instruments, notably in the keyboard and string families, enabled composers to create richer effects than had been possible before. Particularly in Italy, which in the sixteenth and seventeenth centuries was the chief center of new ideas in music, musicians began to explore the potential of a form that first emerged in these years: the opera. Drawing on the

GianLorenzo Bernini
ST. PETER'S SQUARE AND CHURCH, ROME
The magnificent circular double colonnade that Bernini created in front of St. Peter's is one of the triumphs of Baroque architecture. The church itself was already the largest in Christendom (markers in the floor still indicate how far other famous churches would reach if placed inside St. Peter's), and it was topped by the huge dome Michelangelo had designed. The vast enclosed space that Bernini built reinforced the grandeur of a church that was the pope's own.
Joachim Messerschmidt/Corbis Stock Market

Gian Lorenzo Bernini
THE ECSTASY OF ST. TERESA, **1652**
Bernini's sculpture is as dramatic an example of Baroque art as the paintings of Caravaggio. The moment that St. Teresa described in her autobiography at which she attained mystic ecstasy, as an angel repeatedly pierced her heart with a dart, became in Bernini's hands the centerpiece of a theatrical tableau. He placed the patrons who had commissioned the work on two walls of the chapel that houses this altarpiece, sitting in what seem to be boxes and looking at the stage on which the drama unfolds.
Scala/Art Resource, NY

resources of the theater, painting, architecture, music, and dance, an operatic production could achieve splendors that were beyond the reach of any one of these arts on its own. The form was perfectly attuned to the courtly culture of the age, to the love of display among the princes of Europe, and to the Baroque determination to overwhelm one's audience.

The dominant figure in seventeenth-century music was the Italian Claudio Monteverdi (1567–1643), one of the most innovative composers of all time. He has been called with some justification the creator of both the operatic form and the orchestra. His masterpiece, *Orfeo* (1607), was a tremendous success, and in the course of the next century operas gained in richness and complexity, attracting composers, as well as audiences, in ever-increasing numbers.

Stability and Restraint in the Arts

Classicism   **Classicism,** the other major style of the seventeenth century, attempted to recapture (though on a much larger scale than Renaissance imitations of antiquity) the aesthetic values and the strict forms that had been favored in ancient Greece and Rome. Like the Baroque, Classicism aimed for grandiose effects, but unlike the Baroque, it achieved them through restraint and discipline within a formal structure. The gradual rise of the Classical style in the seventeenth century echoed the trend toward stability that was taking place in other areas of intellectual life and in politics. In the arts, the age of striving and unrest was coming to an end.

Poussin   The epitome of disciplined expression and conscious imitation of Classical antiquity was Nicolas Poussin (1594–1665), a French artist who spent much of his career in Rome. Poussin was no less interested than his contemporaries in momentous and dramatic subjects, but the atmosphere is always more subdued than in the work of Velázquez or Rubens. The colors are muted, the figures are restrained, and the settings are serene. Peaceful landscapes, men and women in togas, and ruins of Classical buildings are features of his art.

The Dutch Style   In the United Provinces different forces were at work, and they led to a style that was much more intimate than the grandiose outpourings of a Rubens or a Velázquez. Two aspects of Dutch society, Protestantism and republicanism, had a particular influence on its painters. The Reformed Church frowned on religious art, which reduced the demand for paintings of biblical scenes. Religious works, therefore, tended to express personal faith. And the absence of a court meant that the chief patrons of art were sober merchants, who were far more interested in precise, dignified portraits than in ornate displays. The result,

Classicism in Drama   By the middle of the seventeenth century, the formalism of the Classical style was also being extended to literature, especially drama. This change was most noticeable in France, but it soon moved through Western Europe, as leading critics insisted that new plays conform to the structure laid down by the ancients. In particular, they wanted the three Classical unities observed: unity of place, which required that all scenes take place without change of location; unity of time, which demanded that the events in the play occur within a twenty-four-hour period; and unity of action, which dictated simplicity and purity of plot.

Corneille   The work of Pierre Corneille (1606–1684), the dominant figure in the French theater during the midcentury years, reflects the rise of Classicism. His early plays were complex and involved, and even after he came into contact with the Classical tradition, he did not accept its rules easily. His masterpiece, *Le Cid* (1636), based on the legends of a medieval Spanish hero, technically observed the three unities, but only by compressing an entire tragic love affair, a military campaign, and many other events into one day. The play won immediate popular success, but the critics, urged on by the royal minister Cardinal Richelieu, who admired the regularity and order of Classical style, condemned Corneille for imperfect observance of the three unities. Thereafter, he adhered to the Classical forms, though he was never entirely at ease with their restraints.

Passion was not absent from the Classical play; the works of Jean Racine (1639–1699), the model Classical dramatist, generate some of the most intense emotion ever seen on the stage. But the exuberance of earlier drama was disappearing. Nobody summed up the values of Classicism better than Racine in his eulogy of Corneille:

> You know in what a condition the stage was when he began to write. . . . All the rules of art, and even those of decency and decorum, broken everywhere. . . . Corneille, after having for some time sought the right path and

struggled against the bad taste of his day, inspired by extraordinary genius and helped by the study of the ancients, at last brought reason upon the stage.

Paul Mesnard (ed.), *Oeuvres de J. Racine*, Vol. 4, 1886, p. 366, trans. T. K. Rabb.

This was exactly the progression—from turbulence to calm—that was apparent throughout European culture in this period.

SOCIAL PATTERNS AND POPULAR CULTURE

The new sense of orderliness, of upheaval subdued, was visible throughout European society in the last years of the seventeenth century. After decades of political and religious conflict, of expressions of uneasiness in philosophy, literature, and the arts, stability and confidence were on the rise. Similarly, the end of population decline, the restoration of social order, and the suppression of disruptive forces like witchcraft indicated that the tensions were easing at all levels of society.

Population Trends

The sixteenth-century rise in Europe's population was succeeded by a period of decline that in most areas lasted long after the political and intellectual upheavals subsided. The rise had been fragile, because throughout these centuries only one child in two reached adulthood. Each couple had to give birth to four children merely to replace themselves, and since they had to wait until they were financially independent to marry—usually in their mid-twenties—they rarely had the chance to produce a big family. Before improvements in nutrition in the nineteenth century, women could bear children only until their late thirties; on average, therefore, a woman had some twelve years in which to give birth to four children to maintain the population. Because lactation delayed ovulation, the

EUROPE'S POPULATION, 1600–1700, BY REGIONS			
Region	*1600**	*1700*	*Percentage Change*
Spain, Portugal, Italy	23.6	22.7	−4
France, Switzerland, Germany	35.0	36.2	+3
British Isles, Low Countries, Scandinavia	12.0	16.1	+34
Total	70.6	75.0	+6

*All figures are in millions.

From Jan de Vries, *The Economy of Europe in an Age of Crisis, 1600–1750*, Cambridge, 1976, p. 5.

mean interval between births was almost two and a half years, which meant that most couples were capable of raising only two children to adulthood. As soon as there was outside pressure—such as plague, famine, or war—population growth became impossible.

The worst of these outside pressures in the seventeenth century was the Thirty Years' War, which alone caused the death of more than 5 million people. It also helped plunge Europe into a debilitating economic depression, which, in turn, decreased the means of relieving the regular famines that afflicted all areas. Disasters like these were not easily absorbed, despite government efforts to distribute food and take other measures to combat natural calamities. Only when better times returned could population increase resume. Because England and the Netherlands led in economic recovery, they experienced a demographic revival long before their neighbors; indeed, the rise in their numbers, which began in the 1660s, accounted for most of the slight population increase the whole of Europe was able to achieve in this difficult century. By 1700, though, prosperity and population were again on the rise—both a reflection and a cause of Europe's newfound assurance and stability.

Social Status

The determinants of status in modern times—wealth, education, and family background—were viewed rather differently in the seventeenth century. Wealth was significant chiefly to merchants, education was important mainly among professionals, and background was vital primarily to the nobility. But in this period the significance of these three social indicators began to shift. Wealth became a more general source of status, as ever-larger numbers of successful merchants bought offices, lands, and titles that allowed them to enter the nobility. Education was also becoming more highly prized; throughout Europe attendance at institutions of higher learning soared after 1550, bringing to universities the sons of artisans as well as nobles. And although background was being scrutinized ever more defensively by old-line nobles, who regarded family lineage as the only criterion for acceptance into their ranks, their resistance to change was futile as the "new" aristocrats multiplied.

In general, it was assumed that everyone occupied a fixed place in the social hierarchy and that it was against the order of nature for someone to move to another level. The growing social importance of wealth and education, however, indicates that mobility was possible. Thanks to the expansion of bureaucracies, it became easier to move to new levels, either by winning favor at court or by buying an office.

Contradictions in the Status of Women   At each level of society, women were usually treated as subordinate by the legal system: In many countries, even the widows of aristocrats could not inherit their husbands' estates; an abbess could never become prominent in Church government; and the few women allowed to practice a trade were excluded from the leadership of their guild. Yet there were notable businesswomen and female artists, writers, and even scientists among the growing numbers of successful self-made people in this period. Widows often inherited their husbands' businesses and pursued thriving careers in their own right, from publishing to innkeeping. One of Caravaggio's most distinguished disciples was Artemisia Gentileschi; the Englishwoman Aphra Behn was a widely known playwright; and some of the leading patrons of intellectual life were the female aristocrats who ran literary circles, particularly in Paris. In fiction and drama, female characters often appeared as the equals of males, despite the legal restrictions of the time and the warnings against such equality in sermons and moral treatises.

Mobility and Crime

The Peasants' Plight   The remarkable economic advances of the sixteenth century helped change attitudes toward wealth, but they brought few benefits to the lower levels of society. Peasants throughout Europe were, in fact, entering a time of increasing difficulty at the end of the sixteenth century. Their taxes were rising rapidly, but the prices they got for the food they grew were stabilizing. Moreover, landowners were starting what has been called the "seigneurial reaction"—making additional demands on their tenants, raising rents, and squeezing as much as they could out of the lands they owned. The effects of famine and war were also more severe at this level of society. The only escapes were to cities or armies, both of which grew rapidly in the seventeenth century. Many of those who fled their villages, however, remained on the road, part of the huge bodies of vagrants and beggars who were a common sight throughout Europe.

A few of those who settled in a town or city improved their lot, but for the large majority, poverty in cities was even more miserable and hungry than poverty on the land. Few could become apprentices, and day laborers were poorly paid and usually out of work. As for military careers, armies were carriers of disease, frequently ill fed, and subject to constant hardship.

Crime and Punishment   For many, therefore, the only alternative to starvation was crime. One area of London in the seventeenth century was totally controlled by the underworld. It offered refuge to fugitives and was never entered by respectable citizens. Robbery and violence—committed equally by desperate men, women, and even children—were common in most cities. As a result, social events like dinners and outings, or visits to the theater, took place during the daytime because the streets were unsafe at night.

If caught, Europe's criminals were treated harshly. In an age before regular police forces, however, catching them was difficult. Crime was usually the responsibility of local authorities, who depended on part-time officials (known in England as constables) for law enforcement. Only in response to major outbreaks, such as a gang of robbers preying on travelers, would the authorities recruit a more substantial armed band (rather like a posse in the American West) to pursue criminals. If such efforts succeeded in bringing offenders to justice, the defendants found they had few rights, especially if they were poor, and punishments were severe. Torture was a common means of extracting confessions; various forms of maiming, such as chopping off a hand or an ear, were considered acceptable penalties; and repeated thefts could lead to execution. Society's hierarchical instincts were apparent even in civil disputes, where nobles were usually immune from prosecution and women often could not start a case. If a woman was raped, for example, she had to find a man to bring suit.

Change in the Villages and Cities

Loss of Village Cohesiveness   Over three-quarters of Europe's population still lived in small village communities, but their structure was changing. In Eastern Europe, peasants were being reduced to serfdom; in the West—our principal concern—familiar relationships and institutions were changing.

The essence of the traditional village had been its isolation. Cut off from frequent contact with the world beyond its immediate region, it had been self-sufficient and closely knit. Everyone knew everyone else, and mutual help was vital for survival. There might be distinctions among villagers—some more prosperous, others less so—but the sense of cohesiveness was powerful. It extended even to the main "outsiders" in the village, the priest and the local lord. The priest was often indistinguishable from his parishioners: almost as poor and sometimes hardly more literate. He adapted to local customs and beliefs, frequently taking part in semipagan rituals so as to keep his authority with his flock. The lord could be exploitative and demanding; but he considered the village his livelihood, and he therefore kept in close touch with its affairs and did all he could to ensure its safety, orderliness, and well-being.

Forces of Change   The main intrusions onto this scene were economic and demographic. As a result of the boom in agricultural prices during the sixteenth century, followed by the economic difficulties of the seventeenth, differences in the wealth of the villagers became more marked. The richer peasants began to set themselves apart from their poorer neighbors, and the feeling of village unity began to break down. These divisions were exacerbated by the rise in population during the sixteenth century—which strained resources and forced the less fortunate to leave in search of better opportunities in cities—and by the pressures of taxation, exploitation, plague, and famine during the more difficult times of the seventeenth century.

Another intrusion that undermined the traditional cohesion of the community was the increased presence of royal officials. For centuries, elected councils, drawn from every part of the population, had run village affairs throughout Europe. In the late seventeenth century, however, these councils began to disappear as outside forces—in some cases a nearby lord, but more often government officials—asserted their control over the localities. Tax gatherers and army recruiters were now familiar figures throughout Europe. Although they were often the target of peasant rebellions, they were also welcomed when, for example, they distributed food during a famine. Their long-term influence, however, was the creation of a new layer of outside authority in the village, which was another cause of the division and fragmentation that led many to flee to the city.

As these outside intrusions multiplied, the interests of the local lord, who traditionally had defended the village's autonomy and had offered help in times of need, also changed. Nobles were beginning to look more and more to royal courts and capital cities, rather than to their local holdings, for position and power. The natural corollary was the "seigneurial reaction," with lords treating the villages they dominated as sources of income and increasingly distancing themselves from the inhabitants. Their commitment to charitable works declined, and they tended more and more to leave the welfare of the local population to church or government officials.

City Life   As village life changed, the inhabitants who felt forced to leave headed for the city—an impersonal place where, instead of joining a cohesive population, they found themselves part of a mingling of peoples. The growing cities needed ever wider regions to provide them with food and goods, and they attracted the many who could not make ends meet in the countryside. Long-distance communications became more common, especially as localities were linked into national market and trade networks, and in the cities the new immigrants met others from distant villages.

A city was a far more chaotic place than a rural community. Urban society in general was fragmentary and

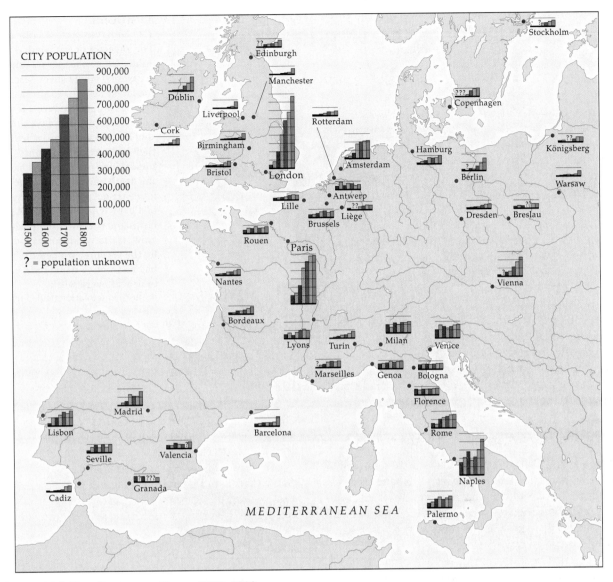

MAP 16.3 THE GROWTH OF CITIES, 1500–1800
In addition to the remarkable rise in the population of Europe's cities, particularly after 1550, this map reveals the northward shift in the distribution of the largest cities: in 1500, three of the four largest were in Italy; in 1700, only one. When did London overtake Paris as the largest city in Europe?
◆ For an online version, go to www.mhhe.com/chambers9 > chapter 16 > book maps

disorganized, even if an individual area, such as a parish, seemed distinct and cohesive—some parishes, for example, were associated with a single trade. A city's craft guilds gave structure to artisans and shopkeepers, regulating their lives and providing welfare, but less than half the population could join a guild. The rest did odd jobs or turned to crime. The chief attraction of cities was the wide variety of economic opportunity: for women, in such areas as selling goods and processing food; for men, in construction, on the docks, and in delivery services. But employment was unpredictable, and citizens did not have community support

to fall back on in hard times as they did in the village. Even forms of recreation and enjoyment were different in the city.

Popular Culture in the City   One major difference between country and town was the level of literacy. Only in urban areas were there significant numbers of people who could read: It has been estimated that in cities perhaps a third of adult males were literate by 1700. Not only was reading necessary for commerce but it had been strongly encouraged by the Reformation, with its insistence that the faithful read the Bible for themselves.

Anonymous
THE NEWSVENDOR, WOODCUT
The ancestor of the regularly published newspaper was the occasional single sheet describing the latest news or rumors. Printers would produce a few hundred copies and have them sold by street vendors whenever they had an event of some importance to describe: a battle, the death of a ruler, or some fantastic occurrence like the birth of a baby with two heads. As cities and the potential readership grew, the news sheets expanded; by the seventeenth century they had distinctive names and began to appear every week.
Bibliothèque Nationale de France, Paris

This stimulus ensured that literacy also rose among women, who increasingly became pupils at the growing number of schools in Europe (although they were still not admitted to universities). As many as 25 percent of the adult women in cities may have been able to read.

These changes had a notable effect on urban life. There was now a readership for newspapers, which became common by the mid-seventeenth century, as did the coffeehouses in which they were often read. Although newspaper stories were regularly inaccurate or untrue, and their writers (relying on informants at courts) could find themselves prosecuted for showing the authorities in a bad light, they were avidly consumed, and they made politics for the first time a subject of wide interest and discussion. Theater and opera also became popular entertainments, with women for the first time taking stage roles and obtaining performances for plays they had written. Sales of books surged, often because they had a popular audience, and they gave broad circulation to traditional favorites, such as travel stories and lives of saints, as well as to the latest ideas of science.

Belief in Magic and Rituals

Although in the countryside cultural patterns looked different—with lower literacy, simpler recreations, and more visible religiosity—there was one area of popular culture in which the outlook of the city and the village was remarkably similar: the belief in magic. The townspeople may have seemed more sophisticated, but the basic assumption they shared with their country cousins was that mysterious forces controlled nature and their own lives and that there was little they could do to ensure their own well-being. The world was full of spirits, and all one could do was encourage the good, defend oneself against the evil, and hope that the good would win. Nothing that happened—a calf dying, lightning striking a house—was accidental. Everything had a purpose. Any unusual event was an omen, part of a larger plan, or the action of some unseen force.

Charivari   To strengthen themselves against trouble, people used whatever help they could find. They organized special processions and holidays to celebrate good times such as harvests, to lament misfortunes, to complain about oppression, or to poke fun at scandalous behavior. These occasions, known as "rough music" in England and *charivari* in France, often used the theme of "the world turned upside down" to make their point. In the set pieces in a procession, a fool might be dressed up as a king, a woman might be shown beating her husband, or a tax collector might appear hanging from a tree. Whether ridiculing a dominating wife or lamenting the lack of bread, the community was expressing its solidarity in the face of difficulty or distasteful behavior through these rituals. They were a form of public opinion, enabling people to let off steam and express themselves.

The potential for violence was always present at such gatherings, especially when religious or social differences became entangled with other resentments. The viciousness of ordinary Protestants and Catholics toward one another revealed a frustration and aggressiveness that was not far below the surface. When food was scarce or new impositions had been ordered by their rulers, peasants and townspeople needed little excuse to show their anger openly. Women often took the

lead, not only because they had firsthand experience of the difficulty of feeding a family but also because troops were more reluctant to attack them.

Magical Remedies   Ordinary people also had other outlets for their frustrations. Recognizing their powerlessness in the face of outside forces, they resorted to their version of the magic that the literate were finding so fashionable at this very time. Whereas the sophisticated patronized astrologers, paying handsomely for horoscopes and advice about how to live their lives, the peasants and the poor consulted popular almanacs or sought out "cunning men" and wise women for secret spells, potions, and other remedies for their anxieties. Even religious ceremonies were thought of as being related to the rituals of the magical world, in which so-called white witches—the friendly kind—gave assistance when a ring was lost or when the butter would not form out of the milk.

Witches and Witch-Hunts   Misfortunes were never just plain bad luck; rather, there was intent behind everything that happened. Events were willed, and if they turned out badly, they must have been willed by the good witch's opposite, the evil witch. Such beliefs often led to cruel persecutions of innocent victims—usually helpless old women, able to do nothing but mutter curses when taunted by neighbors, and easy targets if someone had to be blamed for unfortunate happenings.

This quest for scapegoats naturally focused on the most vulnerable members of society, such as Jews or, in the case of witches, women. Accusations were often directed at a woman who was old and alone, with nobody to defend her. She was feared because she seemed to be an outsider or not sufficiently deferential to her supposed betters. It was believed that witches read strange books and knew magic spells, an indication of what many regarded as inappropriate and dangerous levels of literacy for a woman.

In the sixteenth and seventeenth centuries, the hunt for witches intensified to levels never previously reached. This period has been called the era of the "great witch craze," and for good reason. There were outbursts in every part of Europe, and tens of thousands of the accused were executed. Dozens of men, most of them clerics, made witch-hunting a full-time profession and persuaded civic and other government authorities to devote their resources to stamping out this threat to social and religious stability. Suspects were almost always tortured, and it is not too surprising that they usually "confessed" and implicated others as servants of the devil. The practices that were uncovered varied—in some areas witches were said to dance with the devil, in others to fly on broomsticks, in

Hans Baldung Grien
***WITCHES*, WOODCUT**
This woodcut by the German artist Grien shows the popular image of witches in early modern Europe. One carries a potion while flying on a goat. The others put together the ingredients for a magic potion in a jar inscribed with mystical symbols. The fact that witches were thought to be learned women who could understand magic was another reason they were feared by a Europe that expected women to be uneducated.

others to be possessed by evil spirits who could induce dreadful (and possibly psychosomatic) symptoms—but the punishment was usually the same: burning at the stake. And the hysteria was infectious. One accusation could trigger dozens more until entire regions were swept with fear and hatred.

Forces of Restraint

By the middle of the seventeenth century, the wave of assaults on witches was beginning to recede (see "A Witness Analyzes the Witch Craze," p. 487). Social and political leaders came to realize that the campaigns

A WITNESS ANALYZES THE WITCH CRAZE

Although for most Europeans around 1600 witchcraft was real—a religious problem caused by the devil—there were a few observers who were beginning to think more analytically about the reasons for the rapid spread of accusations. One such observer was a clergyman named Linden, who was attached to the cathedral of the great city of Trier in western Germany. His description of a witch-hunt in the Trier region ignored the standard religious explanations.

"Inasmuch as it was popularly believed that the continued sterility of many years was caused by witches, the whole area rose to exterminate the witches. This movement was promoted by many in office, who hoped to gain wealth from the persecution. And so special accusers, inquisitors, notaries, judges, and constables dragged to trial and torture human beings of both sexes and burned them in great numbers. Scarcely any of those who were accused escaped punishment. So far did the madness of the furious populace and the courts go in this thirst for blood and booty that there was scarcely anybody who was not smirched by some suspicion of this crime. Meanwhile, notaries, copyists and innkeepers grew rich. The executioner rode a fine horse, like a noble of the court, and dressed in gold and silver; his wife competed with noble dames in the richness of her array. A direr pestilence or a more ruthless invader could hardly have ravaged the territory than this inquisition and persecution without bounds. Many were the reasons for doubting that all were really guilty. At last, though the flames were still unsated, the people grew poor, rules were made and enforced restricting the fees and costs of examinations, and suddenly, as when in war funds fail, the zeal of the persecutors died out."

From George L. Burr (ed.), "The Witch Persecutions," *Translations and Reprints from the Original Sources of European History*, Vol. 3, Philadelphia: University of Pennsylvania, 1902, pp. 13–14.

against witches could endanger authority, especially when accusations were turned against the rich and privileged classes. Increasingly, therefore, cases were not brought to trial, and when they were, lawyers and doctors (who treated the subject less emotionally than the clergy) cast doubt on the validity of the testimony. Gradually, excesses were restrained and control was reestablished; by 1700 there was only a trickle of new incidents.

The decline in accusations of witchcraft reflected not only the more general quieting down of conflict and upheaval in the late seventeenth century but also the growing proportion of Europe's population that was living in cities. Here, less reliant on the luck of good weather, people could feel themselves more in control of their own fates. If there were unexpected fires, there were fire brigades; if a house burned down, there might even be insurance—a new protection for individuals that was spreading in the late 1600s. A process that has been called the "disenchantment" of the world—growing skepticism about spirits and mysterious forces, and greater self-reliance—was under way.

Religious Discipline   The churches played an important part in suppressing the traditional reliance on magic. In Catholic countries the Counter-Reformation produced better-educated priests who were trained to impose official doctrine instead of tolerating unusual local customs. Among Protestants, ministers were similarly well educated and denounced magical practices as idolatrous or superstitious. And both camps treated passion and enthusiasm with suspicion. Habits did not change overnight, but gradually ordinary people were being persuaded to abandon old fears and beliefs. There were still major scares in midcentury. An eclipse in 1654 prompted panic throughout Europe; comets still inspired prophecies of the end of the world; and in the 1660s a self-proclaimed messiah named Shabtai Zvi attracted a massive following among the Jews of Europe and the Middle East. Increasingly, though, such visions of doom or the end of time were becoming fringe beliefs, dismissed by authorities and most elements of society. Eclipses and comets now had scientific explanations, and the messiah came to be regarded as a spiritual, not an immediate, promise.

Summary

Even at the level of popular culture, therefore, Europeans had reason to feel, by the late seventeenth century, that a time of upheaval and uncertainty was over. A sense of confidence and orderliness was returning, and in intellectual circles the optimism seemed justified by the achievements of science. In fact, there arose a scholarly dispute around 1700, known as the "battle of the books," in which one side claimed, for the first time, that the "moderns" had outshone the "ancients." Using the scientists as their chief example, the advocates of the "moderns" argued—in a remarkable break with the reverence for the past that had dominated medieval and Renaissance culture—that advances in thought were possible and that one did not always have to accept the superiority of antiquity. Such self-confidence made it clear that, in the world of ideas as surely as in the world of politics, a period of turbulence had given way to an era of renewed assurance and stability.

QUESTIONS FOR FURTHER THOUGHT

1. Are there similarities in the creativity that marks the scientist and the artist?

2. Is it fair to ask whether popular beliefs and rituals do more harm than good?

RECOMMENDED READING

Sources

*Drake, Stillman (tr. and ed.). *Discoveries and Opinions of Galileo.* 1957. The complete texts of some of Galileo's most important works.

*Hall, Marie Boas (ed.). *Nature and Nature's Laws: Documents of the Scientific Revolution.* 1970. A good collection of documents by and about the pioneers of modern science.

Studies

Biagioli, Mario. *Galileo, Courtier: The Practice of Science in the Culture of Absolutism.* 1993. A fascinating study of the political forces at work in Galileo's career.

Braudel, Fernand. *Capitalism and Material Life, 1400–1800.* Miriam Kochan (tr.). 1973. A classic, pioneering study of the structure of daily life in early modern Europe.

*Burke, Peter. *Popular Culture in Early Modern Europe.* 1978. A lively introduction to the many forms of expression and belief among the ordinary people of Europe.

Fara, Patricia. *Newton: The Making of a Genius.* 2002.

*Gutmann, Myron P. *Toward the Modern Economy: Early Industry in Europe, 1500–1800.* 1988. A clear survey of recent work on economic development in this period.

*Ladurie, Emmanuel Le Roy. *The Peasants of Languedoc.* John Day (tr.). 1966. A brilliant evocation of peasant life in France in the sixteenth and seventeenth centuries.

*Levack, Brian P. *The Witch-Hunt in Early Modern Europe.* 1987. An excellent survey of the belief in witchcraft and its consequences.

Oppenheimer, Paul. *Rubens: A Portrait.* 2002.

Rabb, Theodore K. *Renaissance Lives.* 1993. Brief biographies of fifteen people, both famous and obscure, who lived just before and during this period.

*Shapin, S. *The Scientific Revolution.* 1996.

*Shearman, John. *Mannerism.* 1968. The best short introduction to a difficult artistic style.

*Thomas, Keith. *Religion and the Decline of Magic.* 1976. The most thorough account of popular culture yet published, this enormous book, while dealing mainly with England, treats at length such subjects as witchcraft, astrology, and ghosts in a most readable style.

Wiesner, Merry E. *Women and Gender in Early Modern Europe.* 1993.

*Available in paperback.

Nicolas de Largilliére
LOUIS XIV AND HIS FAMILY
**Louis XIV (seated) is shown here in full regal splendor surrounded by three of his heirs. On his
right is his eldest son, on his left is his eldest grandson, and, reaching out his hand, is his eldest
great-grandson, held by his governess. All three of these heirs died before Louis, and thus they
never became kings of France.**
Reproduced by Permission of the Trustees of the Wallace Collection, London

Chapter Seventeen

THE EMERGENCE OF THE EUROPEAN STATE SYSTEM

ABSOLUTISM IN FRANCE • OTHER PATTERNS OF ABSOLUTISM • ALTERNATIVES TO ABSOLUTISM • THE INTERNATIONAL SYSTEM

The acceptance of strong central governments that emerged out of the crisis of the mid-seventeenth century was a victory not merely for kings but for an entire way of organizing society. As a result of huge increases in the scale of warfare and taxation, bureaucracies had mushroomed, and their presence was felt throughout Europe. Yet no central administration, however powerful, could function without the support of the nobles who ruled the countryside. Regional loyalties had dominated European society for centuries, and only a regime that drew on those loyalties could hope to maintain the support of its subjects. The political structures that developed during the century following the 1650s were, therefore, the work not only of ambitious princes but also of a nobility long accustomed to exercising authority and now prepared to find new ways of exerting its influence. To the leaders of society during the century following the crisis of the 1640s and 1650s, it was clear that state building and the imposition of their power on the rest of the world were now ever more central to rulers' ambitions, and required a common effort to establish stronger political, social, military, financial, and religious structures that would support effective government. The institutions and practices they created have remained essential to the modern state ever since.

Locke, *Second Treatise of Civil Government* **1690** ●

"Glorious" Revolution in England **1689** ●

Reign of Peter the Great in Russia **1682–1725** ▬▬▬

Hobbes, *Leviathan* **1651** ●

Reign of Louis XIV in France **1643–1715** ▬▬▬▬▬

ABSOLUTISM IN FRANCE

One way of creating a strong, centralized state was the political system known as **absolutism:** the belief that power emanated from the monarch's unlimited authority. Absolutism was based on a theory known as the **divine right of kings,** derived from the fact that kings were anointed with holy oil at their coronations; it asserted that the monarch was God's representative on earth.

The Rule of Louis XIV

The most famous absolutist state was the Kingdom of France, which became the most powerful regime in Europe. Taken to an extreme, as it was by Louis XIV (1643–1715), absolutism justified unlimited power and treated treason as blasphemy. The leading advocate of the theory, Bishop Bossuet, called Louis God's lieutenant and argued that the Bible itself endorsed absolutism. In reality, the king worked in close partnership with the nobles to maintain order, and he often (though not always) felt obliged to defend their local authority as a reinforcement of his own power. Nevertheless, the very notion that the king not only was supreme but could assert his will with armies and bureaucracies of unprecedented size gave absolutism both an image and a reality that set it apart from previous systems of monarchical rule. Here at last was a force that could hold together and control the increasingly complex interactions of regions and interest groups that made up a state.

Versailles   The setting in which a central government operated often reflected its power and its methods. Philip II in the late 1500s had created, at the Escorial

outside Madrid, the first isolated palace that controlled a large realm. A hundred years later, Louis XIV created at Versailles, near Paris, a far more elaborate court as the center of an even larger and more intrusive bureaucracy than Philip's. The isolation of government and the exercise of vast personal power seemed to go hand in hand.

The king moved the court in the 1680s to Versailles, 12 miles from Paris, where, at a cost of half a year's royal income, he transformed a small chateau his father had built into the largest building in Europe. There, far from Parisian mobs, he enjoyed the splendor and the ceremonies, centered on himself, which exalted his majesty. His self-aggrandizing image as "Sun King" was symbolized by coins that showed the sun's rays falling first on Louis and only then, by reflection, onto his subjects. Every French nobleman of any significance spent time each year at Versailles, not only to maintain access to royal patronage and governmental affairs but also to demonstrate the wide support for Louis' system of rule. Historians have called this process the domestication of the aristocracy, as great lords who had once drawn their status from their lineage or lands came to regard service to the throne as the best route to power. But the benefits cut both ways. The king gained the services of influential administrators, and they gained privileges and rewards without the uncertainties that had accompanied their traditional resistance to central control.

Court Life   The visible symbol of Louis' absolutism was Versailles. Here the leaders of France assembled, and around them swirled the most envied social circles of the time. From the court emanated the policies and directives that increasingly affected the lives of the king's subjects and also determined France's relations with other states.

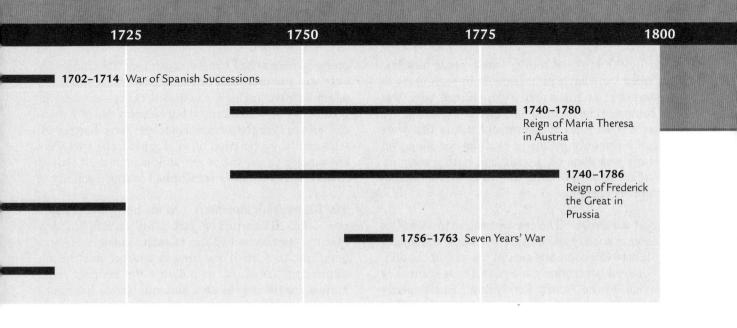

1702–1714 War of Spanish Successions

1740–1780
Reign of Maria Theresa
in Austria

1740–1786
Reign of Frederick
the Great in
Prussia

1756–1763 Seven Years' War

At Versailles, too, French culture was shaped by the king's patronage of those artists and writers who appealed to the royal taste. For serious drama and history, Louis turned to the playwright and writer Racine (1639–1699); for comedy, to the theatrical producer and playwright Molière (1622–1673); and for opera and the first performances of what we now call ballet, to the composer Lully (1632–1687). Moreover, all artistic expression, from poetry to painting, was regulated by royal academies that were founded in the 1600s;

PERSPECTIVE VIEW OF VERSAILLES FROM THE PLACE D'ARMES, **1698**
This painting shows Versailles not long before Louis decided to move there; he was soon to begin an enormous expansion into the gardens at the back that more than doubled the size of the buildings. In this scene, the royal coach, with its entourage, is just about to enter the château.
Giraudon/Art Resource, NY

backed by the king's authority, these academies laid down rules for what was acceptable in such areas as verse forms or architectural style. Official taste was what counted. The dazzling displays at Versailles had to observe strict rules of dignity and gravity that were considered the only means of exalting the king. Yet everything was done on a scale and with a magnificence that no other European ruler could match, though many tried.

Paris and Versailles   The one alternative to Versailles as a center of society and culture was Paris, and indeed the split between court and capital was one of the divisions between government and people that eventually was to lead to the French Revolution. A particularly notable difference was in the role of women. Versailles was overwhelmingly a male society. Women achieved prominence only as royal mistresses in Louis' early years or as the creators of a rigidly pious atmosphere in his last years. They were also essential to the highly elaborate rituals of civility and manners that developed at Versailles. But they were allowed no independent initiative in social or cultural matters.

In Paris, by contrast, women established and dominated the gatherings known as **salons** that promoted easy conversation, a mixture of social backgrounds, and forms of expression—political discussion and ribald humor, for example—that were not acceptable at the staid and sober court. Yet the contrasts were not merely between the formal palace and the relaxed salon. Even before Louis moved to Versailles, he banned as improper one of Molière's comedies, *Tartuffe*, which mocked excessive religious devoutness. It took five years of reworking by Molière before Louis allowed the play to be performed (1669), and it then became a major hit in Paris, but it was never a favorite at court.

Government

Absolutism was more than a device to satisfy royal whims, for Louis was a gifted administrator and politician who used his power for state building. By creating and reorganizing government institutions, he strengthened his authority at home and increased his ascendancy over his neighbors. The longest-lasting result of his absolutism was that the French state won control over three crucial activities: the use of armed force, the formulation and execution of laws, and the collection and expenditure of revenue. These functions, in turn, depended on a centrally controlled bureaucracy responsive to royal orders and efficient enough to carry them out in distant provinces over the objections of local groups.

Nobody could suppress all vested interests and local loyalties, but the bureaucracy was supposed to be insulated from outside pressure by the absolute monarch's power to remove and transfer appointees. This independence was also promoted by training programs, improved administrative methods, and the use of experts wherever possible—both in the central bureaucracy and in provincial offices. Yet the system could not have functioned without the cooperation of local aristocrats, who were encouraged to use the power and income they derived from official positions to strengthen central authority.

The King's Dual Functions   At the head of this structure, Louis XIV carried off successfully a dual function that few monarchs had the talent to sustain: He was both king in council and king in court. Louis the administrator coexisted with Louis the courtier, who hunted, cultivated the arts, and indulged in huge banquets. Among his many imitators, however, the easier side of absolutism, court life, consumed an excessive share of a state's resources and became an end in itself. The effect was to give prestige to the leisure pursuits of the upper classes while sapping the energies of influential figures. Louis was one of the few who avoided sacrificing affairs of state to regal pomp.

Like court life, government policy under Louis XIV was tailored to the aim of state building. As he was to discover, the resources and powers at his disposal were not endless. But until the last years of his reign, they served his many purposes extremely well (see "Louis XIV on Kingship," p. 495). Moreover, Louis had superb support at the highest levels of his administration— ministers whose viewpoints differed but whose skills were carefully blended by their ruler.

Competing Ministers   Until the late 1680s the king's two leading advisers were Jean-Baptiste Colbert and the marquis of Louvois. Colbert was a financial wizard who regarded a mercantilist policy as the key to state building. He believed that the government should give priority to increasing France's wealth. As a result, he believed that the chief danger to the country's well-being was the United Provinces, Europe's great trader state, and that royal resources should be poured into the navy, manufacturing, and shipping. By contrast, Louvois, the son of a military administrator, consistently emphasized the army as the foundation of France's power. He believed that the country was threatened primarily by land—by the Holy Roman Empire on its flat, vulnerable northeast frontier—and thus that resources should be allocated to the army and to border fortifications.

Foreign Policy

Louis tried to balance these goals within his overall aims—to expand France's frontiers and to assert his superiority over other European states. Like the magnifi-

LOUIS XIV ON KINGSHIP

From time to time, Louis XIV put on paper brief accounts of his actions: For example, he wrote some brief memoirs in the late 1660s. These reflections about his role as king were intended as a guide for his son and indicate both his high view of kingship and the seriousness with which he approached his duties. The following are extracts from his memoirs and other writings.

"Homage is due to kings, and they do whatever they like. It certainly must be agreed that, however bad a prince may be, it is always a heinous crime for his subjects to rebel against him. He who gave men kings willed that they should be respected as His lieutenants, and reserved to Himself the right to question their conduct. It is His will that everyone who is born a subject should obey without qualification. This law, as clear as it is universal, was not made only for the sake of princes: it is also for the good of the people themselves. It is therefore the duty of kings to sustain by their own example the religion upon which they rely; and they must realize that, if their subjects see them plunged in vice or violence, they can hardly render to their person the respect due to their office, or recognize in them the living image of Him who is all-holy as well as almighty.

"It is a fine thing, a noble and enjoyable thing, to be a king. But it is not without its pains, its fatigues, and its troubles. One must work hard to reign. In working for the state, a king is working for himself. The good of the one is the glory of the other. When the state is prosperous, famous, and powerful, the king who is the cause of it is glorious; and he ought in consequence to have a larger share than others do of all that is most agreeable in life."

From J. M. Thompson, *Lectures on Foreign History, 1494–1789,* Oxford: Blackwell, 1956, pp. 172–174.

Antoine Watteau
FÊTE IN THE PARK, 1718
The luxurious life of the nobility during the eighteenth century is captured in this scene of men and women in fine silks, enjoying a picnic in a lovely park setting.
Reproduced by Permission of the Trustees of the Wallace Collection, London

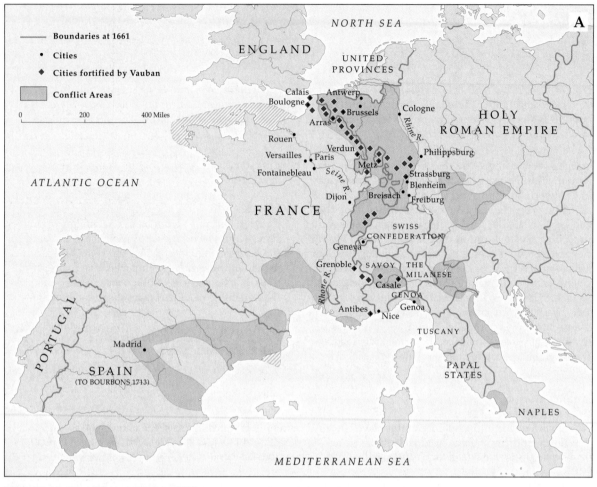

MAP 17.1A THE WARS OF LOUIS XIV
Louis XIV's aggressive aims took his troops to many areas of Europe.
◆ For an online version, go to www.mhhe.com/chambers9 > chapter 17 > book maps

cence of his court, his power on the international scene served to demonstrate *la gloire* (the glory) of France. But his effort to expand that power prompted his neighbors to form coalitions and alliances of common defense, designed to keep him in check. From this response was to emerge the concept of a state system and the notion of a **balance of power** among the states of Europe.

In his early years Louis relied heavily on Colbert, who moved gradually toward war with the Dutch when he was unable to undermine their control of French maritime trade. But the war (1672–1678) was a failure, and so the pendulum swung toward Louvois' priorities. In the early 1680s Louis adopted the marquis's aims and claimed a succession of territories on France's northeast border. No one claim seemed large enough to provoke his neighbors to fight, especially

since the Holy Roman Emperor, Leopold I, was distracted by a resumption in 1682 of war with the Turks in the east. The result was that France was able to annex large segments of territory until, in 1686, a league of other European states was formed to restrain Louis' growing power (see maps 17.1A and 17.1B).

Louis versus Europe   The leaders of the league were William III of the United Provinces and Emperor Leopold. Leopold was prepared to join the struggle because his war with the Turks turned in his favor after 1683, when his troops broke a Turkish siege of Vienna. And six years later William became a far more formidable foe when he gained the English throne. In 1688 the league finally went to war to put an end to French expansion. When Louis began to lose the territories he had gained in the 1680s, he decided to seek peace and

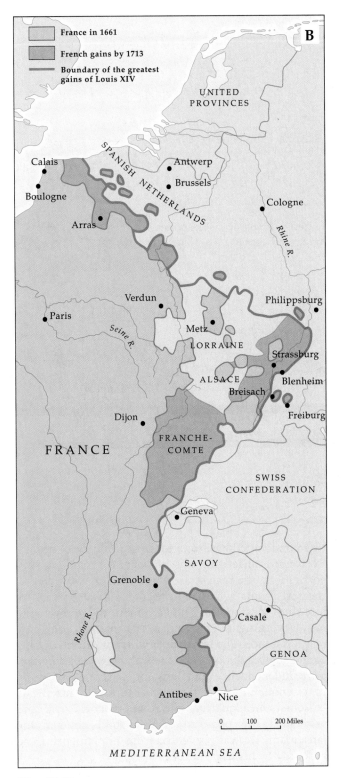

MAP 17.1B
THE WARS OF LOUIS XIV
The main conflict was on France's eastern border, where Louis made small but significant gains. Why was there so much conflict along this border?
◆ For an online version, go to www.mhhe.com/chambers9 > chapter 17 > book maps

remove Louvois from power in 1690, though the war did not end until 1697. But the respite did not last long. Four years later France became involved in a bitter war that brought famine, wretched poverty, and humiliation. This was a war to gain the Spanish throne for Louis' family, regardless of the devastating consequences of the fighting. This final, ruinous enterprise revealed both the new power of France and its limits. By launching an all-out attempt to establish his supremacy in Europe, Louis showed that he felt capable of taking on the whole of the continent; but by then he no longer had the economic and military base at home or the weak opposition abroad to ensure success.

Economic strains had begun to appear in the 1690s, when shattering famines throughout France reduced tax revenues and the size of the workforce, even as enemies began to unite abroad. Louis had the most formidable army in Europe—400,000 men by the end of his reign—but both William and Leopold believed he could be defeated by a combined assault, and they led the attack in the final showdown when the Habsburg king of Spain, Charles II, died without an heir in 1700.

The War of Spanish Succession   There were various claimants to the Spanish throne, but Charles's choice was Philip, Louis XIV's grandson (see "The Spanish Succession, 1700," p. 498). Had Louis been willing to agree not to unite the thrones of France and Spain and to allow the Spanish empire to be opened (for the first time) to foreign traders, Charles's wish might have been respected. But Louis refused to compromise, and in 1701 William and Leopold created the so-called Grand Alliance, which declared war on France the following year. The French now had to fight virtually all of Europe in a war over the Spanish succession, not only at home but also overseas, in India, Canada, and the Caribbean.

Led by two brilliant generals—the Englishman John Churchill, duke of Marlborough, and the Austrian Prince Eugène—the Grand Alliance won a series of smashing victories. France's hardships were increased by a terrible famine in 1709. Although the criticism of his policies became fierce and dangerous rebellions erupted, the Sun King retained his hold over his subjects. Despite military disaster, he was able to keep his nation's borders intact and the Spanish throne for his grandson (though he had to give up the possibility of union with France and end the restrictions on trade in the Spanish empire) when peace treaties were signed at Utrecht in 1713 and 1714. When it was all over, Louis' great task of state building, both at home and abroad, had withstood the severest of tests: defeat on the battlefield.

THE SPANISH SUCCESSION, 1700

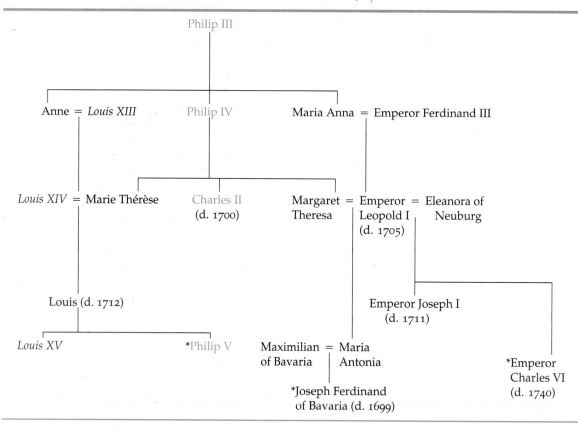

Note: Names in blue = kings of Spain; names in r ed = kings of France.

*People designated at various times as heirs of Charles II.

Domestic Policy

Control and Reform   The assertion of royal supremacy at home was almost complete by the time Louis came to power, but he extended centralized control to religion and social institutions. Both the Protestant Huguenots and the Catholic Jansenists interfered with the religious uniformity that Louis considered essential in an absolutist state. As a result, pressures against these groups mounted steadily. In 1685 Louis revoked the Edict of Nantes, now almost a century old, which had granted Protestants limited toleration, and he forced France's 1 million Huguenots either to leave the country (four-fifths did) or to convert to Catholicism. This was a political rather than a religious step, taken to promote unity despite the economic consequences that followed the departure of a vigorous, productive, and entrepreneurial minority.

Jansenism was more elusive. It had far fewer followers, and it was a movement that emphasized spiritual values within Catholicism. But the very fact that it challenged the official Church emphasis on ritual and was condemned by Rome made it a source of unrest. Even more unsettling was its success in gaining support among the magistrate class—the royal officers in the parlements, who had to register all royal edicts before they became law. The Parlement of Paris was the only governmental institution that offered Louis any real resistance. The issues over which it caused trouble were usually religious, and the link between *parlementaire* independence and Jansenism gave Louis more than enough reason for displeasure. He razed the Jansenists' headquarters, the Abbey of Port-Royal, and persuaded the pope to issue a bull condemning Jansenism. He was prevented from implementing the bull only by his death in 1715.

The drive toward uniformity that prompted these actions was reflected in all of domestic policy. Louis kept in check what little protest arose in the parlements and either forbade or overruled their efforts to block his decrees; major uprisings by peasants in central France in the 1690s and 1700s were ruthlessly suppressed; Parisian publishers came under bureaucratic supervision; and the *intendants*, the government's chief provincial officers, were given increased authority, especially to supply the ever-growing money and recruitment needs of the army.

At the outset of his rule, Louis also used his power to improve France's economy. In these early years, under Colbert's ministry, major efforts were made to stimulate manufacturing, agriculture, and home and foreign trade. Some industries, notably those involving luxuries, like the silk production of Lyons, received considerable help and owed their prosperity to royal patronage. Colbert also tried, not entirely effectively, to reduce the crippling effects of France's countless internal tolls. These were usually nobles' perquisites, and they could multiply the cost of shipped goods. The government divided the country into a number of districts, within which shipments were to be toll-free, but the system never removed the worst abuses. Louis also hoped to boost foreign trade, at first by financing new overseas trading companies and later by founding new port cities as naval and commercial centers. He achieved notable success only in the West Indies, where sugar plantations became a source of great wealth.

The End of an Era

Louis' success in state building was remarkable, and France became the envy of Europe. Yet ever since the Sun King's reign, historians have recalled the famines and wars of his last years and have contrasted his glittering court with the misery of most French people. Taxes and rents rose remorselessly, and in many regions the hardships were made worse by significant declines in the population. Particularly after the famines of the 1690s and 1709, many contemporaries remarked on the dreadful condition of France's peasants.

The reign of Louis XIV can thus be regarded as the end of an era in the life of the lower classes. By pushing his need for resources to its limits, he inflicted a level of suffering that was not to recur, because governments increasingly came to realize that state building depended on the welfare and support of their people. In the eighteenth century, although there was still much suffering to come, the terrible subsistence crises, with their cycles of famine and plague, came to an end, largely because of official efforts to distribute food in starving areas and to isolate and suppress outbreaks of plague. Thus, although the hand of the central government was heavier in 1715 than a hundred years before, it was becoming more obviously a beneficent as well as a burdensome force. The Counter-Reformation Church, growing in strength since the Council of Trent, also had a more salutary influence as religious struggles died away, for it brought into local parishes better-educated and more dedicated priests who, as part of their new commitment to service, exerted themselves to calm the outbreaks of witchcraft and irrational fear that had swept the countryside for centuries. Despite the strains Louis had caused, therefore, his absolutist authority was now firmly in place and could ensure a dominant European role for a united and powerful France.

France after Louis XIV

The Sun King had created a model for absolutism in partnership with his nobility, but the traditional ambitions of the nobles reasserted themselves after he died in 1715, leaving a child as his heir. The duke of Orlèans, Louis XIV's nephew, who became regent until 1723, sought to restore the aristocrats' authority. He also gave the parlements political power and replaced royal bureaucrats with councils composed of leading members of the nobility. The councils were unable to govern effectively, but the parlements would never again surrender their power to veto royal legislation. They became a rallying point for those who opposed centralization and wished to limit the king's powers.

Finance was also a serious problem for the government, because of the debts left by Louis XIV's wars. A brilliant Scottish financier, John Law, suggested an answer: a government-sponsored central bank that would issue paper notes, expand credit, and encourage investment in a new trading company for the French colonies. By tying the bank to this company, the Company of the Occident, a venture that promised subscribers vast profits from the Louisiana territory in North America, Law set off an investment boom. But the public's greed soon pushed prices for the company's stock to insanely high levels. A bust was inevitable, and when it came, in 1720, the entire scheme of bank notes and credit collapsed.

Louis XV and Fleury   Political and financial problems were to plague France throughout the eighteenth century, until the leaders of the French Revolution sought radical ways to solve them in the 1790s. Yet the uncertainties of the regency did give way to a long period of stability after 1726, when Louis XV gave almost unlimited authority to his aging tutor and adviser, Cardinal Fleury. Cautious, dedicated to the monarchy, and surrounded by talented subordinates, Fleury made absolutism function quietly and effectively and enabled France to recover from the setbacks that had marked the end of Louis XIV's reign. Fleury's tenure coincided with abundant harvests, slowly rising population, and increased commercial activity.

Political Problems   Fleury contained the ambitions of the governing class, but when he died in 1743 at the age of 90, the pressures exploded. War hawks plunged

HISTORICAL ISSUES: TWO VIEWS OF LOUIS XIV

Implicit in any assessment of the reign of Louis XIV in France is a judgment about the nature of absolutism and the kind of government the continental European monarchies created in the late seventeenth and eighteenth centuries. From the perspective of Frenchman Albert Sorel, a historian of the French Revolution writing at the end of the nineteenth century, the Revolution had been necessary to save France from Louis' heritage. For the American John Rule, a historian who concerned himself primarily with the development of political institutions during the seventeenth century, the marks of Louis XIV's rule were caution, bureaucracy, and order.

Sorel: "The edifice of the state enjoyed incomparable brilliance and splendor, but it resembled a Gothic cathedral in which the height of the nave and the arches had been pushed beyond all reason, weakening the walls as they were raised ever higher. Louis XIV carried the principle of monarchy to its utmost limit, and abused it in all respects to the point of excess. He left the nation crushed by war, mutilated by banishments, and impatient of the yoke which it felt to be ruinous. Men were worn-out, the treasury empty, all relationships strained by the violence of tension, and in the immense framework of the state there remained no institution except the accidental appearance of genius. Things had reached a point where, if a great king did not appear, there would be a great revolution."

From Albert Sorel, *L'Europe et la rèvolution française,* 3rd ed., Vol. 1, Paris, 1893, p. 199, as translated in William F. Church (ed.), *The Greatness of Louis XIV: Myth or Reality?*, Boston: D. C. Heath, 1959, p. 63.

Rule: "As Louis XIV himself said of the tasks of kingship, they were at once great, noble, and delightful. Yet Louis' enjoyment of his craft was tempered by political prudence. At an early age he learned to listen attentively to his advisers, to speak when spoken to, to ponder evidence, to avoid confrontations, to dissemble, to wait. He believed that time and tact would conquer. Despite all the evidence provided him by his ministers and his servants, Louis often hesitated before making a decision; he brooded, and in some instances put off decisions altogether. As he grew older, the king tended to hide his person and his office. Even his officials seldom saw the king for more than a brief interview. And as decision-making became centralized in the hands of the ministers, [so] the municipalities, the judges, the local estates, the guilds and at times the peasantry contested royal encroachments on their rights. Yet to many in the kingdom, Louis represented a modern king, an agent of stability whose struggle was their struggle and whose goal was to contain the crises of the age."

From John C. Rule, "Louis XIV, *Roi-Bureaucrate,*" in Rule (ed.), *Louis XIV and the Craft of Kingship,* Columbus: Ohio State University Press, 1969, pp. 91–92.

France into the first of several unsuccessful wars with its neighbors that strained French credit to the breaking point. At home royal authority also deteriorated. Having no one to replace Fleury as chief minister, Louis XV put his confidence in a succession of advisers, some capable, some mediocre. But he did not back them when attacks arose from court factions. Uninterested in government, he avoided confrontation, neglected affairs of state, and devoted himself instead to hunting and to court ceremony.

Although Louis XV provided weak leadership, France's difficulties were structural as well as personal. The main problems—special privileges and finance—posed almost impossible challenges. Governments that levy new taxes arbitrarily seem despotic, even if the need for them is clear and the distribution equitable. One of France's soundest taxes was the *vingtième,* or twentieth, which was supposed to tap the income of all

parts of French society roughly equally. But the nobility and clergy evaded most of the tax. Naturally, aggressive royal ministers wanted to remedy that situation. In the 1750s, for example, an effort was made to put teeth into the *vingtième's* bite on the clergy's huge wealth. But the effort failed. The clergy resisted furiously; and the parlements denounced the "despotism" of a crown that taxed its subjects arbitrarily. Thus, the privileged groups not only blocked reforms but also made the monarch's position more difficult by their opposition and rhetoric of liberty.

The Long Term   Despite these special interests, the 1700s were a time of notable advance for Europe's most populous and wealthy state. France enjoyed remarkable expansion in population, in the rural economy, in commerce, and in empire building. No one knew at the time that the failures of reforming royal ministers in

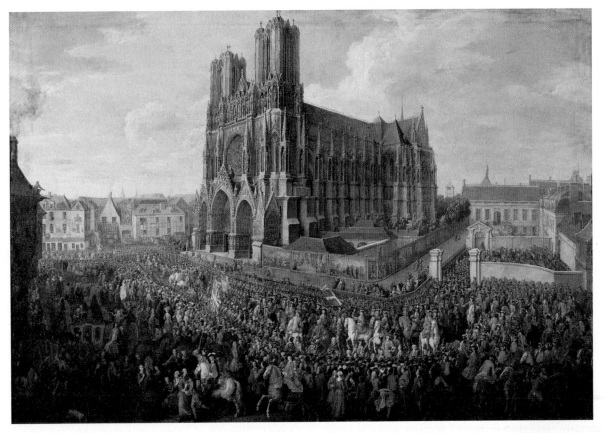

Pierre Denis Martin
PROCESSION AFTER LOUIS XV'S CORONATION AT RHEIMS, 26 OCTOBER 1722, CA. 1724
This magnificent scene, in front of the cathedral in which French kings traditionally were crowned, provides a sense of the throngs who came to celebrate the day in 1722 when Louis XV officially came of age and received his crown. Paintings depicting royal virtue were erected around the cathedral, and Louis himself (in red on a white horse just to the right of center) was preceded by a flag covered with his symbol, the fleur-de-lis. The other flags remind us that this event was an occasion for international pageantry.
Giraudon/Art Resource, NY

the mid-1700s foretold a stalemate that would help bring the old regime crashing down.

OTHER PATTERNS OF ABSOLUTISM

Four other monarchies pursued state building through absolutist regimes in this period, often in imitation of the French model. The governments they created in Vienna, Berlin, Madrid, and St. Petersburg differed in strengths and weaknesses, but all were attempts to centralize power around a formidable ruler.

The Habsburgs at Vienna

The closest imitation of Versailles was the court of the Habsburg Leopold I, the Holy Roman emperor (1658–1705). Heir to a reduced inheritance that gave him control over only Bohemia, Austria, and a small part of

Hungary, Leopold still maintained a splendid establishment. His plans for a new palace, Schönbrunn, that was supposed to outshine Versailles were modified only because of a lack of funds. And his promotion of the court as the center of all political and social life turned Vienna into what it had never been before: a city for nobles as well as small-time traders.

Nevertheless, Leopold did not display the pretensions of the Sun King. He was a younger son and had come to the throne only because of the death of his brother. Indecisive, retiring, and deeply religious, he had no fondness for the bravado Louis XIV enjoyed. He was a composer of some talent, and his patronage laid the foundation for the great musical culture that was to be one of Vienna's chief glories. But he did inherit considerable royal authority, which he sought to expand—though unlike Louis XIV he relied on a small group of leading nobles to devise policy and run his government.

Government Policy   The Thirty Years' War that ended in 1648 had revealed that the elected head of the Holy Roman Empire could no longer control the princes who nominally owed him allegiance. In his own domains, however, he could maintain his control with the cooperation of his nobility. The Privy Council, which in effect ran Leopold's government, was filled largely with members of aristocratic families, and his chief advisers were always prominent nobles. To make policy, he consulted each of his ministers and then, even when all agreed, came to decisions with agonizing slowness.

Unlike the other courts of Europe, Schönbrunn did not favor only native-born aristocrats. The leader of Austria's armies during the Turks' siege of Vienna in 1683 was Charles, duke of Lorraine, whose duchy had been taken over by the French. His predecessor as field marshal had been an Italian, and his successor was to be one of the most brilliant soldiers of the age, Prince Eugène of Savoy. They became members of the Austrian nobility only when Leopold gave them titles within his own dominions, but they all fitted easily into the aristocratic circles that controlled the government and the army.

Eugène and Austria's Military Success   Prince Eugène (1663–1736) was a spectacular symbol of the aristocracy's continuing dominance of politics and society. A member of one of Europe's most distinguished families, he had been raised in France but found himself passed over when Louis XIV awarded army commissions, perhaps because he had been intended for the Church. Yet he was determined to have a military career, and he volunteered to serve the Austrians in the war with the Turks that, following the siege of Vienna, was to expand Habsburg territory in the Balkans by the time peace was signed in 1699 (see map 17.2). Eugène's talents quickly became evident: He was field marshal of Austria's troops by the time he was 30. Over the next forty years, as intermittent war with the Turks continued, he became a decisive influence in Habsburg affairs. Though foreign-born, he was the minister primarily responsible for the transformation of Vienna's policies from defensive to aggressive.

Until the siege of Vienna by the Turks in 1683, Leopold's cautiousness kept Austria simply holding the line, both against Louis XIV and against the Turks. In the 1690s, however, at Eugène's urging, he tried a bolder course and in the process laid the foundations for a new Habsburg empire along the Danube River: Austria-Hungary. He helped create the coalition that defeated Louis in the 1700s, he intervened in Italy so that his landlocked domains could gain an outlet to the sea, and he began the long process of pushing the Turks out of the Balkans. Although Leopold did not live to see the advance completed, by the time of Eugène's death, the Austrians' progress against the Turks had brought them within a hundred miles of the Black Sea.

The Power of the Nobility   Yet the local power of the nobility tempered the centralization of Leopold's dominions. Unlike Louis XIV, who supported his nobles only if they worked for him, Leopold gave them influence in the government without first establishing control over all his lands. The nobles did not cause the Habsburgs as much trouble as they had during the Thirty Years' War, but Leopold had to limit his centralization outside Austria. Moreover, as Austrians came increasingly to dominate the court, the nobles of Hungary and Bohemia reacted by clinging stubbornly to their local rights. Thus, compared to France, Leopold's was an absolutism under which the nobility retained far more autonomous power.

The Hohenzollerns at Berlin

The one new power that emerged to prominence during the age of Louis XIV was Brandenburg-Prussia, and here again state building was made possible by a close alliance between a powerful ruler and his nobles. Frederick William of Hohenzollern (r. 1640–1688), known as the "great elector," ruled scattered territories that stretched seven hundred miles from Cleves, on the Rhine, to a part of Prussia on the Baltic. That so fragmented and disconnected a set of lands could be shaped into a major European power was a testimony to the political abilities of the Hohenzollerns. The process began when, taking advantage of the uncertainties that followed the Thirty Years' War, Frederick William made his territories the dominant principality in northern Germany and at the same time strengthened his power over his subjects.

Foreign Policy   His first task was in foreign affairs, because when he became elector, the troops of the various states that were fighting the Thirty Years' War swarmed over his possessions. Frederick William realized that even a minor prince could emerge from these disasters in a good position if he had an army. With some military force at his disposal, he could become a useful ally for the big powers, who could then help him against his neighbors; while at home he would have the strength to crush his opponents.

By 1648 Frederick William had eight thousand troops, and he was backed by both the Dutch and the French in the Westphalia negotiations that year as a possible restraint on Sweden in northern Europe. With-

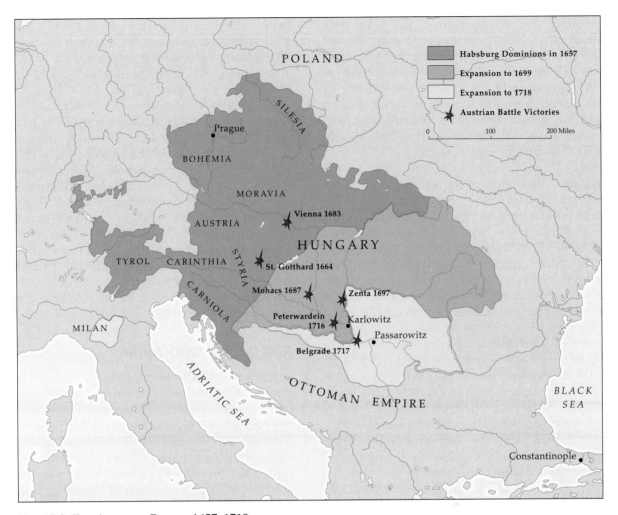

MAP 17.2 THE AUSTRIAN EMPIRE, 1657–1718
The steady advance of the Habsburgs into the Balkans was marked by a succession of victories; their gains were confirmed by treaties with the Turks at Karlowitz (1699) and Passarowitz (1718). How much bigger were Habsburg dominions in 1718 than they were in 1657?
◆ For an online version, go to www.mhhe.com/chambers9 > chapter 17 > book maps

out having done much to earn new territory, he did very well in the peace settlement, and he then took advantage of wars around the Baltic in the 1650s to confirm his gains by switching sides at crucial moments. In the process, his army grew to twenty-two thousand men, and he began to use it to impose his will on his own lands. The fact that the army was essential to Frederick William's success—at home and abroad—was to influence much of Prussia's and thus also Germany's subsequent history.

Domestic Policy   The role of the military in establishing the elector's supremacy was apparent throughout Brandenburg-Prussia's society. In 1653 the Diet of Brandenburg met for the last time, sealing its own fate by giving Frederick William the right to raise taxes without its consent. The War Chest, the office in charge of financing the army, took over the functions of a treasury department and collected government revenue even when the state was at peace. The implementation of policies in the localities was placed in the hands of war commissars—who originally were responsible for military recruitment, billeting, and supply but now became the principal agents of all government departments.

Apart from the representative assemblies, Frederick William faced real resistance only from the long-independent cities of his realm. Accustomed to going their own way because authority had been fragmented in the empire for centuries, and especially during the Thirty Years' War, city leaders were dismayed when the elector began to intervene in their affairs. Yet once again sheer intimidation overcame opposition. The last determined effort to dispute his authority arose in the rich city of Königsberg, which allied with the Estates General of Prussia to refuse to pay taxes. But this resistance was crushed in 1662, when Frederick William marched into the city with a few thousand troops. Similar pressure brought the towns of Cleves into submission after centuries of proud independence.

The Junkers　The main supporters and beneficiaries of the elector's state building were the Prussian nobles, known as **Junkers** (from the German for "young lord," *jung herr*). In fact, it was an alliance between the nobility and Frederick William that undermined the Diet, the cities, and the representative assemblies. The leading Junker families saw their best opportunities for the future in cooperation with the central government, and both in the representative assemblies and in the localities, they worked to establish absolutist power—that is, to remove all restraints on the elector. The most significant indicator of the Junkers' success was that by the end of the century, two tax rates had been devised, one for cities and one for the countryside, to the great advantage of the latter.

As the nobles staffed the upper levels of the elector's army and bureaucracy, they also won new prosperity for themselves. Particularly in Prussia, the support of the elector enabled them to reimpose serfdom and consolidate their land holdings into vast, highly profitable estates. This area was a major grain producer, and the Junkers maximized their profits by growing and distributing their produce themselves, thus eliminating middlemen. Efficiency became their hallmark, and their wealth was soon famous throughout the Holy Roman Empire. These Prussian entrepreneurs were probably the most successful group of European aristocrats in pursuing economic and political power.

Frederick III　Unlike Louis in France, Frederick William had little interest in court life. The Berlin court became the focus of society only under his son, Elector Frederick III, who ruled from 1688. The great elector had begun the development of his capital, Berlin, into a cultural center—he founded what was to become one of the finest libraries in the world, the Prussian State Library—but this was never among his prime concerns. His son, by contrast, had little interest in state building, but he did enjoy princely pomp and encouraged the arts with enthusiasm.

Frederick III lacked only one attribute of royalty: a crown. When Emperor Leopold I, who still had the right to confer titles in the empire, needed Prussia's troops during the War of the Spanish Succession, he gave Frederick, in return, the right to call himself "king in Prussia"; the title soon became "king of Prussia." At a splendid coronation in 1701, Elector Frederick III of Brandenburg was crowned King Frederick I, and thereafter his court felt itself the equal of the other monarchical centers of Europe.

Frederick determinedly promoted social and cultural glitter. He made his palace a focus of art and polite society that competed, he hoped, with Versailles. A construction program beautified Berlin with new churches and huge public buildings. He also established an Academy of Sciences and persuaded the most famous German scientist and philosopher of the day, Gottfried Wilhelm von Leibniz, to become its first president. All these activities obtained generous support from state revenues, as did the universities of Brandenburg and Prussia. By the end of his reign in 1713, Frederick had given his realm a throne, celebrated artistic and intellectual activity, and an elegant aristocracy at the head of social and political life.

Rivalry and State Building

Europe's increasingly self-confident states were in constant rivalry with their neighbors during the eighteenth century. The competition intensified their state building, because the conflicts forced rulers to expand their revenues, armies, and bureaucracies. The counterexample was Poland, which failed to centralize and was partitioned three times by Russia, Austria, and Prussia, until in 1795 it ceased to exist as a sovereign state. Political consolidation, by putting a premium on military and economic power, shaped both the map of modern Europe and the centralization of the major states.

The relationship between international rivalry and internal development is well illustrated by Prussia and Austria. In the mid-eighteenth century these two powers sought to dominate central Europe, and they launched reforms to wage their struggle more effectively. Their absolute rulers built their states by increasing the size of their armies, collecting larger revenues, and developing bureaucracies for the war effort. Whether the ruler was a modern pragmatist like Frederick II of Prussia or a pious traditionalist like Maria Theresa of Austria, both understood the demands of the state system.

The Prussia of Frederick William I

Prussia's Frederick William I (r. 1713–1740) relentlessly pursued a strengthened absolutism at home and Europe-wide influence abroad. Strikingly different from his refined father, this spartan ruler approached affairs of state as all business and little pleasure. He disdained court life, dismissed numerous courtiers, and cut the salaries of those who remained. Uncluttered by royal cere-

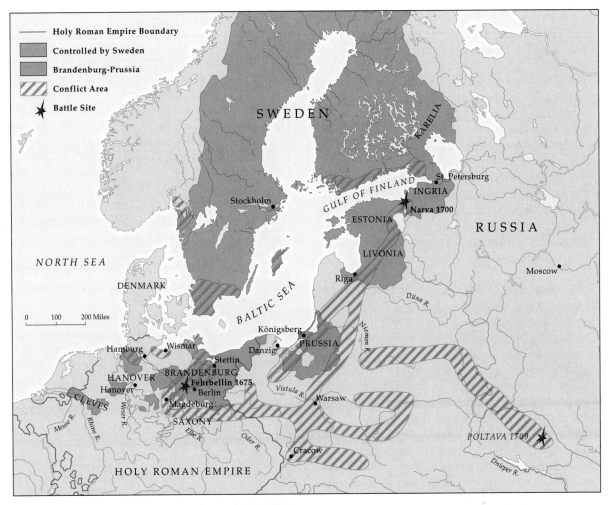

MAP 17.3 CONFLICT IN THE BALTIC AREA, 1660–1721
The fighting around the Baltic eventually destroyed Sweden's power in northern Europe; the new powers were to be Brandenburg-Prussia and Russia. At what point did Sweden no longer dominate the Baltic?
◆ For an online version, go to www.mhhe.com/chambers9 > chapter 17 > book maps

monies, his days were strictly regulated as he attempted to supervise all government activities personally.

Emphasis on the Military   It has been said that Frederick William I organized his state to serve his military power. During his reign the army grew from 38,000 to 83,000, making it the fourth largest in Europe, behind France, Russia, and Austria. And all his soldiers had to undergo intensive drilling and wear standardized uniforms. Determined to build an effective force, he forbade his subjects to serve in foreign armies and compelled the sons of nobles to attend cadet schools to learn martial skills and attitudes. But Frederick William did not intend to die in battle. For all his involvement with military life, he avoided committing his army to battle and was able to pass it on intact to his son.

Centralization kept pace with the growth of the army. In 1723 the General Directory of Finance, War, and Do-mains took over all government functions except justice, education, and religion. A super-agency, it collected revenues and oversaw expenditures (mostly military) and local administration. Even education was seen merely as a way to encourage people to serve the state. Frederick made education compulsory for all children, ordering local communities to set up schools where there were none, though he never enforced these decrees. Uninterested in intellectual pursuits for their own sake, the king allowed the universities to decline; they did not fit his relentless vision of how to build his state.

Frederick the Great

Frederick William I's most notable triumph, perhaps, was the grooming of his successor. This was no mean task. Frederick II (r. 1740–1786) seemed opposite in temperament to his father and little inclined to follow in his footsteps. The father was a God-fearing German Protestant. The son disdained German culture and was a deist (see p. 558). Sentimental and artistically inclined, Frederick II was a composer of music who played the flute, wrote poetry, and greatly admired French culture. He even wrote philosophical treatises and corresponded with leading European intellectuals.

But the young prince was not exempt from the effort to draw all Prussians into the task of state building. On the contrary: His father forced him to work at all levels of the state apparatus so as to experience them directly, from shoveling hay on a royal farm to marching with the troops. The father trained his son for kingship, reshaping his personality, giving him a sense of duty, and toughening him for leadership. Despite Frederick's resistance, this hard apprenticeship succeeded.

Frederick's Absolutism

When he assumed the throne in 1740, Frederick II was prepared to lead Prussia in a ruthless struggle for power and territory. While his intellectual turn of mind caused him to agonize over moral issues and the nature of his role, he never flinched from exercising power. But he did try to justify absolutism at home and aggression abroad. He claimed undivided power for the ruler, not because the dynasty had a divine mission but because only absolute rule could bring results. The king, he said, was the first servant of the state, and in the long run an enlightened monarch might lead his people to a more rational and moral existence. Some of his objectives, such as religious toleration and judicial reform, he could reach at once, and by putting them into effect Frederick gained a reputation as an **"enlightened" absolutist.**

But these were minor matters. The paramount issue, security, provided the best justification for absolutism. Success here required Prussia to improve its vulnerable geographic position by acquiring more territory, stronger borders, and the power to face other European states as an equal. Until that was achieved, Frederick would not consider the domestic reforms that might disrupt the flow of taxes or men into the army, or provoke his nobility. The capture of territory was his most singular contribution to the rise of Prussia and what earned him his title of Frederick the Great. As it happened, a suitable task for his army presented itself in the year Frederick II came to the throne, 1748—an attack on the province of Silesia, which the Habsburgs controlled but were unable to defend. Prussia had no claim to the province; it was simply a wealthy neighboring domain that would expand Prussia's territory. Yet the conquest of Silesia brought to a new level the state building that the great elector had begun in 1648; the reaction also shaped state building in the Habsburg Empire.

The Habsburg Empire

The Habsburg Empire was like a dynastic holding company of diverse territories under one crown: Austria, Bohemia, Hungary, and other possessions such as the Austrian Netherlands, Lombardy, and Tuscany. The emperors hoped to integrate Austria, Bohemia, and Hungary into a Catholic, centralized, German-speaking super-state. But the traditional representative assemblies in these provinces resisted such centralization.

International Rivalry

In the reign of Leopold's successor, Charles VI (r. 1711–1740), yet another problem complicated the destiny of this multinational empire, for his only heir was his daughter, Maria Theresa. In 1713 Charles drafted a document known as the Pragmatic Sanction, declaring that all Habsburg dominions would pass intact to the eldest heir, male or female; and for the next twenty-five years he sought recognition of the Pragmatic Sanction from the European powers. By making all kinds of concessions and promises, he won this recognition on paper. But when he died in 1740, his daughter found that the commitments were worthless: The succession was challenged by force from several sides. Concentrating on diplomacy alone, Charles had neglected the work of state building, leaving an empty treasury, an inadequately trained army, and an ineffective bureaucracy.

In contrast to Austria, Prussia had a full treasury, a powerful army, and a confident ruler, Frederick II, who seized the Habsburg province of Silesia without qualm. His justification was simply **"reasons of state,"** combined with the Habsburgs' faltering fortunes. And Maria Theresa had her hands more than full, because the French declared war on her to support their ally Bavaria's claim to the Habsburg throne. Meanwhile, Spain hoped to win back control of Austria's Italian possessions. Worse yet, Maria Theresa faced a rebellion by the Czech nobles in Bohemia. Her position would probably have been hopeless if Hungary's Magyar nobles had followed suit. But Maria Theresa promised them autonomy within the Habsburg Empire, and they offered her the troops she needed to resist the invaders.

The War of Austrian Succession

In the War of Austrian Succession (1740–1748) that followed, Maria Theresa learned the elements of state building. With her Hungarian troops and with financial help from her one ally, Britain, she fought her opponents to a stalemate. Frederick's conquest of Silesia proved to be the only significant territorial change produced by the war. Even for England and France, who fought the war mainly in overseas colonies, it was a standoff. But Maria Theresa was now determined to recover Silesia

E. F. Cunningham
THE RETURN OF FREDERICK II FROM A MANEUVRE, **1787**
Were it not for the richly embroidered saddle cover and the fine white horse, Frederick the Great would be hard to spot among his officers. Nor is there anything to indicate that the two men on the black and brown horses behind him are his nephew and grandnephew. This sober evocation of a king as a professional soldier contrasts strikingly with earlier glorifications (see painting, p. 419).
Staatliche Museen Preussischer Kulturbesitz Nationalgalerie/BPK Berlin

and humiliate Prussia, and this required a determined effort of state building.

Maria Theresa   The woman whose authority was established not by her father's negotiations but by force of arms was a marked contrast to her archenemy, Frederick. The Prussian king was practical and irreligious; Maria Theresa was moralistic and pious. Her personality and her ruling style were deceptively traditional, however, for she was a shrewd innovator in the business of building and reasserting the power of her state.

Unlike Frederick, Maria Theresa had a strong regard for her dynasty. In this respect, being a woman made no difference to the policies or government of the empire. She believed in the divine mission of the Habsburgs and conscientiously attended to the practical needs of her realm.

Reform in Church and State   It was because she put the state's interests first that this most pious of Catholic sovereigns—who disdained religious toleration and loathed atheists—felt obliged to reform the Church. Responding to waste and self-interest in her monasteries, she forbade the founding of new establishments. She also abolished the clergy's exemptions from taxes, something the French king found impossible to do.

A new bureaucratic apparatus was constructed on the models of French and Prussian absolutism. In Vienna, reorganized central ministries recruited staffs of experts. In the provinces, new agents were appointed who were largely free of local interests, though some concession did have to be made to the regional traditions of the Habsburg realm. The core domains (excluding Hungary and the Italian possessions) were reorganized into ten provinces, each subdivided into

Martin van Meytens
MARIA THERESA AND HER FAMILY, 1750
Although the setting is just as splendid, the portrayal of Maria Theresa with her husband and thirteen of her sixteen children suggests a domesticity that is absent from Louis XIV's family portrait of half a century before (see painting, p. 490).
Galleria Palatina, Palazzo Pitti, Florence, Italy. Scala/Art Resource, NY

districts directed by royal officials. With the help of these officials, the central government could wrest new taxes from the local diets. Meanwhile, Maria Theresa brought important nobles from all her domains to Vienna to participate in its social and administrative life. She also reformed the military, improving the training of troops and establishing academies to produce a more professional officer corps. Thus did international needs help shape domestic political reforms.

Habsburgs and Bourbons at Madrid

In Spain the Habsburgs had little success in state building either at home or abroad. The king who followed Philip IV, Charles II (r. 1665–1700), was a sickly man, incapable of having children; and the War of the Spanish Succession seriously reduced the inheritance he left. Both the southern Netherlands and most of Italy passed to the Austrian Habsburgs, and Spain's overseas possessions often paid little notice to the homeland.

The Spanish nobility was even more successful than the Austrian in turning absolutism to its advantage. In 1650 the crown had been able to recapture Catalonia's loyalty only by granting the province's aristocracy virtual autonomy, and this pattern recurred throughout Spain's territories. Parasitic, unproductive nobles controlled the regime, often for personal gain. The country fell into economic and cultural stagnation, subservient to a group of powerful families, with its former glory visible mainly in its strong navy.

Bourbon Spain   Yet Spain and its vast overseas possessions remained a force in eighteenth-century affairs. When the Bourbons gained the crown, following the War of Spanish Succession, they ended the traditional independence of Aragon, Catalonia, and Valencia and integrated these provinces into the kind of united Spain Olivares had sought eighty years earlier. They imported the position of *intendant* from France to administer the provinces, and although the nobles remained far more independent, the Bourbons did begin to impose uniform procedures on the country. In midcentury the ideas of enlightened absolutism that were visible elsewhere in Europe had their effect, largely because of a liberal reformer, Count Pedro de Campomanes. The most remarkable change concerned the religious order that had been identified with Spain since the days of its founder, Loyola: the Jesuits. They had become too powerful and too opposed to reform, and so they were expelled from Spanish territory in 1767.

In a sense, though, the Jesuits were to have their revenge. Spain's colonies in America were flourishing in the eighteenth century: Their trade with Europe was booming; they were attracting new settlers; and by 1800 they had over 14 million inhabitants. But they were still subject to the same absolutist control as the homeland. It was largely under the inspiration of disgruntled Jesuits that the idea of breaking free from Spain took hold in the empire, an idea that led to the independence movements of the 1800s.

Peter the Great at St. Petersburg

One of the reasons the new absolutist regimes of the late seventeenth and eighteenth centuries seemed so different from their predecessors was that many of them consciously created new settings for themselves. Versailles, Schönbrunn, and Berlin were all either new or totally transformed sites for royal courts. But only one of the autocrats of the period went so far as to build an entirely new capital: Tsar Peter I (the Great) of Russia (1682–1725), who named the new city St. Petersburg after his patron saint.

Peter's Fierce Absolutism   None of the state-building rulers of the period had Peter's terrifying energy or ruthless determination to exercise absolute control. He was only nine when he was chosen tsar, and in his early years, when his sister and his mother were the effective rulers, he witnessed ghastly massacres of members of his family and their associates by soldiers in Moscow. Like little Louis XIV, endangered by Paris mobs during the Fronde, Peter determined to leave his capital city. Soon after he assumed full powers in 1696, therefore, he shifted his court to St. Petersburg, despite thousands of deaths among the peasants who were forced to build the city in a cold and inhospitable swamp. Well over six feet tall—a giant by the standards of the time—Peter terrorized those around him, especially during his many drunken rages. His only son, Alexis, a weak and retiring figure, became the focus of opposition to the tsar, and Peter had him put in prison, where Alexis mysteriously died. Peter refused even to attend his funeral.

Western Models   Early in his reign, Peter suffered a humiliating military defeat at the hands of the Swedes. This merely confirmed his view that, in order to compete with Europe's powers, he had to bring to Russia some of the advances the Western nations had recently made. To observe these achievements firsthand, Peter traveled incognito through France, England, and the Netherlands in 1697 and 1698, paying special attention to economic, administrative, and military practices (such as the functioning of a Dutch shipyard). Many of his initiatives were to derive from this journey, including his importation of Western court rituals, his founding of an Academy of Sciences in 1725, and his encouragement of the first Russian newspaper.

Italian artists were brought to Russia, along with Scandinavian army officers, German engineers, and Dutch shipbuilders, not only to apply their skills but also to teach them to the Russians. St. Petersburg, the finest eighteenth-century city built in Classical style, is mainly the work of Italians. But gradually Russians

PETER THE GREAT AT ST. PETERSBURG
In the eighteenth century Peter the Great of Russia outstripped the grandeur of other monarchs of the period by erecting an entirely new city for his capital. St. Petersburg was built by forced labor of the peasants under Peter's orders; they are shown here laying the foundations for the city.
Tass/Sovfoto

took over their own institutions—military academies produced native officers, for example—and by the end of Peter's reign they had little need of foreign experts.

Bureaucratization In ruling Russia, Peter virtually ignored the Duma, the traditional advisory council, and concentrated instead on his bureaucracy. He carried out countless changes until he had created an administrative apparatus much larger than the one he had inherited. Here again he copied Western models—notably Prussia, where nobles ran the bureaucracy and the army, and Sweden, where a complex system of government departments had been created. Peter organized his administration into similar departments: Each had either a specialized function, such as finance, or responsibility for a geographic area, such as Siberia. The result was an elaborate but unified hierarchy of authority, rising from local agents of the government through provincial officials up to the staffs and governors of eleven large administrative units and finally to the leaders of the regime in the capital. Peter began the saturating bureaucratization that characterized Russia from that time on.

The Imposition of Social Order The tsar's policies laid the foundations for a two-class society that persisted until the twentieth century. Previously, a number of ranks had existed within both the nobility and the peasantry, and a group in the middle was seen sometimes as the lowest nobles and sometimes as the highest peasants. Under Peter such mingling disappeared. All peasants were reduced to one level, subject to a new poll tax, military conscription, and forced

public work, such as the building of St. Petersburg. Below them were serfs, whose numbers were increased by legislation restricting their movement. Peasants had a few advantages over serfs, such as the freedom to move, but their living conditions were often equally dreadful. Serfdom itself spread throughout all areas of Peter's dominions and became essential to his state building because, on royal lands as well as the estates of the nobles, serfs worked and ran the agricultural enterprise that was Russia's economic base.

At the same time, Peter created a single class of nobles by substituting status within the bureaucracy for status within the traditional hierarchy of titles. In 1722 he issued a table of bureaucratic ranks that gave everyone a place according to the office he held. Differentiations still existed, but they were no longer unbridgeable, as they had been when family was the decisive determinant of status. The result was a more controlled social order and greater uniformity than in France or Brandenburg-Prussia. The Russian aristocracy was the bureaucracy, and the bureaucracy the aristocracy.

The Subjugation of the Nobility This was not a voluntary alliance between nobles and government, such as existed in the West; in return for his support and his total subjection of the peasantry, Peter required the nobles to provide officials for his bureaucracy and officers for his army. When he began the construction of St. Petersburg, he also demanded that the leading families build splendid mansions in his new capital. In effect, the tsar offered privilege and wealth in exchange for conscription into public service. Thus, there was hardly any sense of partnership between nobility and throne: The tsar often had to use coercion to ensure that his wishes were followed. On the other hand, Peter helped build up the nobles' fortunes and their control of the countryside. It has been estimated that by 1710 he had put under the supervision of great landowners more than forty thousand peasant and serf households that had formerly been under the crown. And he was liberal in conferring new titles—some of them, such as count and baron, copies of German examples.

Control of the Church   Peter's determination to stamp his authority on Russia was also apparent in his destruction of ecclesiastical independence. He accomplished this with one blow: He simply did not replace the patriarch of the Russian Church who died in 1700. Peter took over the monasteries and their vast income for his own purposes and appointed a procurator (at first an army officer) to supervise religious affairs. The Church was, in effect, made a branch of government.

Military Expansion   The purpose of all these radical changes was to assert the tsar's power both at home and abroad. Peter established a huge standing army, more than three hundred thousand strong by the 1720s, and imported the latest military techniques from the West. One of Peter's most cherished projects, the creation of a navy, had limited success, but there could be no doubt that he transformed Russia's capacity for war and its position among European states. He extended Russia's frontier to the south and west, and, at the battle of Poltava in 1709, reversed his early defeat by the Swedes. This victory began the dismantling of Sweden's empire, for it was followed by more than a decade of Russian advance into Estonia, Livonia, and Poland. The very vastness of his realm justified Peter's drive for absolute control, and by the time of his death he had made Russia the dominant power in the Baltic and a major influence in European affairs.

ALTERNATIVES TO ABSOLUTISM

The absolutist regimes offered one model of political and social organization, but an alternative model—equally committed to uniformity, order, and state building—was also created in the late seventeenth century: governments dominated by aristocrats or merchants. The contrast between the two was noted by contemporary political theorists, especially opponents of absolutism, who preferred **constitutionalism.** And yet the differences were often less sharp than the theorists suggested, mainly because the position of the aristocracy was similar throughout Europe.

Aristocracy in the United Provinces, Sweden, and Poland

In the Dutch republic, the succession of William III to the office of Stadholder in 1672 seemed to be a move toward absolutism. As he led the successful resistance to Louis XIV in war (1672–1678), he increasingly concentrated government in his own hands. Soon, however, the power of merchants and provincial leaders in the Estates General reasserted itself. William did not want to sign a peace treaty with Louis when the French invasion failed. He wanted instead to take the war into France and reinforce his own authority by keeping the position of commander in chief. But the Estates General, led by the province of Holland, ended the war.

A decade later William sought the English crown, but he did so only with the approval of the Estates General, and he had to leave separate the representative assemblies that governed the two countries. When William died without an heir, his policies were continued by his close friend Antonius Heinsius, who held the same position of grand pensionary of Holland that Jan de Witt had once occupied; but the government was in effect controlled by the Estates General. This representative assembly now had to preside over the decline of a great power. In finance and trade, the Dutch were gradually overtaken by the English, while in the war against Louis XIV, they had to support the crippling burden of maintaining a land force, only to hand over command to England.

Dutch Society   The aristocrats of the United Provinces differed from the usual European pattern. Instead of ancient families and bureaucratic dynasties, they boasted merchants and mayors. The prominent citizens of the leading cities were the backbone of the Dutch upper classes. Moreover, social distinctions were less prominent than in any other country of Europe. The elite was composed of hard-working financiers and traders, richer and more powerful but not essentially more privileged or leisured than those farther down the social ladder. The inequality described in much eighteenth-century political writing—the special place nobles had, often including some immunity from the law—was far less noticeable in the United Provinces. There was no glittering court, and although here as elsewhere a small group controlled the country, it did so for largely economic ends and in different style.

Sweden   The Swedes created yet another nonabsolutist model of state building. After a long struggle with the king, the nobles emerged as the country's dominant political force. During the reign of Charles XI (1660–1697), the monarchy was able to force the great lords to return to the state the huge tracts of land they

MAP 17.4 THE EXPANSION OF RUSSIA AND THE PARTITION OF POLAND
All three of the powers in Eastern Europe—Prussia, Russia, and Austria—gained territory from the dismemberment of Poland. Which country was the chief beneficiary of the partition? In addition to the territory it gained from Poland, where else was Russia expanding in the period 1721–1795?
◆ For an online version, go to www.mhhe.com/chambers9 > chapter 17 > book maps

had received as rewards for loyalty earlier in the century. Since Charles stayed out of Europe's wars, he was able to conserve his resources and avoid relying on the nobility as he strengthened the smoothly running bureaucracy he had inherited from Gustavus Adolphus.

His successor, Charles XII (r. 1697–1718), however, revived Sweden's tradition of military conquest. He won land from Peter the Great, but then made the fatal decision to invade Russia. Defeated at the battle of Poltava in 1709, Charles had to retreat and watch helplessly as the Swedish Empire was dismembered. By the

time he was killed in battle nine years later, his neighbors had begun to overrun his lands, and, in treaties signed from 1719 to 1721, Sweden reverted to roughly the territory it had had a century before.

Naturally, the nobles took advantage of Charles XII's frequent absences to reassert their authority. They ran Sweden's highly efficient government while he was campaigning and forced his successor, Queen Ulrika, to accept a constitution that gave the Riksdag effective control over the country. The new structure, modeled on England's political system, gave the nobility the role of the English gentry—leaders of society and the shapers of its politics. A splendid court arose, and Stockholm became one of the more elegant and cultured aristocratic centers in Europe.

Poland Warsaw fared less well. In fact, the strongest contrast to the French political and social model in the late seventeenth century was Poland. The sheer chaos and disunity that plagued Poland until it ceased to exist as a state in the late eighteenth century were the direct result of continued dominance by the old landed aristocracy, which blocked all attempts to centralize the government. There were highly capable kings in this period—notably John III, who achieved Europe-wide fame by relieving Vienna from the Turkish siege in 1683. These monarchs could quite easily gather an army to fight, and fight well, against Poland's many foes: Germans, Swedes, Russians, and Turks. But once a battle was over, the ruler could exercise no more than nominal leadership. Each king was elected by the assembly of nobles and had to agree not to interfere with the independence of the great lords, who were growing rich from serf labor on fertile lands. The crown had neither revenue nor bureaucracy to speak of, and so the country continued to resemble a feudal kingdom, where power remained in the localities.

The Triumph of the Gentry in England

The model for a nonabsolutist regime was England, even though King Charles II (r. 1660–1685) seemed to have powers similar to those of his ill-fated father, Charles I. He still summoned and dissolved Parliament, made all appointments in the bureaucracy, and signed every law. But he no longer had prerogative courts like Star Chamber, he could not arrest a member of Parliament, and he could not create a new seat in the Commons. Even two ancient prerogatives, the king's right to dispense with an act of Parliament for a specific individual or group and his right to suspend an act completely, proved empty when Charles II tried to exercise them. Nor could he raise money without Parliament; instead, he was given a fixed annual income, financed by a tax on beer.

The Gentry and Parliament The real control of the country's affairs had by this time passed to the group of substantial landowners known as the gentry. In a country of some 5 million people, perhaps fifteen to twenty thousand families were considered gentry—local leaders throughout England, despite having neither titles of nobility nor special privileges. Amounting to 2 percent of the population, they probably represented about the same proportion as the titled nobles in other states. Yet the gentry differed from these other nobles in that they

ENGRAVING FROM *THE WESTMINSTER MAGAZINE*, 1774
Political cartoons were standard fare in eighteenth-century newspapers and magazines. This one shows a weeping king of Poland and an angry Turk (who made no gains) after Poland was carved up in 1772 by Frederick the Great, the Austrian emperor, and the Russian empress. Louis XV sits by without helping his ally Poland, and all are urged on by the devil under the table.

had won the right to determine national policy through Parliament. Whereas nobles elsewhere depended on monarchs for power, the English revolution had made the gentry an independent force. Their authority was now hallowed by custom, upheld by law, and maintained by the House of Commons.

Not all the gentry took a continuing interest in affairs of state, and only a few of their number sat in the roughly five-hundred-member House of Commons. Even the Commons did not exercise a constant influence over the government; nevertheless, the ministers of the king had to be prominent representatives of the gentry, and they had to be able to win the support of a majority of the members of the Commons. Policy was still set by the king and his ministers, but the Commons had to be persuaded that the policies were correct; without parliamentary approval, a minister could not long survive.

The Succession   Despite occasional conflicts, this structure worked relatively smoothly throughout Charles II's reign. But the gentry feared that Charles's brother, James, next in line for the succession and an open Catholic, might try to restore Catholicism in England. To prevent this, they attempted in 1680 to force Charles to exclude James from the throne. But in the end the traditional respect for legitimacy, combined with some shrewd maneuvering by Charles, ensured that there would be no tampering with the succession.

Soon, however, the reign of James II (r. 1685–1688) turned into a disaster. Elated by his acceptance as king, James rashly offered Catholics the very encouragement the gentry feared. This was a direct challenge to the gentry's newly won power, and in 1688 seven of their leaders, including members of England's most prominent families, invited the Protestant ruler of the United Provinces, William III, to invade and take over the throne. Though William landed with an army half the size of the king's, James, uncertain of his support, decided not to risk battle and fled to exile in France. Because the transfer of the monarchy was bloodless and confirmed the supremacy of Parliament, it came to be called the Glorious Revolution.

William and Mary   The new king gained what little title he had to the crown through his wife, Mary (see the genealogical table below), and Parliament proclaimed the couple joint monarchs early in 1689. The Dutch ruler took the throne primarily to bring England into his relentless struggles against Louis XIV, and he willingly accepted a settlement that confirmed the essential role of Parliament in the government. A **Bill of Rights** determined the succession to the throne, defined Parliament's powers, and established basic civil rights. An Act of Toleration put an end to all religious persecution, though members of the official Church of England were still the only people allowed to vote, sit in Parliament, hold a government office, or attend a university. In 1694 a statute declared that Parliament had to meet and new elections had to be held at least once every three years.

Despite the restrictions on his authority, William exercised strong leadership. He guided England into an aggressive foreign policy, picked ministers favorable to his aims, and never let Parliament sit when he was out of the country to pursue the war or to oversee Dutch affairs. In his reign, too, the central government grew considerably, gaining new powers and positions, and

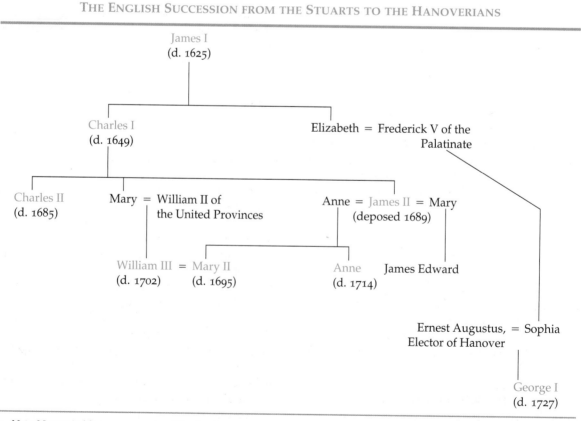

THE ENGLISH SUCCESSION FROM THE STUARTS TO THE HANOVERIANS

Note: Names in blue = monarchs of England.

thus new opportunities for political patronage. But unlike James, William recognized his limits. He tried to have the Bill of Rights reversed and a standing army established, but he gave up when these efforts provoked major opposition. By and large, therefore, the gentry were content to let the king rule as he saw fit, for they had shown by their intervention in 1688 that ultimately they controlled the country.

Politics and Prosperity

The political system in England now reflected the social system: A small elite controlled both the country's policy and its institutions. This group was far from united, however, as was apparent when a party system began to appear in Parliament during Charles II's reign. On one side was the **Whig** party, that opposed royal prerogatives and Catholicism and was largely responsible for the attempt to exclude James II from the throne. The rival **Tory** party stood for the independence and authority of the crown and favored a ceremonial and traditional Anglicanism.

Party Conflict   Because the Whigs had been the main advocates of the removal of James II, they controlled the government for most of William III's reign. They supported his war against Louis XIV (1689–1697), because France harbored both James and his followers (the romantic but ill-fated Jacobites, who kept trying to restore James's line to the throne). This was a fairly nonpartisan issue, but the Tories and Whigs still competed fiercely for voters. Because the qualification for voting—owning land worth forty shillings a year in rent—had become less restrictive as a result of inflation (which made forty shillings a fairly modest sum) and was not to be raised to a higher minimum until the late 1700s, England now had what would be its largest electorate before the 1860s. Almost 5 percent of the population (more than 15 percent of adult males) could vote, and although results were usually determined by powerful local magnates, fierce politicking was common. And in the election of 1700 there was a major upset: The Tories won by opposing renewal of war with Louis XIV, who had seemed restrained since the end of the previous war in 1697.

Within two years, however, and despite William's death in 1702, England was again at war with France, this time over the Spanish succession; and soon the Whigs were again in control of the government. The identification of the parties with their attitude toward war continued until 1710, when weariness over the fighting brought the Tories back into power. They persuaded Queen Anne, William's successor, to make peace with France at Utrecht in 1713; and they lost power only because they made the mistake of negotiating with the rebel Jacobites after Anne died in 1714 without an heir. Anne's successor was a German prince, the elector of Hanover, who founded the new Hanoverian Dynasty as George I (1714–1727). Since they firmly supported his succession, the Whigs regained control of the government when George came to the throne. They then entrenched themselves for almost a century.

The Sea and the Economy   At the same time, England was winning for itself unprecedented prosperity and laying the foundations of its world power. The English navy was the premier force on the sea, the decisive victor over France during the worldwide struggle of the early eighteenth century. Overseas, England founded new colonies and steadily expanded the empire. When England and Scotland joined into one kingdom in 1707, the union created a Great Britain ready to exercise a worldwide influence.

The economic advances were equally remarkable. A notable achievement was the establishment of the Bank of England in 1694. The bank gained permission to raise money from the public and then lend it to the government at a favorable 8 percent interest. Within 12 days its founders raised more than a million pounds, demonstrating not only the financial stability of England's government but also the commitment of the elite to the country's political structure. London was becoming the financial capital of the world, with her merchants gaining control of maritime trade from east Asia to North America. And the benefits of the boom also helped the lower levels of society.

English Society   With the possible exception of the Dutch, ordinary English people were better off than their equivalents elsewhere in Europe. Compared with the sixteenth century, there was little starvation. The system of poor relief may often have been inhumane in forcing the unfortunate to work in horrifying workhouses, but it did provide them with the shelter and food they had long lacked. It is true that thousands still found themselves unable to make a living in their home villages each year and were forced by poverty to take to the roads. And the many who ended up in London hardly improved their situation. The stream of immigrants was driving the capital's population toward half a million, and the city contained frightful slums and miserable crime-ridden sections. Even a terrible fire in London in 1666 did little to improve the appallingly crowded living conditions, because the city was rebuilt much as before, the only notable additions being a series of splendid churches. But the grimness should not be overdrawn.

After more than a century of inflation, the laborer could once again make a decent living, and artisans

William Hogarth
THE POLLING, 1754
Despite the high reputation of the polling day as the central moment in the system of representative government, Hogarth's depiction of it in this scene suggests how corrupt and disheveled the process of voting was. The sick and the foolish are among the mob of voters; the central figure looks bewildered as he is told what to do; on the right a bloated official cannot decide whether a voter should be allowed to take his oath on the Bible with a wooden hand; and all ignore the distress of Britannia, the symbol of Britain, in her coach on the left.
By courtesy of the Trustees of Sir John Soane's Museum, London

were enjoying a growing demand for their work. Higher in the social scale, more men had a say in the political process than before, and more found opportunities for advancement in the rising economy—in trade overseas, in the bureaucracy, or in the expanding market for luxury goods. It has been estimated that in 1730 there were about sixty thousand adult males in what we would call the professions. England also had better roads than any other European country and a more impartial judicial system. Yet none of these gains could compare with those that the gentry made. In fact, many of the improvements, such as fair administration of justice, were indirect results of what the upper classes had won for themselves. The fruits of progress clearly belonged primarily to the gentry.

The Growth of Stability

Like the absolutist regimes, the British government in the 1700s was able to advance state building—to expand its authority and its international power. This was the work not so much of a monarch as of the "political nation": the landowners and leading townsmen who elected almost all the members of Parliament. Their control of the nation was visible in the distribution of the 558 seats in the House of Commons, which bore little relation to the size of constituencies. In 1793, for example, fifty-one English and Welsh boroughs, with fewer than fifteen hundred voters, elected one hundred members of Parliament, nearly a fifth of the Commons. Many districts were safely in the pocket

NEW GALLOWS AT THE OLD BAILEY, ENGRAVING
It was an indication of the severity of English criminal justice that the gallows erected near the chief court in London, the Old Bailey, in the mid-eighteenth century was specially constructed so that ten condemned criminals, both men and women, could be executed at once.
© British Museum

of a prominent local family; and elsewhere elections were often determined by bribery, influence, and intimidation. On the national level, loose party alignments pitted Whigs, who wanted a strong Parliament and usually preferred commercial to agricultural interests, against Tories, who tended to support the king and policies that favored large landholders. But the realities of politics were shaped by small factions within these larger groups, and alliances revolved around the control of patronage and office.

War and Taxes   As the financial and military needs and capabilities of the government expanded, Parliament now created a thoroughly bureaucratized state. Britain had always prided itself on having a smaller government and lower taxes than its neighbors, largely because, as an island, it had avoided the need for a standing army. All that now came to an end. Starting with the struggle against Louis XIV, wars required constant increases in resources, troops, and administrators. A steadily expanding navy had to be supported, as did an army that reached almost two hundred thousand men by the 1770s. Before the 1690s, public expenditures rarely amounted to 2 million a year; by the 1770s, they were almost 30 million, and most of that was

spent on the military. In this period, as a result, Britain's fiscal bureaucracy more than tripled in size. The recruiting officer became a regular sight, and so too did the treasury men who were imposing increasingly heavy tax burdens.

Unlike their counterparts on the Continent, however, the wealthier classes in Britain paid considerable taxes to support this state building, and they maintained more fluid relations with other classes. The landed gentry and the commercial class, in particular, were often linked by marriage and by financial or political associations. Even great aristocrats sometimes had close ties with the business leaders of London. The lower levels of society, however, found the barriers as high as they had ever been. For all of Britain's prosperity, the lower third of society remained poor and often desperate. As a result, despite a severe system of justice and frequent capital punishment, crime was endemic in both country and town. The eighteenth century was the heyday of that romantic but violent figure, the highwayman.

The Age of Walpole   The first two rulers of the Hanoverian Dynasty, George I (r. 1714–1727) and George II (r. 1727–1760), could not speak English fluently. The

Samuel Scott
THE BUILDING OF WESTMINSTER BRIDGE, CA. 1742
The elegance, but not the squalor, of city life in the eighteenth century is suggested by this view of Westminster.
The Metropolitan Museum of Art, Purchase, Charles B. Curtis Fund and Joseph Pulitzer Bequest, 1944. (44.56) Photograph © 1993 The Metropolitan Museum of Art

language barrier and their concern for their German territory of Hanover left them often uninterested in British politics, and this helped Parliament grow in authority. Its dominant figure for over twenty years was Sir Robert Walpole, who rose to prominence because of his skillful handling of fiscal policy during the panic following the collapse of an overseas trading company in 1720. This crash, known as the South Sea Bubble, resembled the failure of John Law's similar scheme in France, but it had less effect on government finances. Thereafter, Walpole controlled British politics until 1742, mainly by dispensing patronage liberally and staying at peace.

Many historians have called Walpole the first prime minister, though the title was not official. He insisted that all ministers inform and consult with the House of Commons as well as with the king, and he continued to sit in Parliament in order to recruit support for his decisions. Not until the next century was it accepted that the Commons could force a minister to resign. But Walpole took a first step toward ministerial responsibility, and to the notion that the ministers as a body or "cabinet" had a common task, and he thus shaped the future structure of British government.

Commercial Interests   In Great Britain as in France, the economic expansion of the eighteenth century increased the wealth and the social and political weight of the commercial and financial middle class. Although Londoners remained around 11 percent of the population, the proportion of the English who lived in other sizable towns doubled in the 1700s; and by 1800 some 30 percent of the country's inhabitants were urbanized. Walpole's policy of peace pleased the large landlords but angered this growing body of merchants and businesspeople, who feared the growth of French commerce and colonial settlements. They found their champion

in William Pitt, later earl of Chatham, the grandson of a man who had made a fortune in India. Eloquent, self-confident, and infused with a vision of Britain's imperial destiny, Pitt began his parliamentary career in 1738 by attacking the government's timid policies and demanding that France be driven from the seas. Though Walpole's policies continued even after his resignation in 1742, Pitt's moment finally came in 1758, when Britain became involved in a European war that was to confirm its importance in continental affairs (see pp. 523–524).

Contrasts in Political Thought

The intensive development of both absolutist and antiabsolutist forms in the seventeenth century stimulated an outpouring of ideas about the nature and purposes of government. Two Englishmen, in particular, developed theories about the basis of political authority that have been influential ever since.

Hobbes   Thomas Hobbes, a brilliant scholar from a poor family who earned his livelihood as the tutor to aristocrats' sons, determined to use the strictly logical methods of the scientist to analyze political behavior. As a young man Hobbes was secretary to Francis Bacon, who doubtless gave him a taste for science. And the almost scientific reasoning is the essence of his masterpiece, *Leviathan* (1651), which began with a few premises about human nature from which Hobbes deduced major conclusions about political forms.

Leviathan   Hobbes's premises, drawn from his observation of the strife-ridden Europe of the 1640s and 1650s, were stark and uncompromising. People, he asserted, are selfish and ambitious; consequently, unless

PORTRAIT OF THOMAS HOBBES
This depiction of the famous philosopher shows him with a twinkle in the eye and a smile that might seem surprising, given the pessimism about human nature in his *Leviathan*.
Art Resource, NY

restrained, they fight a perpetual war with their fellows. The weak are more cunning and the strong more stupid. Given these unsavory characteristics, the **state of nature**—which precedes the existence of society—is a state of war, in which life is "solitary, poor, nasty, brutish, and short." Hobbes concluded that the only way to restrain this instinctive aggressiveness is to erect an absolute and sovereign power that will maintain peace. Everyone should submit to the sovereign because the alternative is the anarchy of the state of nature. The moment of submission is the moment of the birth of orderly society.

In a startling innovation, Hobbes suggested that the transition from nature to society is accomplished by a contract that is implicitly accepted by all who wish to end the chaos. The unprecedented feature of the contract is that it is not between ruler and ruled; it is binding only on the ruled. They agree among themselves to submit to the sovereign; the sovereign is thus not a party to the contract and is not limited in any way. A

government that is totally free to do whatever it wishes is best equipped to keep the peace, and peace is always better than the previous turmoil. The power of Hobbes's logic, and the endorsement he seemed to give to absolutism, made his views enormously influential. But his approach also aroused hostility. Although later political theorists were deeply affected by his ideas, many of Hobbes's successors denounced him as godless, immoral, cynical, and unfeeling. It was dislike of his message, not weaknesses in his analysis, that made many people unwilling to accept his views.

Locke   John Locke, a quiet Oxford professor who admired Hobbes but sought to soften his conclusions, based his political analysis on a general theory of knowledge. Locke believed that at birth a person's mind is a *tabula rasa,* a clean slate; nothing, he said, is inborn or preordained. As human beings grow, they observe and experience the world. Once they have gathered enough data through their senses, their minds begin to work on the data. Then, with the help of reason, they perceive patterns, discovering the order and harmony that permeate the universe. Locke was convinced that this underlying order exists and that every person, regardless of individual experiences, must reach the same conclusions about its nature and structure.

When Locke turned his attention to political thought, he put into systematic form the views of the English gentry and other antiabsolutists throughout Europe. The *Second Treatise of Civil Government,* published in 1690, was deeply influenced by Hobbes. From his great predecessor, Locke took the notions that a state of nature is a state of war and that only a contract among the people can end the anarchy that precedes the establishment of civil society. But his conclusions were decidedly different.

Of Civil Government   Using the principles of his theory of knowledge, Locke asserted that, applying reason to politics, one can prove the inalienability of three rights of an individual: life, liberty, and property. Like Hobbes, he believed that there must be a sovereign power, but he argued that it has no power over these three natural rights of its subjects without their consent. And this consent—for taxes, for example—must come from a representative assembly of men of property, such as Parliament. The affirmation of property as one of the three natural rights (it became "the pursuit of happiness" in the more egalitarian American Declaration of Independence) is significant. Here Locke revealed himself as the voice of the gentry. Only those with a tangible stake in their country have a right to control its destiny, and that stake must be protected as surely as their life and liberty. The concept of liberty remained vague, but it was taken to imply the sorts of

LOCKE ON THE ORIGINS OF GOVERNMENT

The heart of John Locke's Second Treatise of Civil Government, *written in the mid-1680s before England's Glorious Revolution but published in 1690, is its optimism about human nature—as opposed to Hobbes's pessimism. In this passage Locke explains why, in his view, people create political systems.*

"If man in the state of nature be so free, if he be absolute lord of his own person and possessions, equal to the greatest, and subject to nobody, why will he part with his freedom, and subject himself to the dominion and control of any other power? To which it is obvious to answer, that though in the state of nature he hath such a right, yet the enjoyment of it is very uncertain, and constantly exposed to the invasions of others. This makes him willing to quit this condition, which, however free, is full of fears and continual dangers; and it is not without reason that he seeks out and is willing to join in society with others, who have a mind to unite, for the mutual preservation of their lives, liberties, and estates, which I call by the general name, property. The great and chief end, therefore, of men's putting themselves under government, is the preservation of their property.

"But though men when they enter into society give up the equality, liberty, and power they had in the state of nature into the hands of society; yet it being only with an intention in every one the better to preserve himself, his liberty, and property, the power of the society can never be supposed to extend further than the common good. And all this to be directed to no other end but the peace, safety, and public good of the people."

From John Locke, *The Second Treatise of Civil Government,* Thomas P. Peardon (ed.), Indianapolis: Bobbs-Merrill, 1952, chapter 9, pp. 70–73.

freedom, such as freedom from arbitrary arrest, that appeared in the English Bill of Rights. Hobbes allowed a person to protect only his or her life. Locke permitted the overthrow of the sovereign power if it infringed on the subjects' rights—a course the English followed with James II and the Americans with George III.

Locke's prime concern was to defend the individual against the state, a concern that has remained essential to liberal thought ever since (see "Locke on the Origins of Government," above). But it is important to realize that his emphasis on property served the elite better than the mass of society. With Locke to reassure them, the upper classes put their stamp on eighteenth-century European civilization.

THE INTERNATIONAL SYSTEM

While rulers built up their states by enlarging bureaucracies, strengthening governmental institutions, and expanding resources, they also had to consider how best to deal with their neighbors. In an age that emphasized reasoned and practical solutions to problems, there was hope that an orderly system could be devised for international relations. If the reality fell short of the ideal, there were nevertheless many who thought they were creating a more systematic and organized structure for diplomacy and warfare.

Diplomacy and Warfare

One obstacle to the creation of impersonal international relations was the continuing influence of traditional dynastic interests. Princes and their ministers tried to preserve a family's succession, and they arranged marriages to gain new titles or alliances. Part of the reason that those perennial rivals, Britain and France, remained at peace for nearly thirty years until 1740 was that the rulers in both countries felt insecure on their thrones and thus had personal motives for not wanting to risk aggressive foreign policies.

Gradually, however, dynastic interests gave way to policies based on a more impersonal conception of the state. Leaders like Frederick II of Prussia and William Pitt of Britain tried to shape their diplomacy to what they considered the needs of their states. "Reasons of state" centered on security, which could be guaranteed only by force. Thus, the search for defensible borders and the weakening of rivals became obvious goals. Eighteenth-century leaders believed that the end (security and prosperity) justified the means (the use of power). Chasing the impossible goal of complete invulnerability, leaders felt justified in using the crudest tactics in dealing with their neighbors.

"Balance of Power" and the Diplomatic System If there was any broad, commonly accepted principle at work, it was that hegemony, or domination by one

Louis Nicolas Blarenberghe
THE BATTLE OF FONTENOY, **1745**
This panorama shows the English and Dutch assaulting the French position in a battle in present-day Belgium.
The French lines form a huge semicircle from the distant town to the wood on the left. The main attacking force
in the center, surrounded by gunfire, eventually retreated, and news of the victory was brought to Louis XV, in
red on the right, by a horseman in blue who is doffing his hat.
Photo: Gérard Blot. Château de Versailles et de Trianon, Versailles, France. Réunion des Musées Nationaux/Art
Resource, NY. Giraudon/Art Resource, NY

state, had to be resisted because it threatened international security. The concern aroused by Louis XIV's ambitions showed the principle at work, when those whom he sought to dominate joined together to frustrate his designs. The aim was to establish equilibrium in Europe by a balance of power, with no single state achieving hegemony.

The diplomats, guided by reasons of state and the balance of power, knew there were times when they had to spy and deceive. Yet diplomacy also could stabilize: In the eighteenth century it grew as a serious profession, paralleling the rationalization of the state itself. Foreign ministries were staffed with experts and clerks, who kept extensive archives, while the heads of the diplomatic machine, the ambassadors, were stationed in permanent embassies abroad. This routinized management of foreign relations helped foster a sense of collective identity among Europe's states despite their endless struggles. French was now the common language of diplomacy; by 1774 even a treaty between Turks and Russians was drafted in that language. And socially the diplomats were cosmopolitan aristocrats

who saw themselves as members of the same fraternity, even if the great powers dominated international agreements, usually at the expense of the smaller states. Resolving disputes by negotiation could be as amoral as war.

Armies and Navies

Despite the settlement of some conflicts by diplomacy, others led to war. Whereas Britain emphasized its navy, on the Continent the focus of bureaucratic innovation and monetary expenditure was the standing army, whose growth was striking. France set the pace. After 1680 the size of its forces never fell below 200,000. In Prussia the army increased in size from 39,000 to 200,000 men between 1713 and 1786. But the cost, technology, and tactics of armies and navies served to limit the devastation of eighteenth-century warfare. The expenses led rulers to conserve men, equipment, and ships carefully. Princes were quick to declare war but slow to commit armies or navies to battle. Casualties also became less numerous as discipline improved

ENGRAVING OF A MILITARY ACADEMY, FROM H. F. VON FLEMING, *VOLKOMMENE TEUTSCHE SOLDAT*, 1726
This scene, of young men studying fortifications and tactics in a German academy, would have been familiar to the sons of nobles throughout Europe who trained for a military career in the eighteenth century.

and the ferocity that had been caused by religious passions died away.

Tactics and Discipline On land, the building and besieging of fortresses continued to preoccupy military planners, even though the impregnable defenses built by the French engineer Sebastian Vauban to protect France's northeastern border were simply bypassed by the English general Marlborough when he pursued the French army in the War of the Spanish Succession. The decisive encounter was still the battle between armies, where the majority of the troops—the infantry—used their training to maneuver and fire in carefully controlled line formations. The aim of strategy was not to annihilate but to nudge an opposing army into abandoning a position in the face of superior maneuvers. Improved organization also reduced brutality. Better supplied by a system of magazines and more tightly disciplined by constant drilling, troops were less likely to desert or plunder than they had been during the Thirty Years' War. At sea, the British achieved superiority by maneuvering carefully controlled lines of ships and seeking to outnumber or outflank the enemy.

As these practices took hold, some encounters were fought as if they were taking place on a parade ground or in a naval strategy room. Pitched battles were increasingly avoided, for even important victories might be nullified if a winning army or navy returned to its home bases for the winter. And no victor ever demanded unconditional surrender; in almost all cases, a commander would hesitate to pursue a defeated company or squadron.

Officers The officer corps were generally the preserve of Europe's nobility, though they also served as channels of upward social mobility for wealthy sons of middle-class families who purchased commissions. In either case, the officer ranks tended to be filled by men who lacked the professional training for effective leadership. The branches of service that showed the most progress were the artillery and the engineers, in which competent middle-class officers played an unusually large role.

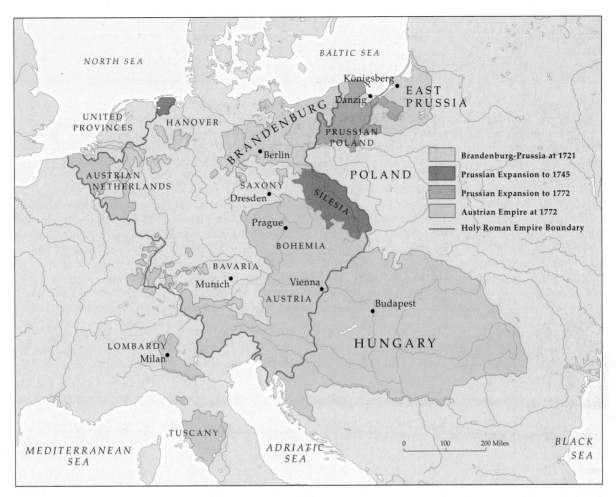

MAP 17.5 PRUSSIA AND THE AUSTRIAN EMPIRE, 1721–1772
The steady territorial advances of Prussia had created a major power in northern and eastern Europe, alongside the Austrian Empire, by the time of the first partition of Poland in 1772. Which was the most extensive of Prussia's gains between 1721 and 1772?

◆ For an online version, go to www.mhhe.com/chambers9 > chapter 17 > book maps

Weak Alliances   A final limit on the scale of war in the eighteenth century was the inherent weakness of coalitions, which formed whenever a general war erupted. On paper these alliances looked formidable. On battlefields, however, they were hampered by primitive communications and lack of mobility even at the peak of cooperation. Moreover, the partnerships rarely lasted very long. The competitiveness of the state system bred distrust among allies as well as enemies.

The Seven Years' War

The pressures created by the competition of states and dynasties finally exploded in a major war, the Seven Years' War (1756–1763). Its roots lay in a realignment of diplomatic alliances prompted by Austria. Previously, the Bourbon-Habsburg rivalry had been the cornerstone of European diplomacy. But by the 1750s two other antago-

nisms had taken over: French competition with the British in the New World and Austria's vendetta against Prussia over Silesia. For Austria, the rivalry with Bourbon France was no longer important. Its position in the Holy Roman Empire depended now on humbling Prussia. French hostility toward Austria had also lessened, and thus Austria was free to lead a turnabout in alliances—a diplomatic revolution—so as to forge an anti-Prussian coalition with France and Russia. Russia was crucial. The pious Empress Elizabeth of Russia loathed Frederick II and saw him as an obstacle to Russian ambitions in Eastern Europe. Geographical vulnerability also made Prussia an inviting target, and so the stage was set for war.

Prussia tried to compensate for its vulnerability. But its countermoves only alienated the other powers. Frederick sought to stay out of the Anglo-French rivalry by coming to terms with both these states. He had been France's ally in the past, but he now sought a

MARIA THERESA IN A VEHEMENT MOOD

The animosities and ambitions that shaped international relations in the eighteenth century were exemplified by the Empress Maria Theresa. Her furious reaction to the event that destroyed Europe's old diplomatic system—England's signing of the Convention of Westminster with Maria Theresa's archenemy, Frederick the Great—suggests how deep were the feelings that brought about the midcentury conflagration. After learning the news and deciding (in response) to ally herself with France, she told the British ambassador on May 13, 1756, exactly where she stood.

"I have not abandoned the old system, but Great Britain has abandoned me and the system, by concluding the Prussian treaty, the first intelligence of which struck me like a fit of apoplexy. I and the king of Prussia are incompatible; and no consideration on earth will ever induce me to enter into any engagement to which he is a party. Why should you be surprised if, following your example in concluding a treaty with Prussia, I should now enter into an engagement with France?

"I am far from being French in my disposition, and do not deny that the court of Versailles has been my bitterest enemy; but I have little to fear from France, and I have no other recourse than to form such arrangements as will secure what remains to me. My principal aim is to secure my hereditary possessions. I have truly but two enemies whom I really dread, the king of Prussia and the Turks; and while I and Russia continue on the same good terms as now exist between us, we shall, I trust, be able to convince Europe, that we are in a condition to defend ourselves against those adversaries, however formidable."

From William Coxe, *History of the House of Austria*, Vol. 3, London: Bohn, 1847, pp. 363–364.

treaty with England, and in January 1756 the English, hoping to protect the royal territory of Hanover, signed a neutrality accord with Prussia, the Convention of Westminster. The French, who had not been informed of the negotiations in advance, saw the Convention as an insult, if not a betrayal: the act of an untrustworthy ally. France overreacted, turned against Prussia, and thus fell into Austria's design (see "Maria Theresa in a Vehement Mood," above). Russia too considered the Convention of Westminster a betrayal by its supposed ally England. English bribes and diplomacy were unable to keep Russia from actively joining Austria to plan Prussia's dismemberment.

The Course of War   Fearing encirclement, Frederick gambled on a preventive war through Saxony in 1756. Although he conquered the duchy, his plan backfired, for it activated the coalition that he dreaded. Russia and France met their commitments to Austria, and the three began a combined offensive against Prussia. For a time Frederick's genius as a general brought him success. Skillful tactics and daring surprise movements brought some victories, but strategically the Prussian position was shaky. Frederick had to dash in all directions across his provinces to repel invading armies whose combined strength far exceeded his own. Disaster was avoided mainly because the Russian army returned east for winter quarters regardless of its gains, but even so, the Russians occupied Berlin.

On the verge of exhaustion, Prussia at best seemed to face a stalemate with a considerable loss of territory; at worst, the war would continue and bring about a total Prussian collapse. But the other powers were also war-weary, and Frederick's enemies were becoming increasingly distrustful of one another. In the end, Prussia was saved by one of those sudden changes of reign that could cause dramatic reversals of policy in Europe. In January 1762 Empress Elizabeth died and was replaced temporarily by Tsar Peter III, a passionate admirer of Frederick. He quickly pulled Russia out of the war and returned Frederick's conquered eastern domains of Prussia and Pomerania. In Britain, meanwhile, William Pitt was replaced by the more pacific earl of Bute, who brought about a reconciliation with France; both countries then ended their insistence on punishing Prussia. Austria's coalition collapsed.

Peace   The terms of the Peace of Hubertusburg (1763), settling the continental phase of the Seven Years' War, were therefore surprisingly favorable to Prussia. Prussia returned Saxony to Austria but paid no compensation for the devastation of the duchy, and the Austrians recognized Silesia as Prussian. In short, the status quo was restored. Frederick could return to Berlin, his dominion preserved partly by his army but mainly by luck and the continuing fragility of international alliances.

Summary

If, amidst the state building of the eighteenth century, Europe's regimes were ready to sustain a major war even if it brought about few territorial changes, that was not simply because of the expansion of government and the disciplining of armies. It was also the result of remarkable economic advances and the availability of new resources that were flowing into Europe from the development of overseas empires. In politics, this was primarily an age of consolidation; in economics, it was a time of profound transformation.

QUESTIONS FOR FURTHER THOUGHT

1. Although Americans naturally prefer regimes that provide for representation and citizen participation in government, are there times when it is advantageous for a state to have an authoritarian or absolutist regime?

2. How important is the development of a capital city or a center of government in the process of state building?

RECOMMENDED READING

Sources

*Hobbes, Thomas. *Leviathan.* 1651. Any modern edition.

*Locke, John. *Second Treatise of Civil Government.* 1690. Any modern edition.

Luvvas, J. (ed.). *Frederick the Great on the Art of War.* 1966.

Studies

*Behrens, C. B. A. *Society, Government, and the Enlightenment: The Experience of Eighteenth-Century France and Prussia.* 1985.

Brewer, John. *The Sinews of Power: War, Money, and the English State, 1688–1783.* 1989. The work that demonstrated the importance of the military and the growth of bureaucracy in eighteenth-century England.

*Hatton, R. N. *Europe in the Age of Louis XIV.* 1969. A beautifully illustrated and vividly interpretive history of the period that Louis dominated.

*Holmes, Geoffrey. *The Making of a Great Power: Late Stuart and Early Georgian Britain, 1660–1722;* and *The Age of Oligarchy: Pre-industrial Britain, 1722–1783.* 1993. The best detailed survey.

Hughes, Lindsey. *Peter the Great: A Biography.* 2002.

Lossky, Andrew. *Louis XIV and the French Monarchy.* 1994.

Mettam, Roger. *Power and Faction in Louis XIV's France.* 1988. An analysis of government and power under absolutist rule.

Oresko, Robert, G. C. Gibbs, and H. M. Scott (eds.). *Royal and Republican Sovereignty in Early Modern Europe.* 1997.

*Plumb, J. H. *The Growth of Political Stability in England, 1675–1725.* 1969. A brief, lucid survey of the development of parliamentary democracy.

Raeff, Marc. *The Well-Ordered Police State: Social and Institutional Change through Law in the Germanies and Russia, 1600–1800.* 1983.

*Tuck, Richard. *Hobbes.* 1989. A clear introduction to Hobbes's thought.

Weigley, R. F. *The Age of Battles: The Quest for Decisive Warfare from Breitenfeld to Waterloo.* 1991. The best military history of the age.

*Available in paperback.

Philip van Dijk
BRISTOL DOCKS AND QUAY, CA. 1780
**Commerce increased dramatically in the Atlantic ports of England and France as ships
embarked for Africa, the Caribbean, North America, and Spanish America as well as other
parts of Europe. Shown here, the port of Bristol in England.**
Bristol City Museum and Art Gallery, UK/Bridgeman Art Library

Chapter Eighteen

THE WEALTH OF NATIONS

DEMOGRAPHIC AND ECONOMIC GROWTH • THE NEW SHAPE OF INDUSTRY •
INNOVATION AND TRADITION IN AGRICULTURE • EIGHTEENTH-CENTURY EMPIRES

In the early eighteenth century the great majority of Europe's people still lived directly off the land. With a few regional exceptions, the agrarian economy remained immobile: It seemed to have no capacity for dramatic growth. Technology, social arrangements, and management techniques offered little prospect of improvement in production. Several new developments, however, were about to touch off a remarkable surge of economic advance. The first sign, and a growing stimulus for this new situation, was the sustained growth of Europe's population. This depended in turn on an expanding and surer food supply. While changes in agrarian output on the Continent were modest but significant, in England innovations in the control and use of land dramatically increased food production and changed the very structure of rural society.

The exploitation of overseas colonies provided another critical stimulus for European economic growth. Colonial trade in slaves and in sugar, tobacco, and other raw materials radiated from port cities like London and Bristol in England and Bordeaux and Nantes in France. An infrastructure of supportive trades and pro-cessing facilities developed around these ports and fed trade networks for the reexport across Europe of finished colonial products. The colonies, in turn, offered new markets for goods manufactured in Europe, such as cotton fabrics. The Atlantic slave trade and plantation slavery in the New World underpinned most of this commerce.

In one small corner of the economy, the growing demand for cotton cloth at home and abroad touched off a quest among English textile merchants for changes in the organization and technology of production. Dramatic structural change in English cotton manufacturing heralded the remarkable economic transformation known as industrialization. By the early nineteenth century, fundamental changes in the methods of raising food and producing goods were under way in Britain and were spreading to the Continent. This chapter explores the character of economic development; the impediments to that process; the nature of eighteenth-century innovations in agriculture, manufacturing, and trade; and some of the social consequences of these economic transformations.

1730s ████████
Sustained population growth begins in Europe;
slave trade monopolies broken

● **1694** Bank of England chartered

DEMOGRAPHIC AND ECONOMIC GROWTH

Perhaps the most basic, long-term historical variable is the movement of population. Historical demographers deal with the migrations of existing populations, from country to city, across national borders or even oceans. More fundamentally, they study the trends over time within populations and chart death rates, birthrates, and the growth or decline of population. Similarly, economic historians analyze macroeconomic trends in production and prices, which in turn can reinforce population growth or deter it. In this section we will consider certain trends in the demography and economy of eighteenth-century Europe, which combined to support economic growth.

A New Demographic Era

In the relationship between people and the land, between demography and agriculture, European life before the eighteenth century showed little change. Levels of population seemed to flow like the tides, in cyclical or wavelike patterns. Population might increase substantially over several generations, but eventually crop failures or the ravages of plague and other contagious diseases would drive the level of population down once again. In extreme cases, a lack of able-bodied workers led to the abandonment of land, and entire villages disappeared altogether. Such dramatic population losses had last occurred in seventeenth-century Germany, Poland, and Mediterranean Europe (the southern parts of Italy, Spain, and France).

For centuries Europe's population had been vulnerable to subsistence crises. Successions of poor harvests or crop failures might leave the population without adequate food and would drive up the price of grain and flour beyond what the poorest people could afford. If actual starvation did not carry them off, undernourishment made people more vulnerable than usual to disease. Such crises could also set off a chain of side effects, from unemployment to pessimism, that made people postpone marriage and childbearing. Thus, subsistence crises could drive down the birthrate as well as drive up the death rate, causing in combination a substantial loss in population.

Population Growth   Although barely perceived by most Europeans at the time, a new era in Europe's demography began around 1730, and by 1800 Europe's population had grown by at least 50 percent. (Since the first censuses were not taken until the early nineteenth century, all population figures prior to that time are only estimates.) Europe's estimated population jumped from about 120 million to about 180 or 190 million. Europe had probably never before experienced so rapid and substantial an increase in the number of its people. Prussia and Sweden may have doubled their populations, while Spain's grew from 7.5 million to about 11.5 million. High growth rates in England and Wales raised the population there from an estimated 5 million people in 1700 to more than 9 million in 1801, the date of the first British census. The French, according to the best estimates, numbered about 19 million at the death of Louis XIV in 1715 and probably about 26 million in 1789. France was the most densely populated large nation in Europe in the late eighteenth century and, with the exception of the vast Russian Empire, the most populous state.

Europe's population growth of the eighteenth century continued and indeed accelerated during the nineteenth century, thus breaking once and for all the tidelike cycles and immobility of Europe's demography.

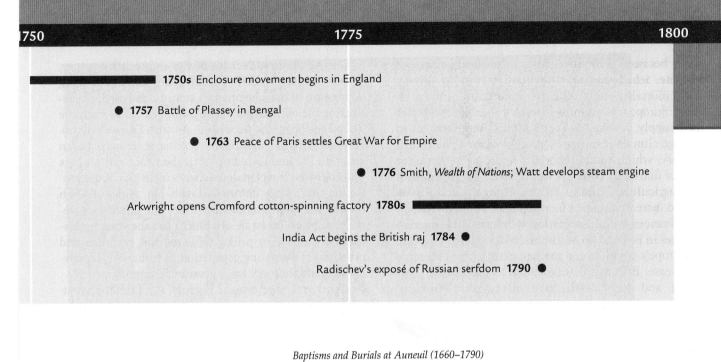

1750s Enclosure movement begins in England

● 1757 Battle of Plassey in Bengal

● 1763 Peace of Paris settles Great War for Empire

● 1776 Smith, *Wealth of Nations*; Watt develops steam engine

Arkwright opens Cromford cotton-spinning factory 1780s

India Act begins the British raj 1784 ●

Radischev's exposé of Russian serfdom 1790 ●

Baptisms and Burials at Auneuil (1660–1790)

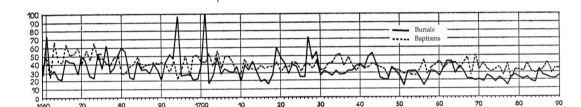

Baptisms and Burials at Saint-Lambert des Levées (1600–1790)

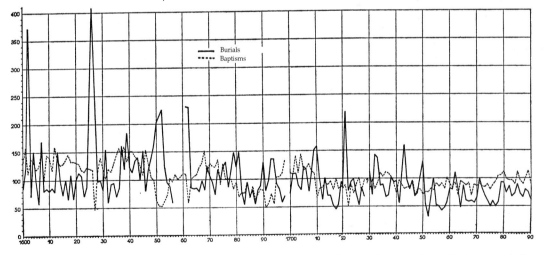

In these two French parishes, the seventeenth century came to a close with severe food shortages and sharp surges of mortality. In a more favorable economic climate, by contrast, the later eighteenth century brought an almost consistent annual surplus of births over deaths.

What caused this fundamental transformation in the underlying structure of European history?

Falling Death Rates There are two possible explanations for rapid population growth: a fall in death rates or a rise in birthrates. The consensus among historians is that a decline in mortality rates, rather than a rise in birthrates, accounts for most of the population growth in the eighteenth century, although England seems to have been an exception. Declines in the death rate did not sea brought coal close to iron, raw materials close to factories, and products close to markets. Above all, the sea gave Britain's merchants access to the much wider world beyond their shores.

Efficiency of transport was critical in setting the size of markets. During the eighteenth century, Britain witnessed a boom in the building of canals and turnpikes by private individuals or syndicates. By 1815 the country possessed some 2,600 miles of canals linking rivers, ports, and other towns. In addition, few institutional obstructions to the movement of goods existed. United under a strong monarchy, Britain was free of internal tariff barriers, unlike prerevolutionary France, Germany, or Italy. Merchants everywhere counted in the same money, measured their goods by the same standards, and conducted their affairs under the protection of the common law. By contrast, in France differences in provincial legal codes and in weights and measures complicated and slowed exchange. As the writer Voltaire sarcastically remarked, the traveler crossing France by coach changed laws as frequently as horses.

The English probably had the highest standard of living in Europe and generated strong consumer demand for manufactured goods. English society was less stratified than that on the Continent, the aristocracy powerful but much smaller. Primogeniture (with the family's land going to the eldest son) was the rule among both the peers (the titled members of the House of Lords) and the country gentlemen or squires. Left without lands, younger sons had to seek careers in other walks of life, and some turned toward commerce. They frequently recruited capital for their ventures from their landed fathers and elder brothers. English religious dissenters, chiefly Calvinists and Quakers, formed another pool of potential entrepreneurs; denied careers in government because of their religion, many turned their energies to business enterprises.

British Financial Management   A high rate of reinvestment is critical to industrialization; reinvestment, in turn, depends on the skillful management of money by both individuals and public institutions. Here again, Britain enjoyed advantages. Early industrial enterprises could rely on Britain's growing banking system to meet their capital needs. In the seventeenth century, the goldsmiths of London had assumed the functions of bankers. They accepted and guarded deposits, extended loans, transferred upon request credits from one account to another, and changed money. In the eighteenth century, banking services became available beyond London; the number of country banks rose from three hundred in 1780 to more than seven hundred by 1810. English businesspeople were familiar with banknotes and other forms of commercial papers,

and their confidence in paper facilitated the recruitment and flow of capital.

The founding of the Bank of England in 1694 marked an epoch in the history of European finance. The bank took responsibility for managing England's public debt, sold shares to the public, and faithfully met the interest payments due to the shareholders, with the help of government revenue (such as the customs duties efficiently collected on Britain's extensive foreign trade). When the government needed to borrow, it could turn to the Bank of England for assistance. This stability in government finances ensured a measure of stability for the entire money market and, most important, held down interest rates in both the public and private sectors. In general, since the Glorious Revolution of 1688, England's government had been sensitive to the interests of the business classes, who in turn had confidence in the government. Such close ties between money and power facilitated economic investment.

In contrast, France lacked a sound central bank, and extensive government borrowing drove up interest rates in the private sector as well. On balance, although limited capital and conservative management held back French business enterprises, they dampened but did not suppress the expansion of the economy. France remained a leader in producing wool and linen cloth as well as iron, but it seemed more inclined to produce luxury items or very cheap, low-quality goods. On the other hand, England (with its higher standard of living and strong domestic demand) seemed more adept at producing standardized products of reasonably good quality.

Cotton: The Beginning of Industrialization

The process of early industrialization in England was extremely complex and remains difficult to explain. What seems certain is that a strong demand for cheap goods was growing at home and abroad in the eighteenth century, and a small but important segment of the English community sensed this opportunity and responded to it.

Specifically, the market for cotton goods became the most propulsive force for change in industrial production. Thanks to slave labor in plantation colonies, the supply of raw cotton was rising dramatically. On the demand side, lightweight cotton goods were durable, washable, versatile, and cheaper than woolen or linen cloth. Cotton, therefore, had a bright future as an item of mass consumption. But traditional textile manufacturing centers in England (the regions of protoindustrialization such as East Anglia and the Yorkshire districts) could not satisfy the growing demand. The organization and technology of the putting-out system had reached its limits. For one thing, the merchant was

Richard Arkwright not only invented this power-driven machine to spin cotton yarn but also proved to be a highly successful entrepreneur with the factory he constructed at Cromford in the Lancashire region.
The Science Museum, London

The engineering firm of Bolton & Watt became famous for its steam engines, whose complex mechanisms of cams, gears, and levers could harness the power of steam to a variety of uses in industry and transportation.
The Science Museum, London

limited to the labor supply in his own district; the farther he went to find cottage workers, the longer it took and the more cumbersome it became to pass the materials back and forth. Second, he could not adequately control his workers. Clothiers were bedeviled with embezzlement of raw materials, poor workmanship, and lateness in finishing assigned work. English clothiers were therefore on the lookout for technological or organizational innovations to help them meet a growing demand for textiles.

Machines and Factories   Weavers could turn out large amounts of cloth thanks to the invention of the fly shuttle in the 1730s, which permitted the construction of larger and faster handlooms. But traditional methods of spinning the yarn caused a bottleneck in the production process. Responding to this problem, inventors built new kinds of spinning machines that could be grouped in large factories or mills. Richard Arkwright's water frame drew cotton fibers through rollers and twisted them into thread. Not simply an inventor but an entrepreneur (one who combined the various factors of production into a profitable enterprise), Arkwright initially housed his machines in a large factory sited

near a river so that his machines could be propelled by waterpower.

At around the same time, James Watt had been perfecting the technology of steam engines—machinery originally used to power suction pumps that would evacuate water from the pits of coal mines. The earliest steam engine had produced a simple up-and-down motion. Watt not only redesigned it to make it far more efficient and powerful but also developed a system of gears to harness the engine's energy into rotary motion that could drive other types of machines. In 1785 Arkwright became one of Watt's first customers when he switched from waterpower to steam engines as the means of driving the spinning machines in his new cotton factory at Cromford. With Arkwright (who became a millionaire) and Watt, the modern factory system was launched (see "Richard Arkwright's Achievement," p. 536).

Spinning factories, however, disrupted the equilibrium between spinning and weaving in the other direction: Yarn was now abundant, but hand-loom weavers could not keep up with the pace. This disequilibrium created a brief golden age for the weavers, but merchants were eager to break the new bottleneck. In 1784 Edmund Cartwright designed a power-driven loom. Small technical flaws and the violent opposition of hand-loom weavers retarded the widescale adoption of power looms until the early nineteenth century, but then both spinning and weaving were totally transformed. Power-driven machinery boosted the output of yarn and cloth astronomically, while merchants could assemble their workers in factories and scrutinize their every move to maximize production. In a factory, one

THE CONDITION OF THE SERFS IN RUSSIA

For publishing this unprecedented critique of the miseries and injustices of serfdom, the author was imprisoned by Catherine II.

"A certain man left the capital, acquired a small village of one or two hundred souls [i.e., serfs], and determined to make his living by agriculture. . . . To this end he thought it the surest method to make his peasants resemble tools that have neither will nor impulse; and to a certain extent he actually made them like the soldiers of the present time who are commanded in a mass, who move to battle in a mass, and who count for nothing when acting singly. To attain this end he took away from his peasants the small allotment of plough land and the hay meadows which noblemen usually give them for their bare maintenance, as a recompense for all the forced labor which they demand from them. In a word, this nobleman forced all his peasants and their wives and children to work every day of the year for him. Lest they should starve, he doled out to them a definite quantity of bread. . . . If there was any real meat, it was only in Easter Week.

"These serfs also received clothing befitting their condition. . . . Naturally these serfs had no cows, horses, ewes, or rams. Their master did not withhold from these serfs the permission, but rather the means to have them. Whoever was a little better off and ate sparingly, kept a few chickens, which the master sometimes took for himself, paying for them as he pleased.

"In a short time he added to his two hundred souls another two hundred as victims of his greed, and proceeding with them just as with the first, he increased his holdings year after year, thus multiplying the number of those groaning in his fields. Now he counts them by the thousands and is praised as a famous agriculturalist.

"Barbarian! What good does it do the country that every year a few thousand more bushels of grain are grown, if those who produce it are valued on a par with the ox whose job it is to break the heavy furrow? Or do we think our citizens happy because our granaries are full and their stomachs empty?"

Alexander Radischev, *A Journey from St. Petersburg to Moscow,* 1790.

across the lands of the village, no matter who owned them; and profited from monopolies on food-processing operations such as flour mills, bread ovens, and wine presses.

Concerned as they were with securing their basic livelihood, few peasants worried about trying to increase productivity with new farming methods. Satisfied with time-tested methods of cultivation, they could not risk the hazards of novel techniques. Along with growing grain for their own consumption, peasant households had to meet several obligations as well: royal taxes, rents, seigneurial dues, the tithe to the local church, and interest payments on their debts. In short, most peasant households in Western Europe were extremely insecure and relied on custom and tradition as their surest guides.

Peasant Survival Strategies Every peasant household in Western Europe hoped to control enough land to ensure its subsistence and meet its obligations. Ideally, it would own this land. But most peasants did not own as much land as they needed and were obliged to rent additional plots or enter into sharecropping arrangements. Peasants therefore hated to see the consolidation of small plots into large farms, for this meant that the small plots that they might one day afford to buy or lease were becoming scarcer. The lords and the most prosperous peasants, on the other hand, were interested in extending their holdings, just like the "improving" landlords across the English Channel.

When the land that small peasants owned and rented did not meet their needs, they employed other survival strategies. Peasants could hire out as laborers on larger farms or migrate for a few months to other regions to help with grain or wine harvests. They might practice a simple rural handicraft or weave cloth for merchants on the putting-out system. Some peasants engaged in illegal activities such as poaching game on restricted land or smuggling salt in avoidance of royal taxes. When all else failed, a destitute peasant family might be forced to take to the road as beggars.

The Family Economy In their precarious situation, peasants depended on strong family bonds. A peasant holding was a partnership between husband and wife, who usually waited until they had accumulated enough resources, including the bride's dowry, to establish their own household. Men looked for physical vigor and domestic skills in their prospective brides. ("When a girl knows how to knead and bake bread, she is fit to wed," went a French proverb.) In peasant households the wife's domain was inside the cottage,

Nicolas-Bernard Lépicié
COUR DE FERME
While changes in agricultural practices transformed the rural population of England and Russia, the small-holding peasant remained the most typical social type in France. In the peasant "family economy," husband and wife each made vital contributions to the household's productivity.
Musée du Louvre, Photo © R.M.N./Art Resource, NY

where she cooked, repaired clothing, and perhaps spent her evenings spinning yarn. Wives were also responsible for the small vegetable gardens or the precious hens and chickens that peasants maintained to raise cash for their obligations. The husband's work was outside: gathering fuel, caring for draft animals (if the family owned any), plowing the land, planting the fields, and nurturing the crops. But at harvest time everyone worked in the fields.

Peasants also drew strength from community solidarity. Many villages possessed common lands open to all residents. Poorer peasants could forage there for fuel and building materials, and could inexpensively graze whatever livestock they owned. Since villagers generally planted the same crops at the same times, after the harvest livestock was allowed to roam over the arable fields and graze on the stubble of the open fields, a practice known as vacant pasture. All in all, insecurity and the scarcity of land in continental villages made it risky and improbable that peasants would adopt innovative methods or agree to the division of common land.

The Limits of Agrarian Change on the Continent
Change, therefore, came more slowly to the continental countryside than it did to England. The Netherlands, the Paris basin and the northeast of France, the Rhineland in Germany, and the Po Valley of Italy experienced the most active development—all areas of dense settlement in which high food prices encouraged landlords with large farms to invest in agricultural improvements and to adopt innovative methods.

Like their English counterparts, innovating continental farmers waged a battle for managerial freedom, though the changes they sought were not as sweeping as the English enclosure movement. Most French villages worked the land under an open-field system in which peasants followed the same rhythms and routines of cultivation as their neighbors, with the village also determining the rights of its members on common lands. From the middle of the century on, the governing institutions of several provinces banned obligatory vacant pasture and allowed individual owners to enclose their land; some authorized the division of communal lands as well. But the French monarchy did not adopt enclosure as national policy, and after the 1760s provincial authorities proved reluctant to enforce enclosure ordinances against the vigorous opposition of peasants. Traces of the medieval village thus lasted longer in France and Western Europe than in England.

In France in 1789, on the eve of the Revolution, probably 35 percent of the land was owned by the peasants who worked it. In this regard, the French peasants were more favored than those of most other European countries. But this society of small peasant farms was vulnerable to population pressures and was threatened by sharp movements in prices—two major characteristics of eighteenth-century economic history, as we have seen.

In the regions close to the Mediterranean Sea, such as southern Italy, difficult geographical and climatic conditions—the often rugged terrain, thin soil, and dearth of summer rain—did not readily allow the introduction of new techniques either, although many peasants improved their income by planting market crops such as grapes for wine or olives for oil instead of grains for their own consumption. Still, most peasants continued to work their lands much as they had in the Late Middle Ages and for the same poor reward. Fertile areas near the Baltic Sea, such as east Prussia, benefited from the growing demand for grains in Western countries, but on the whole, Eastern Europe did not experience structural agrarian change until the next century.

EIGHTEENTH-CENTURY EMPIRES

The economic dynamism of the eighteenth century derived not simply from growing population and consumer demand, or from English innovations in agriculture and textile manufacturing. Europe's favorable position as a generator of wealth owed as much to its mercantile empires across the seas. Colonial trade became an engine of economic growth in Britain and France. Plantation economies in the Atlantic world, fueled by the West African slave trade, provided sugar, tobacco, and cotton for an ever-expanding consumer demand. In the East spices, fine cloths, tea, and luxury goods similarly enriched European merchants. But behind the merchants and trading companies stood the military and naval muscle of the British and French states. Their rivalry finally erupted in a "Great War for Empire"—the global dimension of the Seven Year's War on the Continent. Here British victories came not only in North America and the Caribbean, but also in South Asia, where they ousted the French from their foothold in India. This left the British free to extend their sway in the nineteenth century over India, which became "the jewel in the crown" of British imperial dominion.

Mercantile and Naval Competition

After 1715 a new era began in the saga of European colonial development. The three pioneers in overseas expansion had by now grown passive, content to defend domains already conquered. Portugal, whose dominion over Brazil was recognized at the Peace of Utrecht in 1715, retired from active contention. Likewise, the Dutch could scarcely compete for new footholds overseas and now protected their interests through cautious

neutrality. Although Spain continued its efforts to exclude outsiders from trade with its vast empire in the New World, it did not pose much of a threat to others. The stage of active competition was left to the two other Atlantic powers, France and Britain.

The Decline of the Dutch   The case of Dutch decline is an instructive counterexample to the rise of French and British fortunes. In the seventeenth century the United Provinces, or Dutch Netherlands, had been Europe's greatest maritime power. But this federated state emerged from the wars of Louis XIV in a much weakened position. The country had survived intact, but it now suffered from demographic and political stagnation. The population of 2.5 million failed to rise much during the eighteenth century, thus setting the Dutch apart from their French and British rivals. As a federation of loosely joined provinces, whose seven provincial oligarchies rarely acted in concert, the Netherlands could barely ensure the common defense of the realm.

The Dutch economy suffered when French and English merchants sought to eliminate them as the middlemen of maritime commerce and when their industry failed to compete effectively. Heavy taxes on manufactured goods and the high wages demanded by Dutch artisans forced up the price of Dutch products. What kept the nation from slipping completely out of Europe's economic life was its financial institutions. Dutch merchants shifted their activity away from actual trading ventures into the safer, lucrative areas of credit and finance. Their country was the first to perfect the uses of paper currency, a stock market, and a central bank. Amsterdam's merchant-bankers loaned large amounts of money to private borrowers and foreign governments, as the Dutch became financial brokers instead of traders.

The British and French Commercial Empires   Great Britain, a nation that had barely been able to hold its own against the Dutch in the seventeenth century, now began its rise to domination of the seas. Its one serious competitor was France, the only state in Europe to maintain both a large army and a large navy. Their rivalry played itself out in four regions. The West Indies, where both France and Britain had colonized several sugar-producing islands, constituted the fulcrum of both empires. The West Indian plantation economy, in turn, depended on slave-producing West Africa. The third area of colonial expansion was the North American continent, where Britain's thirteen colonies became centers of settlement whereas New France remained primarily a trading area. Finally, both nations sponsored powerful companies for trade with India and other Asian lands. These companies were supposed to compete for markets without establishing colonies.

The two colonial systems had obvious differences and important similarities. French absolutism fostered a centralized structure of control for its colonies, with intendants and military governors ruling across the seas as they did in the provinces at home. Britain's North American colonies, by contrast, remained independent from each other and to a degree escaped direct control from the home government, although Crown and Parliament both claimed jurisdiction over them. British colonies each had a royal governor but also a local assembly of sorts, and most developed traditions of self-government. Nonetheless, the French and British faced similar problems and achieved generally similar results. Both applied mercantilist principles to the regulation of colonial trade, and both strengthened their navies to protect it.

Mercantilism   Mercantilist doctrine supported the regulation of trade by the state in order to increase the state's power against its neighbors (see chapter 15). **Mercantilism** was not limited to the Atlantic colonial powers. Prussia was guided by mercantilism as much as were Britain and France, for all regarded the economic activities of their subjects as subordinate to the interests of the state.

Mercantilist theory advocated a favorable balance of trade as signified by a net inflow of gold and silver, and it assumed that a state's share of bullion could increase only at its neighbor's expense. (Adam Smith would attack this doctrine in 1776, as we have seen.) Colonies could promote a favorable balance of trade by producing valuable raw materials or staple crops for the parent country and by providing protected markets for the parent country's manufactured goods. Foreign states were to be excluded from these benefits as much as possible. By tariffs, elaborate regulations, bounties, or prohibitions, each government sought to channel trade between its colonies and itself. Spain, for example, restricted trade with its New World colonies exclusively to Spanish merchant vessels, although smugglers and pirates made a mockery of this policy.

Europe's governments sought to exploit overseas colonies for the benefit of the parent country and not simply for the profit of those who invested or settled abroad. But most of the parties to this commerce prospered. The large West Indian planters made fortunes, as did the most successful merchants, manufacturers, and shipowners at home who were involved in colonial trade. Illicit trade also brought rewards to colonial merchants; John Hancock took the risk of smuggling food supplies from Boston to French West Indian planters in exchange for handsome profits.

"Empire" generally meant "trade," but this seaborne commerce depended on naval power: Merchant ships had to be protected, trading rivals excluded, and regula-tions enforced. This reciprocal relationship between the expansion of trade and the deployment of naval forces added to the competitive nature of colonial expansion. Naval vessels needed stopping places for reprovisioning and refitting, which meant that ports had to be secured in strategic locations such as Africa, India, and the Caribbean and denied to rivals whenever possible.

The Profits of Global Commerce

The call of colonial markets invigorated European economic life. Colonial commerce provided new products, like sugar, and stimulated new consumer demand, which in turn created an impetus for manufacturing at home. It is estimated that the value of French commerce quadrupled during the eighteenth century. By the 1770s commerce with their colonies accounted for almost one-third of the total volume of both British and French foreign trade. The West Indies trade (mainly in sugar) bulked the largest, and its expansion was truly spectacular. The value of French imports from the West Indies increased more than tenfold between 1716 and 1788, from 16 million to 185 million livres.

The West Indies seemed to be ideal colonies. By virtue of their tropical climate and isolation from European society, which made slavery possible, the islands produced valuable crops difficult to raise elsewhere: tobacco, cotton, indigo, and especially sugar, a luxury that popular European taste soon turned into a necessity. Moreover, the islands could produce little else and therefore depended on exports from Europe. They could not raise an adequate supply of food animals or grain to feed the vast slave population, they could not cut enough lumber for building, and they certainly could not manufacture the luxury goods demanded by the planter class.

Triangular Trade   Numerous variations of **triangular trade** (between the home country and two overseas

THE GROWTH OF ENGLAND'S FOREIGN TRADE IN THE EIGHTEENTH CENTURY

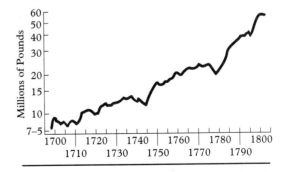

Three-year averages of combined imports and exports
Adapted from Phyllis Dean and W. A. Cole, *British Economic Growth, 1688–1959,* Cambridge University Press, 1964, p. 49.

Pietro Longhi
THE GEOGRAPHY LESSON
This painting of *The Geography Lesson* evokes the interest in exotic places among Europe's educated elites, male and female, during the eighteenth centruy.
Cameraphoto/Art Resource, NY

Chapter Nineteen

THE AGE OF ENLIGHTENMENT

THE ENLIGHTENMENT • EIGHTEENTH-CENTURY ELITE CULTURE • POPULAR CULTURE

Sharp breaks have been rare in Europe's intellectual and religious life—two of the defining themes in the Western experience—but we are about to witness one. During the eighteenth century, the great scientific and philosophical innovations of the previous century evolved into a naturalistic worldview divorced from religion. Scientific knowledge and religious skepticism, previously the concerns of an extremely narrow group of learned people, entered the consciousness of Europe's elites in a way that would have startled Descartes or Newton. Displacing the authority of religion with that of reason, the new outlook offered an optimistic vision of future progress in human affairs. Known as the Enlightenment, this movement formed the intellectual foundation for a new sense of modernity.

Never since pagan times, certainly not during the Renaissance, was religious belief so directly challenged. Many important eighteenth-century intellectuals no longer believed in Christianity and wished to reduce its influence in society. They argued that there was no divine standard of morality, no afterlife to divert humanity from worldly concerns. These writers developed a strong, sometimes arrogant, sense of their own capacity to ignore traditional authority and guide society toward change.

The evolution of cultural institutions and the media of the day gave these writers an increasingly wide forum. While aristocratic patronage and classical culture remained influential, a new kind of middle-class culture was developing alongside a much wider reading public and an expanding sphere of public discussion.

Yet, as we turn to consider the Enlightenment within the varied cultural environments of the eighteenth century, we should not exaggerate. Although they were critics of their society, most eighteenth-century intellectuals lived comfortably amid Europe's high culture. They had scant interest in or understanding of the vibrant popular culture around them. On the contrary, their growing belief in "public opinion" referred solely to the educated elites of the aristocracy and the middle classes.

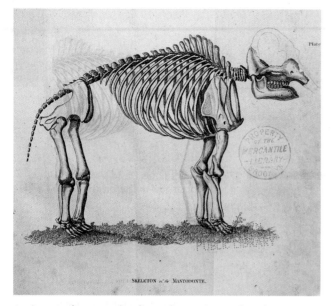

An image of a mastadon from the section on fossil remains in Buffon's *Natural History*.
Courtesy Brooklyn Public Library

Although he was a nonbeliever, Buffon did not explicitly attack religious versions of such events as the Creation; he simply ignored them, an omission of obvious significance to his readers. Similarly, while he did not specifically contend that human beings have evolved from beasts, he implied it. "It is possible," he wrote, "to descend by almost insensible degrees from the most perfect creature to the most formless matter." Buffon's earth did not derive from a singular act of divine creation that would explain the origins of human beings. The readers of his *Natural History* or its numerous popularizations in several languages thus encountered a universe that had developed through evolution.

Beyond Christianity

The erosion of biblical revelation as a source of authority is one hallmark of the Enlightenment. This shift derived some of its impetus from seventeenth-century scientists and liberal theologians who were themselves believing Christians but who opposed religious superstition or "enthusiasm," as they called it. They had hoped to accommodate religion to new philosophical standards and scientific formulations by eliminating the superstitious imagery that could make religion seem ridiculous and by treating the world of nature as a form of revelation in which God's majesty could be seen. The devil, for example, could be considered as a category of moral evil rather than as a specific horned creature with a pitchfork. They hoped to bolster the

Christian religion by deemphasizing miracles and focusing on reverence for the Creator and on the moral teachings of the Bible. Their approach did indeed help educated people adhere to Christianity during the eighteenth century. In the final analysis, however, this kind of thinking diminished the authority of religion in society.

Toleration   One current of thought that encouraged a more secular outlook was the idea of toleration, as propounded by the respected French critic Pierre Bayle. Consciously applying methodical doubt to subjects that Descartes had excluded from such treatment, Bayle's *Critical and Historical Dictionary* (1697) put the claims of religion to the test of critical reason. Certain Christian traditions emerged from this scrutiny as the equivalent of myth and fairy tale, and the history of Christianity appeared as a record of fanaticism and persecution. Bayle's chief target was Christianity's attempts to impose orthodoxy at any cost (for example, the Spanish Inquisition and Louis XIV's revocation of the Edict of Nantes and persecution of French Protestants). Though a devout Calvinist himself, Bayle advocated complete toleration, which would allow any person to practice any religion or none at all. An individual's moral behavior rather than his or her creed is what mattered, according to Bayle.

The most striking success of the eighteenth-century campaign for toleration came with the Edict of Toleration issued by the Habsburg emperor Joseph II on his ascendancy to the throne in 1781. For the first time, a Catholic Habsburg ruler recognized the right of Protestants and Jews in his realm to worship freely and to hold property and public office (see "Joseph II on Religious Toleration," p. 559). Joseph also tried to reduce the influence of the Catholic Church by ordering the dissolution of numerous monasteries on the grounds that they were useless and corrupt. Part of their confiscated wealth was used to support the medical school at the University of Vienna.

Deism   Voltaire became the Enlightenment's most vigorous antireligious polemicist. This prolific writer was one of the century's most brilliant literary stylists, historians, and poets. Those talents alone would have ensured his fame. But Voltaire was also a dedicated antagonist of Christianity. For tactical reasons, much of his attack against *l'infâme* ("the infamous thing"), as he called Christianity, targeted such practices as monasticism or the behavior of priests. His ultimate target, though, was Christianity itself, which, he declared, "every sensible man, every honorable man must hold in horror."

Voltaire's masterpiece, a best seller called *The Philosophical Dictionary* (1764), had to be published

JOSEPH II ON RELIGIOUS TOLERATION

Between 1765 and 1781 Joseph II was joint ruler of the Habsburg Empire with his pious mother, Empress Maria Theresa. Joseph advocated a utilitarian approach to religious toleration (Document 1) but made little headway against Maria Theresa's traditional insistence that the state must actively combat religious dissent. Soon after Maria Theresa's death, Joseph promulgated a series of decrees on religion, including a landmark Toleration Edict for Protestants (Document 2) and even a special, if somewhat less sweeping, edict of toleration for the Jews of his domains.

1. LETTER TO MARIA THERESA, JULY 1777

"The word toleration has caused misunderstanding.... God preserve me from thinking it a matter of indifference whether the citizens turn Protestant or remain Catholics.... I would give all I possess if all the Protestants of your States would go over to Catholicism. The word *toleration* as I understand it, means only that I would employ any persons, without distinction of religion, in purely temporal matters, allow them to own property, practice trades, be citizens if they were qualified and if this would be of advantage to the State and its industry.... The undisturbed practice of their religion makes them far better subjects and causes them to avoid irreligion, which is a far greater danger to our Catholics."

2. TOLERATION EDICT OF OCTOBER 1781

"We have found Ourselves moved to grant to the adherents of the Lutheran and Calvinist religions, and also to the non Uniat Greek religion, everywhere, the appropriate private practice of their faith.... The Catholic religion alone shall continue to enjoy the prerogative of the public practice of its faith.... Non-Catholics are in future admitted under dispensation to buy houses and real property, to acquire municipal domicile and practice as master craftsmen, to take up academic appointments and posts in the public service, and are not to be required to take the oath in any form contrary to their religious tenets.... In all choices or appointments to official posts ... difference of religion is to be disregarded."

From C. A. Macartney (ed.), *The Habsburg and Hohenzollern Dynasties in the 17th and 18th Centuries*, HarperCollins, 1970, pp. 151, 155–157.

anonymously and was burned by the authorities in Switzerland, France, and the Netherlands. Modeled after Bayle's dictionary, it was far more blunt. Of theology, he wrote, "We find man's insanity in all its plenitude." Organized religion is not simply false but pernicious, he argued. Voltaire believed that religious superstition inevitably bred fanaticism and predictably resulted in bloody episodes like the Saint Bartholomew's Day Massacre.

Voltaire hoped that educated Europeans would abandon Christianity in favor of **deism,** a belief that recognized God as the Creator but held that the world, once created, functions according to natural laws without interference by God. Humanity thus lives essentially on its own in an ordered universe, without hope or fear of divine intervention and without the threat of damnation or the hope of eternal salvation. For deists, religion should be a matter of private contemplation rather than public worship and mythic creeds. Although certain figures in the Enlightenment went beyond deism to a philosophical atheism, which rejected any concept of God as unprovable, Voltaire's mild deism remained a characteristic view of eighteenth-century writers. At bottom,

however, this form of spirituality was essentially secular. Broad-minded clergy could accept many of the arguments of eighteenth-century science and philosophy, but they could not accept deism.

The Philosophes

Science and secularism became the rallying points of a group of French intellectuals known as the **philosophes.** Their traditionalist opponents employed this term to mock the group's pretensions, but the philosophes themselves used that label with pride. They saw themselves as a vanguard, the men who raised the Enlightenment to the status of a self-conscious movement. The leaders of this influential coterie of writers were Voltaire and Denis Diderot. Its ranks included mathematicians Jean d'Alembert and the Marquis de Condorcet, the magistrate Baron de Montesquieu, the government official Jacques Turgot, and the atheist philosopher Baron d'Holbach. Thus, the French philosophes came from both the aristocracy and the middle class. Outside of France their kinship extended to a group of brilliant Scottish philosophers, including David Hume and Adam Smith; to the German

In 1745 the Habsburg monarchy expelled an estimated seventy thousand Jews from Prague to appease anti-Semitic sentiment.

playwright Gotthold Lessing and the philosopher Immanuel Kant; to the Italian economist and penal reformer the Marquis of Beccaria; and to such founders of the American Philosophical Society as Benjamin Franklin and Thomas Jefferson.

Intellectual Freedom   The philosophes shared above all else a critical spirit, the desire to reexamine the assumptions and institutions of their societies and expose them to the tests of reason, experience, and utility. Today this might sound banal, but it was not so at a time when almost everywhere religion permeated society. Asserting the primacy of reason meant turning away from faith, the essence of religion. It meant a decisive break with the Christian worldview, which placed religious doctrine at the center of society's values. The philosophes invoked the paganism of ancient Greece and Rome, where the spirit of rational inquiry prevailed among educated people. They ridiculed the Middle Ages as the "Dark Ages" and contrasted the religious spirit of that era to their own sense of liberation and modernity. In *The Decline and Fall of the Roman Empire* (1776–1788), the historian Edward Gibbon declared that Christianity had eclipsed a Roman civilization that had sought to live according to reason rather than myths.

The inspiration of antiquity was matched by the stimulus of modern science and philosophy. The philosophes laid claim to Newton, who made the universe intelligible without the aid of revelation, and Locke, who uncovered the workings of the human mind. From Locke they went on to argue that human

personality is malleable: Its nature is not fixed, let alone corrupted by original sin. People are, therefore, ultimately responsible to themselves for what they do with their lives. Existing arrangements are no more nor less sacred than experience has proved them to be. As the humanists had several centuries before, the philosophes placed human beings at the center of thought. Unlike most humanists, however, philosophes placed thought in the service of change and launched a noisy public movement.

Persecution and Triumph   Philosophes appeared clamorous to their contemporaries because they had to battle entrenched authority. Religious traditionalists and the apparatus of censorship in almost all countries threatened the intellectual freedom demanded by the philosophes. They often had to publish their works clandestinely and anonymously. Sometimes they were pressured into withholding manuscripts from publication altogether or into making humiliating public apologies for controversial books. Even with such caution, almost all philosophes saw some of their publications confiscated and burned. A few were forced into exile or sent to jail: Voltaire spent several decades across the French border in Switzerland, and Voltaire and Diderot both spent time in prison. Although the notoriety produced by these persecutions stimulated the sale of their works, the anxiety took its toll.

By the 1770s, however, the philosophes had survived their running war with the authorities. Some of them lived to see their ideas widely accepted and their works acclaimed. In 1778, the last year of his life, Voltaire

WHAT IS ENLIGHTENMENT?

The most concise formulation of the Enlightenment's spirit is conveyed in an essay of the 1780s by the German philosopher Immanuel Kant. As Kant makes clear, intellectual freedom and the role of public opinion refer not so much to the average person in the street as to the educated classes—serious writers (whom he calls "scholars") and their public. Note that in drawing the distinction between the public realm (where freedom is vital) and the private realm (where obedience is rightly expected), Kant reverses the labels that we would likely assign to the two realms today.

"Enlightenment is man's emergence from his self-imposed nonage. Nonage is the inability to use one's own understanding without another's guidance. This nonage is self-imposed if its cause lies not in lack of understanding but in indecision and lack of courage to use one's own mind without another's guidance. Dare to know. (*Sapere aude*). 'Have the courage to use your own understanding,' is therefore the motto of the Enlightenment.

"Laziness and cowardice are the reasons why such a large part of mankind gladly remain minors all their lives, long after nature has freed them from external guidance. They are the reasons why it is so easy for others to set themselves up as guardians. It is so comfortable to be a minor. If I have a book that thinks for me, a pastor who acts as my conscience, then I have no need to exert myself. . . .

"This enlightenment requires nothing but freedom: freedom to make public use of one's reason in all matters. . . . On the other hand, the private use of reason may frequently be narrowly restricted without especially hindering the progress of enlightenment. By 'public use of reason' I mean that use which man, as a scholar, makes of it before the reading public. I call 'private use' that use which a man makes of his reason in a civic post that has been entrusted to him . . . and where arguing is not permitted: one must obey. . . . Thus it would be very unfortunate if an officer on duty and under orders from his superiors should want to criticize the appropriateness or utility of his orders. He must obey. But as a scholar he could not rightfully be prevented from taking notice of the mistakes in the military service and from submitting his views to his public for its judgement."

returned triumphantly to Paris. When he attended a performance of one of his plays at the national theater, the audience greeted him with tumultuous enthusiasm. Even if the philosophes had contributed little else to the Western experience, their struggle for freedom of expression would merit them a significant place in its history.

Pioneering in the Social Sciences   But the philosophes achieved far more. In their scholarly and polemical writings, they investigated a wide range of subjects and pioneered in several new disciplines. Some philosophes—Voltaire, for example—were path-breaking historians. Moving beyond traditional chronicles of battles and rulers' biographies, they studied culture, social institutions, and government structures in an effort to understand past societies as well as describe major events. Practically inventing the notion of social science, they investigated the theoretical foundations of social organization (sociology) and the workings of the human mind (psychology). On a more practical level, they proposed fundamental reforms in such areas as the penal system and education.

The philosophes embedded their study of social science in questions of morality and the study of ethics. Enlightenment ethics were generally utilitarian. Such philosophers as David Hume tried to define good and evil in pragmatic terms; they argued that social utility should become the standard for public morality. This approach to moral philosophy in turn raised the question of whether any human values were absolute and eternal. Among the philosophers who grappled with this challenge, Kant tried to harmonize the notion of absolute moral values with practical reason.

Political Liberty   The most influential work of social science produced by the Enlightenment was probably *The Spirit of the Laws* (1748) by the French magistrate Montesquieu. The book offered a comparative study of governments and societies. On the one hand, Montesquieu introduced the perspective of relativism: He tried to analyze the institutions of government in relation to the special customs, climate, religion, and commerce of various countries. He thus argued that no single, ideal model of government existed. On the other hand, he deeply admired his own idealized version of the British system of government; he thereby implied that all societies could learn from the British about liberty.

Montesquieu's sections on liberty won a wide readership in Europe and in America, where the book was influential among the drafters of the U.S. Constitution.

An English engraving entitled "Voltaire's Staircase" suggests how the great writer stood at the center of Europe's literary and intellectual life. The fifth figure from the right at the top, Voltaire is bidding good-bye to d'Alembert, coeditor of the *Encyclopedia*.
Bettmann/Corbis

Political liberty, said Montesquieu, requires checks on those who hold power in a state, whether that power is exercised by a king, an aristocracy, or the people. Liberty can thrive only with a balance of powers, preferably by the separation of the executive, the legislative, and the judicial branches of government. Montesquieu ascribed a central role to aristocracies as checks on royal despotism. Indeed, many eighteenth-century writers on politics considered strong privileged groups, independent from both the crown and the people, as the only effective bulwarks against tyranny. To put it another way, Montesquieu's followers thought that the price for a society free from despotism was privilege for some of its members.

Liberal Economics   French and British thinkers of the Enlightenment transformed economic theory with attacks against mercantilism and government regulation. We noted in chapter 18 Adam Smith's critique of artificial restraints on individual economic initiative. In France, the Physiocrats similarly argued that economic progress depended on freeing agriculture and trade from restrictions. Since in their view (unlike Adam Smith's) land was the only real source of wealth, they also called for reforms in the tax structure, with a uniform and equitable land tax. In opposition to a traditional popular insistence on government intervention to maintain supplies of grain and flour at fair prices, the Physiocrats advocated freedom for the grain trade to operate according to the dictates of supply and demand. The incentive of higher prices would encourage growers to expand productivity, they believed, and in this way the grain shortages that plagued Europe could eventually be eliminated, although at the cost of temporary hardship for most consumers.

Diderot and the Encyclopedia

The Enlightenment thus produced not only a new intellectual spirit but also a wide range of critical writings on various subjects. In addition, the French philosophes collectively generated a single work that exemplified their notion of how knowledge could be useful: Diderot's *Encyclopédie* (*Encyclopedia*).

Within a few years of arriving in Paris as a young man, Denis Diderot had published novels, plays, treatises on mathematics and moral philosophy, and critical essays on religion. His most original writings examined the role of passion in human personality and in any system of values derived from an understanding of human nature. Specifically, Diderot affirmed the role of sexuality, arguing against artificial taboos and repression. As an advocate of what was sometimes called "the natural man," Diderot belies the charge leveled against the philosophes that they overemphasized reason to the neglect of feeling.

Diderot's unusual boldness in getting his works published brought him a considerable reputation but also some real trouble. Two of his books were condemned by the authorities as contrary to religion, the state, and morals. In 1749 he spent one hundred days in prison and was released only after making a humiliating apology. At about that time, Diderot was approached by a publisher to translate a British encyclopedic reference work into French. After a number of false starts, he persuaded the publisher to sponsor instead an entirely new and more comprehensive work that would reflect the interests of the philosophes.

The Encyclopedia   The *Encyclopedia, or Classified Dictionary of the Sciences, Arts, and Occupations*, an inventory of all fields of knowledge from the most theoretical to the most mundane, constituted an arsenal of critical concepts. As the preface stated: "Our Encyclopedia is a work that could only be carried out in a

Diderot's *Encyclopedia* focused much of its attention on technology. Illustrations of mechanical processes, such as the one shown here for making plate glass, filled eleven folio volumes.

in the context of the times, it
lution that Diderot sought was
te in a letter to a friend, the en-
moting "a revolution in the
em from prejudice." Judging by
s and government authorities,
ccessful. "Up till now," com-
ishop, "hell has vomited its
Now, he concluded, it could be
en the *Encyclopedia's* covers.
st three volumes to appear, the
ned the *Encyclopedia* in 1759
eller's license to issue the re-
he attorney general of France
t formed, a society organized to
o destroy religion, to inspire a
nd to nourish the corruption of
cyclopedia's contributors pru-
he project, but Diderot went
ued the herculean task until
every promised volume, in-
ent folios of illustrations. By
the persecutions had receded.
was reprinted in cheaper edi-
ed) that sold out rapidly, earn-
blishers. This turn of events
erot's project as the landmark

eau

al and influential eighteenth-
ques Rousseau stood close to
tside the coterie of the
provided in his life and writ-
of the status quo but of the

Enlightenment itself. Obsessed with the issue of moral freedom, Rousseau found society far more oppressive than most philosophes would admit, and he considered the philosophes themselves to be part of the problem.

Young Rousseau won instant fame when he submitted a prize-winning essay in a contest sponsored by a provincial academy on the topic, "Has the restoration of the arts and sciences had a purifying effect upon morals?" Unlike most respondents, Rousseau answered that it had not. He argued that the lustrous cultural and scientific achievements of recent decades were producing pretension, conformity, and useless luxury. Most scientific pursuits, he wrote, "are the effect of idleness which generate idleness in their turn." The system of rewards in the arts produces "a servile and deceptive conformity . . . the dissolution of morals . . . and the corruption of taste." Against the decadence of high culture, he advocated a return "to the simplicity which prevailed in earliest times"—manly physical pastimes, self-reliance, independent citizens instead of fawning courtiers.

Rousseau's Moral Vision   Rousseau had no wish to return to a state of nature, a condition of anarchy in which force ruled and people were slaves of appetite. But the basis of morality, he argued, was conscience, not reason. "Virtue, sublime science of simple minds: are not your principles graven on every heart?" This became one of his basic themes in two popular works of fiction, *Julie, or the New Héloise* (1761), and *Emile, or Treatise on Education* (1762).

In the first novel, Julie is educated in virtue by her tutor St. Preux but allows herself to fall in love with and be seduced by him. In the second half of the novel, Julie breaks away from St. Preux and marries Monsieur de Wolmar, her father's wealthy friend. She maintains a distant friendship with her old lover and rears her children in exemplary fashion, overseeing their education. In the end she overcomes her past moral lapse and sacrifices her own life to save one of her children. Wolmar then brings in the chastened St. Preux to continue the children's education. This tale of love, virtue, and motherhood won an adoring audience of male and female readers who identified with the characters, shed tears over their moral dilemmas, and applauded Rousseau for this superb lesson in the new sensibility.

Emile recounts the story of a young boy raised to be a moral adult by a tutor who emphasized experience over book learning and who considered education a matter of individual self-development. This new kind of man of course required a comparably sensitive wife, attuned to practical matters and without vain aristocratic pretenses. Sophie, the girl in question, received a very different type of education, however, one concerned with virtue but far more limited in its scope. Rousseau depicted men and women liberating themselves from stultifying traditional values, yet in the new relation-

Nicolas Henri Jeaurat de Bertry
Allegory of the Revolution with a Portrait Medallion of J. J. Rousseau
The French revolutionaries acclaimed both Voltaire and Rousseau and transferred their remains to a new Pantheon. But Rousseau was the man considered by many French people to be the Revolution's spiritual father, as suggested by his position in this allegorical painting of 1793, filled with the new symbolism of liberty and equality.
Musée de la Ville de Paris, Musée Carnavalet, Paris, France. Giraudon/Art Resource, NY

ships he portrayed in these novels, women held a decidedly subordinate position. Their virtues were to be exclusively domestic in character, while the men would be prepared for public roles—a distinction that deeply troubled feminist thinkers in the future (see "Mary Wollstonecraft on the Education of Women," p. 565).

The Rebel as Cultural Hero   Rousseau himself was by no means a saint. His personal weaknesses—including the illegitimate child that he fathered and abandoned—doubtless contributed to his preoccupation with morality and conscience. Nonetheless, his rebellious life as well as his writings greatly impressed the generation of readers and writers coming of age in the 1770s and 1780s. Not only did he quarrel with the repressive authorities of Church and state—who repeatedly

MARY WOLLSTONECRAFT ON THE EDUCATION OF WOMEN

The sharpest challenge to Rousseau's widely shared attitude toward women came only in 1792, with the publication of Mary Wollstonecraft's A Vindication of the Rights of Woman. *Inspired by the French Revolution's doctrine of natural rights, this spirited writer deplored the fact that society kept women (in her words) frivolous, artificial, weak, and in a perpetual state of childhood. While men praised women for their beauty and grace, they hypocritically condemned them for a concern with vanity, fashion, and trivial matters, yet refused to treat them as rational human beings who could contribute to society as much as men. Her book emphasized the need for educational reform that would allow women to develop agile bodies and strong minds. Along the way Wollstonecraft took particular aim at Rousseau's* Emile.

"The conduct and manners of women, in fact, evidently prove that their minds are not in a healthy state; for, like the flowers which are planted in too rich a soil, strength and usefulness are sacrificed to beauty. . . . One cause of this barren blooming I attribute to a false system of education, gathered from the books written on this subject by men who, considering females rather as women than human creatures, have been more anxious to make them alluring mistresses than affectionate wives and rational mothers. The understanding of the sex has been so bubbled by this specious homage, that the civilized women of the present century, with a few exceptions, are only anxious to inspire love, when they ought to cherish a nobler ambition, and by their abilities and virtues exact respect.

"[T]he most perfect education, in my opinion, is such an exercise of the understanding as is best calculated to strengthen the body and form the heart. Or, in other words, to enable the individual to attain such habits of virtue as will render it independent. In fact, it is a farce to call any being virtuous whose virtues do not result from the exercise of its own reason. This was Rousseau's opinion respecting men: I extend it to women, and confidently assert that they have been drawn out of their sphere by false refinement, and not by an endeavor to acquire masculine qualities. Still the regal homage which they receive is so intoxicating, that till the manners of the times are changed, and formed on more reasonable principles, it may be impossible to convince them that the illegitimate power, which they obtain by degrading themselves, is a curse, and that they must return to nature and equality."

From Sandra M. Gilbert and Susan Gubar (eds.), *The Norton Anthology of Literature by Women: The Tradition in English*, W. W. Norton Co, 1985.

banned his books—but he also attacked the pretensions of his fellow philosophes, whom he considered arrogant, cynical, and lacking in spirituality.

By the 1770s the commanding figures of the Enlightenment, such as Voltaire and Diderot, had won their battles and had become masters of the most prestigious academies and channels of patronage. In a sense, they had themselves become the establishment. For younger writers frustrated by the existing distribution of influence and patronage, Rousseau became the inspiration.

Rousseau's Concept of Freedom   What proved to be Rousseau's most enduring work, *The Social Contract*, published in 1762, became famous only after the French Revolution dramatized the issues that the book had raised. (The Revolution, it could be said, did more for the book than Rousseau did for the Revolution, which he neither prophesied nor advocated.) *The Social Contract* was not meant as a blueprint for revolution but rather as an ideal standard against which readers might measure their own society. Rousseau did not expect that this standard could be achieved in practice, since existing states were too large and complex to allow the kind of participation that he considered essential.

For Rousseau, a government distinct from the individuals over whom it claims to exercise authority has no validity. Rousseau denied the almost universal idea that some people are meant to govern and others to obey. In the ideal polity, Rousseau said, individuals have a role in making the law to which they submit. By obeying it, they are thus obeying themselves as well as their fellow citizens. For this reason, they are free from arbitrary power. To found such an ideal society, each citizen would have to take part in creating a social contract laying out the society's ground rules. By doing so, these citizens would establish themselves as "the sovereign." This sovereign—the people—then creates a government that will carry on the day-to-day business of applying the laws.

Rousseau was not advocating simple majority rule but rather a quest for consensus as to the best interests of all citizens. Even if it *appears* contrary to the welfare of some or even many citizens, Rousseau believed, the best interest of the community must be every individual's best interest as well, since that individual is a member of the community. Rousseau called this difficult concept the **"general will."** Deferring to the general will means that an individual ultimately must do what

ROUSSEAU'S CONCEPT OF THE GENERAL WILL

"The essence of the social compact reduces itself to the following terms: Each of us puts his person and all his power in common under the supreme direction of the general will, and, in our collective capacity, we receive each member as an indivisible part of the whole. . . .

"In fact, each individual, as a man, may have a particular will contrary or dissimilar to the general will which he has as a citizen. His particular interest may speak to him quite differently from the common interest: his absolute and naturally independent existence may make him look upon what he owes to the common cause as a gratuitous contribution, the loss of which will do less harm to others than the payment of it is burdensome to himself. . . . He may wish to enjoy the rights of citizenship without being ready to fulfill the duties of a subject. The continuance of

such an injustice could not but prove the undoing of the body politic.

"In order then that the social compact may not be an empty formula, it tacitly includes the undertaking, which alone can give force to the rest, that whoever refuses to obey the general will shall be compelled to do so by the whole body. This means nothing less than that he will be forced to be free; for this is the condition which, by giving each citizen to his country, secures him against all personal dependence. In this lies the key to the working of the political machine."

From Jean-Jacques Rousseau, *The Social Contract*, Book 1, David Campbell Publishers.

---

one *ought*, not simply what one *wants*. This commitment derives from conscience, which must do battle within the individual against passion, appetite, and mere self-interest. Under the social contract, to use Rousseau's most striking phrase, the individual "will be forced to be free" (see "Rousseau's Concept of the General Will," above). Thus, for Rousseau, individual freedom depends on a political framework involving consent and participation as well as subordination of individual self-interest to the commonweal. More than any of the philosophes, Rousseau argued that individual freedom depends on the arrangements governing the collectivity.

EIGHTEENTH-CENTURY ELITE CULTURE

The Enlightenment was merely one dimension of Europe's vibrant cultural life in the eighteenth century. An explosive increase in publishing activity, legal and underground, served diverse audiences. New cultural forums and institutions, such as salons and freemasons lodges, combined with new media to create a **"public sphere"** for the uninhibited exchange of ideas. Meanwhile, the realm of literature saw remarkable innovation, including the rise of the novel. Royal courts and aristocracies still dominated most activity in music and the fine arts through their patronage, but here too the presence of a growing middle-class audience made itself felt and offered new opportunities of recognition for composers and artists.

Cosmopolitan High Culture

As the expansive, cosmopolitan aspects of European high culture are described here, it must be remembered that the mass of Europe's peasants and workers remained virtually untouched by these developments, insulated within their local environments and traditions. But the educated and wealthy, the numerically small and influential elites, enjoyed a sense of belonging to a common European civilization. French was the international language of this culture; even King Frederick II of Prussia favored French over German. Whatever the effects of Frederick's attitude might have been—the German dramatist Lessing, for one, considered it a deplorable cultural prejudice—the widespread knowledge of French meant that ideas and literature could circulate easily past language barriers.

The Appeal of Travel Europeans sharpened their sense of common identity through travel literature and by their appetite for visiting foreign places. Although transportation was slow and uncomfortable, many embarked on a "grand tour," whose highlights included visits to Europe's large cities (such as London, Paris, Rome, and Vienna) and to the ruins of antiquity—to the glories of the modern and the ancient worlds.

Kings, princes, and municipal authorities were embellishing their towns with plazas, public gardens, theaters, and opera houses. Toward the end of the century, amenities such as street lighting and public transportation began to appear in a few cities, with London leading the way. From the private sector came two notable additions to the urban scene: the coffeehouse and the storefront window display. Coffeehouses, where customers

Anicet Charles G. Lemonnier
READING OF VOLTAIRE'S TRAGEDY "L'ORPHELIN DE LA CHINE" AT THE SALON OF MADAME GEOFFRIN, **1755**
This 1814 painting of Mme. Geoffrin's Salon in 1755 reflects the artist Lemonnier's imagination rather than historical reality. His canvas depicts an assemblage of all the major philosophes and their patrons that never actually took place. Yet it does accurately convey the social atmosphere and serious purpose of the Parisian salons. At the center is a bust of Voltaire, who lived in exile at the time.
Giraudon/Art Resource, NY

could chat or read, and enticing shop windows, which added to the pleasures of city walking (and stimulated consumer demand), enhanced the rhythms of urban life for tourists and residents alike. When a man is tired of London, Samuel Johnson remarked, he is tired of life.

Travelers on tour invariably passed from the attractions of bustling city life to the silent monuments of antiquity. As the philosophes recalled the virtues of pagan philosophers like Cicero, interest grew in surviving examples of Greek and Roman architecture and sculpture. Many would have agreed with the German art historian Johann Winckelmann that Greek sculpture was the most worthy standard of aesthetic beauty in all the world.

The Republic of Letters Among writers, intellectuals, and scientists, the sense of a cosmopolitan European culture devolved into the concept of a "republic of letters." The phrase, introduced by sixteenth-century French humanists, was popularized by Pierre Bayle (noted earlier as a proponent of religious toleration), who published a critical journal that he called *News of the Republic of Letters.* The title implied that the realm of culture and

ideas stretched across Europe's political borders. In one sense, it was an exclusive republic, limited to the educated; but it was also an open society to which people of talent could belong regardless of their social origins.

Aside from the medium of the printed word, the republic of letters was organized around the salons and the academies. Both institutions encouraged social interchange by bringing together socially prominent men and women with talented writers. The philosophes themselves exemplified this social mixture, for their "family" was composed in almost equal measures of nobles (Montesquieu, Holbach, Condorcet) and commoners (Voltaire, Diderot, d'Alembert). Voltaire, while insisting that he was as good as any aristocrat, had no desire to topple the aristocracy from its position; rather, he sought amalgamation. As d'Alembert put it, talent on the one hand and birth and eminence on the other both deserve recognition.

The Salons and Masonic Lodges Usually organized and led by women of wealthy bourgeois or noble families, the **salons** sought to bring together important writers with the influential persons they needed for favors and patronage. The salon of Madame Tencin, for example, helped launch Montesquieu's *Spirit of the Laws* in the 1740s, while the salon of Madame du Deffand in the 1760s became a forum in which the philosophes could test their ideas (see figure, p. 567). The salons also helped to enlarge the audience and contacts of the philosophes by introducing them to a flow of foreign visitors, ranging from German princes to Benjamin Franklin. Private newsletters kept interested foreigners and provincials abreast of activities in the Parisian salons when they could not attend personally, but salons also operated in Vienna, London, and Berlin.

The salons placed a premium on elegant conversation and wit. The women who ran them insisted that intellectuals make their ideas lucid and comprehensible, which increased the likelihood that their thought and writings would have some impact. The salons were also a forum in which men learned to take women seriously, and they constituted a unique cultural space for women between the domestic and public spheres. But the salons' emphasis on style over substance led Rousseau to denounce them as artificial rituals that prevented the display of genuine feeling and sincerity.

Throughout Europe, freemasonry was another important form of cultural sociability that often crossed the lines of class and (less commonly) of gender. Operating in an aura of secretiveness and symbolism, the masonic lodges fostered a curious mixture of spirituality and rationalism. Originating as clubs or fraternities dedicated to humane values, they attracted a wide range of educated nobles, commoners, and liberal clergy, while some lodges accepted women as well. But toward the end of the century, freemasonry was torn by sectarian controversies, and its influence seemed to be diminishing.

The Learned Academies   As important for the dissemination of ideas in the eighteenth century as the salons were the learned academies. These ranged from the Lunar Society in Birmingham, a forum for innovative British industrialists and engineers, to state-sponsored academies in almost every capital of Southern and Central Europe, which served as conduits for advanced scientific and philosophical ideas coming from Western Europe. In France, moreover, academies were established in more than thirty provincial cities, most of which became strongholds of advanced thinking outside the capital.

These provincial academies were founded after the death of Louis XIV in 1715, as if in testimony to the liberating effect of his demise. Most began as literary institutes, concerned with upholding the purity of literary style. A few academies adhered to such goals well into midcentury, but most gradually shifted their interests from literary matters to scientific and practical questions in such areas as commerce, agriculture, and local administration. They became offshoots, so to speak, of the *Encyclopedia's* spirit. Indeed, when a Jesuit launched an attack against the *Encyclopedia* in the Lyons Academy, many members threatened to resign unless he retracted his remarks.

By the 1770s the essay contests sponsored by the provincial academies and the papers published by their members had turned to such topics as population growth, capital punishment and penology, education, poverty and welfare, the grain trade, the guilds, and the origins of sovereignty. A parallel shift in membership occurred. The local academies began as privileged corporations, dominated by the nobility of the region. Associate membership was extended to commoners from the ranks of civil servants, doctors, and professionals. Gradually, the distinction between regular and associate participants crumbled. The academies admitted more commoners to full membership, and a fragile social fusion took place.

Publishing and Reading

The eighteenth century saw a notable rise in publishing geared to several kinds of readers. Traveling circulating libraries originated in England around 1740 and opened untapped markets for reading material; by the end of the century almost one thousand traveling libraries had been established. "Booksellers," or publishers—the intermediary between author and reader—combined the functions of a modern editor, printer, salesperson, and (if need be) smuggler. Their judgment and marketing techniques helped create as well as fill the demand for books, since they conceived and financed a variety of works. The *Encyclopedia* originated as a bookseller's project; so, too, did such enduring masterpieces as Samuel Johnson's *Dictionary*, a monumental lexicon that helped purify and standardize the English language. Booksellers commissioned talented stylists to write popular versions of serious scientific, historical, and philosophical works. Recognizing a specialized demand among women readers, they increased the output of fictional romances and fashion magazines and also began to publish more fiction and poetry by women.

Journals and Newspapers   The eighteenth century saw a proliferation of periodicals. In England, which pioneered in this domain, the number of periodicals increased from 25 to 158 between 1700 and 1780. In one successful model, Addison and Steele's *Spectator* (1711), each issue consisted of a single essay that sought in elegant but clear prose to raise the reader's standards of morality and taste. Their goal was "to enliven Morality with Wit, and to temper Wit with Morality. . . . To bring Philosophy . . . to dwell in clubs and assemblies, at tea-tables and coffeehouses." Eliza

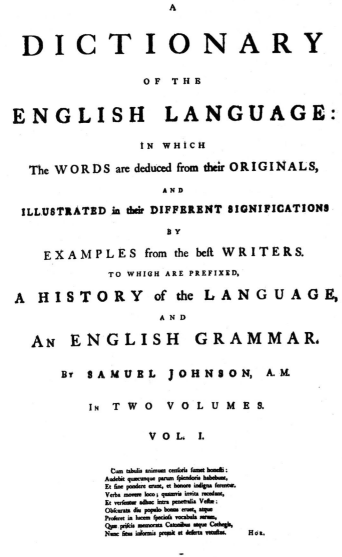

A

DICTIONARY

OF THE

ENGLISH LANGUAGE:

IN WHICH

The WORDS are deduced from their ORIGINALS,

AND

ILLUSTRATED in their DIFFERENT SIGNIFICATIONS

BY

EXAMPLES from the beſt WRITERS.

TO WHICH ARE PREFIXED,

A HISTORY of the LANGUAGE,

AND

AN ENGLISH GRAMMAR.

BY SAMUEL JOHNSON, A.M.

IN TWO VOLUMES.

VOL. I.

Cum tabulis animum cenſoris ſumet honeſti :
Audebit quæcunque parum ſplendoris habebunt,
Et ſine pondere erunt, et honore indigna ferentur.
Verba movere loco; quamvis invita recedant,
Et verſentur adhuc intra penetralia Veſtæ :
Obſcurata diu populo bonus eruet, atque
Proferet in lucem ſpecioſa vocabula rerum,
Quæ priſcis memorata Catonibus atque Cethegis,
Nunc ſitus informis premit et deſerta vetuſtas.   HOR.

LONDON
Printed by W. STRAHAN,
For J. and P. KNAPTON; T. and T. LONGMAN; C. HITCH and L. HAWES;
A. MILLAR and R. and J. DODSLEY.
MDCCLV.

The title page of Samuel Johnson's pioneering *Dictionary of the English Language* (1755 edition), one of the masterpieces of eighteenth-century literature.
The Mary Evans Picture Library

Haywood adapted this format in her journal, *The Female Spectator* (1744–1756), in which she advocated improvement in the treatment of women and greater "opportunities of enlarging our minds." Another type of journal published extracts and summaries of books and covered current events and entertainment; one such journal, the *Gentleman's Magazine,* reached the impressive circulation of fifteen thousand in 1740. More learned periodicals specialized in book reviews and serious articles on science and philosophy.

Most important for the future of reading habits in Europe was the daily newspaper, which originated in England. Papers like the *London Chronicle* at first provided family entertainment and then took on classified advertisements (thereby spurring consumerism and the notion of fashion). English newspapers of course published news of current events, but only after strenuous battles for permission from a reluctant government did they win the right to report directly on parliamentary debates. In France, a handful of major Parisian newspapers enjoyed privileged monopolies in exchange for full compliance with government censorship. This arrangement severely restricted their ability to discuss government and politics, although other periodicals published outside France's borders helped satisfy the demand for such coverage in France.

"Bad Books"   The demand for books and the dynamism of the publishing industry created new employment opportunities for men and women. Although the number of would-be writers swelled, relatively few could achieve financial independence without patronage. Many remained poverty-stricken and frustrated.

Publishers thus could hire legions of otherwise unemployed writers to turn out the kinds of books for which they sensed a great demand: potboilers, romances, salacious pamphlets, and gossip sheets, which pandered to low tastes. Paid for quantity and speed rather than quality, these hack writers led a precarious, humiliating existence. Booksellers and desperate writers saw money to be made in sensational pamphlets assailing the character of notorious aristocrats; in partisan pamphlets attacking a particular faction in court politics; and in pornography. Sometimes they combined character assassination and pornography in pamphlets dwelling on the alleged perversions of rulers or courtiers. For all its wild exaggeration, such material helped "desacralize" monarchy and created a vivid image of a decadent aristocracy.

To satisfy the public's demand for gossip, character assassination, and pornography in violation of laws regulating the book trade in France, publishers located just across the French border marketed such books and pamphlets clandestinely. They smuggled this material into France, along with banned books by writers like Voltaire and Rousseau, using networks of couriers and distributors. In their sales lists of what they called Philosophic Books, the clandestine publishers lumped together banned books by serious writers along with such illicit publications as *The Scandalous Chronicles*, *The Private Life of Louis XV*, and *Venus in the Cloister* (a pornographic account of the alleged perversions of the clergy). The police made the same judgment. In attempting to stop the flow of "bad books," they scarcely distinguished between a banned work by Voltaire assaulting religious bigotry and a libelous pamphlet depicting the queen as a corrupt pervert.

Literature, Music, and Art

Unlike the artistic style of the seventeenth century, generally classified as baroque, the artistic style of the eighteenth century cannot be given a single stylistic label. The nature of the audience and the sources of support for writers and composers also varied considerably. But several trends proved to be of lasting importance: the rise of the novel in England, the birth of Romantic poetry, the development of the symphony in Austria, and the changing social context of French painting late in the century.

The Rise of the Novel   The modern novel had its strongest development in England, where writers and

booksellers cultivated a growing middle-class reading public. The acknowledged pioneer of this new genre was Samuel Richardson. With a series of letters telling the story, Richardson's *Pamela, or Virtue Rewarded* (1740) recounted the trials and tribulations of an honest if somewhat hypocritical servant girl. Pamela's sexual virtue is repeatedly challenged but never conquered by her wealthy employer, Mr. B., who finally agrees to marry her. An instant success, this melodrama broke from the standard forms and heroic subjects of most narrative fiction. Richardson dealt with recognizable types of people.

Pamela's apparent hypocrisy, however, prompted a playwright and lawyer named Henry Fielding to pen a short satire called *Shamela*, which he followed with his own novel *Joseph Andrews*. Here comedy and adventure replaced melodrama; Fielding prefaced *Joseph Andrews* with a manifesto claiming that the novel was to be "a comic epic in prose." Fielding realized the full potential of his bold experimentation with literary forms in *Tom Jones* (1749), a colorful, robust, comic panorama of English society featuring a gallery of brilliantly developed characters and vivid depictions of varied social environments.

The novel was thus emerging as a form of fiction that told its story and treated the development of personality in a realistic social context. It seemed to mirror its times better than other forms of fiction. Like the dramas that filled the stage in the second half of the century, most novels focused on family life and everyday problems of love, marriage, and social relations. Novelists could use broad comedy, or they could be totally serious; they could experiment endlessly with forms and techniques and could deal with a wide range of social settings.

In *Evelina, or A Young Lady's Entrance into the World* (1778), the writer Fanny Burney used the flexibility of the novel to give a woman's perspective on eighteenth-century English social life. In the form of letters, like *Pamela* and Rousseau's *Julie*, *Evelina* traces a provincial girl's adventures in London as she discovers her true father and finds a suitable husband. While falling back on conventional melodrama, in which marriage is the only happy ending for a young woman, Burney also uses social satire to suggest how society restricts, and even endangers, an independent woman's life. If Burney was ambivalent about the possibilities for female independence in the social world, her own writing, together with that of other women writers of the period, demonstrated the opportunities for female artistic achievement.

The Birth of Romantic Poetry   During most of this century of innovation in prose fiction, poetry retained its traditional qualities. Still the most prized form of literary expression, poetry followed unchanging rules

on what made good literature. Each poetic form had its particular essence and rules, but in all types of poems diction was supposed to be elegant and the sentiments refined. Poets were expected to transform the raw materials of emotion into delicate language and references that only the highly educated could appreciate. In this neoclassical tradition, art was meant to echo eternal standards of truth and beauty. Poets were not permitted to unburden their souls or hold forth on their own experiences. The audience for poetry was the narrowest segment of the reading public—"the wealthy few," in the phrase of William Wordsworth, who criticized eighteenth-century poets for pandering exclusively to that group.

By the end of the century, however, the restraints of **Neoclassicism** finally provoked rebellion in the ranks of English and German poets. Men like Friedrich von Schiller and Wordsworth defiantly raised the celebration of individual feeling and inner passion to the level of a creed, which came to be known as **Romanticism.** These young poets generally prized Rousseau's writings, seeing the Genevan rebel as someone who had forged a personal idiom of expression and who valued inner feeling, moral passion, and the wonders of nature. Hoping to appeal to a much broader audience, these poets decisively changed the nature of poetic composition and made this literary form, like the novel, a flexible vehicle of artistic expression.

Goethe   The writer who came to embody the new ambitions of poets, novelists, and dramatists was Johann von Goethe, whose long life (1749–1832) spanned the beginnings and the high point of the Romantic movement. A friend of Schiller and many of the German writers and philosophers of the day, he soon came to tower over all of them. Goethe first inspired a literary movement known as *Sturm und Drang* (Storm and Stress), which emphasized strong artistic emotions and gave early intimations of the Romantic temperament. The best-known work of Sturm und Drang was Goethe's *The Sorrows of Young Werther* (1774), a novel about a young man driven to despair and suicide by an impossible love.

Courted by many of the princes and monarchs of Germany, Goethe soon joined the circle of the duke who ruled the small city-state of Weimar, where he remained for the rest of his life. There flowed from his pen an astonishing stream of works—lyrical love poetry, powerful dramas, art and literary criticism, translations, philosophic reflections, an account of his travels in Italy, and studies of optics, botany, anatomy, and mathematics. Even though he held official posts in the duke's court, Goethe's literary output never flagged. His masterpiece, *Faust*, occupied him for nearly fifty years and revealed the progress of his art. The first part (published in 1808) imbued with romantic longing the story of a

man who yearns to master all of knowledge and who makes a pact with the devil to achieve his goal. But the second part (1831) emphasized the determination that came to be Goethe's credo. The final lines are:

He only earns his freedom and existence
Who daily conquers them anew.

What had begun in the youthful exuberance and energy of Romanticism ended in an almost classical mood of discipline. No wonder that Goethe seemed to his contemporaries to be the last "universal man," the embodiment of conflicting cultural values and Western civilization's struggle to resolve them.

The Symphony   For Europe's elites, music offered the supreme form of entertainment, and the development of the symphony in music paralleled the rise of the novel in literature. For much of the century, composers still served under royal, ecclesiastical, or aristocratic patronage. They were bound by rigid formulas of composition and by prevailing tastes tyrannically insistent on conventions. Most listeners wanted little more than pleasant melodies in familiar forms; instrumental music was often commissioned as background fare for balls or other social occasions.

The heartland of Europe's music tradition shifted during the eighteenth century from Italy and France to Austria. Here a trio of geniuses transformed the routines of eighteenth-century composition into original and enduring masterpieces. True, the early symphonies of Franz Joseph Haydn and young Wolfgang Amadeus Mozart were conventional exercises. As light and tuneful as its audience could wish, their early music had little emotional impact. By the end of their careers, however, these two composers had altered the symphonic form from three to four movements, had achieved extraordinary harmonic virtuosity, and had brought a deep if restrained emotionalism to their music. Haydn and Mozart had changed the symphony radically from the elegant trifles of earlier years.

Beethoven   Ludwig van Beethoven consummated this development and ensured that the symphony, like the novel and Romantic poetry, would be an adaptable vehicle for the expression of creative genius. In each of his nine symphonies, as well as in his five piano concertos, Beethoven progressively modified the standard formulas, enlarged the orchestra, and wrote movements of increasing intricacy. His last symphony burst the bonds of the form altogether. Beethoven introduced a large chorus singing one of Schiller's odes to conclude his *Ninth Symphony* (1824), making it a celebration in music of freedom and human kinship. Laden with passion, the music is nevertheless recognizable as an advanced form of the classical symphony. Thus, it provides a bridge between the music of two periods:

Jean-Baptiste Greuze
THE FATHER'S CURSE, **1777**
Instead of the aristocrats or classical figures that most artists chose for their subjects, Jean-Baptiste Greuze painted ordinary French people. His portraits and dramatic scenes (such as *The Father's Curse*) seemed to echo Rousseau's call for honest, "natural" feeling.
Louvre, Paris, France. Giraudon/ Arts Resource, NY

Élisabeth Vigée-Le Brun
MARIE ANTOINETTE WITH A ROSE
One of the leading French portrait painters, and the most successful female artist of the era anywhere, was Élisabeth Vigée-Le Brun, who enjoyed the patronage of Queen Marie Antoinette. Shown here is one of several portraits that she painted of the French queen.
Giraudon/Art Resource, NY

eighteenth-century classicism and nineteenth-century Romanticism.

Aristocratic and court patronage remained the surest foundation for a career in music during the eighteenth century. Haydn, for example, worked with mutual satisfaction as the court composer for one prince from 1761 to 1790. At the end of his long life, however, Haydn moved out on his own, having won enough international recognition to sign a lucrative contract with a London music publisher who underwrote performances of his last twelve symphonies. In contrast, Mozart had an unhappy experience trying to earn his living by composing. After a few miserable years as court composer for the Archbishop of Salzburg, Mozart escaped to Vienna but could not find a permanent employer. He was obliged to eke out an inadequate living by teaching, filling private commissions, and giving public concerts. Beethoven did much better at freeing himself from dependence on a single patron through individual commissions and public concerts.

The Social Context of Art Unlike the situation in literature and music, there were no notable innovations in the field of painting during most of the eighteenth century. With the exception of the Frenchman Jacques-

Jacques-Louis David
THE OATH OF THE HORATII
The greatest innovation in French painting came in reaction to the artificiality of the rococo style and subject matter, with a return to favor of "noble simplicity and calm grandeur." This Neoclassical style found its supreme expression in the work of Jacques-Louis David. Such history paintings as *The Oath of the Horatii* evoked the ideal of civic virtue in ancient Greek and Roman civilization.
Louvre, Paris, France. Erich Lessing/ Art Resource, NY

a dismal status quo. C
ular literature helps u
hope of extending his

Oral Tradition   Ora
told at the fireside on
on from generation to
bodied the convention

Themes touching o
more likely to turn u
booklets. Songs and t
ness of ordinary men
present hardships and
drudgery of work in th
empty stomach, the cru
stepparents, the desper
most fantastic tales e
which strangers might
fairies but might just
witches. Oral tradition
and cunning of ordinar
in the spirit of the sayin

Literacy and Prim

The wars of religion ha
and elementary schoolir
plicitly promoted literac
their Bibles directly; strc
as Scotland, Switzerland
high rates of literacy by
Catholic Church, as well

Louis David, eighteenth-century painters were over-shadowed by their predecessors. Neoclassicism re-mained a popular style in the late eighteenth century, with its themes inspired by antiquity and its timeless conceptions of form and beauty, comparable to the rules of Neoclassical poetry.

The social context of painting, however, was chang-ing. Most commissions and patronage still depended on aristocrats and princes, but the public was beginning to claim a role as the judge of talent in the visual arts. Public opinion found its voice in a new breed of art critics, unaffiliated with official sources of patronage, who reached their new audience through the press in the second half of the century. The Royal Academy of Art in France created the opening for this new voice by sponsoring an annual public exhibition, or "salon," starting in 1737. People could view the canvases cho-sen by the Academy for these exhibitions and could reach their own judgments about the painters.

David and Greuze   David, a brilliant painter in the Neoclassical style, won the greatest renown in this arena of public opinion during the 1780s. He skillfully celebrated the values of the ancient world in such his-torical paintings as *The Oath of the Horatii* (see figure, above), *The Death of Socrates*, and *Brutus*. Discarding many of the standard conventions for history painting (and thereby drawing criticism from the Academy), David overwhelmed the public with his vivid imagery and the emotional force of his compositions. His paint-

ings of the 1780s unmistakably conveyed a yearning for civic virtue and patriotism that had yet to find its polit-ical outlet in France. Not surprisingly, David became the most engaged and triumphant painter of the French Revolution.

In an entirely different vein, a few eighteenth-century artists chose more mundane and "realistic" subjects or themes for their canvases, parallel in some respects to what novelists and playwrights were doing. Jean-Baptiste Greuze, for example, made a hit in the Parisian exhibitions of the 1770s with his sentimentalized paint-ings of ordinary people in family settings caught in a dramatic situation, such as the death of a father or the banishment of a disobedient son. William Hogarth, a superb London engraver who worked through the medium of prints and book illustrations, went further down the social pyramid with his remarkable scenes of life among the working classes and the poor.

POPULAR CULTURE

While the cultural world of aristocratic and middle-class elites has been extensively studied, the culture of artisans, peasants, and the urban poor remains more dimly known. In those sectors of society, culture prima-rily meant recreation, and it was essentially public and collective. Despite traditions of elementary schooling in certain regions and the spread of literacy among some groups, literacy rates remained generally low. Popular

**A page from
likely weath...
New York Pub...**

culture did have its w...
prevalent than the ora...
folktales, and proverbs...
of popular culture in th...
to suggest the rich varie...
practice among working...

Popular Literature

Far removed from the ...
Gentleman's Magazine e...
ular literature—the read...
neymen and peasants, t...
those who could barely ...
read at all. From the se...
nineteenth century, publ...
ence small booklets writ...
cheap paper, costing only...
itinerant peddlers who k...
tomers. Presumably the b...
by those who could read t...

This popular literature t...
gious material included de...

educating their young. Education could seem a waste of time when their children could be contributing to the family's livelihood; they might especially begrudge spending the money on tuition that most elementary schooling required.

A village usually hired a schoolmaster in consultation with the pastor or priest; schools usually straddled community and church, since the schoolmaster often served as the pastor's aide. Except in towns that had charitable endowments to support schooling, the parents, the village, or some combination of the two paid the schoolmaster, and for that reason numerous villages did without any schooling. Even a modest tuition could deter impoverished parents from hiring a master, enrolling their children, or keeping them in school for a sufficient time. Since schoolmasters taught reading first and writing separately and later, many pupils, especially girls, were not kept in school long enough to learn how to write anything but their names. Schooling, in other words, was largely demand-driven, the product of a community's level of wealth and interest.

Schooling in Central Europe

While England and France left primary schooling entirely to the chance of local initiative, the Habsburg monarchy seriously promoted primary education and thereby became the first Catholic realm to do so. The Habsburg General School Ordinance of 1774 authorized state subsidies, in combination with local funds, for the support of a school in almost every parish. Attendance was supposed to be compulsory, though the state had no way to enforce it. The state also intended to train future teachers at institutions called normal schools. A similar two-pronged strategy was adopted in Prussia under Frederick II at about the same time, although little was done to implement it.

In Prussia, as in most of Europe, schoolmasters remained barely competent and poorly paid. Frederick II indeed had a limiting vision of popular education: "It is enough for the country people to learn only a little reading and writing. . . . Instruction must be planned so that they receive only what is most essential for them but which is designed to keep them in the villages and not influence them to leave." As elsewhere in Europe, the goals of elementary schooling were to inculcate religion and morality, propagate the virtues of hard work, and promote deference to one's superiors.

Sociability and Recreation

If the educated elites had their salons, masonic lodges, and learned academies, the common people also formed organized cultural groups. Many artisans, for example, belonged to secret societies that combined fraternal and trade-union functions. Young unmarried artisans frequently traveled the country, stopping periodically to work with comrades in other towns in order to hone their skills. Artisans also relied on their associations for camaraderie and ritual celebrations. Married artisans often joined religious confraternities, which honored a patron saint and ensured a dignified funeral when they died, or mutual aid societies to which they contributed small monthly dues to pay for assistance if illness or accident should strike.

Taverns and Festivals

Corresponding to the coffeehouses of the urban middle classes were the taverns in working-class neighborhoods. These noisy, crowded places catered to a poor clientele, especially on Sunday and on Monday, which workingmen often took as a day off, honoring (as they put it) "Saint Monday." The urban common people were first beginning to consume wine in the eighteenth century, still something of a luxury except in its cheapest watered form. In England gin was the poor person's drink, cheap and plentiful until the government levied a hefty excise tax after realizing that too many people were drinking themselves into disability and death—a concern depicted in Hogarth's etchings, p. 577.

More commonly, drinking was not done in morbid fashion but as part of a healthy and vibrant outdoor life. Popular pastimes followed a calendar of holidays that provided occasions for group merrymaking, eating, drinking, dressing-up, contests, and games. Local festivals were particularly comfortable settings for single young men and women to meet each other. The highlight of a country year usually came in early autumn after the summer harvest was in, when most villages held a public feast that lasted several days. In Catholic countries similar festivities were often linked with church rituals. Popular observances included the commemoration of local patron saints, pilgrimages to holy places, and the period of Carnival before Lent. More generally, a growing "commercialization of leisure" in the eighteenth century supported new spectator sports, such as horse racing and boxing matches.

In early modern Europe, gentlefolk and commoners had been accustomed to mixing in recreational and religious settings: fairs and markets, sporting events, village or town festivals, Carnival in Catholic countries. But in the eighteenth century, as aristocrats and bourgeois alike became more concerned with good manners and refinement, these elite groups began to distance themselves from the bawdy and vulgar behavior of ordinary people. With growing intolerance, they censured popular recreational culture in the hope of "reforming" the people into a more sober and orderly lifestyle. Social status was based on birth or wealth, but cultural taste was becoming its behavioral marker.

William Hogarth

GIN LANE AND *BEER STREET*

In his *Gin Lane* etching of 1750, Hogarth depicted the results of excessive gin drinking by the English common people as death, apathy, and moral decay. A cheerful companion piece called *Beer Street*, however, suggested that drinking in moderation was an acceptable practice.

Hogarth, *Gin Lane.* The Metropolitan Museum of Art, Harris Brisbane Dick Fund, 1932. Photography © 2002 The Metropolitan Museum of Art, New York.

Hogarth, *Beer Street.* The Metropolitan Museum of Art, Harris Brisbane Dick Fund, 1932. [32.35 (123)]. Photograph © 2002 The Metropolitan Museum of Art, New York.

Summary

The philosophes, celebrated members of Europe's cultural establishment by the 1770s, hoped that their society would gradually reform itself under their inspiration. Although these writers criticized their society, they were not its subverters. Distrustful of the uneducated masses and afraid of popular emotion, superstition, and disorder, the philosophes were anything but democrats. Nonetheless, the Enlightenment challenged basic traditional values of European society: from Voltaire's polemics against Christianity through the sober social science of Diderot's *Encyclopedia* to the impassioned writings of Rousseau. Along with a flood of "bad books"—the pornography and scandal sheets of the clandestine publishers—booksellers, writers, and journalists disseminated critical ideas among Europe's educated men and women. The philosophes challenged the automatic respect for convention and authority, promoted the habit of independent reflection, and implanted the conviction that the reform of institutions was both necessary and possible. They promoted a climate that put the status quo on the defensive and in which revolution—when provoked under particular circumstances—would not be unthinkable.

QUESTIONS FOR FURTHER THOUGHT

1. What were the core values of the Enlightenment and how would you assess their strengths and weaknesses? What might have produced a backlash against Enlightenment values in subsequent periods? How might one defend them today?

2. How does the music, painting, and literature of the eighteenth century compare to the high culture of earlier periods you have studied, such as the Renaissance or the seventeenth century? Has the social or political context of cultural life changed? Were there comparable changes in the realm of popular culture?

3. What do you make of Jean-Jacques Rousseau?

RECOMMENDED READING

Sources

Gay, Peter (ed.). *The Enlightenment: A Comprehensive Anthology.* 1973.

Gendzier, Stephen (ed.). *Denis Diderot: The Encyclopedia: Selections.* 1967.

*Jacob, Margaret C. *The Enlightenment: A Brief History with Documents.* 2001.

Mohl, Mary R., and Helene Koon (eds.). *The Female Spectator: English Women Writers Before 1800.* 1977.

Vigée-Le Brun, Marie-Louise . . . Élisabeth. *Memoirs.* S. Evans (ed.). 1989. Memoirs of the most notable female painter in eighteenth-century France.

Studies

*Brewer, John. *The Pleasures of the Imagination: English Culture in the Eighteenth Century.* 1997. A lively, panoramic survey of the production and consumption of high culture in all its forms.

Bruford, W. H. *Germany in the Eighteenth Century: The Social Background of the Literary Revival.* 1952. A useful survey.

Buchan, James. *Crowded with Genius: The Scottish Enlightenment: Edinburgh's Moment of the Mind.* 2003. A popular history of the remarkable circle of Scottish philosophes, including Adam Smith and David Hume.

Capp, Bernard. *English Almanacs, 1500–1800: Astrology and the Popular Press.* 1979. A probing study of the most important genre of popular literature.

*Chartier, Roger. *The Cultural Origins of the French Revolution.* 1991. A synthesis of recent research on publishing, the public sphere, and the emergence of new political attitudes.

Cranston, Maurice. *Jean-Jacques, The Noble Savage,* and *The Solitary Self.* 1982, 1991, and 1995. A three-volume study of the life and work of Rousseau, critical but sympathetic.

*Crow, Thomas. *Painters and Public Life in Eighteenth-Century Paris.* 1985. A pioneering work on the development of a public sphere of critical discourse about art.

*Darnton, Robert. *The Forbidden Best Sellers of Pre-Revolutionary France.* 1995. A pathbreaking work on the circulation, content, and impact of banned books.

*Gay, Peter. *The Enlightenment: An Interpretation.* 2 vols. 1966 and 1969. A masterly, full-bodied exposition of Enlightenment thought.

*Goodman, Dena. *The Republic of Letters: A Cultural History of the French Enlightenment.* 1994. Focuses on the salons and the roles of women in cultural and intellectual life.

*Isherwood, Robert. *Farce and Fantasy: Popular Entertainment in Eighteenth-Century Paris.* 1986. A cultural and institutional history of fairs and popular theater.

Malcolmson, R. W. *Popular Recreations in English Society, 1700–1850.* 1973. A good survey of a neglected subject.

May, Gita. *Elisabeth Vigée-Le Brun: The Odyssey of an Artist in an Age of Revolution.* 2005. The public and private life of the period's most prominent female painter.

*Maza, Sarah. *Private Lives and Public Affairs: The Causes Célèbres of Pre-Revolutionary France.* 1993. An original analysis of scandals and lawsuits that raised social consciousness in the later eighteenth century.

McClellan, James. *Science Reorganized: Scientific Societies in the Eighteenth Century.* 1985.

Melton, James Van Horn. *Absolutism and the Eighteenth-Century Origins of Compulsory Schooling in Prussia and Austria.* 1988.

———. *The Rise of the Public in Enlightenment Europe.* 2001. An excellent comparative survey of the developing "public sphere" in Europe.

Palmer, Robert R. *Catholics and Unbelievers in Eighteenth-Century France.* 1939. The response of Catholic intellectuals to the century's philosophic thought.

Porter, Roy, and Mikulas Teich (eds.). *The Enlightenment in National Context.* 1981. A comprehensive geographic overview.

*Roche, Daniel. *France in the Enlightenment*. 1998. A masterly synthesis, especially on the Enlightenment and French society.

*Spencer, Samia (ed.). *French Women and the Age of Enlightenment*. 1984. A pioneering collection of essays on a variety of literary and historical themes.

Venturi, Franco. *Italy and the Enlightenment*. 1972. Essays on important Italian philosophes by a leading historian.

*Watt, Ian. *The Rise of the Novel: Studies of Defoe, Richardson, and Fielding*. 1957. The view from England.

Wilson, Arthur. *Diderot*. 1972. An exhaustive, reliable biography of the consummate French philosophe.

*Available in paperback.

Jean Duplessis-Bertaux
STORMING OF THE TUILERIES, COURS DU CAROUSSEL, AUGUST 10, 1792
The armed assault on the Tuileries Palace of August 10, 1792, brought an end to the monarchy and led directly to the founding of the first French Republic.
Giraudon/Art Resource, NY

Chapter Twenty

THE FRENCH REVOLUTION

REFORM AND POLITICAL CRISIS • 1789: THE FRENCH REVOLUTION •
THE RECONSTRUCTION OF FRANCE • THE SECOND REVOLUTION

Well into the eighteenth century, the long-standing social structures and political institutions of Europe were securely entrenched. Most monarchs still claimed to hold their authority directly from God. In cooperation with their aristocracies, they presided over realms composed of distinct orders of citizens, or *estates* as they were sometimes known. Each order had its particular rights, privileges, and obligations. But pressures for change were building during the century. In France, the force of public opinion grew increasingly potent by the 1780s. A financial or political crisis that could normally be managed by the monarchy threatened to snowball in this new environment. Such vulnerability was less evident in Austria, Prussia, and Russia, however, where strong monarchs instituted reforms to streamline their governments. Similarly, in Britain the political system proved resilient despite explosions of discontent at home and across the Atlantic.

Unquestionably, then, the French Revolution constituted the pivotal event of European history in the late eighteenth century. From its outbreak in 1789, the Revolution transformed the nature of sovereignty and law in France. Under its impetus, civic and social institutions were renewed, from local government and schooling to family relations and assistance for the poor. Soon its ideals of liberty, equality, and fraternity resonated across the borders of other European states, especially after war broke out in 1792 and French armies took the offensive.

The French Revolution's innovations defined the foundations of a liberal society and polity. Both at home and abroad, however, the new regime faced formidable opposition, and its struggle for survival propelled it in unanticipated directions. Some unforeseen turns, such as democracy and republicanism, became precedents for the future even if they soon aborted. Other developments, such as the Reign of Terror, seemed to nullify the original liberal values of 1789. The bloody struggles of the Revolution thus cast a shadow over this transformative event as they dramatized the brutal dilemma of means versus ends.

Civil Constitution of the Clergy **1790** ●

Peasant revolts and August 4 decree **July–August 1789** ●

Storming of the Bastille **July 1789** ●

Estates General become National Assembly **June 1789** ●

Failed Assembly of Notables in France **1787** ●

1780s
Joseph II's authoritarian reforms in Habsburg Empire

● **1776** American Declaration of Independence

REFORM AND POLITICAL CRISIS

To put the French Revolution into perspective, it helps to compare political tensions and conflicts elsewhere in Europe. Strong monarchs with reputations for being "enlightened" reigned in Prussia, Austria, Spain, and even Russia. Their stature seemingly contrasts with the mediocrity of Louis XV and Louis XVI, who ruled in France. Yet the former did not get far in reforming their realms or granting rights and freedom to their subjects. The limits of "enlightened absolutism," therefore, should be kept in mind when considering the crisis that confronted France. Meanwhile, in Britain energetic movements for political reform ran into determined opposition. This rigidity had a particular impact across the Atlantic, where Britain's thirteen colonies in North America were driven to rebellion and a revolutionary war for independence.

Enlightened Absolutism in Central and Eastern Europe

During the late nineteenth century, German historians invented the concept of enlightened absolutism to describe the Prussian and Habsburg monarchies of the eighteenth century. Critical of the ineptitude and weakness of French monarchs in that period, these historians argued that the strength of an enlightened ruler had been the surest basis for progress in early modern Europe. A king who ruled in his subjects' interest, they implied, avoided violent conflicts like those of the French Revolution. Earlier strong monarchs, such as Philip II of Spain and France's Louis XIV (who had once declared: "I am the state"), had been irresponsible; in contrast, these German historians argued, Frederick II of Prussia symbolized the enlightened phase of absolutism with his comment that the ruler is the "first servant of the state."

Previous chapters, however, have demonstrated that monarchs dealt with the same fundamental issues during all stages of absolutism. They always strove to assert their authority over their subjects and to maximize the power of their state in relation to other realms, principally by means of territorial expansion. Any notion that Enlightenment thinking caused monarchs to abandon these efforts is misleading. Still, several eighteenth-century monarchs did initiate reforms and did modify their styles of ruling in order to appear more modern or enlightened. Frederick II of Prussia and Catherine II of Russia, for example, lavished praise on Voltaire and Diderot, and those philosophes returned the compliment. These rulers may simply have been engaging in public relations. Yet the fact that they seemed supportive of such writers suggests that absolutism had indeed adopted a new image.

Catherine the Great (r. 1762–1796) played this game to its limit. In 1767 she announced a new experiment in the direction of representative government—a policy hailed as a landmark by her philosophe admirers, who were too remote from St. Petersburg to see its insincerity. Catherine convened a Legislative Commission, a body of delegates from various strata of Russian society who were invited to present grievances, propose reforms, and then debate the proposals. In the end, however, she sent the delegates home under the pretext of having to turn her attention to a war with Turkey. Little came of the Legislative Commission except some good publicity for Catherine. In fact, she later promulgated a Charter of the Nobility, which, instead of limiting the nobility's privileges, strengthened their corporate status and increased their control over their serfs in exchange for their loyalty to the throne.

- **April 1792** French war against Austria and Prussia
- **August 1792** French monarchy overthrown
- **January 1793** Execution of Louis XVI
- **March 1793** Vendée rebellion begins
- **June 1793** Purge of the Girondins
- **August 1793** *Levée en masse*
- **September–October 1793** Jacobin dictatorship and Reign of Terror begin
- **July 1794** Fall of Robespierre

Conceptions of Enlightened Rule in Germany In justification of absolute monarchy, eighteenth-century German writers depicted the state as a machine and the ruler as its mainspring. Progress came from sound administration, through an enlightened monarch and well-trained officials. In keeping with this notion, German universities began to train government bureaucrats, and professors offered courses in the science of public finance and administration called *cameralism.*

The orders for the bureaucracy came from the monarchs, who were expected to dedicate themselves to the welfare of their subjects in return for their subjects' obedience. The framework for this command-obedience chain was to be a coherent body of public law, fairly administered by state officials. According to its advocates, this system would produce the rule of law, without the need for a written constitution or a representative parliament. The ruler and his or her officials, following their sense of public responsibility and rational analysis, would ensure the citizens' rights and well-being.

Joseph II and the Limits of Absolutism

Joseph II, coruler of the Habsburg Empire with his mother, Maria Theresa, from 1765 and sole ruler in the 1780s, vigorously promoted reform from above. Unlike Frederick or Catherine, he did not openly identify with the philosophes, and he maintained his own Catholic faith. But Joseph proved to be the most innovative of the century's major rulers as well as one of its most autocratic personalities. It was a problematic combination.

Sound rule for Emperor Joseph involved far more than the customary administrative and financial reform necessary for survival in the competitive state system. With startling boldness he implemented several reforms long advocated by Enlightenment thinkers: freedom of expression, religious toleration, greater state control over the Catholic Church, and legal reform. A new criminal code, for example, reduced the use of the death penalty, ended judicial torture, and allowed for no class differences in the application of the laws. By greatly reducing royal censorship, Joseph made it possible for Vienna to become a major center of literary activity. And we have already noted Joseph's remarkable Edicts of Religious Toleration for Protestants and for Jews. But Joseph's religious policies did not stop there. To make the Catholic Church serve its parishioners better, Joseph forced the clergy to modernize its rituals and services. Most of his Catholic subjects, however, preferred their traditional ways to Joseph's streamlined brand of Catholicism. These "reforms" proved extremely unpopular.

Agrarian Reform Joseph's most ambitious policies aimed to transform the economic and social position of the peasants. Elsewhere, agrarian reform was generally the weak side of enlightened absolutism, since Frederick II and Catherine II did little to improve the lot of the peasants or serfs in their realms. Joseph, however, set out to eradicate serfdom and to convert Habsburg peasants into free individuals in command of their persons and of the land they cultivated.

By royal decree, Joseph abolished personal servitude and gave peasants the right to move, marry, and enter any trade they wished. He then promulgated laws to secure peasants' control over the land they worked. Finally and most remarkably, he sought to limit the financial obligations of peasant tenants to their lords and to the state. All land was to be surveyed and subject to a uniform tax. Twelve percent of the land's annual yield would go to the state and a maximum of 18 percent would go to the lord. This tax replaced

Joseph II, shown here visiting a peasant's field, actually promulgated his momentous agrarian reform edicts without any significant consultation with the peasants before or after the fact.
Austrian Press & Information Service

previous seigneurial obligations in which peasants owed service to their lord that could consume more than one hundred days of labor a year.

Joseph ordered these reforms in an authoritarian fashion, with little consultation and no consent from any quarter. Predictably, these reforms provoked fierce opposition among the landowning nobles. But they also perplexed most peasants, who already distrusted the government because of its arbitrary religious policies. Joseph made no effort to build support among the peasants by carefully explaining the reforms, let alone by modifying their details after getting feedback from the grass roots.

His arbitrary manner, however, was not incidental. Joseph acknowledged no other way of doing things, no limitation on his own sovereignty. In reaction to the opposition that his reforms aroused, he moved to suppress dissent in the firmest possible way. Not only did he restore censorship in his last years, but he elevated the police department to the status of an imperial ministry and gave it unprecedented powers. By the time he died, in 1790, Joseph was a disillusioned man. His realm resembled a police state, and his successors quickly restored serfdom.

Upheavals in the British Empire

An aggressive monarch, George III, helped ignite political unrest in Great Britain. He was intent on advancing royal authority, but rather than bypass Parliament altogether, he simply tried, as Whig ministers had before him, to control its members through patronage and influence. The Whig aristocrats saw this operation as a threat to their own traditional power. Not only did they oppose the king and his ministers in Parlia-

ment, but they enlisted the support of citizens' groups outside of Parliament as well. These organizations were calling for political reform, including representation in Parliament proportionate to population, stricter laws against political corruption, and greater freedom of the press.

"Wilkes and Liberty"   John Wilkes, a member of Parliament and a journalist, became the center of this rising storm. Wilkes viciously attacked the king's prime minister, and by implication the king himself, over the terms of the Treaty of Paris, which ended the Seven Years' War in 1763. The government arrested him for seditious libel on a general warrant. When the courts quashed the indictment, the government then accused Wilkes of having authored a libelous pornographic poem, and this time he fled to France to avoid prison. He stayed in France for four years; but in 1768, still under indictment, he returned to stand once more for Parliament. Three times he was reelected, and three times the House of Commons refused to seat him. With the ardent support of radicals and to the acclaim of crowds in London, who marched to the chant of "Wilkes and Liberty," Wilkes finally took his seat in 1774.

Agitation for parliamentary reform drew support primarily from shopkeepers, artisans, and property owners, who had the franchise in a few districts but were denied it in most others. Thus, even without a right to vote, English citizens could engage in politics and mobilize the power of public opinion, in this case by rallying to Wilkes. Most radicals called only for political reform, not for the overthrow of the British political system. They retained a measure of respect for the nation's political traditions, which ideally guaranteed the rights of "freeborn Englishmen."

The committee that drafted the American Declaration of Independence included John Adams, Thomas Jefferson, and Benjamin Franklin, all shown here standing at the desk.
The Library of Congress

Rebellion in America   Great Britain did face revolutionary action in the thirteen North American colonies. George III and his prime minister, Lord North, attempted to force the colonies to pay the costs, past and present, of their own defense. The policy would have meant an increase in taxes and a centralization of authority in the governance of the British Empire. Colonial landowners, merchants, and artisans of the eastern seaboard organized petitions and boycotts in opposition to the proposed fiscal and constitutional changes.

The resistance in North America differed fundamentally from comparable movements in Europe. American political leaders did not appeal to a body of privileges that the actions of the monarchy were allegedly violating. Instead, they appealed to traditional rights supposedly enjoyed by all British subjects, regardless of status, and to theories of popular sovereignty and natural rights advanced by John Locke and other English libertarian writers. When conciliation and compromise with the British government failed,

the American Declaration of Independence in 1776 gave eloquent expression to those concepts. The lack of a rigid system of estates and hereditary privileges in American society, the fluid boundaries that separated the social strata, and the traditions of local government in the colonies—from town meetings in New England to the elected legislatures that had advised colonial governors—blunted the kinds of conflicts between aristocrats and commoners that derailed incipient revolutionary movements in Ireland, Belgium, and the Dutch Netherlands.

These differences help to explain the unique character of the American rebellion, which was simultaneously a war for independence and a political revolution. The theories that supported the rebellion, and the continuing alliance between social strata, made it the most democratic revolution of the eighteenth century before 1789. The American Revolution created the first state governments, and ultimately a national government, in which the exercise of power was grounded not on royal sovereignty or traditional privilege but on the participation and consent of male citizens (apart from the numerous black slaves, whose status did not change). Even more important as a historical precedent, perhaps, it was the first successful rebellion by overseas colonies against their European masters.

1789: THE FRENCH REVOLUTION

Although the rebellion in America stirred sympathy and interest across the Atlantic, it seemed remote from the realities of Europe. The French Revolution of 1789 proved to be the turning point in European history. Its sheer radicalism, creativity, and claims of universalism made it unique. Its ultimate slogan—"Liberty, Equality, Fraternity"—expressed social and civic ideals that became the foundations of modern Western civilization. In the name of individual liberty, French revolutionaries swept away the institutionalized constraints of the old regime: seigneurial charges upon the land, tax privileges, guild monopolies on commerce, and even (in 1794) black slavery overseas. The revolutionaries held that legitimate governments required written constitutions, elections, and powerful legislatures. They demanded equality before the law for all persons and uniformity of institutions for all regions of the country, denying the claims to special treatment of privileged groups, provinces, towns, or religions. The term *fraternity* expressed a different kind of revolutionary goal. Rousseauist in inspiration, it meant that all citizens, regardless of social class, or region, shared a common fate in society and that the nation's well-being could override the interests of individual citizens.

Origins of the Revolution

Those who made the Revolution believed they were rising against despotic government, in which citizens had no voice, and against inequality and privilege. Yet the government of France at that time was no more tyrannical or unjust than it had been in the past. On the contrary, a process of modest reform had been under way for several decades. What, then, set off the revolutionary upheaval? What had failed in France's long-standing political system?

An easy answer would be to point to the incompetence of King Louis XVI (r. 1774–1792) and his queen, Marie Antoinette. Louis was good-natured but weak and indecisive, a man of limited intelligence who lacked self-confidence and who preferred hunting deer to supervising the business of government. By no stretch of the imagination was he an enlightened absolutist. Worse yet, his young queen, a Habsburg princess, was frivolous, meddlesome, and tactless. But even the most capable French ruler could not have escaped challenge and unrest in the 1780s.

The Cultural Climate   In eighteenth-century France, as we have seen, intellectual ferment preceded political revolt. For decades the philosophes had questioned accepted political and religious beliefs. They undermined confidence that traditional ways were the best ways. But the philosophes harbored deep-seated fears of the uneducated masses and did not question the notion that educated and propertied elites should rule society; they wished only that the elites should be more enlightened and more open to new ideas. Indeed, the Enlightenment had become respectable by the 1770s, a kind of intellectual establishment. Rousseau damned that establishment and wrote of the need for simplicity, sincerity, and virtue, but the word *revolution* never flowed from his pen either.

More subversive perhaps than the writings of Enlightenment intellectuals were several sensational lawsuits centered on the scandalous doings of high aristocrats. The melodramatic legal briefs published by the lawyers in such cases were eagerly snatched up by the reading public along with prohibited "bad books"—the clandestine gossip sheets, libels, exposés, and pornography—discussed earlier. All this material—indirectly, at least—portrayed the French aristocracy as decadent and the monarchy as a ridiculous despotism. Royal officials and philosophes alike regarded the authors of this material as "the excrement of literature," as Voltaire put it. And writers forced to earn their living by turning out such stuff were no doubt embittered at being stuck on the bottom rung in the world of letters. Their resentment would explode once the Revolution began in 1789, and many became radical journalists either for or against the new regime. In itself, however, the "literary underground" of the old regime did not advocate, foresee, or directly cause the Revolution.

Class Conflict?   Did the structure of French society, then, provoke the Revolution? Karl Marx, and the many historians inspired by him, certainly believed so. Marx saw the French Revolution as the necessary break marking the transition from the aristocratic feudalism of the Middle Ages to the era of middle-class capitalism. In this view, the French bourgeoisie, or middle classes, had been gaining in wealth during the eighteenth century and resented the privileges of the nobility, which created obstacles to their ambition. Though they framed their ideology in universal terms in 1789, the middle classes led the Revolution in order to change the political and social systems in their own interests.

Three decades of research have rendered this theory of the Revolution's origins untenable. Whether a sizable and coherent capitalist middle class actually existed in eighteenth-century France is questionable. In any case, the leaders of the Revolution in 1789 were lawyers, administrators, and liberal nobles, and rarely merchants or industrialists. Moreover, the barrier between the nobility of the Second Estate and the wealthy and educated members of the Third Estate was porous, the lines of social division frequently (though not always) blurred. Many members of the middle class identified themselves on official documents as "living nobly," as substantial property owners who did not work for a living. Conversely, wealthy nobles often invested in mining, overseas trade, and finance—activities usually associated with the middle classes. Even more important, the gap between the nobility and the middle classes was nothing compared with the gulf that separated both from the working people of town and country. In this revisionist historiography, the bourgeoisie did not make the Revolution so much as the Revolution made the bourgeoisie (see "On the Origins of the French Revolution," p. 588).

Yet numerous disruptive pressures were at work in French society. A growing population left large numbers of young people in town and country struggling to attain a stable place in society. New images and attitudes rippled through the media of the day, despite the state's efforts to censor material it deemed subversive. The nobility, long since banished by Louis XIV from an independent role in government, chafed at its exclusion, although it continued to enjoy a near monopoly on positions in the officer corps. The prosperous middle classes too aspired to a more active role in government. The monarchy struggled to contain these forces within the established social and political systems. Until the 1780s it succeeded, but then its troubles began in earnest.

Fiscal Crisis and Political Deadlock

When he took the throne in 1774, Louis XVI tried to conciliate elite opinion by recalling the parlements, or sovereign law courts, that his grandfather had banished in 1770 for opposing his policies. This concession to France's traditional "unwritten constitution" did not suffice to smooth the new sovereign's road. Louis' new controller-general of finances, Jacques Turgot, encountered a storm of opposition from privileged groups to the reforms he proposed.

The Failure of Reform   Turgot, an ally of the philosophes and an experienced administrator, hoped to encourage economic growth by a policy of nonintervention, or *laissez-faire,* that would give free play to economic markets and allow individuals maximum freedom to pursue their own economic interests. He proposed to remove all restrictions on commerce in grain and to abolish the guilds. In addition, he tried to cut down on expenses at court and to replace the obligation of peasants to work on the royal roads (the *corvée*) with a small new tax on all landholders. Privately, he also considered establishing elected advisory assemblies of landowners to assist in local administration. Vested interests, however, viewed Turgot as a dangerous innovator. When agitation against him mounted in the king's court at Versailles and in the Paris parlement, Louis took the easy way out and dismissed his contentious minister. With Turgot went perhaps the last hope for significant reform in France under royal leadership.

Deficit Financing   The king then turned to Jacques Necker, a banker from Geneva who had a reputation for financial wizardry. Necker had a shrewd sense of public relations. To finance the heavy costs of France's aid to the rebellious British colonies in North America, Necker avoided new taxes and instead floated a series of large loans at exorbitant interest rates as high as 10 percent.

By the 1780s royal finances hovered in a state of permanent crisis. Direct taxes on land, borne mainly by the peasants, were extremely high but were levied inequitably. The great variations in taxation from province to province and the numerous exemptions for privileged groups were regarded by those who benefited from them as traditional liberties. Any attempt to revoke these privileges therefore appeared to be tyrannical. Meanwhile, indirect taxes on commercial activity (customs duties, excise or sales taxes, and royal monopolies on salt and tobacco) hit regressively at consumers, especially in the towns. At the same time, the cycle of borrowing—the alternative to increased taxes—had reached its limits. New loans would only raise the huge interest payments already being paid out. By the 1780s those payments accounted for about half the royal budget and created additional budget deficits each year.

Calonne and the Assembly of Notables   When the king's new controller-general, Charles Calonne, pieced all this information together in 1787, he warned that, contrary to Necker's rosy projections, the monarchy was facing outright bankruptcy. Though no way had yet been found to win public confidence and forge a consensus for fiscal reform, the monarchy could no longer rely on old expedients. Calonne accordingly proposed to establish a new tax, called the *territorial subvention,* to be levied on the yield of all landed property without exemptions. At the same time, he proposed

HISTORICAL ISSUES: ON THE ORIGINS OF THE FRENCH REVOLUTION

A long-held view of the French Revolution's origins attributed the starring role to the middle class, "the rising bourgeoisie." Liberal historians of the nineteenth century regarded the middle class as the carrier of liberal ideals—individual freedom, civil equality, representative government—that finally came to fruition in the French Revolution. Marxists considered the triumph of capitalism to be the pivotal issue in modern history and linked it to the political ascendancy of the middle class in the French Revolution. In a sense, both versions of this "social interpretation" of the French Revolution read its causes back from its results. In his classic synthesis of 1939 embodying the social interpretation, for example, Georges Lefebvre begins with these observations:

"The ultimate cause of the French Revolution of 1789 goes deep into the history of France and of the western world. At the end of the eighteenth century the social structure of France was aristocratic. It showed the traces of having originated at a time when land was almost the only form of wealth, and when the possessors of land were the masters of those who needed it to work and to live. It is true that in the course of age-old struggles the king had been able gradually to deprive the lords of their political powers and subject nobles and clergy to his authority. But he had left them the first place in the social hierarchy.

"Meanwhile the growth of commerce and industry had created, step by step, a new form of wealth, mobile or commercial wealth, and a new class, called in France the bourgeoisie. . . . In the eighteenth century commerce, industry and finance occupied an increasingly important place in the national economy. It was the bourgeoisie that rescued the royal treasury in moments of crisis. . . . The role of the nobility had correspondingly declined; and the clergy, as the ideal which it proclaimed lost prestige, found its authority growing weaker. These groups preserved the highest rank in the legal structure of the country, but in reality economic power, personal abilities and confidence in the future had passed largely to the bourgeoisie. Such a discrepancy never lasts forever. The Revolution of 1789 restored the harmony between fact and law."

From Georges Lefebvre, *The Coming of the French Revolution*, R. R. Palmer (trans.), Princeton University Press, 1989.

Since the 1950s, revisionist historians have challenged this "social interpretation" of the French Revolution. In his synthesis, William Doyle summarizes some of their research and arguments.

"Money, not privilege, was the key to pre-revolutionary society in France. Wealth transcended all social barriers and bound great nobles and upper bourgeois together into an upper class unified by money. . . . Eighteenth-century capitalism was far from a bourgeois monopoly. One of its basic features was the heavy involvement of nobles. . . . [On the other hand,] the wealth of all social groups in pre-revolutionary France was overwhelmingly non-capitalist in nature. Capitalism had not become the dominant mode of production in the French economy before 1789. . . . there was between most of the nobility and the proprietary sectors of the middle class, a continuity of investment forms and socioeconomic values that made them, economically, a single group.

"If the nobility and the bourgeoisie had so much in common, why did they become such implacable enemies in 1789? [Since] the Revolution could not be explained in economic terms as a clash of opposed interests. . . . it was time to revert to a political explanation of the Revolution's outbreak. The radical reforms of 1789 were products of a political crisis, and not the outcome of long-maturing social and economic trends. [As historian George Taylor concluded:] 'It was essentially a political revolution with social consequences and not a social revolution with political consequences.' "

From William Doyle, *Origins of the French Revolution*, Oxford University Press, 1988.

to convene *provincial assemblies* elected by large landowners to advise royal officials on the collection and allocation of revenues.

Certain that the parlements would reject this scheme, Calonne convinced the king to convene an Assembly of Notables, comprising about 150 influential men, mainly but not exclusively from the aristocracy, who might more easily be persuaded to support the re-

forms. To Calonne's shock, the Assembly of Notables refused to endorse the proposed decrees. Instead, they denounced the lavish spending of the court and insisted on auditing the monarchy's financial accounts. Moreover, when the government now submitted Calonne's proposals to the parlement, it not only rejected them but demanded that Louis convene the **Estates General,** a body representing the clergy, nobility, and Third

Estate, which had not met since 1614. Louis responded by sending the members of the parlements into exile. But a huge outcry in Paris and in the provinces against this arbitrary act forced the king to back down: After all, the whole purpose of Calonne's proposals had been to build public confidence in the government.

Facing bankruptcy and unable to float new loans in this atmosphere, the king recalled the parlements, reappointed Necker, and agreed to convene the Estates General in May 1789. In the opinion of the English writer Arthur Young, who was visiting France, the kingdom was "on the verge of a revolution, but one likely to add to the scale of the nobility and clergy." The aristocracy's determined opposition was putting an end to absolutism in France. But it was not clear what would take its place.

From the Estates General to the National Assembly

The calling of the Estates General in 1789 created extraordinary excitement across the land. The king invited his subjects to express their opinions about this great event, and thousands did so in pamphlet form. Here the "patriot," or liberal, ideology first took shape. Self-styled patriots came from the ranks of the nobility and clergy as well as from the middle classes; they opposed traditionalists, whom they labeled as "aristocrats." Their top priority was the method of voting to be used in the Estates General. While the king accorded the Third Estate twice as many delegates as the two higher orders, he refused to promise that the deputies would all vote together (by head) rather than separately in three chambers (by order). Voting by order would mean that the two upper chambers would outweigh the Third Estate no matter how many deputies it had. Patriots had hoped that the lines dividing the nobility from the middle class would crumble in a common effort by France's elites at reform. Instead, it appeared as if the Estates General might sharpen the lines of separation between the orders.

The Critique of Privilege   It did not matter that the nobility had led the fight against absolutism. Even if they endorsed new constitutional checks on absolutism and accepted equality in the allocation of taxes, nobles would still hold vastly disproportionate powers if the Estates General voted by order. In the most influential pamphlet about the Estates General, Emmanuel Sieyès posed the question, "What is the Third Estate?" and answered flatly, "Everything." "And what has it been until now in the political order?" he asked. Answer: "Nothing." The nobility, he claimed, monopolized all the lucrative positions in society while doing little of its productive work. In the manifestos of Sieyès

THE AWAKENING OF THE THIRD ESTATE
Thousands of pamphlets discussed the calling of the Estates General in 1789, but the grievances of the Third Estate translated most readily into vivid imagery and caricature.
Roger-Viollet/Bibliothèque Nationale de France, Paris

and other patriots, the enemy was no longer simply absolutism but privilege as well.

Unlike reformers in England or the American revolutionaries of 1776, the French patriots did not simply claim that the king had violated historic traditions of liberty. Rather, they contemplated a complete break with a discredited past. As a basis for reform, they would substitute reason for tradition. It is this frame of mind that made the French Revolution so radical.

Cahiers and Elections   For the moment, however, patriot spokesmen stood far in advance of opinion at the grass roots. The king had invited all citizens to meet in their local parishes to elect delegates to district electoral assemblies and to draft grievance petitions (*cahiers*) setting forth their views. The great majority of rural cahiers were highly traditional in tone and complained only of particular local ills or high taxes, expressing confidence that the king would redress them. Only a few cahiers from cities like Paris invoked concepts of natural rights and popular sovereignty or demanded that France must have a written constitution, that sovereignty belonged to the nation, or that feudalism and regional privileges should be abolished. It is impossible, in other words, to read in the cahiers the future course of the Revolution. Still, these gatherings of citizens promoted reflection on France's problems and encouraged expectations for change. They thereby raised the nation's political consciousness.

So too did the local elections, whose royal ground rules were remarkably democratic. Virtually every

When the king opened the meeting of the Estates General, the deputies for each estate were directed to sit in three separate sections of the hall.
Bulloz/© Photo RMN/Art Resource, NY

adult male taxpayer was eligible to vote for electors, who, in turn, met in district assemblies to choose representatives of the Third Estate to the Estates General. The electoral assemblies were a kind of political seminar, where articulate local leaders emerged to be sent by their fellow citizens as deputies to Versailles. Most of these deputies were lawyers or officials, without a single peasant or artisan among them. In the elections for the First Estate, meanwhile, parish priests rather than Church notables formed a majority of the deputies. And in the elections for the Second Estate, about one-third of the deputies could be described as liberal nobles or patriots, the rest traditionalists.

Deadlock and Revolution Popular expectation that the monarchy would provide leadership in reform proved to be ill-founded. When the deputies to the Estates General met on May 5, Necker and Louis XVI spoke to them only in generalities and left unsettled whether the estates would vote by order or by head. The upper two estates proceeded to organize their own chambers, but the deputies of the Third Estate balked. Vainly inviting the others to join them, the Third Estate took a decisive revolutionary step on June 17 by proclaiming that it formed a "National Assembly." A few days later more than a third of the deputies from

the clergy joined them. The king, on the other hand, decided to cast his lot with the nobility and locked the Third Estate out of its meeting hall until he could present his own program. But the deputies moved to an indoor tennis court and swore that they would not separate until they had given France a constitution.

The king ignored this act of defiance and addressed the delegates of all three orders on June 23. He promised equality in taxation, civil liberties, and regular meetings of the Estates General at which, however, voting would be by order. France would be provided with a constitution, he pledged, "but the ancient distinction of the three orders will be conserved in its entirety." He then ordered the three estates to retire to their individual meeting halls, but the Third Estate refused to move. "The assembled nation cannot receive orders," declared its spokesman. Startled by the determination of the patriots, the king backed down. For the time being, he recognized the National Assembly and ordered deputies from all three estates to join it.

Thus, the French Revolution began as a nonviolent, "legal" revolution. By their own will, delegates elected by France's three estates to represent their own districts to the king became instead the representatives of the entire nation. As such, they claimed to be the sovereign power in France—a claim that the king now

Jacques-Louis David
OATH OF THE TENNIS COURT, THE 20TH OF JUNE, 1789
Jacques-Louis David's depiction of the Tennis Court Oath, one of the great historical paintings, captures the deputies' sense of idealism and purpose.
Giraudon/Art Resource, NY

seemed powerless to contest. In fact, however, he was merely biding his time until he could deploy his army to subdue the capital and overwhelm the deputies at Versailles. The king ordered twenty thousand royal troops into the Paris region, due to arrive sometime in July.

The Convergence of Revolutions

The political struggle at Versailles was not occurring in isolation. The mass of French citizens, politically aroused by elections to the Estates General, was also mobilizing over subsistence issues. The winter and spring of 1788–1789 had brought severe economic difficulties, as crop failures and grain shortages almost doubled the price of flour and bread on which the population depended for subsistence. Unemployed vagrants filled the roads, angry consumers stormed grain convoys and marketplaces, and relations between town and country grew tense. Economic anxieties merged with rage over the obstructive behavior of aristocrats in Versailles. Parisians believed that food shortages and royal troops would be used to intimidate the people into submission. They feared an "aristocratic plot" against the National Assembly and the patriot cause.

The Fall of the Bastille When the king dismissed Necker on July 11, Parisians correctly assumed that a counterrevolution was about to begin. They prepared to resist, and most of the king's military units pulled back in the face of determined crowds. On July 14 Parisian crowds searching for weapons and ammunition laid siege to the **Bastille,** an old fortress that had once served as a royal prison and in which gunpowder was stored. The small garrison resisted, and a fierce firefight erupted. Although the troops soon capitulated, dozens of citizens were hit, providing the first martyrs of the Revolution, and the infuriated crowd massacred several soldiers as they left the fortress. Meanwhile, patriot electors ousted royal officials of the Paris city government, replaced them with a revolutionary municipality, and organized a citizens' militia to patrol the city. Similar municipal revolutions occurred in twenty-six of the thirty largest French cities, thus ensuring that the defiance in the capital would not be an isolated act.

THE STORMING OF THE BASTILLE
The fall of the Bastille was understood at the time to be a great turning point in history, and July 14 eventually became the French national holiday. Numerous prints and paintings evoke the daunting qualities of the fortress, the determination of the besieging crowd, and the valor of individuals in that crowd.
Bulloz/© Photo RMN/Art Resource, NY

The Parisian insurrection of July 14 not only saved the National Assembly but altered the Revolution's course by giving it a far more popular dimension. Again the king capitulated. He traveled to Paris on July 17 and, to please the people, donned a ribbon bearing three colors: white for the monarchy and blue and red for the capital. This *tricolor* would become the emblem of the new regime.

Peasant Revolts and the August 4 Decree These events did not pacify the anxious and hungry people of the countryside. Peasants had numerous and long-standing grievances. Population growth and the parceling of holdings reduced the margin of subsistence for many families, while the purchase of land by rich townspeople further shrank their opportunities for economic advancement. Seigneurial dues and church tithes weighed heavily on many peasants. Now, in addition, suspicions were rampant that nobles were hoarding grain in order to stymie the patriotic cause. In July peasants in several regions sacked the houses of the nobles and burned the documents that recorded their seigneurial obligations.

This peasant insurgency blended into a vast movement known to historians as "the Great Fear." Rumors abounded that the vagrants who swarmed through the countryside were actually "brigands" in the pay of nobles, who were marching on villages to destroy the new harvest and cow the peasants into submission. The fear was baseless, but it stirred up the peasants' hatred and suspicion of the nobles, prompted armed mobilizations in hundreds of villages, and set off new attacks on manor houses.

Peasant revolts worried the deputies of the National Assembly, but they decided to appease the peasants rather than simply denounce their violence. On the night of August 4, therefore, certain deputies of the nobility and clergy dramatically renounced their ancient privileges. This action set the stage for the Assembly to decree "the abolition of feudalism" as well as the end of the church tithe, the sale of royal offices, regional tax privileges, and social privilege of all kinds. Later, it is true, the Assembly clarified the August 4 decree to ensure that property rights were maintained. While personal servitudes such as hunting rights, manorial justice, and labor services were suppressed outright, the Assembly decreed that most seigneurial dues would end only after the peasants had paid compensation to their lords. Peasants resented this onerous requirement, and most simply refused to pay the dues; pressure built until all seigneurial dues were finally abolished without compensation by a more radical government in 1793.

THE RECONSTRUCTION OF FRANCE

The summer of 1789 had seen a remarkable sequence of unprecedented events. A bloodless, juridical revolution from above (engineered by the patriot deputies to the Estates General) combined with popular mobilization from below in town and country made the French Revolution seem irresistible. After the clearing operations of August 4, the National Assembly set out not simply to enact reforms but to reconstruct French institutions on entirely new principles. With sovereignty wrested from the king and vested in the people's deputies, no aspect of France's social or political system was immune to scrutiny, not even slavery in the colonies. First, the Assembly adopted a set of general principles known as the Declaration of the Rights of Man and Citizen. Then it proceeded to draft a constitution, settle the question of voting rights (where the issue of women's citizenship first came up), reorganize the structures of public life, and determine the future of the Catholic clergy. None of this occurred without intense disagreement, especially over the religious issue and the role of the king. Moreover, Austria and Prussia eventually decided on armed intervention against revolutionary France. In 1792 war broke out, which led directly to the fall of the monarchy and to a new, violent turn in the Revolution.

The Declaration of the Rights of Man and Citizen

By sweeping away the old web of privileges, the August 4 decree permitted the Assembly to construct a new regime. Since it would take months to draft a constitution, the Assembly drew up a Declaration of the Rights of Man and Citizen to indicate its intentions (see "Two Views of the Rights of Man," p. 594). The Declaration was the death certificate of the old regime and a rallying point for the future. It affirmed individual liberties but also set forth the basic obligation of citizenship: obedience to legitimate law. The Declaration enumerated **natural rights,** such as freedom of expression and freedom of religious conscience, but (unlike the America Bill of Rights) stipulated that even these rights could be circumscribed by law. It proclaimed the sovereignty of the nation and sketched the basic criteria for a legitimate government, such as representation and the separation of powers. The Declaration's concept of natural rights meant that the new regime would be based on the principles of reason rather than history or tradition.

In his *Reflections on the Revolution in France,* published in 1790, the Anglo-Irish statesman Edmund Burke condemned this attitude, as well as the violence of 1789. In this influential counterrevolutionary tract, Burke argued that France had passed from despotism to anarchy in the name of misguided, abstract principles. Burke distrusted the simplicity of reason that the Assembly celebrated. In his view, the complexity of traditional institutions served the public interest. Burke attacked the belief in natural rights that guided the revolutionaries; something was natural, he believed, only if it resulted from long historical development and habit. Trying to wipe the slate of history clean was a grievous error, he wrote, since society "is a contract between the dead, the living, and the unborn." Society's main right, in Burke's view, was the right to be well-governed by its rulers. Naturally this argument did not go unchallenged, even in England. Mary Wollstonecraft countered with *A Vindication of the Rights of Man,* followed shortly by her seminal *Vindication of the Rights of Woman,* while Thomas Paine published *The Rights of Man* in 1792 to refute Burke.

The New Constitution

Representative Government   From 1789 to 1791, the National Assembly acted as a Constituent Assembly to produce a constitution for France. While proclaiming equal civil rights for all French citizens, it effectively transferred political power from the monarchy and the privileged estates to the body of propertied citizens; in 1790 nobles lost their titles and became indistinguishable from other citizens. The new constitution created a limited monarchy with a clear separation of powers. Sovereignty effectively resided in the representatives of the people, a single-house legislature to be elected by a system of indirect voting. The king was to name and dismiss his ministers, but he was given only a suspensive or delaying veto over legislation; if a bill passed the Assembly in three successive years, it would become law even without royal approval.

Two Views of the Rights of Man

The radical theoretical and practical implications of French revolutionary ideology are suggested in a comparison of two essentially contemporaneous documents. The Prussian General Code, a codification initiated by Frederick the Great and issued in its final form in 1791 after his death, reinforced the traditional prerogatives of the nobility under an umbrella of public law. The French National Assembly's Declaration of the Rights of Man and Citizen (1789) established the principle of civil equality alongside the doctrines of national sovereignty, representation, and the rule of law. While the Prussian General Code exemplifies the old order against which French revolutionary ideology took aim, the Declaration became a foundational document of the liberal tradition.

EXCERPTS FROM THE PRUSSIAN GENERAL CODE, 1791

- This general code contains the provisions by which the rights and obligations of inhabitants of the state, so far as they are not determined by particular laws, are to be judged.
- The rights of a man arise from his birth, from his estate, and from actions and arrangements with which the laws have associated a certain determinate effect.
- The general rights of man are grounded on the natural liberty to seek and further his own welfare, without injury to the rights of another.
- Persons to whom, by their birth, destination or principal occupation, equal rights are ascribed in civil society, make up together an *estate* of the state.
- The nobility, as the first estate in the state, most especially bears the obligation, by its distinctive destination, to maintain the defense of the state. . . .
- The nobleman has an especial right to places of honor in the state for which he has made himself fit.
- Only the nobleman has the right to possess noble property.
- Persons of the burgher [middle-class] estate cannot own noble property except by permission of the sovereign.
- Noblemen shall normally engage in no burgher livelihood or occupation.

From R. R. Palmer (trans.), *The Age of Democratic Revolution*, Princeton University Press, 1959, pp. 510–511.

EXCERPTS FROM THE FRENCH DECLARATION OF THE RIGHTS OF MAN AND CITIZEN, 1789

1. Men are born and remain free and equal in rights. Social distinctions may be based only on common utility.
3. The principle of all sovereignty rests essentially in the nation. No body and no individual may exercise authority which does not emanate expressly from the nation.
4. Liberty consists in the ability to do whatever does not harm another; hence the exercise of the natural rights of each man has no limits except those which assure to other members of society the enjoyment of the same rights. These limits can only be determined by law.
6. Law is the expression of the general will. All citizens have the right to take part, in person or by their representatives, in its formation. It must be the same for all whether it protects or penalizes. All citizens being equal in its eyes are equally admissible to all public dignities, offices and employments, according to their capacity, and with no other distinction than that of their virtues and talents.
13. For maintenance of public forces and for expenses of administration common taxation is necessary. It should be apportioned equally among all citizens according to their capacity to pay.
14. All citizens have the right, by themselves or through their representatives, to have demonstrated to them the necessity of public taxes, to consent to them freely, to follow the use made of the proceeds, and to determine the shares to be paid, the means of assessment and collection and the duration.

Under the French Constitution of 1791, every adult male of settled domicile who satisfied minimal taxpaying requirements (roughly two-thirds of all adult males) gained the right to vote, with a higher qualification needed to serve as an elector. Although it favored the propertied, France's new political system was vastly more democratic than Britain's. Still, the National Assembly considered the vote to be a civic function rather than a natural right. "Those who contribute nothing to the public establishment should have no direct influence on government," declared Sieyès. In the same frame of mind the Assembly excluded all women from voting.

Women in the Revolution That the Assembly even debated political rights for women testifies to the potential universalism of the Revolution's principles. A brief but spirited drive for women's suffrage advanced through pamphlets, petitions, and deputations to the Assembly—most notably the "Declaration of the Rights of Women" (1791) drafted by the playwright Olympe de Gouges. But the notion of gender difference

In October 1789 Parisian women were furious over the high cost of bread and suspicious of the king and queen. In concert with the National Guard, they set out on an armed march to confront the royal couple in Versailles. To appease the menacing crowd, Louis XVI agreed to return to Paris and to cooperate with revolutionary authorities.
Giraudon/Art Resource, NY

and separate spheres, popularized by Rousseau, easily prevailed. The great majority of deputies believed women to be too emotional. Too easily influenced to be independent, they must be excluded from the new public sphere—the more so because of the deputies' belief that elite women had used their sexual powers nefariously behind the scenes during the old regime to influence public policy. Now public life would be virtuous and transparent, uninfluenced by feminine wiles. Instead, women would devote themselves to their crucial nurturing and maternal roles in the domestic sphere.

This type of discourse has prompted some feminist scholars to claim that the revolutionary public sphere "was constructed not merely without women but against them." Balanced against this argument, however, is an offsetting consideration. Male revolutionaries may have distrusted women, and some were overt misogynists, yet their own ideology and political culture created unprecedented public space for women. True, women could not vote or hold office, but otherwise *citoyennes* had extensive opportunity for political participation. Women actively engaged in local conflicts over the Assembly's religious policy (discussed later in this chapter). In the towns they agitated over

food prices, and in October 1789 Parisian women led a mass demonstration to Versailles that forcibly returned the king and queen to Paris. Combining traditional concerns over food scarcities with antiaristocratic revolutionary ideology, women frequently goaded authorities like the national guard into action.

In unprecedented numbers women also took up the pen to publish pamphlets and journals. Their physical presence in public spaces was even more important. Women helped fill the galleries of the Assembly, of the Paris Jacobin Club, and later of the Revolutionary Tribunal—shouting approval or disapproval and in general monitoring their officials. In at least sixty towns women formed auxiliaries to the local Jacobin club, where they read newspapers, debated political issues, and participated in revolutionary festivals.

Nor did Rousseauian antifeminism prevent the revolutionaries from enacting dramatic advances in the civil status of women. Legislation between 1789 and 1794 created a more equitable family life by curbing paternal powers over children, lowering the age of majority, and equalizing the status of husbands and wives in regard to property. Viewing marriage as a contract between a free man and a free woman, the revolutionaries

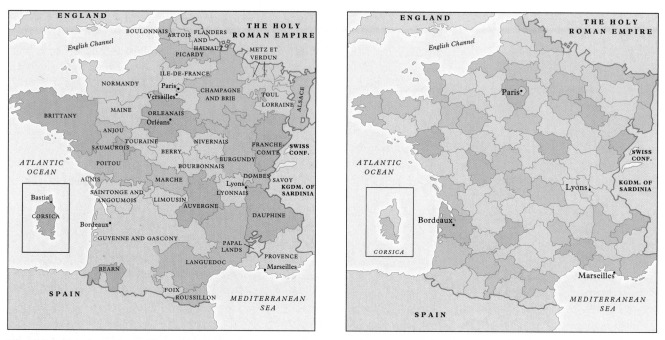

MAP 20.1 REDIVIDING THE NATION'S TERRITORY IN 1789
The old regime provinces (left) were replaced by revolutionary departments (right). What advantages did this change bring for the French state?
◆ For an online version, go to www.mhhe.com/chambers9 > chapter 20 > book maps

provided the right of divorce to either spouse should the marriage go sour. A remarkably egalitarian inheritance law stipulated that daughters as well as sons were entitled to an equal share of a family's estate. Finally, in the domain of education—central to the feminist vision of Mary Wollstonecraft that the French Revolution had crystalized—an unprecedented system of universal and free primary schooling in 1794 extended to girls as well as boys and provided for state-salaried teachers of both sexes.

Race and Slavery   As the Assembly excluded women from voting citizenship without much debate, other groups posed challenges on how to apply "the rights of man" to French society. In eastern France, where most of France's forty thousand Jews resided amid discrimination, public opinion scorned them as an alien race not entitled to citizenship. Eventually, however, the Assembly rejected that argument and extended civil and political equality to Jews. A similar debate raged over the status of the free Negroes and mulattoes in France's Caribbean colonies. White planters, in alliance with the merchants who traded with the islands, were intent on preserving slavery and demanded local control over the islands' racial policy as their best defense. The planters argued that they could not maintain slavery, which was manifestly based on race, unless free people of color were disenfranchised.

When the Assembly accepted this view, the mulattoes rebelled. But their abortive uprising had the unintended consequence of helping ignite a slave rebellion. Led by Toussaint-L'Ouverture, the blacks turned violently on their white masters and proclaimed the independence of the colony, which became known as Haiti. In 1794 the French revolutionary government abolished slavery in all French colonies. (For further discussion see "The Fight for Liberty and Equality in Saint-Domingue," p. 598.)

Unifying the Nation   Within France the Assembly obliterated the political identities of the country's historic provinces and instead divided the nation's territory into eighty-three departments of roughly equal size (see map 20.1). Unlike the old provinces, each new department was to have exactly the same institutions. The departments were, in turn, subdivided into districts, cantons, and communes (the common designation for a village or town). On the one hand, this administrative transformation promoted local autonomy: The citizens of each department, district, and commune elected their own local officials, and in that sense political power was decentralized. On the other hand, these local governments were subordinated to the national legislature in Paris and became instruments for promoting national integration and uniformity.

The new administrative map also created the boundaries for a new judicial system. Sweeping away the parlements and law courts of the old regime, the revolutionaries established a justice of the peace in each canton, a civil court in each district, and a criminal court in each department. The judges on all tribunals were to be elected. The Assembly rejected the use of juries in civil cases but decreed that felonies would be tried by juries; also, criminal defendants for the first time gained the right to counsel. In civil law, the Assembly encouraged arbitration and mediation to avoid the time-consuming and expensive processes of formal litigation. In general, the revolutionaries hoped to make the administration of justice faster and more accessible.

Economic Individualism   The Assembly's clearing operations extended to economic institutions as well. Guided by the dogmas of laissez-faire theory and by its uncompromising hostility to privileged corporations, the Assembly sought to open up economic life to individual initiative, much as Turgot had attempted in the 1770s. Besides dismantling internal tariffs and chartered trading monopolies, it abolished merchants' and artisans' guilds and proclaimed the right of every citizen to enter any trade and conduct it freely. The government would no longer concern itself with regulating wages or the quality of goods. The Assembly also insisted that workers bargain in the economic marketplace as individuals, and it therefore banned workers' associations and strikes. The precepts of economic individualism extended to the countryside as well. At least in theory, peasants and landlords were free to cultivate their fields as they saw fit, regardless of traditional collective practices. In fact, those deep-rooted communal restraints proved to be extremely resistant to change.

The Revolution and the Church

To address the state's financial problems, the National Assembly acted in a way that the monarchy had never dared contemplate. Under revolutionary ideology, the French Catholic Church could no longer exist as an independent corporation—as a separate estate within the state. The Assembly, therefore, nationalized Church property (about 10 percent of the land in France), placing it "at the disposition of the nation," and made the state responsible for the upkeep of the Church. It then issued paper notes called ***assignats,*** which were backed by the value of these "national lands." The property was to be sold by auction at the district capitals to the highest bidders. This plan favored the bourgeois and rich peasants with ready capital and made it difficult for needy peasants to acquire the land, though some pooled their resources to do so.

The sale of Church lands and the issuance of assignats had several consequences. In the short run, they eliminated the need for new borrowing. Second, the hundreds of thousands of purchasers gained a strong vested interest in the Revolution, since a successful counterrevolution was likely to reclaim their properties for the Church. Finally, after war broke out with an Austrian-Prussian coalition in 1792, the government made the assignats a national currency and printed a volume of assignats way beyond their underlying value in land, thereby touching off severe inflation and new political turmoil.

Religious Schism   The issue of Church reform produced the Revolution's first and most fateful crisis. The Assembly intended to rid the Church of inequities that enriched the aristocratic prelates of the old regime. Many Catholics looked forward to such healthy changes that might bring the clergy closer to the people. In the **Civil Constitution of the Clergy** (1790), the Assembly reduced the number of bishops from 130 to 83 and reshaped diocesan boundaries to conform exactly with those of the new departments. Bishops and parish priests were to be chosen by the electoral assemblies in the departments and districts and were to be paid according to a uniform salary scale that favored those currently at the lower end. Like all other public officials, the clergy was to take an oath of loyalty to the constitution.

The clergy generally opposed the Civil Constitution because it had been dictated to them by the National Assembly; they argued that such questions as the selection of bishops and priests should be negotiated either with the Pope or with a National Church Council. But the Assembly asserted that it had the sovereign power to order such reforms, since they affected temporal rather than spiritual matters. In November 1790 the Assembly demanded that all clergy take the loyalty oath forthwith; those who refused would lose their positions and be pensioned off. In all of France only seven bishops and about 54 percent of the parish clergy swore the oath; but in the west of France only 15 percent of the priests complied. A schism tore through French Catholicism, since the laity had to take a position as well: Should parishioners remain loyal to their priests who had refused to take the oath (the nonjuring, or refractory, clergy) and thus be at odds with the state? Or should they accept the unfamiliar "constitutional clergy" designated by the districts to replace their own priests?

The Assembly's effort to impose reform in defiance of religious sensibilities and Church autonomy was a grave tactical error. The oath crisis polarized the nation. It seemed to link the Revolution with impiety and the Church with counterrevolution. In local

A PORTRAIT OF THE PARISIAN SANS-CULOTTE

"A Sans-Culotte is a man who goes everywhere on his own two feet, who has none of the millions you're all after, no mansions, no lackeys to wait on him, and who lives quite simply with his wife and children, if he has any, on the fourth or fifth floor. He is useful, because he knows how to plough a field, handle a forge, a saw, or a file, how to cover a roof or how to make shoes and to shed his blood to the last drop to save the Republic. And since he is a working man, you will never find him in the Cafe de Chartres where they plot and gamble. . . . In the evening, he is at his Section, not powdered and perfumed and all dolled up to catch the eyes of the *citoyennes* in the galleries, but to support sound resolutions with all his power and to pulverize the vile faction [of moderates]. For the rest, a Sans-Culotte always keeps his sword with a sharp edge, to clip the ears of the malevolent. Sometimes he carries his pike and at the first roll of the drum, off he goes to the Vendée, to the Army of the Alps or the Army of the North."

From a pamphlet attributed to the Parisian militant Vingternier: "A Reply to the Impertinent Question: But What Is a Sans-Culotte?" 1794.

At the height of a radical "dechristianization" movement (which lasted for about eight months in 1793–1794), more than eighteen thousand priests renounced their vocations under pressure from militant revolutionaries. About a third also agreed to marry as a way of proving the sincerity of their resignations. (The print's caption states: "They shave me in the morning and have me married by evening.")
Bibliothèque Nationale de France, Paris

Within this upsurge of activism, the Society of Revolutionary-Republican Women, founded in Paris in the spring of 1793, constituted a vanguard of female radicals. The members of this club were undeterred by their exclusion from the vote, which did not much concern them at this point. Even without voting rights, women considered themselves citizens in revolutionary France.

In agitating for severe enforcement of price controls and the compulsory use of republican symbols, however, these women irritated the revolutionary government. Before long the ruling Jacobins perceived them as part of an irresponsible ultra-left opposition, whom they denounced as *enragés*, rabid ones. In October the government arrested the most prominent *enragés*, male and female, closed down the Society of Revolutionary-Republican Women, and forbade the formation of female political clubs in the future. The government's spokesman derided these activists as "denatured women," viragos who neglected their maternal duties. Behind this bitter antifeminist rhetoric lay a

The radical activists of the aris sections—the sans-culottes and their female counterparts—made a point of their plebeian forms of dress, their freedom to bear arms, and their egalitarian insignias, such as the red liberty cap.
Bulloz/© Photo RMN/Art Resource, NY

sense of anxiety. In the virile and punitive world of radical republicanism (see the illustration of Hercules on p. 610), the Jacobins yearned for an offsetting feminine virtue to soften the severity required in the public sphere.

To Robespierre, in any case, the notion of direct democracy appeared unworkable and akin to anarchy. The Convention watched the sans-culottes with concern, supportive of their democratic egalitarianism but fearful of the unpredictability, disorder, and inefficiency of this popular movement. The Mountain attempted to encourage civic participation yet control it. From the forty-eight sections of Paris, however, came an endless stream of petitions, denunciations, and veiled threats to the government. In the spring of 1794 the Convention finally curbed the power of the sections by drastically restricting their rights and activities. But in forcibly cooling down the ardor of the sans-culottes, the revolutionary government necessarily weakened its own base of support.

The Revolutionary Wars

Ultimately, the Revolution's fate rested in the hands of its armies, although no one had thought in such terms in 1789. France's revolutionary ideology had initially posed no direct threat to the European state system. Indeed, the orators of the National Assembly had argued that the best foreign policy for a free society was peace, neutrality, and isolation from the diplomatic intrigues of monarchs. But peaceful intentions did not imply pacifism. When counterrevolution at home coalesced with threats from abroad, the revolutionaries vigorously confronted both. As in most major wars, however, the initial objectives were soon forgotten. As the war expanded, it brought revolution to other states.

The revolutionary wars involved standard considerations of international relations as well as new and explosive purposes. On the one hand, France pursued the traditional aim of extending and rounding off its frontiers. On the other hand, France now espoused revolutionary principles such as the right of a people to self-determination. As early as September 1791, the National Assembly had declared that "the rights of peoples are not determined by the treaties of princes."

Foreign Revolutionaries and French Armies   Even before 1789 "patriots" in Geneva, the Dutch Netherlands, and the Austrian Netherlands (Belgium) had unsuccessfully challenged the traditional arrangements that governed their societies, and the French Revolution rekindled those rebellious sentiments. Foreign revolutionaries were eager to challenge their governments again, and they looked to revolutionary France for assistance. Refugees from these struggles had fled to France and now formed pressure groups to lobby French leaders for help in liberating their own countries during France's war against Austria and Prussia. Some revolutionaries from areas contiguous to France (Belgium, Savoy, and the Rhineland) hoped that the French Republic might simply annex those territories. Elsewhere—in the Dutch Netherlands, Lombardy, Ireland, and the Swiss Confederation—insurgents hoped that France would help establish independent republics by overthrowing the ruling princes or oligarchies.

Few French leaders were interested in leading a European crusade for liberty, but practical considerations led them to intervene. As the war spilled over into Belgium and the Rhineland, the French sought to establish support abroad by incorporating the principles of the Revolution into their foreign policy. Thus, in December 1792 the Convention decided that feudal practices and hereditary privileges would be abolished wherever French armies prevailed. The people thus liberated, however, would have to pay for their liberation with special taxes

MAP 21.1 FRANCE AND ITS SISTER REPUBLICS, 1798
Notice the locations of France's sister republics. Which republics were likely to be the most viable?
◆ For an online version, go to www.mhhe.com/chambers9 > chapter 21 > book maps

ministry. There he advocated a new strategy: opening a front in Italy to strike at Austrian forces from the south, while French armies on the Rhine pushed as usual from the west. The strategy was approved, and Bonaparte gained command of the Army of Italy in 1796.

The Making of a Hero   Austria's forces outnumbered the French in Italy, but Bonaparte moved his troops rapidly to achieve surprise and numerical superiority in specific encounters. The end result was a major victory that brought the French into the Habsburg domain of Lombardy and its capital, Milan. Bonaparte's overall plan almost miscarried, since the Army of the Rhine did not advance as planned. But this mishap made his own triumphs all the more important to the Directory. And Bonaparte ensured his popularity with the government by making his campaign self-supporting through organized levies on the Italians.

Bonaparte brought a great sense of excitement and drama to the French occupation of Lombardy. His personal magnetism and his talent in manipulating people attracted many Italians. The general encouraged the Italians to organize their own revolutionary movement; the liberation of northern Italy, he believed, would solidify support for his army and enhance his own reputation. This policy distressed the Directory, since it had intended to trade back conquests in Italy in exchange for security on the Rhine frontier. But in the end the Directory endorsed the Treaty of Campo Formio, in which Bonaparte personally negotiated a peace settlement with Austria in October 1797. Austria recognized a new, independent state in northern Italy, the Cisalpine Republic, and left the Rhine question to future negotiations. The Directory regime had found the hero it desperately needed.

The French now focused their patriotic aspirations on defeating the last member of the coalition: the hated British enemy. Bonaparte naturally yearned for the glory of accomplishing this feat, and he was authorized to prepare an invasion force. Previous seaborne landings directed at Ireland had failed, however, and Bonaparte too finally had to abandon the scheme because of France's insufficient naval force.

Instead, in the spring of 1798 Bonaparte launched an expedition to Egypt intended to strike at Britain's approaches to India. But British naval superiority, in the form of Admiral Horatio Nelson's fleet, turned the expedition into a debacle. The British destroyed the French fleet at the Battle of the Nile, thereby marooning a French army in North Africa. Worse yet, the French were beaten back in several engagements with Turkish forces. Only cynical news management prevented the full story of this defeat from reaching France. Instead, the expedition's exotic details and scientific explorations held the attention of the French public. Bonaparte extricated himself from this mess by slipping off through the British blockade, in effect abandoning his army as he returned to France.

The Brumaire Coup

While Bonaparte floundered in Egypt, the Directory was faltering under political pressures at home. Charges of tyranny and ineptitude accumulated against the directors. Further French expansion into Italy, which produced new sister republics centered in Rome and Naples, precipitated a new coalition against France, consisting of Britain, Russia, and Austria. In June 1799 ill-supplied French forces were driven out of most of Italy and Switzerland.

The legislature ousted four of the five directors and named Sieyès, a respected leader of the patriots in 1789, among the replacements. Sieyès and his supporters secretly wished to alter the constitution itself, for they had lost confidence in the regime's institutions, especially its annual elections. These "revisionists" wanted to redesign the Republic along more oligarchic lines, as opposed to the Neo-Jacobins, who wished to democratize the Republic. The centrist position had virtually disappeared. The revisionists blocked emergency measures proposed by the Neo-Jacobins in reaction to the new war crisis and breathed a sigh of relief as French armies rallied and repulsed Anglo-Russian forces in the Batavian Republic and Switzerland. Most of Italy was lost for the time being, but the threat to France itself had passed. Sieyès and the revisionists moved against the Neo-Jacobins by closing their clubs and newspapers and prepared for a coup.

A General Comes to Power Although no dire military threat remained to propel the country into the arms of a general, the revisionists wished to establish a more centralized, oligarchic republic, and they needed a general's support. Generals were the only national heroes in France, and only a general could organize the force necessary to ensure the coup's success. Bonaparte's return to France from Egypt thus seemed most timely. Bonaparte was not the revisionists' first choice, but he proved to be the best available one.

Contrary to the intentions of Sieyès and his fellow conspirators, Bonaparte became the tail that wagged the dog. Once the coup began, he proved to be far more ambitious and energetic than the other conspirators and thrust himself into the most prominent position. Bonaparte addressed the legislature to denounce a mythical Jacobin plot and to demand emergency powers for a new provisional government. Intimidated into submission, a cooperative rump of the legislature approved the new arrangements. Along with Sieyès, Bonaparte was empowered to draft a new constitution. Thus unfolded the coup of 18 Brumaire (November 9, 1799).

The **Brumaire** coup had not been intended to install a dictatorship, but that was its eventual result. In the maneuvering among the revisionists, Bonaparte's ideas and personality prevailed. The plotters agreed to eliminate meaningful elections, which they saw as promoting political instability. They agreed also to enshrine the social ideals of 1789, such as civil equality, and to bury those of the year II, such as popular democracy. The vague notion of popular sovereignty gave way to concentrated authority. The general came out of the coup as the regime's strongman, and Sieyès' elaborate plans for a republican oligarchy ended up in the wastebasket. On one other point, the plotters were particularly deceived. With General Bonaparte's leadership they hoped to achieve durable peace through military victory. Instead, the Napoleonic regime promoted unbounded expansion and endless warfare.

THE NAPOLEONIC SETTLEMENT IN FRANCE

Bonaparte's prime asset in his rapid takeover of France was the apathy of its citizens. Most French people were so weary politically that they saw in Bonaparte what they wished to see.[1] The Committee of Public Safety had won grudging submission through its terroristic policies; Bonaparte achieved the same result almost by default. As a brilliant propagandist for himself and a man of great personal appeal, he soothed a divided France. Ultraroyalists and dedicated Jacobins never warmed to his regime, but most citizens fell between those positions. They relished the prospect of a strong, reliable government, a return to order and stability, a codification of basic revolutionary gains, and settlement of the religious conflict.

The Napoleonic Style

Napoleon Bonaparte was not a royalist or a Jacobin, not a conservative or a liberal, though his attitudes were flavored by a touch of each viewpoint. Authority, not ideology, was his great concern, and he justified his actions by their results. The revolutionaries of 1789 could consider Napoleon one of theirs because of his hostility toward the unjust and ineffective institutions of the old regime. He had little use for seigneurialism, the cumbersome institutions of Bourbon absolutism, or the congealed structures of aristocratic privilege, which the Revolution had destroyed. Napoleon valued the Revolution's commitment to equality of opportunity and continued to espouse that liberal premise. Other rights and liberties of 1789 he curtailed or disdained.

Ten years of upheaval had produced a grim paradox: The French Revolution had proceeded in the name of liberty, yet successive forms of repression had been mounted to defend it. Napoleon fit comfortably into this history; unlike the Directory, he made no pretense about it. The social gains of the Revolution would be preserved through political centralization and authoritarian control. Napoleon's field of action was in fact far greater than that of the most powerful eighteenth-century monarch, for no entrenched aristocracy existed to resist him. Thanks to the clearing operations of the Revolution, he could reconstruct at will.

Tragically, however, Napoleon drifted away from his own rational ideals. Increasingly absorbed in his personal power, he began to force domestic and foreign policies on France that were geared to his imperial ambitions. Increasingly he concentrated his government on raising men and money for his armies and turned his back on revolutionary liberties.

Political and Religious Settlements

Centralization   Bonaparte gave France a constitution, approved in a plebiscite, that placed almost unchecked authority in the hands of a First Consul (himself) for ten years. Two later constitutional revisions, also approved overwhelmingly in plebiscites, increased executive power and diminished the legislative branch until it became simply a rubber stamp. The first revision, in 1802, converted the consulship into a lifetime post; the second, in 1804, proclaimed Napoleon hereditary emperor. The task of proposing new laws passed from elected representatives to appointed experts in the Council of State. This new body advised the ruler, drafted legislation under his direction, and monitored public officials. Such government by experts stood as an alternative to meaningful parliamentary democracy for the next century.

The system of local government established by Bonaparte in 1800 came ironically close to the kind of royal centralization that public opinion had roundly condemned in 1789. Bonaparte eliminated the local elections that the Revolution had emphasized. Instead, each department was now administered by a **prefect** appointed by the ruler. The four-hundred-odd subprefects on the district level as well as the forty thousand mayors of France's communes were likewise appointed. With minor changes, the unquestionably efficient prefectorial system survived in France for 150 years, severely limiting local autonomy and self-government.

Police-state methods finished what constitutional change began: the suppression of independent political activity. From the legislature to the grass roots, France was depoliticized. The government permitted no organized opposition, reduced the number of newspapers drastically, and censored the remaining ones. The free journalism born in 1789 gave way to government press releases and news management. In 1811 only four newspapers remained in Paris, all hewing to the official line. Political clubs were prohibited, outspoken dissidents deported, and others placed under police surveillance. All these restrictions silenced liberal intellectuals as well as former political activists.

The Concordat   Napoleon's religious policies promoted tranquillity at home and a good image abroad. Before Brumaire the Republic tolerated Catholic worship in theory but severely restricted it in practice. Continued proscription of the refractory clergy; insistence on the republican calendar, with its ten-day weeks that made Sunday a workday; and a drive to keep religious instruction out of elementary schools

---

[1] It is customary to refer to him as Bonaparte until 1804, when the general crowned himself Emperor Napoleon I.

Antoine Jean Gros
PORTRAIT OF BONAPARTE AS FIRST CONSUL
**Napoleon Bonaparte as First Consul, at the height of his
popularity, painted by his admirer J.-B. Gros.**
Bulloz/© Photo RMN/Art Resource, NY

the state. Though nominated by the ruler, bishops would again be consecrated by the pope. But as a major concession to the Revolution, the Concordat stipulated that land confiscated from the Church and sold during the Revolution would be retained by its purchasers. On the other hand, the government dropped the ten-day week and restored the Gregorian calendar.

The balance of church-state relations tilted firmly in the state's favor, for Napoleon intended to use the clergy as a major prop of his regime. The pulpit and the primary school became instruments of social control, to be used, as a new catechism stated, "to bind the religious conscience of the people to the august person of the Emperor." As Napoleon put it, the clergy would be his "moral prefects." Devout Catholics came to resent this subordination of the Church. Eventually Pope Pius renounced the Concordat, to which Napoleon responded by removing the pontiff to France and placing him under house arrest.

The Era of the Notables

With civil equality established and feudalism abolished, Napoleon believed that the Revolution was complete. It remained to encourage an orderly hierarchical society to counteract what he regarded as the excessive individualism of revolutionary social policy. Napoleon intended to reassert the authority of the state, the elites, and, in family life, the father.

In the absence of electoral politics, Napoleon used the state's appointive powers to confer status on prominent local individuals, or **notables,** thus associating

curtailed the free and familiar exercise of Catholicism. These policies provoked wide resentment among the mass of citizens whose commitment to Catholicism remained intact throughout the Revolution.

Though not a believer himself, Napoleon judged that major concessions to Catholic sentiment were in order, provided that the Church remained under the control of the state. In 1801 he negotiated a **Concordat,** or agreement, with Pope Pius VII. It stipulated that Catholicism was the "preferred" religion of France but protected religious freedom for non-Catholics. The Church was again free to operate in full public view and to restore the refractory priests. Primary education would espouse Catholic values and use Catholic texts, as it had before the Revolution, and clerical salaries would be paid by

FAMILY AND GENDER ROLES UNDER THE NAPOLEONIC CIVIL CODE

"Art. 148. The son who has not attained the full age of 25 years, the daughter who has not attained the full age of 21 years, cannot contract marriage without the consent of their father and mother; in case of disagreement, the consent of the father is sufficient.

"Art. 212. Married persons owe to each other fidelity, succor, assistance.

"Art. 213. The husband owes protection to his wife, the wife obedience to her husband.

"Art. 214. The wife is obliged to live with her husband, and to follow him to every place where he may judge it convenient to reside: the husband is obliged to receive her, and to furnish her with everything necessary for the wants of life, according to his means and station.

"Art. 215. The wife cannot plead [in court] in her own name, without the authority of her husband, even though she should be a public trader . . . or separate in property.

"Art. 217. A wife . . . cannot give, alienate, pledge, or acquire by free or chargeable title, without the concurrence of her husband in the act, or his consent in writing.

"Art. 219. If the husband refuses to authorize his wife to pass an act, the wife may cause her husband to be cited directly before the court of first instance . . . which may give or refuse its authority, after the husband shall have been heard, or duly summoned.

"Art. 229. The husband may demand a divorce on the ground of his wife's adultery.

"Art. 230. The wife may demand divorce on the ground of adultery in her husband, when he shall have brought his concubine into their common residence.

"Art. 231. The married parties may reciprocally demand divorce for outrageous conduct, ill-usage, or grievous injuries, exercised by one of them towards the other."

---

them with his regime. These local dignitaries were usually chosen from among the largest taxpayers: prosperous landowners, former nobles, businessmen, and professionals. Those who served the regime with distinction were honored by induction into the Legion of Honor, nine-tenths of whose members were military men. "It is with trinkets that mankind is governed," Napoleon once said. Legion of Honor awards and appointments to prestigious but powerless local bodies were precisely such trinkets.

Napoleon offered more tangible rewards to the country's leading bankers when he chartered a national bank that enjoyed the credit power derived from official ties to the state. In education, Napoleon created elite secondary schools, or *lycées*, to train future government officials, engineers, and officers. The *lycées* embodied the concept of careers open to talent and became part of a highly centralized French academic system called the *University*, which survived into the twentieth century.

The Civil Code Napoleon's most important legacy was a civil code regulating social relations and property rights. Baptized the Napoleonic Code, it was in some measure a revolutionary law code that progressives throughout Europe embraced. Wherever it was implemented, the **Civil Code** swept away feudal property relations and gave legal sanction to modern contractual notions of property. The code established the right to choose one's occupation, to receive equal treatment under the law, and to enjoy religious freedom. At the same time, it allowed employers to dominate their

workers by prohibiting strikes and trade unions. Nor did the code match property rights with popular rights like the right to subsistence.

Revolutionary legislation had emancipated women and children by establishing their civil rights. Napoleon undid most of this by restoring the father's absolute authority in the family. "A wife owes obedience to her husband," said the code, which proceeded to deprive wives of property and juridical rights established during the 1790s. The code curtailed the right to divorce, while establishing a kind of double standard in the dissolution of a marriage (see "Family and Gender Roles under the Napoleonic Civil Code," above). The code also expanded the husband's options in disposing of his estate, although each child was still guaranteed a portion.

The prefectorial system of local government, the Civil Code, the Concordat, the University, the Legion of Honor, and the local bodies of notables all proved to be durable institutions. They fulfilled Napoleon's desire to create a series of "granite masses" on which to reconstruct French society. His admirers emphasized that these institutions contributed to social stability as skillful compromises between revolutionary liberalism and an older belief in hierarchy and central authority. Detractors point out that these institutions were class oriented and excessively patriarchal. Moreover, they fostered overcentralized, rigid structures that might have sapped the vitality of French institutions in succeeding generations. Whatever their merits or defects, these institutions took root, unlike Napoleon's attempt to dominate all of Europe.

Nicolas Andre Monsiau
Deputies from the Cisalpine Republic of Italy proclaim Napoleon Bonaparte their president in 1802.
Chateaux de Versailles et de Trianon, Versailles, France. Erich Lessing/Art Resource, NY

NAPOLEONIC HEGEMONY IN EUROPE

After helping to give France a new government, Bonaparte turned to do battle against the second anti-French coalition in northern Italy. The outcome of his campaign against Austria would either solidify or destroy his regime. Within a few years, in the arena of international relations his ambitions lost all semblance of restraint. Bonaparte evolved from a winning general of the Republic to an imperial conqueror. After defeating his continental opponents on the battlefield in a series of ever more murderous campaigns, he still faced an implacable enemy in Britain. Unable to invade Britain, he resorted to economic warfare and blockade, but Britain withstood that assault as well. Meanwhile, the raw militarism of Napoleon's rule became evident in the relentless expansion of military conscription within the empire.

Military Supremacy and the Reorganization of Europe

Bonaparte's strategy in 1800 called for a repeat of the 1797 campaign: He would strike through Italy while the Army of the Rhine pushed eastward against Vienna. Following French victories at Marengo in Lombardy and in Germany, Austria sued for peace. The Treaty of Lunéville (February 1801) essentially restored France to the position it had held after Bonaparte's triumphs in Italy in 1797.

In Britain a war-weary government now stood alone against France and decided to negotiate. The Treaty of Amiens (March 1802) ended hostilities and reshuffled territorial holdings outside Europe, such as the Cape Colony in South Africa, which passed from the Dutch to the British. But this truce proved precarious since it did not settle the future of French influence in Europe or of commercial relations between the two great powers. Napoleon abided by the letter of the treaty but soon violated its spirit. Britain and Austria alike were dismayed by further expansion of French influence in Italy and Switzerland. Most important, perhaps, France seemed determined to exclude British trade rather than restore normal commercial relations. Historians agree that the Treaty of Amiens failed to keep the peace because neither side was ready to abandon its century-long struggle for predominance.

The Third Coalition   A third anti-French coalition soon took shape, a replay of its predecessors. France ostensibly fought to preserve the new regime at home and

Nicholas Pocock
***NELSON'S FLAGSHIPS AT ANCHOR,
1807***
**Admiral Nelson's heavily armed
three-decker ship of the line,
which inflicted devastation on
the French fleet at Trafalgar.**
National Maritime Museum,
Greenwich, London

its sister republics abroad. The coalition's objectives included the restoration of the Netherlands and Italy to "independence," the limitation of French influence elsewhere, and, if possible, a reduction of France to its prerevolutionary borders. Like most such alliances, the coalition would be dismembered piecemeal.

French hopes of settling the issue directly by invading Britain proved impossible once again. At the Battle of Trafalgar (October 1805), Admiral Nelson's fleet crushed the combined naval forces of France and its ally Spain. Nelson, an innovative tactician who broke rule-book procedures on the high seas just as French generals did on land, died of his wounds in the battle but ensured the security of the British Isles for the remainder of the Napoleonic era.

Napoleon, meanwhile, had turned against the Austro-Russian forces. Moving 200,000 French soldiers with unprecedented speed across the Continent, he took his enemies by surprise and won a dazzling succession of victories. After occupying Vienna he proceeded against the coalition's main army in December. Feigning weakness and retreat at the moment of battle, he drew his numerically superior opponents into an exposed position, crushed the center of their lines, and inflicted a decisive defeat. This Battle of Austerlitz was Napoleon's most brilliant tactical achievement, and it forced the Habsburgs to the peace table. The resulting Treaty of Pressburg (December 1805), extremely harsh and humiliating for Austria, imposed a large indemnity and required the Habsburgs to cede their Venetian provinces.

France and Germany   By now the French sphere of influence had increased dramatically to include most of southern Germany, which Napoleon reorganized into the Confederation of the Rhine, a client realm of France (see map 21.2). France had kept Prussia neutral during the war with Austria by skillful diplomacy. Only after Austria made peace did Prussia recognize its error in failing to join with Austria to halt Napoleon. Belatedly, Prussia mobilized its famous but antiquated army; it was rewarded with stinging defeats by France in a number of encounters culminating in the Battle of Jena (October 1806). With the collapse of Prussian military power, the conquerors settled in Berlin and watched the prestige of the Prussian ruling class crumble. Napoleon was now master of northern Germany as well as the south. For a while it appeared that he might obliterate Prussia entirely, but he restored its sovereignty—after amputating part of its territory and imposing a crushing indemnity.

Napoleon was free to reorganize central Europe as he pleased. After formally proclaiming the end of the Holy Roman Empire in 1806, he liquidated numerous small German states and merged them into two new ones: the Kingdom of Westphalia, with his brother Jérôme on the throne, and the Grand Duchy of Berg, to be ruled by his brother-in-law Joachim Murat. His ally Saxony became a full-scale kingdom, while a new duchy of Warsaw was carved out of Prussian Poland. This "restoration" of Poland had propaganda value; it made the emperor appear as a champion of Polish aspirations, compared to the rulers of Prussia, Russia, and Austria, who had dismembered Poland in a series of partitions between 1772 and 1795. Moreover, Napoleon could now enlist a Polish army and use Polish territory as a base of operations against his remaining continental foe, Russia.

France and Russia   In February 1807 Napoleon confronted the colossus of the east in the Battle of Eylau; the resulting carnage was horrifying but inconclusive.

Charles Meynier
THE DAY AFTER THE BATTLE OF EYLAU, 9 FEBRUARY 1807
Napoleon amidst the carnage on the battlefield of Eylau, the bloodiest engagement to date of the revolutionary-Napoleonic era, where the French and Russians fought each other to a stalemate in 1807.
Versailles, France. Giraudon/Art Resource, NY

When spring came, only a dramatic victory could preserve his conquests in central Europe and vindicate the extraordinary commitments of the past two years. The Battle of Friedland in June was a French victory that demoralized Russia's Tsar Alexander I and persuaded him to negotiate.

Meeting at Tilsit, the two rulers buried their differences and agreed, in effect, to partition Europe into eastern and western spheres of influence. Each would support the other's conquests and mediate in behalf of the other's interests. The Treaty of Tilsit (July 1807) sanctioned new annexations of territory directly into France and the reorganization of other conquered countries. The creation of new satellite kingdoms became the vehicle for Napoleon's domination of Europe. Like the French Republic, the sister republics became kingdoms between 1805 and 1807. And it happened that Napoleon had a large family of brothers ready to wear those new royal crowns.

The distorted shape of Napoleonic Europe is apparent on maps dating from 1808 to 1810 (see map 21.2). His chief satellites included the Kingdom of Holland, with brother Louis on the throne; the Kingdom of Italy, with Napoleon himself as king and his stepson Eugène de Beauharnais as viceroy; the Confederation of the Rhine, including brother Jérôme's Kingdom of Westphalia; the Kingdom of Naples, covering southern Italy, with

brother Joseph the ruler until Napoleon transferred him to Spain and installed his brother-in-law Murat; and the Duchy of Warsaw. Belgium, the Rhineland, Tuscany, Piedmont, Genoa, and the Illyrian provinces had been annexed to France. Switzerland did not become a kingdom, but the Helvetic Republic (as it was now called) received a new constitution dictated by France. In 1810, after yet another war with Austria, a marriage was arranged between the house of Bonaparte and the house of Habsburg. Having divorced Joséphine de Beauharnais, Napoleon married princess Marie Louise, daughter of Francis II, who bore him a male heir the following year.

Naval War with Britain

For a time it seemed that Britain alone stood between Napoleon and his dream of hegemony over Europe. Since Britain was invulnerable to invasion, Napoleon hoped to destroy its influence by means of economic warfare. Unable to blockade British ports directly, he could try to close off the Continent: keep Britain from its markets, stop its exports, and thus ruin its trade and credit. Napoleon reasoned that if Britain had nowhere to sell its manufactured goods, no gold would come into the country and bankruptcy would eventually ensue. Meanwhile, overproduction would cause unemployment and labor unrest, which would turn the

MAP 21.2 EUROPE AROUND 1810
Note the extent of the French Empire as well as its satellite territories and allies. Was it plausible that the Napoleonic Empire could sustain its military power from Madrid to Warsaw?
◆ For an online version, go to www.mhhe.com/chambers9 > chapter 21 > book maps

British people against their government and force the latter to make peace with France. At the same time, French advantages in continental markets would increase with the elimination of British competition.

The Continental System Napoleon therefore launched his **Continental System** to prohibit British trade with all French allies. Even neutral ships were banned from European ports if they carried goods coming from the British Isles. Britain responded in 1807 with the Orders in Council, which in effect reversed the blockade: It *required* all neutral ships to stop at British ports to procure trading licenses and pay tariffs. In other words, the British insisted on regulating all

trade between neutral states and European ports. Ships that failed to obey would be stopped on the high seas and captured. In an angry response, Napoleon, in turn, threatened to seize any neutral ship that obeyed the Orders in Council by stopping at British ports.

Thus, a total naval war between France and Britain enveloped all neutral nations. Indeed, neutral immunity virtually disappeared, since every ship was obliged to violate one system or the other and thus run afoul of naval patrols or privateers. While the British captured only about forty French ships a year after 1807 (for few were left afloat), they seized almost three thousand neutral vessels a year, including many from the United States.

Jean-Auguste-Dominique Ingres
NAPOLEON ON HIS IMPERIAL THRONE, 1806
Emperor Napoleon I on his imperial throne in 1806, by the great portrait painter Ingres. Note the dramatic contrast in appearance with the young, intense military hero of the Republic in David's portrait at the beginning of this chapter.
Musée des Beaux-Arts, Rennes, France. Erich Lessing/Art Resource, NY

CHRONOLOGY
Napoleon and Europe

June 1800	Battle of Marengo and defeat of the Second Coalition.
Feb. 1801	Treaty of Lunéville with Austria.
March 1802	Treaty of Amiens with Britain.
Sept. 1802	Annexation of Piedmont.
1805–1806	Third Coalition forms.
Oct. 1805	Battle of Trafalgar and defeat of French fleet.
Dec. 1805	Battle of Austerlitz; defeat of Austria.
1806	Battle of Jena and humiliation of Prussia.
1807	Battles of Eylau and Friedland; stalemate with Russia.
July 1807	Treaty of Tilsit with Russia. Consolidation of satellite kingdoms.
1807	Launching of Continental System against British trade.
Feb. 1808	Invasion of Spain.
July 1809	Battle of Wagram; Austria defeated again.
April 1810	Napoleon weds princess Marie Louise of Austria.
Dec. 1810	Annexation of Holland.
July 1812	Invasion of Russia.
Oct. 1812	Retreat and destruction of Grand Army.
Oct. 1813	Battle of Leipzig and formation of Fourth Coalition.
March 1814	Battle of France and Napoleon's abdication.

The Continental System did hurt British trade. British gold reserves dwindled, and 1811 saw widespread unemployment and rioting. France was affected, in turn, by Britain's counterblockade, which cut it off from certain raw materials necessary for industrial production. But the satellite states, as economic vassals of France, suffered the most. In Amsterdam, for example, shipping volume declined from 1,350 ships entering the port in 1806 to 310 in 1809, and commercial revenues dropped calamitously. Out of loyalty to the people whom he ruled, Holland's King Louis Bonaparte tolerated smuggling. But this action so infuriated Napoleon that he ousted his brother from the throne and annexed the Kingdom of Holland directly to France. Smuggling

was, in fact, the weak link in the system, for it created holes in Napoleon's wall of economic sanctions that constantly needed plugging. This problem drove the emperor to ever more drastic actions.

The Napoleonic Conscription Machine

One key to Napoleon's unrestrained ambitions in Europe was the creation of an efficient administrative state in France and its annexed territories with the ability to continuously replenish the ranks of the imperial army.

The National Convention's mass levy of August 1793 had drafted all able-bodied unmarried men between the ages of eighteen and twenty-five. But this unprecedented mobilization had been meant as a one-time-only emergency measure, a temporary "requisition." There was no implication that subsequent cohorts of young men would face conscription into the army as part of their civic obligations. When the war resumed in 1798, however, the Directory passed a conscription law that made successive "classes" of young men (that is, those born in a particular year) subject to a military draft should the need arise. The Directory immediately implemented this law and called up three classes, but local officials reported massive draft evasion in most of the departments. Many French youths found the prospect of military service repugnant. From this shaky foundation, however, the Napoleonic regime developed a remarkably successful conscription system.

The Rules of the Game   After much trial and error with the details, timetables, and mechanisms, the system began to operate efficiently within a few years. The government assigned an annual quota of conscripts for each department. Using parish birth registers, the mayor of every community compiled a list of men reaching the age of nineteen that year. These youths were then led by their mayor to the cantonal seat on a specified day for a draft lottery. Panels of doctors at the departmental capitals later verified or rejected claims for medical exemptions. In all, about a third of French youths legally avoided military service because they were physically unfit—too short, lame, or suffering from poor eyesight, chronic diseases, or other infirmities.

In the draft lottery, youths picked numbers out of a box; marriage could no longer be used as an exemption, for obvious reasons. Those with high numbers were spared (for the time being), while those who drew low numbers filled the local induction quota. Two means of avoiding service remained: The wealthy could purchase a replacement, and the poor could flee. True, the regime had a bad conscience about allowing draftees to hire replacements, because the practice made its rhetoric about the duties of citizenship sound hollow. But to placate wealthy notables and peasants with large holdings (who were sometimes desperate to keep their sons on the farm), the government permitted the hiring of a replacement under strict guidelines that made it difficult and expensive but not impossible. The proportion of replacements was somewhere between 5 and 10 percent of all draftees.

Draft Evasion   For Napoleon's prefects, conscription levies were always the top priority among their duties, and draft evasion was the number one problem. Dogged persistence, bureaucratic routine, and various forms of coercion gradually overcame this chronic resistance. From time to time, columns of troops swept through areas in which evasion and desertion were most common and arrested culprits by the hundreds. But draft evaders

L'Ogre Dévorateur du Genre humain

Royalist caricatures often depicted Napoleon as an ogre whose conscription machine devoured the nation's young men.
Bibliothèque Nationale de France, Paris

usually hid out in remote places—mountains, forests, marshes—so coercion had to be directed against their families as well. Heavy fines assessed against the parents did little good, since most were too poor to pay anything. A better tactic was to billet troops in the draft evaders' homes; if their families could not afford to feed the troops, then the community's wealthy taxpayers were required to do so. All these actions created pressure on the youths to turn themselves in. By 1811 the regime had broken the habit of draft evasion, and conscription was grudgingly becoming accepted as a disagreeable civic obligation, much like taxes. Just as draft calls began to rise sharply, draft evasion fell dramatically.

Napoleon had begun by drafting 60,000 Frenchmen annually, but by 1810 the annual quotas had risen steadily to 120,000, and they continued to climb. Moreover, in 1810 the emperor ordered the first of many "supplementary levies," calling up men from earlier classes who had drawn high lottery numbers. In January 1813, to look ahead, Napoleon replenished his armies by calling up the class of 1814 a year early and by making repeated supplementary calls on earlier classes.

RESISTANCE TO NAPOLEON

By 1808, with every major European power except Britain vanquished on the battlefield, Napoleon felt that nothing stood in his way. Since Spain and, later, Russia seemed unable or unwilling to stop smuggling from Britain, thus thwarting his strategy of economic warfare, the emperor decided to deal with each by force of arms. His calculations proved utterly mistaken, and in both places he ultimately suffered disastrous defeats. More generally, Napoleon's intrusion into Italy, Germany, Spain, and Russia set in motion various responses and movements of resistance. French expansion sparked new forms of nationalism in some quarters, but also liberalism and reaction. Finally, all his opponents coalesced, defeated Napoleon on the battlefield, and drove him from his throne.

The "Spanish Ulcer"

Spain and France shared a common interest in weakening British power in Europe and the colonial world. But the alliance they formed after making peace with each other in 1795 brought only troubles for Spain, including the loss of its Louisiana Territory in America and (at the Battle of Trafalgar) most of its naval fleet. The Spanish royal household, meanwhile, was mired in scandal. Prime Minister Manuel de Godoy, once a lover of the queen, was a corrupt opportunist and extremely unpopular with the people. Crown Prince Ferdinand despised Godoy and

Godoy's protectors, the king and queen, while Ferdinand's parents actively returned their son's hostility.

Napoleon looked on at this farce with irritation. At the zenith of his power, he concluded that he must reorganize Spain himself to bring it solidly into the Continental System. As a pretext for military intervention, he set in motion a plan to invade Portugal, supposedly to partition it with Spain. Once the French army was well inside Spain, however, Napoleon intended to impose his own political solution to Spain's instability.

Napoleon brought the squabbling king and prince to France, where he threatened and bribed one and then the other into abdicating. The emperor then gathered a group of handpicked Spanish notables who followed Napoleon's scenario by petitioning him to provide a new sovereign, preferably his brother Joseph. Joseph was duly proclaimed king of Spain. With 100,000 French troops already positioned around Madrid, Joseph prepared to assume his new throne, eager to rule under a liberal constitution and to believe his brother's statement that "all the better Spanish people are on your side." As he took up the crown, however, an unanticipated drama erupted.

Popular Resistance   Faced with military occupation, the disappearance of their royal family, and the crowning of a Frenchman, the Spanish people rose in rebellion. It began on May 2, 1808, when an angry crowd in Madrid rioted against French troops, who responded with firing squads and brutal reprisals. This bloody incident, known as the Dos de Mayo and captured in

Francisco Goya
THE THIRD OF MAY, 1808
The great Spanish artist Francisco Goya memorably captured the brutality of French reprisals against the citizens of Madrid who dared to rebel against the Napoleonic occupation on May 2, 1808.
Painted in 1814. Museo del Prado, Madrid, Spain. Erich Lessing/Art Resource, NY

Francisco de Goya
THE DISASTERS OF WAR: POPULACHO
In a relentlessly bleak series of drawings collectively entitled *The Horrors of War*, Goya went on to record the savagery and atrocities committed by both sides of the struggle in Spain.
The Norton Simon Art Foundation, Pasadena, CA

SPANISH LIBERALS DRAFT A CONSTITUTION, 1812

"The general and extraordinary Cortes of the Spanish nation, duly organized . . . in order duly to discharge the lofty objective of furthering the glory, prosperity and welfare of the Nation as a whole, decrees the following political Constitution to assure the well-being and upright administration of the State.

"Art. 1: The Spanish Nation is the union of all Spaniards from both hemispheres.

"Art. 3: Sovereignty resides primarily in the Nation and because of this the right to establish the fundamental laws belongs to it exclusively.

"Art. 4: The Nation is obligated to preserve and protect with wise and just laws civil liberty, property and the other legitimate rights of all the individuals belonging to it.

"Art. 12: The religion of the Spanish Nation is and always will be the Catholic, Apostolic, Roman and only true faith. The Nation protects it with wise and just laws and prohibits the exercise of any other.

"Art. 14: The Government of the Spanish Nation is an hereditary limited Monarchy.

"Art. 15: The power to make laws resides in the Cortes with the King.

"Art. 16: The power to enforce laws resides in the King.

"Art. 27: The Cortes is the union of all the deputies that represent the Nation, named by the citizens.

"Art. 34: To elect deputies to the Cortes, electoral meetings will be held in the parish, the district, and the province.

"Art. 59: The electoral meetings on the district level will be made up of the electors chosen at the parish level who will convene at the seat of every district in order to name the electors who will then converge on the provincial capital to elect the deputies to the Cortes.

"Art. 338: The Cortes will annually establish or confirm all taxes, be they direct or indirect, general, provincial or municipal. . . .

"Art. 339: Taxes will be apportioned among all Spaniards in proportion to their abilities [to pay], without exception to any privilege."

From *Political Constitution of the Spanish Monarchy*, proclaimed in Cádiz, March 19, 1812, James B. Tueller (tr.).

Goya's famous paintings, has remained a source of Spanish national pride, for it touched off a sustained uprising against the French. Local notables created committees, or *juntas*, to organize resistance and to coordinate campaigns by regular Spanish troops. These troops were generally ineffective against the French, but they did produce one early victory: A half-starved French army was cut off and forced to surrender at Bailén in July 1808. This defeat broke the aura of Napoleonic invincibility.

The British saw a great opportunity to attack Napoleon in concert with the rebellious Spanish people. Landing an army in Portugal, the British bore the brunt of anti-French military operations in Spain. In what they called the Peninsular War, a grueling war of attrition, their forces drove the French out of Portugal. After five years of fighting and many reversals, they pushed the French back across the Pyrénées in November 1813. The British commander, the Duke of Wellington, grasped the French predicament when he said: "The more ground the French hold down in Spain, the weaker they will be at any given point."

About 30,000 Spanish **guerilla** fighters helped wear down the French and forced the occupiers to struggle for survival in hostile country. The guerillas drew French forces from the main battlefields, inflicted casualties, impeded the French access to food, and punished Spanish collaborators. Their harassment kept the in-

vaders in a constant state of anxiety, which led the French to adopt harsh measures in reprisal. But these "pacification" tactics only escalated the war's brutality and further enraged the Spanish people.

Together, the Spanish regulars, the guerillas, and the British expeditionary force kept a massive French army of up to 300,000 men pinned down in Spain. Napoleon referred to the war as his "Spanish ulcer," an open sore that would not heal. Though he held the rebel fighters in contempt, other Europeans were inspired by their example of armed resistance to France.

The Spanish Liberals The war, however, proved a disaster for Spanish liberals. Torn between loyalty to Joseph, who would have liked to be a liberal ruler, and nationalist rebels, liberals faced a difficult dilemma. Those who collaborated with Joseph hoped to spare the people from a brutal war and to institute reform from above in the tradition of Spanish enlightened absolutism. But they found that Joseph could not rule independently; Napoleon gave the orders in Spain and relied on his generals to implement them. The liberals who joined the rebellion organized a provisional government by reviving the ancient Spanish parliament, or Cortes, in the southern town of Cádiz. Like the French National Assembly of 1789, the Cortes of Cádiz drafted a liberal constitution in 1812 (see "Spanish Liberals Draft a Constitution, 1812," above), which pleased the

British and was therefore tolerated for the time being by the juntas.

In reality, most nationalist rebels despised the liberals. They were fighting for the Catholic Church, the Spanish monarchy, and the old way of life. When in 1814 Wellington finally drove the French out of Spain and former crown prince Ferdinand VII took the throne, the joy of the Cádiz liberals quickly evaporated. As a royalist mob sacked the Cortes building, Ferdinand tore up the constitution of 1812, reinstated absolutism, restored the monasteries and the Inquisition, revived censorship, and arrested the leading liberals. Nationalist reactionaries emerged as the victors of the Spanish rebellion.

Independence in Spanish America   The Creoles, descendants of Spanish settlers who were born in the New World, also profited from the upheaval in Spain. Spain had been cut off from its vast empire of American colonies in 1805, when the British navy won control of the Atlantic after the Battle of Trafalgar. In 1807 a British force attacked Buenos Aires in Spain's viceroyalty of the Río de la Plata (now Argentina). The Argentines—who raised excellent cattle on the *pampas*, or grassy plains—were eager to trade their beef and hides for British goods, but Spain's rigid mercantilism had always prevented such beneficial commerce. The Argentines welcomed the prospect of free trade, but not the prospect of British conquest. With Spain unable to defend them, the Creoles organized their own militia and drove off the British, pushed aside the Spanish viceroy, and took power into their own hands. The subsequent upheaval in Spain led the Argentines to declare their independence. After Ferdinand regained the Spanish throne in 1814, he sent an army to reclaim the colony, but the Argentines, under General José de San Martín, drove it off, and Argentina made good on its claim to full independence.

Rebellion spread throughout Spanish America, led above all by Simón Bolívar, revered in the hemisphere as "The Liberator." After Napoleon removed the king of Spain in 1808, the Creoles in Spain's viceroyalty of New Granada (encompassing modern-day Venezuela, Colombia, and Ecuador) elected a congress, which declared independence from Spain. An arduous, protracted war with the Spanish garrisons followed, and by 1816 Spain had regained control of the region.

Bolívar resumed the struggle and gradually wore down the Spanish forces; in one campaign his army marched six hundred miles from the torrid Venezuelan lowlands over the snow-capped Andes Mountains to Colombia. Finally in 1819 the Spanish conceded defeat. Bolívar's dream of one unified, conservative republic of Gran Colombia soon disintegrated under regional pres-

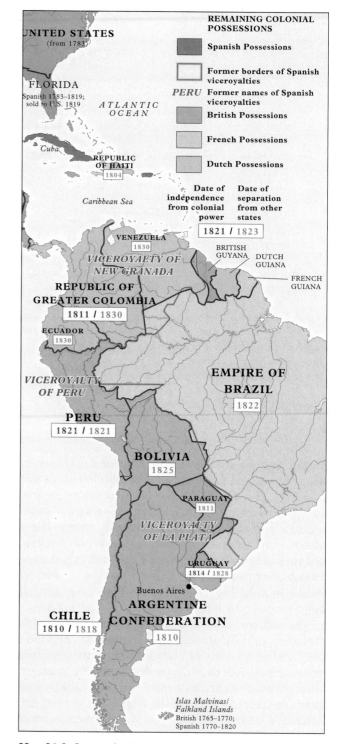

MAP 21.3 SOUTH AMERICA AFTER INDEPENDENCE
◆ For an online version, go to www.mhhe.com/chambers9 > chapter 21 > book maps

sures into several independent states, but not before Bolívar launched one final military campaign and liberated Peru, Spain's remaining colony in South America (see map 21.3).

MAP 21.4 THE RUSSIAN CAMPAIGN OF 1812
◆ For an online version, go to www.mhhe.com/chambers9 > chapter 21 > book maps

The Russian Debacle

Napoleon did not yet realize in 1811 that his entanglement in Spain would drain French military power and encourage resistance in Central Europe. On the contrary, never were the emperor's schemes more grandiose. Surveying the crumbling state system of Europe, he imagined that it could be replaced with a vast empire, ruled from Paris and based on the Napoleonic Code. He mistakenly believed that the era of the balance of power among Europe's states was over and that nationalist sentiments need not constrain his actions.

Russia now loomed as the main obstacle to Napoleon's imperial reorganization and domination of Europe. Russia, a restive ally with ambitions of its own in Eastern Europe, resented the restrictions on its trade under the Continental System. British diplomats, anti-Napoleonic exiles such as Baron Stein of Prussia, and nationalist reactionaries at court all pressured the tsar to resist Napoleon. Russian court liberals, more concerned with domestic reforms, hoped on the contrary that Alexander would maintain peace with France, but by 1812 their influence on the tsar had waned. For his part, Napoleon wanted to enforce the Continental System and humble Russia. As he bluntly put it: "Let Alexander defeat the Persians, but don't let him meddle in the affairs of Europe."

Napoleon prepared for his most momentous military campaign. His objective was to annihilate Russia's army or, at the least, to conquer Moscow and chase the army to the point of disarray. To this end he marshaled a "Grand Army" of almost 600,000 men (half of them French, the remainder from his satellite states and allies) and moved them steadily by forced marches across Central Europe into Russia. The Russians responded by retreating in orderly fashion and avoiding a fight. Many Russian nobles abandoned their estates and burned their crops to the ground, leaving the Grand Army to operate far from its supply bases in territory stripped of food. At Borodino the Russians finally made a stand and sustained a frightful 45,000 casualties, but the remaining Russian troops managed to withdraw in order. Napoleon lost 35,000 men in that battle, but far more men and horses were dying from hunger, thirst, fatigue, and disease in the march across Russia's unending, barren territory. The greatly depleted ranks of the Grand Army staggered into Moscow on September 14, 1812, but the Russian army was still intact and far from demoralized.

The Destruction of the Grand Army   In fact, the condition of Moscow demoralized the French. They found the city deserted and bereft of badly needed supplies. The next night Moscow was mysteriously set ablaze, causing such extensive damage as to make it unfit to be the Grand Army's winter quarters. Realistic advisers warned the emperor that his situation was dangerous, while others told him what he wished to hear—that

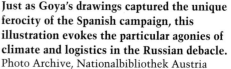
Just as Goya's drawings captured the unique ferocity of the Spanish campaign, this illustration evokes the particular agonies of climate and logistics in the Russian debacle.
Photo Archive, Nationalbibliothek Austria

Russian resistance was crumbling. For weeks Napoleon hesitated. Logistically it was imperative that the French begin to retreat immediately, but that would constitute a political defeat. Only on October 19 did Napoleon finally order a retreat, but the order came too late.

The delay forced an utterly unrealistic pace on the bedraggled army as it headed west. Supplies were gone, medical care for the thousands of wounded nonexistent, horses lacking. Food shortages compelled foraging parties to sweep far from the main body of troops, where these men often fell prey to Russian guerillas. And there was the weather—Russia's bitter cold and deep snow, in which no commander would wish to find himself leading a retreat of several hundred miles, laden with wounded and loot but without food, fuel, horses, or proper clothing. Napoleon's poor planning, the harsh weather, and the operation of Russian guerilla bands made the long retreat a nightmare of suffering for the Grand Army. No more than 100,000 troops survived the ordeal. Worse yet, the Prussian contingent took the occasion to desert Napoleon, opening the possibility of mass defections and the formation of a new anti-Napoleonic coalition.

German Resistance and the Last Coalition

Napoleon was evidently impervious to the horror around him. On the sleigh ride out of Russia, he was already planning how to raise new armies and set things aright. Other European statesmen, however, were ready to capitalize on Napoleon's defeat in Russia and demolish his empire once and for all. Provocative calls for a national uprising in various German states to throw off the tyrant's yoke reinforced the efforts of diplomats like Prussia's Baron Stein and Austria's Klemens von Metternich to revive the anti-Napoleonic coalition.

Reform from Above in Prussia   In Prussia after the defeat of 1806, the government had introduced reforms intended to improve the quality of the bureaucracy by offering nonnobles more access to high positions and by reducing some of the nobility's privileges. The monarchy hoped thereby to salvage the position of the nobility and the authority of the state. Prussian military reformers adopted new methods of recruitment to build up a trained reserve force that could be rapidly mobilized, along with a corps of reserve officers to take command of these units. Prussia, in other words, hoped to achieve French-style efficiency and military mobilization without resorting to new concepts of citizenship, constitutions, legislatures, or the abolition of seigneurialism. On the level of propaganda and the symbolic gesture, writers in Prussia and other German states called for a popular war of liberation under the slogan "With God for King and Fatherland."

Against this background of Prussian military preparation and growing nationalist sentiment, the diplomats maneuvered and waited. Finally, in March 1813, King Frederick William III of Prussia signed a treaty with Russia to form an offensive coalition against Napoleon. A great struggle for Germany ensued between the Russo-Prussian forces and Napoleon and his allies. Austria continued to claim neutrality and offered to mediate the dispute, but at a meeting in Prague, Napoleon rejected an offer of peace in exchange for restoring all French conquests since 1802.

In August, as Napoleon learned of new defeats in Spain, Habsburg Emperor Francis finally declared war on his son-in-law. Napoleon called up underage and overage conscripts and was able to field one last army, but his major southern German ally, Bavaria, finally changed sides. A great battle raged around Leipzig for three days in October, and when the smoke cleared, Napoleon was in full retreat. German states were free from Napoleon's domination, but Prussia's rulers were also free from the need to concede further reforms in the political and social order.

The Fall of Napoleon   In the belief that he could rely on his conscription machine, Napoleon had rebuffed offers by the allies to negotiate peace in 1813. In fact, however, he reached the end of the line in November 1813 with a desperate call for 300,000 more men to defend France against the allies. Difficulties were inevitable, wrote one prefect, "when the number of men required exceeds the number available." Another reported: "There is scarcely a family that is not oppressed by conscription." Alongside sizable contingents of Italians, Germans, and other foreigners from the annexed territories and satellite states, nearly 2.5 million Frenchmen had been drafted by Napoleon. At least 1 million of those conscripts never returned.

With Napoleon driven back into France, British troops reinforced the coalition to ensure that it would not disintegrate once Central Europe had been liberated. The coalition offered final terms to the emperor: He could retain his throne, but France would be reduced to her "normal frontiers." (The precise meaning of this term was left purposely vague.) Napoleon, still hoping for a dramatic reversal, chose to fight, and with some reluctance the allies invaded France. Napoleon led the remnants of his army skillfully but to no avail. The French had lost confidence in him, conscription had reached its limits, and no popular spirit of resistance to invasion developed as it had in 1792. Paris fell in March 1814. The price of this defeat was unconditional surrender and the emperor's abdication. Napoleon was transported to the island of Elba, between Corsica and Italy, over which he was granted sovereignty. After twenty-two years of exile, the Bourbon Dynasty returned to France.

The Napoleonic Legend

For Napoleon, imperial authority—originating with him in France and radiating throughout Europe—represented the principle of rational progress. In his view, the old notion of balance of power among European states merely served as an excuse for the British to pursue their selfish interests. While paying lip service to the notion of Italian, Spanish, and Polish nationhood, Napoleon generally scorned patriotic opposition to his domination as an outmoded, reactionary sentiment—exemplified by the "barbaric" guerillas in Spain fighting for king and religion. Modern-minded Europeans, he believed, would see beyond historic, parochial traditions to the prospect of a new European order. Indeed, Napoleon's credibility with some reformers in Europe was considerable. The Bavarian prime minister, for instance, justified his collaboration with France in 1810 in these words: "The spirit of the new age is one of mobility, destruction, creativity. . . . The wars against France offer the [unfortunate] possibility of bringing back old constitutions, privileges, and property relations."

During his final exile, however, Napoleon came to recognize that nationalism was not necessarily reactionary—as one could plainly see in the nationalistic but liberal Cortes of Cádiz of 1812. Progressive thinking and nationalist aspirations could coexist. From exile Napoleon rewrote his life story to portray his career as a series of defensive wars against selfish adversaries (especially Britain) and as a battle in behalf of the nations of Europe against reactionary dynasties. In this way, Napoleon brilliantly (if falsely) put himself on the side of the future.

These memoirs and recollections from exile formed the basis of the Napoleonic legend, as potent a force historically, perhaps, as the reality of the Napoleonic experience. The image they projected emphasized how General Bonaparte had consolidated what was best about the French Revolution while pacifying a bitterly divided nation and saving it from chaos. They cast the imperial experience in a deceptively positive light, glossed over the tyranny and unending military slaughter, and aligned Napoleon with reason, efficiency, and modernity (see "Napoleon Justifies Himself in 1815," p. 638).

The Napoleonic legend also evoked a sense of grandeur and glory that moved ordinary people in years to come. Napoleon's dynamism and energy became his ultimate inspirational legacy to succeeding generations. In this way, the Napoleonic legend fed on the Romantic movement in literature and the arts. Many young romantics (including the poet William Wordsworth and

NAPOLEON JUSTIFIES HIMSELF IN 1815

"I have cleansed the Revolution, ennobled the common people, and restored the authority of kings. I have stirred all men to competition, I have rewarded merit wherever I found it, I have pushed back the boundaries of greatness. Is there any point on which I could be attacked and on which a historian could not take up my defense? My despotism? He can prove that dictatorship was absolutely necessary. Will it be said that I restricted freedom? He will be able to prove that license, anarchy, and general disorder were still on our doorstep. Shall I be accused of having loved war too much? He will show that I was always on the defensive. That I wanted to set up a universal monarchy? He will explain that it was merely the fortuitous result of circumstances and that I was led to it step by step by our very enemies. My ambition? Ah, no doubt he will find that I had ambition, a great deal of it—but the grandest and noblest perhaps, that ever was: the ambition of establishing and consecrating at last the kingdom of reason and the full exercise, the complete enjoyment, of all human capabilities!"

From B. Las Cases (ed.), *Mémorial de Sainte-Hélène.*

the composer Ludwig van Beethoven) saw in the French Revolution a release of creativity and a liberation of the individual spirit. Napoleon's tyranny eventually alienated most such creative people. But the Napoleonic legend, by emphasizing the bold creativity of his career, meshed nicely with the sense of individual possibility that the romantics cultivated. Napoleon's retrospective justifications of his reign may not be convincing, but one can only marvel at the irrepressible audacity of the man.

Summary

In the confrontations between Napoleon and his European adversaries, France still embodied the specter of revolution. Even if the revolutionary legacy in France amounted by that time to little more than Napoleon's contempt for the inefficiency and outmoded institutions of the old regime, France after Brumaire remained a powerful challenge to the status quo. Napoleon intended to abolish feudalism, institute centralized administrations, and implant the French Civil Code in all of France's satellite states. But by 1808 his extravagant international ambitions relied on increasingly tyrannical and militaristic measures. These in turn provoked a range of responses, including nationalist rebellions. Britain and Russia, then Prussia and Austria, joined forces once more to bring the Napoleonic Empire down, to restore the balance of power in Europe, and to reinstall the Bourbons in France. But the clock could not really be set back from Europe's experience of revolution and Napoleonic transformation. The era of modern political and social conflicts had begun.

QUESTIONS FOR FURTHER THOUGHT

1. Apart from Jesus, more books have probably been written about Napoleon than any other historical figure. What accounts for this enduring fascination? Compare Napoleon to dominant leaders of the past whom you have studied (e.g., Alexander the Great, Caesar, Philip II, and Louis XIV).

2. Was Napoleon a revolutionary? Did he consolidate or betray the French Revolution?

3. Using the boxed excerpt in which Napoleon justifies his conduct as a starting point, what is *your* assessment of his reign?

RECOMMENDED READING
(SEE ALSO CHAPTER 20)

Sources

De Caulaincourt, Armand. *With Napoleon in Russia.* 1935. A remarkable account of the diplomacy and warfare of the 1812 debacle by a man at Napoleon's side.

Herold, J. C. (ed.). *The Mind of Napoleon.* 1961.

Thompson, J. M. (ed.). *Napoleon Self-Revealed.* 1934.

*Walter, Jakob. *The Diary of a Napoleonic Foot Soldier.* M. Raeff (ed.). 1991. A vivid and appalling account of the Russian campaign.

Studies

*Bergeron, Louis. *France under Napoleon.* 1981. A fresh and insightful evaluation of the Napoleonic settlement in France.

*Broers, Michael. *Europe under Napoleon, 1799–1815.* 1996. An incisive and up-to-date synthesis on French expansion in Europe.

Chandler, David. *Napoleon's Marshals.* 1986. By a leading expert on Napoleonic military history.

*Connelley, Owen. *Blundering to Glory: Napoleon's Military Campaigns.* 1988. An irreverent but incisive account of Napoleon's military leadership.

———. *Napoleon's Satellite Kingdoms.* 1965. A study of the states conquered by France and ruled by the Bonaparte family.

*Dwyer, Philip (ed.). *Napoleon and Europe.* 2001. A well-focused yet wide-ranging collection of essays with a comprehensive bibliography.

*Ellis, Geoffrey. *Napoleon.* 1997. A concise profile of the era.

Elting, John. *Swords around a Throne: Napoleon's Grande Armee.* 1988. An eminently readable military history.

*Englund, Steven. *Napoleon: A Political Life.* 2004. The most recent, and perhaps the best, one-volume biography in English.

Esdaile, Charles. *Fighting Napoleon: Guerrillas, Bandits, and Adventurers in Spain, 1808–1814.* 2004.

Forrest, Alan. *Conscripts and Deserters: The Army and French Society during the Revolution and Empire.*

1988. A study of popular resistance to revolutionary and Napoleonic conscription.

Gates, David. *The Spanish Ulcer: A History of the Peninsular War.* 1986. On the Spanish rebellion, the French response, and Wellington's expeditionary force.

*Geyl, Pieter. *Napoleon, For and Against.* 1949. Napoleon and the historians, as reviewed by a Dutch scholar with no illusions.

Hazareesingh, Sudhir. *The Legend of Napoleon.* 2004. A lively and suggestive study of an elusive subject.

*Lynch, John. *The Spanish American Revolutions, 1808–1826.* 1986. A comprehensive account of the independence movements in Spanish America and their aftermath.

Lyons, Martyn. *France under the Directory.* 1975. A brief topical survey of the Revolution's later, unheroic phase.

*———. *Napoleon Bonaparte and the Legacy of the French Revolution.* 1994. A good recent textbook.

Marcus, G. J. *A Naval History of England, II: The Age of Nelson.* 1971. The standard history of British naval supremacy.

Palmer, Robert R. *The World of the French Revolution.* 1971. Emphasizes the interplay of French power and revolutionary movements outside of France.

Rothenberg, Gunther. *The Art of Warfare in the Age of Napoleon.* 1978. A good analysis of strategy and tactics.

*Sheehan, James. *German History, 1770–1866.* 1989. An outstanding overview of this and other periods in German history.

*Sutherland, D. M. G. *France, 1789–1815: Revolution and Counter-revolution.* 1985. A fine general history of France in this period.

Tulard, Jean. *Napoleon: The Myth of the Savior.* 1984. A synthesis by the leading French expert on Napoleon.

*Woloch, Isser. *Napoleon and His Collaborators: The Making of a Dictatorship.* 2001.

Woolf, Stuart. *A History of Italy, 1700–1860.* 1979. An authoritative general history, with fine chapters on this period.

*Available in paperback.

Leander Russ
THE AUSTRIAN SOUTHERN RAILWAY FROM VIENNA TO BADEN, 1847
The contrast of new and old: The train from Vienna to Baden frightened the horses in this watercolor done in 1847.
AKG London

Chapter Twenty-Two

FOUNDATIONS OF THE NINETEENTH CENTURY: POLITICS AND SOCIAL CHANGE

THE POLITICS OF ORDER • THE PROGRESS OF INDUSTRIALIZATION • THE SOCIAL EFFECTS

After twenty-five years of war, peace was a dramatic change. The first concern of the powers that had opposed Napoleon was to guarantee that no one state would be able to dominate the Continent again.

The wars against France had been about more, however, than territory or the balance of power. The allies had fought to preserve monarchy and social hierarchy, and they sought a peace that would prevent events like the French Revolution in the future. The first step was to impose regimes that would be safely conservative. For the most part, they restored the dynasties that had been overturned. These restored regimes were nonetheless new, and establishing them raised classical questions about the body politic—how power should be organized, what institutions should direct society, and who should participate in deciding policy. The possibility of revolution thus remained a fact of life, dreaded by

some and hoped for by others, reinvoked in each country by the risings, acts of repression, and major reforms of the next thirty years.

The challenge to the restoration experiment was not just political. Enforced stability was expected to bring social peace and economic benefits. In some parts of Europe, however, industrialization was under way and beginning to transform society. The technologies that stimulated economic development and the changing economy's impact on social structure and family were also part of the political and social system of the restoration and are treated in this chapter. Coming after the French Revolution and Napoleon, these changes opened the way to a new era of passionate politics and pervasive social change. How Europeans dealt with the resulting tensions is the subject of chapter 23.

coal to become the Continent's first industrialized nation. Belgium extracted more coal than did France or Germany and was the first country to complete a railway network. The French railway system, on the other hand, was not finished until after Germany's, for it was slowed by political conflict despite early and ambitious plans. France's production of iron, coal, and textiles increased severalfold between 1815 and 1848. This growth would have been impressive a generation earlier, but Britain's expansion in each of these sectors was several times greater. In iron production, for example, the two countries were about equal in 1800, but by 1850 Britain's output was six or seven times greater. Britain outstripped France still more in textiles and coal, producing by midcentury half the world total of these items.

Everywhere, increased production led to more commerce and closer international ties as capital, techniques, workers, and managers moved from Britain across the channel and spread from Belgium and France into the rest of Europe. Finance became so internationally linked that the Bank of France granted an emergency loan to the Bank of England in 1825, only a decade after Waterloo. The domestic banking policies of the United States, in response to a financial panic in 1837, led to a wave of crises in the financial centers of Europe.

State Politics　Although many writers argued that the new prosperity followed from natural economic laws that worked best unimpeded by government, by midcentury the state was centrally involved in the process of economic growth even in Britain. Railroads required franchises and the power of eminent domain before a spike was pounded. Inevitably, routes, rates, and even the gauge of the track became political matters to be settled by parliaments or special commissions. In Belgium and in most of Germany, railroads were owned as well as planned by the state.

Tariffs, the dominant issue in British politics in the 1840s, became a critical question in every country. In 1846, after a wrenching public campaign, Britain abolished the tariff on imported grain, known as the Corn Laws. In doing so, the nation expressed confidence in its position as the world's greatest center of manufacture and sided with those who favored trade and a lower price for bread rather than with the landowners who benefited from higher, protected grain prices. Equally important to economic development was the role of government in banking and currency. Just before the middle of the century, Parliament granted the Bank of England a monopoly on issuing money and required companies to register with the government and publish their annual budget as a guide to investors. Similar steps were taken across Europe. Before industries could effectively tap private wealth, investors needed assurance that they risked only the money they invested, without being liable (as in a partnership) for all a firm's debts. That assurance required new legislation establishing limited liability and encouraging the formation of corporations, and every major country passed such measures.

The Role of Government　The growth of cities and the benefits of new technology created additional social demands on government. By the 1840s most cities had a public omnibus, some sidewalks, and gas lighting in certain areas. Such services, usually provided by private companies, had to be subsidized, regulated, and given legal protection by the government. As the cost and importance of these services increased, so did the state's participation in them, often extending to full ownership.

The growing role of government was exemplified by the postal service, which most states had provided since the seventeenth and eighteenth centuries. These postal systems proved inadequate for an industrial era. In Britain demands for improvement led a little-known inventor to propose a solution that captured the thinking of the new age. He called for standard envelopes and payment in advance by means of an adhesive stamp. These innovations would not only eliminate graft and reduce costs, he argued, but the service would pay for itself because lower rates would increase volume. His reforms, denounced as dangerous and impractical, passed nevertheless in 1840; and within twenty years the volume of mail in Britain increased sixfold. By then, money orders, savings accounts, and the telegraph had been added to postal services. In France mail delivery was extended to rural areas, and by the 1850s every major government was adopting the new system, including the postage stamp.

Effective government, in short, was now expected to further economic development—by subsidizing ports, transportation, and new inventions; by registering patents and sponsoring education; by encouraging investment and enforcing contracts; and by maintaining order and preventing strikes. In the 1840s the leaders of Britain, France, and Belgium busily did these things—in Great Britain the number of government employees increased about fourfold in the first half of the century—and the desire in other countries to have governments similarly foster economic development was an important element in the revolutions of 1848 and the nationalist movements of the period that followed.

The Crystal Palace　The British celebrated their position as the masters of industrialization in 1851 with the first international industrial exhibition. Prominent people from the aristocracy, business, and gov-

Henry Thomas Alken
A VIEW OF THE WHITECHAPEL ROAD, 1828
By 1830 it was possible to conceive of life transformed by technology, as in this imagined view of what London's important White Chapel road might soon become, with traffic jams and smog but on an unpaved road with room for dogs.
National Railway Museum, York, UK/Bridgeman Art Library

ernment joined in the planning, and a specially designed pavilion was built in London, a sort of giant greenhouse called the Crystal Palace, which proved to be an architectural milestone. Many governments feared that Britain risked revolution by attracting huge throngs to London, but the admiring crowds proved well behaved.

The exhibition provided a significant comparison of the relative economic development of the participating countries. Russia displayed primarily raw materials; Austria showed mainly luxury handicrafts. So did the German *Zollverein* and the Italian states, whose appearance as single economic units foretold the advantages of national unification. Although unable to fill all the space it had demanded, the United States impressed viewers with collections of fossils, cheap manufactured products for use in the home, mountains of dentifrice and soap, and a series of new

inventions, including Colt revolvers, a sewing machine, and McCormick's reaper. French machines, which ranged from a much-admired device for folding envelopes to a submarine, were generally considered the most elegant. But British machines surpassed everyone's in quantity, size, and variety. It is, explained London's *Morning Chronicle*, "to our wonderful industrial discipline—our consummately arranged organization of toil, and our habit of division of labour—that we owe all the triumph." By 1850 Great Britain was the wealthiest nation in history,[3] and over the next twenty years, it would continue to increase its lead in goods produced.

[3]Although all estimates for this period are uncertain, it seems likely that by 1860 the per capita wealth of the French was about two-thirds and of the Germans about two-fifths that of the British.

J. Leonard
The Doctor for the Poor
Hopelessness dominates J. Leonard's painting of the poor coming to the charitable doctor in an endless stream.
Musée des Beaux-Arts, Valenciennes/Giraudon/Bridgeman Art Library

Purchasing Power   Although most workers everywhere suffered from the changing conditions of employment, workers in some trades and places were distinctly better off. Overall, real wages—measured, that is, in terms of what they could buy—may have begun to increase somewhat even before the general rise in wages in the mid-1840s and notably again in the 1850s, though these gains meant less in new factory towns, where workers could be forced to buy shoddy goods at high prices in company stores. Alcoholism was so extensive that in many a factory town paydays were staggered in order to reduce the dangerous number of drunks, a sign of alienation that may also have reflected an increase in available money. Technology brought benefits as well. The spread of the use of soap and cotton underwear was a boon to health, and by midcentury brick construction and iron pipes had improved housing even for many of the relatively poor. Luxuries such as sugar, tea, and meat were becoming available to the lower-middle class and to the more prosperous artisans.

The vigorous debate among historians over whether industrialization raised or lowered workers' standard of living in the first half of the century has become in large measure a judgment about the effects of capitalism (see "Industrialization and the Standard of Living," p. 665). But historians generally agree that whatever improvements occurred reached the masses slowly and often could not compensate for the added burdens of industrial employment or the growing chasm between the destitute and the regularly employed. In industrial Europe the urban poor remained a subject of baffled concern. The more fortunate workers and the middle classes were unquestionably more prosperous than they had been in the recent past, which made the contrast with the poverty of those beneath them even more striking. A luxury restaurant in Paris (by 1830 Paris had more than three thousand restaurants of every type, in contrast to only fifty or so before the Revolution) might charge twenty-five or thirty times an average worker's daily wage for a single meal; even modest restaurants charged twice a worker's daily wage—to a clientele that ate three or four times a day, in contrast to the two meals of many workers. From the top to the bottom of society, the gradations in status and wealth were subtle, but the differences between the comfortable minority and the poor majority were palpable in every aspect of daily life.

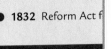

HISTORICAL ISSUES: INDUSTRIALIZATION AND THE STANDARD OF LIVING

These excerpts show the diverse emphases and shifting conclusions in this debate but not the careful reasoning and the extraordinary range of the research that makes this literature still worth reading. The first four excerpts are anthologized in Philip A. M. Taylor (ed.), The Industrial Revolution in Britain: Triumph or Disaster?, *D. C. Heath, 1970.*

JOHN L. AND BARBARA HAMMOND

"The apologies for child labour were precisely the same as the apologies for the slave trade. This was no travesty of their argument. The champions of the slave trade pointed to the £70,000,000 invested in the sugar plantations, to the dependence of our commerce on the slave trade. . . . The argument for child labour followed the same line. . . . Sir James Graham thought that the Ten Hours Bill would ruin the cotton industry and with it the trade of the country. . . . Our population, which had grown rapidly in the Industrial Revolution was no longer able to feed itself; the food it bought was paid for by its manufactures: those manufactures depended on capital: capital depended on profits: profits depended on the labour of the boys and girls who enabled the manufacturer to work his mills long enough at a time to repay the cost of the plant and to compete with foreign rivals. This was the circle in which the nation found its conscience mangled.

". . . Thus England asked for profits and received profits. Everything turned to profit. The towns had their profitable dirt, their profitable smoke, their profitable slums, their profitable disorder, their profitable ignorance, their profitable despair. The curse of Midas was on this society. . . . For the new town was not a home where man could find beauty, happiness, leisure, learning, religion, the influences that civilize outlook and habit, but a bare and desolate place. . . . The new factories and the new furnaces were like the Pyramids, telling of man's enslavement, rather than of his power, casting their long shadow over the society that took such pride in them."

From John L. and Barbara Hammond, *The Rise of Modern Industry*, M. S. G. Haskell House, 1925.*

THOMAS S. ASHTON

"Let me confess at the start that I am of those who believe that, all in all, conditions of labour were becoming better, at least after 1820, and that the spread of the factory played a not inconsiderable part in the improvement. . . . One of the merits of the factory system was that it offered, and required, regularity of employment and hence stability of consumption. During the period 1790–1830 factory production increased rapidly. A greater proportion of the people came to benefit both as producers and as consumers. The fall in the price of textiles reduced the price of clothing. Government contracts for uniforms and army boots called into being new industries, and after the war the products of these found a market among the better-paid artisans. Boots began to take the place of clogs and hats replaced shawls, at least for wear on Sundays. Miscellaneous commodities, ranging from clocks to pocket handkerchiefs, began to enter into the scheme of expenditure, and after 1820 such things as tea and coffee and sugar fell in price substantially. The growth of trade-unions, friendly societies, savings banks, popular newspapers and pamphlets, schools, and nonconformist chapels—all give evidence of the existence of a large class raised well above the level of mere subsistence."

From Thomas S. Ashton, "The Standard of Life of the Workers in England, 1790–1830," *Journal of Economic History*, Vol. 9, 1949.*

ERIC J. HOBSBAWM

"We may consider three types of evidence in favour of the pessimistic view: those bearing on (a) mortality and health, (b) unemployment and (c) consumption. . . . The rise in mortality rates in the period 1811–41 is clearly of *some* weight for the pessimistic case, all the more as modern work . . . tend[s] to link such rates much more directly to the amount of income and food consumption than to other social conditions.

". . . It is too often forgotten that something like 'technological' unemployment was not confined to those workers who were actually replaced by new machines. It could affect almost all pre-industrial industries and trades. . . . Doubtless the general expansion of the early industrial period (say 1780–1811) tended to diminish unemployment except during crises: doubtless the decades of difficulty and adjustment after the wars tended to make the problem more acute. From the later 1840s, the working classes began to adjust themselves to life under a new set of economic rules . . . but it is highly probable that the period 1811–42 saw abnormal problems and abnormal unemployment. . . . These notes on unemployment are sufficient to throw doubt upon the less critical statements of the optimistic view, but not to establish any alternative view. . . . Per capita consumption can hardly have risen. The discussion of food consumption thus throws considerable doubt on the optimistic view."

From Eric J. Hobsbawm, "The British Standard of Living, 1790–1850," *Economic History Review*, 1957.*

continued

yearning fo
Schlegel an
(heavily inf
among the
through inte
lectuals as w
etry, drama,

Coleridge
great long p
tion, and th
lore, the poe
albatross ar

Augustus Pugin
A convert to Catholicism and a leading student of Gothic architecture, Augustus Pugin was one of the architects of the Houses of Parliament. These illustrations, part of a book on *Contrasts* comparing Catholic and Protestant society, sum up the romantic and conservative critique of modern society for replacing church spires with smokestacks, cottages and artisanship with massive tenements and factories, and charities with prisons. (The new prison in the foreground is Jeremy Bentham's Panopticon, designed so that a single guard can see down all the cellblocks.)
New York Public Library

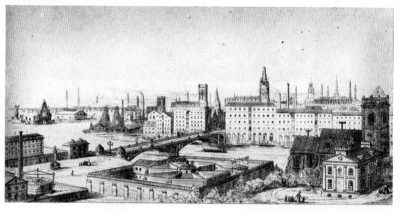

IDEAS OI

Political idea
the arts wer
nineteenth
painted pictu
lyzed society
Several elem
versity and ir
artists, and p
tial increasir
place in socie
Primarily ma
depended les
to establishe
ties, publish
Through exh
they sought t
broader audi
ety, like thei
tion, produce
fact, debates
sources of hi

Romantic

Romanticisn
cannot be cap
with the grea
ter part of th
Jean-Jacques
movement,
gland, rapidly
America. Ro:
and in such a
as a set of a
than as a de

Hear the voice of the Bard,
Who present, past, and future, sees
The Holy Word
That walk'd among the ancient trees.

The anguish, depression, and despair experienced in their personal lives became for Romantic poets a sign of their own sensitivity and a summons to a higher vision of the meaning of life.

In France, where Romanticism developed somewhat later, Madame Anne-Louise de Staël's essays on the German thinkers stimulated a whole generation of philosophers, historians, and novelists. These ranged from the young Victor Hugo, whose plays and novels (*The Hunchback of Notre Dame* and *Les Misérables* are the best known) made him the towering figure of French letters through most of the century, to the swashbuckling stories of Alexander Dumas' *Three Musketeers*. Novelists and dramatists in Italy and Russia, as well as in England, France, and Germany, often set their tales in the distant past and tended to favor vivid description and singular settings appropriate to occurrences beyond rational understanding. Turning from the Enlightenment and its veneration for the Renaissance, they preferred the rougher, sprawling picture of human experience in seventeenth-century writers like Shakespeare and Cervantes (stimulating an important revival of interest in their work). They felt a kinship with the Middle Ages as an age of faith and spontaneity that produced such achievements as Dante's poetry and Gothic architecture.

Joseph Mallord William Turner
INTERIOR OF TINTURN ABBEY, EXHIBITED 1794
The evocation of nature and time, favorite Romantic themes, made the ruins of Tintern Abbey the subject of a poem by Wordsworth and of this watercolor by Turner.
Watercolor. Victoria and Albert Museum, London/Art Resource, NY

Wordsworth on the Role of the Poet

Wordsworth was one of England's most popular poets, and the success of his Lyrical Ballads *may have encouraged him to write a preface to the second edition, explaining what he was up to. He points out that his poems differ from classical poetry with its greater formality and lofty themes, and he justifies his use of ordinary speech. In making his case, he touches on many of the themes characteristic of the Romantic movement.*

"The principle object of these Poems was to choose incidents and situations from common life, and to relate or describe them, throughout, as far as was possible in a selection of language really used by men, and, at the same time, to throw over them a certain colouring of imagination, whereby ordinary things could be presented to the mind in an unusual aspect. . . . Humble and rustic life was generally chosen because, in that condition, the essential passions of the heart find a better soil in which they can attain their maturity, are less under restraint, and speak a plainer and more emphatic language; because in that condition of life our elementary feelings co-exist in a state of greater simplicity, and, consequently, may be more accurately contemplated and more forcibly communicated; because the manners of rural life germinate from those elementary feelings . . . ; and, lastly, because in that condition the passions of men are incorporated with the beautiful and permanent forms of nature. . . .

" . . . For all good poetry is the spontaneous overflow of powerful feelings: and though this be true, Poems to which any value can be attached were never produced on any variety of subjects but by a man who, being possessed of more than usual organic sensibility, had also thought long and deeply. . . .

"The Man of science seeks truth as a remote and unknown benefactor; he cherishes and loves it in his solitude; the Poet, singing a song in which all human beings join with him, rejoices in the presence of truth as our visible friend and hourly companion. Poetry is the breath and finer spirit of all knowledge; it is the impassioned expression which is the countenance of all Science. Emphatically may it be said of the Poet, as Shakespeare hath said of man, 'that he looks before and after.' He is the rock of defence for human nature; an upholder and preserver, carrying everywhere with him relationship and love . . . ; the Poet binds together by passion and knowledge the vast empire of human society, as it is spread over the whole earth, and over all time."

From William Wordsworth, "Preface to the Second Edition of *Lyrical Ballads*," in *William Wordsworth: Selected Poems and Prefaces*, Jack Stillinger (ed.), Houghton-Mifflin, 1965.

The Wider Influence of Romanticism   The fairy tales of Hans Christian Andersen combined the Romantic delight in folk culture and affection for childhood. Throughout the Western world there was a new taste for tales of ghostly spirits (Edgar Allen Poe was one of the first American writers to achieve international recognition) and paintings of storms and ruins that evoked unseen powers, as in the landscapes of William Constable and J. M. W. Turner in England and Caspar David Friedrich in Germany.

Literary and artistic works thus burst beyond classical forms. Romantic painters like Théodore Géricault in France emphasized vibrant color and swirling lines without the sharp outlines and balanced composition so important to their predecessors. Like Eugène Delacroix (see his paintings on p. 699), they were drawn to exotic scenes from the past and from North Africa and the Middle East.

Romantic values came together with particular power in music, admired for its ability to communicate an ineffable understanding deeper than words. The response to the works of Beethoven had brought a self-conscious seriousness to music. Critics wrote of his symphonies and string quartets in terms of their philosophic profundity, and audiences listened in reverent silence, finding in that shared experience something akin to religion. Subsequent Romantic composers appealed even more directly to the heart, emphasizing melody and using freer harmonies. When words and music were combined, as in the song cycles of Franz Schubert and Robert Schumann, or in grand opera (often hailed as the highest of the arts), it was the music that mattered most.

Both conservatives and radicals drew upon the Romantic movement, for it was both a call for change and a response to it, attentive to politics as well as to philosophy and the arts. Conservatives found in Romantic values powerful arguments for rejecting the French Revolution and considered it the lamentable result of Enlightenment rationalism and of the universalism that ignored local variety and tradition. Stability, they argued, was possible only in a society organically connected, held together as it had been in the Middle Ages by respect for custom and religion. They contrasted their vision of an organic society with the competition and selfish individualism of modern capitalism.

Radicals, however, used Romantic themes to argue that a new era required shattering old institutional constraints, much as creativity in the arts fostered the breaking of established art forms. Romantic thinkers tended to see folk culture and language as natural expressions of the nation. For conservatives these values validated rural life and custom; for radicals the promise of this culture would be realized when the people spontaneously arose to achieve new freedoms. In Germany and England many Romantics had, like Wordsworth, initially welcomed the French Revolution only to turn away from it in disgust. Victor Hugo, on the other hand, turned from conservatism to become a lifelong advocate of radical change. A younger generation of English poets, led by Lord Byron, Percy Bysshe Shelley, and John Keats, were persistent critics of church and state drawn to the promise of revolution. In its aspirations and its tumultuousness Romanticism expressed the preoccupation with change that marked the age.

Social Thought

Conservatism   Conservatism grew from opposition to the French Revolution to become what today would be called an ideology—a coherent view of human nature, social organization, and political power that generally justified the status quo. This conservatism was not mere nostalgia for the past. Rather, like the restoration regimes established in 1815, conservatives advocated changes when designed to strengthen the kind of society they favored.

Not that conservatives always agreed. But in arguing for social order, they tended to emphasize the limitations of human understanding, the wisdom of established customs, the value of hierarchy, and the social importance of religion. From those concerns, conservatives mounted a powerful critique not just of radical programs but of modern society itself as perilously inclined toward antisocial individualism, materialism, and immorality. More than a matter of temperament or interest, conservatism would remain a vigorous part of European intellectual life and political discourse throughout the nineteenth century.

From the late eighteenth century on, the powerful English prose of Edmund Burke (see discussion on p. 593) provided what was perhaps the most influential formulation of the conservative position. Society, he argued, exists through continuity. By granting special privileges to certain groups, it fulfills social needs in a way that sustains order, achieving a delicate arrangement in which rank is related to social function and in which differences of status, having evolved through time, are acceptable to all. This "natural" historical order, Burke argued, was far wiser than the "artificial" plans of radicals, no matter how well intentioned. The Burkean view thus allowed for gradual change, at least in theory; in practice, such arguments could be used against any plan for general reform. This tendency was

George Cruikshank
***DEATH OR LIBERTY*, 1819**
This cartoon by George Cruikshank, the most famous cartoonist of the day, reflects the vitriolic quality of political debate in the early nineteenth century. A satanic figure of Reform (the Phrygian cap on a pike behind him was a symbol of the French Revolution) assaults Britannia, who relies on religion to save her. The cartoon is sarcastically entitled "Death or Liberty," but the subtitle is more straightforward: "or Britannia and the Virtues of the Constitution in Danger of Violation from the Great Political Libertine, Radical Reform."
Private Collection/Bridgeman Art Library

strengthened by a distrust of reason that rejected the ideas of the Enlightenment as dangerously abstract. No social schemes or written constitutions could reconstitute society, because it was a great interconnecting web, and slogans about rights or equality merely concealed selfish interests and encouraged false hopes.

Conservatives found in history the record of how painfully civilization had developed and how fragile it remained, and many saw evidence not only of human error but of divine will in events since the French Revolution. Christianity was the source of Europe's strength, and Christian fear a necessary restraint on humanity's selfish and prideful nature. Without it, society dissolved into revolution and anarchy. Political battles were part of a far larger millennial conflict.

Such views gave conservative thought both militancy and depth. Europeans were used to receiving radical ideas from France, and two of the most pungent exponents of conservatism were men who wrote in French, Joseph de Maistre and Louis de Bonald. Society's first task, they argued, is self-preservation. Only authority can check the selfish wills of individuals, and authority requires undivided sovereignty, social hierarchy, close links between church and state, and the vigilant suppression of dangerous ideas. These writers thus connected religion to politics and tied the Church to aristocracy and monarchy. Revolution, Maistre explained, is divine retribution for

MAISTRE'S OPPOSITION TO REFORM

Over the course of the past twenty years, most European governments had adopted constitutions when Joseph de Maistre, writing from exile in Russia, set forth his objections to them in his Essay on the Generative Principle of Political Constitutions. *First published in Russia in 1810 and in Paris in 1814, the essay was reprinted many times.*

"Every thing brings us back to the general rule—*man cannot create a constitution; and no legitimate constitution can be written.* The collection of fundamental laws, which must essentially constitute a civil or religious society, never has been written, and never will be, *a priori.* It is only when society finds itself already constituted, without being able to say how, that it is possible to make known, or explain, in writing, certain special articles; but in almost every case these declarations or explanations are the effect of very great evils, and always cost the people more than they are worth.

" . . . Not only does it not belong to man to create institutions, but it does not appear that his power, *unassisted,* extends even to change for the better institutions already established. . . . *Nothing* [says the philosopher, Origen] . . . *can be changed for the better among men, without God.* All men have a consciousness of this truth, without being

in a state to explain it to themselves. Hence that instinctive aversion, in every good mind, to innovations. The word *reform,* in itself, and previous to all examinations, will be always suspected by wisdom, and the experience of every age justifies this sort of instinct.

" . . . To apply these maxims to a particular case . . . the great question of parliamentary reform, which has agitated minds in England so powerfully, and for so long a time, I still find myself constrained to believe, that this idea is pernicious, and that if the English yield themselves too readily to it, they will have occasion to repent."

From Joseph de Maistre, *Essay on the Generative Principle of Political Constitutions,* Boston: Little and Brown, 1847; reprint: Scholars' Facsimiles & Reprints, New York: Delmar, 1977.

false ideas (see "Maistre's Opposition to Reform," above). This hard-line conservatism, very different from Burke's, contained little that was humane or tolerant. With its praise of hangmen and censors, it spoke only to those who already shared its fears. Terrified of weakening the dikes that held back revolution, it left little room for compromise, divided while calling for unity, and relied on power while speaking of the social good. Nevertheless, as a way of understanding change, mobilizing opposition to liberal demands, and criticizing modern life, conservatism would be a profoundly influential element in modern thought.

Liberalism   Liberalism, like conservatism, was not so much a compact doctrine as a set of attitudes. Whereas conservatism emphasized tradition and hierarchy, liberalism was associated with ideas of social progress, belief in economic development, and values associated with the middle class. Confident that their ideas would triumph, liberals generally welcomed change.

They appraised society primarily in terms of freedom for individual choice and opportunities for individual growth, an emphasis that gave some ethical dignity to the pain of industrialization and lent promise to the process of social change. They believed their principles were universally valid; yet, to the perpetual surprise of its adherents, liberalism proved a creed of limited appeal, forever subject to attack and internal di-

vision. Enthusiasm for limited constitutional reform produced disagreements over how limited it should be. In practice, reconciling liberty with order or equal rights with private property proved contentious and led to attacks on liberalism and divisions among liberals themselves. Some theorists reduced liberalism to little more than the narrow justification of individual success. Others expanded it until the demand for social justice overshadowed its founding principles of competition and individualism. In each country the temper of liberalism was different, shaped by a national history liberals never wholly dominated.

Political Liberalism   Liberal political thought was rooted in the writings of John Locke and of the philosophes. Liberals in the nineteenth century believed that their programs would benefit individuals and society as a whole. A leading French liberal, Benjamin Constant, put the case succinctly: "The liberty of the individual is the object of all human association; on it rest public and private morality; on it are based the calculations of industry and commerce, and without it there is neither peace, dignity, nor happiness for men." By this creed, freedom would lead to morality, prosperity, and progress. The freedom that liberals sought was primarily political and legal, and they generally favored a constitution and representative institutions, freedom of the press and of assembly, an extension of the jury

In Prussia, the most influential aristocrats were the **Junkers** of east Prussia, owners of large estates, some of which included sizable villages. The Junkers maintained their traditional position even when the state became the instrument of dramatic and rapid change. Considered crude and ignorant by most of the aristocracies of Europe—which set great store by polished manners, elegant taste, and excellent French—the Junkers had a proud tradition of service to the state and loyalty to their king. In local government, in the bureaucracy, in the army, and at the court, their manners and their values—from rectitude to fondness for dueling, from arrogance to loyalty—set the tone of Prussian public life.

France is thus the European exception, for there the old aristocracy was reduced to a minor role in national politics after the revolution of 1830. Its members retained major influence in the Church, army, and foreign service, but those institutions were also on the defensive. Yet even in France, aristocrats maintained a strong voice in local affairs and were a major influence on manners and the arts. Everywhere, however, aristocrats were in danger of being isolated from important sources of political and economic power. Lineage was once of such importance that tracing family lines had been a matter of state; now, pride of family was becoming a private matter.

Peasants   The overwhelming majority of all Europeans were peasants, a social class as firmly tied to the land and to tradition as the aristocracy. Praised by conservatives for simple virtues and solid values, disparaged by progressives for their ignorance, peasants struggled to make ends meet in a changing world.

An important change occurred with the emancipation of peasants from traditional obligations to the lord whose land they worked. These "feudal" obligations typically might have required the peasant to give the lord a number of days of labor or to use the lord's grain mill at rates the lord set. The French Revolution abolished such requirements, a policy carried to much of Western Europe by Napoleon and spread to most of Eastern Europe with the revolutions of 1848. These changes encouraged peasant producers to enter the commercial market; but they also deprived peasants of such traditional protections against hard times as the use of a common pasture, the right to glean what was left after the first harvest, and the practice of foraging for firewood in forests owned by others.

Similarly, the decline of the putting-out system in textiles and of local industries took away critical income, especially during the winter months. Agriculture became more commercial, its production increasingly intended for market rather than for mere subsistence or local consumption. Profits increased with the cultivation of one or two cash crops and with the use of improved fertilizers and machinery, but these changes were easier for those farmers with more capital and bigger holdings than most peasants enjoyed. Because larger farms were more likely to be profitable, landed nobles, bourgeois investors, and richer peasants sought to expand and consolidate their holdings.

Peasant Activism   Peasants, however, were not just passive victims of outside forces. They tenaciously maintained old loyalties to their region, their priests, and their habitual ways; and they were the despair of reformers, who were often defeated by peasant suspicion of outsiders and opposition to change. But peasants also used elaborate ties of family and patronage to build effective social networks, and they were frequently shrewd judges of their interests, cooperating with measures that promised immediate benefits while resisting all others with the skepticism of experience.

Their hunger for land, resentment of taxes and military service, and sense of grievance against those above them could also become a major political force. Peasant involvement made a crucial difference in the early days of the French Revolution, in the Spanish resistance to Napoleon, in the wars of German liberation, and in the strength of nationalism in Germany and Italy. Rulers were kept on edge by eruptions of peasant violence in southern England in the 1820s; Ireland in the 1830s and 1840s; Wales, Silesia, and Galicia in the 1840s; and on a smaller scale in most other countries. The outbreaks of 1848 would topple the system of feudal service in the Austrian Empire and eastern Prussia, though rural indifference to constitutional claims and to workers' demands undermined the urban revolutions there.

The peasantry was deeply divided between those who owned land and those who were forced to sell their labor. Some of the former, especially in the West, grew relatively prosperous and joined the influential notables of their region. In most of Europe peasants were tenants who received only a part of the crops they raised, with the rest going to their landlords. Such arrangements could provide security, but they also tended to be inflexible, discouraging adaptation to changes in prices, markets, and technology. Rural laborers were the poorest and most insecure of all, the tinder of violence and the recruits for factory work.

Peasants and Social Change   A central problem for nineteenth-century European society was how to integrate the agricultural economy and the masses dependent on it into the developing commercial and

industrial economy. By the 1850s the process had gone farthest in France and Great Britain but by opposite means. In Britain the peasantry was largely eliminated as the continuing enclosures of great estates reduced the rural poor to laborers, shifting from place to place and hiring out for the season or by the day (see chapter 18). The concentration of landholding in Great Britain was one of the highest in Europe: Some 500 aristocratic families controlled half the land; and some 1,300 others, most of the rest. In France, on the other hand, peasants owned approximately one-third of the arable land and were gradually gaining more. They made the most of their situation by favoring crops that required intense cultivation, such as grapes and sugar beets, and by maintaining small-scale craft industries.

Patterns elsewhere lay between these two extremes. Small landholding persisted in western Germany, northern Italy, Switzerland, the Netherlands, Belgium, and Scandinavia alongside a trend toward the consolidation of larger farms that reduced millions to becoming day laborers. In Germany emancipation from personal obligations to the lord usually required peasants to pay for their freedom with part (often the best part) of the land they had previously cultivated.

The clear distinction remained, however, between these western and central regions and Eastern Europe, where peasants were more directly subject to the power of the lord, most of all under Russian serfdom. In the West, developments that increased agricultural productivity often made the life of peasants more precarious. In the East, the landowners' authority over their peasants included claims to their unpaid labor, which in

Russia ranged from a month or so of work each year to several days a week. The disadvantages of such a system were many, and the eventual emancipation of Russian serfs in the 1860s proved necessary for economic growth and minimal military and administrative efficiency. As urbanization and industrialization advanced, many writers waxed nostalgic for the bucolic purity and sturdy independence of peasant life, but the social and economic problems of the peasantry were, in fact, some of the gravest and most intractable of European society.

Workers and Artisans   Industrial workers attracted far more attention than did the peasantry; yet even in Britain industrial workers were a minority among paid laborers (there were more domestic servants than factory hands). Industrial workers, however, were taken to be indicative of the new age because of the environment in which they lived and worked and because of their absolute dependence on wages set by employers, who could fire them at will and who determined the tasks performed as well as the conditions of work and the length of the workday.

Most factory workers earned too little to sustain a family even when work was steady, and the employment of women and children became as necessary to the family's survival as it was advantageous to employers, who appreciated their greater dexterity and the lower wages they would accept. Awakened before dawn by the factory bell, they tramped to work, where the pace of production was relentless and the dangers from machinery and irate foremen were great. Any lapse of attention during a workday of fourteen hours or more,

An etching of Dean Mills in 1851 shows cotton spinning as contemporaries liked to think of it: women working together with nimble industriousness under the watchful but gentle eye of a sturdy foreman, all in the iron grandeur of an immaculate, orderly, huge new factory.
Mansell/TimePix/Getty Images

even stopping to help a neighbor, brought a fine and a harsh reprimand.

Industrial workers were set apart by the conditions of their labor, the slums in which they lived, and special restrictions such as the *livret*, or passport, that all French workers were required to present when applying for a job and on which previous employers recorded comments on the worker's conduct and performance. Life was still more precarious for the millions without regular employment, who simply did such tasks as they could find, hauling or digging for a few pence. Understandably, the powerful worried about the social volcano on which they lived.

The most independent workers were the artisans, who had been stripped of their tight guilds and formal apprenticeships by the French Revolution, by a series of laws passed in Britain in the years before the 1830s, and by a similar process in Germany that was completed by the revolutions of 1848. Nevertheless, artisans continued to ply their crafts in a hierarchy of masters, journeymen, and apprentices, working in small shops in which conditions varied as much ac-

cording to the temper of the master as to the pressures of the market. Skilled or semiskilled workers, from carpenters and shoemakers to mechanics, were distinctly better paid than the masses of the unskilled. Although they were vulnerable to unemployment during the frequent economic slumps, in general their real wages tended slowly to increase, and they could expect to earn enough to support their families in one or two bare rooms on a simple diet.

Uneducated and exhausted industrial workers, often strangers to one another, for the most part lacked the means necessary for effective concerted action to improve their lot. Their frequent outbursts of resentment and intermittent strikes usually ended in some bloodshed and sullen defeat. Most worker protests were led by artisans, who felt most keenly the threat of economic change and held clearer visions of their rights and dignity.

Early Labor Movements Trade unions were banned everywhere except in England after 1824, and even there the laws against conspiracy restricted their activity. But various local organizations had developed in the eighteenth century for mutual aid. By 1850 more than 1.5 million British workers may have belonged to such groups, called friendly societies in England and confraternities in France, which tended to form around skilled workers and to meet in secret, often of necessity but also as a sign of brotherhood and trust. Although their members were fond of elaborate rituals, these societies served specific purposes, such as providing burial costs for members or assistance in times of illness. There were also movements that aimed to increase the workers' control over their lives, such as consumers' cooperatives and artisans' production cooperatives. Such programs sometimes became associated with radical politics, a specter likely to rouse crushing opposition even from liberal governments. For the most part, however, these expressions of workers' insistence on their rights and dignity remained small in scale and local in influence.

The hundreds of strikes that occurred throughout Western Europe in the first half of the century suggested what unions might accomplish; but without funds, organizational experience, or effective means of communication, these labor movements usually petered out after a few years or sometimes a few months. Not even the Workingman's Association for Benefiting Politically, Socially, and Morally the Useful Classes, launched with some fanfare in England in 1836, managed to survive for long or bring off the general strike its more radical members dreamed of. Yet these organizations did influence Parliament to favor factory legislation.

The meetings, torchlight parades, and special workers' tracts all contributed to the growing sense of belonging to a distinctive class. So, above all, did the repression by police and courts that usually followed. By midcentury millions of workers in Britain, somewhat fewer perhaps in France, and smaller numbers elsewhere shared heroes and rituals, believed they faced a common enemy, and adopted organization as the prime means of defending themselves in a hostile world. In Britain the national trade unions of skilled workers formed in the 1830s and 1840s (with only some 100,000 members then) steadily increased their size and influence, reaching more than a million members a generation later.

The vast majority of the working class, however, remained essentially defenseless, possessing meager skills, dependent on unstable employment, and living in the isolation of poverty. Ideas of *fraternité* and *egalité*, of the rights of freeborn English people, and of simple patriotism, often expressed in Biblical prose, communicated a common sense of hope and outrage to the millions of men and women who attended rallies,

met in dingy cafés, and read the working-class press (or listened as it was read to them). Newspapers and pamphlets intended for workers were numerous in England after 1815, less widespread in France in the 1830s and 1840s, and present everywhere in 1848. The common themes were people's natural rights, pride of work, and the claims of social justice.

The Middle Classes   Of all the social classes, the most confident and assertive was the middle class. At the top stood the great bankers, who in London and Paris were often closely connected to the liberal aristocracy and whose political influence after 1830 was considerable. Just below them in status, the great industrialists and the wealthiest merchants were more separate from and a little contemptuous of the traditional elites. The bottom of the middle class consisted of office clerks, schoolteachers, and small shopkeepers, often distinguishable from artisans only by their pretensions. This petite bourgeoisie constituted most of the middle class numerically, but the class was epitomized by those neither at the top nor bottom but in between: most merchants, managers, and upper bureaucrats and nearly all lawyers, doctors, engineers, and professors. The view that such disparate groups made up a social class resulted as much from ideas shared as from common interests. Opposed to aristocratic privilege, they saw themselves as the beneficiaries of social changes that allowed talented people to gain security and influence.

They were primarily an urban class and intimately connected with the commerce and politics of city life. In Paris they constituted nearly all of that part of the population (between one-fourth and one-fifth) that was prosperous enough to pay some taxes, have at least one maid, and leave an estate sufficient to cover the costs of private burial. In other cities their proportion was probably somewhat smaller. Among nations, they were most numerous in Great Britain, a sizable fraction in France and Belgium, and a smaller minority elsewhere. The middle class was the only social class that it was possible to fall out of, and people established their membership in it by economic self-sufficiency, literacy, and respectability. Their manner, their dress, and their homes were thus symbols of their status and were meant to express values of probity, hard work, fortitude, prudence, and self-reliance. No matter how favored by birth or fortune, they tended to think of themselves as self-made.

Middle-Class Values   While industrial centers were notoriously drab, the middle-class home became more ornate, packed with furnishings that boasted of elaborate craftsmanship. Women's fashions similarly

Fashion magazines like *La Mode Illustré* kept middle-class women informed of the latest styles and elegant touches to which they might aspire.
Bulloz/© RMN/Art Resource, NY

need to blush on finding themselves called by a London paper in 1807 "those persons . . . always counted the most valuable, because the least corrupted, members of society," or on hearing John Stuart Mill speak a generation later of "the class which is universally described as the most wise and the most virtuous part of the community, the middle rank." Society was understood in terms of social class at a time when the hallmarks of the era—flourishing commerce, science, and technology; great works of art and institutions of culture; triumphant movements of liberalism and nationalism—were seen as achievements of the middle class.

The Changing Population

While Europeans grappled with political, economic, and social changes, they also faced the fact that there were more and more people—more people to feed, more seeking work, and more living in cities.

Demographic Growth   The effects of population growth were particularly visible in areas in which industrialization was under way, and historians used to think that industrialization had stimulated a rising birthrate with new opportunities for employment, particularly of children. But demographic research has challenged that view, and current explanations emphasize a decline in disease-carrying germs, an increase in the food supply, a lowering of the age at which people married, and, after 1870, some improvement in public sanitation.

Admittedly spotty data suggest that the world experienced a decline in some common diseases beginning in the eighteenth century. Microbes have cycles (like those of locusts but less regular), and remissions had undoubtedly occurred many times before. Now, however, better supplies of food allowed the larger number of babies surviving the perilous years of infancy to reach adulthood and form families of their own.

The food supply rose because of better transportation, more effective agricultural techniques, and the potato. Agricultural associations, usually led by enlightened aristocrats, campaigned for more scientific farming; and the humble potato, not common on the Continent before 1750, was a staple of the peasant's diet in most of Europe by 1830. Potatoes are easy to cultivate in a small space and can yield more calories per acre than any other crop. While infant mortality remained enormously high by modern standards, even a slight decline in death rates could make a great difference in the total number of people, so close to subsistence did most Europeans live.

Population and Society   The reasons for the trend toward earlier marriage are less clear, but peasants freed

featured ornamental frills, and shops translated Parisian elegance into forms available to more modest purses. Masculine garb, by contrast, grew plainer, a point of some pride in a practical age; and clerk and banker tended to dress alike. Those who forged great industries out of daring, foresight, and luck; those who invented or built; and those who taught or tended shop or wrote for newspapers came to share a certain pride in one another's achievements as proof that personal drive and social benefit were in harmony and as a harbinger of progress yet to come.

More than any other, the middle class was associated with an ideology; and the triumph of the middle class in this period—so heralded then and by historians since—related as much to constitutionalism and legal equality, individual rights, and economic opportunity as it did to any explicit transfer of power. The conquests of the middle class were measured not just by its rise in importance but also by a more general adoption of values associated with it. Even being in the middle, between the extremes of luxury and power and of poverty and ignorance, was seen as an advantage, a kind of inherent moderation. Most of Europe's writers, scientists, doctors, lawyers, and businesspeople would have felt no

Jean-Auguste-Dominique Ingres
LOUIS FRANCOIS BERTIN, 1832
This painting portrays the entrepreneur Louis Francois Bertin as the very epitome of the self-reliant, aggressive man of the industrial middle class.
Giraudon/Art Resource, NY

immeasurable importance, for it reduced the isolation of country folk and stimulated a pattern of migration to the Americas that would become a flood. Young people constituted a greater proportion of the population, which may have made for increased restiveness and a larger pool of potential radical leaders.[2] There was also a distinction in birthrates by social class, which demographers call *differential fertility*. On the whole, the higher a man stood on the social scale, the fewer the children in his family, which led some to interpret the lower classes' fertility as a lack of foresight and moral restraint and to worry that they would eventually overwhelm society.

The most influential analysis of population was Thomas R. Malthus' *An Essay on the Principle of Population as It Affects the Future Improvement of Society*, first published in 1798 and reissued in many revisions. Observing the Britain of his time, Malthus argued that human population, unless checked by death (through war, famine, or pestilence) or deliberate sexual continence, increases faster than the supply of food. A clergyman, he advocated continence; but he remained pessimistic that human beings were capable of such restraint. An economist as well, Malthus presented demography as a science closely attached to liberal economic theory, with the convenient corollary that the misery of the poor resulted from their own improvidence.

Urbanization   At the turn of the century, greater London reached 1 million in population. No European city since imperial Rome had ever approached this size. Paris, with about half that number, would reach 1 million a generation later. The third largest European city in 1800, Naples, had some 350,000 inhabitants; and in all Europe there were then only twenty-two cities with populations of more than 100,000. By midcentury there were forty-seven. Great Britain was the leader, with six cities over the 100,000 mark; London's population had surpassed 2.5 million by 1856, Liverpool had grown from 80,000 to almost 400,000, and Manchester and Glasgow each had more than 300,000 people. By the 1850s, half of Britain's population lived in towns or cities, making it the most urbanized society since the Classical era.

On the Continent most old cities increased by at least 50 percent in the first half of the century, and many a town became a city. The major capitals burgeoned. Paris reached a population of nearly 1.5 million

from servile obligations apparently tended to marry and form new households at a younger age. Early marriage was facilitated by the spread of cottage industry, which preceded the new factories and enabled families to add to their income by spinning or weaving at home.

The increased number of people in a single generation multiplied in the next generation and led to an enormous increase in the aggregate. As population grew, the proportion who were in the childbearing years grew still faster, which increased the ratio of births to the total population. The net result was that the 180 to 190 million Europeans of 1800 had become 266 million by 1850 and 295 million by 1870.

The effects of a larger population were far-reaching. More people consumed more food, which necessitated more intensive cultivation and the use of land previously left fallow. An increasing population also meant an expanding market for goods other than food, an element of growth that would have stronger impact later in the century. More people meant a larger potential workforce readier to leave the countryside for industrial jobs; and this mobility became a social change of

[2] The nationalist organization Young Italy limited membership to those under forty, and probably most of the leaders of the revolutions of 1848 would have met that standard. The relation of youth to revolution is interestingly discussed in Herbert Moller, "Youth as a Force in the Modern World," *Comparative Studies in Society and History*, April 1968.

Gustave Doré
In this famous engraving of London, the rhythmic sameness and cramped efficiency of new housing suggest a machine for living appropriate to the age of the railroad.
New York Public Library

by 1850; Berlin almost trebled, to 500,000; and a similar growth rate pushed Brussels to 250,000. St. Petersburg, Vienna, and Budapest all had populations between 400,000 and 500,000.

By the 1860s the English countryside was actually losing people, as were some sections of France. The tide of urbanization was overwhelming, and nearly all the subsequent increase in European population would end up in cities swelling with immigrants, as rural folk moved to nearby villages, villagers to towns, and town dwellers to cities. Clearly, the tide of urbanization was strongest where industry was great, but the growth of ports and national capitals demonstrated the importance of great commercial, financial, and political centers as well.

Urban Problems   Society had neither the experience nor the means to cope very well with such an expansion. Urban conditions for all but the reasonably pros-

perous were unspeakable. Narrow alleys were littered with garbage and ordure that gave off an overpowering stench. The water supply in Paris, better than in most large cities, offered access to safe water only at fountains that dotted the city (the affluent paid carriers by the bucket), and in London the private companies that provided water allowed it to flow only a few hours a day. In most cities the water supply came from dangerously polluted rivers. Sewage was an even more serious problem. A third of Manchester's houses used privies in the 1830s, and a decade later the ratio of inside toilets to population was 1 to 212. In London cesspools menaced health only slightly less than still more public means of disposal.

The most dramatic inadequacy, however, was in housing. A third of Liverpool's citizens lived crowded into dark, cold cellars, and conditions in Lille were similar. In every city the poor of both sexes crowded into filthy, stuffy, unheated rooms; and over the cities,

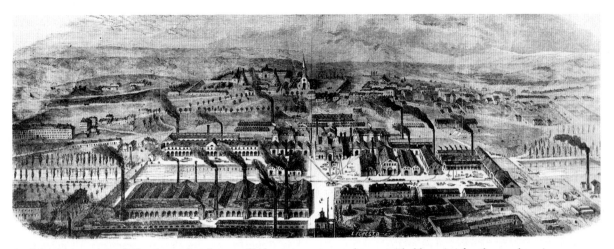

Le Creusot was a carefully planned and controlled company town that provided housing for the workers in its foundries.
Roger-Viollet/Getty Images

especially manufacturing and mining towns, chemical smog and coal smoke darkened the sky. It is hardly surprising that crime was rampant, that often more than a third of the births were illegitimate, and that the number of prostitutes soared (reaching perhaps 80,000 in London, where 9,000 were officially registered; 3,600 were registered in Paris).

Maintaining public order became a new kind of problem. The protection of lives and property in great cities, the effective handling of crowds, and the enforcement of local ordinances required new police forces. London's force was established by Sir Robert Peel in 1829, and the Paris Municipal Guard was created under Guizot a few years later. The role played by Sir Robert Peel led to the nickname "Bobbies," by which the police are still called in London.

For all their misery, cities continued to grow; and through the century the worst conditions were slowly alleviated by housing codes, public sewers, and reliable water supplies. These improvements were made possible in part by industrialization, which gradually provided iron pipes, water closets, gas lighting, better heating, and sounder buildings. Urban life developed a style of its own, increasingly distinct from life in the countryside. Towns clustered around factories and railway stations, but cities teeming with the poor and indigent were also the thriving centers of communication, commerce, politics, and culture.

Social Welfare

Social questions were debated in hundreds of speeches and pamphlets and in newspaper articles that worried about public health and morals, class division, and pauperism. These discussions were filled with the appalling facts uncovered through parliamentary and private inquiries in Britain and scholarly investigations in France. These humanitarian attempts to improve the lot of the lower class had discouragingly modest results, although individual employers, especially in Britain and Alsace, improved conditions somewhat by building special housing for their workers, drab barracks that nonetheless seemed marvels of cleanliness and decency.

Charity   Middle-class radicals supported efforts like those of England's Society for the Diffusion of Useful Knowledge, founded in 1826 to carry enlightenment to the lower classes. They contributed to and gave lectures for workers at night schools, many of which were run by the Mechanics' Institutes (of which there were more than 700 in Great Britain by 1850) and by the Polytechnic Association of France (which had more than 100,000 participants by 1848). Thousands of middle-class people personally carried the lamp of truth to the poor in the form of Bibles, pious essays, moral stories, and informative descriptions of how machines worked. Ambitious members of the lower-middle class were, however, more likely than workers to take advantage of these opportunities.

For the truly poverty-stricken, charities were established at an astounding rate; more than 450 relief organizations were listed in London alone in 1853, and whole encyclopedias cataloging these undertakings were published in France. A revival of Christian zeal provided powerful impetus to such groups in Britain, and on the Continent new Catholic religious orders, most with specific social missions, were founded by the hundreds. They sponsored lectures, organized wholesome recreation to compete with the temptations of the tavern, set up trade apprenticeships, provided expectant

The visitation of the poor by charitable members of the middle class was expected to bring a good example as well as food and clothes.
Jean-Loup Charmet/Bridgeman Art Library

mothers with a clean sheet and a pamphlet on child care, opened savings banks that accepted even the tiniest deposit, campaigned for hygiene and temperance, gave away soup and bread, supported homes for abandoned children and fallen women, and ran nurseries, schools, and hostels. These good works were preeminently the province of women. Catholic nuns and Protestant matrons in the middle class were expected to uplift the poor by example as well as charity. The Society of St. Vincent de Paul believed that pious men could have a similar effect. Organized in Paris in 1835, it soon spread to all of Catholic Europe, requiring thousands of educated and well-to-do men to visit the poor regularly so that they might teach thrift and give hope by their very presence. Although these efforts were important for some lucky individuals and were a significant means of informing the comfortable about the plight of the poor, they were never adequate to the social challenge. Most of Europe's urban masses remained largely untouched by charity or religion.

Public Health In matters of public health, standards of housing, working conditions, and education, governments were forced to take a more active role. By modern standards the official measures were timid and hesitant. Vaccination, enforced by progressive governments, made smallpox less threatening. Beyond that, advances in medicine contributed little to public health. The great work of immunization would come later in the century. The most important medical gain of the 1840s was probably the use of anesthesia in surgery, dentistry, and childbirth.

Serious epidemics broke out in every decade. Typhus, carried by lice, was a constant threat, accounting for one death in nine in Ireland between 1816 and 1819, and infected water spread typhoid fever in city after city. A cholera epidemic, which apparently began along India's Ganges River in 1826, spread through East Asia, reaching Moscow and St. Petersburg by 1830; 100,000 people died of cholera in Russia in two years. From Russia it spread south and west, to Egypt and North Africa, to Poland, Austria, and into Germany, where it was reported in Hamburg in 1831. Despite efforts to put ports in quarantine (a move opposed by shipping interests), the disease reached northern England and then France in that same year and continued slowly to the south, taking a ninth of Palermo's population in the period from 1836 to 1837.

Reaction to the cholera epidemic in Britain, France, and Germany revealed much about social change. An official day of fasting, prayer, and humiliation in England and warnings of the archbishop of Paris that the cholera was divine retribution expressed the strength of traditional faith and revealed widespread distrust of an era of materialism and its claims to progress.

But governments were expected to act. Torn between two inaccurate theories of how the disease spread, governments mobilized inspectors to enforce such sanitary regulations as existed. (Not infrequently the inspectors faced riots by a populace fearful of medical body snatchers eager to dissect corpses.) In Paris and Lille, tenements were whitewashed by the tens of thousands, foods inspected, and streets and sewers cleaned by official order; similar steps were taken in the German states and in Britain, where the demonstrated inadequacy of local government prompted establishment of a national Public Health Commission with extraordinary powers over towns and individuals.

Carefully collected statistics led to a new understanding of how disease spread and of the importance of social factors for public health. Over the years, doctors and inspectors reported with troubled consciences on the terrible conditions they had found among lower-class neighbors whose quarters they had never visited before. Another cholera epidemic followed in the 1840s and lesser ones thereafter, but the shock and uncertainty of what to do was never again so great. Gradually, hospitals, too, came under more direct state supervision as the cost and complexity of medical treatment increased. By midcentury housing and sanitary codes regulated most of urban construction throughout the West, and inspectors were empowered to enforce these rules.

The Irish Famine Liberalism showed its other face in England's handling of the terrible potato famine in Ireland. As the potato blight struck late in 1845, disaster for a population so dependent on a single crop was not hard to predict. By winter hundreds of thousands of families sold what little they had to survive, were forced off the land, and began to suffer the diseases that accompany famine. Hope rested on a good harvest the following year. In spring and summer the potato plants emerged promisingly; but when desperate peasants dug them up, there was only stinking rot. In 1846 the blight was nearly total. In that year and the next, millions died, about a quarter of the population—the exact number will never be known. Roads were lined with bodies, huts abandoned. For several years some of England's ablest officials struggled with bureaucratic earnestness to collect information, organize relief, and maintain order in a corpse-strewn land; yet they were so inhibited by respect for the rules of liberal economics and the rights of property that their efforts had limited effect. In England, even those public figures most concerned to provide help to the Irish tended to view the famine as a natural disaster rather than a failure of policy; and many blamed Irish laziness for the country's dependence on potatoes, an easy crop to grow.

Ireland did produce grain, but that brought a better price in Britain. The landowners, mainly English and absentee, followed market principles and continued to export most of their wheat to England even as famine spread. Most Irish farmers rented the tiny plots they worked and paid for them principally by selling the pig or two they could raise on the same potatoes that provided their subsistence. When that crop failed and they had no money for rent, landlords usually forced them off the land. The relief law that denied aid to anyone who farmed more than a quarter acre of land had a similar effect, forcing tenants to abandon farming so their families might have food. The Irish famine, which made migration to the United States a part of Irish life and stimulated increased hatred of English rule, also fostered debate about what the responsibilities of a liberal government should be.

Government Regulation   In the 1830s and 1840s governments began reluctantly to regulate child labor, banning employment of those under nine years old in textile mills in Britain and factories in Prussia, under eight in factories in France, and under ten in mines in Britain. By the end of the 1840s, similar measures had been adopted in Bavaria, Baden, Piedmont, and Russia. Generally, the laws variously held the workday to eight or nine hours for children under twelve or thirteen years old and to twelve hours for those under sixteen or eighteen. Britain and France included additional requirements that the very young be provided with a couple of hours of schooling each day. To be effective, such regulations required teams of inspectors, provided for only in Britain, where earnest disciples of Jeremy Bentham applied the laws diligently. This expansion of government authority had been vigorously opposed by industrialists and many liberals; but mounting evidence of the harmful effects of industrial work made the need apparent, and the ability to gather such evidence became one of government's most important functions.

The most bitterly controversial welfare measure of the period was Britain's Poor Law of 1834. The old parish system of relief permitted each county to supplement local wages up to a level of subsistence determined by the price of bread. The system, expensive and inadequate to changing needs, was attacked by liberal economists, who charged that it cost too much and discouraged workers from migrating to new jobs. An extensive campaign for reform led to the Poor Law of 1834, based on the Benthamite notion that unemployment had to be made as unattractive as possible. Those receiving relief were required to live in workhouses, where discipline was harsh, conditions were kept suitably mean, and the sexes were separated. Workers bitterly resented the new law, and referred to the new institutions as Bastilles. On the Continent welfare measures kept more traditional forms while gradually shifting the responsibility for directing them from local and religious auspices to the state.

Education   Public education also became a matter of national policy. Prussia had declared local schooling compulsory in 1716, and efforts to enforce and regulate that requirement culminated in 1807 with the creation of a bureau of education. In the following decades the government, with the cooperation of the Lutheran clergy, established an efficient system of universal primary instruction with facilities now needed to train the teachers and to guarantee that the subject matter taught would remain rudimentary and politically safe. The network of secondary schools was also enlarged but kept quite separate, generally not admitting graduates of the ordinary primary schools. Most of the German states had similar arrangements, establishing nearly universal elementary education.

In France the French Revolution had provided the framework for a national system of free public schools meant as a substitute for the extensive but more informal and largely religious schools of the old regime. Slowly that vision of a national system of public schools took effect. By 1833 every commune was required to support a public school, and schooling steadily expanded while the quality of teachers improved and the power of inspectors over tightfisted local authorities increased. By the revolution of 1848, three-fourths of France's school-age children were receiving some formal instruction.

In Britain conflict between the Church of England and other Protestant churches prevented creation of a state-controlled system of elementary schools, a lack welcomed by those conservatives who opposed educating the masses. Nevertheless, Parliament voted in 1833 to underwrite the construction of private schools, and subsidies for education gradually increased in amount and scope each year thereafter. From Spain to Russia, elementary schools were favored by every government and passionately demanded by liberals. The public schools of Europe, inadequate and impoverished, offered little chance of social advancement to those forced to attend them, but few doubted that they could be a major instrument for improving society as well as a force for social peace.

THE SPREAD OF LIBERAL GOVERNMENT

These limited social programs were part of the great age of liberalism that began in 1830, made England its model, and spread to the Continent with revolution in France and the revolt that created Belgium. With the establishment of liberal governments, these representative monarchies of the West stood in sharp contrast to the autocratic governments of Central and Eastern Europe.

Great Britain

Britain's withdrawal in the 1820s from Metternich's Concert of Europe represented more than insular habit. The world's leading example of liberalism, Britain was coming to favor liberal programs in other countries, too. But the triumph of liberalism at home had not come without serious conflict.

Pressure for Change The turmoil of the postwar years was heightened by the economic crisis that resulted from demobilization and the collapse of wartime markets, and popular meetings echoed with cries of class resentment. The government's economic policies—removal of the wartime income tax and a higher tariff on grains, which made bread more expensive—favored the rich. To change policies required reform of the political system; heated agitation for that reform swept the country.

The government at first responded with repression. Habeas corpus was suspended for the first time in English history in 1817. A mass meeting for reform at St. Peter's Field, Manchester, in 1819 so terrified the local magistrates that they called out troops. In the ensuing charge, hundreds of demonstrators, including women and children, were wounded, and several were killed. With bitter mockery people called it the Peter-

loo Massacre (see the illustration on p. 695). Parliament responded by passing the Six Acts of 1819, which restricted public meetings, facilitated the prosecution of radicals, and imposed a stamp tax intended to cripple the radical press. Support for the established order continued to ebb, and the scandal of George IV's personal life earned public contempt. Old restrictions on Protestant dissenters and Roman Catholics (they could not hold public office, for example) now brought rising criticism of the special privileges accorded the Church of England.

Even an unreformed Parliament could be sensitive to public opinion, however, and it began to support compromises on some critical issues. The government reduced some tariffs and repealed the Combination Acts that had banned unions, although an amendment effectively outlawing strikes was soon added. As the minister in charge of the Home Office, Sir Robert Peel ceased the prosecution of newspapers and the use of political spies, halved the list of capital crimes, and put domestic order in the hands of civil authority by creating a police force. The Tories, who opposed such measures, looked to the conservative Duke of Wellington, the prestigious victor over Napoleon at Waterloo, to resist further change. Yet as prime minister even he saw the need to push through Parliament a measure he himself disliked, allowing Catholics and religious dissenters to vote and to hold public office.

All of these issues—religious freedom, the legitimacy of labor unions, tariffs, restrictions on the press—led to agitation that from London to Ireland increasingly focused on the need to reform Parliament itself. Elections in 1830, required by the death of King George IV and the accession of William IV, raised the political temperature. In the countryside, disenfranchised laborers set haystacks afire by night; by day, stern magistrates ordered laborers accused of seditious activity transported to Australia.

The Reform Bill of 1832 As public turmoil rose (and British leaders watched with concern the revolution of 1830 in France), a new cabinet presented a bill to reform the electoral system. The measure was approved in the House of Commons only after a new election and was then rejected in the Lords until the king reluctantly threatened to create enough new peers to get it through. Each defeat made the public mood uglier, and the king's intervention came amid demonstrations, the burning of the town hall and the bishop's palace in Bristol, and much dark talk about the French example.

The bill itself offered a good deal less than the more outspoken radicals had wanted, but it marked a fundamental change in Britain's electoral system. Suffrage was increased, allowing some 800,000 well-to-do men to vote, based on the property they owned or the rents

This cartoon of the 1819 Peterloo Massacre captures the sense of class hatred it evoked. Citizens, peaceably seeking reform, are wantonly trampled by His Majesty's overfed officials.
The Granger Collection, New York

they paid.[3] More important was the elimination of local variation in favor of a uniform national standard which, as many Tories warned, could easily be broadened in the future. Before the Reform Bill was passed, many boroughs that sent representatives to Parliament were barely villages (the most notorious, Old Sarum, was uninhabited), and the bustling cities of Birmingham and Manchester had had no representatives at all. Perhaps a third of the members of Parliament owed their seats to the influence of some lord. Now representation was at least crudely related to population, and the voices of commerce and manufacturing would be more numerous.

[3] This electorate was considerably broader than that established in either France or Belgium in 1830, though Belgium, the only country to give elected representatives a salary, had in many respects Europe's most liberal constitution. About 1 Frenchman in 160 could vote in 1830; 1 Briton in 32, after the Reform Bill of 1832. About 1 Belgian in 95 could vote by 1840; and 1 in 20 by 1848. Universal male suffrage permits approximately one-fifth of the total population to go to the polls.

Although restricted suffrage and social tradition (and open voting) guaranteed the continued dominance of the upper classes, Parliament was ready after 1832 to turn to other reforms. Slavery was abolished in Britain's colonies in 1833, a victory for Protestant reformers and humanitarian radicals. The Factory Act, limiting the hours children worked,[4] soon followed, as did the much-despised Poor Law of 1834. A law granting all resident taxpayers the right to vote in municipal elections challenged aristocratic influence even more directly than the Reform Bill of 1832. When young Victoria ascended the throne in 1837, representative government was stronger than ever. Her reign of more than six decades would rival that of Queen Elizabeth I as a period of British glory and power, but she would remain subordinate (often against her wishes) to an increasingly flexible political system.

[4] The work week was limited to 48 hours for children between the ages of six and thirteen, and to 69 hours for those between ages fourteen and eighteen.

Joseph Nash
INTERIOR OF THE HOUSE OF COMMONS
The British House of Commons sat in a new building of Gothic splendor that made parliamentary liberty seem ancient and the two-party system inevitable.
Houses of Parliament, Westminster, London, UK/Bridgeman Art Library

Chartism and the Corn Laws   Two great popular movements helped define the limits of that political system. **Chartism** was a huge, amorphous workers' movement, the central aim of which was political democracy, spelled out in what was called the People's Charter.[5] With articulate leaders and a working-class base, Chartists propagandized widely; held huge demonstrations in 1839, 1840, and 1848; and were accused of causing riots that ended with scores of deaths. Although treated by the state as dangerous revolutionaries, their principal tactic was to present Parliament with petitions containing tens of thousands of signatures (see "The Great Charter," p. 697). These petitions were summarily rejected, however, and by 1842 the movement was weakening. It failed, despite its size, to find a program that could for long mobilize the masses struggling for survival. And it failed, despite its emphasis on political rather than more threatening economic goals, to stir the consciences of those in power. Angry or desperate workers could riot here or there, but in England they were too isolated from one another and from other classes to gain their political, let alone their social, goals.

The other great popular movement, against the grain tariff, was victorious. The Anti-Corn Law League grew out of urban resentment over the high cost of bread resulting from grain tariffs—the **Corn Laws**—that bene-

fited the landowning classes. From Manchester the movement spread throughout the country, becoming a kind of crusade, an attack on the privileges of aristocracy in the name of the "productive orders" of society, the middle and working classes. The league's propaganda used the new techniques of popular politics: parades and rallies, songs and speeches, pamphlets and cartoons. Its slogans were printed on trinkets for children, ribbons for women, drinking cups for men. Two manufacturers, Richard Cobden and John Bright, proved effective spokesmen who became influential figures in public life, spreading the gospel of free trade across the land. To the upper classes, such activity seemed in terrible taste; and conservatives argued that the nation's greatness was rooted in its landed estates.

In the face of this sort of coalition of the middle and working classes, however, British politics proved responsive. Twice Sir Robert Peel's government lowered duties on a wide range of items, including grain, but the league demanded more. Finally, in 1845, Peel an-

[5] The six points of the People's Charter were universal male suffrage, a written ballot, abolition of property qualifications for members of Parliament, payment of the members, constituencies of equal population, and annual elections. All but the last of these points had been adopted by 1918.

THE GREAT CHARTER

The Chartist movement reached its peak in 1842 with the presentation to the House of Commons of the Great Charter. There were more than 3 million signatures on this petition calling for universal male suffrage, annual parliaments, lower taxes, and greater attention to the needs of the poor.

TO THE HONOURABLE THE COMMONS OF GREAT BRITAIN AND IRELAND, IN PARLIAMENT ASSEMBLED.

"The petition of the undersigned people of the United Kingdom. . . .

"That as Government was designed for the benefit and protection of, and must be obeyed and supported by all, therefore all should be equally represented.

"That any form of Government which fails to effect the purposes for which it was designed, and does not fully and completely represent the whole people, who are compelled to pay taxes to its support, and obey the laws resolved upon by it, is unconstitutional, tyrannical, and ought to be amended or resisted.

"That your honourable House, as at present constituted, has not been elected by, and acts irresponsibly of, the people; and hitherto has only represented parties, and benefited the few, regardless of the miseries, grievances, and petitions of the many. Your honourable House has enacted laws contrary to the expressed wishes of the people, and by unconstitutional means enforced obedience to them, thereby creating an unbearable despotism on the one hand, and degrading slavery on the other. . . .

"That the existing state of representation is not only extremely limited and unjust, but unequally divided, and gives preponderating influence to the landed, and monied interests, to the utter ruin of the small-trading and labouring classes.

"That bribery, intimidation, corruption, perjury, and riot, prevail at all parliamentary elections, to an extent best understood by the Members of your honourable House. . . .

"That your petitioners would direct the attention of your honourable House to the great disparity existing between the wages of the producing millions, and the salaries of those whose comparative usefulness ought to be questioned, where riches and luxury prevail amongst the rulers, and poverty and starvation amongst the ruled. . . .

"That your petitioners believe all men have a right to worship God as may appear best to their consciences, and that no legislative enactments should interfere between man and his Creator.

"That your petitioners maintain that it is the inherent, indubitable, and constitutional right, founded upon the ancient practice of the realm of England, and supported by well approved statutes, of every male inhabitant of the United Kingdom, he being of age and of sound mind, non-convict of crime, and not confined under any judicial process, to exercise the elective franchise in the choice of Members to serve in the Commons House of Parliament."

---

nounced his support for outright repeal of the Corn Laws. In 1846 he shepherded the measure through both the Commons and the Lords. The grain tariff was reduced to almost nothing, and nearly all duties were abolished or greatly lowered. As in 1832, the political system had bent when demands for reform gained widespread support among the middle class, but Peel's courage split his party and ended his ministry. He was jeered by angry Tories as a young newcomer, Benjamin Disraeli, rose to decry Peel's treachery to the great landlords. Yet the growing weight of public opinion and the liberal creed had triumphed; the sphere of political debate had expanded to include vexing social issues.

The Revolutions of 1830

Uprisings across Europe   The cause of reform in Britain had benefited from fear of revolution, following a wave of revolutions on the Continent in 1830. The first of these occurred in France. Brief and largely limited to Paris, it was a revolution nevertheless, and any uprising in France was a European event. Minor revolts stimulated by the French example occurred in central Italy, Spain, Portugal, some of the German principalities, and Poland. Austria once again extinguished revolt in Italy, and the Russian army crushed Poland's rebels; elsewhere, the results were more lasting.

Belgium   In the southern Netherlands, Catholics and liberals took the occasion to rise against Dutch rule. This revolt was a direct challenge to the provisions of the Congress of Vienna. Britain opposed any intervention by the great powers, however, once convinced that France had no territorial designs on the Netherlands; and Britain led in arranging international guarantees for the independence of the southern Netherlands, which became Belgium. The British and French then pressured the Dutch to acquiesce.

The Belgian monarchy established in 1830 was one of the triumphs of liberal constitutionalism. The new

Mass meetings had been one of the Chartists' most effective devices, and this one held on Kensington Common in London, April 10, 1848, was one of the most publicized. With revolution on the Continent and famine in Ireland, radical hopes were as high as conservative fears. The twenty thousand who attended this meeting had passed armed soldiers, policemen, and special constables. The expectation of violence explains the small number of women and children in this photograph. What might have been the beginning of a revolution in England was instead the Chartists' last national demonstration.
The Royal Archives © 2002 Her Majesty Queen Elizabeth II

state, which owed its existence both to French restraint and British protection, took as its king Leopold I, who had lived long in England (he was an uncle of Queen Victoria) and who soon married the daughter of Louis Philippe. The constitution went further than France's in guaranteeing civil rights and the primacy of the Chamber of Deputies. Politics revolved around a coalition—rare in Europe—of Catholics and liberals, aristocrats and members of the upper-middle class.

Rapidly becoming the most industrialized nation on the Continent, Belgium was prosperous. Self-confident and satisfied with the new order of things, the Belgians built on the administrative traditions left from earlier Austrian and French rule as well as that of the Dutch and proved themselves remarkably adept at planning railroads, reforming taxes and schools, and making timely political concessions.

France's July Monarchy   In France, Charles X's abdication led not to the succession of his son, as the king had hoped, but to a provisional government. Organized largely in newspaper offices, it soon settled for a liberal monarchy. Most of France was ready to accept that compromise when the Marquis de Lafayette, still a republican and a popular hero, stepped out on the balcony of the town hall to present the candidate for the throne. Louis Philippe, head of the House of Orleáns, the liberal branch of the royal line, whose father had voted with the Jacobins for the death of his cousin, Louis XVI. The symbols of revolution and moderation were neatly combined in France's new monarchy.

Louis Philippe's posters proclaimed him citizen-king, and the Revolution's tricolor replaced the Bourbon flag. Known as the **July Monarchy,** the new regime began with a constitution presented as a contract the king swore to keep, not as a gift he granted. Similar to the one it replaced, the contract offered stronger guarantees of political freedom, lowered property requirements for voters (nearly doubling their number to some 170,000, safely restricted to men of means), and replaced the hereditary upper house with lifetime peers. Because most of the old aristocracy resigned their offices, never to return to public life, there was an important change in government personnel. Those who replaced the aristocracy were professional people and bearers of newer (often Napoleonic) titles. In his appeal to the people of Paris, Louis Philippe sounded more radical than he was, and the new government hastened to assure Europe's other monarchs that this French revolution would send no militants to sponsor or support revolution elsewhere.

The overriding political question of the 1830s in France was the July Monarchy itself, which was attacked from left and right. Louis Philippe presented himself as a good bourgeois, while the regime's opponents on both sides sought broader support. With strong Catholic support, legitimists (those in favor of the Bourbons) campaigned in the countryside and the newspapers. In 1832 the duchess of Berry, whose infant son was now the legitimist claimant to the throne, tried to stage an uprising. Republicans were active, too, often in secret groups that had provocative names like

Eugène Delacroix
LIBERTY LEADING THE PEOPLE,
28 JULY 1830
Delacroix's painting presents the revolution of 1830 in France as the heroic rising of the people, poor and middle class together, being led by Liberty into a new era.
Louvre, Paris, France/Peter Willi/
Bridgeman Art Library

Jeanron's depiction of a Parisian barricade in 1830 (later used to illustrate Louis Blanc's socialist history of the period) presents a more realistic scene of the fighting than Delacroix's more famous version, but a similar heroic vision of workers and middle class together.
Roger-Viollet/Getty Images

the Society of the Rights of Man. When the silk workers of Lyons went on strike in 1834, it was viewed as a republican revolt and was suppressed with the bitterness of class hatred by the bourgeois National Guard.

Limited Liberalism in France   Despite such turbulence, the July Monarchy presented itself as a center of stability and patriotism, even laying claim to the cult

of Napoleon I by bringing the emperor's body back from St. Helena and placing it with nationalist pomp in the marble crypt of the Invalides. The government built on the administrative system that had developed under the Revolution and Napoleon to promote public education, new if limited social services, and industrialization. With time (and restrictions on the press) opposition quieted, and many of the

Carefully staged ceremonies marked the return of Napoleon's ashes from St. Helena for internment in Paris on December 15, 1840, as a national, patriotic event.
AKG London

middle-class notables of France rallied to a government of cautious moderation that talked of progress.

A regime largely isolated from workers, peasants, and the old aristocracy had found in nationalism its most effective means of propaganda. Yet it remained divided between those who wanted further reform and wider suffrage and those, like the king himself, who believed the proper balance between liberty and order had been achieved. The former were led by Adolphe Thiers; the latter, by François Guizot. Both were journalists and historians of great talent; but their skillful verbal duels in parliament failed to mobilize opinion in France as agitation over the Corn Laws had done in England. From 1840 to 1848 the government was dominated by Guizot. A Protestant in a Catholic country, an intellectual in politics, a man who held broad principles rigidly, Guizot had in excess failings common to many liberals of the nineteenth century. He spoke of liberty, progress, and law in eloquent terms that made his cautious practices seem hypocritical. In 1848 the whole regime fell as easily as incumbents losing an election.

The two freest and most prosperous of Europe's great nations had developed similarly since 1830. In both, liberal governments led by able men sought through reasonable compromise, the rule of law, and parliamentary politics to unify their nations and to make "progress" compatible with stability. Discontent and workers' misery, though frightening, were understood in the councils of government primarily as a threat to order. In England reform had to be wrung from a powerful aristocracy that was, in the end, secure enough to cede under pressure. In France the aristocracy counted for little after 1830; but the government, fearful of the more radical hopes for democracy and social justice that it excluded, remained uncertain of its popular support.

Spain   The victories of French and British liberalism seemed part of a general trend. In Spain the monarchy itself wooed liberals. When King Ferdinand VII died in 1833, he had carefully arranged for his three-year-old daughter, Isabella, to succeed him. But the king's brother, Don Carlos, denounced the arrangement as illegal and began an uprising that lasted until 1839. The Carlists, who favored autocracy and the traditional claims of Spanish Catholicism, found their greatest support in rural areas and regions of the north that were resentful of rule from Madrid. Despite eventual defeat, Don Carlos won a place in Spanish legend as a dashing and chivalric hero, protector of old Spanish virtues. Carlism would remain a conservative rallying cry in every subsequent Spanish revolution.

To win liberal support, the regency ruling in Isabella's name granted a constitution in 1834. Cautiously modeled on the French constitution of 1814, with narrow suffrage and protection of royal power, it established representative institutions as a lasting feature of Spanish politics. Even so modest a step placed Spain in the liberal camp, and Isabella's government relied on extensive support from Britain and France against threats from abroad. Internal war brought generals into politics and conflict between two camps: the moderates (who supported the constitution of 1834 and admired Guizot's France) and the anticlerical progressives (who demanded a democratic constitution and the election of local officials). Only after a couple of military coups did moderates establish a regime in the 1840s strong enough to hold power for a decade. Everywhere, the changes that brought constitutions, limited suffrage, and circumscribed freedoms were based on a delicate balance that proved difficult to maintain.

Summary

Clusters of ideas about the nature of historical change, about how to prevent revolutions or achieve them, and about the kind of future that industrialization might bring had grown into the ideologies that have divided Western social thought ever since. In the arts and philosophy, Romanticism pointed nostalgically to the past but also toward the new, hailing individual genius yet yearning for community. Conservatives sustained standards critical of the new age; liberals gained strength from their confidence in the future; and socialists envisioned an alternative to capitalist industrialization. From 1815 on, a variety of political experiments, each claiming to be permanent, had been tried in Europe. The problem for conservative regimes was to increase their political effectiveness while preserving as much of the old social order as possible. Although liberal regimes fostered the benefits of uniform justice, legal equality, individual rights, and broader political participation, they faced the question of how far such principles could be taken without creating instability. They, like the conservative regimes they replaced, were a compromise. In fact, all available ideas, institutions, and policies were challenged by the social changes that accompanied industrialization, factory labor, demographic growth, and urbanization. Living with change had become a definition of modernity. There was an explosive mixture in these intellectual, social, and political trends; and they came together in the revolutions that swept across Europe in 1848 and in the increased emphasis on the importance of the state, especially a national state that could demand the loyalty of its citizens.

QUESTIONS FOR FURTHER THOUGHT

1. What explains the relevance, two centuries later, of political and cultural ideologies that took shape during the French Revolution and early years of industrialization?
2. How is it that society can still be described in terms of social classes despite all the social and political changes that have occurred?
3. What kinds of people are most likely to be drawn to liberalism or to reject its appeal? Does that change over time?

RECOMMENDED READING

Sources

Engels, Friedrich. *The Condition of the Working Class in England.* Written in 1844 and available in many modern editions, this influential work by Karl Marx's friend and coauthor paints a dark picture of the working-class slum and conveys the moral outrage radicals felt.

Novels are important sources for understanding nineteenth-century society. Elizabeth Gaskell (*Mary Barton* and *North and South*) and Charles Dickens (*Hard Times* and *Oliver Twist*) provided contemporaries with an influential picture of social conditions in England; Honoré de Balzac's *Père Goriot* set the tone for criticisms of the selfishness of the middle class.

Studies

*Bellamy, Richard. *Liberalism and Modern Society: A Historical Argument.* 1992. Treats the changes over time and the national differences in the meanings of liberalism.

Berdahl, Robert M. *The Politics of the Prussian Nobility: The Development of a Conservative Ideology.* 1988. Shows how political interests and social structure led to the formation of a conservatism that dominated much of German history.

*Briggs, Asa. *Victorian Cities.* 1970. Colorful studies of the urban politics and social life of individual cities.

Brock, Michael. *The Great Reform Act.* 1974. Analyzes the significance of the Reform Bill of 1832 through a close examination of the political and social forces that brought it about.

Church, Clive H. *Europe in 1830: Revolution and Political Change.* 1983. A study that emphasizes the significance of the revolutions of 1830 by noting their transnational connections and impact.

Coffin, Judith G. *The Politics of Women's Work: The Paris Garment Trades, 1750–1915.* 1996. The quintessential women's work was in the garment industry, and this study reveals the long evolution of women in the labor movement and of ideas about gender.

*Davidoff, Leonore, and Catherine Hall. *Family Fortunes: Men and Women of the English Middle Class, 1780–1850.* 1985. A rich and concrete picture of the aspirations and concerns of middle-class life.

Dennis, Richard. *English Industrial Cities of the Nineteenth Century.* 1984. A comprehensive study of the special problems of this new kind of city.

Foster, R. F. *Modern Ireland 1600–1972.* 1988. A magisterial, well-written synthesis.

Franklin, S. H. *The European Peasantry: The Final Phase.* 1969. These essays on different countries reveal not only the striking differences in peasants' lives but the importance of the peasantry for understanding the general history of European nations.

*Hamerow, Theodore S. *Restoration, Revolution, and Reaction: Economics and Politics in Germany, 1815–1871.* 1958. A complex analysis of the relationship of social classes and the state to economic change in this revolutionary period.

Harrison, J. F. C. *The Early Victorians, 1832–1851.* 1971. A lively account of the personalities and issues that marked the beginning of a new era.

*Heilbroner, Robert L. *The Worldly Philosophers.* 1972. A good introduction to the ideas of the economic liberals.

Holmes, Stephen. *Benjamin Constant and the Making of Modern Liberalism.* 1984. The biographical focus offers a valuable insight into the evolution of liberalism on the Continent.

*Hopkins, Eric. *Industrialisation and Society: A Social History, 1830–1951.* 2000. A wide-ranging discussion of the impact of industrialization on British society through the nineteenth century and on to the welfare state.

Johnson, Douglas. *Guizot: Aspects of French History.* 1963. Essays on the dominant figure of the July Monarchy reveal the tensions between aspirations for a liberal society and conservative fear for order.

Katznelson, Ira, and Artistide R. Zolberg (eds.). *Working-Class Formation: Nineteenth-Century Patterns in Western Europe and the United States.* 1986. Interpretive essays by some leading scholars take a fresh look at how working-class awareness was formed.

*Lichtheim, George. *A Short History of Socialism.* 1975. Well-constructed treatment of the evolution of socialist ideas in their historical context.

*Lindemann, Albert S. *A History of European Socialism.* 1984. Establishes the line of continuity from the early socialists through labor movements and the eventual dominance of Marxism.

*Lukács, Georg. *The Historical Novel.* Hannah and Stanley Mitchell (trs.). 1962. Insightful study of the social significance of the nineteenth-century novel by one of Europe's leading Marxist scholars.

Perkin, Harold. *The Origins of Modern English Society, 1780–1860.* 1969. Provides a clear picture of the diverse sectors of English society and how they adapted to the changes of the period.

Porter, Roy, and Mikul Teich (eds.). *Romanticism in National Context.* 1988. Particularly useful for the student because this volume of interpretive essays includes many on smaller European nations.

Price, Roger. *A Social History of Nineteenth-Century France.* 1987. A clear synthesis of recent research that provides an excellent introduction.

*Riasanovsky, Nicholas V. *The Emergence of Romanticism.* 1992. An introduction to the origins of European Romanticism that emphasizes its importance for rising nationalism.

Saville, John. *1848: The British State and the Chartist Movement.* 1987. Why Chartism failed to win its aims.

Segalen, Martine. *Love and Power in the Peasant Family: Rural France in the Nineteenth Century.* J. C. Whitehouse and Sarah Mathews (trs.). 1983.

*Sewell, William H., Jr. *Work and Revolution in France: The Language of Labor from the Old Regime to 1848.* 1980. An important study that shows the radical potential and continuing strength of a preindustrial working-class culture.

*Thompson, Dorothy. *The Chartists: Popular Politics in the Industrial Revolution.* 1984. A lively and sympathetic account that relates working-class action to the larger social context.

*Thompson, Edward P. *The Making of the English Working Class.* 1964. A remarkable work of sympathetic insight and exhaustive research that continues to influence studies of the working class in all societies.

Walker, Mack. *German Home Towns: Community, State, and General Estate, 1648–1871.* 1971. Sensitive treatment of the response of small-town life to political and social change.

*Weiss, John. *Conservatism in Europe, 1770–1945: Traditionalism, Reaction, and Counter-Revolution.* 1977. A valuable survey of the rich variety and social insight in conservative thought and of its political importance.

*Available in paperback.

Anton von Werner
PROCLAMATION OF THE GERMAN EMPIRE ON JANUARY 18, 1871 AT THE HALL OF MIRRORS IN VERSAILLES, 1885
Victory and the birth of a new Germany: The halls of Versailles ring as Prussian officers hail the proclamation of Prussia's King Wilhelm as German Kaiser.

Chapter Twenty-Four

NATIONAL STATES AND NATIONAL CULTURES

THE REVOLUTIONS OF 1848 • THE POLITICS OF NATIONALISM •
NINETEENTH-CENTURY CULTURE

In the spring of 1848, revolution swept across Europe from France to Hungary. Popular uprisings seemed to transform Europe in a few dramatic months; yet the revolutionary regimes were soon suppressed. They nevertheless demonstrated that revolution could erupt at any time, that demands for political freedom could win passionate support, that class conflict could be explosive, that military power could be decisive, and that nationalism could make the broadest appeal of all. In the next thirty years, two new national states, Italy and Germany, came into being and governments everywhere took increased responsibility for shaping public life. That included supporting a formal culture that was both an expression of national identity and a means of defining and propagating it.

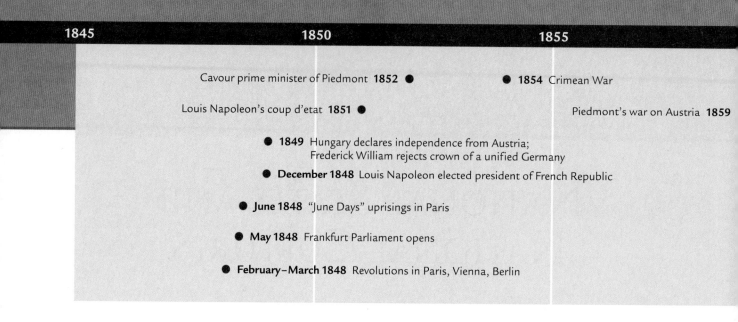

1845   1850   1855

Cavour prime minister of Piedmont **1852** ●

Louis Napoleon's coup d'etat **1851** ●

● **1854** Crimean War

Piedmont's war on Austria **1859**

● **1849** Hungary declares independence from Austria;
Frederick William rejects crown of a unified Germany

● **December 1848** Louis Napoleon elected president of French Republic

● **June 1848** "June Days" uprisings in Paris

● **May 1848** Frankfurt Parliament opens

● **February–March 1848** Revolutions in Paris, Vienna, Berlin

THE REVOLUTIONS OF 1848

The revolutions of 1848 spread by a kind of spontaneous imitation from city to city, their causes, early successes, and ultimate defeat somewhat different in each case. Yet all of them went through comparable phases in which easy victory and initial euphoria was followed by rising social conflict and, ultimately, by the triumph of the forces of order.

Two years of poor harvests and industrial recession in most of Europe preceded these outbreaks, but economic crisis alone does not make a revolution. In Ireland more than a million people died from starvation during the famine years from 1846 to 1849, yet that tragedy did little more to shake British rule than the Chartist movement. In Switzerland, Belgium, and the Netherlands, major liberalization occurred without a serious revolt. Revolutions occurred where governments were distrusted and where the fear and resentment fed by rising food prices and unemployment found focus in specific political demands.

The Opening Phase

France In France Guizot's government refused to widen the suffrage, and that led to the fall of the July Monarchy. The parliamentary opposition launched a protest movement that staged large banquets across the country. When a nervous government, aware of its unpopularity, banned the banquet scheduled for Paris in late February 1848, some members of the Chamber of Deputies announced they would attend anyway. Crowds gathered in the streets, and workers who could never have afforded banquet tickets started to build barricades. The rituals of revolution had begun. Louis Philippe, ever sensitive to middle-class opinion, held a review of his citizen militia, the National Guard. When

they sullenly refused to cheer him, Louis Philippe knew his days were numbered. He abdicated in favor of his grandson and left for England, much as Charles X had done just eighteen years before.

A provisional government of men chosen by two rival newspapers appeared at the Hôtel de Ville and declared France a republic. The Paris crowds cheered, and political clubs organized. The new cabinet—led by Alphonse de Lamartine, a handsome and much-admired Romantic poet—was dominated by moderates who at first cooperated with more radical members, including a socialist, Louis Blanc. They agreed that the republic should adopt universal male suffrage, a degree of democracy allowed in no other large nation. They proclaimed the citizens' right to work as a principle of government and established a commission to hold public hearings on problems of labor.

At the same time, the new regime was careful to demonstrate its restraint. It refused to intervene on behalf of revolutions in other countries, rejected proposals for adopting a red flag as the symbol of socialism and kept the familiar tricolor, and levied new taxes to balance the budget. Relations with the Catholic Church were the best in a generation, and April elections for a constituent assembly took place in good order. Nearly 85 percent of the eligible electorate voted, giving moderate republicans an overwhelming majority. The Second Republic seemed solidly established.

Revolution Spreads As news of the events in France sped across Europe, a conservative nightmare became a reality. Nearly every capital had citizens who found exciting promise in words like *constitution, rights, liberty,* and *free press.* In Hungary the Diet cheered Lajos Kossuth, the Magyar leader, as he called on March 3 for representative government. In the same week, demon-

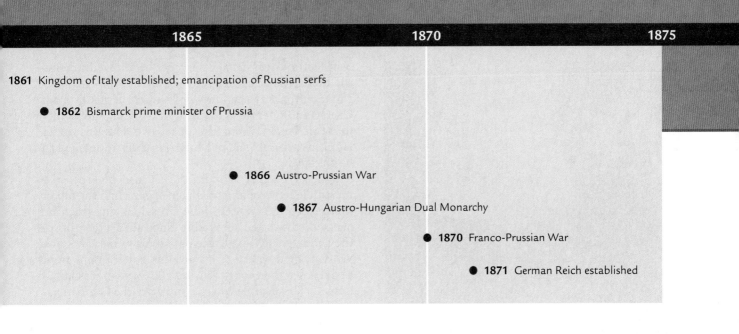

1861 Kingdom of Italy established; emancipation of Russian serfs

● **1862** Bismarck prime minister of Prussia

● **1866** Austro-Prussian War

● **1867** Austro-Hungarian Dual Monarchy

● **1870** Franco-Prussian War

● **1871** German Reich established

Felix Philippoteaux
LAMARTINE REJECTS THE RED FLAG, 1848
Lamartine persuades the crowd to reject the red flag and let the new French republic keep the tricolor.
Musée du Petit Palais, Paris. Giraudon/Bridgeman Art Library

strations with similar demands erupted in the cities of the Rhineland, soon giving way to revolution there and then in Vienna (March 12), Berlin (March 15), Milan (March 18), and Venice (March 22). Each of these revolutions followed a similar pattern. The news from France would attract excited crowds; groups of men—especially journalists, lawyers, and students—would meet in cafés to discuss rumors and newspaper reports. Governments that did not quickly grant constitutions (as they had tended to do in Italy) would call out troops to maintain order; and with a kind of inevitability,

some incident would occur—a shot fired by a soldier insulted once too often or by someone in the crowd with an unfamiliar gun.

Then barricades would rise in the style that came from Paris, constructed of paving stones, a passing coach ceremoniously overturned, nearby trees, and furniture. Barricades became the people's voice, threatening but vague, as workers and professional people, men, women, and children labored together. When blood was shed, the crowd had its martyrs. In Paris corpses were carried around on a cart as a spur to revolutionary

In one of the early triumphs of the 1848 revolutions, the citizens of Milan forced the Austrian Army to leave the city. Everyone now knew how to build barricades, and the whole family helped, using whatever was available.
Museo del Risorgimento, Milan. © G. Costa/Index

determination; in Berlin the king, supporting his fainting queen, acceded to the crowd's demands and paid his respects, bareheaded, to the subjects his own troops had killed. When new concessions were won, the atmosphere would grow festive. New flags would fly, often a tricolor, an echo of the French Revolution but with colors symbolizing some other nation. In the almost universal dedication to politics, newspapers and pamphlets appeared in floods (one hundred new newspapers in Vienna, nearly five hundred in Paris). Radicals would seek ever after to recapture the unanimity and joy of those early days of revolution. Others, and not just conservatives, would never forget fearsome crowds, fanatical faces, and ugly threats.

Central Europe   In the Austrian Empire, the Hungarian Diet had by mid-March established a free press and a national guard, abolished feudal obligations (with compensation to the lords), and required nobles to pay taxes. Everyone noticed the parallel to 1789. Reluctantly Vienna agreed that Hungary could levy its own taxes and direct its own army. The Hungarian example encouraged students in Vienna to demand representative government for Austria as well, and crowds soon clashed with the troops and formed specific demands. In rapid order Metternich resigned, censorship was abolished, a constitution was promised, and firearms were passed out to the students. When students rejected the proposal that all men ex-

cept factory workers and servants be allowed to vote, the monarchy conceded universal male suffrage. Hungarian autonomy then brought similar demands from Czechs in Bohemia, Croatians in Croatia, and Romanians in Transylvania (these last two domains under Hungarian rule). The old Austrian Empire seemed to be collapsing.

When Frederick William IV of Prussia learned the incredible news of an uprising in Vienna and the fall of Metternich, he granted the concessions on which he had stalled, relaxed censorship, and called a meeting of the Landtag. Fighting broke out anyway, and Frederick William then agreed to remove his hated troops from Berlin, used the evocative word *Germany* in proclamations to "my dear Berliners," and wore the German national colors: black, gold, and red. A constituent assembly was elected in May by universal but indirect male suffrage, and when it met in Berlin, where a civic guard now kept order, revolution seemed to have triumphed in Prussia, too.

Events in the rest of Germany confirmed that victory. In May, 830 delegates elected in the various German states convened the **Frankfurt Parliament** to write a constitution for all of Germany. Mostly liberals, more than half of them were lawyers and professors, but there were also businessmen, members of the liberal gentry, and even nobles. The great majority favored a monarchical German state under a liberal constitution as the brilliant, difficult, and noisy assembly set about to write a constitution for a united Germany.

The arrangements contrived in 1815 at the Congress of Vienna were under siege in Italy as well, where in the 1820s and 1830s the kingdoms of Piedmont in the north and Naples (including Sicily) in the south had barely weathered earlier revolts, which had also threatened the smaller duchies in between. A well-organized rising in Palermo against rule from Naples was actually the first of the revolutions in 1848; but it was news of the revolution in Paris that made it possible to demand constitutions in Naples, Tuscany, and Piedmont. Even the Papal States got a constitution, though it awkwardly preserved a veto for the pope and the College of Cardinals. Lombardy and Venetia had been ruled as part of the Habsburg Empire since 1815, but shortly after the revolution in Vienna, a revolt broke out in Milan against the Austrian forces there. The Austrians were forced to retreat, and the "Five Glorious Days of Milan" were added to the heroic legends of March. Then Venice rose up to reestablish the Venetian republic of old, and the possibility that the Italian peninsula might be freed from foreign rule stimulated a nationalist fervor that forced Piedmont to join the war against Austria.

CHRONOLOGY
The Opening Phase
1848

France	German States		Italian States
	Habsburg Empire	*Prussia*	
Feb. 22 Barricades in Paris.	**Mar. 3** Hungarian demands.	**Mar. 15** Berlin rising.	**Jan. 12** Palermo revolt.
Feb. 23 Louis Philippe abdicates; Republic proclaimed.	**Mar. 12** Student risings in Vienna.	**Mar. 18–21** Prussian king calls Landtag.	**Feb. 10** King in Naples grants constitution.
Apr. 23 French elections.	**Mar. 13** Metternich resigns.	**May 18** Frankfurt national assembly meets.	**Mar. 4** Constitution granted in Piedmont.
	Mar. 15–31 Liberal legislation; Hungarian autonomy.	**May 22** Prussian constituent assembly meets.	**Mar. 14** Pope grants constitution.
	Apr. 25 Emperor proclaims constitution for Austria.		**Mar. 18–22** Milan revolt: Five Glorious Days.
	May 15 Demonstrators in Vienna demand democracy.		**Mar. 22** Venice declares republic.
			May 30 Italian troops defeat Austrians.

The Fatal Dissensions

Social Class   Everywhere, however, the new freedom exposed divisions among those who had fought for it. In France these divisions were primarily social—between Paris and the countryside, between the middle class and the workers. Workers agitated for a social program and pinned their hopes on the national workshops that had been established as an echo of ideas popularized by the socialist Louis Blanc. Imagined as cooperatives in which workers would work for themselves and share the profits, the workshops that the Republic established were in practice little more than a program of temporary public relief. Unemployed men from Paris and the countryside nevertheless enrolled by the tens of thousands. To moderate republicans the workshops represented a dangerous principle and outrageous waste. The government ordered them disbanded in June. To workers the workshops represented a symbolic promise and the beginning of a new era. They responded by building barricades in the working-class sections of Paris. For three days workers fought with the ferocity of hopelessness before the Republic's troops under General Cavaignac systematically crushed the threat to order.

More than a thousand people died; thousands more would be sent to prison or into exile. The **June Days** re-mained the very symbol of class conflict for socialists, and radicals never quite recaptured their faith that democracy alone would lead to social justice. Given almost dictatorial powers, Cavaignac took steps to restrict the press, suppress radical societies, and discipline workers. Yet Cavaignac remained a convinced republican, and the assembly continued to write a constitution that maintained universal suffrage and provided for a president directly elected by popular vote. But after June there was something a little hollow about the Second Republic.

National Ambitions   In Germany and Austria, also, revolution uncovered latent conflicts between workers and the middle class and among artisans, peasants, and nobles. But the outcome was determined more by competing nationalisms and the fact that kings still had their armies. The Frankfurt parliament felt little sympathy for uprisings by other nationalities against German rule. Instead of protesting the repression of revolution, it congratulated the Austrian field marshal who bombarded Prague (where Czechs had staged a Pan-Slav conference) on his German victory; and it applauded the Austrian forces that regrouped in northern Italy and fought their way back into Milan. It called on the Prussian army to put down a Polish uprising in Posen and to fight against Danes in

Ernest Meissonier
The Barricade in Rue Mortellerie, Paris, June 1848
A silent street in Paris after the June Days, its rubble, bodies, and blood—the emblems of revolution defeated.
Louvre, Paris, France. Erich Lessing/Art Resource, NY

Venice and France were also republics, and assemblies were still busy drafting constitutions in Vienna, Berlin, and Frankfurt, but there could be no doubt that conservative forces were gaining ground.

The Final Phase

New Leaders In December, France elected a president, and the candidates who had been prominent in the new republic finished far behind Louis Napoleon Bonaparte, who won 70 percent of the votes. The ambitious nephew of Emperor Napoleon, he had campaigned as a republican. He had written more about social questions and workers' needs than any other candidate, and he was supported by the Catholic Church and the monarchists, for want of anyone else, as a man of order. Above all, he had his name.[1]

Austria, too, found a strong new leader in Prince Felix von Schwarzenberg, who filled the place Metternich left vacant. In December he persuaded the emperor to abdicate in favor of his eighteen-year-old nephew, Franz Joseph I, who could promise a fresh start. In Prussia the king felt confident enough to dissolve the Landtag and promulgate a constitution of his own. Ten months of turmoil had led back to the arrangements of February.

Military Force One by one, the remaining revolutionary regimes were subdued. The Frankfurt Assembly, having completed its constitution for a unified Germany, in March 1849 elected the Prussian king as German emperor, only to have him reject this "crown from the gutter," declaring that the ones he recognized came by grace of God. The Frankfurt constitution—with its list of old abuses to be abolished, its universal male suffrage and promises of civil rights and education—would never be tested (see "The Frankfurt Constitution," p. 713). New revolutions broke out in the Rhineland, Saxony, and Baden, but all were quashed in June and July with the aid of Prussian troops. The Habsburgs' multinational armies bombarded the revolutionaries of Vienna into submission and soon turned on Hungary, where a republic had been declared because Schwarzenberg refused to permit Hungary to have a constitution. The Hungarians battled for months against the armies of Austria and against Croatians and Romanians until Russia

Schleswig. In September, when riots broke out in Frankfurt itself, the assembly invited Prussian troops to restore order. Conflicts among multiple nationalities were also strengthening the Habsburgs at home, as the emperor mobilized Croatians demanding autonomy from Hungary much as Hungary had from Austria. In parts of the empire, Austrian officials were also able to win peasant support by abolishing serfdom and by playing on their distrust of local revolutionaries.

The armies that soon moved on Frankfurt and Vienna confronted resistance that, like the June Days in Paris, revealed popular fury and more radical demands than the risings of February and March. Politics turned more radical in Rome, too, where the pope had proved not to be an Italian nationalist; economic conditions worsened, and a government that had promised much accomplished little. When his prime minister was assassinated, Pius IX slipped across the border into the Kingdom of Naples, and a representative assembly gave the eternal city its ancient title of Roman Republic.

---

[1] On trial for his attempted coup in 1840, Louis Napoleon had concluded his defense with these words: "I represent before you a principle, a cause, and a defeat: the principle is sovereignty of the people; the cause, that of the Empire; the defeat, Waterloo. The principle you have recognized; the cause you have served; the defeat you want to avenge."

CHRONOLOGY
Fatal Dissensions
1848

France	German States		Italy
	Habsburg Empire	*Prussia*	
June 23–26 June Days insurrection.	**June 12** Prague bombarded; Pan-Slav congress dissolved.	**June–Sept.** Frankfurt assembly supports Prussia against Danes in Schleswig.	**July 24** Austrians defeat Italian army.
Nov. 4 Constitution.	**June 22** Assembly in Vienna adopts constitution, peasants emancipated.		**Nov. 25** Pope flees Rome.
	Sept. 17 Habsburg army from Croatia invades Hungary.		
	Oct. 31 Vienna bombarded, occupied.		

An engraving of the violence in Frankfurt in September 1848 contrasts the fighting styles of troops and the defenders of revolution.
The Granger Collection, New York

intervened in June to seal the fate of the Hungarian republic.

In Italy, too, military force was decisive. Austria defeated Piedmont one more time, leaving it nothing to show for its support of Italian independence except an enormous debt, an unpopular government, a new ruler, a cautious constitution, and the red, white, and green flag of Italian nationalism. Ten years later the constitution and the flag would seem quite a lot; for the time being, Austrian power once again dominated

CHRONOLOGY
The Final Phase
1848–1849

France	German States		Italy
	Habsburg Empire	*Prussia*	
Dec. 20 Louis Napoleon elected president.	**Dec. 2.** Francis Joseph, emperor.	**Dec. 5** Prussian assembly dissolved.	**Feb. 9** Roman Republic established.
	Jan. 5 Budapest occupied.	**Mar. 27** Frankfurt constitution completed; rejected by Prussia on Apr. 21.	**Mar. 23** Decisive defeat of Piedmont by Austria.
	Mar. 4 Austrian Assembly dissolved.	**July** Last insurgents crushed in Baden.	**Apr. 24** French army lands in Papal States.
	Apr. 13 Hungary declares a republic.		**June 30** Rome falls to French.
	June 17 Russia invades Hungary.		**Aug. 28** Venice surrenders.
	Aug. 13 Hungary capitulates.		

the Italian peninsula. There was soon a further foreign presence in the center of Italy, for Louis Napoleon sent French armies to restore the pope and defeat the Roman Republic, which fought with heroic tenacity for three months before being overrun. The Kingdom of Naples did not reconquer Sicily until May 1849 and only after a bombardment of the city of Messina that gave Ferdinand II the nickname King Bomba. The last of the revolutionary regimes to fall was the Venetian republic, defeated in August 1849 more by starvation and cholera than by the Austrian artillery that accomplished the unprecedented feat of lobbing shells three miles from the mainland into the island city.

The Results A famous liberal historian, G. M. Trevelyan, called 1848 "the turning-point at which modern history failed to turn," and his epigram captures the sense of destiny thwarted that still colors the liberal view of 1848. Current historical analysis of the failures of 1848 generally makes five broad points. First, liberal constitutions and increased civil rights failed to pull strong and lasting support from artisans, peasants, and workers, whose more immediate needs were neither met nor understood. Second, the revolutions of February and March were made primarily by the middle classes, strengthened by popular discontent; but when radicals sought more than representative government and legal equality, the middle classes worried about order and private property. Isolated from the

masses, they were too weak to retain power except in France; and there order came only after repression of the urban poor and erosion of constitutional liberties. Third, the leaders of the revolutions, inexperienced in practical politics, often mistook parliaments for power and left intact the established authorities that would soon turn on them. Fourth, nationalism divided revolutionaries and prevented the cooperation that was essential for durable success. Fifth, no major nation was ready to intervene in behalf of change. Britain was sympathetic, France encouraging, and the United States (its consulates centers of republicanism) enthusiastic; but none of that sympathy matched the military assistance Russia gave the Austrian emperor or the formidable armies of Austria and Prussia.

The events of 1848 had significant effects nonetheless. Revolution so widespread reflected the failures of restoration, displayed again the power of political ideas, and uncovered the effects of a generation of social change. Many of the gains won in that year endured: The peasants of eastern Prussia and the Austrian Empire were emancipated from serfdom in 1848 and remained free of servile obligations; Piedmont and Prussia kept their new, limited constitutions. The monarchs triumphant in 1849 punished revolutionaries with execution, prison, and exile, but they also learned that they must pay more attention to winning some popular support. Liberals would never again depend so optimistically on the spontaneous power of the

THE FRANKFURT CONSTITUTION

The Frankfurt Parliament completed its work on a constitution for Germany in 1849. It was a long and detailed document, carefully proscribing the repressive acts that had been most common in the preceding years. Its proud assertions of German freedom remain significantly vague, however, about the enforcement of its provisions and what the boundaries of the German nation will be.

THE FUNDAMENTAL RIGHTS OF THE GERMAN PEOPLE

Article 1

¶ 131. The German people consists of the citizens of the states, which make up the Reich.

¶ 132. Every German has the right of German Reich's citizenship. He can exercise this right in every German land. Reich's franchise legislation shall provide for the right of the individual to vote for members of the national assembly.

¶ 133. Every German has the right to live or reside in any part of the Reich's territory, to acquire and dispose of property of all kinds, to pursue his livelihood, and to win the right of communal citizenship. . . .

¶ 134. No German state is permitted to make a distinction between its citizens and other Germans in civil, criminal, and litigation rights which relegates the latter to the position of foreigners.

¶ 135. Capital punishment for civil offenses shall not take place, and, in those cases where condemnation has already been made, shall not be carried out, in order not to infringe upon the hereby acquired civil law.

¶ 136. Freedom of emigration shall not be limited by any state; emigration levies shall not be established.

All matters of emigration remain under the protection and care of the Reich.

Article 2

¶ 137. There are no class differences before the law. The rank of nobility is abolished.

All special class privileges are abolished.

All Germans are equal before the law.

All titles, insofar as they are not bound with an office, are abolished and never again shall be introduced.

No citizen shall accept a decoration from a foreign state.

Public office shall be open to all men on the basis of ability.

All citizens are subject equally to military service; there shall be no draft substitutions.

Article 3

¶ 141. The confiscation of letters and papers, except at an arrest or house search, can take place with a legally executed warrant, which must be served on the arrested person at once or within the next twenty-four hours.

¶ 142. The secrecy of letters is inviolable.

Necessary exceptions in cases of criminal investigation and in the event of war shall be established by legislation.

Article 4

¶ 143. Every German shall have the right freely to express his opinion through speech, writing, publication, and illustration.

The freedom of the press shall be suspended under no circumstances through preventive measures, namely, censorship, concessions, security orders, imposts, limitation of publication or bookselling, postal bans, or other restraints.

From Louis L. Snyder (ed.), *The Documents of German History*, Rutgers University Press, 1958.

---

people, and advocates of social reform would be more skeptical of political liberalism. International power clearly constrained domestic policy, but political leaders of every hue now also recognized the potential force of nationalism.

THE POLITICS OF NATIONALISM

Why **nationalism** assumed such importance in the nineteenth century and has retained it to the present day remains one of the important questions of modern history. As an ideology, it represents itself as a natural, age-old sentiment arising spontaneously; yet national-

ism is essentially a modern phenomenon and often seems to require persistent propaganda. Associated with liberalism in the first part of the nineteenth century, nationalism came to be embraced and used by both the left and the right. And it affected politics on every level: international relations; the unification of Italy and Germany, which changed the map of Europe; and domestic policies in every sort of government.

The Elements of Nationalism

Nationalism's deepest roots lie in a shared sense of regional and cultural identity, especially as those roots are expressed in custom, language, and religion. This

Mazzini's Nationalism

"On the Duties of Man" is one of Giuseppe Mazzini's most famous essays. It was first written in 1844 for Italian workers living in England; the excerpts here are from the fifth chapter, which was added for a new edition in 1858. Despite the events of the intervening years, Mazzini's romantic faith had changed little. The essay's title was meant to contrast with the French Revolution's "Declaration of the Rights of Man," which Mazzini criticized for encouraging selfishness and materialism.

"Your first duties—first as regards importance—are, as I have already told you, towards Humanity. . . . If you do not embrace the whole human family in your affection, . . . if, wheresoever a fellow-creature suffers, or the dignity of human nature is violated by falsehood or tyranny—you are not ready, if able, to aid the unhappy, and do not feel called upon to combat, if able, for the redemption of the betrayed or oppressed—you violate your law of life, you comprehend not that Religion which will be the guide and blessing of the future.

"But what can each of you, singly, *do* for the moral improvement and progress of Humanity? . . . The watchword of the faith of the future is *Association*, and . . . [the] means was provided for you by God when he gave you a country; when, even as a wise overseer of labour distributes the various branches of employment according to the different capacities of the workmen, he divided Humanity into distinct groups or nuclei upon the face of the earth, thus creating the germ of Nationalities. Evil governments have disfigured the divine design. Nevertheless you may still trace it, distinctly marked out—at least as far as Europe is concerned—by the course of the great rivers, the direction of the higher mountains, and other geographical

conditions. They have disfigured it by their conquests, their greed, and their jealousy even of the righteous power of others. . . .

"These governments did not, and do not, recognize any country save their own families or dynasty, the egotism of caste. But the Divine design will infallibly be realized. Natural divisions, and the spontaneous, innate tendencies of the peoples, will take the place of the arbitrary divisions sanctioned by evil governments. The map of Europe will be redrawn. The countries of the Peoples, defined by the vote of free men, will arise upon the ruins of the countries of kings and privileged castes. . . .

"O my brothers, love your Country! Our country is our Home, the house that God has given us, placing therein a numerous family that loves us, and whom we love. . . . Our country is our common workshop, whence the products of our activity are sent forth for the benefit of the whole world. . . . In labouring for our own country on the right principle, we labour for Humanity."

From Giuseppe Mazzini, *On the Duties of Man*, Greenwood Publishing Group.

---

found in free trade, sound finances, and railroads a power that could remake Piedmont.

Cavour pursued his liberal goals with tactical brilliance, skillfully using newspapers and parliamentary debate to mold public opinion. He created a centrist parliamentary coalition with which he dominated both king and parliament from 1852 until his death in 1861. In that brief time he established himself as one of the outstanding statesmen of the century. Piedmont's internal strength was Cavour's first concern, but he also sought to make his state the center of Italy's resurgence, the ***risorgimento***.[2] He welcomed exiles from other parts of the peninsula, encouraged the nationalist press, and sought every opportunity for symbolic gestures of patriotism. He was aided in this goal by the Italian National

Society, one of whose founders was the president of the Venetian republic in 1848. The National Society propagandized for Italian unity under Piedmont's king and established secret committees in most of the cities of Italy. Its members were predominantly liberal aristocrats, local lawyers, and professors; and in calling for Italian unity, the society combined Mazzinian rhetoric with hardheaded insistence on the need for international alliances and military force. Economic liberalism largely replaced more generous and vaguer social theories.

War against Austria   Most of all, Cavour depended on astute foreign policy. He had pushed for Piedmont's participation in the Crimean War and was rewarded with the discussion of the Italian question at the Congress of Paris. Using his state's enhanced international position, he argued that Italy repressed would remain a danger to European order. He appealed for liberal sympathy throughout Western Europe, and he courted Napoleon III. At last, in July 1858, Cavour and Napoleon III met

---

[2] *Risorgimento*, now the historian's label for the whole period of Italian unification, was a term meaning "resurgence," often used by nationalists and made the title of a liberal newspaper that Cavour helped to found and edit.

secretly. It was easy to argue that war was inevitable, given Austria's resentment of Piedmont's growing prominence. If France would support Piedmont against Austria, Cavour promised to accept a complicated set of arrangements designed to benefit France and limit Piedmont's expansion.

Austria, watching young Lombards and Venetians escape conscription by streaming to Piedmont as volunteers, determined to end the nationalist threat once and for all. It sent Piedmont an ultimatum so strong that Cavour needed only to reply with cautious dignity in order to have his war. On April 29, 1859, Austria invaded Piedmont, and France went to the rescue of a small state attacked by her giant neighbor. The rapid movement of large French armies was impressive, but thereafter the war was fought with little tactical brilliance on either side. As the Austrians retreated to the fortresses controlling the Lombard plain, Napoleon suddenly lost his taste for war and unilaterally assented to a truce. The emperors of France and Austria agreed that Piedmont should have Lombardy but not Venetia and that the other Italian states should remain as before.

Formation of the Italian Kingdom

Those other Italian states, however, were not immune to the excitement of a national war. Gentle revolutions accompanied the march of Piedmontese troops throughout northern Italy. When local patriots gathered in the streets, the dukes of Modena, Parma, and Tuscany simply fled, to be replaced by provisional governments led by members of the National Society. These governments quickly adopted Piedmontese laws and held elections to representative assemblies. The terms of the truce arranged by France and Austria could not be carried out; and after a few months, the provisional governments held plebiscites—a device Napoleon could hardly reject—on the question of annexation to Piedmont. Italians trooped to the polls with bands playing and flags waving, peasants behind their lords and workers with their guilds. The result was as one-sided as in the plebiscites in France. Piedmont's King Victor Emmanuel ruled from the Alps to Rimini on the Adriatic. To compensate Napoleon III, the province of Savoy and the city of Nice were turned over to France.

Moderate liberals had united half of Italy. Sputtering revolts in Sicily gave more democratic nationalists a chance to lead a different sort of risorgimento. Former Mazzinians, eager to promote a Sicilian uprising, gathered guns in Genoa and planned an expedition that Cavour dared neither support nor oppose. Its leader was Giuseppe Garibaldi, Italy's most popular hero. Exiled for his Mazzinian activity in the 1830s, Garibaldi had spent ten years fighting for democratic causes in South America, returning to Italy in time to take part in the wars of 1848. He had directed the heroic defense of the Roman Republic in 1849 and led the most effective corps of volunteers in 1859. In his greatest exploit of all, he set sail for Sicily one night in May 1860 with a thousand men, mainly middle-class youths from Lombardy, Venetia, and the Romagna.

Garibaldi Goes South

No event in the nineteenth century so captured the popular imagination as that daring venture. The Expedition of the Thousand was like some ancient epic come to life in an industrial age. Untrained men, wearing the red shirts Garibaldi had adopted in South America, fought with bravery and discipline, enthusiastically supported in the Sicilian countryside. Garibaldi's tactics confused and defeated the Neapolitan generals, despite their far larger and better-equipped forces. In two weeks the Red Shirts occupied Palermo and within two months almost all of Sicily. Volunteers flocked from all over Italy to join Garibaldi, and money was raised in his behalf in all the towns of northern Italy and from New York to Stockholm.

The epic continued when, against all odds, Garibaldi sailed across the strait and landed on the Italian mainland. He declared his goal to be Rome itself and not just Naples. That worried Cavour, who considered Garibaldi irresponsible and believed that an attack on Rome might lead Austria and France to intervene on behalf of the pope. So Cavour encouraged uprisings in the Papal States and then sent Piedmontese troops to preserve

The handshake of Victor Emmanuel and Garibaldi, which sealed the unification of Italy as their armies met in 1860, became a favorite subject for illustrations of the risorgimento. This engraving is English.
Culver Pictures, Inc.

MAP 24.2 THE UNIFICATION OF ITALY
Dreams of Italian unification began during the French revolutionary era, when "sister republics" were briefly established up and down the peninsula. What were the major obstacles to Italian unification? How was it that the Kingdom of Piedmont became the engine that drove the process to success?
◆ For an online version, go to www.mhhe.com/chambers9 > chapter 24 > book maps.

order. Carefully skirting the area around Rome, they moved south to meet Garibaldi. On September 18, between lines of suspicious men, Giuseppe Garibaldi and

Victor Emmanuel rode out to shake hands and unite Italy. Garibaldi added to his legend by thus giving way in the interests of union, and the Piedmontese took

A demonstration in Florence's historic Piazza della Signoria in 1866 for the annexation of Venetia to the new Kingdom of Italy.
Scala/Art Resource, NY

over. Plebiscites confirmed the union, and in March 1861 the Kingdom of Italy was proclaimed.

United Italy   The Kingdom of Italy included almost all of Italy except for Rome and Venetia. Catholics throughout the world opposed the annexation of Rome, which Napoleon III was pledged to protect, and Austrian troops were massed in Venetia. Italy acquired Venetia in 1866 as a by-product of war between Austria and Prussia. Austria offered it in return for Italy's neutrality; Prussia had promised it to Italy if Prussia defeated Austria with Italy's support. Italy kept its prior pledge to Prussia, went to war, fought poorly, but got Venetia following Prussia's rapid victory. Rome was annexed when French troops withdrew during the Franco-**Prussian War** of 1870; the new nation finally had its ancient capital.

More lasting problems remained. To many Italians, especially in the south, unification felt like a foreign occupation, and Italy's leaders were appalled at the poverty and corruption they could not overcome. Pius IX forbade Catholics to take part in national elections and rejected the indemnity and guarantees of protection the government offered. United Italy was poor and overwhelmingly agricultural. It had no coal or iron, and three-quarters of the population was illiterate. With liberal conviction, the Italian government assumed the debts of all the former governments and struggled to balance the annual budget. Despite taxes that were among the highest in Europe, Italy continued to lag in schools, railways, and roads. The sale of Church lands failed to benefit peasants as much as hoped, and the lower Piedmontese tariffs brought instant distress to hundreds of small producers in the rest of the peninsula. It took years of sporadic fighting to enforce order in the south. For millions of artisans and peasants, few tangible benefits followed from replacing reactionary dukes with a liberal national state.

A New Nation: The Unification of Germany

German cultural identity had grown throughout the first half of the nineteenth century, from the battles against Napoleon to the statements of the Frankfurt Parliament. It was strengthened by achievements in philosophy, science, literature, and music that were seen as German accomplishments no matter what German kingdom, principality, or free city they occurred in. The open question was what the political expression of that identity should be. The German Confederation was ineffectual, none of the schemes for unification in 1848 had been adopted, and Austria had blocked Prussian plans for leadership in 1850. Yet it was Prussia that created modern Germany.

The Dominance of Prussia   Several factors account for Prussia's eventual dominance. One was economic.

Sand in France, to be recognized as influential thinkers. For a middle-class public faced with so much new work to choose from, critics became important as professional intellectuals who guided taste much as the popular books on etiquette and gastronomy taught manners to people of new means.

The Content of Culture

Varied Forms   The most admired artistic works were valued for a moral seriousness and formality that distinguished them from popular culture. In painting, great historical scenes were the most admired, ranked considerably above genre painting or portraits. Music was increasingly treated as a kind of spiritual essay, to be heard reverentially in concerts suitable to its distinctive forms—symphony, concerto, quartet, and sonata. The novel's great popularity was related to the social panorama it presented. Balzac attempted in his novels to encompass all the "human comedy" (the phrase contrasted with Dante's divine concerns), showing the wealthy, the ambitious, and the poor in their roles as husbands, wives, soldiers, bankers, politicians, and writers. Novelists used social types to analyze society and challenge the public conscience, and no reformer was more influential than Dickens. Scott's swashbuckling stories of romance and chivalry in an earlier age probed the connection between personal character and social tension in a way that influenced writers throughout Europe. Theater and opera featured historical settings; and Hugo, Alexander Pushkin, and Alessandro Manzoni promulgated patriotism by connecting high ideals to the national past, painting in words monumental interpretations of historical events. The novel's most common theme, the conflict between personal feeling (especially romantic love) and social convention, explored critical contemporary issues of individualism and social change.

Conceptions of culture were also strongly gendered. Women were held to have qualities—including a natural sense of beauty and openness to emotion—that made them especially responsive to art. Women were thought to be the principal readers of novels, and novels presented women's lives in ways that underscored the inequities of their social subordination and ultimately enlarged the perception of women's abilities. Women were especially associated with the intimate side of middle-class culture, the popularity of poetry, lithographs, watercolor paintings, and piano music—all to be savored in the parlor, with the woman of the house at the center.

Changing Styles   In culture as in philosophy there was also a strong desire for synthesis, for ideas and forms that would tie everything together. In the arts

this urge gave lyric opera special resonance. Opera was first of all theater, combining popular appeal with aristocratic elegance. It featured elaborate plots, often in historical settings, flowery poetic texts, varied, tuneful, and complex music, the whole further enriched by ballet, colorful sets, and special effects. The two leading operatic composers of the period were Giuseppe Verdi and his exact contemporary Richard Wagner. Verdi, an Italian national hero, wrote compelling and often patriotic music that explored human emotion and character in diverse contexts, often historical ones explicitly about politics. Wagner carried the search for an artistic synthesis still further. He wrote his own texts and increasingly used Germanic myths with nationalist intent. In his operas recurrent musical themes were identified with major ideas and characters to create a whole in which voices, instruments, words, and visual experience moved inseparably to a powerful climax.

By the 1840s rapidly changing and competing artistic styles had become a characteristic of modern culture, a response to social change and new audiences but also an expression of the creative artist's sense of self. Some artists adapted Romanticism's emphasis on individual genius to claim that the merit of a piece of art was independent of any social or moral purpose and to adopt, therefore, the cry of "art for art's sake." For others, the goal of the artist should be to capture the essence of "modernity." By midcentury, **realism** was becoming the dominant style, as writers and painters reemphasized close observation in a socially concerned effort to portray ordinary people, sometimes with shocking directness, as in Gustave Flaubert's *Madame Bovary* (1857), an acid account of a young middle-class wife's aimless existence in a small French town, or J. F. Millet's paintings of rural workers and villages. Innovation was often taken for a sign of genius, and the belief that artists must be in an *avant-garde*, ahead of their duller public, became a cliché. Often disturbing to their audiences, the arts were never more honored nor artists more critical of their own society than in the nineteenth century.

Religious Thought   In some respects the nineteenth century was a very religious age, for thoughtful people cared greatly about religion. Protestant and Catholic missions campaigned with an intensity not seen since the seventeenth century, and the pious became more militant and turned to social action, preaching temperance, teaching reading, and establishing charities. This focus on the problems of modern life was connected, however, to the fear that religion was losing its social importance. Some intellectuals became bitter anticlericals, seeing in the church the barrier to progress. More typically, especially in England, stern morality and propriety were substituted for theology.

Jean Francois Miller
THE GLEANERS, **1857**
Splendid example of realism in nineteenth-century French painting.
Musée d'Orsay, Paris, France.
Réunion des Musées Nationaux/
Art Resource, NY

The impact of historical research on religion created a sensation across Europe when the Protestant David Strauss published his *Life of Jesus* in 1835, for it cast erudite doubt on the accuracy of the Gospels, frightening many with the apparent need to choose between scholarship and Christ. In Denmark the writings of Soren Kierkegaard starkly explored ethical dilemmas in a passionate search for faith; his intense, semiautobiographical essays that interweave biblical stories and personal symbols have continued to fascinate twentieth-century thinkers.

The Sense of History   Nineteenth-century intellectual life emphasized historical thinking. A romantic respect for the past, nationalists' claims, explanations of revolution, economic theory, and preoccupation with change all underscored the importance of history. Its systematic study became an admired profession. In England, France, and Germany, national projects were launched for publishing historical documents and for training scholars to interpret them. Some historians were as widely read as novelists, among them Jules Michelet, for whom French history was a dramatic story of the people's fight for freedom, and Thomas B. Macaulay, for whom the history of England was a record of progressive change through moderation and compromise. In each country certain events and themes—in England, the Glorious Revolution of 1688; in France, the Revolution; in Germany, the rise of Prussia—were favored as part of an intense search for national roots, heroes, and patterns of development significant for the present.

Summary

In 1848 a wave of revolutions, the most spontaneous and widespread Europe had ever known, brought new governments to power. Defeated before they could complete their democratic and egalitarian programs, these revolutionary regimes left important legacies not only in measures passed but lessons learned. In the future, radicals would not rely on middle-class support and political reform, while liberals would be more willing to sacrifice democracy for social order. In these circumstances the most effective governments of the 1850s were those that adopted parts of the revolutionaries' programs and some of their techniques for reaching a broader public while keeping the forces of order on their side. Thus, the Second Empire of Napoleon III was the principal guarantor of that social order and economic growth important to the properted classes. Piedmont and Prussia, as the focus of nationalist movements, won significant followings and triumphed dramatically in creating national states in Italy and Germany. In this Europe of the modern national state, astute political leaders from England to Prussia found ways to undertake new social responsibilities, facilitate industrialization, and mobilize popular support without giving way to full democracy or radical programs. Closely associated with the nation, cultural institutions flourished, supporting a diverse and dynamic culture that was one of the great achievements of the age. By the 1870s, European nations had the means to generate unprecedented power and the will to spread their influence around the world.

QUESTIONS FOR FURTHER THOUGHT

1. What is the historical significance of revolutions in which the revolutionaries are defeated?
2. Why did nationalism become so important in the nineteenth century?
3. Nationalist ideologies have much in common, but what accounts for the important differences among them?

4. When you look at art, listen to music, or read works written in the nineteenth century, what characteristics do you identify with the period in which they were created?

RECOMMENDED READING

Sources

Marx, Karl. *The Class Struggles in France, 1848–1850* and *The Eighteenth Brumaire of Louis Napoleon.* Early and polemical applications of Marx's ideas to contemporary political events, the revolution of 1848 in France and Napoleon's coup d'état.

Treitschke, Heinrick. *History of Germany in the Nineteenth Century.* Written shortly after German unification, this vast work exemplifies the importance of history as nationalist propaganda.

Studies

*Agulhon, Maurice. *The Republican Experiment, 1848–1852.* Janel Lloyd (tr.). 1983. An authoritative study of politics and society during the Second French Republic, sensitive to popular attitudes and concerns.

*Alter, Peter. *Nationalism.* 1989. A valuable introduction to the different kinds of nationalism.

*Anderson, Benedict. *Imagined Communities: Reflections on the Origin and Spread of Nationalism.* 1983. An important analysis of modern nationalism worldwide, stressing its origins in European culture and capitalism.

*Beales, Derek. *The Risorgimento and the Unification of Italy.* 1982. Concise, skeptical introduction to the history of Italian unification.

*Chadwick, Owen. *The Secularization of the European Mind.* 1975. Perceptive, introduction to changing patterns of thought about religion.

Freifel, Alice. *Nationalism and the Crowd in Liberal Hungary, 1848–1914.* 2000. Demonstrates the unique aspects of Hungarian nationalism.

*Gellner, Ernest. *Nations and Nationalism.* 1983. An effort to build a theory by analyzing the relation of industrialization to nationalism.

Greenfield, Kent R. *Economics and Liberalism in the Risorgimento: A Study of Nationalism in Lombardy, 1814–1848.* 1978. A classic study of the connection between economic change and nationalism.

*Hamerow, Theodore S. *The Social and Economic Foundations of German Unification, 1858–1871.* 2 vols. 1969 and 1972. The politics and ideas of unification placed in the context of a developing economy.

Hemmings, F. W. J. *Culture and Society in France, 1789–1848.* 1987. *Culture and Society in France, 1848–1898.* 1971. A literary scholar's provocative and comprehensive analysis of the relationship between cultural styles and social context.

*Howard, Michael. *The Franco-Prussian War.* 1969. Exemplary study of how war reflects (and tests) an entire society.

*Jelavich, Barbara. *History of the Balkans.* 2 vols. 1983. A thorough survey of society and politics, from the eighteenth century to the present.

*Mack Smith, Denis. *Cavour.* 1985. An expert and well-written assessment of the personalities and policies that created an Italian nation.

*Mosse, George L. *The Nationalization of the Masses: Political Symbolism and Mass Movements in Germany from the Napoleonic Wars through the Third Reich.* 1975. One of the most complete efforts to find the roots of Nazism in popular nationalism.

Olsen, Donald J. *The City as a Work of Art: London, Paris, Vienna.* 1986. Combines an analysis of how ordinary people really lived with an appreciation of the aesthetics of the modern city and the economic and political realities behind it.

Pflanze, Otto. *Bismarck and the Development of Germany: The Period of Unification, 1815–1871.* 1963. Places each of Bismarck's actions in its larger context.

*Pinkney, David. *Napoleon III and the Rebuilding of Paris.* 1958. Studies the political background to one of the most extensive, influential, and successful examples of urban policy.

*Plessis, Alain. *The Rise and Fall of the Second Empire, 1852–1871.* Jonathan Mandelbaum (tr.). 1985. A balanced assessment of this important political experiment.

*Poovey, Mary. *Making a Social Body: British Cultural Formation, 1830–1864.* This study of how the public was conceived in literature and politics exposes the ways in which public institutions helped construct categories of gender and class.

*Read, Donald. *England 1868–1914: The Age of Urban Democracy.* 1979. Political change presented in terms of economic and social conditions.

Reardon, B. M. G. *Religion in the Age of Romanticism: Studies in Early Nineteenth-Century Thought.* 1985. An excellent introduction to the formation of one of the most important intellectual traditions of the century.

Rich, Norman. *Why the Crimean War? A Cautionary Tale.* 1985. A concise synthesis and engaging interpretation of the political and diplomatic problems involving the major powers.

Salvemini, Gaetano. *Mazzini.* 1957. Still the best introduction to Mazzini's thought and its relationship to his revolutionary activities.

*Sperber, Jonathan. *The European Revolutions, 1848–1851.* 1994. A fresh synthesis that pays attention to popular attitudes and symbolic actions as well as political and social conflict.

*Stearns, Peter N. *1848: The Revolutionary Tide in Europe.* 1974. Assesses conflicting interpretations in bringing together accounts of these diverse revolutions.

Wandycz, Piotyr S. *The Lands of Partitioned Poland, 1795–1918.* 1974. An excellent overview of the history of divided Poland.

*Available in paperback.

Ernst Ludwig Kirchner
STREET, DRESDEN, 1908
Kirchner's stark painting of Dresden's Königstrasse evokes the sensory barrage of modern urban life. In the midst of the crowd, the individual figures appear anguished and cut off from one another.
Digital Image © The Museum of Modern Art/Licensed by Scala/Art Resource, NY

Chapter Twenty-Five

PROGRESS AND ITS DISCONTENTS

ECONOMIC TRANSFORMATIONS • UNDERSTANDINGS OF NATURE AND SOCIETY •
THE BELLE EPOQUE • ATTACKS ON LIBERAL CIVILIZATION • DOMESTIC POLITICS

In the second half of the nineteenth century, economic growth became an expectation for the first time in history. New technologies, large-scale industry, better communication, and greater capital investment made unprecedented productivity possible and seemingly self-sustaining, and these gains were in turn a triumph of social organization and new knowledge. Large-scale institutions—business corporations, government agencies, political parties, labor unions, national associations, and newspapers—became essential to a new society characterized by rapid economic growth and broader political participation. Most observers hailed this period as an age of progress, marked by a rising standard of living, greater democracy, new opportunities for education and employment, and greater leisure.

Yet as European power reached its peak, the weaknesses inherent in liberalism and capitalism began to show. Although millions shared in Europe's consumer culture, contemporaries worried about rampant materialism and its corrupting effects on moral standards, the erosion of community by widespread urbanization, and the poverty and hopelessness that persisted among the lower classes. Many organized movements, both radical and religious, stepped up their attacks on this confident society, and new intellectual currents questioned the basis for its optimism. Groups that felt most neglected or threatened—women, the lower classes, and those who feared political or economic change—sometimes turned to violence and revolution or encouraged racial hatred for political gain. Just as ominous were rising international tensions. Britain and France, historically the most powerful European nations, found themselves economically eclipsed by American and German industrial growth, and the expansionist ambitions of Germany and Japan threatened Britain's and Russia's global influence. An age that would be remembered for its optimism and peaceful prosperity was also a time of division and conflict.

attacked Jews as part of the liberal, capitalist world alien to national traditions. Conspiracy theories and racist distortions of Darwinism gave concrete and simple explanations for the baffling pace of social change, offering the hope that by circumscribing specific groups—and especially Jews—society could resist change itself.

Late-nineteenth-century anti-Semitism was no mere continuation of medieval prejudices. Social Darwinists of the era despised Jews not so much on the basis of religion as on their status as a biologically inferior "race." In Germany, Austria, and France, anti-Semitism emerged within a new politics of mass appeal; its prominence in France, where French Jews had long been recognized as equal citizens, was especially shocking. For Theodor Herzl, who became the leading spokesperson of Zionism, the lesson was clear: Jews must have a homeland of their own.

The Revival of the Right   Neither irrationalism nor anti-Semitism belongs inherently to a single political persuasion, but both were used primarily by the political right in the decades preceding World War I. Rightist movements revived notably in these years, building among those social groups that felt most harmed by the changes of the century: aristocrats, rural people, members of the lower-middle class whose status was threatened, and many Christians. A reinvigorated right also voiced concerns about the materialism of middle-class culture and the evils of unchecked capitalism. Right-wingers tried, frequently with success, to use patriotism and national strength as their battle cry, learning to make the effective mass appeal that had often eluded them in the past. Yet as critical as they were of liberal centrists, they saw socialists as their primary foes, declaring socialism the menace of the hour and the natural consequence of liberal error.

Thus, critics from the right and the left gained by addressing the discontents that liberalism tended to ignore and by criticizing the modern changes that most people still labeled progress. So many simultaneous assaults created grave political crises in many states. How those assaults were dealt with in each country reshaped the political system that would guide it through the challenges ahead.

DOMESTIC POLITICS

In many respects political systems were more similar at the end of the nineteenth century than they had been since before the French Revolution, and everywhere they faced many of the same issues. Yet each nation evolved its own distinctive response to the pressures for continuity and change.

Common Problems

There were certain issues that every political system confronted. One was who should participate in political life. The trend was to increase suffrage until every adult male had the right to vote, but extending that right to women became a divisive issue in many countries by the turn of the century. Each political system also found its own ways of constraining democracy, through royal prerogatives, a conservative second chamber, or limits on what legislatures could do.

The state was now a participant in social and economic life, but its precise role was often hotly contested, especially its responsibility for social welfare and its economic policies that affected banks, commerce, and labor unions. Powerful groups, such as the church, the military, or the aristocracy, sought to enlist the state on their side. Sometimes these competing interests could be balanced, but often these conflicts reinforced older ideological divisions that threatened to undermine the political system itself.

Large-Scale Organizations   These tensions emerged as states and social groups throughout Europe were increasingly represented by large bureaucracies. As governments took on increased responsibilities for public health, transportation, communications (the post and telegraph), their bureaucratic organization expanded, as did that of larger business companies. In response, smaller firms organized in associations that could represent their interests in dealings with government and with other lobbying groups.

Workers, too, were increasingly organized in national trade unions that negotiated for particular industries and mobilized major strikes in every industrial country from the 1880s. Political parties also adopted some form of national organization and a permanent staff, especially where universal male suffrage made such efforts worthwhile. The massive Marxist German Social Democratic party was the most impressive example of this.

New professional associations set standards, lobbied governments, and conferred prestige on the physicians, lawyers, engineers, and teachers that belonged to them. Like political parties, associations offered a means whereby scattered groups and new interests could make their presence felt in public life. This institutionalization of society was in many respects a source of stability, providing rapidly expanding occupations with norms, internal discipline, and a means for negotiating conflicts. But the very size of these organizations often promoted the growth of factions within them.

Nearly every country also struggled with the definition of national community and whether some groups—ethnic minorities, foreigners, Catholics, Jews, anarchists, or socialists—should be excluded as alien or of uncertain loyalty. The way each society responded to this challenge became an important test of its political system.

France: The Third Republic

In France political conflict revolved around the form of government following the fall of the Second Empire.

Monarchy or Republic Shortly after Louis Napoleon surrendered in the Franco-Prussian War of 1870, Parisian crowds cheered the proclamation of a republic, and new leaders sought to mobilize the nation as an earlier republic had done in 1792. German forces quickly surrounded Paris, but French forces, strengthened by newly recruited peasants, still made some gains until, overmatched, they were pushed back in December.

Paris remained under German siege. Refusing to surrender, its citizens held out for four months. They cut down the trees of the boulevards for fuel, slaughtered pets, and emptied the zoo as a starving city continued to resist during a winter as severe as any on record. But heroism and patriotic fervor could not defeat a modern army, and at the end of January Paris capitulated.

France's newly elected assembly met at Versailles and quickly accepted peace on German terms. The assembly, divided between monarchists and republicans, could not agree, however, on the form of government. It compromised by naming Adolphe Thiers, a moderate politician who had been prominent in the July Monarchy thirty years earlier, as chief of the "Executive Power," thereby postponing the issue of whether France was to have a king or a president.

The Paris Commune Thiers knew that his government must establish control of Paris, which had been cut off from the rest of France. As a first step, he decided to disarm the city's National Guard. When troops from Versailles tried to remove some cannons, however, they were confronted by an angry crowd. Shots were fired; by day's end, two generals lay dead. Faced with insurrection, Thiers withdrew his army, determined first to isolate the revolution and then to crush it. The municipal council of Paris, in another echo of the French Revolution of 1789, declared the city a self-governing commune and prepared to fight. The Paris Commune included moderate and radical republicans, militant socialists, and a few members of the Marxist First International. Its program, favoring democracy and federalism, was not very specific on other matters, and it had little time to experiment.

Scenes of the Paris Commune and the destruction that resulted were in great demand afterward. One dramatic moment was the execution of Generals Clément-Thomas and Lecomte by the communards on March 18, 1871. That scene was reconstructed a few months later in this composite photograph. Created for its commercial possibilities (in books and on postcards, for example), the image echoed traditional scenes of comparable historical episodes.
Roger-Viollet/Getty Images

Civil War While German armies idly watched, the French engaged in civil war. The conservative assembly in Versailles sent its armies to assault the Paris Commune. The mutual hatred in this civil war was exacerbated by the recent anguish of siege and defeat as well as by the long-standing differences, ideological and social, between rural France and the capital. The two camps fought for competing visions of what the nation should become, and they fought with rising fury. On both sides, hostages were taken and prisoners shot. It took almost two months of bloodshed before government troops broke into the city in May.

Even then the fighting continued, barricade by barricade, into the working-class quarters, where the group commanded by the anarchist Louise Michel was among the last to fall. Among the most famous of hundreds of militant communards, she would later tell her captors, "I belong entirely to the Social Revolution." Solid citizens shuddered at revolutionary excess (and especially at the part played by women), but on the whole, the victors were more brutal. Tens of thousands of Parisians died in the streets, and summary court martials ordered execution, imprisonment, or deportation for tens of thousands more.

Throughout Europe, the Commune raised the specter of revolution. From the first, Marxists hailed it as a proletarian rising, the dawning of a new era, though Marx was indignant with the communard's lack of revolutionary daring and their respect for property and legality. Former communards became the heroes of socialist gatherings for the next generation, and to this day the cemetery where many of them were executed remains a shrine honored by socialists and communists.[5] Historians have been at great pains to show how little socialism, still less Marxism, there was in the Paris Commune (it respectfully left the Bank of Paris intact); yet myth has its historical importance, too. The Commune was indisputably a class conflict, and the rage on both sides was more significant than mere differences of program. After 1871 a proletarian revolution became a credible possibility to radical and conservative alike, and working-class movements across Europe pointed to the martyrs of the Commune as evidence of the cruelty of bourgeois rule.

The Founding of the Third Republic   Remarkably, a stable republic gradually emerged from this unpromising beginning. The administrative structure of the French state remained strong, and Thiers used it effectively. The loan needed to pay the indemnity to Germany was soon oversubscribed. As elections produced victories for moderate republicans, monarchists feared that their chance was slipping away. They ousted Thiers, put a monarchist in his place, and looked for a chance to restore the monarchy. They never found it.

The monarchists themselves were divided between the conservative supporters of the grandson of Charles X and those who favored the grandson of Louis Philippe. Meanwhile, moderate republicans continued to gain in popularity, and in 1875 the assembly passed a law declaring that "the president of the republic" should be elected by the two legislative houses. The Third Republic was thus quietly established as the government that, as Thiers put it, divided Frenchmen least.

There was a Chamber of Deputies, elected by direct universal male suffrage, and a Senate, indirectly elected by local officials. In elections the following year, republicans captured two-thirds of the seats in the Chamber and almost half those in the Senate. The presidency, which had been so strong under Thiers, was still in monarchist hands, but its authority continued to decline. That established a further precedent: The Republic would have a weak executive. Made acceptable by having crushed the Commune and by having a conservative Senate, this republic was a regime of compromise; it would last longer than any French regime since 1789.

Successive republican governments guaranteed political freedom and deferred to the middle class, while France's public institutions preserved the remarkable

---

[5] A century later a Russian sputnik proudly carried to the moon not only a Soviet flag but a red flag from the Commune of 1871.

CHRONOLOGY
Radicalism and Violent Protest in the Belle Epoque

1864–1872	First International.
1871	Paris Commune.
1887	Assassination of the prime minister of Spain.
1889	Strike of London dockworkers; formation of the Second International.
1894	Assassination of the president of France; Dreyfus affair.
1898	Assassination of the empress of Austria; left-wing riots in Milan.
1901	Assassination of the president of the United States.
1905	Russian Revolution of 1905.
1909	Left-wing riots in Barcelona.
1910–1914	Strikes in London.
1912	Social Democrats gain majority in Reichstag.

administrative continuity that had characterized them since 1800. For twenty years, from 1879 to 1899, the leading politicians were moderates who recognized unions and made elementary education in state schools compulsory but initiated few projects of public works or social welfare. Economic growth, less dramatic than in Great Britain or Germany, was also less disruptive. France found its own balance between the demand for order and the need for change.

Nevertheless, there were threats to the republic's moderate politics in the last years of the nineteenth century. In 1889, France escaped the threat of a coup d'etat by the authoritarian General Georges Boulanger, whose anti-German diatribes and speeches expressing concern for workers attracted public attention and support. Then the republic faced a scandal after companies financing a canal through Panama went bankrupt and investigations uncovered political graft. There followed a stormy campaign against republican politicians, liberal newspapers, and Jewish financiers. Only when the regime seemed close to toppling did its defenders pull together.

The Dreyfus Affair   The Third Republic's greatest trial came with the Dreyfus case. In 1894 a court-martial convicted Captain Alfred Dreyfus, a Jew and a member of the General Staff, of providing the German

Every stage of the Dreyfus affair was the occasion for public demonstrations. *Le Petit Journal*, which had the largest circulation of any Paris newspaper, printed this scene of a crowd of magistrates and ordinary citizens hailing the news in February 1898 that Zola has been convicted of libel.
Edimedia

military attaché with secret French documents. Although the sensational press denounced Jewish treachery, the issue only became the center of public attention three years afterward, when evidence appeared implicating another officer as the guilty party.

The army's principal officers, refusing to reopen the case, spoke darkly of honor and state secrets, and the right-wing press hailed their patriotism. The controversy escalated with charges and countercharges in parliament and the press, a series of sensational trials, and huge public demonstrations. The nation was divided. The majority of Catholics, monarchists, and conservatives joined in patriotic indignation against Jews and socialists who were allegedly conspiring to sell out France and weaken a loyal army. The left—intellectuals, socialists, and republicans—came to view Dreyfus as the innocent victim of a plot against republican institutions.

Figures like the novelist Émile Zola, who was twice convicted of libel for his efforts, led in demanding a new trial. The military courts, however, were reluctant to admit past mistakes. A court-martial in 1898 instead acquitted the man who forged the principal evidence against Dreyfus, and a year later it convicted Dreyfus a second time but "with extenuating circumstances," a confusing ruling that led to a presidential pardon. The defenders of Dreyfus narrowly won the battle for public opinion,[6] yet that victory set the tone of subsequent French politics, cementing traditions of republican unity on the left and greatly reducing the political influence of the Church and monarchists.

A Stable Republic   From 1900 until World War I, government was in the hands of firm republicans who called themselves the Radical party. They purged the

---

[6] A few Dreyfusards continued collecting evidence and finally won acquittal in a civil trial in 1906. Dreyfus was then decorated and promoted to the rank of major.

At a mine entrance in the Ruhr in 1912, striking German mine workers read an official proclamation warning that the police are authorized to shoot.
Ullstein Bilderdienst

army of the most outspoken opponents of the republic and passed a law separating church and state in 1905. Yet these so-called radicals also solidified support for the republic through reform and conciliation, reaching out, for example, to small businessmen and peasant farmers, traditionally defenders of the status quo. At the same time, although the trade union movement doubled its membership during this period, frequent strikes never culminated in the revolutionary general strike so much talked about. On the eve of world war, France, prosperous and stable, appeared to have surmounted its most dangerous divisions.

Germany: The Reich

Bismarck had given Germany a constitution that established representative institutions but left power in the hands of a conservative monarchy, and throughout its history the Reich would be haunted by the question of whether this awkward system could hold together or must veer sharply toward autocracy or democracy. Until 1890 Bismarck dominated German public life with an authority few modern figures have equaled. Scornful of criticism, he made many enemies but remained untouchable until William II ascended the throne in 1888 and subsequently forced Bismarck's resignation.

The Army and the Conservative Leagues   Bismarck's policies had allowed for great concentrations of political and economic power in a rapidly expanding society, one in which court, army, bureaucracy, and business were treated as semiautonomous interests. Holding the system together while balancing the demands of parliament and public opinion was a growing challenge, especially as the decline in agriculture

threatened the power base of the Junker ruling elite. Bismarck's successors tried to match his dazzling successes in foreign policy and followed him in attending to the army. Yet military appropriations were a constant, intense source of conflict between right and left, and each time the army expanded and government rhetoric grew more nationalistic, German society became increasingly divided.

Germany's conservatives had learned from Bismarck the value of appealing to the public, and they did so through the strident propaganda of political leagues—the Landlords', Peasants', Pan-German, Colonial, and Naval Leagues—organized in the 1890s. Well-financed by Prussian Junkers and some industrialists, these leagues campaigned for high tariffs, overseas empire, and the military, with attacks on socialists, Jews, and foreign enemies. As pressure groups, they won significant victories, including the naval bill of 1898, which proposed to create a fleet that could compete with Britain's. In addition to building railroads, roads, and schools, the government extended the comprehensive social welfare programs begun under Bismarck, and William II was hailed as "the Labor Emperor" for supporting social security, labor arbitration, the regulation of workers' hours, and provisions for their safety.

The Social Democrats   But Bismarck's hope that such measures would weaken the socialists was not realized. The well-organized Social Democrats continued to gain in the 1890s, and they became the largest party in the Reichstag in 1912 (and the strongest socialist party in Europe) despite the distortions of the electoral system. Socialists also dominated Germany's vigorous labor unions, which had 2.5 million members by 1912, and the Social Democratic party sustained an influential subculture that had its own newspapers, libraries, and recreation centers.

In theory, at least, the Social Democrats remained firm revolutionaries, formally rejecting the revisionism of Eduard Bernstein, who in his book *Evolutionary Socialism* (1897), argued for less emphasis on economic determinism or revolution and a greater focus instead on improving working conditions and strengthening democracy. The subject of international debate, Bernstein's criticism of Marx and his alternative theory implied a less militant socialism willing to cooperate with other democratic parties, and it was an important moment in the history of socialism when Germany's powerful Social Democrats chose instead to make a rigorous Marxism their official policy.

The uncompromising stance of the left was matched in vigor and fury by conservatives. The royal court spoke openly of using the army against radicals. As the chancellor still remained responsible to the crown and not to the Reichstag, Germany's experiment with liberal institutions seemed to be coming to an end. Europe's other powers, facing economic competition from Germany, watched with anxiety as in the last years before World War I, its politicians emphasized militarism and risked imperial clashes with foreign powers to avoid facing political problems at home.

Italy: The Liberal Monarchy

Italy's liberal monarchy was committed to modernizing the nation while balancing the budget and steadily sponsoring modest reforms, but the political system in which only the well-to-do could vote and in which the government kept its parliamentary majority by means of political favors made it hard to win broad popular support.

The Crisis of the 1890s   As a hero of Italian unification and a former radical, Francesco Crispi, prime minister in the late 1880s and 1890s, tried to change that. His policies—which included anticlericalism, a trade war with France, and a disastrous imperial adventure in Ethiopia—proved divisive instead.

Domestic unrest increased both in the poverty-stricken agrarian south and in the rapidly industrializing north, where anarchist bombs, socialist demonstrations, and waves of strikes culminated in riots that reached revolutionary scale in Milan in 1898. The government restored order but at the cost of bloodshed, the suppression of scores of newspapers, and a ban on hundreds of socialist, republican, and Catholic organizations. Many conservatives argued for still firmer measures; yet the Chamber of Deputies, although frightened, refused further restriction of civil liberties, a stand supported in the elections of 1900. In Italy, as in France at the same time,

the political campaign of a revitalized right was defeated by parliament and public opinion.

Limited Liberalism   The political system acquired a broader base of support under Giovanni Giolitti, prime minister from 1903 to 1914. He acknowledged the right to strike, nationalized railroads and life insurance, sponsored public health measures, and in 1911 supported universal male suffrage. Giolitti also encouraged Catholics to enter the national politics they had boycotted since 1870. Like Crispi, he pursued imperial ambitions, waging war on the Ottomans for control of some of their Mediterranean holdings, including Tripoli in Libya. But in contrast to Crispi, whose military debacle in Ethiopia forced him from office, Giolitti's successful war earned his government fervent popular support. Although the economic problems of the south remained grave and the discontent of more and more militant workers went largely unappeased, the Italian economy, less developed than that of the great industrial powers, experienced the fastest growth rate in Europe during the decade ending in 1914. Italy appeared firmly set on a liberal, democratic course.

Russia: Defeat and Revolution

In Russia the pressures for political change were held in check for a generation by official policies that centered on a program of "Russification," meant to create a united nation. But defeat in war and the first stages of industrialization produced a revolution.

Reaction   Alexander III had become tsar in 1881 on his father's assassination, an event that he believed resulted from too much talk about further reform following the abolition of serfdom. He sought to achieve stability by using the Orthodox Church and the police to extend an official reactionary ideology through public life, and he gave nobles an increased role in regional councils, the *zemstvos*, and in rural administration. Local governors were authorized to use martial law, to restrict or ban the religions and languages of non-Russian peoples, and to persecute Jews.[7] These policies were continued with equal conviction but less energy by Tsar Nicholas II, who ascended the throne in 1894. As unrest increased in cities and in the countryside, many in the government searched for other ways of achieving the solidarity that repression had failed to create.

---

[7] One of history's famous forgeries, the *Protocols of the Elders of Zion*, was published (and written) by the Russian police in 1903. The protocols purported to be the secret minutes of a Jewish congress that revealed a conspiracy to control the world.

Studies

Abrams, Lynn. *The Making of Modern Woman: Europe 1789–1918*. 2002. Provides a thorough and wide-ranging examination of both the changing role of women throughout the nineteenth century and the extensive historiography on this subject.

Agulhon, Maurice. *The French Republic 1879–1992*. Antonia Nevill (tr.). 1993. The first part of this comprehensive history of France discusses the Third Republic, with special emphasis paid to political developments.

*Avineri, Shlomo. *The Social and Political Thought of Karl Marx*. 1971. There are dozens of excellent introductions to Marx's thought; this one stands out for its clarity and freshness.

Berghahn, Volker R. *Germany, 1871–1914: Economy, Society, Culture, and Politics*. 1993. A thematic survey unusual in its breadth, particularly attentive to public culture and social structure.

Berlanstein, Lenard R. *The Working People of Paris, 1871–1914*. 1984. Looks at the important changes in the lives of wage earners, in the nature of work, and in the workplace, as well as their impact on working-class movements.

Bowler, P. *Evolution: The History of an Idea*. 1989. Combining recent work in the history of science with more general intellectual history, this book traces the various conceptions of evolution in different fields.

Canning, Kathleen. *Languages of Labor and Gender: Female Factory Work in Germany, 1850–1914*. 1996. Connects social changes in the nature of work to changes in women's lives and to the shifting discourse on gender.

Derfler, Leslie. *Socialism since Marx: A Century of the European Left*. 1973. Thoughtful discussion of the movements that stemmed from Marx, showing their variety, creativity, and contradictions.

Evans, Richard J. (ed.). *Society and Politics in Wilhelmine Germany*. 1979. An important collection of essays applying the "history from below" approach to the study of German history and society.

*Gullickson, Gay L. *Unruly Women of Paris: Images of the Commune*. 1997. A richly illustrated study of the newspaper accounts of the role of women in the Commune.

Hughes, H. Stuart. *Consciousness and Society: The Reorientation of European Social Thought, 1890–1930*. 1958. A gracefully written and indispensable analysis of the currents of modern thought in this time of transition from midcentury certitudes.

Johnson, Douglas. *France and the Dreyfus Affair*. 1966. A cogent account of the affair that explains its extraordinary impact.

*Joll, James. *The Second International, 1889–1914*. 1966. A general history of the socialist movement in this period, with striking portraits of the major figures.

Kaplan, Marion. *The Making of the Jewish Middle Class: Women, Family, and Identity in Imperial Germany*. 1991. An engaging analysis of the position and priorities of Jewish women in late-nineteenth-century Germany.

Kennedy, Paul. *The Rise of the Anglo-German Antagonism, 1860–1914*. 1980. This massive study of international relations includes economic and political rivalry as well as imperialism in accounting for the rising tension between the two nations.

Kocka, Jürgen, and Allan Mitchell (eds.). *Bourgeois Society in Nineteenth-Century Europe*. 1993. A collection of essays examining and comparing the rise of the middle class in Britain, France, Germany, and Italy.

Lidtke, Vernon. *The Alternative Culture: Socialist Labor in Imperial Germany*. 1985. A significant analysis of how German socialists created Europe's best-organized working-class subculture.

*Löwith, Karl. *From Hegel to Nietzsche: The Revolution in Nineteenth-Century Thought*. 1964. A sober essay on the pessimistic and irrationalist transformations in modern thought and the powerful insights that resulted.

McLellan, David. *Karl Marx: His Life and Thought*. 1977. Considers the more youthful writings as well as *Das Kapital,* bringing out their essential unity.

Milward, Alan S., and S. B. Saul. *The Development of the Economies of Continental Europe, 1850–1914*. 1977. A study of the second great wave of industrialization, which underscores the difference between this later continental experience and the earlier English one.

Moses, Claire. *French Feminism in the Nineteenth Century*. 1984. Reveals the vigor of a feminist movement quite different from its British and German counterparts.

*Mosse, George L. *The Crisis of German Ideology*. 1964. Looks for the currents of Nazi ideology in the views of nation and race embodied in the popular ideas and movements of the late nineteenth century.

Nord, Philip. *Paris Shopkeepers and the Politics of Resentment*. 1986. Explores the antimodern militancy of lower-middle-class shopkeepers seen in response to the rise of mass-produced goods and the prominence of the department store.

Paret, Peter. *The Berlin Secession: Modernism and Its Enemies in Imperial Germany*. 1980. Examines the Berlin Secessionist movement, which was a major cultural force in German politics and culture between 1898 and 1918.

Pick, Daniel. *Faces of Degeneration: A European Disorder, c. 1848–1918.* 1989. Comparative study of the cultural preoccupation with "degeneration" in Great Britain, Italy, and France in the decades before the First World War.

Ralston, David B. *The Army of the Republic, 1871–1914.* 1967. Treats the role of the military in France both before and after the Dreyfus affair.

Reddy, William M. *Money and Liberty in Modern Europe: A Critique of Historical Understanding.* 1987. A critical look at the social impact of the expansion of capitalism in England, France, and Germany, probing the nature of the inequality that resulted.

Schivelbusch, Wolfgang. *The Railway Journey: The Industrialization of Time and Space in the 19th Century.* 1986. Explores the psychological and technological impact of the introduction and expansion of rail travel throughout later nineteenth-century Europe.

*Schorske, Carl E. *Fin-de-Siècle Vienna: Politics and Culture.* 1980. Sensitive and imaginative assessment of one of the important moments in European cultural history.

Seton-Watson, Christopher. *Italy from Liberalism to Fascism.* 1967. A general political account of Italy in its first period of rapid industrialization.

Sheehan, James J. *German Liberalism in the Nineteenth Century.* 1978. A detailed assessment of a much disputed and critical issue, the place of liberalism in German intellectual and political life.

Showalter, Elaine. *Sexual Anarchy: Gender and Culture at the Fin de Siècle.* 1990. Analyzes the myths and images of sexual crisis that were dominant in both Europe and the United States at this time.

Smith, Helmut Walser, *The Butcher's Tale: Murder and Anti-Semitism in a German Town.* 2002. Engaging analysis of an unsolved murder, committed in 1900 in the easternmost part of the German empire, that testifies to both the strength and irrationality of European anti-Semitism at the turn of the century.

*Weber, Eugen. *Peasants into Frenchmen: The Modernization of Rural France, 1880–1914.* 1976. A provocative treatment stressing how resistance in rural France to pressures for change delayed modernization efforts.

*Available in paperback.

Thomas Jones Barker
The Secret of England's Greatness, CA. 1863
Painted by Thomas Jones Barker in 1863, this painting, entitled *The Secret of England's Greatness*, epitomizes the nineteenth-century liberal conception of empire. Prince Albert and the statesmen Lord Palmerston and Lord John Russell look on as Queen Victoria gives a Bible to a kneeling African. The queen represents empire as a benevolent, paternalist force, bestowing European civilization and Christianity on the colonies. The African symbolizes the colonial subject, who embraces his subordinate position and gratefully receives these gifts.
The National Portrait Gallery, London

Chapter Twenty-Six

NINETEENTH-CENTURY EMPIRES

THE BIRTH OF THE LIBERAL EMPIRE • EUROPEAN EXPANSION IN THE MIDCENTURY •
THE NEW IMPERIALISM, 1870–1914 • IMPERIALISM AT ITS PEAK

Since the first invasions of the Spanish conquistadors in the early sixteenth century, Europeans had amassed a vast New World empire. A flourishing plantation economy, sustained by African slave labor, formed the economic base of this world, the hub of which was the prosperous sugar colonies of the West Indies. The New World colonies served the mercantilist goal to enrich the monarchical state through the creation of advantageous trade monopolies with its colonies and found moral justification in the religious mission of saving the immortal souls of "heathens."

In the early nineteenth century, a new liberal empire supplanted this older religious-mercantilist colonial regime. Abandoning the New World, European entrepreneurs, merchants, missionaries, and explorers staked claims in Asia and Africa. European governments frequently followed in their wake, carving out spheres of influence to protect their interests and activities. Operating increasingly within the context of a market economy, nineteenth-century Europeans perceived the non-Western world as untapped markets for European manufactures and capital investment and as sources of raw materials for Europe's

burgeoning industries. Steeped in the culture of the Enlightenment and principles of liberal universalism, moreover, Europeans saw empire not just as a means of benefiting themselves, but as an opportunity to bring the fruits of European civilization to the non-Western world.

In the late nineteenth century, empire's foundations shifted once more. The "new imperialism" of this period was characterized by the aggressive expansionism of competing European nation-states. In the space of a few decades, Europeans conquered and colonized virtually all of Africa and vast regions of Asia. European attitudes toward colonial subjects changed as well, shaped by anticolonial insurgence and, after Darwin, the ascendancy of biological determinism in thinking about culture and race. These developments undermined the liberal aims of the early nineteenth century, raising new doubts about both the desirability and the feasibility of Europeanizing non-European peoples. The turn of the century was thus a moment of intense contradictions: the peak moment of Europe's global power, but also one in which Europeans began to rethink the scope and future of empire.

Indian Rebellion **1857**

Taiping Rebellion in China **1850–1864** ▶

The Great Trek of the Afrikaners in southern Africa **1835–1845** ▬▬▬▬

Britain abolishes slavery **1834** ●

● **1807** Britain abolishes the slave trade

▬▬▬▬▬▬▬ **1804–1825** Latin American liberation from colonial rul

● **1791** Haitian Revolution

THE BIRTH OF THE LIBERAL EMPIRE

In the nineteenth century, Europeans lost their Atlantic empires and built new ones in Asia and Africa. Although the first two-thirds of the century saw little outright colonization, Europeans steadily expanded their influence overseas. As European merchants, missionaries, explorers, and settlers penetrated different parts of the world, European governments provided them with support and, in so doing, became increasingly involved in the affairs of foreign polities. The expansionism of this period had its economic foundation in the growth of a capitalist market economy and its philosophical roots in the Enlightenment culture of liberal universalism. Europeans thus saw the acquisition of overseas spheres of influence as a way to secure new sources of raw materials and new markets for their industrial manufacturers and, equally important, as an opportunity to "civilize" the non-Western world by making it over in the European image.

The Decline of the Mercantile Colonial World

The mercantile colonial world sustained an unprecedented series of external and internal challenges during the late eighteenth and early nineteenth centuries. Outside of Europe, the threat to empire came primarily in the form of independence movements and slave revolts. Simultaneously, within Europe, the gradual rise of a market economy and the cultural revolution sparked by the Enlightenment undermined the foundations of the old empire.

External Challenges Independence movements, starting with the American Revolution of 1776, drove Euro-

pean colonial powers from much of the New World at the turn of the nineteenth century. From 1804 to 1824, France lost control of Haiti (then known as Saint-Domingue); Portugal of Brazil; and Spain the rest of Latin America except for Cuba and Puerto Rico (see chapter 21). Led by landed Creole elites (American-born people of European descent), Latin American independence movements were influenced by Enlightenment thought and the examples of the French and American Revolutions.

Slave agitation constituted a central part of the assault on the mercantile colonial world. From the late eighteenth through the early nineteenth centuries, runaway slaves called *Maroons*, living in outlaw societies behind the lines of colonial settlement in South America, the Caribbean, and Spanish Florida, waged sporadic guerilla attacks against local plantations, a phenomenon known as the Maroon Wars. Simultaneously, a series of increasingly well-planned and militant slave revolts from Dutch Surinam to British Jamaica erupted in the second half of the eighteenth century, culminating in the Haitian Revolution in the French colony of Sainte-Domingue in 1791 (see "The Fight for Liberty and Equality in Saint-Domingue," p. 598).

The Antislavery Movement in Europe A rapidly expanding European movement to end slavery further threatened the Atlantic colonial system during the late eighteenth century. Although abolitionists organized in the Netherlands and France as well, the British campaign was by far the strongest and most effective.

Religious antislavery sentiment served as the catalyst to abolitionism. In spite of the fact that most world religions had historically sanctioned slavery, by the eighteenth century newer forms of Protestantism—Quakerism among them—condemned slavery as a sin antithetical to religious tenets of brotherly love and

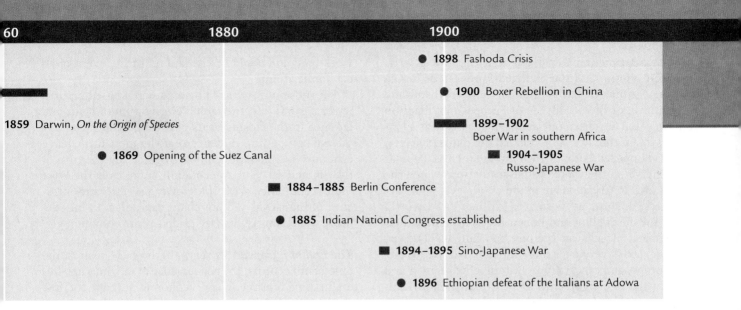

● **1898** Fashoda Crisis

● **1900** Boxer Rebellion in China

1859 Darwin, *On the Origin of Species*

■ **1899–1902**
Boer War in southern Africa

■ **1904–1905**
Russo-Japanese War

● **1869** Opening of the Suez Canal

■ **1884–1885** Berlin Conference

● **1885** Indian National Congress established

■ **1894–1895** Sino-Japanese War

● **1896** Ethiopian defeat of the Italians at Adowa

spiritual equality. These religious dissenters sparked the movement and established its emotive tone and ethic of benevolence, but antislavery soon spread from there to the religious mainstream, including well-connected Evangelicals, such as the parliamentary member William Wilberforce.

The Influence of the Enlightenment Secular reformers joined forces with religious abolitionists. Although philosophers had debated the morality of slavery well before sustained Christian opposition to slavery burgeoned, most had found ways to justify slavery as a rational and efficient economic and social system. Such justifications became more difficult to make in the humanist intellectual climate of the Enlightenment. Thus, while the seventeenth-century political theorist John Locke himself condoned slavery, his ideas—in particular, his critique of arbitrary power, appeal to rule by reason, and championing of natural and universal human rights—shaped arguments mounted against slavery by Enlightenment humanists such as Baron Montesquieu and Denis Diderot a century later.

Most fundamentally, Enlightenment universalism, or belief in the basic sameness of all humans, undermined the acceptance of slavery and allowed eighteenth-century thinkers to link oppressed Africans to the disenfranchised poor of Europe. Values and principles rooted in this universalist framework, including belief in the individual's natural and inalienable right to freedom, ownership of one's self and labor, and equality before the law, also clashed deeply with the concept of human bondage. Finally, the Enlightenment's optimism and emphasis on the inner goodness and malleability of human beings made it difficult to defend slavery as a necessary evil for less "civilized" peoples. This view was perhaps best encapsulated in Rousseau's cult of the noble savage, which contrasted the natural

Illustration from a nineteenth-century British children's book of a slave being flogged. Part of the abolitionist campaign against British slavery, the image was intended to stir compassion for the slaves' suffering in young readers. The British Library, London

virtues of the so-called primitive with the moral flaws of civilized Europeans and further fostered popular sympathy for enslaved Africans. Taken together, these ideas persuaded Enlightenment thinkers across Europe to soundly reject slavery as an unreasonable, unnatural, and immoral system.

Enlightened philosophical and religious arguments also influenced a romantically oriented popular culture of feeling in the late eighteenth century. This helped make antislavery a pervasive, even fashionable, position among the European elite, especially among well-to-do women, who came to play a pivotal role in the British movement. Religious emphasis on the goodness of humans and the importance of compassion fit with a secular, sentimental worldview that cast the slave as innocent victim and the civilized European as heroic savior. Similarly, Enlightenment universalism and recognition of the decadence of European civilization fed educated European outrage against slavery as a barbaric system that not only violated the rights of slaves, but also impeded Europe's own moral progress. Popular primitivism in the wake of Rousseau also elevated the status of the African slave in the public eye, while acclaimed Romantic poets such as William Wordsworth, Percy Bysshe Shelley, and Robert Burns fashioned their own poetic attacks on tyranny and human bondage, making antislavery ever more modish. All over Western Europe, and especially in Britain, elite women and men of the late eighteenth and early nineteenth century inspired by these trends joined abolitionist circles, signed antislavery petitions, and circulated tracts and images that exposed the cruelties of human bondage.

The Free-Trade Lobby   By themselves these intellectual and cultural developments probably would not have had the force to abolish slavery. However, antislavery sentiment was strongly reinforced by merchants and industrialists seeking to replace the mercantile colonial system—and its system of protective tariffs intended to privilege trade between colony and mother country—with free trade. By the early nineteenth century, European manufacturers objected increasingly to the protective tariffs levied on foreign imports in the mercantile marketplace. These tariffs effectively prevented domestic manufacturers and consumers from buying cheaper foreign goods, compelling them instead to purchase goods exclusively from domestic producers, at home or in the colonies. British sugar refiners, for example, felt exploited by a system that forced them to buy high-priced raw sugar from Jamaica, while shielding Jamaican sugar producers from competition from French sugar producers in Sainte-Domingue and Spanish sugar producers in Cuba.

Capitalists in favor of free trade based their arguments on both theory and real-world experience. For theoretical support, they drew on critiques of **mercantilism** and the slave economy elaborated by Enlightenment classical economists such as Adam Smith and David Ricardo. Smith and Ricardo contended that the mercantile colonial economy was an inefficient, irrational system that flouted the natural law of rational utility by preventing most people from pursuing their economic self-interest. In contrast, they argued, market competition was both natural and rational because it afforded economic liberty to individuals and benefited the majority by generating lower prices all around. Smith also censured the built-in inefficiency and inflexibility of the slave economy, pointing out that slaves, unlike wage laborers, lacked the incentive to work hard and could not be laid off in the event of an economic slump.

For those unconvinced by arguments based on utility or natural law, the rapid deterioration of Haiti and Jamaica in the closing years of the eighteenth century offered compelling evidence that the mercantile slave economy was economically retrograde. By the turn of the nineteenth century, economic troubles in the West Indies, combined with the growing wealth and influence of industrial and merchant capitalists in Europe, made the claims of the free traders more convincing.

The End of European Slavery   In the early years of the nineteenth century, the convergence of religious and humanitarian sentiment and economic support for free market competition led to the abolition of the European slave trade. Denmark outlawed the Atlantic slave trade first in 1803, followed by Britain and the United States in 1807. Although Spain, Portugal, France, and the Netherlands agreed to abolish the slave trade in 1815, they did little to eliminate it. Britain, by contrast, embarked on a zealous antislaving mission, searching ships in the Atlantic suspected of carrying slave cargo and rescuing slaves along the West African coast. They provided the latter with passage to Liberia, an African settlement created for and partly by freed American slaves in 1821. By 1850 the European slave trade had essentially ended.

Britain abolished slavery itself in 1834, emancipating the remaining 780,000 British-owned slaves in the West Indies. The British government paid £20 million to slave owners to compensate them for their loss of property. While France and Denmark followed suit in 1848, slavery continued until 1863 in the Dutch New World colonies, 1865 in the United States, 1886 in Spanish Cuba, and 1888 in Brazil. These dates often mattered more to Europeans than to freed slaves, however, who in some cases continued to be treated as slaves for several decades after emancipation.

New Sources of Colonial Legitimacy

Just as the economic, religious, and intellectual forces of the Enlightenment undermined the mercantile colonial world, they also built the new liberal empire that replaced it.

The Growth of the Market Economy   The continued growth of industrial capitalism and the market economy brought a new economic rationale to empire. Free-trade advocates in the business world became richer and more influential during the early nineteenth century. By the 1830s, their belief in the individual pursuit of profit in a free, self-regulating market as efficient, natural, and moral was considered common sense. Yet, while free market competition was the mantra of early-to-mid-nineteenth-century capitalists, economic practice sometimes contradicted imperial rhetoric. From 1830 to 1870—the peak era of economic liberalism—European nation-states competed with one another for spheres of economic influence abroad. Europeans were quick to abandon free trade, in other words, when they perceived their own economic interests to be threatened by indigenous and other European competitors.

Enlightenment Universalism   The liberal empire's philosophical underpinnings also differed fundamentally from those of early modern empire. Liberal empire had roots in Enlightenment theories of human biological and cultural sameness and belief in human improvement through the application of reason to social reform. While pre-Enlightenment Europeans had emphasized the irreconcilable, permanent gap between themselves and others, eighteenth-century philosophers from Montesquieu to Voltaire claimed the similarities between human societies to be far more significant than the differences. Likewise, although Enlightenment natural scientists like the Swede Carolus Linnaeus or the Frenchman Georges-Louis Leclerc de Buffon sought to classify the varieties of human physical types, they assumed that the "races" of man belonged to a single species. Enlightened Europeans posited that, while different societies had attained different levels of civilization, all of them occupied positions along a common developmental path. This belief meant not only that change was possible, but that the process of development could be guided and accelerated through reasoned social intervention.

Cultural Relativism   Europeans at the turn of the nineteenth century were also less firmly convinced of their own superiority and more critical about the colonial enterprise than their forebears. The universalist framework of the eighteenth century allowed for a new cultural relativism that recognized the value and achievements of other societies. Voltaire's respect for ancient Chinese and Islamic civilizations and the English historian Edward Gibbon's admiration for Islam exemplify this trend, as does the rhetoric of Christian brotherhood preached by evangelical missionaries. Similarly, cultural relativism permitted Rousseau and his followers to exalt New World societies as models of virtue and freedom for a decadent Europe. In the main, however, European cultural relativists still insisted on their own supremacy, even while acknowledging the achievements of other cultures.

These Enlightenment ideas had radical implications for the colonial project. During the sixteenth and seventeenth centuries, colonizers had concerned themselves primarily with the "heathen" nature of "savage" societies and the future of their immortal souls. Assim-

ilation to a European way of life had occurred largely as an unintended consequence of missionary efforts to impart Christian faith to New World peoples. By the turn of the nineteenth century, in contrast, universalism had humanized the colonial subject, and assimilation, rather than exclusion or outright exploitation, emerged as the dominant model for confronting the difference of the non-European. The majority of Europeans, both secular and religious, saw the assimilation of other peoples to European political, economic, and cultural models as a moral imperative and colonial domination as the ideal means to achieve this end. At the same time, a powerful new sense of instrumentality—of the ability of humans to shape the world around them—lent confidence to their civilizing endeavors.

The Case of Captain Cook   The new ideological underpinnings of the emergent liberal empire were exemplified by Captain James Cook's expeditions to the South Pacific. The prototypical colonialist of the Enlightenment, Cook's explicit goals were not merely commercial but also scientific: his voyage was part of a series of eighteenth-century expeditions to explore this region, the last maritime frontier for Europeans, and, in particular, to locate the missing continent, known as *Terra Australis*. Toward this end, a team of more than twenty ethnographers, geographers, botanists, and other scientific experts, accompanied Cook on his South Seas voyages.

Cook's voyages to the South Pacific also bore traces of Europeans' new moral scruples in their interactions with non-Europeans. Unlike earlier generations of colonizers, Cook and his contemporaries were self-conscious about the delicate nature of their enterprise and sought to justify their intrusion with the lofty goals of advancing science and spreading civilization. As universalists, they accorded rights to non-Europeans; as cultural relativists, they ascribed value to cultural difference. In practical terms, this meant that King George III authorized Cook to establish British authority in Hawaii in 1779, for example, but cautioned him to do so only with the express consent of the natives; similarly, the Royal Scientific Society, one of the chief backers of the voyage, instructed Cook to treat the local customs and culture with the utmost respect. In ways such as these, late-eighteenth-century colonizers sought not only to legitimize their role as civilizers in the eyes of the colonized but to reinforce their own identities as the civilized by divorcing themselves from the brutality of their imperial precursors.

The Civilizing Mission in India   In the early nineteenth century, India was the laboratory in which Britain conducted its most ambitious civilizing experiments. While evangelical missionaries such as Charles Grant

Johann Zoffany
***The Death of Captain James Cook*, 1779**
Zoffany's painting depicts the prototypical explorer-scientist of the Enlightenment, Captain James Cook (lying on the ground in the center of the image), and his men being attacked by angry, armed Hawaiians in Kealakekua Bay in 1779. Cook was killed in the fracas. His death helped call into question the popular myth of the noble savage, marking a turning point in European views of "primitive" people.
National Maritime Museum, Greenwich, London

Thomas Rowlands
***The Burning System*, 1815**
This engraving shows an Indian woman committing sati, or burning herself on the funeral pyre of her dead husband. On one side are native musicians. On the other, Englishmen debate the pros and cons of abolishing sati, the practice of which was considered a sign of India's backwardness.
The British Library, London

and William Wilberforce sought to bring religious enlightenment and to stamp out Indian "superstition," secular liberal reformers like Jeremy Bentham, James Mill, his son, John Stuart Mill, and Thomas Macaulay determined to rid India of "Oriental despotism" by eradicating "barbaric" Indian laws and customs and introducing a British-style educational system (see "Macaulay's Minute on Indian Education," p. 779). Macaulay claimed that the "entire native literature of India and Arabia" was not worth "a single shelf of a good European library," asserting that a British model of education was

needed to produce "a class of persons Indian in blood and color, but English in taste, in opinions, in morals and intellect." The potent triad of law, education, and free trade, British reformers believed, would bring the hopelessly backward Indians into the modern world.

Liberal reformers sought to apply liberal ideas to eliminate the barriers of custom and tradition and managed to bring about several important policy changes in India. One of the controversial reforms was to prohibit *sati*, the practice of the widow burning herself to death on the funeral pyre of her dead husband.

MACAULAY'S MINUTE ON INDIAN EDUCATION

Thomas Macaulay (1800–1859) was the Law Member of the Governor General's Council and an important example of the British liberal voice in India. He believed that "backward" societies like India's could be transformed through the introduction of law, free trade, and education. In the early part of the nineteenth century, Orientalist scholars and administrators felt that India should be ruled through its own laws and through indigenous institutions and languages. British liberals like Macaulay thought otherwise. In 1835 a major debate took place as to what kind of education the British should promote and finance. Macaulay argued that Indians should be taught Western subjects and the English language instead of Arabic and Sanskrit. This was seen as imperative to disseminate moral values as well as maintain and strengthen British rule in India. On Macaulay's advice, English was made the medium of education in secondary schools established in major cities across India.

"How, then, stands the case? We have to educate a people who cannot at present be educated by means of their mother-tongue. We must teach them some foreign language. The claims of our own language it is hardly necessary to recapitulate. It stands pre-eminent even among the languages of the west. It abounds with works of imagination not inferior to the noblest which Greece has bequeathed to us; with models of every species of eloquence; with historical compositions, which, considered merely as narratives, have seldom been surpassed, and which, considered as vehicles of ethical and political instruction, have never been equalled; with just and lively representations of human life and human nature; with the most profound speculations on metaphysics, morals, government, jurisprudence, and trade; with full and correct information respecting every experimental science which tends to preserve the health, to increase the comfort, or to expand the intellect of man. Whoever knows that language has ready access to all the vast intellectual wealth, which all the wisest nations of the earth have created and hoarded in the course of ninety generations. It may safely be said, that the literature now extant in that language is of far greater value than all the literature which three hundred years ago was extant in all the languages of the world together. Nor is this all. In India, English is the language spoken by the ruling class. It is spoken by the higher class of natives at the seats of Government. It is likely to become the language of commerce throughout the seas of the East. It is the language of two great European communities which are rising, the one in the south of Africa, the other in Australasia; communities which are every year becoming more important, and more closely connected with our Indian empire. Whether we look at the intrinsic value of our literature, or at the particular situation of this country, we shall see the strongest reason to think that, of all foreign tongues, the English tongue is, that which would be the most useful to our native subjects. . . .

"To sum up what I have said, I think it clear that we are not fettered by the Act of Parliament of 1813; that we are not fettered by any pledge expressed or implied; that we are free to employ our funds as we choose; that we ought to employ them in teaching what is best worth knowing; that English is better worth knowing than Sanscrit or Arabic; that the natives are desirous to be taught English, and are not desirous to be taught Sanscrit or Arabic; that neither as the languages of law, nor as the languages of religion, have the Sanscrit and Arabic any peculiar claim to our engagement; that it is possible to make natives of this country thoroughly good English scholars, and that to this end our efforts ought to be directed.

"In one point I fully agree with the gentlemen to whose general views I am opposed. I feel with them, that it is impossible for us, with our limited means, to attempt to educate the body of the people. We must at present do our best to form a class who may be interpreters between us and the millions whom we govern; a class of persons, Indian in blood and colour, but English in taste, in opinions, in morals, and in intellect. To that class we may leave it to refine the vernacular dialects of the country, to enrich those dialects with terms of science borrowed from the Western nomenclature, and to render them by degrees fit vehicles for conveying knowledge to the great mass of the population."

G. M. Young (ed.), *Speeches by Lord Macauley with His Minute on Indian Education*, Oxford University Press, 1935.

For the British, *sati* epitomized both the moral weakness of Indian men, who degraded rather than protected their women, and the general backwardness of Indian civilization as a whole. Although *sati* became a key public symbol of the liberal reform agenda, it was not, in fact, a widespread practice, but was actually limited only to certain groups of upper-caste Hindus.

British civilizing efforts came to an abrupt halt, however, with the Indian Rebellion of 1857 (see "The Indian Rebellion of 1857," pp. 800–802). Hereafter, British officials ceded issues of Indian reform to Indian social reformers, since they saw their interference in Indian religion and ritual as one of the key causes of the discontent that had sparked the rebellion.

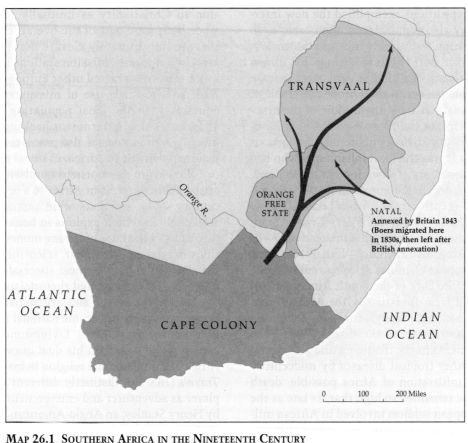

MAP 26.1 SOUTHERN AFRICA IN THE NINETEENTH CENTURY
Friction between Afrikaner and British settlers in southern Africa sparked Afrikaner emigration from the Cape Colony during the 1830s and 1840s (the Great Trek) and led to the establishment of independent Afrikaner republics. British expansionist aspirations, intensified by the discovery of diamond and gold in Afrikaner territory in the late nineteenth century, threatened the long-term survival of the republics. They were absorbed into British South Africa after the Boer War of 1889–1902. How did conflict between Europeans and Africans in the region affect the intra-European conflict?
◆ For an online version, go to www.mhhe.com/chambers9 > chapter 26 > book maps

In southern Africa, fifteen thousand Afrikaners migrated north of the Orange River in the Great Trek of 1835–1845, fleeing British control and seeking land of their own. Despite ongoing battles over territory with Bantus, in particular the Zulus (a southern Bantu people), the Afrikaners flourished as cattle ranchers and, by the late 1830s, had established independent Afrikaner republics in the Natal, the Orange Free State, and the Transvaal. For the British, however, Afrikaner expansionism threatened their own sovereignty and plans for further expansion in southern Africa. To cut the Afrikaners off from strategic coastal access, they annexed the Natal province outright in 1843 and, although the British eventually recognized the sovereignty of the Orange Free State and the Transvaal in 1854, they meddled continually in Bantu-Afrikaner conflicts.

Clashes with African Powers These European incursions did not meet with a passive, quiescent Africa. Parallel to the European infiltration of Africa, widespread internal war and conquest destabilized African politics and economic life in large parts of the continent during the early to mid-nineteenth century. In particular, Zulu political ambitions in southern Africa and the theocratic aims of Islamic jihad states in West Africa during this period created political and economic upheaval across broad swathes of Africa. In many cases, African polities on the move collided with expansionist Europeans, often ending in violent confrontation.

The sudden ascendancy of the Zulus in South Africa in the early nineteenth century was a case in point. In the 1820s, the military genius Shaka Zulu built a powerful and extensive Zulu empire in the Natal region, sparking major disturbances in Southern Africa. Although many inhabitants of the area capitulated outright to Shaka's dominion, his raiding armies also drove many other Bantu peoples, including the Ndebele, to seek refuge elsewhere. As huge numbers of Bantus fled the Zulus south into British territory and north into the Afrikaner republics, Bantus and Afrikaners warred continually over land. The Zulus themselves also battled Afrikaners who migrated north into Zulu dominions in 1837–1838, as well as the British, most notably in the Anglo-Zulu War of 1878–1879. Although the latter marked the first defeat of a European power by an African force in the Battle of Isandhlwana, the British ultimately crushed the Zulus.

The expansion of Islam in Africa during this period also triggered great turmoil. In the late eighteenth century and early nineteenth century, a fundamentalist Islamic revival emerged among the Fulani people in West Africa. The Fulani reviled indigenous religious beliefs and practices as well as European Christianity as threats to the purity of Islam. Overthrowing the local Hausa chieftains, the Fulani established an enduring decentralized state structure known as the Sokoto caliphate in 1809, which waged *jihad*—holy war—to impose Islam throughout the region. By midcentury, expansionist Fulani jihadists came into conflict with French colonizers moving east out of Senegal.

European Encroachment in Egypt   Europeans sought control of Egypt, an Ottoman province since the sixteenth century, because of its strategic location on the Red Sea en route to India. When Ottoman control wavered in the late eighteenth century, Napoleon seized the opportunity to invade Egypt in 1798, although British forces, backed by Ottoman Turks, ultimately destroyed his fleet in the Battle of the Nile. Although the Ottomans regained nominal rule of the province, the Sultan lost control when Mohammed Ali, an Albanian officer in the Ottoman army of reoccupation, seized power. Mohammed Ali's efforts to establish Egyptian autonomy were thwarted, however, by the Sultan's continued resistance and British and French commercial interests in Egypt. By midcentury, Europeans controlled a large portion of Egypt's trade and European bankers were financing modernization projects. These included constructing an Egyptian railway system from Alexandria to Cairo and building the Suez Canal connecting the Red Sea to the Mediterranean Sea under Ferdinand Lesseps's direction from 1859 to 1869.

THE NEW IMPERIALISM, 1870–1914

In the closing decades of the nineteenth century, Europeans remapped the contours of empire. By the 1870s, the piecemeal expansionism of the earlier part of the century gave way to a systematic campaign of explicit conquest and occupation of much of Africa and Asia. This global conquest is often described as the "new imperialism" to differentiate it from earlier forms of empire. Indeed, while late-nineteenth-century imperialism was built on many of the same ideological foundations as the midcentury empire and endorsed the liberal civilizing mission at the outset, it soon metamorphosed into a distinctive intellectual and material enterprise.

Four features of the new imperialism stand out as novel. First, late-nineteenth-century European nations adopted imperialism as an official policy for the first

In 1897, the British troops attacked and looted the Edo capital of Benin, in present-day southern Nigeria. The Benin expedition was a punitive one, responding to the ambush of a British military party sent to force trade concessions from the Edo king a year earlier. This photograph shows British officers of the expedition surrounded by booty, including the famed Benin bronzes, seized from the royal compound. The plundered objects ended up in European and American art museums.
Courtesy of the Trustees of The British Museum

time, replacing empires governed largely by traders with those ruled by expansionist states. Although European nation-states had sponsored imperial expansion earlier in the century, they had most often done so after the fact, in an effort to protect and promote the activities of their missionaries and merchants overseas; now it was the state that took the imperial initiative. Second, the entrance of a new group of nations into the race for territory during this period changed the rules of the imperial game. In Europe, Germany, Belgium, and Italy appeared on the imperial scene, while outside Europe, the United States and Japan emerged as major imperial powers. As multiple players competed aggressively for territory and power, Britain's longstanding global sovereignty began to fade. Third, the more competitive imperial climate changed the political objectives of imperial nations. No longer content with informal influence, they now sought explicit territorial occupation and political conquest. Finally, the new imperialism defined its own distinctive ideological mission, gradually abandoning the universalist premise of the liberal empire for a belief in the unbreakable gap between Europe and its colonial subjects. As that happened, Europeans began to retreat from the civilizing goals of the early to midcentury and to seek increasingly to secure and consolidate imperial rule through force. Unfettered by the moral constraints of early nineteenth-century colonizers, the new imperialism brought Europe to the peak of its power.

Europe Transformed: Explaining the New Imperialism

No single factor can explain the new imperialism. Rather, it emerged out of a number of significant changes that occurred in Europe during the second half of the nineteenth century.

Technology   By the late nineteenth century, Europeans had access to new and astonishingly efficient technologies that would change the course of colonial conquest and domination. To be sure, technology had played a major role in spreading European influence abroad throughout the nineteenth century and earlier; steamships, industrial weaponry, and the use of quinine to treat malaria had allowed Europeans to penetrate continental Africa, and the arrival of gunboats—armed steamboats—had played decisive roles, for example, in the conquest of Burma and the opening of China. Nevertheless, the advent of the second industrial revolution (see chapter 25) in the late nineteenth century made technology an even more important factor in the speed, extent, and vigor of the conquests. Ironclad warships with steam turbines now spread the power of far more advanced and

deadly European weaponry overseas, while the invention of the telegraph radically simplified the logistics of military mobilization from afar. After conquest, dynamite lessened the difficulty of building roads, and modern medicine significantly reduced the dangers of fighting and living in the tropics.

Nationalism   While turn-of-the-century technologies made possible conquest on a global scale, they did not create new incentives to conquer. Most historians would agree that it was nationalism—understood in the broadest sense of the term—that propelled the new imperialism forward. Although nationalism was hardly new, it developed in strikingly new ways during this period. The ideological tenor of nationalism changed, moving away from its early-nineteenth-century romantic and liberal origins and tilting toward a more strident, aggressive, and exclusionary variant. Nationalism was transformed, in other words, from a phenomenon associated with the democratic and liberal left to one linked to the emergence of a new mass politics on the right. Based on emotional appeals to community and history, the new nationalism challenged the liberal politics of the midcentury based on the rational individual and the possibilities of societal progress. Imperial domination, in this context, was seen as a sign of national vigor and a marker of prestige.

Nationalism also played an integral role in the rise of a new political and economic order of nation-states in this period. Germany's national unification transformed it overnight into one of the foremost continental powers. Its meteoric economic and political ascent, along with the emergence of Japan and the United States as industrial giants, fundamentally reconfigured the global balance of power and in so doing changed the stakes of empire. The new order sharply challenged British global sovereignty, unrivaled since the late eighteenth century, and demoted Britain's lagging rival, France, to a third-rate power. On the economic and political defensive, Britain and France sought to expand their empires to compensate for their loss of economic primacy and political prestige. Germany, Japan, and the United States responded in turn by carving out their own colonial empires.

Economic Factors   Within this charged nationalist framework, economic, political, and cultural forces each played their role in promoting the imperial scramble. Economic factors were critical. As they had done earlier in the century, turn-of-the-century imperial nations viewed their colonies as vital markets for selling European industrial goods, buying raw materials and cash crops, and investing surplus capital. But now the economic context had changed. One new factor was the presence of Germany and the United States as leading industrial powers. By 1890 both Germany and the United States had surpassed British steel and iron production and Germany was outselling the British in certain overseas markets (Latin America, China, and the Ottoman Empire). A lengthy industrial depression from 1873 to the early 1890s played a significant role as well. This unstable economic context promoted the view that colonial markets could act as buffers against the fluctuations of global commerce. As a consequence, the Western European nations started to abandon the rhetoric of free trade in the 1880s and 1890s, once again endorsing mercantilist policies that—in addition to raising trade barriers in the domestic market—explicitly demarcated the colonies as protected economic spheres. Finally, the advent of a new, more advanced phase of industrial capitalism in the late nineteenth century brought with it fears of saturation of the domestic market and, with that, industrial overproduction. In this context, many Europeans came to view empire as an essential outlet for surpluses of goods and capital.

As scholars of empire have pointed out, however, economic incentives alone cannot account for the new imperialism, and nation-states often pursued imperial objectives even when their economic costs appeared to outweigh their benefits. Undoubtedly, the colonies furnished attractive markets for Europe's industrial manufactures in the late nineteenth century; in 1890 Britain exported one-third of its industrial goods and one-quarter of its investment capital to India. However, strictly in terms of trade volume, European nations traded far more with other independent countries, including their European neighbors, than they did with their colonies. Britain, the largest overseas investor and trader, traded more with Latin America and the United States, for example, than with its African or even its Asian colonies. Moreover, it was not always the most industrialized, economically powerful nations that took the imperial initiative. Although France lagged far behind Germany as an industrial producer, for example, it was the French who amassed the world's second largest empire.

Political Motives   The primacy of the nation-state during this period also put strategic and territorial ambitions at center stage. The actions of European nations within the imperial arena were taken as much to jockey for political power and to preempt the territorial claims of other nations as they were to pursue economic gain. For Kaiser Wilhelm II, the German ruler from 1888 to 1918, for example, a central motivation for building up a strong German navy was to contest Britain's global power, so dependent on its naval strength, in North Africa, China, and the Ottoman Empire. The new nation of Italy likewise sought a colonial empire in North and East Africa as part of its quest to achieve great-power status.

Cultural Incentives   In the cultural realm, too, late-nineteenth-century nation-states mobilized imperialism to assist with internal processes of state-building. Newly unified nation-states, in particular, but older and established ones as well, actively sought to fully unify their citizens, in large part by inducing them to transfer their primary loyalties from their local community to the far more abstract, "imagined" community of the nation. This process met with significant resistance, particularly since it entailed a loss of regional identity, and national leaders used the attractions of empire as one means of appealing to its citizens. Empire was presented as the shared symbolic property of the nation, an asset that in theory (but not in practice) transcended social class and allowed peasants and workers—as much as members of the upper classes—to cast themselves as superior to the nation's colonial subjects. Governments also encouraged their citizens to conceive of empire as a measure of the nation's virile masculinity, seen in favorable contrast to the supposedly weak, "effeminate" colony. Imperialism and, more specifically, imperial racism helped to consolidate the nation-state, in other words, by substituting race hierarchies for the hierarchies of class.

The Scramble for Africa

The Scramble for Africa constituted by far the most remarkable chapter of the European expansion of the late nineteenth century. Between 1880 and 1912, seven European states partitioned most of the African continent, leaving only Abyssinia (Ethiopia) and Liberia independent.

The Berlin Conference   By the mid-1880s, a number of European governments had begun to object to the haphazardness with which conflicts over African territory were being settled. The Berlin Conference of 1884–1885, presided over by the German Prime Minister Otto von Bismarck, was convened to sort out the conflict between the Portuguese and the Belgians over control of the Congo River in particular and, more generally, to lay the ground rules for colonization. A watershed in European diplomacy, the conference brokered conflicting claims without recourse to intra-European violence, even as it came to inflict bloodshed and suffering on Africa. European cooperation at Berlin owed a great deal to Bismarck's diplomatic shrewdness. Seeking to compensate France and Britain for their loss of power in the European arena and, at the same time, to fuel Franco-British imperial rivalry, he conceded the bulk of African territories to Britain and

This is an image of a popular French children's board game from the late nineteenth century, the objective of which was to conquer Africa. Popular culture proved a powerful tool for propagating ideas about the "natural inferiority" of Africans and the legitimacy of the European conquest.

France. Despite its small number of African colonies, Germany's foreign policy thus decisively influenced the Scramble.

Since the lines of partition had been drawn long before the Berlin Conference, its main role was to formally ratify the principle that coastal settlement by a European nation also gave it claim to the hinterlands beyond as long as it could establish authority in the region. Although the Berlin participants legitimized some new claims in central Africa—such as those of Belgium's King Leopold II in the Congo—in the main, the African partition extended European control from older coastal enclaves into the interior of the continent.

For Africans, the carving up of the continent redrew the African map in ways that consolidated previously separate polities and ethnic groups in new, European-made units—a single new colony, for example, could comprise three hundred smaller political units. The Berlin Conference thus centralized power in a previously decentralized political landscape. In addition, by using the artificial entity of the "tribe" to designate previously distinct groups of the same region, it permanently reconfigured ethnic and cultural identities in African society. While colonial rule and the work of Christian missionaries in standardizing related language dialects ultimately strengthened the cultural bonds between disparate groups, many of the African "tribes" of the present day are at least partial inventions of the Berlin Conference.

The Berlin Conference also extended the European abolition of slavery and the slave trade to Africa. Missionaries such as David Livingstone had campaigned ardently against the slave trade in East Africa since midcentury without making much headway. As formal colonizers, however, Europeans could enforce abolitionism to a much greater extent than before. Their desire to abolish African slavery emerged both from a genuine humanitarianism and from the understanding that it was politically expedient as a justification for conquest. In spite of partial successes, clandestine slav-

As African guides clear their path through thick vegetation, French and German negotiators consult their maps and renegotiate the boundaries of French Equatorial Africa and German Cameroon. European powers frequently came into conflict with one another on African soil, but for the most part were able to resolve their differences peacefully.

ery and slave trading in Africa continued into the early twentieth century and new forms of forced labor, heavily relied upon by European colonizers themselves, also replaced slavery in many regions.

The Wars of Conquest   In the aftermath of the Berlin Conference, the conquest of Africa unfolded in a series of bloody wars that took place between the 1880s and the first decade of the twentieth century. Although European powers faced fierce African resistance, they enjoyed several advantages in these conflicts. Their footholds on the African coast and, in many cases, longstanding commercial connections with coastal communities provided them with a base of operations and a ready source of supplies. Europeans also benefited from, and sometimes ruthlessly exploited, the divi-

sions between local communities. In their expansion into West Africa (Nigeria) in the 1890s, for example, the British profited from local enmity by mobilizing the subjugated Nupe against their Fulani overlords, only to conquer the Nupe soon afterward.

Most important in facilitating the conquest was the immense and growing technological advantage enjoyed by the Europeans, especially in weaponry. To be sure, the weapons gap was nothing new. But the new military equipment produced by the second industrial revolution magnified the inequality between African and European forces. By the time Africans acquired rifles in the late nineteenth century, Europeans were deploying, first, rapid-firing breechloaders (repeating rifles) and, later, machine guns. In fact, most of the new weaponry of the First World War was first tested in the laboratory of late-nineteenth-century colonial warfare. One example of the devastation wrought by these new technologies was in the Battle of Omdurman in Sudan in 1898, where field artillery and hand-driven Gatling machine guns allowed Anglo-Egyptian forces to kill 11,000 and wound 16,000 Sudanese soldiers, with only 49 dead and 382 wounded among their own ranks. In the few cases where Africans had access to equally advanced technology, they were often able to thwart conquest. In part of French West Africa (Mali), for example, the troops of Islamic Malinké ruler Samori Touré, armed with up-to-date European weaponry, staved off French conquest from the mid-1880s to the late 1890s. These exceptions further underscore how critical advanced weaponry was to the European conquest.

New Imperial Nations   While France and Britain dominated the conquest, other European nations carved out significant African territories as well. After the Berlin Conference had recognized King Leopold II's claims in the Congo in exchange for free trading and shipping rights in the region for other European states, Belgium emerged as a major African power. The full-scale subjugation of the massive Congo Free State (Democratic Republic of the Congo)—76 times as large as Belgium—took over ten years and met with continued insurgence, particularly from Arab slave traders of the Lualaba River region.

Germany also played a central role in the Scramble. At Berlin, Bismarck had ceded dominance in Africa to Britain and France, claiming a few protectorates in the areas where German traders and missionaries were most active, such as Togoland (Togo), Cameroon, South West Africa (Namibia), and East Africa (Tanzania). In 1888, however, the accession of Wilhelm II to the German throne and the subsequent dismissal of Bismarck ushered in a new era of aggression in German foreign policy. Thereafter, Germany posed an active threat to

CHRONOLOGY
Scramble for Africa

1881	French occupy Tunisia.
1882	Revolt in Egypt (against British and French financial influence by Arabi Pasha) prompts occupation by British.
1883	Start of French conquest of Madagascar.
1884	Germany acquires South West Africa, Togo, Cameroon. Berlin Conference.
1885	King Leopold II of Belgium acquires Congo.
1886	Germany and Britain divide East Africa.
	Discovery of gold in South Africa.
1889	Italy establishes colonies in Eritrea and Somaliland.
	Cecil Rhodes's British South Africa Company begins colonization of Rhodesia.
1894	Britain occupies Uganda.
1896	Abyssinian (Ethiopian) army defeats invading Italian army.
1898	Fashoda Crisis.
1899–1902	Boer War.
1905–1906; 1911	Morocco Crises.

France and Britain in the imperial arena. The Moroccan Crisis of 1905–1906 developed, for example, when Germany protested against the Franco-Spanish division of power in the region and demanded a sphere of its own. A second crisis, the Agadir Incident of 1911, erupted when the Kaiser sent a gunboat to the Moroccan port of Agadir in a display of German power meant to intimidate the French. Although both crises were resolved diplomatically, with France retaining effective control of Morocco, episodes like these signal the belligerent diplomatic stance of post-Bismarckian Germany and the consequent heightening of imperial competition.

Worried about Belgian and German encroachment on its colonial borders, Portugal managed to enlarge its Angolan holdings on the West African coast and to establish Portuguese East Africa (Mozambique) on the southeastern coast of Africa. These incursions sparked extended wars of resistance, especially in the Zambezi Valley. Meanwhile, the new nation-state of Italy, seeking to enhance its international standing by staking out terrain in East Africa, faced the unique humiliation of being defeated by an African polity. On the Horn of Africa, Italy seized Eritrea and Somaliland (Somalia) as colonies

in 1889, but failed to conquer Abyssinia (Ethiopia), when King Menelik II's troops—about 100,000 soldiers armed with European breechloaders, a few machine guns, and field artillery—soundly defeated an Italian force of 14,500, equipped with inaccurate maps, at the Battle of Adowa in 1896. Italy fared better in Tripoli (Libya), declaring a protectorate there in 1912.

France   French and British expansion in Africa overshadowed that of all other powers. Although the British denigrated the French Empire as a large "sandbox," France clearly dominated West Africa and North Africa. From Algeria, where they had been entrenched since 1830, France expanded in virtually every direction. To the east, it squeezed out Italian and British interests, using the growing indebtedness of the ruling bey as the pretext for making Tunisia a French protectorate in 1881. To the west, France moved on Morocco, thwarting German interests and appeasing Spain with a small zone of control. By 1895 they dominated an enormous swath of sub-Saharan territories known as French West Africa (Ivory Coast, Senegal, Guinea, Mali). In 1897, France seized the French Congo in central Africa (Republic of the Congo) and, three years later, invaded the Lake Chad region, thereby linking up its possessions in the west and the north with those in central Africa. In 1911 it combined Chad and French Congo to form French Equatorial Africa. On the east coast, the French also claimed part of Somaliland and, in 1896, conquered the island of Madagascar, where they established a prosperous sugar plantation economy based on the forced labor of the local population.

Britain and the Boer War   British imperialists envisioned a railway from Capetown to Cairo that would span their African Empire. Starting in the 1880s, Britain moved to consolidate its hold on Egypt and Sudan. Although Britain had shared financial control with France over an increasingly bankrupted Egypt during the late nineteenth century and the French had financed the construction of the Suez Canal, the British finally edged the French out of Egypt in the 1870s and 1880s, claiming it as a protectorate in 1882 (see "The Earl of Cromer: Why Britain Acquired Egypt," p. 794).

Once entrenched in Egypt, the British moved to extend their power south into Turco-Egyptian-controlled Sudan. There they clashed with the millenarian jihadist Mahdist state, which had sought repeatedly to overthrow Egyptian rule during the 1880s. In 1885, the armies of the Mahdi (the Guided One) attacked Khartoum, the Egyptian capital of Sudan and, after a ten-month siege, annihilated Anglo-Egyptian troops led by General Charles Gordon (known as "Chinese" Gordon because of his role in suppressing the Taiping Rebellion). At nearby Omdurman, the Mahdi established an Islamic

Image of the Battle of Adowa of 1896, in which the troops of Menelik II, armed with European weaponry, routed the Italian army and effectively saved Abyssinia (Ethiopia) from colonial conquest.
The Mary Evans Picture Libary

state, which thrived for the next twelve years. But the British did not forget the defeat at Khartoum and in 1896 launched a new campaign to take the Sudan. In 1898 British troops led by Lord Kitchener handed the Mahdist State a fatal defeat at the battle of Omdurman.

The expansion into Sudan allowed Britain to link up Egypt with its territories to the southeast, British East Africa (Kenya) and Buganda (Uganda), seized in 1888 and 1894, respectively. At the same time, in West Africa, the British expanded from trading forts along the Gold Coast, purchased earlier from the Dutch and the Danes, and defeated the Asante to colonize Ghana. In an effort to protect the commercial interests of British palm oil merchants in the Niger River delta, the British-chartered Royal Niger Company, under the leadership of George Goldie, also expanded into Nigeria between 1886 and 1899.

Pressing north from the British Cape Colony, the British fought the Zulus in the Anglo-Zulu War of 1878–1879. Led by the archetypal expansionist Cecil Rhodes, they took Bechuanaland (Botswana) in 1885, Rhodesia (Zimbabwe) in 1889, and Nyasaland (Malawi) in 1893. In so doing, the British managed to create a wedge separating German South West Africa (Namibia) and German East Africa (Rwanda, Burundi, continental Tanzania, part of Mozambique) and to approach the southern border of the Congo Free State. More importantly, this expansion threatened the independent Afrikaner republics north of the Cape Colony, a conflict that ultimately led to the Boer War of 1899–1902, in which approximately 75,000 lives were lost.

The British encroachment on the Afrikaner republics had been fueled by the discovery there of diamonds in the 1860s and gold in the 1880s. By 1890 the Afrikaner republics were overrun by British citizens and surrounded by British colonies. Conflicts between the two groups grew more heated, and in 1899 the Afrikaners declared war. British forces rapidly occupied

THE EARL OF CROMER: WHY BRITAIN ACQUIRED EGYPT

Evelyn Baring (1871–1917), First Earl of Cromer, was the first British Commissioner of the Egyptian Public Debt Office and then British Agent and Consul General after Egypt became a British colony in 1882. Ruling Egypt with an iron hand, Cromer reorganized its financial, judicial, and administrative system as well as defended it from the incursions of other European powers. Although he brought about important changes in Egypt and virtually rescued it from bankruptcy, the Egyptians disliked his autocratic ways and his willingness to subordinate the interests of Egypt to that of Britain. He ignored demands by middle-class Egyptians for higher education, for instance, for fear that it would lead to the emergence of nationalist sentiment, as it had in India. Likewise, the primary objective of his successful agricultural experiments to promote the growth of Egyptian cotton was to provide British industries with raw materials. Still, Cromer was greatly admired in the West. When he died in 1917, the London Times called him the "Maker of Modern Egypt." In this excerpt, Cromer explains why the British and not any other European power could—and did—take over Egypt.

"History, indeed, records some very radical changes in the forms of government to which a state has been subjected without its interests being absolutely and permanently shipwrecked. But it may be doubted whether any instance can be quoted of a sudden transfer of power in any civilized or semi-civilized community to a class so ignorant as the pure Egyptians, such as they were in the year 1882. These latter have, for centuries past, been a subject race. Persians, Greeks, Romans, Arabs from Arabia and Baghdad, Circassians, and finally, Ottoman Turks, have successively ruled over Egypt, but we have to go back to the doubtful and obscure precedents of Pharaonic times to find an epoch when, possibly, Egypt was ruled by Egyptians. Neither, for the present, do they appear to possess the qualities which would render it desirable, either in their own interests, or in those of the civilized world in general, to raise them at a bound to the category of autonomous rulers with full rights of internal sovereignty.

"If, however, a foreign occupation was inevitable or nearly inevitable, it remains to be considered whether a British occupation was preferable to any other. From the purely Egyptian point of view, the answer to this question cannot be doubtful. The intervention of any European power was preferable to that of Turkey. The intervention of one European power was preferable to international intervention. The special aptitude shown by Englishmen in the government of Oriental races pointed to England as the most effective and beneficent instrument for the gradual introduction of European civilization into Egypt. An Anglo-French, or an Anglo-Italian occupation, from both of which we narrowly and also accidentally escaped, would have been detrimental to Egyptian interests and would ultimately have caused friction, if not serious dissension, between England on the one side and France or Italy on the other. The only thing to be said in favor of Turkish intervention is that it would have relieved England from the responsibility of intervening.

"By the process of exhausting all other expedients, we arrive at the conclusion that armed British intervention was, under the special circumstances of the case, the only possible solution of the difficulties, which existed in 1882. Probably also it was the best solution. The arguments against British intervention, indeed, were sufficiently obvious. It was easy to foresee that, with a British garrison in Egypt, it would be difficult that the relations of England either with France or Turkey should be cordial. With France, especially, there would be a danger that our relations might become seriously strained. Moreover, we lost the advantages of our insular position. The occupation of Egypt necessarily dragged England to a certain extent within the arena of Continental politics. In the event of war, the presence of a British garrison in Egypt would possibly be a source of weakness rather than of strength. Our position in Egypt placed us in a disadvantageous diplomatic position, for any power, with whom we had a difference of opinion about some non-Egyptian question, was at one time able to retaliate by opposing our Egyptian policy. The complicated rights and privileges possessed by the various powers of Europe in Egypt facilitated action of this nature."

From The Earl of Cromer, *Modern Egypt*, vol. 1, New York: Macmillan, 1908, pp. xvii–xviii.

the major cities of the Afrikaner republics, but it took two years to subdue the Afrikaners' skillful guerrilla resistance. The rest of Europe watched Britain's slow progress with surprise and then shock as farmhouses were destroyed and homeless Afrikaners herded together in guarded areas called concentration camps, where disease and starvation killed at least 20,000 of them. In Great Britain, the Boer War initially produced patriotic fervor, but politicians and the public alike grew disillusioned as the war dragged on. British victory allowed the establishment in 1910 of the Union of South Africa, a partial fulfillment of Rhodes's ambitions. To appease the disaffected Afrikaner minorities, British leaders implemented Afrikaner policies of

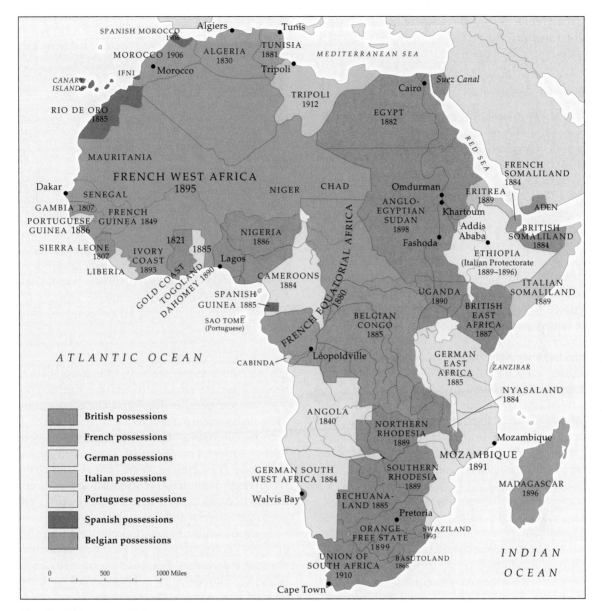

MAP 26.2 AFRICA, 1914
This map shows the European partition of Africa. Only Liberia and Ethiopia were independent after the turn of the century. Notice how the west-east axis of French territories runs into the north-south axis of British holdings. How were the European powers able to overrun an entire continent in such a short period of time?
◆ For an online version, go to www.mhhe.com/chambers9 > chapter 26 > book maps

Apartheid, and the legal segregation of white and black Africans became the law of the land.

Intra-European Conflict in Africa   By the turn of the century, the extent of European expansion, compounded by the heightened tension within Europe, led to a growing number of intra-European imperial clashes. The Boer War, in which Afrikaners were armed with German weapons, was one of these. Another important confrontation occurred between Britain and

France at Fashoda, on the Nile, in 1898. With the French driving inland across Africa from west to east and the British expanding south from Egypt and north from the Cape Colony, such conflict was inevitable. At Fashoda, British troops marching south from Omdurman met French expeditionary forces advancing east from the Congo. Both sides declared that their national honor was at stake, but after several weeks of threats the French government backed down, distracted by the Dreyfus affair at home. After the French retreat from

Fashoda, the French agreed to recognize British control of the Nile in return for British recognition of French West Africa.

Conquest in Asia

While Africa was the main theater of late-nineteenth-century imperial expansion, Asia was the second key site of aggressive expansionism at the turn of the twentieth century.

The Middle East   In the late nineteenth century, the British began to withdraw their support from the Ottoman Empire. Although the empire had been strategically and commercially important to the British as the gateway to Asia, it no longer played that role after the opening of the Suez Canal in 1869. Bankrupted, in commercial decline, and riven by internal dissent, the empire ceased to be the attractive ally the British had made use of earlier in the century.

South and Central Asia   India, ruled directly by the British crown after 1857, remained the jewel of the British Empire. It continued to be invaluable, both in terms of trade and capital investment. During the last quarter of the nineteenth century, London financiers invested more than £2.5 million in India, most of it in railways. By the eve of the First World War, India also had emerged as the chief export market for British industrial goods.

The security of India continued to obsess British politicians, who sought to protect her borders from other expansionist powers, in particular Russia. The British, allied with the French and the Ottoman Turks, had fought the Russians directly in the Crimean War (1854–1856) but otherwise grappled with the Russian threat through a combination of formal and informal diplomacy known as the "Great Game." The political maneuverings of the Great Game finally ended with the Anglo-Russian Entente of 1907, which resolved British and Russian differences over Persia, Tibet, and Afghanistan, dividing Persia into British and Russian spheres of influence and effectively consolidating Russian power in Central Asia.

Southeast Asia and the South Pacific   In Southeast Asia, the Dutch strengthened their hold over the Dutch East Indies (Indonesia), including Sumatra, Java, Borneo, and the western half of New Guinea, and continued to prosper from a colonial plantation economy based largely on rubber and coffee. The British, meanwhile, expanded their territories in Southeast Asia, annexing upper Burma in 1886 and a part of Malaya (Malaysia) in 1896. The French, who had established commercial interests in Indochina at the turn of the

Russian postcard (ca. 1902), showing the United States and Britain pushing Japan, the only imperial Asian state, into a confrontation with Russia. Japan would defeat Russia shortly thereafter in the Russo-Japanese War of 1904–1905.
© British Museum

nineteenth century, steadily increased their holdings there in the late nineteenth century, taking Tonkin and Annam (Vietnam) in 1883 and Cambodia and Laos in 1893. Although a militant and well-organized Vietnamese resistance movement, known as the "Black Flags," fought French infiltration (even appealing for help from the Chinese, their former colonial masters) the French prevailed. Following a series of protracted military campaigns, France formed the French Indochina Union in 1894.

From the mid-nineteenth century on, the South Pacific also emerged as an arena for competition among the colonial powers. Europeans perceived South Pacific Islanders, like Africans, to be childlike "primitives," in need of European protection and divided the many islands of the region among themselves. While Britain and Germany split the western half of New Guinea, France seized New Caledonia and Tahiti. Germany also acquired the Marshall Islands, and the British took Fiji and Tonga. The Germans, British, and Americans fought for dominance in Samoa, resulting in a split between German and American Samoa, while the Germans and the British divided up the Solomon Islands. In addition to a highly prosperous sugar economy centered in Fiji, the region also provided cheap labor for Australian sugar plantations.

As the European powers snatched up Pacific islands, the generally isolationist United States became involved in the imperial politics of the region. In 1898 it annexed Hawaii, a strategic Pacific naval base and a profitable sugar cane and pineapple producer. After defeating Spain in the Spanish-American War, ignited by conflict over the control of Cuba, the United States re-

Chinese woodblock print showing Western soldiers being humiliated in a battle during the Boxer Rebellion of 1900 directed against Western exploitation of China. Although China was battered by the Rebellion and the Western powers emerged with still more influence over Chinese affairs, the Rebellion influenced the establishment of the first Chinese nationalist movement, led by Sun Yat-sen.
The British Library, London

ceived a number of Spanish territories, including the Philippines, Cuba, Puerto Rico, and Guam. In the Philippines, the Americans faced a fierce indigenous resistance movement that sought Filipino independence, but after three years of fighting and the capture of the insurrection leader, Emilio Aguinaldo, the United States declared the Philippines its territory. These conquests, combined with growing American influence and economic power in Latin America during this period, transformed the United States into a formidable global power.

East Asia The continued decline of China and rise of Japan were the central developments in East Asia during the late nineteenth century. Although some Chinese reformers favored economic and technological modernization, including the building of railways, as a way to strengthen the nation, considerable conservative opposition to the process existed. The pattern of the midcentury thus continued unabated, with the European powers and the United States forcing trade concessions, annexing territory, and lending money to the Chinese government on disadvantageous terms. In the aftermath of the Sino-Japanese War of 1894–1895, fought over control of Korea, the Chinese were forced to borrow money from Europe to pay a war indemnity to Japan and, in return, the Europeans exacted more trade privileges and concessions to build railways. The 1897 murder of two German missionaries in China led to further concessions. The Germans received a lease of the port of Quingdao and the right to build railways in Shandong Province, the Russians took Port Arthur, and the French acquired a lease on Canton Bay and a sphere of influence in southern China. To prevent the further partitioning of China, the United States initiated the Open Door policy in 1898, agreed upon by all colonizing nations with the exception of Japan. Allowing all nations equal trading rights in all parts of China, the Open Door policy also protected China's territorial integrity.

Foreign encroachment and exploitation sparked the Boxer Rebellion in 1900. A clandestine society called the "Patriotic Harmonious Fists"—known as Boxers because of the martial arts training of its members—

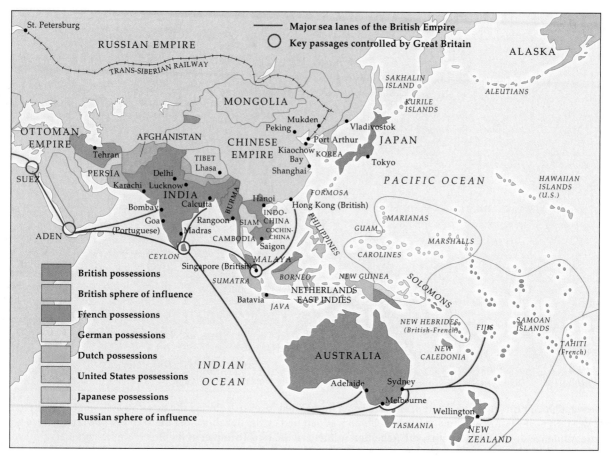

MAP 26.3 IMPERIALISM IN ASIA, 1900
This map shows the European colonies in Asia. Notice British dominance in this part of the world, centered largely on India. How did the entry of Japan and the United States into the Asian imperial arena change the power balance in the region?

◆ For an online version, go to www.mhhe.com/chambers9 > chapter 26 > book maps

organized to protest the corrupting influence of "foreign devils," including missionaries, traders, and soldiers. The Boxer Rebellion erupted in northern China, where Boxers attacked European, American, and Chinese Christians in Shandong Province, sabotaged rail lines, and besieged foreign embassies in Beijing for almost two months. A force of twenty thousand British, French, German, Russian, Italian, American, and Japanese troops viciously suppressed the Boxer Rebellion and imposed a huge indemnity on the Qing regime. Continued degradation and economic exploitation at the hands of the Europeans, Americans, and Japanese (often in the form of disadvantageous railway leases) fueled the Chinese nationalist movement led by Sun Yat-sen, which finally overthrew the beleaguered Qing Dynasty in 1911.

Japan's fate differed dramatically from that of China. An industrial giant after the Meiji Restoration of 1868, Japan sought an empire to reflect its global

standing. A Korean insurrection against Chinese influence in 1894 offered the Japanese an opportunity to establish a foothold in Korea. The ensuing Sino-Japanese War of 1894–1895 ended in Chinese defeat, the Japanese annexation of Taiwan, and increased Japanese trade privileges and political influence in Korea. Japan's expansionist ambitions brought it into direct conflict not only with China, but also with Russia. Its victory in the Russo-Japanese War of 1904–1905 stunned the world. A clash over influence in Chinese-held Manchuria and Korea, the war broke out following Russian maneuvers to take the Chinese province of Liaotung (and, in particular, the ice-free harbor of Port Arthur), controlled by the Japanese since the Sino-Japanese War. Japan not only kept Liaotung after victory, but took over the Russian sphere of influence in Chinese Manchuria, as well as half of Sakhalin Island, and seized Russian-controlled railways in Manchuria. The Japanese triumph over Russia marked a turning point for both European imperialists, who suddenly perceived the limits to their power, and for colonial subjects from Bombay to Cairo, who rejoiced and found hope in the European defeat. Undermining the credibility of Tsar Nicholas' regime, it also contributed to the failed first Russian Revolution of 1905. In 1910 a triumphant Japan annexed Korea.

The New Imperial Mission

New ideological foundations also distinguished the new imperialism from the liberal empire. Responding to anticolonial insurgency in India and to the Darwinian revolution at home, Europeans reconsidered the nature of their political, cultural, and biological relationship to subject peoples.

The Failure of the Liberal Vision   Europeans at the end of the nineteenth century confronted their vast global empire with a transformed sense of mission. Gradually abandoning the liberal conceit of Europeanizing the non-Western world for the more modest goal of improving the "natives" within their own cultural context, Europeans increasingly replaced paternalist justifications of empire with the unabashed consolidation of imperial rule by force. The new mission did not appear overnight. In fact, the self-critical attitude and eagerness to legitimize Europe's imperial presence characteristic of colonial encounters of the late eighteenth and early nineteenth centuries were already fading by midcentury, supplanted by a growing intolerance of cultural difference.

By the late nineteenth century, attitudes had further hardened. Europeans still believed in the flagrant inferiority of subject peoples, but, unlike previous generations of colonizers, they were far more inclined to see this inferiority as biological and, therefore, irremediable. While they continued to vaunt their own superiority as the justification for empire, Europeans thus increasingly questioned the extent of their responsibilities as civilizers and the likelihood that such efforts would succeed. The concrete experience of imperial rule contributed significantly to the new cynicism. In the case of Britain, for example, the Indian Rebellion of 1857 (see p. 800–802) irrevocably changed not only the conception of imperial duty but British expectations of their colonial subjects.

By the end of the century, many took the pessimistic view of the British poet Rudyard Kipling, captured in his poem of 1898, "The White Man's Burden." In it Kipling described the unrewarding task of bringing civilization to "new-caught, sullen peoples," whose response to European benevolence was not gratitude but intransigent hostility:

Take up the White Man's burden—
And reap his old reward:
The blame of those ye better,
The hate of those ye guard—

In Kipling's depiction, the civilizing mission was not only thankless, but futile, because subject peoples inevitably backslid into barbarism:

And when your goal is nearest
The end for others sought,
Watch sloth and heathen Folly
Bring all your hopes to nought

Darwinian Challenges to the Enlightenment   Even more than the politics of imperial rule, ideological developments within Europe profoundly influenced the civilizing mission. The Darwinian revolution of the late nineteenth century irrevocably changed what it meant to be human and, therefore, to be European. Although decades of nineteenth-century scientific research on race difference and racial development had seriously weakened the Enlightenment conception of a single human species developing largely through environmental influence, it was Darwin's particular formulation of the theory of evolution—and its distortion by social Darwinists (see chapter 25) to explain cultural difference—that most affected late-nineteenth-century European views about the capacity of "primitives" to become civilized.

Darwinian theory undermined several key tenets of liberal Enlightenment thought. First, in linking humans to a common ape ancestor, Darwin raised the specter of the animal nature—and thus, the fundamental primitivity—of all humans. Scandalized Europeans responded by accentuating the gap between their own civilized nature and the primitive nature of other "races." Although they disagreed intensely as to whether the gap was wide enough to warrant the classification of other races as separate species (and Darwin himself favored the idea of a single species), most came to view the differences between the races as more significant than the similarities. As a consequence, some abandoned the Enlightenment notion of a single human trajectory along which all cultures developed at varied paces and came to believe in the separate and incommensurable developmental paths of different cultures. Social Darwinian thought thus dealt the liberal universalism of the Enlightenment a serious blow.

Second, Darwin's theory of **natural selection,** which held that the natural selection of traits best adapted to survival served as the prime motor of human development, also challenged European understandings of human agency. In contrast to Europeans of the Enlightenment, who believed that environment—both natural and social—shaped culture, their late-nineteenth-century

as rulers who had remained loyal to them during the revolt, while treating those who had been active in the rebellion as traitors, including many Muslims. By deepening the divisions in Indian society, these policies helped the British maintain control over Indian subjects and prevent future uprisings.

Antagonistic feelings toward Indians ran high not just among the British in India, but in Britain itself. In spite of the extreme brutality with which the rebellion had been suppressed, the popular press and literature depicted British rule as a noble and benign one that had been attacked by savages. Particularly offensive to the British imagination was the idea that Englishwomen had been "defiled" by the rebels, and Victorian paintings and mass market novels were filled with lurid accounts and images of white women being raped and mutilated by Indians. Such images contributed to an enduring British view of the Indian as barbaric and uncivilized.

In the final analysis, how does one judge the Rebellion of 1857? Depending on the perspective, the Rebellion of 1857 has been regarded as a "Mutiny" or the "First War of Indian Independence." As we have seen, British colonial officials perceived the uprising as mindless violence by an ungrateful native population. Indian nationalist leaders and historians have glorified the rebellion as representing the first stirrings of nationalist sentiment in India. Most modern historians, however, emphasize that it is somewhat anachronistic to see the Rebellion of 1857 in terms of the emergence of Indian nationalism. No sense of a shared mission united the local rulers who rose up in rebellion against the British. The loyalty of these rulers was to their own kingdoms, not to the Indian nation. Even the Mughal emperor was seen as the supreme head of a feudal system, not as a representative of a modern state. In their turn, peasants did not always understand that many of their difficulties emerged out of colonial exploitation and attacked the most visible manifestations of oppression such as local landlords and moneylenders. In fact, peasant nationalism was not to emerge in India until the twentieth century.

In spite of its ultimate failure, however, the Rebellion of 1857 remains extremely important for many reasons. It was certainly the largest anticolonial movement that had taken place so far in British India. Moreover, its emphasis on Hindu-Muslim unity made it a powerful symbol for later nationalist leaders. Although many Muslims felt the end of Mughal rule meant that their fortunes and prestige would be under threat, there was also a real recognition that Muslims and Hindus suffered together under British oppression, and in many places they fought side by side against what they perceived as a common foreign enemy. In addition, although led by the landed elite and feudal chieftains, the rebellion saw the participation of different classes, including tribal peoples and low castes. In many ways, therefore, the rebellion marked a crucial turning point in the history of colonial India. Perhaps its greatest legacy is that it served as an inspiration to anticolonial movements, not just in India, but also in Asia and Africa in the late nineteenth and twentieth centuries.

counterparts took Darwin's theory to mean that biology determined culture. Darwin's influence thus undercut the liberal Enlightenment belief in the human mastery of nature and the possibility of socially engineered progress.

Finally, whereas Enlightenment thinkers stressed the mutability of human beings, Darwin's theory of race differentiation lent itself to belief in the permanence of racial traits. Unlike all other human traits, which evolved continually under the pressures of natural selection, Darwin argued, the superficial physical distinctions between the races emerged early in human history through the process of **sexual selection,** preferences marked out in the sexual competition for mates. Because these sexually selected traits—such as hair texture or skin color—provided no benefit for survival, moreover, they tended either not to change or to evolve much more slowly than other traits. While Darwin himself never said that racial traits were fixed, many race scientists of the late nineteenth century made that mental leap themselves and erroneously used Darwin to assert that racial difference was permanent. Social Darwinian misinterpretations of Darwin in this way eroded the liberal Enlightenment belief in mutability and progress.

Popular Views of Race   Darwinian and social Darwinian ideas had an astonishingly broad impact on European conceptions of race and empire. Racist tracts influenced by Darwin, in tandem with newspapers, periodicals, and imperial adventure novels, shaped popular conceptions of the colonial "native," inculcating the widespread belief that non-Western peoples were biologically—and not simply culturally—retrograde and lacked the capacity to improve. Although racist propagandists had been disseminating their ideas for decades (two of the most influential racist writers of the nineteenth century, Count Gobineau and Robert Knox, published their works almost ten years before Darwin), Darwinian theory seemed to many to grant them new legitimacy and authority.

Africa and black Africans occupied a special place in post-Darwinian racist hierarchies because of their presumed proximity to apes. While these links had been made much earlier, they were now widely regarded as having been verified by scientific inquiry and therefore to constitute a sound basis for imperial policy. Some of the most extreme arguments—like those made by social Darwinist imperialist propagandists such as Benjamin Kidd, author of *Social Evolution* (1894)—cast Africans as biologically defective and asserted the inevitability of black extinction and white rule in Africa. Similarly, the ideas of social Darwinist Herbert Spencer propagated the notion that the domination and ultimate biological elimination of less fit African societies was the natural—and therefore evolutionarily desirable—outcome of the struggle for survival of the fittest. While Europeans had viewed African blacks as lesser beings for centuries, for many blackness now became the mark of innate and unchanging biological inferiority.

Race Science and Eugenics   Darwin's work decisively influenced scholarly views of the "native" as well. Race scientists, for example, used—and distorted—his ideas to support theories of race hierarchy. Like Darwin, the race scientists of the late nineteenth century believed in the animal nature of humans and the biological, rather than social, determinants of civilization. Unlike Darwin, however, they believed in the permanent character of race traits and in the unbreachable gap between different race-culture groups. These theories were far from new. Polygenism, or the belief in many human species, had been on the rise in the scientific community since 1800 and dominant since 1850.

This photograph was taken around the turn of the twentieth century by Harry Hamilton Johnson (1858–1927), a colonial administrator, geographer, and naturalist. Like many contemporaries, Johnston was preoccupied with the "racial" classification of colonial subjects and used anthropometry, the measurement of differences in the body types of the human "races," as a tool toward this end.
Royal Geographical Society, London

But Darwin's work lent new conviction and credibility to this theoretical foundation for race science.

The new field of **eugenics** was also an outgrowth of Darwin's influence. Both a science of human heredity and a social program of selective breeding, eugenics was founded in 1883 by Darwin's cousin, Francis Galton, and Galton's colleague, Karl Pearson. Believing that biological differences between races and individuals determined the social order, eugenicists sought to control the process of natural selection and, thereby, to engineer the production of a fitter race. Using the techniques of **biometry,** early eugenicists such as Pearson and Galton tried to apply statistical analysis to identify the salient traits of the races. But Galton soon realized that the eugenicist project required more research into the laws of heredity. That recognition led to the acceptance of the new science of genetics, which identified the gene as the unit of inheritance. Although the Austrian scientist Gregor Mendel had first elaborated the gene-based theory of heredity in the 1860s, it was not until Galton and Pearson made use of Mendelian genetics around 1900 that genetic theory gained scientific respectability.

By the turn of the century, the eugenics movement was a highly prestigious scientific movement in Europe, the United States, and Japan. As such, it influenced public policy, including the forced sterilization of "unfit" groups (people with mental impairment, for example) and the introduction of immigration quotas limiting the influx of "racial undesirables." Despite the nefarious connotations of the movement, especially in the aftermath of Hitler, the eugenicists of the early twentieth century were a motley political group. While Galton himself was a Victorian liberal committed to human progress, for example, Pearson embraced social Darwinist views and argued in his work *National Life from the Standpoint of Science* (1901) that Africans must be eliminated from British South Africa for the biological and moral purification of the colony (see "Karl Pearson on National Life from the Standpoint of Science," p. 805).

The Rise of Anthropology   Darwinian theory also had a formative impact on the view of the "native" adopted by the new field of anthropology, which emerged as a formal academic discipline in the late nineteenth century to chart the stages of human cultural evolution and to identify the universal cultural traits of humankind through the comparative study of cultures. Anthropologists and archaeologists of the period fiercely debated whether contemporary "savages" were remnants of the European past, whether they had degenerated from a higher level of civilization, and whether they had the capacity to improve. A dominant model was expounded by the social evolutionary anthropologist Edward Burnett Tylor. His **doctrine of survivals** argued that contemporary "savages" were evolutionary atavisms whose cultural life provided a window onto the European past. A liberal universalist and relativist himself, Tylor admired many of the moral traits he observed in "savage" culture and acknowledged certain defects in European society. Nevertheless, his social evolutionary paradigm reinforced the view that contemporary "savage" culture—especially that of black Africans—had developed outside of the evolutionary mainstream and, therefore, would always remain inferior to European civilization.

If nineteenth-century anthropology created images of innate or cultural primitivity that seemed to invite European domination, European colonizers also made use of anthropological study to implement imperial rule. Believing that knowledge of "primitive culture" was the key to the consolidation of colonial rule, European governments were frequently the sponsors of ethnographic research in the late nineteenth century. They had also done this earlier, of course, and the late-nineteenth-century application of scientific study to political control was in a sense merely a continuation of the Enlightenment project of systematically studying the world in order to master it; Captain James Cook's scientific voyages to the Pacific had embodied this project, as had Mungo Park's African expeditions. Two key ideas, however, frequently distinguished the project in the late nineteenth century: first, the conviction that European cultural superiority stemmed from biological roots and, second, that this superiority—and with it the mandate to rule the world—was a permanent feature of the global order.

IMPERIALISM AT ITS PEAK

By the turn of the century, Europeans had transformed the constructed environment, the economic life, the social order, and the cultural practices of their colonial subjects. The emergence of the first anticolonial nationalist movements in this period responded to this upheaval. At the same time, ordinary Europeans were becoming more aware of the empire. By the eve of the First World War, the colonies permeated European consciousness and culture as never before. Just as empire imposed European culture on the non-Western world, it brought that world into the heart of Europe.

The Reordering of Colonial Life

Once Europeans had secured control over their colonies, they moved to consolidate and exploit that power to its fullest. In so doing, they transformed every aspect of colonial life, from building colonial cities and establishing a cash crop economy to introducing Western education and remapping indigenous social hierarchies.

Building Colonial Infrastructure   With the global conquest completed by the turn of the twentieth century, European colonizers embarked on the massive enterprise of building colonial infrastructure and implementing colonial administration. In less urbanized parts of the empire they erected colonial cities, towns, and ports, and in them schools, hospitals, clock towers, and ceremonial gateways. In places where cities and ports existed, such as Cairo, Lagos, Singapore, and Bombay, Europeans undertook ambitious modernization projects, including clearing slums and

KARL PEARSON ON NATIONAL LIFE FROM THE STANDPOINT OF SCIENCE

Karl Pearson (1857–1936) was an English, Cambridge-educated mathematician who also studied law and social and political philosophy. He held the first chair of eugenics at University College, London, and became the director of the eugenics laboratory there. He was a disciple of Francis Galton, the founder of eugenics, which sought to improve the human race through selective breeding. Pearson, in his turn, applied statistical methods to the study of biological problems, especially evolution and heredity, a science he called biometrics. Pearson's views on eugenics are seen as deeply problematic and racist today. He claimed that he was a socialist, committed to uplifting the masses, but in fact, his "scientific" view of a nation, as presented in National Life from the Standpoint of Science, *claimed that a country's progress and well-being depended on constantly replenishing its "better" stock at the expense of its "inferior races." The twentieth century was to see many undesirable applications of the principles of eugenics in the Western world, including the mass exterminations carried out by Nazi Germany.*

"History shows me one way, and one way only, in which a high state of civilization has been produced, namely, the struggle of race with race, and the survival of the physically and mentally fitter race. . . . The struggle means suffering, intense suffering, while it is in progress; but that struggle and that suffering have been the stages by which the white man has reached his present stage of development, and they account for the fact that he no longer lives in caves and feeds on roots and nuts. This dependence of progress on the survival of the fitter race, terribly black as it may seem to some of you, gives the struggle for existence its redeeming features; it is the fiery crucible out of which comes the finer metal. You may hope for a time when the sword shall be turned into the plowshare, when American and German and English traders shall no longer compete in the markets of the world for their raw material and for their food supply, when the white man and the dark shall share the soil between them, and each till it as he lists. But, believe me, when that day comes mankind will no longer progress; there will be nothing to check the fertility of inferior stock; the relentless law of heredity will not be controlled and guided by natural selection. Man will stagnate; and unless he ceases to multiply, the catastrophe will come again; famine and pestilence, as we see them in the East, physical selection instead of the struggle of race against race, will do the work more relentlessly, and, to judge from India and China, far less efficiently than of old. . . .

"There is a struggle of race against race and of nation against nation. In the early days of that struggle it was a blind, unconscious struggle of barbaric tribes. At the present day, in the case of the civilized white man, it has become more and more the conscious, carefully directed attempt of the nation to fit itself to a continuously changing environment. The nation has to foresee how and where the struggle will be carried on; the maintenance of national position is becoming more and more a conscious preparation for changing conditions, an insight into the needs of coming environments.

"We have to remember that man is subject to the universal law of inheritance, and that a dearth of capacity may arise if we recruit our society from the inferior and not the better stock. If any social opinions or class prejudices tamper with the fertility of the better stocks, then the national character will take but a few generations to be seriously modified. . . . You will see that my view—and I think it may be called the scientific view of a nation—is that of an organized whole, kept up to a high pitch of internal efficiency by insuring that its numbers are substantially recruited from the better stocks, and kept up to a high pitch of external efficiency by contest, chiefly by way of war with inferior races, and with equal races by the struggle for trade-routes and for the sources of raw material and of food supply. This is the natural history view of mankind, and I do not think you can in its main features subvert it."

From Karl Pearson, *National Life from the Standpoint of Science,* 1900, available at housatonic.net/Documents/333.htm.

constructing new housing and roadways. They also brought new modes of transportation to their empires, in the form of highway systems, bridges, canals, and railway networks, as well as new systems of communication, notably the telegraph. By 1865 telegraph lines connected India to Europe; by 1871 a cable ran from Vladivostok to Shanghai, Hong Kong, and Singapore. In addition to constructing a new built environment, colonial rulers imposed European models of administration in many spheres of colonial life. Colonial ad-

ministrators reorganized the police, army, judiciary, and postal service along European lines and, to varying degrees, introduced European models of education—including European language instruction—and Western-style medicine.

Europeans regarded these projects as central to the task of colonial rule. The use of grid layouts in colonial cities and ports and the laying of railway lines were intended to efficiently transport goods to both domestic and metropolitan markets and thus to facilitate

THE TERMS OF THE TRIPLE ALLIANCE

These articles are from the treaty of 1912 in which Austria-Hungary, Germany, and Italy renewed the Triple Alliance for the fifth time since 1882. This version essentially continued earlier ones, except for articles VI through XI, not printed here, which dealt rather vaguely with the Balkans, Ottoman territories, Egypt, and North Africa. With respect to those regions, the signatories reassured each other that they preferred to maintain the status quo but promised mutual understanding and even support if Austria-Hungary or Italy found it necessary temporarily to occupy territory in the Balkans or if Italy had to take measures against French expansion in North Africa. The promises of support to Italy indicated the higher price now required to keep Italy in the Alliance.

"Article I. The High Contracting Parties mutually promise peace and friendship, and will enter into no alliance or engagement directed against any one of their States.

"They engage to proceed to an exchange of ideas on political and economic questions of a general nature which may arise, and they further promise one another mutual support within the limits of their own interests.

"Article II. In case Italy, without direct provocation on her part, should be attacked by France for any reason whatsoever, the two other Contracting Parties shall be bound to lend help and assistance with all their forces to the Party attacked.

"This same obligation shall devolve upon Italy in case of any aggression without direct provocation by France against Germany.

"Article III. If one, or two, of the High Contracting Parties, without direct provocation on their part, should chance to be attacked and to be engaged in a war with two or more Great Powers nonsignatory to the present Treaty, the *casus foederis* will arise simultaneously for all the High Contracting Parties.

"Article IV. In case a Great Power nonsignatory to the present Treaty should threaten the security of the states of one of the High Contracting Parties, and the threatened Party should find itself forced on that account to make war against it, the two others bind themselves to observe towards their Ally a benevolent neutrality. Each of them reserves to itself, in this case, the right to take part in the war, if it should see fit, to make common cause with its Ally.

"Article V. If the peace of one of the High Contracting Parties should chance to be threatened under the circumstances foreseen by the preceding Articles, the High Contracting Parties shall take counsel together in ample time as to the military measures to be taken with a view to eventual cooperation.

"They engage, henceforth, in all cases of common participation in a war, to conclude neither armistice, nor peace, nor treaty, except by common agreement among themselves.

"Article XII. The High Contracting Parties mutually promise secrecy as to the contents of the present Treaty."

From Sidney Bradshaw Fay, *The Origins of the World War*, Macmillan, 1930.

Treaty with Russia lapse, France pressed Russia for an understanding. By 1894 that became a full alliance. France and Russia promised that each would support the other if either were attacked by Germany or by another member of the Triple Alliance that was aided by Germany. Such an accord between the Russian autocracy and the French Republic had seemed politically impossible, despite Russia's having already turned to France for loans and arms purchases. Now the tsar greeted French delegates while a band played the "Marseillaise," previously outlawed in Russia as a song of revolution.

In response, German diplomats were determined to reassert Germany's importance in world affairs. They did so in inconsistent, even contradictory, ways. On the one hand, the Kaiser attempted to reach some understanding with Great Britain and spoke of a "natural" alliance between the Teutonic and Anglo-Saxon races. On the other hand, the Germans antagonized and alienated the British. When, in 1896, the South African Boers foiled an attack on the republic of the Transvaal mounted by the British Cape Colony (the Jameson Raid), Kaiser William II sent a telegram congratulating the president of the Boer republic (the Kruger telegram). The British public responded with anger. The Kaiser also explored the possibility of organizing a continental coalition against Great Britain. Above all, the massive expansion of the German navy, vigorously lobbied for by the German Navy League, roused the hostility of the British.

Anglo-French Understanding Relations between Great Britain and France had centered on their colonial competition, in which they had seemed ready to risk war. Instead, they settled for defined spheres of influence. Following the confrontation at Fashoda in 1898, the French set about turning humiliation into good relations. They accepted British domination in Egypt in return for Britain's recognition of French interests in North Africa, particularly Morocco. Further understandings followed, culminating in the Anglo-French Entente Cordiale of 1904, in which France and Great Britain eliminated their major issues of imperial conflict. Those issues stretched from Asia to the Atlantic (from Siam to Newfoundland) and across the African continent (from the Niger River to North Africa). Formally a mere understanding, the Entente implied much more, as the exchange of public visits between Edward VII and the president of France was meant to demonstrate.

Germany's diplomatic position remained strong, and German leaders reasoned that an assertive foreign policy would demonstrate that strength. But the tenor of international relations was changing. As armaments increased and treaties proliferated, each power became more obsessed with its own security, and public opinion grew more sensitive to questions of national honor.

Testing Alliances: Three International Crises
From 1905 to 1911 three diplomatic crises—each of which initially seemed a German victory—in fact drew Germany's opponents closer together. The first of these crises arose over Morocco. France, with well-known designs on Morocco, had carefully won acquiescence from the powers except for Germany. The German chancellor, Bernhard von Blow, demanded that an international conference settle Morocco's future. He aimed to demonstrate that France was isolated, and in fact his warnings forced the resignation of Théophile Delcassé, France's foreign minister and the architect of French policy. When in 1906 the conference met at Algeciras, it confirmed that Morocco had special international status but recognized the primacy of French interests. The crisis was a disaster for German diplomacy. Only Austria-Hungary loyally voted with its ally. Italy, Russia, Great Britain, and the United States (now a regular participant in such international agreements) supported France, and Germany's threatening tactics led French and British officials to begin talks about their mutual military interests.

The second crisis arose over the Balkans. Austria was concerned that Serbia, led by a new king and a radical nationalist government, had become a dangerous antagonist. Austria also feared that Turkey's influence in the Balkans would grow following the 1908 revolution in Turkey—led by a group known as the Young Turks, who were determined to modernize their nation. In response, Austria-Hungary decided to annex Bosnia and Herzegovina. That move, which threatened Serbia, in turn outraged Russian Slavophiles. They were nationalists who believed that Russia should defend the interests of Slavs everywhere, and they demanded an international conference. Britain and France agreed. Germany supported Austria-Hungary, although angered by the sudden annexation.

Diplomatic crises were becoming tests of alliances (and significantly, Italy expressed resentment at not being consulted by Austria-Hungary rather than loyalty to the Triple Alliance). There had been earlier signs that Italy might drift away. In 1902 France recognized Italian ambitions in Libya, and France and Italy pledged neutrality if either was attacked by a third power (i.e., Germany). Although the Triple Alliance was renewed in the same year, Italy now sat on the fence between the Franco-Russian and the Austro-German alliances. Only time would tell on which side Italy might end up.

The third major crisis once again involved Morocco, which France now wanted to annex. It had consulted all the European powers, and talks with Germany seemed to be going well when suddenly in 1911 the Germans sent the gunboat *Panther* to the Moroccan port of Agadir (a show of power and a classic imperialist gesture) and then asked for all of the French Congo as the price for accepting France's annexation of Morocco. Both the demands and the method seemed excessive, and in Great Britain David Lloyd George publicly denounced them. Once again, eventual compromise (France would cede parts of its Congo lands and bits of its other African territories adjacent to German colonies) counted for less than the rising tension and growing international distrust of the Germans.

The Arms Race
The standing armies of France and Germany doubled between 1870 and 1914, and all able-bodied men had some military responsibilities from the age of twenty to their late fifties. In 1889 Great Britain adopted the principle that its navy must equal in size the two next-largest fleets combined, and in 1906 it had launched the *Dreadnought*, the first battleship armed entirely with big guns. By 1914 Britain had twenty-nine ships of this class afloat and thirteen under construction. The German navy had eighteen, with nine being built. With the dangers of a European arms race ever more apparent, especially the growing naval competition between Britain and Germany, the major powers agreed to two great conferences on disarmament and compulsory arbitration. The conferences met at The Hague in 1899 and again in 1907, but no country was willing to sacrifice any of its strength. At the second conference German delegates bluntly rejected any limitation on their sovereign right to make war, while at that very moment Kaiser William complained to the British press that England should be grateful to Germany for having remained neutral in the Boer War. This time, British recriminations against the outspoken Kaiser reflected an important shift in policy as well as anger.

The Triple Entente
In 1902 Britain ended its long tradition of refusing peacetime alliances and did so by signing a treaty with Japan, the rising power in the East. It was a first step toward reducing conflicts over

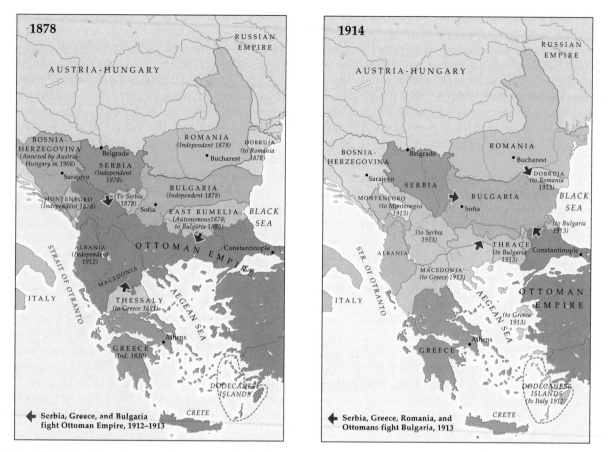

MAP 27.1 THE BALKANS, 1878–1914
These two maps of southeastern Europe show the new nations created in the period between the Congress of Berlin in 1878 and the beginning of the First World War. Notice which of these nations had gained considerable territory by the end of this period. What developments and events led to such geographical changes in the region, and which of these new countries do you suppose were most aggrieved by these various settlements?
◆ For an online version, go to www.mhhe.com/chambers9 > chapter 27 > book maps

imperial claims. That agreement was followed in 1907 by an accord among France, Russia, and Japan. It delimited each nation's areas of interest and, by guaranteeing the integrity of China, sought to reduce their competition there. Such understandings opened the way for further agreement between Great Britain and Russia, old imperial antagonists. They resolved points of contention reaching from the Black Sea to Persia, Afghanistan, and Tibet. The treaty between Britain and Russia, each already allied with France, brought into being the Triple Entente as an informal coalition of France, Russia, and Britain. It was clearly intended to counterbalance the Triple Alliance of Germany, Austria, and Italy, and its implications became clear when Britain decided in 1912 to withdraw its battleships from the Mediterranean, leaving the French navy to defend Britain's interests there while the British fleet concentrated on the German threat in the North Sea.

The Outbreak of World War

The Triple Alliance and the Triple Entente glared menacingly at each other, increasing their armament and measuring every international event as a gain or loss for their side.

The Balkan Threat Turmoil in the Balkans became a test of strength for the two sides. The ferment there of nationalism, modernization, militarism, and shaky parliamentarism echoed Europe-wide trends, but it was complicated by centuries of oppression, by disputed boundaries (most of recent invention), and by social, ethnic, and religious rivalries. The privileged role of Hungarians in Austria-Hungary and the Hungarian policy of enforced "Magyarization"—both consequences of the Compromise of 1867 (see chapter 24) fostered resentment and stoked nationalist aspirations among other ethnic groups living in the Habsburg Empire. The competition between Russia and Austria-Hungary quickly became enmeshed in these conflicts, and so did the Balkan ambitions of Germany (with railway and economic interests in the peninsula) and of Italy.

Italy's defeat of Turkey in 1912, when Italy gained Libya and important Mediterranean islands, triggered what came to be known as the first Balkan War. In the fall of that year Bulgaria, Serbia, and Greece also declared war on Turkey. In a few months they drove the Ottomans from all their remaining holdings in Europe except Constantinople. After a partial truce and months of border skirmishes, the great powers hammered out the terms of peace at the end of May 1913.

One month later Serbia and Greece, quickly joined by Romania and Turkey, declared war on Bulgaria, the big winner in the previous war. This conflict ended in a few weeks, but local anger and international concern did not. The great powers pressured the belligerents to accept peace, but they were watching each other more closely still.

The Assassination of an Austrian Archduke   In this atmosphere of growing distrust, tension between Austria-Hungary and Serbia increased. Groups of Serbian nationalists scattered throughout the Balkan region agitated on behalf of their fellow Slavs living under Austrian rule in Bosnia and Herzegovina, and Austria threatened to use force against Serbia if it did not abandon some of its nationalist claims. Against this background, Archduke Francis Ferdinand, the heir to the Austrian and Hungarian thrones, chose to parade in Sarajevo, the capital of Bosnia, on June 28, 1914. If the archduke wished to display Habsburg authority, others were eager to demonstrate against Austria. As the archduke's car moved down the street, a bomb just missed him. Then other conspirators lost their courage and failed to fire as his car passed by. At that point his driver made a wrong turn, started to back up, and yet another young Bosnian revolutionary fired point-blank, killing both the archduke and his wife.

The leaders of Austria-Hungary, convinced that the Serbian government was involved, believed it essential to respond strongly. They dispatched a special emissary to Berlin, where he was promised Germany's full support, and on July 23 Austria sent an ultimatum to Serbia. Meant to be unacceptable, it gave Serbia forty-eight hours in which to apologize, ban all anti-Austrian propaganda, and accept Austria-Hungary's participation in investigations of the plot against Francis Ferdinand.

Serbia replied with great tact, accepting all terms except those that diminished its sovereignty and offering to submit even these to arbitration. Great Britain proposed an international conference, to which France and Russia reluctantly agreed, and Germany hinted that Serbia and Austria-Hungary alone should settle the

The assassination of Archduke Francis Ferdinand and his wife in Sarajevo, painted as a dramatic moment when a single act affected the course of history.
Bettmann/Corbis

matter. Another crisis seemed about to pass when, on July 28, Austria-Hungary declared war on Serbia.

Stumbling into War   The system of alliances, increasing armament, bluster, and compromise had become a trap. Austria-Hungary was in reality not yet ready to fight. Germany and Great Britain still hoped the Austrians would limit themselves to occupying Belgrade, the Serbian capital, and then agree to an international conference. But Russia could not appear to abandon its role as protector of the Slavs nor let Austria-Hungary unilaterally extend its sway in the Balkans.

On July 29 Russia ordered partial mobilization, making clear that its move was aimed at Austria-Hungary only. The following day, however, the Russians discovered they lacked the organization for a partial call-up and so announced a general mobilization instead. On uncertainty, increased by inflation and unemployment, tended, like the disillusionment over reparations or the specter of Bolshevism, to favor caution.

Changes in Women's Lives

Women's suffrage, once hotly debated, had been adopted in the Scandinavian countries (Finland, 1906; Norway, 1907; Denmark, 1917; Sweden, 1919) and in Great Britain (1918) and was part of the new constitutions of Austria and Germany. The effects on public life were less dramatic than either advocates or opponents had predicted, but there was significance in the growing sense that for women to vote was a natural extension of democracy.

The most fundamental social changes of the period were usually not the result of deliberate policy. Employment in services such as sales and office work increased more rapidly than in industry, and the number of domestic servants continued to decline. These changes affected unmarried women especially. In most countries more women were gainfully employed than before the war despite a sharp decline from the wartime peak and despite the strong tendency for women to leave work upon marriage. Everywhere, women received more years of schooling than before, and the number of middle-class male youths enrolled in universities increased sharply. A rising standard of living and the automobile began to alter middle-class life.

Limited Recovery in France

Life in France quickly returned to prewar patterns. The nation had become par excellence the land of the middle class, the artisan, and the peasant proprietor fiercely attached to a tiny plot of land. Though the expected cornucopia of reparations never materialized, ordinary people accomplished miracles of reconstruction, carefully making their new buildings look as much as possible like those destroyed. The Chamber of Deputies elected in 1919 at the height of patriotic pride in victory was the most conservative since the founding of the Third Republic; and politics, too, focused on restoration.

The depreciation of the franc, for a century one of the world's most stable currencies, was the principal concern of President Raymond Poincaré's conservative program. Inadequate taxation during the war lay at the root of the problem, and budgetary contraction was the preferred solution. The rigid focus on a stable franc and military security reflected the psychological as well as the economic and demographic costs of war.

In the subsequent prosperity, competent leaders presided over governments content with policies that permitted domestic stagnation and encouraged inflexibility in foreign affairs. Poincaré's concern for national honor and a stable currency appealed to a cautious middle class but avoided more difficult long-term issues of working conditions, social inequality, cultural change, or international peace.

The Altered Circumstances of the United Kingdom

In the United Kingdom, also, the elections of 1919—the first in which women were allowed to vote—produced an overwhelming victory for leaders who promised to extract enough from Germany to make winning the war worthwhile. Lloyd George remained prime minister, but his government was essentially conservative. The breakup of the wartime coalition exposed the Liberal party's decline, and in 1924 new elections brought the Labour party briefly to power. Except for recognizing the Soviet Union, Labour did little to recall its leftist origins. For most of that decade, Britain was led with dull caution by the Conservatives and Stanley Baldwin, who inherited problems of unemployment, Irish nationalism, and a changing empire.

A crisis in the coal industry led to a ten-day general strike in 1926 that became a lightning rod for social division. Frightened by the bitter class conflict, many of the well-to-do volunteered in maintaining essential services, thus helping to break the strike. That response and the antilabor legislation that followed did much to deepen the resentments of British workers and heighten the angry rhetoric of public life.

Irish Independence

The Irish question was equally explosive. The promise of home rule had been suspended during the war, and the Easter Rebellion of 1916 had been firmly suppressed. In 1919, however, the most militant Irish nationalists, led by the Sinn Fein

Demonstrations and parades were banned in Dublin and Belfast, where an armored car stands ready to put down any trouble; violence had become an expected part of political struggle in Ireland.
Bettmann/Corbis

(meaning "We Ourselves") party, refused to take their seats in the House of Commons and met instead at Dublin in a parliament of their own, the Dail Eireann. There, they declared Ireland an independent nation.

To this defiance the London government responded slowly and ineptly, finally choosing to suppress the Sinn Fein party and with it Irish independence. The government then sent armed reinforcements in numbers sufficient to spread the fighting without ending it, troops that soon became the most hated symbol of British repression. Violent civilian resisters called themselves the Irish Republican Army. By the 1920s the two sides were fighting a bloody war.

With pressure mounting at home and abroad for some settlement, the British government in 1920 passed the Ireland Act, creating two Irish parliaments, one in the predominantly Catholic areas of the south and west, and the other in the predominantly Protestant counties of the northeast. Sinn Fein warred against this division of the island during almost two more years of fighting. Nevertheless, in December 1922 the Irish parliament sitting in Dublin in the Catholic south proclaimed, with British acquiescence, the existence of the Irish Free State, which included all Ireland except the six northern counties of Ulster. As Northern Ireland, these counties maintained the traditional union with Great Britain in an uneasy peace.

The British Commonwealth   Only in imperial affairs did flexible compromise still seem to work. Canadian complaints led the Imperial Conference of 1926 to a significant new definition of all dominions as "autonomous communities . . . equal in status . . . united by a common allegiance to the crown and freely associated as members of the British Commonwealth of Nations." Autonomous in all domestic and foreign affairs, dominions accepted ties to the British crown as the expression of their common traditions and loyalties. Given legal sanction by the Statute of Westminster in 1931, this conception of empire proved a skillful adaptation to new conditions crowned by the stability, prosperity, and loyalty of dominions such as Canada, New Zealand, and Australia.

International Relations

From 1924 to 1930 the conduct of international relations reflected some of the idealism of the Paris Peace Conference. The League of Nations, formally established in 1920, successfully resolved a number of disputes, despite the absence of the United States, Britain's greater concern for its empire, and France's tendency to use the League for its own security. The League's special commissions helped restructure the disjointed economies of new states, aided refugees, and set international standards for public health and working conditions. To further the rule of law, the League also established the Permanent Court of International Justice in The Hague, and in the late 1920s its decisions were treated with great respect.

Debt Payments   Crises over debt payments were dealt with directly by the major powers. As Germany fell behind in its payments, the Allies took the position that they, in turn, could not pay their war debts to the United States. Some compromise was essential, and in 1924 the nations involved accepted the proposals of an international commission of financial experts, headed by the American banker Charles G. Dawes. The Dawes Plan fixed Germany's reparations payments on a regular scale, established an orderly mode of collection, and provided loans to Germany equal to 80 percent of the reparations payment Germany owed in the first year of the plan.

The Dawes Plan did not admit any connection between Allied debts to the United States and German reparations to the European victors, but it did end the worst of the chaos. For the next six years, Germany, fed by loans largely from the United States, made its reparations payments on schedule. The issue seemed forever resolved with the adoption of the Young Plan in 1929, which finally set a limit to Germany's obligations, reduced annual payments, and ended foreign occupation of the Rhineland. Under the leadership of American bankers, the interests of international capital had come to shape policy.

The Locarno Era   International efforts to outlaw war led to a series of treaties in 1925 known as the Locarno Pact. In the major agreement—entered into by Germany, Belgium, France, Great Britain, and Italy—all parties accepted Germany's western frontier as defined by the Versailles Treaty and promised to arbitrate their disagreements. In addition, France pursued a more traditional diplomacy, signing a mutual-defense alliance with Poland and Czechoslovakia. A continental war caused by German aggression now seemed impossible.

The optimism of the Locarno era was capped by the Kellogg-Briand pact of 1928. The French had suggested that the American entry into World War I be commemorated by a friendship pact, and the Americans proposed to include others as well. More than a score of nations signed the pact, which, though unenforceable, renounced war "as an instrument of national policy."

Disarmament   From 1921 on, some League commission was always studying the problem of disarmament. Given the enormous cost of capital ships, naval disarmament seemed especially promising. At the Washington Conference of 1921–1922, the United States, Great

This idealized image of Lenin addressing the people conveys the power of Lenin's oratory skills and the sense that his leadership began a new era. The portrait of impassioned workers, soldiers and sailors, men and women—all inspired by their leader—and the careful placement of Stalin just behind Lenin reveal the painting as the subsequent official view of the Soviet government. One of the marks of the new era in Europe was, in fact, the effective propaganda of single-party states.
Sovfoto

Chapter Twenty-Eight

THE GREAT TWENTIETH-CENTURY CRISIS

TWO SUCCESSFUL REVOLUTIONS • THE DISTINCTIVE CULTURE OF THE TWENTIETH
CENTURY • THE GREAT DEPRESSION AND THE RETREAT FROM DEMOCRACY •
NAZI GERMANY AND THE USSR • THE DEMOCRACIES' WEAK RESPONSE

The 1920s and 1930s opened an era of intense hope and great fear. As the prosperity and consumerism of the 1920s gave way to economic depression, Europe's liberal governments had difficulty responding. Domestic divisions grew sharper, reinforced by the example of radical alternatives; for, although most of the revolutions in the aftermath of World War I had failed, new political systems emerged in Communist Russia and Fascist Italy. Relatively isolated at first, these new regimes became influential models. The possibility of communist revolution and the potential of fascist nationalism reshaped political life throughout Europe.

Cultural life was unsettling, too. A flourishing popular culture, flippant and commercial, undermined nineteenth-century standards of propriety (and the confidence that went with them). Europe's most interesting artists and intellectuals disdained the prosperity of the 1920s, and provocative theories, in both the physical and social sciences, invited skepticism about absolute truths and traditional values. Politics and culture both struggled with questions about the nature of modern mass society.

There were also immediate reasons for discontent among workers who had expected the postwar world to bring greater improvements in their way of life, among peasants who found it hard to make a living from small but often inefficient holdings, among ethnic groups resentful of sudden minority status as a result of the boundary changes in Eastern Europe, among nationalists angry that their new states had not gained more territory, and among all those who disliked the altered lifestyle of the postwar era. Then economic depression drove home the failures of capitalism, the limitations of liberalism, and the weaknesses of democracy.

Two nations seemed to rise above the economic crisis: Communist Russia under Stalin and Nazi Germany under Hitler. Their apparent escape from the Great Depression, their capacity to mobilize popular support, and their brutal use of force contrasted with the hesitant compromises of more democratic governments. In the 1930s that contrast sharpened as they began asserting their authority in international relations.

the importance of religion, although they were concerned not with its metaphysical truth but with its contribution to the development of the state and of capitalism. Both stressed the threat to society when group norms broke down, and both saw a danger of that breakdown in modern trends. Through this emphasis on the function of communal values rather than their validity and on the role of myth and ritual in all societies including our own, anthropology, sociology, and history have tended to share psychology's insistent relativism.

Public Culture

To the public at large, developments in science and the arts were associated with the prosperity and brash excitement of the twenties. Science meant the spread of automobiles, radios, and airplanes; new trends were known through colorful stylish advertising, risqué literature, and vibrant theater. The surprising crisp architecture and applied design of Walter Gropius' Bauhaus school in Germany, with its emphasis on relating form to function, began to win a following, and there was curiosity about the still more daring endeavors in France of Le Corbusier to envision a wholly modern city as a machine for living.

Cinema   During the 1920s, motion pictures became more popular and more profitable than any form of entertainment had ever been. Germany, Britain, France, and Italy each built thousands of theaters, often on the most elegant streets of major cities. Many of these theaters gaudily combined the exoticism of a world's fair with reassuring luxury. Egyptian and Greek motifs, marble columns, fountains, and statues reinforced the fantasies on the screen.

People from every stratum of society attended the same films, and women often attended without male escorts. Influenced by the movies, middle-class and working-class families increasingly discussed the same topics and began to imagine different and better lives for themselves. Reviews and movie magazines helped to provide the publicity essential to success in a business that relied on stars and vast distribution networks. American companies did all this very effectively, filling screens around the world. The United States made the most films, followed by Japan and Germany.

The rapid transition to talking pictures between 1929 and 1930 underscored national differences, and every country had some ministry empowered to restrain the presentation on the screen of sex and violence. In 1919 an English Watch committee condemned a film of the Johnson-Jeffries fight, fearing it could "demoralize and brutalize the minds of young persons." Sunday showings were an issue for years. Pol-

Gaudy movie palaces like this Parisian theater, one of the first, became prominent monuments in every city, offering the masses an exotic luxury previously associated with the great opera houses.
Editions Tallandier

itics was present, too. Many countries restricted or banned German films in the 1920s; France, generally the most tolerant, in effect proscribed films made in the Soviet Union where, with Lenin's encouragement, the director Sergei Eisenstein brilliantly showed how well suited the medium was to depicting official views of the revolutionary power of the masses.

Consumerism   While moralists worried about the cynicism of mass entertainment and the amoral excess of nightlife in cabarets and theaters, millions joined a kind of dizzying celebration. Middle-class families bought their first car; millions from every class, their first radio. Sophistication was a kind of shibboleth, used to justify lipstick, short skirts, alcohol, and one brash fad after another but also to underscore the cosmopolitanism that valued American jazz, openly learned from African art, and welcomed the new. For

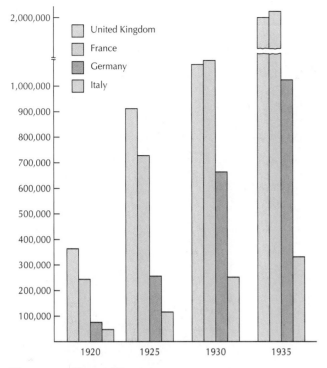

NUMBER OF MOTOR VEHICLES
The number of automobiles in a society reflects its general wealth, adaptation to a consumer economy, and changing patterns of communication. (Note that the United Kingdom, France, and Italy each had about 40 million people; Germany had 65 million.) This graph gives evidence of impressive prosperity and change; by 1935 France and the United Kingdom had one vehicle for every 20 people.

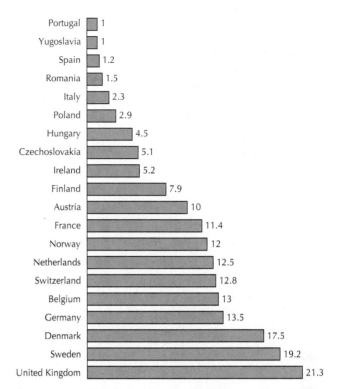

APPROXIMATE NUMBER OF RADIOS LICENSED FOR EVERY 100 PEOPLE IN 20 SELECTED COUNTRIES (1938)
Radio was an important new instrument of communication and propaganda. These statistics suggest that most families in the United Kingdom had a radio, that nearly everyone could sometimes listen to the radio in Finland and Austria, and that from Italy to Portugal millions of people heard the radio only on special occasions when speakers blared in public places.

perhaps the only time, Berlin rivaled Paris as a European artistic center, more famous as the home of acid satire in art and theater than for its thriving cultural institutions of a more traditional sort. Modernism turned its back on gentility.

THE GREAT DEPRESSION AND THE RETREAT FROM DEMOCRACY

Within less than a decade after the Paris Peace Conference, democracy was in retreat across Europe. By 1929 authoritarian regimes had violated or eliminated the liberal constitutions of Hungary, Spain, Albania, Portugal, Lithuania, Poland, and Yugoslavia as well as Italy. By 1936 political liberty had also been suppressed in Romania, Austria, Bulgaria, Estonia, Latvia, and Greece as well as Germany. Most of these countries were among the poorest in Europe, but their political difficulties illustrate the broader trend. Divided over issues of social reform, nationality, and religion—

differences amplified by new and angry socialist and peasant parties—they suffered increased disruption with each economic crisis and foreign threat.

Authoritarian Regimes

Authoritarian leaders often flirted with fascism on the Italian model, only to find it dangerously uncontrollable. They sought through decisiveness and force to achieve stability in societies riven by social conflict and where religious and ethnic loyalties could be readily fanned into anger and hatred by ambitious politicians.

The Monarchies of Central and Eastern Europe   During the 1920s and 1930s, many Eastern European nations experimented with fascist policies and tactics. In Hungary, for example, a series of anti-Semitic governments, beginning with the regime of Admiral Miklos Horthy in 1920, discouraged democracy and introduced many fascist trappings. In Romania the government of King Carol

Police in Vienna prepare to confront socialists in 1927. The socialists were protesting the release of men believed to have murdered a socialist. In the ensuing riots, the palace of justice was burned and a hundred people were killed, part of the cycle of violence shaking the Austrian republic.
Bettmann/Corbis

II—an admirer of Mussolini—stripped most Jews of land and citizenship, tightened censorship, and imposed martial law. A 1934 coup by the military in Bulgaria abolished parliamentary government and free speech in that country. Similarly, in 1929 King Alexander I of Yugoslavia assumed dictatorial powers in an effort to tame the divisive forces of Serbian, Croatian, and Slovenian nationalism.

By the end of the 1930s, however, all of these countries had taken major steps to limit or suppress fascist activities. One reason for these policy shifts was opposition from France, on whose support these countries depended. In addition, the Eastern European authoritarian leaders found themselves threatened by both the ambitions of the fascists themselves and popular backlashes against fascism. Although these governments moved away from fascism, however, most of them remained authoritarian.

The Republics of Poland and Austria Events in Poland followed a somewhat different course. Like other European nations, Poland was wracked by internal conflicts: Catholics versus socialists, conservative landowners versus radical peasants. In 1926 Marshall Jozef Pilsudski assumed power in a military revolt. Once his followers attained a majority in parliament, Pilsudski resigned. However, men from the military continued to run the country.

In Austria the republic was undermined by the sharp division between a Catholic German countryside and a cosmopolitan imperial Vienna. The left-wing Social Democrats had little strength beyond Vienna. Meanwhile, the conservative Christian Socialists—whose nineteenth-century programs of welfare, nationalism, and anti-Semitism had influenced the young Hitler—moved steadily toward fascism. As violent clashes between the parties intensified, Chancellor Engelbert Dollfuss, a Christian Socialist, responded by suspending parliament, outlawing communists, and eventually banning all parties except his own Fatherland Front, a coalition of conservative groups. In 1934 he used military force to crush the Social Democrats. That same year, however, a group of Austrian Nazis assassinated Dollfuss, an act they hoped would lead to *Anschluss,* or union with Germany. Although the *Anschluss* did not take place until 1938, Austria's authoritarian government, having repressed the left, found if difficult to mobilize opposition to growing Nazi pressure.

International Fascism Whether they won power or not, Europe's fascist movements had much in common. Generally influenced by Italian Fascism, they looked and sounded similar. They liked uniforms, starting with a shirt of one color. Cheap to buy and easy to adopt, it made a group of supporters (however few or poor) look like a movement, a historical force. They used paramilitary organization that promised decisive action to remake society through discipline and force. They created drama in the streets—noise, marches, colorful demonstrations, symbolic acts, and real violence—that undermined conventional standards of public behavior while advertising fascism as something new and powerful. They borrowed heavily from working-class movements and used all the devices of democratic politics, while seeming to stand outside the corrupting process of compromise and responsibility. Populist tactics were thus attached to the promise of order.

Fascists nostalgically evoked the enthusiastic patriotism of World War I to offer simple solutions to real problems. The disruption and inequity of capitalism, class conflict, a faltering economy, and aimless governments were the fault of enemies—liberal politicians, Marxist revolutionaries, Jews, and foreigners. Those enemies, although ridiculed and denounced in fascist propaganda, were credited with hidden powers that only the force of fascism could overcome. Fascism promised to create a united, orderly, prosperous community.

There was more to these movements than their simple myths, camaraderie, and sinister attraction to violence. Fascists addressed real fears. They spoke to a rural society that felt threatened by urbanization, to small-business people threatened by the competition of large corporations and to all business people threatened by workers' demands and government intervention, to a middle class threatened by socialism, to the privileged threatened by democracy, to the unemployed threatened by continuing economic depression, to the religious threatened by a secular society. Everywhere, they played on fear of a communist revolution.

The Appeal of Fascism Fascists could do all this by borrowing freely from ideas current throughout Europe. They used socialist criticisms of liberalism and capitalism, conservative values of hierarchy and order, and intellectual denunciations of modern culture. They amplified a widespread contempt for parliamentary ineffectiveness, used doctrines of race made familiar by war and imperialism, and laid claim to the nationalism that every government liked to invoke. At the same time, as admirers of technology and organization, fascists promised to create more modern societies. And they laid claim to corporatism, which Mussolini's Italy advertised as the wave of the future.

Corporatist thought had a long and respectable history. Organizing society as well as parliament according to occupation promised to do away with the selfish competition of interests and parties characteristic of liberalism, to preserve social hierarchy, and to eliminate class conflict. The idea of so integrated a society gained attractiveness in the years of economic depression and prestige with Pope Pius XI's encyclical *Quadragesimo Anno* ("In the Fortieth Year") issued in 1931 on the fortieth anniversary of Leo XIII's *Rerum Novarum.* The new encyclical went further in rejecting the injustices of capitalism and the solutions of Marxism, and it called instead for harmony based on religion and cooperation through corporative organization. Many anxious people found in that papal pronouncement a sympathy for fascism that seemed to justify overlooking its deeply antireligious qualities.

The appeal of fascism was not limited to poor nations. Its ambiguities made it applicable everywhere. In Britain Sir Oswald Mosley, once considered a likely Labour prime minister, founded the British Union of Fascists. In Belgium fascism benefited from the antagonism between Catholics and anticlericals and between French-speaking Walloons and Dutch-speaking Flemings, who were increasingly sympathetic to fascism and to the Nazis. In the Netherlands a National Socialist movement rose to prominence in the 1930s, and there were a number of fascist and protofascist movements in France, including *Action Française,* which had become prominent in the furor of the Dreyfus case.

The Great Depression

Above all, fascist and Marxist movements benefited from a worldwide economic depression that undermined social and political stability and seemed to many the death knell of capitalism.

The Stock Market Crash   On October 24, 1929, the price of stocks on the New York Exchange began to plummet. Suspecting that speculation had pushed stock prices too high, nervous investors sold their shares. Day after day tens of millions of dollars in paper assets disappeared. Such panics were not new, and they had spread from New York to Europe in the previous century. Now, however, the United States was the world's wealthiest nation and greatest creditor, and this panic settled into full-scale depression as banks failed, businesses cut back, consumption declined, factories closed, and unemployment rose. Its banks and exchanges shaken, the European economy suffered further from the decline in world trade and the withdrawal of American investments and loans. Financial panic hit Europe in May 1931 when Austria's largest bank nearly went under. The panic started a run on Austrian and German banks and then spread, as it had in the United States, to other sectors of the economy and to other nations.

The late 1920s had been years of boom in the United States and of general prosperity in much of Europe, but the Great Depression exposed deep-seated problems. Not all industries had recovered after the war. Coal and textile industries had long been sliding toward chronic depression. Former trade patterns had not revived, especially among the underdeveloped new countries of Eastern Europe, and economic difficulties were increased by Germany's inflation and Russia's withdrawal from commerce. Europe, which lost huge amounts of foreign investments during the war, had not regained its prewar percentage of world trade (about half), and American investments in Europe increased dramatically throughout the 1920s. Too much of the international economy rested on the unproductive passing of paper from the United States to Germany as loans, from Germany to the Allies as reparations, and from the Allies to the United States as payment of war debts; and the United States raised tariffs in 1922 and again in 1930 to levels that made it nearly impossible for Europeans to earn dollars by selling to Americans. Much of the prosperity of the 1920s rested on new processes and on new products, such as automobiles and synthetic fabrics, which proved vulnerable to the withdrawal of American investment and the decline in consumer confidence. The Great Depression underscored how uneven and artificial much of the preceding prosperity had been and showed that, for Europe, a decade had not been long enough to overcome the effects of World War I.

The Repercussions   By 1932 the world's industrial production was two-thirds of what it had been in 1929. Unemployment climbed to more than 13 million in the United States, 6 million in Germany, and nearly 3 million in Great Britain. Among leading industrial nations, only France, with its balanced economy and lower fertility rate, escaped a crisis of unemployment. Since the war, and especially in democracies, governments were expected to provide solutions to economic problems. They looked first for international help. Because the reparations system had broken down amid the world economic crisis, European nations declared that they could no longer make debt payments to the United States. The United States refused to acknowledge the connection. Instead, President Hoover proposed that all intergovernment payments be suspended; his proposal, quickly accepted in 1932, was supposed to be temporary but in fact marked the end of both kinds of payments.

Other crises loomed. Austria's banking system had been saved from bankruptcy with British loans; but the deepening depression and other financial burdens forced Great Britain to abandon the gold standard, which meant it no longer guaranteed the value of the pound sterling. The important bloc of countries that traded in sterling followed suit. Tantamount to devaluation, these moves threatened chaos for international monetary exchanges and trade; and so the League of Nations sponsored a World Economic Conference that met in London in 1933. Begun with visions of high statesmanship, it ended in failure. When the United States also went off the gold standard, the structure of credit and exchange that had been one of the signal achievements of liberal finance fell apart. For a century, nations, like so many bankers, had supported international financial stability by honoring these rules of liberal economics, and that historic era had ended.[6]

National Responses   In this crisis democracies responded first to domestic pressures. Austria and Germany sought a customs union, which was opposed by France and rejected by the World Court. Nearly everyone raised tariffs and import quotas, further reducing trade, while domestic programs protected political interests. Liberals were at a loss as to what else to do, and socialists were no better prepared to solve the problems of declining commerce, insufficient capital, and—most pressing of all—unemployment. Socialists could find some vindication in the evident weakness of capitalism, but their favorite nostrum, the nationalization of industry, was barely relevant. In practice, they adopted rather orthodox measures of budget reduction while supporting whatever palliatives for unemployment could be suggested, though the dole, the most common one, strained the budgets they wanted to balance.

---

[6] Karl Polanyi elaborated on the significance of abandoning the gold standard in a famous essay, *The Great Transformation: The Political and Economic Origins of Our Time.*

Most government policies, then, did little to help and may have made the situation worse; bankers and financiers, desperate to stem their losses, gave little attention to the international or social effects of their actions. And the millions of unemployed were more helpless still, standing in line for the dole, eating whatever they could get, taking any bits of work available. Growing communist parties let no one forget that while a whole international system had been collapsing, Soviet production advanced at a steady pace.

Gradually, economic conditions did improve; and by 1937 production in Germany, Britain, and Sweden was well above the 1929 level, though it remained below the 1929 level in the United States, Italy, Belgium, and France. Subsequent government intervention to shore up industries and provide employment did alleviate distress and improve morale. It also changed economic and political life and, at least in democracies, was often as socially divisive as the Depression itself. Democracies faced the dual threat of communism and fascism with a heavy burden of economic and social failure.

Nazi Germany and the USSR

In the 1930s Nazi Germany and the Soviet Union acquired unprecedented power over their own populations and used it in ways that changed the world. Understanding how these regimes evolved, their techniques of rule, and the policies they pursued remains a central challenge of twentieth-century history. Dictatorship has been recognized since ancient times as a specific political form. The most important dictatorships of this century, however, were different enough from previous examples to merit a separate term. They relied on a single political party, absolute devotion to a leader, domination of mass communications, direction of the economy, and the ruthless use of force—all in the name of an explicit, official ideology. The term **totalitarianism** refers to the combination of these characteristics and describes a system of rule more than specific policies, a system inclined to use oppression and terror to force citizens to participate in the regime's activities and belief system. In principle totalitarianism seeks to shape every aspect of life and to crush "enemies" identified by their race, occupation, region, or religion. Such a vision and the institutions that would attempt to carry it out did not develop all at once but evolved, primarily in Communist Russia, Fascist Italy, and Nazi Germany.

Useful as the concept of totalitarianism is, it has also come under heavy criticism for a number of reasons. In practice, none of the totalitarian regimes achieved total control. They often gave way before customs and institutions they could not afford to offend and negotiated with entrenched interests. Inefficiency and duplication were characteristic, even endemic, for these regimes, were not monolithic. Officials and party members often bickered among themselves. No totalitarian ideology was entirely coherent or unanimously embraced, and there were important differences among totalitarian systems. The values promulgated and policies pursued in Soviet Russia were not at all the same as those of Nazi Germany. Italy's claim to be totalitarian was largely propaganda, and that is the point. *Totalitarianism* is a useful term not for describing how these regimes actually functioned but rather for describing the ambitions and techniques that made Europe's leading twentieth-century tyrannies a fundamentally new political form.

Hitler's Germany

The Nazi regime won power in a democracy with an advanced economy and a strong administrative tradition. It played upon selected elements of German history, from militarism and nationalism to the weakness of the Weimar Republic, and it took advantage of the social shocks Germany had recently suffered: defeat in war, failed revolutions, inflation, clashing ideologies, and a depression that brought the most extensive unemployment in Europe.

The Rise of Hitler   As a young man, Adolf Hitler was undistinguished, his ambition to be an artist thwarted when the Academy in Vienna rejected his application. Service in World War I had been a kind of salvation, providing comradeship and some accomplishment: He was promoted in the field. In Munich after the war, he found brief employment spying on the small German Worker's party, which the army considered dangerous. He also took to addressing political rallies in the beer halls, where he learned the potential of a movement that combined the personal loyalty of a paramilitary corps with mass appeal and where he molded the speaking style that would make him the most powerful figure in Germany.

His speeches combined crude accusations, a messianic tone, and simple themes repeated in a spiraling frenzy. Race and universal struggle were the core of his message. Germans were victims of vast conspiracies mounted by foreign powers, capitalists, Marxists, Freemasons, and (above all) Jews—the gutter anti-Semitism that Hitler had absorbed in Vienna. Jews were behind war profits, reparations, inflation, and depression; but Marxism was also Jewish, and communists were agents of the Jewish conspiracy. Internationalism and pacifism were Jewish ideas intended to destroy Germany as the bastion of Western civilization.

To Hitler, Western civilization was Aryan, an old term for the prehistoric peoples of Eurasia that he used to describe race. Germans and Nordic peoples were the purest Aryans, Jews their enemy. Life was a desperate struggle won by the ruthless, and Germany's destiny was victory over enemies who threatened the nation by means of the Versailles Treaty, economic disasters, communists, Jews, moral decay, and abstract art. All attacked the Germanic *Volk*, the German people whose primitive virtues must be welded into an irresistible force.

The Growth of the Nazi Party   Hitler named his party the National Socialist German Workers' party. *Nazi* was its acronym. The party was one of many such nationalist movements when in 1923 Hitler led them in the Munich *Putsch*, or rising. After it failed and Hitler was sent to prison, the book he wrote there, *Mein Kampf*, won little notice, for it was a turbulent, repetitive outpouring of his political views interlarded with demoniac statements about how human beings are manipulated by fear, big lies, and simplistic explanations. In prison and after his release in 1925, Hitler worked to reorganize and strengthen the party. To the SA, his street army of brown-shirted storm troopers, he added the SS, an elite corps in black uniforms who served as his bodyguards and special police.

Hitler's intensity and bad manners offended many, but others felt the fascination of a personality that radiated power. He soon gathered a group of absolutely loyal men: Hermann Göring, an air ace; Joseph Goebbels, journalist and party propagandist; and Heinrich Himmler. They worked ceaselessly to enlarge the party, orchestrate impressive rallies, and terrorize their opponents. The Nazis were gaining attention and support. In 1930 they became the second-largest party in the Reichstag, and the following year a group of Rhineland industrialists promised the Nazis financial support.

By the 1930s, the party was broadly based, and the issue of what social groups were first drawn to the Nazis has been the subject of historical controversy, because different interpretations of **Nazism** follow from the answer. Workers were probably the biggest single group of members, but most workers continued to favor socialists and communists. Disproportionately large numbers of Nazi supporters were small-business people and tradespeople, civil service employees, and (to a lesser extent) farmers—all groups fearful of losing income and status.

In the Depression, promises of recovery, higher agricultural prices, and more employment (tens of thousands found jobs in the SA and SS) had concrete appeal. Many people were drawn to the call to rebuild the army and to save society from socialism. In 1931 an array of right-wing nationalists joined the Nazis in a manifesto denouncing the "cultural Bolshevism" of the Weimar Republic and hinting that, once they seized power, the Nazis would protect only those who had joined them now. The Nazis spoke simultaneously like a government in office and like an underworld gang, and they demonstrated their seriousness by beating up Jews and socialists.

Collapse of the Weimar Republic   The Social Democrats led the government that faced the Great Depression and did the best they could with a shaky parliamentary majority and an uncooperative president. In 1930 the government resigned, to be replaced by the Center party and Heinrich Brüning, a cautious man with little popular appeal.

The elections of 1930 gave Nazis more than a hundred new seats, from which they contemptuously disrupted parliamentary proceedings. His confidence growing, Hitler became a candidate for president in 1932, when Hindenburg's term expired. Worried politicians persuaded the nearly senile field marshal to run for reelection. Ludicrously cast as the defender of the constitution, the eighty-four-year-old Hindenburg won handily, but Hitler got more than 13 million votes. When Brüning proposed a financial reform that included expropriation of some East Prussian estates, Hindenburg dismissed him and turned to Franz von Papen, a friend of important army officers and Junkers.

Hoping to create a right-wing coalition, von Papen lifted Brüning's ban on the SA and SS, named four barons and a count to his cabinet, and declared martial law in Prussia so he could unseat the socialist government there. The outcry led Hindenburg to call another election. This one resulted in a Nazi landslide. With 40 percent of the Reichstag's seats, the Nazis were by far its largest party. Hindenburg avoided naming Hitler chancellor by refusing to grant him the full decree powers he insisted on. The nation was sent to the polls again, and although the Nazis lost a little, they remained the largest party.

Hitler Takes Office   Hindenburg then named another chancellor, General Kurt von Schleicher, a conventional army officer. He made an easy target for the Communists, the disgruntled von Papen (who thought he saw his chance to regain power), and the Nazis. Von Papen, confident he could use Hitler but contain him, persuaded the men around Hindenburg to appoint Hitler the head of a coalition government. In fact Hitler was the only leader acceptable to the right who could also command a popular following. He took office in January 1933.

Hitler almost immediately called another election. Previous campaigns had been ugly, but this one was marked by systematic terror, especially in Prussia, where Hermann Göring was now minister-president and the police acted like electoral agents. The climax came with the burning of parliament, the Reichstag fire that the Nazis loudly blamed on the Communists. Hindenburg agreed to issue special laws—Ordinances for the Protection of the German State and Nation—that ended most civil liberties, including freedom of the press and assembly. The voters gave the Nazis 44 percent of the seats, enough, with the Nazis' nationalist allies, for a bare majority. Hitler pressed on. Communists were expelled from the Reichstag, conservatives wooed with calls to nationalism, and the Center party enticed with promises to respect the privileges of the Catholic Church. By March Hitler dared demand a special enabling act that gave him, as chancellor, the right to enact all laws and treaties independent of constitutional restraints for four years. Of the 566 deputies left in the Reichstag, only 94 Social Democrats (out of 121) voted no. Blandishment and terror had done their work, but the tragedy went deeper: German politics offered no clear alternative to Hitler.

Consolidating Nazi Rule   Hitler's regime moved quickly to destroy the potential for opposition. It established concentration camps, first on private estates and then in larger and more permanent institutions. The new order appeared to enjoy all but unanimous support. A campaign to boycott Jewish businesses was followed in April by laws eliminating most Jews from public service and limiting Jews to 1.5 percent and women to 10 percent of university enrollment. On May Day 1933, workers arrayed by occupation marched beside Nazi banners and slogans. By July all parties except the National Socialist had been outlawed, and soon all competing political organizations disappeared.

In the elections of November 1933, the Nazis won more than 90 percent of the vote. They restructured government, purged the civil service and judiciary, outlawed strikes, and clamped stricter controls on the press. In a few months Hitler had achieved fuller power than Mussolini had managed in years, and in the next few years Nazi policies on racial purity would be extended step by step throughout public life by ordinances, official policies, and police brutality.

Hitler's most serious potential rivals were within his own party, and his solution was barbarically simple.

Nazi party troops march out of the rally on Nuremberg Party Day, 1933, carrying victory banners proclaiming "Germany Awake."
AKG London

On a long weekend in June 1934, leaders of the Nazi left wing were shot or stabbed. Among hundreds of others, so were General von Schleicher and his wife, some Catholic leaders, some socialists, and some taken by mistake. Hitler admitted to seventy-four deaths; subsequent estimates raise the figure to as many as a thousand. The Night of the Long Knives proved that any horror was possible; and the purge, like the noisy accusations of homosexuality that accompanied it, established the tone of Germany's new order. When Hindenburg died in August, Germans voted overwhelmingly to unite presidency and chancellorship in the person of Adolf Hitler, who took the official title of *Führer* ("Leader").

Administrative and Economic Policies   The federal states lost their autonomy through a policy of *Gleichschaltung*, or coordination, and all government employees were made appointees of the Führer. New people's courts heard secret trials for treason, now very broadly defined, and rewritten statutes allowed prosecution for intent as well as for overt acts. Arrest and detention without charge or trial became a regular practice. At the same time, the Nazi party was restructured to parallel the state, with administrative *Gaue* ("regions") headed by a party *Gauleiter*. The party also had its own office of foreign affairs and its own secret police, the Gestapo, which infiltrated both the bureaucracy and the army.

Economic policies scored impressive successes. Unemployment dropped steadily thanks to great public works projects—government offices, highways, public housing, reclamation, and reforestation. Many of these projects used special labor battalions, in which one year's service was soon compulsory. Later the burgeoning armaments industry and growing armed forces eliminated the problem of joblessness entirely. By spending money when more traditional governments thought it essential to balance their budgets, the Nazis reduced unemployment more effectively than any other Western nation.

Paying the Cost   Such programs were expensive, and they were paid for in several ways. A currency scheme largely designed by Hjalmar Schacht, a brilliant economist, required that payments for foreign trade be made with special marks whose value changed according to the products and the nations involved. Goods that Germany bought were paid for in marks redeemable only through purchases in Germany. Tantamount to barter, this system increased Germany's self-sufficiency and its influence in countries that depended on German markets. Additional revenues came from property confiscated from Jews, high taxes, forced loans, and carefully staged campaigns urging patriotic Germans to contribute their personal jewelry to the state. Ultimately, costs would be covered by printing paper currency, with effects long hidden by a war economy and the exploitation of conquered lands. By 1945 the mark had fallen to about 1 percent of its 1933 value.

Labor policies met related goals. Strikes were outlawed and the mobility of workers regulated. The National Labor Front, which represented all workers and management, froze wages and directed personnel in the

The six-pointed star and the word *Jude* scrawled on this Berlin department store in 1938 were a warning to good Aryans not to shop there.
Bettmann/Corbis

interests of business and government. Industrialists were relieved of the uncertainties of the Weimar years.

Winning Approval Meanwhile, the regime advertised the new benefits provided workers, including the summer camps and special cruises that were part of the Nazi program of Strength Through Joy. Nazi propaganda also reassured those ordinary people fearful of contemporary trends by denouncing modern art, the decadence of Berlin nightlife (and especially of homosexuality), and new roles for women. Special benefits to new families aided young couples in a depressed economy. Along with improved prenatal care and special honors for the most prolific mothers, such measures were part of the Nazi obsession with biology.

Initially, women were discouraged from working outside the home as a way to reduce unemployment among men, but the concern with women went far deeper. Wifely subordination was presented as a principle of social order and the foundation of the family. Women could not be lawyers or judges and could not constitute more than 10 percent of the learned professions. Social policies, schools, and clinics reinforced propaganda praising the role of Aryan women as breeders of a pure race. Severe penalties for performing abortions on healthy Aryans were accompanied by forced sterilization of the "unfit." Boys and girls were required to join the Hitler Youth.

The military had clear reasons for gratitude. Disregarding the disarmament clauses of the Treaty of Versailles (which Germany formally repudiated in 1935), Hitler pushed rearmament from the first. With the return of universal compulsory service in 1935 and the creation of an air force, Germany was soon spending several times as much on arms as Britain and France combined. All military officers were required to take an oath of personal loyalty to Hitler. By 1938 Hitler had removed the minister of war, chief of staff, and more than a dozen generals, thereby consolidating his control over the military and the foreign service.

The Nazis and the Churches The churches presented a different challenge. A concordat with the Vatican in 1933 gave the state some voice in the appointment of bishops while assuring the Church of its authority over Catholic orders and schools. Protestant denominations agreed to form a new body, the Evangelical Church, under a national bishop whom Hitler named; but when the bishop declared a need to "Aryanize" the church, dissidents formed the separate Confessional Church. The Minister for Church Affairs was authorized to confiscate ecclesiastical property, withhold funds, and have pastors arrested; but in practice the state kept religion in line more through the local harassment of individual clergy. Some priests and ministers cooperated with the regime—enthusiastically supporting war, race, and Reich. Most resisted at least the more outrageous demands made of them, and some individuals spoke out courageously. In 1937 Martin Niemoeller, the leader of the Confessional Church, was arrested for his opposition to Nazism; and Pope Pius XI condemned both the deification of the state and Nazi racial doctrine. In the following years some Catholic churches were burned, and members of religious orders were frequently tried on morals charges.

Anti-Semitism Anti-Semitism was central to Nazi ideology and practice, and the Nuremberg laws of 1935 codified and extended previous regulations. Jews (anyone with one or more Jewish grandparents was consid-

GOEBBELS' POPULIST VIEW OF GERMAN CULTURE

As minister of propaganda in the German government, Joseph Goebbels was also president of the Reich Chamber of Culture, an organization divided into separate sections for the various arts and for film, radio, and the press. Artists had to belong in order to exhibit, perform, or be published. The speech quoted here was an address given by Goebbels to the annual Congress of the Chamber and of the Strength Through Joy organization held in Berlin in November 1937. Goebbels' efforts were at their peak, and he reported proudly on the campaign against decadent art (which included much of the modern art most admired today), on the abolition of art criticism, and on the new recreation homes for veterans and the elderly, saying, "Nothing similar has even been tried ever or anywhere else in the world."

"My Führer! Your excellencies!

"My racial comrades!

"Organization plays a decisive role in the lives of people. . . . For every organization must demand that its members surrender certain individual private rights for the benefit of a greater and more comprehensive law of life. . . .

"The purging of the cultural field has been accomplished with the least amount of legislation. The social estate of creative artists took this cleansing into its own hands. Nowhere did any serious obstructions emerge. Today we can assert with joy and satisfaction that the great development is once again set in motion. Everywhere people are painting, building, writing poetry, singing, and acting. The German artist has his feet on the ground. Art, taken out of its narrow and isolated circle, again stands in the midst of the people and from there exerts its strong influences on the whole nation.

". . . True culture is not bound up with wealth. On the contrary, wealth often makes one bored and decadent. It is frequently the cause of uncertainty in matters of the mind and of taste. Only in this way can we explain the terrible devastations of the degeneration of German art in the past. Had the representatives of decadence and decline turned their attention to the masses of the people, they would have come up against icy contempt and cold mockery. For the people have no fear of being scorned as out of step with the times and as reactionary by enraged Jewish literati. Only the wealthy classes have this fear. . . . These defects are familiar to us under the label 'snobbism.' The snob is an empty and hollow culture lackey. . . . He goes in black tie and tails to the theater in order to breathe the fragrance of poor people. He must see suffering, which he shudderingly and shiveringly enjoys. This is the final degeneration of the rabble-like amusement industry. . . . The Volk visits the theater, concerts, museums, and galleries for other reasons. It wants to see and enjoy the beautiful and the lofty. That which life so often and stubbornly withholds from the people . . . here ought to unfold before their eyes gleaming with astonishment. The people approach the illusions of art with a naïve and unbroken joyousness and imagine themselves to be in an enchanted world of the Ideal. . . . The people seek joy. They have a right to it.

". . . 'Hence bread and circuses!' croak the wiseacres. No: 'Strength Through Joy!' we reply to them.

"This is why we have thus named the movement for the organization of optimism. It has led all strata of the people by the million to the beauties of our country, to the treasures of our culture, our art, and our life. . . . The German artist of today feels himself freer and more untrammeled than ever before. With joy he serves the people and the state. . . . National Socialism has wholly won over German creative artists. They belong to us and we to them.

". . . In this hour, we all look reverently upon you, Führer, you who do not regard art as a ceremonial duty but as a sacred mission and a lofty task, the ultimate and mightiest documentation of human life."

From Salvator Attanasio et al. (trs.), "Speech of Goebbels," in George L. Mosse, *Nazi Culture: Intellectual, Cultural, and Social Life in the Third Reich*, Grosset & Dunlap, 1966.

ered a Jew) were declared to be mere subjects but no longer citizens. The Law for the Protection of German Blood and Honor prohibited marriage or sexual intercourse between Aryans and Jews, "Gypsies, negroes or their bastards." Subsequently, Jews were expelled from one activity after another, required to register with the state, and ordered to give their children identifiably Jewish names.

In 1938 the murder of a German diplomat by a young Jewish boy touched off a new round of terror. Many Jews were arrested, and the SS led an orgy of violence (named *Kristallnacht*, the "night of broken glass") in which Jews were beaten and murdered, their homes and businesses smashed, and synagogues burned. A fine of 1 billion marks was levied on the Jews of Germany, and they were barred from the theater and concerts, forbidden to buy jewelry, forced to sell their businesses or property, denied access to certain streets, and made to wear a yellow star. Worse would come.

For most Germans, life went on much as before but a little better, and there was a new excitement in the air. From the beginning, the Nazis' publicity had been flamboyant, their posters striking, and their rallies well staged; after the movement came to power, propaganda became a way of life. Torchlight parades, chorused shouts of *Sieg Heil!* ("Hail to victory!"), book burnings, the evocation of Norse gods, schoolyard calisthenics, the return to Gothic script—a thousand occasions offered Germans a feeling of participating, of being swept up and implicated in some great historical transformation. At the Reich Chamber of Culture, Joseph Goebbels saw to it that cinema, theater, literature, art, and music all promoted Nazism (see "Goebbels' Populist View of German Culture," p. 888). Things primitive and brutal were praised as Aryan; any who opposed or even doubted the Führer ceased to be German. For this new regime, warfare was its natural condition.

Stalin's Soviet Union

Communists held that dictatorship in the Soviet Union was incidental and supposedly temporary. The reality proved different. Communist rule became more systematically brutal and bloody after Lenin's death, but in the last decade historians have uncovered substantial evidence in newly opened Russian archives that Lenin had already laid the groundwork for such policies.

The Succession to Lenin   No one knew who Lenin's successors would be when he died in 1924 or even how the succession would be determined. For more than a year, Lenin had been ill and nearly incapacitated, but his prestige had precluded any public scramble for power, and many expected a more relaxed government by committee to follow. In a famous letter, Lenin had assessed two likely successors: Trotsky, whom he called overconfident but the best man in the Politburo, and Stalin, whom Lenin found "too rude" though an able organizer.

Over the next three years, Russia's leaders publicly debated complex issues of Communist theory and practical policy. Trotsky led those who clung to the traditional vision that revolution would spread across Europe, and he favored an uncompromisingly radical program at home and abroad. Stalin declared that the Soviet Revolution must survive alone, a "revolution in one country." No theoretician, and little informed about the world outside Russia, Stalin was not wholly at ease in these debates with more intellectual and experienced opponents. But they, in turn, underestimated his single-minded determination. When the Politburo formally adopted his position in December 1925, his victory rested on more than ideas.

The Rise of Stalin   As general secretary of the party's Central Committee, Stalin was the link between the Politburo and the party organization below it, and he could count on the loyalty of party officials, many of whom he had appointed. He played effectively on personal antagonisms and on resentment of Trotsky's tactless arrogance. When the Politburo elected three new members at that December meeting, all were Stalin's associates. He then effectively eliminated his opponents. When leading figures publicly sided with Trotsky, Stalin labeled the break in party solidarity a threat to communism. Trotsky and Grigori Zinoviev—the head of the Comintern, the organization of the Third International intended to lead communists around the world, whose prominence made him dangerous—were expelled from the Politburo in 1926 and from the party in 1927.

The left was broken, and the following year Zinoviev recanted his "mistake" in having supported Trotsky. Nikolai Bukharin, perhaps the party's subtlest theoretician and a leader of the right, recanted too. Trotsky, who refused to change his mind, was deported, continuing from abroad his criticism of Stalin's growing dictatorship. None of these veterans of the October Revolution had attempted to oust Stalin; even Trotsky, who built the Red Army, never tried to use it against him. Old Bolsheviks fervently accepted the need for party loyalty, and Stalin made sure that the open debates of those early years would not recur.

The First Five-Year Plan: Agriculture   In aims and enforcement, the First **Five-Year Plan** reflected some of the qualities that had brought Stalin to the top. It shamelessly incorporated ideas Stalin had denounced just months before, but it was thoroughly his in the bold assumption that Russia could be transformed into an industrial power by mobilizing every resource. By 1928, when the plan was launched, Russian production had regained prewar levels in most sectors. Lenin's New Economic Policy had depended heavily on private entrepreneurs in commerce and peasant owners in agriculture. The task now was to create a socialist economy, and the first step was to collectivize agriculture.

Using the improved techniques and the mechanization that peasants had on the whole resisted, Soviet agriculture could produce enough both to feed industrial workers and to export grain that in turn would pay for importing the machinery that industrialization required. The problem was that Russian peasants continued to withhold their goods from market when agricultural prices fell. Some 4 or 5 percent of them had the means to hire labor and lend money within their villages, which gave them a further hold over the local economy.

As famine threatened, the government mounted a sweeping campaign of propaganda and police action against these wealthier peasants, calling them *kulaks*—the old, pejorative term for grasping merchants and usurers. Their grain was seized (informers were given a quarter of any hoard uncovered), hundreds of thousands of people killed, and untold numbers deported to till the unbroken soil of Siberia. Peasants destroyed crops and animals rather than let the government have them.

The explosive antagonisms of rural society raged out of control, and Stalin had to intervene in 1930 to halt a virtual civil war. By then, more than half the peasants belonged to collective farms, but the strife had badly hurt production, which contributed to serious famine in 1932–1933. A kind of compromise followed. Even on collective farms peasants were permitted individual plots and privately owned tools. Larger machinery was concentrated at Machine Tractor Stations, which became the rural base for agricultural agents and party officials. By 1933 output was sufficiently reliable to permit the state to concentrate on the most massive and rapid industrialization in history.

The First Five-Year Plan: Industry   According to the five-year forecast, industrial production was to double in less than five years, and in some critical areas, such as electrical power, it was to increase sixfold. More than 1,500 new factories were to be put into operation, including large automobile and tractor plants. Projects on a still grander scale included a Dnieper River power station and a great coal and iron complex in a whole new city, Magnitogorsk. These goals were met somewhat ahead of schedule, and there was only slight exaggeration in the government's proud claim to have made Russia an industrial nation almost overnight.

To pay for that achievement, indirect taxes were levied, wages allowed to increase only slightly, planned improvements postponed, peasants displaced, and peasant land collectivized. Food and most consumer items were rationed, with allotments varying according to one's contribution to the plan. Success required much more than money. Unskilled or poorly trained, laborers were unaccustomed to the pace now required: Turnover was high; output and quality, low. The state resorted to a continuous work week and moved special "shock brigades" of abler workers from plant to plant. Women and young people were urged into industrial jobs. "Socialist competition" pitted groups of workers and whole factories against each other for bonuses and prizes; piecework payment, once a hated symbol of capitalism, became increasingly common. Violators of shop rules were fined; malingering, pilfering, and sabotage (often loosely defined) became crimes against the state. "Corrective" labor camps, initially a mode of prison reform,

became another way to get more work done. Special courses within factories and enlarged technical schools trained new managers and engineers to replace the foreigners who were still essential to efficient industrial production.

In effect, an entire nation was mobilized, and the need for social discipline replaced an earlier emphasis on revolutionary enthusiasm. In schools, the formal examinations, homework, and academic degrees, recently abolished, began to return; classroom democracy gave way to greater authority for the teacher. The state stressed the importance of the family and praised the virtues of marriage, and the earlier emphasis on freedom for women gradually gave way to an emphasis on their contribution to Soviet productivity. Divorce was discouraged, and regulations on abortion, which had been legalized in 1920, became increasingly restrictive. Associations of writers, musicians, and artists worked on propaganda for the plan. Mass organizations of youth and workers met for indoctrination. Within the party, criticism or even skepticism was akin to treason. Hundreds of thousands of party members were expelled, and new recruits were carefully screened. "Overfulfillment" was triumphantly announced in 1932; the miracle of industrialization came with creation of a Russian totalitarianism.

Growth in the 1930s   The Second (1933–1937) and Third (1938–1942) Five-Year Plans continued the push for industrialization at somewhat lower pressure. Consumer goods were more available, and rationing was eliminated by 1936. Standards of quality rose, and dramatic improvement in transportation, especially domestic aviation, made previously remote territories accessible. By 1939 Soviet Russia ranked third among the world's industrial producers behind only the United States and Germany, producing twenty-four times more electrical power and five times more coal and steel than in 1913. Literacy among people older than school age rose from below 50 percent in 1926 to more than 80 percent in 1939. As millions moved to cities, the number of higher schools, libraries, and hospitals doubled or tripled. In these years one-seventh of the population moved to the cities, making the country more urban than ever before. More than 90 percent of peasant households were on collective farms serviced by the Machine Tractor Stations.

Announcing that the stage of socialism had been reached, the Soviet Union adopted a new constitution in 1936. The changes it made were mainly formal. Direct voting by secret ballot replaced the cumbersome indirect elections for the Soviet of the Union. The other house, the Soviet of the Nationalities, represented the republics, which on paper had considerable autonomy. The two houses together elected the Coun-

Villagers watch with anticipation for the first light bulb in Bryansk Province to be switched on, an achievement of the First Five-Year Plan.
Novosti/Sovfoto

This Soviet poster of 1930 hails the International Day of Women Workers, part of the government's extended campaign to encourage women to work in factories.
Edimedia

cil of Ministers (the term *Commissars* thus passed away) as well as the Presidium, which legislated and whose chairman was head of state. The constitution recognized the Communist party as "the vanguard of the working people" and provided social and political guarantees that Communists hailed as the most democratic in the world. Ninety-six percent of the population voted in the next elections, 98 percent of them for the list the party presented.

Stalinism A more confident government showed signs of relaxing its campaigns against potential enemies. Some political prisoners were amnestied in 1935, and a more controlled political police, the NKVD, replaced the sinister secret police. The campaign against religion abated. Opportunities for advancement in this expanding economy were great. White-collar classes got more respect, officers were restored to the army and navy, and supervisors were reinstalled in factories. Expression of opinion remained tightly controlled, however. Writers, Stalin commented ominously, were "engineers of human souls." Although harassed less than during the First Five-Year Plan, intellectuals had

long since learned the necessity of caution. The Russian Academy of Science, an important source of money and prestige, was never far from politics.

At the center of Soviet society stood Stalin, adulated as leader in every activity. Works of art were dedicated to him, factories named after him. His picture was everywhere. Patriotism overshadowed the socialist internationalism of an earlier generation, and Stalin was placed with Ivan the Terrible and Peter the Great as one of the molders of Russia. Although he held no official position other than party secretary, he demonstrated his awful power in the great purges of the late 1930s. Directed against engineers, Ukrainian separatists, former Mensheviks, and party members accused of being counterrevolutionaries, the purges were touched off by the assassination in 1934 of Sergei Kirov, a member of the Politburo who had been a close associate of Stalin's (in fact, Stalin himself was war in the context of Spanish history and international relations.

Carsten, F. L. *The Rise of Fascism.* 1967. The careful synthesis of a distinguished scholar that looks at the varieties of fascist regimes.

Colton, Joel C. *Léon Blum: Humanist in Politics.* 1966. The biography of this appealing figure is particularly useful for the period of the Popular Front.

Fitzpatrick, Sheila. *The Russian Revolution, 1917–1932.* 1982. A valuable, fresh overview that emphasizes social conditions.

*Kershaw, Ian. *The Nazi Dictatorship: Problems and Perspectives of Interpretation.* 2000. A significant assessment that provides an excellent introduction to and interpretation of a vast literature.

*Kershaw, Ian, and Moshe Lewin (eds.). *Stalinism and Nazism: Dictatorships in Comparison.* 1997.

Kindleberger, Charles P. *The World in Depression, 1929–1939.* 1973. A study of the origins of the Depression and of responses to it in different countries.

*Kolb, Eberhard. *The Weimar Republic.* P. S. Falla (tr.). 1988. A comprehensive account of the difficulties and failures of Germany's experiment with democracy.

Koonz, Claudia. *Mothers in the Fatherland: Women, the Family, and Nazi Politics.* 1987. Shows the importance of gender policies to Nazi ideology and rule.

Lee, Stephen J. *The European Dictatorships: 1918–1945.* 1987. A comprehensive and systematic comparison of Communist Russia, Fascist Italy, and Nazi Germany.

Mack Smith, Denis. *Mussolini.* 1981. An informed, skeptical account by the leading English scholar of modern Italy.

*Nolte, Ernst. *Three Faces of Fascism.* Leila Vennewitz (tr.). 1965. A learned effort to place the intellectual history of fascism in France, Germany, and Italy in the mainstream of European thought.

Peukert, Detlev J. K. *Inside Nazi Germany: Conformity, Opposition, and Racism in Everyday Life.* 1987. Makes use of a great deal of recent research to explore the effects of Nazi tyranny on ordinary life and the difficulties of opposition to it.

*Pipes, Richard. *The Formation of the Soviet Union.* 1964. A clear, comprehensive, and very critical treatment of Soviet rule.

Tannenbaum, Edward R. *The Fascist Experience: Italian Society and Culture, 1922–1945.* 1972. A wide-ranging effort to recapture the meaning in practice of Fascist rule.

Thompson, John M. *Revolutionary Russia, 1917.* 1989. A good overview of what the revolution meant for ordinary life throughout the country.

*Ulam, Adam B. *Lenin and the Bolsheviks.* 1969. Combines the study of ideas and of policy to explain Lenin's triumph.

Weinberg, Gerhard L. *The Foreign Policy of Hitler's Germany.* 1970. A major study by a leading American diplomatic historian that helps explain Hitler's early successes.

*Available in paperback.

Leonard Henry Rosoman
A House Collapsing on Two Firemen, Shoe Lane London EC4
This painting of a collapsing building captures the frightful devastation of aerial bombardment during World War II. The scene could have occurred in dozens of cities across Europe, such as Warsaw, Rotterdam, Liverpool, Hamburg, Dresden, or (in this case) London.
The Art Archive/Imperial War Museum

Chapter Twenty-Nine

THE NIGHTMARE: WORLD WAR II

THE YEARS OF AXIS VICTORY • THE GLOBAL WAR, 1942–1945
• BUILDING ON THE RUINS • EUROPEAN RECOVERY

World War II was the centerpiece of a long trial of European civilization. The outbreak of war followed a series of international crises, but in a larger sense it resulted from the kinds of governments brought to power by the social tensions of the era. For more than a decade a kind of ideological civil war undermined established institutions and exposed every weakness in the social fabric. New communist, fascist, and Nazi regimes carried those conflicts into international affairs, challenging the status quo and the democracies that defended it. The result was World War II, a war more total and more worldwide than its predecessor.

The war required massive organization, challenged national economies, and altered social relations. At first Germany gained everywhere, its preparations farther along, its tactics more ruthless. Slowly the Allies gained the upper hand, and the terrors of the battlefield were exceeded by the deliberate, systematic horrors of genocide, torture, and concentration camps. When peace finally came, Europe was a continent devastated, where millions had lost homes, family, health, and hope. It was a struggle just to make society function, and the achievement of stability and prosperity by the 1950s was a European miracle.

MAP 29.1 EUROPE ON THE EVE OF WORLD WAR II

◆ For an online version, go to www.mhhe.com/chambers9 > chapter 29 > book maps

nations. During an afternoon and evening of discussions, Hitler was granted all he asked. Neither the Soviet Union nor Czechoslovakia was consulted. The next day Czechoslovakia submitted to Hitler's terms and accepted last-minute demands from Poland and Hungary for additional pieces of Czechoslovak territory that they had long coveted. At a single stroke, Czechoslovakia surrendered one-third of its population, its best military defenses, and much of its economic strength. Central Europe's strongest democracy was reduced to a German dependency, and a keystone of France's continental security was shattered. As the French prime minister's plane circled the Paris airport on his return from Munich, he watched the crowd below with dread. But it cheered him, and in Britain, Chamberlain became a hero. Peace, the newspapers trumpeted, had been preserved.

Poland and the Hitler-Stalin Pact German might, Hitler's speeches, virulent anti-Semitism, goose-stepping troops marching through central Europe, and news of what life was like in the newly annexed lands and in Germany itself—all gave Jews, ethnic groups the Nazis labeled inferior, peoples living along the German borders, and whole nations reason to be terrified. Early in 1939 German troops occupied Czechoslovakia and annexed the seaport of Memel from a frightened Lithuania. The pretext of absorbing only German peoples had now been abandoned.

Well-coordinated armored and mechanized infantry units spearheaded Germany's *blitzkrieg* (lightening war) against Poland.
AP/Wide World Photos

Chamberlain, believing that not even Nazis could want world war, was one of many in Europe who hoped concessions would appease Hitler; but most people in England and France had finally become resigned to the fact that Germany could only be stopped by force. Italy, inspired by Hitler's success, began a noisy campaign to get Nice and Corsica from France and in the summer of 1939 invaded and annexed Albania. The Rome-Berlin Axis was formally tightened into the "Pact of Steel," and Germany kept European chancelleries quaking with demands for nonaggression pacts. Late in August the leader of the Nazi party in German-speaking Danzig declared that his city, which the Versailles treaties had assigned to Poland, must be returned to the fatherland. The denunciations of the Versailles boundaries that poured from Germany, along with claims that Germans living within the Polish corridor were being persecuted, made it clear that Poland was next. As they had all summer, Britain and France renewed their pledges to protect Poland.

The summer's most important contest was for some alliance with the Soviet Union, and Hitler won that, too. Germany and the Soviet Union announced a nonaggression pact. The USSR had made overtures to Britain and France, suggesting that the territorial integrity of all the states between the Baltic and Black seas be guaranteed. The Western powers, reluctant to grant a communist nation such extensive influence, had responded weakly. Since 1935 the Soviet Union had advocated disarmament, supported the League of Nations, supplied Loyalist Spain, and offered support to

Czechoslovakia, but Stalin feared that the democracies would welcome a war between Germany and the Soviet Union. In May 1939 he replaced his foreign minister, Maxim Litvinov, the eloquent spokesman for a pro-Western policy, with Vyacheslav Molotov, a tougher old ally. Hitler offered the Soviet Union a free hand in Finland, Estonia, Latvia, eastern Poland, and part of Romania should Germany seek any changes in its own eastern border. That became the basis for a nonaggression pact between the international sponsor of antifascist fronts and the creators of the Anti-Comintern Pact, a masterpiece of cynicism (and very old-fashioned diplomacy) that shocked a world still unaccustomed to totalitarian opportunism.

The last days of August resounded with formal warnings and clarifications from the major powers. On September 1, Germany invaded Poland. Britain and France mobilized, sent Germany an ultimatum, and declared war on September 3, 1939. One year after surrendering democratic Czechoslovakia, they would fight for authoritarian Poland.

The Last European War, 1939–1941

One argument for the policy of **appeasement** was that it had enabled Britain and France to buy time. They had been vigorously strengthening their armed forces, and the domestic consensus that war required was slowly taking shape. But much remained to be done; Germany had gained, too, in territory and power, and now there was no time left.

Blitzkrieg and Phony War For two years the Axis scored one victory after another. Having carefully prepared the invasion, Germany attacked Poland with overwhelming force in September 1939, the first ***blitzkrieg***, or "lightning war." Poland fell in less than a month, and Hitler suggested that the war could now end. Few were tempted by his hints of peace. Concerned to strengthen its frontiers against Germany, the Soviet Union attacked Finland in November and met such fierce resistance that the war lasted until the following spring. Having regained boundaries close to those of the last tsars, Russia could afford to wait. The Western powers had been waiting, too. Hitler refrained from attacking along the French border, and the Allied commanders resolved not to risk precious planes too soon or to repeat the pointless assaults of World War I. This was the period of the so-called phony war, during which arms production and mobilization speeded up, the world waited, and little happened. The strain was bad for morale.

With the Soviet Union standing aside from the conflict, French communists now said the war was a mistake; their party was suppressed. Paul Reynaud, energetic and determined, replaced Daladier as premier, and the Allies prepared to defend Norway, an obvious German target. But on April 9, 1940, Germany attacked Denmark, taking it in a day, and captured Norway's most important strategic points in short order, giving Germany bases for numerous assaults on British ships and cities. In Britain, Chamberlain resigned after a wide-ranging and often angry parliamentary debate, and Winston Churchill became prime minister of an all-party government on the day that the Germans attacked on the Western front. A Conservative who believed in empire and an opponent of appeasement, Churchill was a political maverick given his chance in the face of disaster. His decisiveness and eloquence made him one of England's greatest leaders.

The Fall of France On May 10, and without warning, German troops flooded the Netherlands and Belgium. The Dutch, who had expected to escape this war as they had all others since the Napoleonic wars, surrendered in five days. The better-prepared and larger Belgian army held out for eighteen days. On May 14 a skillfully executed German offensive broke through the Ardennes forest, thought to be impervious to tanks, reached Sedan, and drove to the English Channel, trapping the Belgian and British forces fighting there along with much of the French army. The German air force, the Luftwaffe, controlled the skies, and the Allies' proudest achievement in the battle for France was the evacuation from the port town of Dunkirk of 340,000 troops pinned against the sea. They left for Britain in a motley flotilla of naval vessels, commercial ferries, and

French refugees with all the possessions they can carry clog the roads, expecting to be able to escape the German armies in 1940 as their parents had twenty-five years before.
Roger-Viollet/Getty Images

private sailboats, a symbol of heroism and inferior preparation.

The Allied defense of France was broken. German forces renewed the attack on June 5 and took Paris in a week. Anxious lest he miss the war entirely, Mussolini attacked France on June 10. France surrendered on June 16, 1940. The armistice was signed in the railway car used for Germany's surrender in 1918. More ironic still, the man who chose to sign for France was the World War I hero of Verdun, Marshal Henri Philippe Pétain.

Germany's Victory over France Hitler seemed invincible and the blitzkrieg some terrible new Teutonic force, a totalitarian achievement other societies could not hope to equal. In fact, however, many of the tactical ideas on which it rested were first put forward by British and French experts, including a French officer, Charles de Gaulle. The blitzkrieg was the result not so much of new technology as new strategy. It combined air attacks with rapid movements of motorized columns to overcome the advantages that defensive positions had previously enjoyed. Tanks roared through and behind enemy lines, a maneuver requiring speed and precision that were alien to older theories. In the flat terrain of Poland, Germany's panzer tank divisions quickly encircled the enemy; in France, they often assaulted troops so far in the rear that they were not yet prepared for battle. The aim was less to capture ground than to break up communications. Then the Germans used air power to disorient and terrify the retreating army. The strafing of French roads clogged with civilian refugees and the bombing of Rotterdam had their place in the campaign to demoralize.

French strategy had relied too much on the defensive strength of the Maginot Line, a system of fortifications extending from the Belgian border to Switzerland, and on the assumption that Germany would respect the neutrality of Belgium and the Netherlands. The French had numerous tanks of their own but had been slow to deploy them; their air force was momentarily weakened because it was changing models. During the phony war, morale sagged with memories of the previous war and policy was undermined by politics rife with suspicion of the British, of the army, of the politicians, and of the left. Pétain, who believed France must now make its way in Hitler's Europe, blamed the Third Republic, and for a moment the nation turned to the octogenarian marshal with stunned unanimity.

He accepted terms of surrender that put three-fifths of the country under Nazi occupation and allowed 1.5 million French prisoners of war to be kept in Germany. The unoccupied southeastern part of France could have its own government, and that was established at Vichy. There, a reconvened parliament maneuvered by Pierre Laval named Pétain chief of state. The new regime, known as Vichy France, relied on a confused coalition of militant fascists and the traditional right and would never really be independent of Germany. After adopting bits of corporatism and some fascist trappings, it settled into a lethargy of its own, an often willing collaborator in Hitler's new order, ruling a truncated state as rife with intrigue, personal ambition, and shifting alliances as the Third Republic it so heartily denounced.

The Battle of Britain   Great Britain now stood alone. Unprepared for such enormous victories so soon, German officers planned their invasion of Britain while, beginning in June 1940, their bombers roared over England in sustained attacks that many believed would be enough to force surrender. Instead, in September the projected invasion was postponed, while the air attacks continued. The German navy had suffered enough damage in encounters with the British to favor caution, and by the next spring even the air raids were letting up.

Londoners sheltering in an underground subway station from the lethal destruction and sleep-destroying din of the German "Blitz" in 1940–1941.
© Corbis

The waves of German planes flying across the channel sustained losses far greater than those of Britain's Royal Air Force. British fighter planes, particularly the newer designs, proved at least the equal of the German; and they were aided by new techniques of antiaircraft defense, including radar, an English development that was the most critical addition to military technology in these years. At first the air raids concentrated on ports and shipping, then on airfields, and finally on cities, leaving great burning holes in London and completely destroying the industrial city of Coventry. But the diversity of targets dissipated the economic and military effects of the bombing, and the terror from the skies seemed to raise morale in a nation ever better organized and more fiercely determined to carry on. Merely to survive from June 1940 to June 1941 was a kind of victory in what Churchill memorably called Britain's "finest hour."

The Balkans   With all the Continent from Norway to Sicily and the Atlantic in their own hands or under friendly dictators in Spain and Portugal, the Axis powers looked eastward. In October 1940 Italian forces moved from Albania into Greece only to be pushed back, and Hitler had to bail out Mussolini by sending

The invading Germans laid siege to Moscow and Leningrad but finally met unyielding resistance. Soviet troops often engaged the enemy in ferocious close-quarter combat.
The Art Archive

in German troops and further squeezing the Balkan states, which were rapidly losing their independence. In June 1940 the Soviet Union, stretching the terms of its pact with Germany, took Bessarabia from Romania. Hungary and Bulgaria then took some of Romania for themselves, and Hitler announced that he would protect the rest of the country. In fact, all three Eastern European nations, already implicated in Hitler's mapmaking, were closely tied to Germany. It was no great step for them to join the Axis, welcome German troops in March 1941, and cooperate with Germany in invading Yugoslavia (which had hesitated too long over whether to join the Axis) and in attacking Greece, which had fought Mussolini too well.

The invasion was launched in April 1941 and swept through both countries within the month. Some Greek and British forces pulled back to Crete, only to be forced out almost immediately by German gliders and paratroops. The Allies retreated to Egypt, where British forces had held off an attack from Italy's neighboring colony of Libya. The Axis now threatened to dominate the Mediterranean, too.

The Invasion of the Soviet Union Having conquered so much, Hitler decided to complete his domination of the Continent. On June 22 German forces attacked the Soviet Union. The Soviets had long feared such a move, yet they appeared genuinely surprised, at least by the timing and the size of the German invasion. The assault, in three broad sectors, was the largest concentration of military power that had ever been assembled, and once more the blitzkrieg worked its magic. Germany's armored divisions ripped through Russian lines

and encircled astonishing numbers of troops. It looked to many observers as if the Soviet Union might collapse. Stalin, apparently in a state of shock, was silent for the first week after German forces invaded the Soviet Union. Finally, on July 3, 1941, he spoke by radio to the Soviet people. His address acknowledged initial defeats, invoked the example of Russian victories over invaders in the past, and emphasized that the Allies were fighting together against Nazi tyranny. But he also called in striking detail for ordinary citizens to continue the fight by destroying anything that might be helpful to the invaders (which became known as the "scorched earth" policy) and by constant sabotage.

German armies crossed the lands Russia had acquired since 1939, taking Riga and Smolensk in July, reaching the Dnieper in August, claiming Kiev and the whole Ukraine in September. Then the pace slowed, but while one German force lay siege to Leningrad in the north, a second hit Sevastopol in the south and moved into the Crimea. By December still another had penetrated to the suburbs of Moscow. There the German advance stopped temporarily, halted by an early and severe winter, by strained supply lines, and (at last) by sharp Russian counterattacks. The territory now held by Germany had accounted for nearly two-thirds of Russia's production of coal, iron, steel, and aluminum, as well as 40 percent of its grain and hogs.

As the war engulfed all of Europe,[1] German power at the end of 1941 was at its height, encompassing between 7 and 10 million soldiers, a superb air force, and a navy

[1]Only Sweden, Spain, Portugal, Switzerland, and Eire remained even technically neutral by grace of geography.

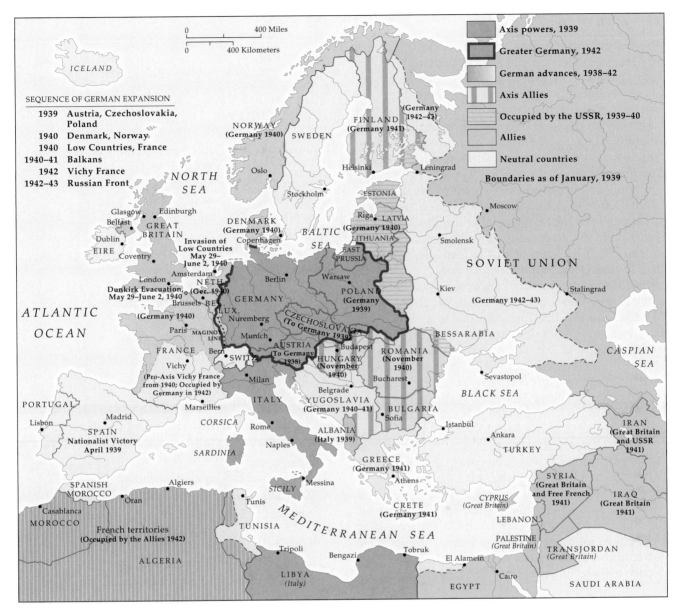

MAP 29.2 THE HEIGHT OF AXIS POWER, 1942
After the sweeping Axis conquests depicted in this map, the Battle of Britain (the struggle for supremacy in the air) thwarted Hitler's next invasion plan. But in actually turning the tide, how crucial do you suppose were the battles of El Alamein in North Africa and Stalingrad in Russia?
◆ For an online version, go to www.mhhe.com/chambers9 > chapter 29 > book maps

that included more than 150 submarines, which would sink nearly 400 Allied ships in the summer of 1942. Italy added sizable forces that were especially important in Africa. And yet Axis dominance was short-lived.

THE GLOBAL WAR, 1942–1945

From the 1930s on, the fascist powers had held the initiative in politics, international relations, and war. Germany's invasion of the Soviet Union extended the war across Europe and the Allied retreat carried it to North

Africa. Japan's attack on the United States in 1941 continued the pattern of Axis surprises, but it also marked the beginning of a significant change. War in the Pacific made this a truly global war—involving Asia, the Middle East, and North Africa—and the addition of American power helped tip the balance toward the Allies, whose industrial capacity was far greater than their enemies'. Axis propaganda was losing effect in the face of the realities of German rule, which gave weight to Allied claims that they were fighting for civilization as Russia, the Americas, and the British Empire set out to reconquer Europe.

The Turn of the Tide

The United States Enters the War   Despite its deep partisanship for France and Britain, the United States had remained technically at peace, even as the American government sold weapons to private firms for transfer to Great Britain and traded fifty old American destroyers for the lease of British bases in the western Atlantic. The United States, which Roosevelt called "the arsenal of democracy," also extended loans to Britain and then the Soviet Union. In August, Churchill and Roosevelt met at sea to draft the Atlantic Charter, which envisioned a world "after the destruction of the Nazi tyranny" that included collective security and self-determination for all nations, a world in which "all the men of all the lands may live out their lives in freedom from fear and want."

Ideological commitment, however, did not bring the United States into the war. Japan did that. Its attack on Manchuria in 1931 had been followed by a series of aggressive actions, from war with China starting in 1937 to the conquest of French Indochina in 1941. Tension between the United States and Japan increased with each new act of Japanese aggression, and America replied to the assault on Indochina with sanctions. Anticipating more, Japan gambled that the United States could be rendered nearly harmless in one blow, an attack on the American Pacific fleet at Pearl Harbor. The raid, on December 7, was devastating, and the United States declared it an act of war. All sides immediately recognized that the wars in Asia, Europe, and North Africa were one. Germany and Italy declared war on the United States three days later. Unless the Allies were driven from the seas, the industrial and military power of the United States might make a decisive difference in a war fought around the world.

Stalingrad   Winter snows raised the specter of a continuing two-front war for Germany, which Hitler had sworn to avoid. For all its losses, Russia's Red Army was intact, and its scorched-earth policy in retreat left the German army little to live on. To secure its massive victories, Germany had to knock Russia out of the war. But the siege of Leningrad, the attacks on Moscow, and even a drive into southern Russia in the summer of 1942 that took Sevastopol (and desperately needed grain) did not accomplish that goal. The crucial battle of the Eastern front began around **Stalingrad** (now Volgograd) in August 1942. A breakthrough for the Germans at that strategic center would open the way to the oilfields of southern Russia.

By September the Germans had penetrated the city and fighting continued from building to building. The heroic defense gave Russia time to amass more troops than the Germans thought were available, and in the

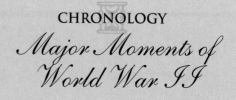

CHRONOLOGY
Major Moments of World War II

March 1938	*Anschluss:* Germany annexes Austria.
September 1938	Munich Agreement, Germany takes Sudetenland.
August 1939	Hitler-Stalin Pact.
September 1939	Germany invades Poland; beginning of World War II.
April 1940	Germany invades Denmark, Norway.
May 1940	Germany invades Belgium, France, Netherlands.
June 1940	France surrenders.
October 1940	Italy invades Albania and Greece.
April 1941	Romania, Bulgaria, Hungary, and Germany invade Yugoslavia.
June 1941	Germany invades the USSR.
August 1941	Atlantic Charter.
December 1941	Japan attacks Pearl Harbor.
August 1942–February 1943	Battle of Stalingrad.
November 1942	Allies land in North Africa.
July 1943	Allies land in Sicily; Mussolini ousted.
November–December 1943	Teheran Conference.
June 1944	Allies land in Normandy.
February 1945	Yalta Conference.
May 1945	Germany surrenders.
July–August 1945	Potsdam Conference.
August 1945	U.S. drops atomic bombs and Japan surrenders.

meantime Germany's supplies dwindled. A Russian counterattack encircled the German army, which Hitler frantically ordered to stand its ground. When it finally surrendered, in February 1943, fewer than one-third of its 300,000 men were left. The giant Russian pincers had cost the Germans more than half a million casualties. Stalingrad was the turning point of the war on the Eastern front.

Strategic Bombing and the Invasion of North Africa
In the West, too, the Axis position was eroding. The

American servicemen survey the ruins on an airfield at Pearl Harbor; the United States had entered the war.
National Archives

losses that German submarines inflicted were less crippling after 1942, and Allied air supremacy extended to the Continent, where thousands of tons of explosives were dropped on Germany each month in 1942, a rate that would increase fivefold in 1943. The Americans bombed strategic targets during the day; the British preferred nighttime area bombing, with a city itself as the target. The inferno created by the firebombing of Hamburg in 1943 was a horror to be exceeded two years later in a yet more massive raid that leveled Dresden, a cultural center without important industry. Meanwhile, the Germans were unaware that the secret codes they believed unbreakable had been cracked in London as early as 1940, giving the Allies an advantage that would grow as the war progressed.[2]

[2]The code was cracked in a project named Ultra, using devices that foreshadowed the computer. The secret of Ultra was not revealed until long after the war, and historians are still assessing its impact. The information that the Allies gained through Ultra appears to have been especially important in the Battle of Britain, the protection of Atlantic shipping, later in the war in Egypt, and in the Normandy landing.

The Allies also regained control of the Mediterranean. Fighting had spread to Libya as soon as Italy entered the war, and battle lines then ebbed and flowed as each side balanced military needs elsewhere against the chance for victory in North Africa. In April 1941 Germany sent significant reinforcements, and General Erwin Rommel, the German "desert fox," began a drive toward the Egyptian border. In October 1942 his *Afrikakorps* reached El Alamein but was defeated there, allowing Britain's General Bernard Montgomery to launch a counteroffensive as British and American forces landed in Morocco and Algeria. That November invasion, the largest amphibious action yet attempted, and the campaign that followed was an important test of green American troops and of Allied coordination under an American commander, General Dwight D. Eisenhower. It succeeded. By May 1943, after heavy losses, the Axis powers had been pushed out of Africa.

Halting the Japanese Advance in the Pacific After costly stands at Bataan and Corregidor, the United States lost the Philippine Islands early in 1942. By March, the Japanese had conquered Malaya and the

Dutch East Indies (today's Indonesia), defeating the British and the Dutch in costly naval and land battles. The fall of Singapore, Britain's Pacific naval bastion, was a crippling blow. The rest of the war against Japan would be fought primarily by Australia and the United States. Stopping further Japanese expansion in the summer of 1942 was thus an important turning point. Although a naval engagement in the Coral Sea in May brought no clear-cut victory to either side, the United States was better able than Japan to replace its losses. A month later the Japanese suffered heavy losses of aircraft carriers at Midway in a naval battle they had sought.

In August American forces launched a relatively small invasion of their own in the Solomon Islands. Each side poured in reinforcements, and the fighting on Guadalcanal, which was especially bloody, continued for six months before the Japanese were defeated. The war was far from won, but these victories ended the threat that Japan might invade Australia or cut off supply lines from India to the Middle East. The Allies could feel comfortable with their agreement that the war in Europe should have priority—an acknowledgement of fear that the Soviet Union might not survive without massive help, of the importance of European industrial power, and of the bonds of Western culture.

Competing Political Systems

War on this scale required the coordination of entire economies and cooperation from every sector of society. After their slow start, Britain and the United States achieved that with impressive effect. The Soviet Union proved far stronger than expected, and Germany, the state that in theory was most devoted to militarism, managed in practice less well than its enemies.

The Allied Effort at Home As bombs rained down on Britain, support for the war effort was nearly unanimous. Civilians accepted sacrifice and welcomed the end of unemployment. One-third of all males between 14 and 64 were in uniform, and unmarried women were mobilized. More women were employed in industry than ever before in both Britain and the United States. Labor unions signed a no-strike pledge, as they did in the United States. With tight rationing and government control of the economy, no society mobilized more thoroughly. Civilians accepted blackouts and suffered air raids and the temporary evacuation of 3.5 million women and children to the safer countryside. Even with that effort and that bravery, Britain increasingly depended on American aid. With its economic resources fully mobilized, the United States by the end of 1942 was producing more war matériel than all its enemies combined. Ships, planes, arms, and munitions

from American factories and food from American farms flowed across the oceans to Britain and the Soviet Union.

Even before 1939 Stalin had adopted the policy of industrializing the more backward regions east of the Urals, a safe distance from Russia's western border, and in the months preceding Hitler's attack in 1941 hundreds of factories were moved there piece by piece. Despite its enormous losses of productive capacity, the Soviet Union was able throughout the war to produce most of the military supplies it needed. Central planning, rationing, military discipline, and the employment of women were not such a dramatic change in this communist regime, but the acceptance of rationing, the increased hours of labor, the destruction of homes, the death of loved ones, and the loss of men and territory required patriotism of a rather old-fashioned sort. Patriotism became the dominant theme of Soviet public life.

Nazi Rule Until 1943 German civilians did not experience hardships comparable to the sacrifices of the Soviets or the lowered standard of living of the British. Nor was German output much greater than at the war's outset. The illusion, fed by military success and propaganda, that the war would soon be over encouraged interim measures. Competing elements of the Nazi party worked at cross purposes with each other and the government. Mutual distrust made it difficult for the Nazis to cooperate consistently with science and industry. Only when Albert Speer was given increased powers over the economy did coordination improve. In mid-July 1943 German production was twice what it had been in 1939, despite Allied bombing. A year later it was three times the prewar level.

Germany certainly benefited from its vast gains of territory rich in resources, industry, and personnel, but the system that took so naturally to ruthless conquest was less well adapted to ordinary life. The Nazis alienated those they conquered with their labor conscription, racial policies, and oppressive brutality. A high percentage of Ukrainians, for example, had welcomed liberation from Russian rule, but brief acquaintance with Nazi treatment of the "racially inferior" Slavs discouraged their cooperation. Nazi rule was most severe and most destructive in Eastern Europe and less harsh among the "Aryan" populations of the Nordic lands. But even in France food rations provided only about half the minimum that decent health requires. Germany's most crucial need was for workers, and slave labor was an answer in accord with Nazi racial theory. Eventually some 5 million Slavs were shipped like cattle to labor in Germany. By 1944 the 8 million foreign workers in Germany constituted one-fifth of the workforce.

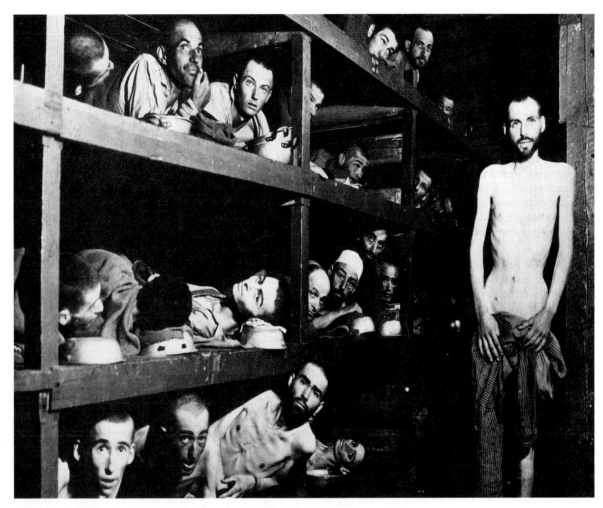

The laborers' barracks at Buchenwald at the end of the war.
Bettmann/Corbis

Genocide   The hysteria of racial hatred got the better of rational planning. Brutalized and starving workers could hardly be efficient. Transporting and guarding slave laborers became an enormous, corrupting, and expensive enterprise. Many millions of people died in forced labor, perhaps 3 million Soviet prisoners of war were killed, and millions more Slavs in occupied territory starved to death. These deaths, evidence of massive brutality and consonant with Nazi ideas about inferior races, could be said to have had some connection with the exigencies of war, as could the German practice of killing large numbers of civilian hostages in occupied lands as a means of demoralizing resistance while reducing unworthy populations. Hounding Jews and Gypsies, cramming them into concentration camps, and killing them had less to do with the brutality of war (the massacre of prisoners taken on the Eastern front may have been a precedent) than with the implementation of Nazi racial theory. Throughout the fall of 1941 mobile SS squads executed Jews who had

been rounded up on the Eastern front. Men and women, old and young were lined up, made to undress, and marched toward ditches to be shot by the SS (one squad reported having killed more than 200,000 people). The orders, equipment, and reports this slaughter required establish that many people had to have known about it.

The Holocaust   In January 1942, at a secret meeting of high officials held just outside Berlin, it was agreed that the systematic and efficient extermination of Jews should be made a general policy, "the **final solution** of the Jewish question" (see "A Gas Chamber," p. 914). By 1945, nearly 6 million Jews and as many other people (Poles, Gypsies, and Magyars especially) had died in concentration camps like Buchenwald and Dachau and the more recently constructed death camps like Auschwitz. Some of these camps were also supposed to be centers of production: A Krupp arms factory, an I. G. Farben chemical plant, and a coal mine were part of the Auschwitz

HISTORICAL ISSUES: THE HISTORIANS' DEBATE ON GERMAN GENOCIDE

Over the past decade historians of Germany, particularly in Germany itself, have sustained a heated debate about the ways of understanding Nazi genocide. Among the issues in this debate, known as the Historikerstreit, are the role of racial theories, the example of the Soviet Union, and whether genocide had distinctly German roots. The citations here, from three well-known scholars, illustrate these positions.

HENRY FRIEDLANDER

"Historians investigating Nazi genocide have long debated who gave the order to commit mass murder, when it was issued, and how it was transmitted. Although the specific mechanism has been a matter of contention between rival groups of historians . . . , there now appears to be a general agreement that Hitler had a deciding voice, although no one has ever discovered, or is likely to discover, a smoking gun. Recently historians have focused on the specific dates when the idea to launch the physical annihilation of the European Jews was first advanced and when the decision to do so became irrevocable. . . . My own approach is somewhat different. I am not particularly interested in exact dates. Instead, I want to trace the sequential development of mass murder.

"I define Nazi genocide, what is now commonly called the Holocaust, as the mass murder of human beings because they belonged to a biologically defined group. Heredity determined the selection of victims. Although the regime persecuted and often killed men and women for their politics, nationality, religion, behavior, or activities, the Nazis applied a consistent and inclusive policy of extermination only against three groups of human beings: the handicapped, Jews, and Gypsies.

"The attack on these targeted groups drew on more than fifty years of political and scientific arguments hostile to the belief in the equality of man. Since the turn of the century, the German elite, that is the members of the educated professional classes, had increasingly accepted an ideology based on human inequality. Geneticists, anthropologists, and psychiatrists had advanced a theory of human heredity that had merged with the racist doctrine of *völkisch* nationalists to form a political ideology of a nation based on race. The Nazi movement both absorbed and advanced this ideology. After 1933 they created the political framework that made it possible to translate this ideology of inequality into a policy of exclusion, while the German bureaucratic, professional, and scientific elite provided the legitimacy the regime needed for the smooth implementation of this policy."

From Henry Friedlander, "Step by Step: The Expansion of Murder, 1939–1941," *German Studies Review* 17, October 1994.

ERNST NOLTE

"Auschwitz is not primarily a result of traditional anti-Semitism and was not, in its essential core, mere 'genocide'; rather, it was, above all, a reaction—born out of anxiety—to the annihilations which occurred during the Russian Revolution. This copy was far more irrational than the earlier original (because it was simply an absurd notion to imagine that 'the Jews' had ever wished to annihilate the German bourgeoisie or even the German people), and it is difficult to attribute to it even a perverted ethos. It was more horrifying than the original because it carried out the annihilation of human beings in a quasi-industrial manner. It was more repulsive than the original because it was based on mere suppositions, and was almost completely free of that mass hatred which, within the midst of horror, remains nonetheless an understandable—and thus, to a limited extent, reconciling—element. All this supports the notion of singularity, yet does not alter the fact that the so-called annihilation of the Jews during the Third Reich was a reaction or a distorted copy—and not a first act, not the original."

From Ernst Nolte, "Between Historical Myth and Revisionism," *Yad Vashem Studies* 19, 1988.

HANS-ULRICH WEHLER

"Nolte's thesis concerning the fatal consequences of the Bolsheviks' anxiety-producing class warfare is directed above all against a well-grounded interpretation: that Hitler and National Socialism were products of German and Austrian history. Only after factors rooted in that past have been assessed should the broader European context be considered. Nolte has sought to undermine this hard-won insight by displacing the 'primary historical guilt' onto Marx, the Russian Revolution, and the extermination policy of the Bolsheviks. I shall emphasize below the main points of the opposing view—a view that is better grounded empirically and more convincing in its interpretive approach than Nolte's theory:

"—Hitler and countless other National Socialists had internalized a fanatical anti-Marxism long before the First World War: that is, before the Russian Revolution, the civil war, and class warfare in the new Soviet Union could confirm and strengthen their hatred of the 'Reds.'

"—Social Darwinism in its vulgar (racist) form was one of the strongest forces driving the highly ideological 'worldview' of Hitler and many other Nazis well before 1917. Contemporary developments thereafter only served as confirmation to these confused minds.

continued

"—The poisonous morass of German and Austrian anti-Semitism was the source of the crazed ideas associated with the Nazi hatred of the Jews. The new racist, political anti-Semitism that flourished in the late 1870s quickly led to the explicit idea of extermination. For example, in its Hamburg resolutions of September 1899, the German Social Reform Party claimed publicly and without any embarrassment that 'in the course of the twentieth century, the Jewish question must be solved . . . once and for all by the complete separation and (if necessary for defensive purposes) the definitive extermination of the Jewish people.' What was new in the 1930s was 'only' that Hitler and his cohorts took this program literally—and brought with them the will to carry out the deed itself.

"—The Nazis effortlessly adopted the widespread, fully developed antidemocratic, antiliberal, and antiparliamentary political ideology that had already been fully developed by the German Right before 1917/18.

"—The Nazis were able to exploit the deeply corrosive anticapitalist resentments of the Protestant, provincial bourgeoisie and of peasant society. They were also able to counter the difficult conflicts of a modern class society with the hypertrophied idealization of an oft-evoked *Volksgemeinschaft* (national community).

"—National Socialism benefitted from long-term conditions in Germany: the antagonisms of Germany's social structure, an authoritarian mentality, the peculiarities of Prussian militarism, the Protestant subservience to the state, the national susceptibility to charismatic leaders, a particular kind of political philosophy, etc. Hitler's regime also profited from more recent conditions that stemmed from the experiences of the period 1914–33. Among these were 'the experience of war,' 'the nation in arms,' the 'total war' of 1916–18, the beginning of the defeat, the renunciation of all war aims, the stab-in-the-back myth, the 'disgraceful peace' at Versailles, the war reparations and postwar hyperinflation, and the destructive force of the Depression. These events belong to a long list of favorable factors with fatal consequences.

"Above all, the traditions and burdens of Germany's past influenced the course of National Socialism. Only after these have been identified should historians proceed to analyze the influence of the wider European and world-historical context."

From Hans-Ulrich Wehler, "Unburdening the German Past? A Preliminary Assessment," in Peter Baldwin (ed.), *Reworking the Past: Hitler, the Holocaust, and the Historians' Debate,* Beacon Press, 1990.

great odds, organized resistance movements formed. Some developed around neighborhood groups; many were connected to prewar political parties. Always composed of a small minority, these partisan movements achieved particular strength in Denmark and Norway, the Netherlands, France, and Yugoslavia. Many of them received material aid and guidance from governments-in-exile operating from London, the most notable being the Free French, headed by General de Gaulle.

Nazi reprisals for acts of resistance were meant to be horrible. When Czechs assassinated their new Nazi governor, Reinard Heydrich, in June 1942, the Germans retaliated by wiping out the village of Lidice, which they suspected of hiding the murderers: Every man was killed; every woman and child deported. On a single day in 1943, the Germans put 1,400 men to death in a Greek village. Hundreds of towns across occupied Europe have their memorials, a burned-out building or a ditch where clusters of civilians were massacred.

Yet the underground movements continued to grow, and their actions became a barometer of the course of the war. In France, partisan activities expanded from single exploits—smuggling Allied airmen out of the country, dynamiting a bridge, or attacking individual German officers—to large-scale intelligence and propaganda operations coordinated from London. Norway's resistance helped force the Germans to keep 300,000 troops there and away from more active fronts. In Yu-

goslavia, two groups of partisans maintained an active guerrilla war, although the British decision to support the group led by the communist Tito all but ensured his control of the country at the end of the war. After the Allied invasion of Italy, partisan groups there maintained an unnerving harassment of Fascist and Nazi forces. Even in Germany itself, some members of the army and the old aristocracy began to plot against Hitler. In July 1944 a group of conspirators planted a bomb under the table as the Führer conducted a conference with his staff. Hitler escaped serious injury, but the sense that he was doomed had spread to the heart of Germany.

These partisan movements were important for more than their immediate contribution to the war. The memory of their bravery partially eased the painful reality of defeat, and in countries like France, Italy, and Norway, where many had acquiesced in fascist regimes, the militant opposition of the resistance could be taken to express the real will of the people. In fact, many of the major political parties of the postwar era were formed in the resistance, and the ideas of democracy, freedom, and equality that circulated so passionately then would be repeated in constitutions and party platforms later. Most resistance fighters were young men, but many women, too, experienced the camaraderie of activism as secret couriers, provisioners, and occasionally group commanders. By joining in the resistance, women were being drawn into the rudimentary renewal of national political life.

Allied Strategy

By 1943 the Axis was on the defensive although it had the advantage of shorter, direct lines of supply. While Hitler continued to imagine that some daring thrust or miracle weapon would bring him victory, the Allies continued to disagree as to how they should attack Hitler's "fortress Europe."

A Second Front   The Soviet Union had repeatedly urged opening a **second front** on the Continent, and most of the American military command favored an immediate invasion. The British warned against the high cost of such an expedition, and, with Roosevelt's support, Churchill prevailed. The Allies invaded North Africa instead, ending the threat to Egypt. When that was not followed by landings on the Continent, the Soviets suspected that they and the Germans were being left to annihilate each other. The Americans continued to favor such an attack, but the British argued for tightening the blockade of Germany and for making more limited assaults in the Eastern Mediterranean and Southern Europe, on what Churchill called the "soft underbelly."

More than military strategy was at stake. The Allies had been less specific about their long-range goals than during World War I, and they were divided. Stalin looked forward to regaining the Polish territory lost in 1939 (Poland could be compensated with territory taken from a defeated Germany). The British recalled the earlier communist aim of revolution across the Continent (as well as imperial Russia's efforts before that to expand into Eastern Europe). The British hoped to place Anglo-American troops in such a way that, after the war, they could have a voice in the disposition of Eastern Europe. In London the exiled leaders of the Eastern European countries agitated for their own nationalist goals, alarmed by Stalin's references to the need for "friendly" governments along Russia's borders.

With such issues before them, Roosevelt and Churchill met at Casablanca in January 1943. There they decided (to the Soviets' disgust) to invade Sicily and agreed to demand the unconditional surrender of Italy, Germany, and Japan, an expression of moral outrage against fascism that was also meant to prevent the Soviet Union and the Western Allies from making any separate deals with the enemy. Welcomed by Allied public opinion at the time, the refusal to negotiate with the Axis was subsequently criticized for strengthening their desperate defense after defeat was inevitable.

The Invasion of Italy   In July a mammoth amphibious assault carried Anglo-American forces into Sicily. A victim of his own propaganda, Mussolini had consistently overestimated Italian strength. As the invaders advanced, the Fascist Grand Council in a secret session voted Mussolini out of office. The Duce was arrested, and Marshal Pietro Badoglio was named prime minister. A coalition of monarchists and moderate Fascists then sought an armistice. But Committees of National Liberation had sprung up throughout Italy; composed of anti-Fascists from liberals to communists, these Committees wanted nothing to do with Badoglio, a Fascist hero of the campaign in Ethiopia, or with the king, who had bowed to Mussolini for twenty years. Again the Allies were divided. Britain favored the monarchy and feared leftist influence in the Committees. The Americans leaned toward the Committees but agreed that representatives of the Soviet Union should be excluded from the Allied military government that would be installed in Italy.

In September Allied forces in Sicily invaded southern Italy, where they were well dug in by the end of the month. The German army, however, had snatched control of the rest of the peninsula. Although the Allies captured Naples in October, their campaign in Italy soon bogged down in difficult terrain and in the face of fierce German resistance. In a daring rescue, German paratroops snatched Mussolini from his mountaintop prison and took him to northern Italy, where he proclaimed a Fascist republic that was blatantly a German puppet. At the same time, Italy's anti-Fascist partisans were becoming increasingly effective. Italians, their country a battleground for foreign armies, were caught in civil war.

The Free French   Italy was not the first place in which the Allies indicated they might compromise with tainted regimes. At the moment of the North African invasion, Admiral Jean François Darlan, a former vice premier of Vichy France and commander of its armed forces, happened to be in Algiers. Eisenhower's staff quickly agreed to make him governor-general of French Africa provided his forces would not resist the Allied invasion. De Gaulle was outraged. He had claimed to represent a free France since his first call for continued resistance in 1940 when, from London, he organized French forces fighting with the Allies. His hauteur, his insistence on a voice in Allied policy, and his success in winning support in the French colonies had made his relations with Britain and the United States difficult at best. The assassination of Darlan in December 1942 eased the situation, and Germany's decision to occupy all of France in response to the Allied invasion of North Africa reduced de Gaulle's fears that the Allies might choose to deal with the Vichy regime. Monitoring events in Italy, the European governments-in-exile shared Stalin's concerns about the consistency and true aims of Allied policy.

Stalin, Roosevelt, and Churchill, meeting for the first time at Teheran, reached an understanding that laid the groundwork for Allied cooperation in pursuing the war.
Bettmann/Corbis

The Teheran Conference Finally, at the end of November 1943, Roosevelt, Churchill, and Stalin met for the first time, at Teheran. The conversations were not easy. Previously, the British had mediated between the United States and the Soviet Union, but now the Americans took a middle position. The Allies reached a tentative understanding that the Soviet Union would accept a border with Poland similar to the one proposed in 1919, and they left open the question of what kind of government a liberated Poland might have. Their unity thus preserved by postponing the most difficult issues, the Allies could plan vigorous prosecution of the war. Stalin promised to declare war on Japan as soon as Germany surrendered, and Churchill's proposal for an invasion of the Dardanelles was rejected. The British and Americans agreed instead to land in France in the following year to open a true second front.

The Road to Victory

The Italian Front The Allies progressed slowly in Italy, taking five months to fight their way past a costly new beachhead at Anzio. In December 1943, King Victor Emmanuel III announced that he would abdicate in favor of his son, and Badoglio gave way to a cabinet drawn from members of the Committees of National Liberation. Italy then officially joined the Allies. The Germans, however, held the advantage of entrenched positions on one mountain ridge after another. Northern Italy became another German-occupied country in which Jews were rounded up for death camps, and captured Italian soldiers were sent to slave labor in Ger-

many. The Allies slowly pushed northward, aided by partisan risings, while the main forces were held aside for the invasion of France. Only in May 1944 did Anglo-American armies finally seize the old Benedictine abbey of Monte Cassino, north of Naples, after a destructive bombardment. Rome, the first European capital to be liberated, was taken in June.

The Soviet Union Soviet successes were more spectacular. In the spring of 1943 the Germans could still launch an offensive of their own, but it slowed within weeks. In July the Soviet army began a relentless advance that continued, with few setbacks, for almost two years. With armies now superior in numbers and matériel, Soviet forces reached the Dnieper and Kiev by November. In February 1944 they were at the Polish border. They retook the Crimea in the spring, Romania surrendered in August, and Finland and Bulgaria fell a few weeks later. Soviet power loomed over Eastern Europe.

The Western Front For months Germany was subjected to constant pounding from the air, and the Germans knew an invasion across the English Channel was imminent. They believed it would come in the area around Calais, the shore closest to England, as a series of calculated feints seemed to indicate. Instead, on June 6, 1944, the Allies landed in Normandy. The largest amphibious landing in history, it put 150,000 men ashore within two days, supported by 5,000 ships and 1,500 tanks. In a complex series of landings, Eisenhower's Allied force poured onto the French beaches. Made

CHURCHILL SEES AN IRON CURTAIN

On March 5, 1946, Winston Churchill gave a speech at Westminster College in Fulton, Missouri, that immediately received worldwide attention. After years of official emphasis on the cooperation among the wartime Allies, its directness was shocking. In effect, it announced the Cold War.

"A shadow has fallen upon the scenes so lately lighted by the Allied victory. Nobody knows what Soviet Russia and its Communist international organization intends to do in the immediate future, or what are the limits, if any, to their expansive and proselytizing tendencies. I have a strong admiration and regard for the valiant Russian people and for my wartime comrade, Marshal Stalin. There is deep sympathy and goodwill in Britain—and I doubt not here also—towards the peoples of all the Russias and a resolve to persevere through many differences and rebuffs in establishing lasting friendships. We understand the Russian need to be secure on her western frontiers by the removal of all possibility of German aggression. We welcome Russia to her rightful place among the leading nations of the world. We welcome her flag upon the seas. Above all, we welcome constant, frequent and growing contacts between the Russian people and our own people on both sides of the Atlantic. It is my duty, however, for I am sure you would wish me to state the facts as I see them to you, to place before you certain facts about the present position in Europe.

"From Stettin in the Baltic to Trieste in the Adriatic, an iron curtain has descended across the Continent. Behind that line lie all the capitals of the ancient states of Central and Eastern Europe. Warsaw, Berlin, Prague, Vienna, Budapest, Belgrade, Bucharest and Sofia, all these famous cities and the populations around them lie in what I must call the Soviet sphere, and all are subject in one form or an-

other, not only to Soviet influence but to a very high and, in many cases, increasing measure of control from Moscow.

". . . An attempt is being made by the Russians in Berlin to build up a quasi-Communist party in their zone of Occupied Germany by showing special favours to groups of left-wing German leaders. At the end of the fighting last June, the American and British Armies withdrew westwards, in accordance with an earlier agreement, to a depth at some points of one hundred and fifty miles upon a front of nearly four hundred miles, in order to allow our Russian allies to occupy this vast expanse of territory which the Western Democracies had conquered.

"If now the Soviet Government tries, by separate action, to build up a pro-Communist Germany in their areas, this will cause new serious difficulties in the British and American zones, and will give the defeated Germans the power of putting themselves up to auction between the Soviets and the Western Democracies. Whatever conclusions may be drawn from these facts—and facts they are—this is certainly not the Liberated Europe we fought to build up. Nor is it one which contains the essentials of permanent peace."

Reprinted in Brian MacArthur, The Penguin Book of Twentieth-Century Speeches, *New York: Viking, 1992, and available in many other places.*

pre-Nazi Weimar Republic. Everywhere social programs received much attention, but reconstruction took precedence over reform.

Ironically, at war's end Germany's industry was in better shape than that of any other continental nation, and the Allies soon relaxed restrictions on its economic activity. Early in 1949 they acknowledged the division of Germany and recognized the western sectors that Britain, France, and the United States had occupied as the Federal Republic of Germany. For the next fourteen years, Konrad Adenauer, the head of the Christian Democrats, served as chancellor. Mayor of Cologne from 1917 to 1933, he was seventy-three years old in 1949, a firm and conservative leader closely allied with the United States, who promoted an atmosphere of efficient calm.

Italy, too, became a republic when a majority of the electorate voted in 1946 to replace a monarchy tainted

by Fascism. As the largest party, the Christian Democrats gave Alcide De Gasperi, prime minister from 1945 to 1953, a solid basis from which to govern. A wily politician, he successfully ostracized the Communists—the largest Communist party in the West—and took advantage of a split among Socialists to bring Italy into close alliance with the United States. Winning the crucial elections of 1948, with the help of heavy American pressure, he launched a program of moderate reform intended to lessen poverty in southern Italy and to stimulate industry in the north. Italian politics had returned to the unheroic tradition of parliamentary maneuver the Fascists had overturned.

France's Fourth Republic looked much like the Third. The new constitution kept the president subordinate to the legislature as in the past, and the domineering de Gaulle was soon pushed from office as provisional president. Although an effective program of

Family allowance payments for children of the working class began to arrive at local post offices in August 1946—a first installment on Britain's postwar "cradle to grave" welfare state.
Hulton Archive/Getty Images

massive reconstruction got quickly under way, the problems of unstable governments, labor agitation, and communist intransigence got more attention. The parliamentary maneuvers necessary to win thin and uncertain majorities soon fostered disillusionment with the Fourth Republic.

Without constitutional change, Britain's postwar politics brought dramatic innovation. Churchill, revered as a war leader, nonetheless lost the election of July 1945. With an enormous majority, the Labour party under Clement Attlee launched a massive program of **nationalization,** taking over the Bank of England and a wide range of major industries, including coal, transportation, electricity, and iron and steel. It also instituted extensive welfare programs and established public housing, national insurance, and free medical care for all. True to its principles, the Labour government also began Britain's withdrawal from the empire to which men like Churchill had been so attached.

The Cold War   A turning point came in 1947 when distrust between the Soviet Union and the United States hardened into a worldwide military, political, and ideological conflict quickly dubbed the Cold War. As Russia tightened its grip on Eastern Europe, the American president announced the Truman Doctrine, promising military and economic aid to nations in danger of communist takeover. His immediate concern was the civil war in Greece, where local communists were aided by neighboring Yugoslavia. The United States also sought bases in Turkey, for Britain could no longer sustain its power and influence in the Eastern

Mediterranean, and the United States replaced Britain as the leading anticommunist force there. American money and supplies poured into Greece, and this, combined with Yugoslavia's break with Russia, enabled the Greek government to crush the opposition by 1949. Turkey, slowly moving toward democracy, received similar assistance. Opposing communism and Soviet influence had become the focus of American policy.

A few months after the announcement of the Truman Doctrine, Secretary of State George Marshall unveiled a bold plan to stimulate European recovery and overcome the postwar economic crisis in which communism was likely to prosper. The United States would offer massive economic aid to all nations still recovering from the war. Remarkably, communist governments were eligible, too, but Russia forbade their participation and established its own Council of Mutual Economic Assistance (Comecon) instead. Even aid was a Cold War issue. In the West, communist parties opposed the Marshall Plan despite its obvious benefits, and the United States used its growing influence to see that communists were excluded from coalition governments in France and Italy. That happened in 1947, and West Germany banned the party itself in 1956. The two halves of Europe followed the lead of their powerful patrons.

Escalating Confrontation   Fearful of the growing German economy and of American support for anticommunist movements everywhere, the Soviet Union tightened its hold over the states of Eastern Europe. Suddenly, in June 1948, the Soviets closed off overland access to Berlin, which they saw as a dangerous outpost of Western power. War seemed imminent. The United States responded with an extraordinary airlift: For nearly a year, until the Soviets backed down, a steady stream of flights ferried in all of West Berlin's supplies.

When the Soviet Union tested its own atomic bomb in 1949, the United States announced that work had begun on the even more devastating hydrogen bomb. But the loss of a monopoly on atomic weapons made ground forces that did not depend on using them an essential deterrent to Soviet aggression. Consequently, in 1949 the **North Atlantic Treaty Organization (NATO)** was created to coordinate the military planning of the United States, Canada, and ten Western European nations,[3] which now received U.S. military aid. The Soviets replied with the **Warsaw Pact** of communist states in 1955.

[3]Great Britain, France, Belgium, the Netherlands, Luxemburg, Italy, Portugal, Denmark, Norway, and Iceland were the European members. Greece and Turkey would be added in 1952; West Germany, in 1955.

serves as president, and a tendency developed for presidents of the European Council to seek some new accomplishment to mark their term, another stimulus to expanded activity. New legislation proposed by the Commission must be approved by a Council of Ministers, specialists in the relevant fields, such as agriculture or finance, appointed by and responsible to the member governments. Clearly intended as a check on the EC's autonomy, the Council of Ministers was nevertheless empowered in the 1980s to set some policies by majority vote rather than unanimity.

At the same time the European Parliament has gradually become more assertive. Despite its very limited powers, the creation of an elected parliament was hailed as "the birth of the European citizen." In 1979 the citizens of each member nation began voting directly for delegates to the Community's parliament, where the representatives sit according to political party rather than nationality. Over the years the European Parliament has begun to assert itself and to supervise the Commission more closely. The process of integration continued, with creation of a mechanism for regulating exchange rates and through the rulings of the EC's court. Thus, uniform regulations have spread to many fields (on standards of product quality, insurance, and environmental issues, for instance) and common legal rights (in the case, for example, of migrant workers).

Agricultural policy was especially controversial. The EC's subsidies, which had strong domestic support from farmers, resulted in costly stockpiles of unsold produce. Because Britain imports most of its food and has a smaller farm population, it contributed far more toward these costs than the EC spent in Britain. Its vigorous protests forced adjustments and then some reform of agricultural policies in 1981; but the issue was complicated by the further enlargement of the Community to include Greece in 1981 and Spain and Portugal in 1986, all countries with competing agricultural interests. Special grants to poorer regions—including the northwestern part of the British Isles, southern Italy, and the poorer members generally (Ireland, Portugal, Spain, and Greece)—have helped to bring those regions closer to the EC's general level of prosperity. As the Community gained a voice in matters traditionally considered the exclusive concern of national governments, especially social issues, domestic opposition to the EC tended to become more vocal.

Toward European Union

The Single Europe Act   In 1986 Jacques Delors, the president of the Commission, succeeded in winning support for the Single European Act, an agreement to create a single market. The act declared that by the end of 1992 there would no longer be any restrictions within the Community on the movement of goods, services, workers, or capital. These terms were met, with minor exceptions, and they brought striking changes in the lives of ordinary people. Most of the border checkpoints between member states on the continent have disappeared. All citizens of the member states carry a community passport, crossing national boundaries without restriction. Any of them can open a bank account, take out a mortgage, receive medical care, or practice a profession anywhere in the EC, for, in principle at least, the licenses and university degrees of one country are recognized in all the others.

The Single European Act required that vast arrays of national regulations be made uniform. Social practice, however, was as important as any new directives. Anticipating European integration, businesses, government agencies, and schools set about on their own to bring their practices in line with those of the EC, forming ties with colleagues in other countries. Organizations and individuals began to think and operate in terms of the Community as a whole; and sensing this momentum, the leaders of the EC pressed for more.

The European Union   The **Maastricht Treaty** of 1992 changed the name of the EC to the European Union (EU) to indicate its greater integration. The treaty also enlarged the powers of its parliament and called for a coordinated foreign policy and the adoption of a common European currency by 1999. The public found all these changes and requirements a little overwhelming. Attitudes toward the EU tended to turn more negative wherever domestic economies faltered, and public opinion on the complex Maastricht Treaty was so evenly divided in most countries that many questioned support for the EU itself. Within member states, opposition to the EU was joined by those opposed to any surrender of national sovereignty, by opponents of the EU's bureaucratic regulations, by those fearful of foreign immigrants, and by a variety of special interests. Advocates of the EU, on the other hand, have tended to include the most prominent political leaders, economic interests, and intellectuals.

In 1995 Austria, Finland, and Sweden joined the EU, and, remarkably, all of the fifteen member states except Greece met the Maastricht Treaty's stringent requirements. That willingness to raise taxes and cut budgets is testimony to widespread faith in the future of the EU. Great Britain, Denmark, and Sweden opted, however, not to join the common currency on the first wave. In the rest of the EU, banks, businesses, and governments began in 1999 to keep accounts in Euros, and in 2002 the traditional coins and bills emblazoned with national symbols gave way to currency in Euros (only the coins have national emblems, on one side).

MAP 30.1 GROWTH OF THE EUROPEAN UNION TO 2005
**Established in 1967 as the European Economic Community (or Common Market), the European Union
originally comprised six nations and by 2004 had grown to twenty-five. In what year did these nations adopt
one common currency? What other nations do you suppose may join?**
◆ For an online version, go to www.mhhe.com/chambers9 > chapter 30 > book maps

for passenger travel as well as for transport (and usually considered a service to be provided by the state) have been extensively modernized. In 1981 French trains, which hold world speed records, began to carry passengers from Paris to Lyons at 165 miles per hour. A tunnel under the English Channel, a project considered for centuries, opened in 1994 to provide direct automobile and rail links between Britain and the Continent. Water transport along Europe's coasts, rivers, and canals is relatively inexpensive, and air travel, dense throughout the Continent, is especially important across the expanses of Russia.

In the face of American and Japanese competition, Western European nations remain among the technological leaders in electronic communication, especially wireless telephones and satellite communication. On average, one-third of EU households are connected to the Internet. Europe's banks and stock markets, important sources of stability, began in the 1980s to become more flexible and in the 1990s to join international and global mergers. In 2000 the Frankfurt and London stock markets joined forces. Until the 1980s, in much of Western Europe as well as the communist nations outside the USSR, economic growth rested on mixed economies, with an important role for state planning in the West and some room for private enterprise in Eastern Europe. Since then, a strong trend toward privatization has brought more rapid growth and painful social adjustments that include cost cutting, rising unemployment, and international competition. The emphasis on productive efficiency, new products, marketing, and personal consumption that once seemed characteristically American now dominates most of Europe.

In the West agricultural productivity has increased as well, while the number of people who work on the land has continued to decline (in Ireland, until very recently one of the West's least developed nations, 60 percent of the workforce were employed in agriculture in 1960 and fewer than 8 percent are today). Modern farming, too, requires new investment and mechanization. With only about 3 percent of the world's farmland, Western Europe produces nearly one-third of the world's dairy products and 15 percent of the world's eggs, potatoes, and wheat (of which France is one of the world's largest producers).

Education   Modern societies require citizens to be more highly educated than ever before. That has led to extensive and controversial reforms that in the late 1960s and early 1970s often led to angry demonstrations and even riots. Traditionally in Europe, secondary education has been the great mark of social difference. A small fraction of students went to secondary schools noted for their demanding and usually classical curriculums. These schools were the gateway to a univer-

The skyscrapers of Frankfurt, one of Europe's greatest commercial centers, loom over the statue of Schiller, Germany's great eighteenth-century playwright.
Liaison International/Getty Images

sity. A larger proportion of students went to vocational secondary schools, and half or more of the youths beyond the ages of twelve and fourteen went directly to work. Despite efforts to make this segregation an effect of academic performance, in practice social class made a critical difference.

Educational reforms intended to make the system more democratic were offensive to defenders of the older curriculum, while not going far enough to satisfy student radicals, but they instituted important changes. In the West enrollments in the more prestigious forms of secondary education doubled and trebled, and a trend toward "comprehensive" schools more like the American high school allowed many of the graduates of those schools to go on to higher education. The number of university students has increased enormously, and more women than men now receive postsecondary education in most developed countries. In communist societies the children of workers and party members had priority for admission to such schools, but total enrollments increased more slowly than in the West before 1989. This expansion in the years of schooling and access to it requires increased state expenditure and families able to support children for a longer period before they begin to work. It helps to make social mobility become a more universal goal and makes education the subject of intense debate about fairness, culture, and employment.

Educational systems have tended to become more similar across Western Europe, although important differences in national traditions remain. Despite the creation of hundreds of new institutions of higher education, often with American-style campuses, enrollments in many countries swelled beyond capacity. Among European nations, the Scandinavian countries, France, Italy, Belgium, and the Netherlands have the highest proportion of young adults in some form of postsecondary education, with the proportion somewhat lower in Great Britain and Germany.

The Changing Roles of Women As women's lives changed even more than men's, European institutions have gradually adapted. Women have become more prominent in all the professions and in politics. Most European women over the age of fifteen engage in economic activity (the proportion ranges from about half in Italy, Spain, and Ireland to more than 80 percent of them in the Czech Republic, Poland, and the Scandinavian countries). Women make up from one-fifth to half of all managers in most countries, especially in smaller enterprises and rarely in top positions. Labor unions thus pay more attention to their needs: in Italy, for example, pressing employers to grant released time with pay to take special courses. Women constitute from one-half to nearly two-thirds of professional and technical workers. European governments and employers have made child care available to most women, in effect, encouraging mothers to have careers. On the average, however, women workers continue to earn less than men (between two-thirds as much in Britain and four-fifths as much in France).

Young women expect to have a freedom of movement that their mothers did not as they train, travel, work, and socialize outside their families. The availability of contraception and, by the 1970s, abortion (changes more accepted in Europe than in the United States) has added to this sense that women have the right to plan their life course. Gender discrimination nevertheless remains a serious problem and source of tension. The EU and many governments have adopted strong statements for equality and against sexual harassment, but their effect is limited, making the difference between ideal and reality all the more apparent as women wrestle with the pressure of multiple responsibilities.

Urban Planning Postindustrial society is heavily urban, and Europe has long experience in making its well-organized cities function well. The threat was clear: As urban agglomerations expanded across the surrounding suburbs, the inner core of older cities tended to lose population as people with greater wealth and leisure sought more space and privacy. The new highways, extended subways, and bus lines that push the cities outward rarely keep pace with the congestion of traffic at their heart. As similar-looking skyscrapers rise in the city centers and in new business centers around what had been the periphery, similar residential districts sprawl across the outskirts. One-fifth of the population of France lives within an hour's drive of Paris, and nearly that proportion of Britain's population is similarly close to London. Volgograd stretches for forty-five miles along the river after which it was named, and some fourteen cities of the former Soviet Union have a population of more than a million.

European states were accustomed to spending money to maintain city services, but governments were unsure how best to build. In the 1950s new housing in both the East and West tended to look like dreary concrete barracks and often provided few of the services necessary to create a sense of community. In nearly every country, whole new cities, often bleak and artificial, surround the metropolis: Five towns of 24,000 people each were placed around Paris; twenty-four such towns surround Moscow. Since the 1970s the trend has shifted to new urban hubs on a smaller scale, carefully planned to have shopping, recreational, and cultural centers of their own as well as some light industry so that much of the working population need not commute. Many of these ventures—those in Scandinavia were among the first—have proved to be attractive models, widely imitated, mixing large and small modern buildings, pleasant streets, and restful green spaces. War damage forced German governments into expensive projects of urban renewal, and from the 1960s on governments across much of Western Europe have invested in refurbishing urban centers and creating some of the world's most interesting experiments in urban planning, often with stunning effects.

Cities like Rome and Vienna found that banning traffic from the narrow, medieval streets of their old centers made them more attractive (and expensive) for shops and housing. Loud laments were heard at the who combined American influences with those of the British music hall, were by far the most influential popular music group of the 1960s and, along with the Rolling Stones, helped to create a transatlantic style that was at home on the Continent and in Latin America as well as in Britain and the United States. By the 1980s an international tour was a normal part of star status in pop music. In each country, performances were usually preceded by local groups, adding to the sense of a single culture with national variants. When in 1997 the Irish band U2 performed in Rome and Sarajevo, or when Bob Dylan and gospel singers appeared with the pope at a eucharistic congress, national origin hardly seemed to matter.

Globalization   These trends were part of a larger pattern known as globalization, in which communications, cultural exchanges, and economic activity increasingly take place on a worldwide scale. The last decades of the twentieth century witnessed a global revolution in communications and information technology. New inventions such as desktop and laptop computers, the In-

Inspired by American musicians such as Chuck Berry, Little Richard, and Elvis Presely, the Beatles took the United States by storm in the 1960s.
© Hulton-Deutsch Collection/Corbis

Once the imperial palace to Ming and Qing Dynasty emperors, the Forbidden City now hosts a Starbucks coffee shop.
© Macduff Everton/Corbis

ternet, cellular telephones, personal digital assistants (PDAs), CD and DVD players, digital photography, and satellite-based systems dramatically enhanced the flow of ideas, making information available instantaneously across the globe. One consequence of the communications revolution was that Western culture, whether based in the United States or in Europe, became accessible to people on every continent.

Global economic activity became more tightly integrated as well. Jobs, goods and services, and capital increasingly flowed over and beyond national borders. One key element in economic globalization was the emergence of large-scale enterprises that are based in one country but have operations in many countries. Known as multinational corporations (MNCs) or transnational corporations (TNCs), these firms increasingly dominated many sectors of the global economy. Significantly, more than 90 percent of the largest TNCs were based in either Western Europe, the United States, or Japan. Among the most prominent European-based TNCs were BP (Great Britain), Nestlé (Switzerland), Siemens (Germany), and Nokia (Finland). Of course, the globalization of economic activity encouraged greater cultural and ideological exchanges between Western and non-Western peoples.

New Directions   The arts had never been more international than after World War II, and they were necessarily affected by the energy of new forms of popular culture. One response was to turn away from the fast-paced plots of American cinema in favor of a more reflective mood. The novels of Alain Robbe-Grillet and the films of Jean François Truffaut and Ingmar Bergman were contemplative personal essays, held together by the sensitivity and imagination of a single creator and by images simultaneously surreal and real. Identified in France as the *nouvelle vague* of the 1960s, this style had its counterpart in all the arts.

Postmodernism   The change of attitude as the arts tended to become less austere and less concerned with the formal principles that academies taught and critics favored was dramatically obvious in architecture. Modern architecture, influenced by the Bauhaus school, had developed an international style that favored the pure and simple, geometric forms and unadorned walls of glass. By the 1970s, however, newer styles rejected that aesthetic and instead deliberately featured unexpected shapes, pitched roofs with gables, echoes of many older styles, and whimsical ornamentation. Because the element that this eclectic architecture most obviously shared was its rejection of modernism, it came to be called *postmodern*, a term soon applied to many other fields as well.

A monument of a postmodern and international age, this Guggenheim museum was designed by the American architect Frank Gehry and opened in 1997 in Bilbao, Spain, a city once known primarily as a grim industrial town.
J. Pavlovsky/Corbis Sygma

A preference for playful attitudes and individualistic innovation more than a formal school of thought, **postmodernism** reflected important cultural tendencies. Labeling regularity, rigid logic, and the control of nature or human beings as modern made postmodernism a convenient way to describe a new direction in the arts and social sciences.

Social Thought

Following World War II, the major schools of social thought had generally assumed that rational analysis could explain social behavior with a certain objectivity that would lead to beneficial policies. From the 1970s on, however, students of society have been increasingly inclined to show instead how programs for social improvement, how claims to objective knowledge, and how the promotion of high culture may actually be exercises that preserve the dominance of elites.

Modernization and Marxism   Social and political thought in the 1950s used historical and social analysis to prescribe solutions for current problems. Theories of modernization traced a line of development from the era of absolute monarchy to a modern age of liberal democracy, and in doing so sought to explain what went wrong in nations like Germany, Italy, and Spain that had not sustained democracy. The answers to these historical questions were then offered as a guide for developing nations around the world as the means to democratic stability.

Writings on modernization, especially pervasive in the United States, influenced the social sciences throughout the West. They demonstrated the connection between political freedom and economic growth and showed that these developments in turn were intricately related to social changes, such as literacy and urbanization. Discussions of modernization tended to advocate for all societies the values, legal systems, and social practices identified as characteristic of Western Europe and the United States. Studies of modernization fostered greater attention to the non-Western world and favored interdisciplinary research that used sophisticated social scientific theories and methods (including quantitative analysis and opinion surveys). By the 1970s, however, these theories had come under heavy attack for creating an idealized description of Western (often American) society and then applying it everywhere, for stressing consensus and compromise while largely ignoring social conflicts and injustice, and for serving as a Cold War ideology in competition with Soviet Marxism.

Marxist thought, which also incorporated ideas of progress, provided the principal alternative to theories of modernization. Varieties of Marxism less rigid than Soviet communism were influential throughout European intellectual life, especially in England and Italy in the late 1960s and 1970s. In their flexibility and subtle insights, these neo-Marxist analyses made lasting contributions to the understanding of society and culture, especially through ideas associated with the so-called Frankfurt school and with Antonio Gramsci. A group of innovative and Marxian social scientists and philosophers had flourished in Frankfurt under Germany's Weimar republic until Hitler forced its leaders into exile. Although their writings were rigorous and difficult, they gained a wide readership in the postwar period. And their analyses, whether of the arts or social structure, interlaced modern sociology and psychology (especially Freudian ideas) with a profound distaste for mass culture and contemporary society. One of their members, Herbert Marcuse, became a hero to leaders of the student revolts of 1968 because of his powerful criticism of the commercialism and illusory freedom of modern society.

The pervasiveness of Marxist thinking also owed a great deal to the work of Antonio Gramsci. Like the more doctrinaire Hungarian Georg Lukács, Gramsci was a communist intellectual who took culture seriously, not simply as a reflection of society's material structure but as the collection of values that held it together. One of Italy's leading communist activists, Gramsci was imprisoned by the Fascist authorities; most of his writing consists of notebooks and letters written in prison during the 1920s and 1930s and published after the war. Gramsci, while recognizing the importance of religion and the arts, sought to explain why peasants and workers accept inequality. He developed the concept of cultural hegemony, exploring how the values and styles invented and promulgated by elites come to be shared across social classes and thus shape the thought and action of entire societies. Radicals, Gramsci argued, must provide an alternative culture that matches the qualities of the culture they wish to overturn.

Cultural Studies   English, French, German, and American scholars applied these ideas to their own histories and to current political debates, exposing a bias toward the status quo in liberal ideology and elitism in much current scholarship. The field of cultural studies has evolved from this line of attack on dominant ideologies while distancing itself from Marxism and gaining momentum from worldwide changes in politics as well as culture. Decolonization invited a new look at how imperialism functions and provoked renewed interest in how non-Western societies wrestle with Western cultural and economic domination. The self-serving assumptions built into European assessments of non-European cultures (a topic that dominates anthropology today) had become easier to identify. Movements in behalf of ethnic minorities—African Americans in the United States and other ethnic groups in the United States and Europe—undermined claims that society's established institutions and authorities were neutral. Cultural studies has also made popular culture the object of serious study, especially in Britain, welcoming its irreverence and finding within it a yearning for freedom and the creative expression of marginalized people alienated from consumer society.

Michel Foucault   The methods, insights, and vocabulary of cultural studies owe a great deal to the work of the Frenchman Michel Foucault, perhaps the most influential thinker of the 1980s, particularly in the United States and England. Foucault was trained as a philosopher, and his work achieved international resonance much as Sartre's had done a generation earlier. Foucault consistently acknowledged his debt to Nietzsche and was clearly influenced by Marx, the new social history,[4] and the work of the French anthropologist Claude Lévi-Strauss. Lévi-Strauss believed that every aspect of a supposedly primitive society—its kinship systems, customs, rituals, and myths—can be understood as the extension of unstated, complex, and integrated structures of thought. These hidden structures, he declared, reflect the nature of the human mind, a view that led him to an admiration of premodern societies comparable to that felt by many modern artists.

All these currents were present in Foucault's thought, but most of all he built on the rising science of semiotics, the study of the signs by which human beings communicate. In Foucault's hands, semiotics provided the means for reinterpreting modern history and civilization. His periodization was conventional: Modernity emerged in the late eighteenth century and was heralded by the French Revolution. But he upended the conventional interpretations of what modernity meant. Medicine, psychology, and prison reform were not simply the progressive results of increased knowledge but instruments of a new social discipline. The scientific observation of other people, however neutral or objective it claims to be, is a means of controlling behavior through shared *discourse*—a crucial Foucauldian term. By *discourse* Foucault means a framework of understanding used consciously and unconsciously that automatically excludes some possibilities and urges others. To talk about certain behavior as an illness, for example, is a form of power, and power is one of Foucault's central concerns. Discourse functions within society to make power diffuse and pervasive, independent of public intent. Foucault's ideas (like his witty, perceptive, and involuted style) provided a new and effective way to challenge not just the acknowledged evils of modern society but the laws, institutions, practices, and conception of knowledge on which society rests. Without proffering solutions, Foucault's works offer an arsenal of weapons with which to unmask intellectual claims to authority or objectivity.

Poststructuralism   A further powerful attack on the apparent neutrality of scientific categories and logical reason is heavily indebted to French intellectual Jacques Derrida. Like Foucault, Derrida uses the tools of semiotics and philosophy and has more followers in the United States than in Europe. The two have been called the philosophers of 1968 because of their ties to the student movement of those years. Derrida studies

[4] French historians centered around the journal *Annales* began before World War II to develop approaches to social history that influenced historical study around the world in the 1960s and 1970s and continue to make important contributions to the social sciences and humanities. Foucault himself was close to, although not part of, the *Annales* group.

literature by concentrating on the text and subjecting it to a technique he named *deconstruction*. For deconstructionists, texts contain linguistic signs that are not straightforward—not *transparent*, to use their term—but instead carry multiple associations with individual words, with style and syntax, and with all the literary, cultural, social, and personal contexts from which a given text has emerged. Necessarily, the signs on the page must be (mis)translated in the mind of the reader. Thus, no text has one stable meaning but communicates differently to different people and on many levels at once. Deconstruction, the exploration of multiple and hidden signification, directly denies the existence of absolutes and any pretense to objectivity.

These currents of contemporary thought, obviously related to postmodernism, are often referred to as *poststructuralism* because they have moved beyond logical structures, scientific models, and fixed categories. Under the influence of poststructuralism, the techniques of literary analysis have become important to contemporary writings about society. Social custom, forms of courtesy and dress, organizations and law, education and religion can all be studied like a text for the multiple messages they convey.

Gender Studies   In no field has the large body of poststructuralist theory had greater impact than in gender studies, which looks beyond biological or sexual differences to the social construction of different roles for men and women, differences fabricated from custom, from views about the nature of women and men, and above all, from seemingly neutral dichotomies such as strength/weakness, rationality/irrationality, and public/private, which when associated with male/female become constraints on the roles thought proper for women. Such studies have made it necessary to rethink and rewrite a great deal of history, anthropology, and sociology. If the theoretical base has been heavily European, its application has been more extensive in the United States, where the structure of universities, the rapid opening of careers to women, and public preoccupation with oppressed groups have fostered the development of gender studies. In Europe, too, however, similar reinterpretations of society and culture have given new strength to feminist movements and to campaigns in behalf of groups previously marginalized (see "A Reflection on Contemporary Feminism," pp. 980).

Europe's admired, established culture and the institutions that sustain it have come under attack from many quarters, and those attacks have made their own contributions to culture. That established culture, which remains at the core of education, religion, and much of public life, meanwhile draws millions of people each year to museums and concert halls.

Questions for

1. How do you explain Union despite hesit disagreements, and along the way have predict its failure?
2. Are postindustrial s really so different fr

Recommended

Sources

Ash, Timothy Garton. *T Revolution of '89 Wii Berlin, and Prague.* 1 particularly keen and

de Beauvoir, Simone. *M* James Kickup (tr.). 19 O'Brian (tr.). 1974. Im contemporary femini a sense of the intellec

Gorbachev, Mikhail. *Per Country and the Wor* Gorbachev's vision of issues it does not add recommendations.

Studies

*Albertini, Rudolf von. *I Administration and F 1919–1960.* Francisca account that focuses especially valuable fo

*Ash, Timothy Garton. *Solidarity.* 1984. Rich techniques, ideas, and captured worldwide a

*Burgess, Michael. *Feder 2000.* Reviews the his make the case for the national states within

psychoanalysis A method of analyzing psychic phenomena and treating emotional disorders that involves treatment sessions during which the patient is encouraged to talk freely about personal experiences and especially about early childhood and dreams.

public sphere Forums outside the royal court, such as newspapers, salons, and academies, in which the educated public could participate in debate on the issues of the day.

Puritans Devout Protestants who believed in a stern moral code and rejected all hints of Catholic ritual or organization.

raj British rule in India, which had spread through most of the subcontinent by the mid-nineteenth century.

realism The depiction of ordinary, everyday subjects in art and literature as part of a broader social commentary; a reaction against the themes and styles typical of Romanticism or of academic painting.

reasons of state Often known by its French name, *raison d'état,* the doctrine that, especially in foreign affairs, a state is bound by no restraint when pursuing its interests.

Reformation The period of major change and variance in the fundamental beliefs of Christianity. The demands of the faithful varied and intensified throughout Western Europe, making it difficult for the Roman Catholic Church alone to accommodate all of them.

relativity Einstein's theory that all aspects of the physical universe must be defined in relative terms.

Renaissance Rebirth of classical culture that occurred in Italy after 1350.

Restorations Attempts by the powers in Europe to restore the dynasties and monarchical institutions (including the Bourbons in France) disrupted by the revolutionary and Napoleonic upheavals.

risorgimento A term meaning "resurgence," used to describe the liberal nationalist movement that led to the unification of Italy by 1870.

Roman Catholic "Universal" church; Christian church headed by a pope.

Romanesque Style of Western European architecture and art developed after 1000; the style is characterized by rounded arches, massive walls, and relatively simple ornamentation.

Romanticism An artistic movement that rejected classical aesthetic forms and norms, and which emphasized personal experience, emotion, or spirituality.

sacrament Means by which God distributes grace. Luther retained only baptism and the Eucharist.

Sadducees Conservative Jewish sect that did not believe in angels or resurrection because such teachings were not found in the five books of the Old Testament, known as the Pentateuch.

sagas Adventure stories told in prose that cover the Viking period to about 1000, when Iceland converted to Christianity.

Saint-Simonians A nineteenth-century movement that called for the reorganization of society by scientists and industrialists to achieve planned progress and prosperity.

salons Social gatherings, usually organized by elite women, that sought to promote discussion of Enlightenment ideas.

sans-culottes Parisian militants, mainly artisans and shopkeepers, who called for repression of counter-revolutionaries, price controls, and direct democracy; helped bring the Jacobins to power in 1793.

satyr play Comic, often vulgar, play performed after an ancient Greek tragedy.

Schlieffen Plan In World War I, the German military plan specifying how the army would fight a two-front war: Germany would invade Belgium and the Netherlands on its way to France, score a quick defeat in the west, and then concentrate its forces against Russia in the east.

Scholasticism A form of argument, or dialectic, developed in the Middle Ages, particularly with Abelard and Thomas Aquinas.

Scientific Revolution The succession of discoveries and the transformation of the investigation of nature that was brought about in the fields of astronomy, physics, and anatomy during the sixteenth and seventeenth centuries.

Second Empire The reign of Napoleon III in France from 1852 to 1870; while authoritarian in nature, the regime fostered popular support through social programs and nationalist sentiment.

second front In World War II, the establishment of an Allied front in Western Europe to match the Russians battling the Nazis in the East; after several delays, the Allies launched the second front with the Normandy invasion in June 1944.

seigneurialism A system prevalent in Western Europe by which peasants owed various fees and dues to the local lord even if the peasants owned their land.

serf or villein Peasant who was personally free, but bound to the lord of a manor and worked the land on the manor.

serfdom A feudal system of agricultural exploitation in which peasants were bound to their lord's estate and owed him forced labor.

sexagesimal System of mathematics based on the number 60.

sexual selection The theory that the traits that increase an organism's (typically male's) success in mating and transmitting its genes are selected and perpetuated. Differs from natural selection, which focuses only on traits that influence survival.

shell shock New psychological diagnosis applied to those soldiers exhibiting signs of psychic distress during the First World War, thought to be caused by the near-constant shelling experienced in the trenches.

sister republics States and territories that fell under French control during the Directory and were reconstituted as republics in collaboration with native revolutionaries.

Skepticism Philosophy that questions whether human beings can ever achieve certain knowledge.

Slavophiles Russian intellectuals who opposed Westernization and saw Russia's unique institutions and culture as superior; some supported autocracy but also favored emancipation of the serfs.

social Darwinism The application of Darwin's scientific theory of evolution to society, often in the service of reactionary and even racist ideas.

social welfare State-run programs for social security, education, medical care, and family benefits.

Sophists Teachers of rhetoric in classical Greece, especially in Athens.

Stalingrad The place where Russians fought ferociously, street by street, to halt the German advance in 1942; marked the turning point of the war on the Eastern front.

state of nature Description in political theory of the condition of humanity before the creation of governments.

steam engine A machine patented in 1782 that converted steam into mechanical energy; provided a cheap and flexible source of power critical for early industrialization.

Stoics Followers, in Greece and Rome, of thought of Zeno, who taught that the wise man leads a life of moderation, unmoved by joy or grief, and stands by his duty according to natural law.

strategic bombing A military doctrine of aerial bombardment of populated and industrial areas; intended to destroy morale and the industrial capacity to fight. Initiated by the Germans on Britain, but most fully used by the British and U.S. air forces.

Sturm und Drang A literary and artistic movement in Germany that emphasized strong artistic emotion; a precursor of the Romantic movement.

subinfeudation The grant of a fief by a vassal to a subordinate who becomes his vassal.

Sunni-Shiite schism Division within the Islamic religion over who should rule after Mohammad's death.

syndicalism A movement in which worker's organizations attempted to destroy bourgeois capitalism and gain control of industry by general strikes.

Talmud General body of Jewish tradition.

tariff A duty or custom fee imposed on imports, often to protect local agriculture or industry from competition.

Tetrarchy Rule of four co-emperors of Rome under Diocletian.

Thermidorian reaction The period between the fall of Robespierre and the establishment of the Directory during which the Convention dismantled the Terror and attacked egalitarian politics.

thermodynamics The study of the relationships between heat and other forms of energy; becomes one of the bases of nineteenth-century physics.

three-field system Agricultural system in which two-thirds of the land was cultivated on a rotating basis; it replaced the two-field system and resulted in increased productivity.

Tory English political party committed to a strong monarch and a strong Anglican Church.

total war Unprecedented type of warfare in which all segments of society, civilians and soldiers, men and women, were mobilized in the hope of ensuring victory.

totalitarianism A twentieth-century form of authoritarian government using force, technology, and bureaucracy to effect rule by a single party and controlling most aspects of the lives of the population.

tragedy The supreme dramatic form in ancient Greece, usually treating a mythological theme and leading to catastrophe for some of the characters.

transubstantiation Belief that bread and wine are transformed into the body and blood of Christ during the Eucharist.

Treaty of Paris (1763) Peace treaty ending the British and French war for empire in which France surrendered Canada to the British and lost its foothold in India.

Treaty of Tordesillas Signed in 1494, the treaty confirmed the pope's division of the world between the Portuguese and Spanish for exploration and conquest. Under its terms, a line was drawn some 1,200 miles west of the Cape Verde Islands, with Portugal granted all lands to the west and Spain granted all lands to the east.

trench warfare Static, defensive type of combat seen mostly on the Western front of World War I, where a war of attrition was fought in a complex system of underground trenches and supply lines.

triangular trade A complex pattern of colonial commerce between the home country (Britain or France) and its colonies in which refined or manufactured goods were exchanged for raw materials or slaves from West Africa.

tribunes Ten Roman plebeians, elected to protect the common people; some of them became powerful political activists.

triremes Greek warship, powered by three banks of oars.

triumvirate "Body of three men," a term applied to two such cabals in the Roman Republic.

trivium and quadrivium School curriculum that became the standard program of study in universities. The trivium comprised the verbal arts (grammar, rhetoric, and logic), while the quadrivium comprised the mathematical arts (arithmetic, astronomy, geometry, and music).

troubadour A writer of vernacular romantic lyrics or tales who enjoyed the patronage of nobles around Europe in the twelfth through fifteenth centuries.

tsar Title adopted by the Russian king; the term was the Slavic equivalent of the Latin term *caesar*.

tyrant In ancient Greek states, a powerful man who ruled in a polis without legal sanction, not necessarily a cruel despot.

ultraroyalists French reactionaries who not only supported divine-right monarchy but called for the return of lands taken from the émigrés during the Revolution.

usury Interest of profit on a loan; it was prohibited by the Church.

Utilitarianism British reform movement that believed that society should be based on "the greatest happiness for the greatest number," and that sound governments could make such calculations.

utopian Having to do with an ideal society, as presented in Sir Thomas More's book *Utopia*, which means "nowhere" in Greek.

vassal A free warrior who places himself under a lord, accepting the terms of loyal service, fighting in times of war, and counseling in times of peace.

Vatican II Vatican council called by Pope John XXIII in 1962. Vatican II made the leadership of the Church more international, directed attention to the concerns of developing nations, and ordered that Masses be conducted in the vernacular instead of Latin.

Vulgate The Latin translation of the Bible in the fourth century, identified with St. Jerome, which became the medieval Church's standard text and was deemed holy in the sixteenth century.

war guilt clause Article 231 of the Treaty of Versailles, specifying that Germany alone was responsible for causing the First World War.

Warsaw Pact The Russian response to NATO; an international military organization established in 1955 that included the Soviet Union and Eastern European communist states.

Weimar Republic Left-liberal German government established after the war, named for the city where German politicians formed the republic; instituted universal suffrage, and wrote a new democratic constitution.

Wergeld Literally, "man-payment"; in Germanic tribes, as a means to prevent feuds, payments given in compensation for crimes committed; the amount of compensation depended on the social rank of the individual.

Whig English political party committed to a strong Parliament and religious toleration.

Yalta Conference In February 1945, the meeting between Roosevelt, Churchill, and Stalin to set the postwar order in Europe. The conference agreed on the creation of the United Nations but was unable to counter future Soviet dominance in Eastern Europe.

Zeus Sky god; the chief god in Greek myth.

ziggurat Terraced tower built of baked brick in Mesopotamia.

Zollverein A customs union established by Prussia among most states in the German Confederation that allowed for free movement of goods; promoted the economic unification of Germany.

Text Credits

Chapter 15

Page 450 From Louis André (ed.), *Testament politique* (Editions Robert Laffont, 1947), pp. 347–348 and 352; translated by Theodore K. Rabb. **Page 453** Adapted from J. H. Elliott, *Imperial Spain, 1469–1716*, Edward Arnold, The Hodder Neadling PLC Group, 1964, p. 175.

Chapter 16

Page 465 From Giorgio de Santillana, "Galileo and Kepler on Copernicus", from *The Crime of Galileo*, Chicago: University of Chicago Press, 1955, pp. 11 and 14–15. Reprinted by permission of the University of Chicago Press. **Page 480** From Jan de Vries, *The Economy of Europe in an Age of Crisis, 1600–1750*, Cambridge University Press, 1976, p. 5. Reprinted by permission.

Chapter 17

Page 495 From J. M. Thompson, *Lectures on Foreign History, 1494–1789*, Oxford: Blackwell, 1956, pp. 172–174.
Page 500 From Albert Sorel, *L'Europe et la révolution française*, 3rd ed., vol. 1, Paris, 1893, p. 199, as translated in William F. Church, *The Greatness of Loius XIV: Myth or Reality?* Copyright © 1959 by D.C. Heath and Company. Used with permission. **Page 500** From John C. Rule, "Louis XIV, Roi-Bureaucrate," in Rule (ed.), *Louis XIV and the Craft of Kingship*, Columbus: Ohio State University Press, 1969, pp. 91–92. Reprinted by permission. **Page 520** From John Locke, *The Second Treatise of Civil Government*, Thomas P. Peardon (ed.), Indianapolis: Bobbs-Merrill, 1952, chapter 9, pp. 70–73.

Chapter 18

Page 543 Adapted from Phyllis Dean and W. A. Cole, *British Economic Growth, 1688–1959*, Cambridge University Press, 1964, p. 49. Reprinted by permission. **Page 544** From Philip D. Curtin, *The Atlantic Slave Trade.* © 1969. Reprinted by permission of The University of Wisconsin Press.

Chapter 19

Page 559 From C. A. Macartney (ed.), *The Habsburg and Hohenzollern Dynasties in the 17th and 18th Centuries*, pp. 151 and 155–157. Copyright © 1970 by C. A. Macartney. Reprinted by permission of HarperCollins Publishers. **Page 565** From Sandra M. Gilbert and Susan Gubar (eds.), *The Norton Anthology of Literature by Women: The Tradition in English*, W. W. Norton Co., 1985. Reprinted by permission.
Page 566 From Jean-Jacques Rousseau, *The Social Contract*, Book 1, David Campbell Publishers. Reprinted by permission.

Chapter 20

Page 588 Georges Lefebvre, *The Coming of the French Revolution.* © 1947 Princeton University Press, 1975 renewed PUP. Reprinted by permission of Princeton University Press. **Page 588** From William Doyle, *Origins of the French Revolution*, 1988. Reprinted by permission of Oxford University Press. **Page 594** R. R. Palmer, *The Age of Democratic Revolution.* © 1959 Princeton University Press, 1987 renewed PUP. Reprinted by permission of Princeton University Press. **Page 594** From R.R. Palmer (trans.), *The Age of Democratic Revolution*, Princeton University Press, 1959, pp. 510–511.

Chapter 21

Page 633 From *Political Constitution of the Spanish Monarchy*, proclaimed in Cadiz, March 19, 1812, (trans. James B. Tueller). **Page 638** From B. Las Cases (ed.), *Mémorial de Sainte-Hélène.*

Chapter 22

Page 650 From Louis L. Snyder (ed.), *Documents of German History*, Rutgers University Press, 1958, pp. 158–159. **Page 655** From B. R. Mitchel, *European Historical Statistics, 1750–1970*, 1975, Columbia University Press. Reproduced with permission of Palgrave Macmillan. **Page 663** From Sidney Pollard and Colin Holmes (eds.), *Documents of European Economic History, Vol. 1*, St. Martin's Press. Reprinted by permission of Palgrave Macmillan. **Page 665** From Thomas S. Ashton, "The Standard of Life of the Workers in England, 1790–1830," *Journal of Economic History*, Vol. 9, 1949. Reprinted by permission. **Page 665** From Eric J. Hobsbawm, "The British Standard of Living, 1790–1850," *Economic History Review*, 1957. Reprinted by permission. **Page 666** From Ronald M. Hartwell, "The Rising Standard of Living in England, 1800–1850," *Economic History Review*, 1961. Reprinted by permission. **Page 666** From Theodore S. Hamerow, *The Birth of a New Europe, State and Society in the Nineteenth Century*, University of North Carolina Press, 1983, pp. 140–141. Reprinted by permission.

Chapter 24

Page 713 From Louis L. Snyder (ed.), *The Documents of German History*, New Brunswick: Rutgers University Press, 1958. **Page 720** From Giuseppe Massini, *On the Duties of Man*, Greenwood Publishing Group. **Page 728** From Louis L. Snyder (ed.), *The Documents of German History*, New Brunswick: Rutgers University Press, 1958.

Chapter 25

Page 740 From Karl Wittgenstein, "Kartelle in Österreich," in Gustav Schmoller (ed.), Über wirtschaftliche Kartelle in Deutschland und im Auslande (Leipzig, 1894), as quoted in Carroll and Embree, Readings in European History since 1814 (1930). **Page 742** From P. Bairoch et al., The Working Population and Its Structure, Gordon V. Breach, 1968, p. 119. Reprinted by permission. **Page 748** From Thomas H. Huxley, Evolution and Ethics and Other Essays, New York: D. Appleton and Company, 1916. **Page 757** From Richard Levy, Antisemitism in the Modern World. Copyright © 1991 by D.C. Heath and Company. Used with permission of Houghton Mifflin Company.

Chapter 27

Page 824 Reprinted with the permission of Scribner, an imprint of Simon & Schuster Adult Publishing Group from Origins of the World War, Volume II, Revised Edition by Sidney B. Fay. Copyright © 1930 by The Macmillan Company; copyright renewed © 1958 by Sidney Bradshaw Fay. **Page 840** From Harold Owen and John Bell (eds.), Wilfred Owen: The Collected Letters, Oxford University Press, 1967. Reprinted by permission. **Page 853** From Sidney Pollard and Colin Holmes (eds.), Documents of European Economic History, Vol. 3: The End of Old Europe, 1914–1939 (St. Martin's Press, 1972). Reprinted by permission of Palgrave Macmillan.

Chapter 28

Page 872 From S. William Halperin (ed.), Mussolini and Italian Fascism (Van Nostrand, 1964). **Page 889** From Salvator Attanasio et al. (trs.), Speech of Goebbels, in George L. Mosse, Nazi Culture: Intellectual, Cultural, and Social Life in the Third

---

Reich, University of Wisconsin Press, 1966. Reprinted by permission.

Chapter 29

Page 914 From J. Noakes and G. Pridham (eds.), Nazism 1919–1945 Volume Two, State Economy and Society 1933–1939: A Documentary Reader. ISBN: 0 85989 599 8 Reprinted by permission of the University of Exeter Press. **Page 916** From Henry Friedlander, "Step by Step: The Expansion of Murder, 1939–1941," German Studies Review 17, October 1994. Reprinted by permission. **Page 916** From Ernst Nolte, "Between Historical Myth and Revisionism," Yad Vashem Studies 19, 1988. Reprinted by permission. **Page 917** From Peter Baldwin, Reworking the Past. Copyright © 1990 by Peter Baldwin. Reprinted by permission of Beacon Press, Boston. **Page 928** From Winston Churchill speech at Westminster College, Fulton, MO, March 5, 1946. Reproduced with permission of Curtis Brown Ltd., London on behalf of Winston S. Churchill. Copyright Winston S. Churchill. **Page 931** Speech by Andrei Y. Vishinsky to the United Nations, November 1, 1948, from Vital Speeches of the Day, Vol. 15, No. 2 (New York: City News Publishing Co., 1949). Reprinted by permission.

Chapter 30

Page 952 From Akural Aynur (tr.), in Ilhan Başgöz and Norman Furniss (eds.), Turkish Workers in Europe, Turkish Studies Publications, 1985. Reprinted by permission. **Page 964** From Brian MacArthur (ed.), The Penguin Book of Twentieth-Century Speeches, New York: Viking, 1992. **Page 980** From Julia Kristeva, New Maladies of the Soul. Copyright © 1995 by Columbia University Press. Reprinted with the permission of the publisher.

Volume II Index

Evolutionary Socialism (Bernstein), 763
Existentialism, 974
Expedition of the Thousand, 721
Expressionists, 875
Extermination camps, 913–914

Factory Act, 695
Factory model, 658–660
Factory system, 536*b*
Falange, 896
Falkland Islands, 958
Fall of Berlin Wall, 940*f*, 953
Fall of the Bastille, 591–592
Family, early nineteenth century, 660–662
Family economy, 540–541
Family Shakespeare (Bowdler), 662
Famine march, 883*f*
Faraday, Michael, 745
Fascism
    international, 881
    Italy, 869–873
Fascist salute, 871
Fashoda crisis, 795–796
Fatherland Front, 881
Father's Curse, The (Greuze), 572*f*
Faust (Goethe), 571
Fauves, 875
February Revolution, 862–863
Female Spectator, The (Haywood), 569
Feminine Mystique, The (Friedan), 954
Feminism, 980*b*
Ferdinand II, 438, 712
Ferdinand VII, 631, 631*f*, 633, 650, 700
Ferry, Jules, 811, 813
Festivals, 576
Fichte, Johann Gottlieb, 714
Fielding, Henry, 570
Fifth Monarchists, 447
Fifth Republic, 935
Final solution, 913, 914*b*
First Balkan War, 827
First International, 754
First Reich, 727*n*
Fischer, Fritz, 828
Fite in the Park (Watteau), 495*f*
Fiume, 869
Five Glorious Days of Milan, 708
Five-year plan, 889–890
Fleming, Sir Alexander, 877
Fleurus, 610
Fleury, Cardinal, 499, 500
Florey, Sir Howard, 877
Foch, Marshall, 842
Forbidden City, 976*f*
Ford, Henry, 892
Fordism, 892
Foreign workers, 951
Foucault, Michel, 978–979
Foundations of nineteenth century, 640–668
    Belgium, 655–656
    Carlsbad Decrees, 649, 650*b*
    coal, 652, 655*f*
    Concert of Europe, 646
    Congress of Vienna, 642–647
    cotton, 654, 655*f*
    Crystal Palace, 656–658
    factory model, 658–660
    family, 660–662
    France, 651–652
    German Confederation, 648–649
    Habsburg Empire, 648
    housing crisis, 663*b*
    industrialization, 652–658
    iron, 652–653, 655*f*

Italy, 650–651
    middle-class women, 661–662
    railroads, 640*f*, 654–655
    Russian Empire, 647–648
    Spain, 650
    standard of living, 662–666
    steam engine, 653
    timeline, 642–643, 647*b*
Fourier, Charles, 680–681
Fourteen Points, 845
Fourth Republic, 928–929, 934
France
    absolutism, 495–499
    African imperialism, 792
    Algeria, 934–935
    aristocracy, 684
    Charles X, 651–652
    civil war, 435–437
    colonial empire, 542–543, 546–549
    confraternities, 687
    Dreyfus affair, 760–761
    education, 693
    Fifth Republic, 935
    Fourth Republic, 928–929, 934
    Fronde, 451
    Henry IV, 449–450
    housing crisis, 663*b*
    July Monarchy, 698–699
    July Ordinances, 652
    kings (sixteenth century), 436
    literacy, 575
    Louis XIV, 490*f*, 492–499
    Monnet Plan, 934
    Napoleon, 614*f*. *See also* Age of Napoleon
    nuclear energy, 956
    Paris Commune, 759–760
    Popular Front, 895
    post–de Gaulle era, 956–957
    post-WWI period, 894–895
    revolution. *See* French Revolution
    revolutions (1830), 698–700
    Richelieu, 450–451
    Second Empire, 715–716
    Third Republic, 759–762
France, Anatole, 812
Francis Ferdinand, 827
Francis II, 601
Franco, Francisco, 896, 955
Franco-Prussian War, 725–727
Frankfurt Constitution, 710, 713*b*
Frankfurt Parliament, 708
Frankfurt school, 978
Franklin, Benjamin, 560, 585*f*
Franz Joseph I, 710, 729, 766
Frederick II of the Palatinate, 437
Frederick II the Great, 505–506, 524, 576
Frederick III, 504
Frederick William I, 504–505
Frederick William III, 637
Frederick William IV, 708
Frederick William of Hohenzollérn,
        502–504
Free French, 917
Free-trade lobby, 776
Freemasonry, 568
Freikorps, 843
French and Indian War, 549
French Constitution of 1791, 594
French Indochina Union, 796
French philosophes, 559
French Revolution, 580–613
    anti-Jacobin rebellion (Lyons), 604
    Assembly of Notables, 588
    assignats, 597

August 4 decree, 592–593
Brunswick Manifesto, 601
cahiers, 589
Church, 597, 600, 608*b*
citizen-soldiers, 610
conflicts, 604*m*
constitution, 593–594
décadi, 607
dechristianization movement, 608*b*
Declaration of the Rights of Man and
        Citizen, 593, 594*b*
deficit financing, 587
execution of Louis XVI, 602, 603*f*
fall of the Bastille, 591–592
Girondins, 602, 603–604
Great Fear, 592
Jacobin dictatorship, 604–606
last uprising, 617, 618*f*
Law of Suspects, 604, 606
Law of the Maximum, 604, 607
levée en masse, 610
Mountain, 602, 604, 609
origins, 586–587, 588*b*
peasant revolts, 592
purge of Girondins, 603–604
race, 596
redividing the territory (1789), 596*m*
Reign of Terror, 606
revolutionary wars, 609–611
Robespierre, 604, 606*b*, 609, 616–617
sans-culottes, 601, 604, 607–609
second revolution, 601–611
slavery, 596
slogan, 586
Tennis Court Oath, 591*f*
Thermidorian reaction, 616–617
timeline, 582–583, 607*b*
Tuileries, 580*f*
Vendée revolt, 603, 605*f*
women, 594–596
Freud, Sigmund, 873–874
Friedan, Betty, 954
Friedland, 627
Friedlander, Henry, 916*b*
Friedrich, Caspar David, 675
Friendly societies, 687
Fronde, 451
Fulant, 787
Fundamental Laws, 765

Galen, 460
Galilei, Galileo, 463–464, 465*b*, 466
Galton, Francis, 803, 804
Gambetta, Leon, 811
Gandhi, Mohandas K., 932
Garibaldi, Giuseppe, 720–721, 722
Garibaldi Brigade, 896
Gaskell, Elizabeth, 731
Gauguin, Paul, 751, 815
Gehry, Frank, 977*f*
Gender studies, 979
*General Theory of Employment, Interest, and
        Money* (Keynes), 893
General will, 565, 566*b*
Generation of 1898, 766
Genocide, 913–915, 916–917*b*
Gentile, Giovanni, 872*b*
Gentileschi, Artemisia, 474*f*, 481
Gentleman's Magazine, 569
Gentry, 444, 448, 513
George I, 515, 517
George II, 517
George III, 584, 585, 777
George IV, 694